The Allyn & Bacon Guide to Writing

Eighth Edition

The Allyn & Bacon Guide to Writing

Eighth Edition

John D. Ramage
Arizona State University

John C. Bean
Seattle University

June Johnson
Seattle University

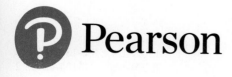
Pearson

330 Hudson Street, NY NY 10013

VP & Portfolio Manager: Eric Stano
Development Editor: Steven Rigolosi
Managing Editor: Cynthia Cox
Marketing Manager: Nick Bolt
Program Manager: Rachel Harbour
Project Manager: Nathaniel Jones
Cover Designer: Pentagram
Cover Illustration: Anuj Shrestha
Manufacturing Buyer: Roy L. Pickering, Jr.
Printer/Binder: LSC Communications/Crawfordsville
Cover Printer: Phoenix Color/Hagerstown

Acknowledgments of third-party content appear on page[s] 607 – 608, which constitute an extension of this copyright page.

Library of Congress Cataloging-in-Publication Data
Names: Ramage, John D., author. | Bean, John C., author. | Johnson, June,
    author.
Title: The Allyn & Bacon guide to writing / John D. Ramage, John C. Bean,
    June Johnson.
Description: Eighth edition. | [New York] : Pearson Education, [2017]
Identifiers: LCCN 2016054973 | ISBN 9780134424521
Subjects: LCSH: English language--Rhetoric--Handbooks, manuals, etc. | Report
    writing--Handbooks, manuals, etc. | College readers.
Classification: LCC PE1408 .R18 2017 | DDC 808/.042--dc23
LC record available at https://lccn.loc.gov/2016054973

2   17

 **Pearson**

ISBN-13: 978-0-134-42452-1
ISBN-10:   0-134-42452-2

Contents

13 Writing a Synthesis of Ideas Essay   247

14 Writing a Classical Argument   269

WRITING PROJECTS

BRIEF PROJECT OPTIONS

CHAPTER 1   Reflect on how your previous writing and reading experiences have prepared you for the demands of college writing as explained in Chapter 1.

CHAPTER 2   Use the "believing and doubting game" to explore a controversial assertion.

CHAPTER 3   Write two messages with different audiences, purposes, and genres.

CHAPTER 4   Write contrasting descriptions of the same place and then analyze how you achieved these different rhetorical effects.

CHAPTER 5   Describe a multimodal text that you have created and reflect on your thinking processes as you designed it.

MAJOR PROJECT OPTIONS

CHAPTER 6   Write an abstract or summary of a reading.

Write a strong response to a text by analyzing its rhetorical strategies and engaging its ideas.

Multimodal or Online Options: Compose a summary and strong response to a blog post, or write an online book review.

CHAPTER 7   Write an autobiographical or literacy narrative shaped by contrary experiences or opposing tensions.

Multimodal or Online Options: Compose a podcast, video photo essay, or graphic story.

CHAPTER 8   Write an exploratory narrative of your engagement with a problem and your attempts to resolve it.

Write an annotated bibliography for a research project.

Multimodal or Online Option: Compose an oral presentation with visual aids explaining your exploratory process.

CHAPTER 9   Write an informative report for a "need-to-know" audience.

Write an informative article for a general audience using the surprising reversal strategy.

Multimodal or Online Options: Create an informative poster, oral presentation with visual aids, video, or Pechakucha presentation.

CHAPTER 10   Analyze and compare two photographs, paintings, or print advertisements.

Multimodal or Online Options: Compose a museum audioguide or a lecture with visual aids comparing advertising campaigns for the same product in different countries.

THEMATIC CONTENTS

The Allyn & Bacon Guide to Writing contains a wealth of readings by professional writers and by students. In addition, the text has many visual texts (such as advertisements, news photographs, posters, and Web sites) that can lead to productive thematic discussions.

ENERGY, ENVIRONMENT, SUSTAINABILITY, AND HEALTH

THE INTERNET, TECHNOLOGY, AND EDUCATION

VIOLENCE, PUBLIC SAFETY, AND INDIVIDUAL RIGHTS

PUBLIC POLICY AND SOCIAL ISSUES

POPULAR CULTURE, MEDIA, AND ADVERTISING

PARENTS, CHILDREN, AND FAMILY

Preface

From its inception as the flagship rhetoric of the Allyn & Bacon publishing house (which has since merged with Pearson), *The Allyn & Bacon Guide to Writing* has been informed by research in writing studies, learning theory, critical thinking, and related fields. Through seven editions, *The Allyn & Bacon Guide to Writing* has been praised for its groundbreaking integration of composition pedagogy and rhetorical emphasis. In regular, brief, and concise editions, the text has been adopted at a wide range of two- and four-year institutions where instructors admire its appeal to students, its distinctive emphasis on reading and writing as rhetorical acts, its focus on shared problems as the starting point for academic writing, its engaging classroom activities that promote critical thinking, and its effective writing assignments. Reviewers have consistently praised the book's theoretical coherence and explanatory power, which help students produce engaged, idea-rich essays and help composition instructors build pedagogically sound, intellectually stimulating courses shaped by their own strengths, interests, and course goals.

What's New in the Eighth Edition?

While retaining the signature strengths of earlier editions, the eighth edition features the following key improvements:

- **A re-organized Part 1 ("A Rhetoric for Writers") incorporates recent research in transfer of learning, threshold concepts, and metacognition** to help learners apply "big picture" concepts to new rhetorical situations.
  - **A new Chapter 1, "Posing Problems: The Demands of College Writing, Reading, and Critical Thinking," introduces students to this "big picture."** It shows how the threshold concepts of problem-posing, knowledge-making, and rhetorical reading promote deep learning, which in turn promotes the transfer of skills from first-year composition to students' study of other disciplines and to their professions.

- **A revised Chapter 2, "Exploring Problems: Making Claims," includes a new module on analysis.** "Playing the Analysis Game" teaches students to analyze an artifact, object, or phenomenon by slowing down, describing the object in detail, and then finding what is puzzling by asking why something is this way rather than some other way (following Ludwig Wittgenstein's dictum: "Everything we see could be otherwise").

- **A reorganized Chapter 3, "Thinking Critically About Rhetorical Problems," provides a richer introduction to rhetorical thinking as a threshold concept.** The explanations of purpose, audience, and genre are now linked to explanations of closed- and open-form prose and to the rhetoric of online environments.

- **A newly designed Chapter 5, "Thinking Critically About Document Design, Visual Rhetoric, and Multimodal Messages," focuses on non-verbal rhetoric.** The persuasive power of document design, of images, and of multimodal messages is now discussed in a single chapter.

- **Part 2 ("Writing Projects") has been significantly streamlined for easier** navigation and includes many refreshed, expanded, or updated chapters.

- **A revised Chapter 6, "Reading Rhetorically: The Writer as Strong Reader,"** includes more coverage of summary writing. A new reading on Internet trolling (along with related student examples and a model essay) replaces Michael Pollan's "Why Bother?"

- **A revised Chapter 9, "Writing an Informative (and Surprising) Essay or Report,"** includes new student examples of informative reports for different purposes and audiences.

- **A revised Chapter 10, "Analyzing Images,"** has many new images and examples, including new mock advertisements and advocacy posters on respect for underrepresented cultures and on environmentalism. The 7th edition's section on European impressionistic painting has been replaced with a sample analysis of Haitian-Puerto Rican American Jean-Michel Basquiat's 1983 piece *Museum Security (Broadway Meltdown)* and a painting, *Reload* (2007), by Native American artist Natalie Ball.

- **A revised Chapter 13, "Analyzing and Synthesizing Ideas,"** includes more emphasis on analysis in the synthesis process.

- **Many new, high-interest student model essays, images, and updated examples appear throughout the text.**

  - **New student essays include** a student's exploratory analysis of a surrealist painting by Dorothea Tanning; a "summary/strong response" essay examining Internet trolling; a solicited informative report on the funding of Planned Parenthood; another informative report on people's misconceptions about Islam and violence;

a zine arguing for improved museum programs for children; an evaluation essay on PETA2's Facebook appeal to youth; and two new reflective pieces emphasizing metacognition and rhetorical awareness.

- **Updated examples and visuals** focus on current issues: driverless cars, gun control, banned books, Europe's refugee crisis, "Black Lives Matter," prescription drug controversies, social media, climate change, and many others.

- **A revised introduction to research in Chapter 21, "Asking Questions, Finding Sources,"** increases the emphasis on rhetorical reading and rhetorical purpose to help students understand research as a knowledge-making activity.

- **A revised Chapter 24, "Citing and Documenting Sources,"** includes updated information on MLA format based on the 8th edition of the *MLA Handbook*.

- **A substantially revised chapter on reflective writing (Chapter 26, "Using Reflective Writing to Promote and Assess Learning")** focuses on metacognition and reinforces the importance of reflection for enabling deep learning and transfer of knowledge.

What Hasn't Changed? The Distinctive Features of *The Allyn & Bacon Guide to Writing*

The Allyn & Bacon Guide to Writing takes a distinctive pedagogical approach that integrates composition research with rhetorical theory and insights from writing across the curriculum. It treats writing and reading both as rhetorical acts and as processes of problem posing, inquiry, critical thinking, analysis, and argument. Its aim is to evoke the kind of deep learning that allows students to transfer compositional and rhetorical skills across disciplines and professional fields. What follows are the text's distinctive features aimed at achieving these goals.

- **Focus on transfer of learning into the disciplines.** Recent cognitive research shows that transfer of knowledge and skills from one course to another depends on deep rather than surface learning. *The Allyn & Bacon Guide to Writing* promotes deep learning in a variety of ways. As one example, the text emphasizes four underlying skills that novice academic writers must acquire: (1) how to pose a problem that engages targeted readers, (2) how to summarize the conversation that surrounds the problem, (3) how to produce a thesis that adds something new, challenging, or surprising to the conversation, (4) how to support the thesis with appropriate forms of reasons and evidence. Armed with knowledge of these principles (deep learning), a student entering a new discipline can ask, "How does this discipline ask questions? How does it summarize the scholarly conversation surrounding this problem (literature reviews)? What constitutes evidence in this discipline?"

- **Classroom-tested assignments that guide students through all phases of the reading and writing processes and make frequent use of collaboration and peer review.** The Writing Projects in Parts 1 and 2 promote intellectual growth and stimulate the kind of critical thinking valued in college courses. Numerous "For Writing and Discussion" exercises make it easy to incorporate active learning into a course while deepening students' understanding of concepts. The text's focus on the subject-matter question that precedes the thesis helps students see academic disciplines as fields of inquiry rather than as data banks of right answers.

- **Easy navigation through the text with headings linked to learning outcomes and with numbered take-away points**

highlighted as "Concepts" or "Skills." These concepts and skills help students build big-picture understanding—by emphasizing transferable principles that promote metacognitive reflection and give students control over their own solutions to subject-matter or rhetorical problems.

- **Placement of nonfiction writing on a continuum from closed to open forms.** This innovative pedagogical strategy introduces students to the rhetorical concepts of purpose, audience, and genre and shows why the "rules" for good writing depend on rhetorical context. The text focuses on closed-form writing for entering most academic, civic, and professional conversations and on open-form writing for communicating ideas and experiences that resist closed-form structures and for creating stylistic surprise and pleasure.

- **Coverage of a wide range of genres and aims, including academic, civic, and professional genres as well as multimodal, personal, and narrative forms.** The text presents students with a wide range of genres and aims, and it clearly explains their rhetorical function and stylistic features. The range of genres is extended to multimodal texts that combine features of closed-form and open-form prose with visual or aural elements to produce powerful new media compositions.

- **Use of reader-expectation theory to explain how closed-form prose achieves maximum clarity and how open-form prose achieves its distinctive pleasures.** Our explanations of closed-form prose show students why certain closed-form strategies— such as identifying the problem before stating the thesis, forecasting structure, providing transitions, placing points before details, and linking new information to old information— derive from readers' cognitive needs rather than from the arbitrary rules of English teachers. Conversely, the skills explained in Chapter

19, "Strategies for Writing Open-Form Prose," show how writers can create pleasurable surprise through purposeful disruptions and violations of the conventions of closed-form prose.

- **Treatment of research as a knowledge-making activity requiring rhetorical reading.** An often-noted strength of *The Allyn & Bacon Guide to Writing* is its method of teaching rhetorical reading so that students can summarize complex readings and speak back to them through their own analysis and critical thinking. This skill is crucial for summarizing the conversation surrounding a subject-matter problem (literature review) and for any research project that uses verbal, visual, or multimodal texts as primary sources. Our instructional approach to research teaches students to understand the differences between print and cyberspace sources; to analyze the rhetorical occasion, genre, context, intended audience, and angle of vision of sources; to evaluate sources according to appropriate criteria; and to negotiate the World Wide Web with confidence.

- **An organizational structure that offers flexibility to instructors.** The modular organization gives instructors maximum flexibility in designing courses. Numbered concepts and skills are designed as mini-lessons that are easy for students to navigate and can be assigned in an order chosen by the instructor. Instructors can select, mix, and match writing assignments to fit their own course goals (or design their own assignments). In Parts 3 and 4, modularized lessons teach students to develop an effective writing process while gaining expert knowledge for composing closed-form, open-form, and multimodal texts. In Part 4, modularized lessons teach students expert strategies for conducting academic research in a rhetorical environment. Part 4 particularly reinforces the rhetorical concepts learned in Part 1 and is closely integrated with Chapter 6's focus on summary writing and formulating strong responses to readings. Finally, Part 5 offers instruction in writing essay exams and doing reflective writing to promote self-assessment, metacognition, and deep learning.

- **Full coverage of outcome goals for first-year composition from the Council of Writing Program Administrators (WPA).** The correlation of the WPA Outcomes Statement with the eighth edition of *The Allyn & Bacon Guide to Writing* appears on the inside back covers of the book and in the Instructor's Resource Manual. In addition to helping instructors plan their courses, these correlations help with program-wide internal and external assessments.

The Eighth Edition of *The Allyn & Bacon Guide to Writing* is Available in Both Print and REVEL Editions

REVEL: Educational Technology Designed for the Way Today's Students Read, Think, and Learn
When students are engaged deeply, they learn more effectively and perform better in their courses. This simple fact inspired the creation of REVEL: an interactive learning environment designed for the way today's students read, think, and learn.

REVEL enlivens course content with media interactives and assessments—integrated directly within the authors' narrative—that provide opportunities for students to read, practice, and study in one continuous experience. This immersive educational technology replaces the textbook and is designed to measurably boost students' understanding, retention, and preparedness.

Learn more about REVEL at http://www.pearsonhighered.com/revel/.

Resources for Instructors and Students

The Instructor's Resource Manual, Eighth Edition, integrates emphases for meeting the Council of Writing Program Administrators' guidelines for outcome goals in first-year composition courses. It continues to offer detailed teaching suggestions to help both experienced and new instructors; practical teaching strategies for composition instructors in a question-and-answer format; suggested syllabi for courses of various lengths and emphases; chapter-by-chapter teaching suggestions; answers to Handbook exercises; suggestions for using the text with nonnative speakers; suggestions for using the text in an electronic classroom; and annotated bibliographies.

Acknowledgments

We give special thanks to the composition scholars and instructors who reviewed the seventh edition, helping us understand how they use *The Allyn & Bacon Guide to Writing* in the classroom and offering valuable suggestions for improving the text.

We are particularly grateful for our new Development Editor Steven Rigolosi, who guided us through our first experience with Pearson's new REVEL template and who also took on the challenging task of updating all the student essays in the text to reflect the guidelines in the eighth edition of the *MLA Handbook*. Steve's patience, professionalism, editorial skill, and broad knowledge of textbook publishing were invaluable to us.

We would also like to thank our Seattle University students who made special contributions as researchers and writers to this edition: Scott Lindquist, Kirsten Smock, Madeline Williams, Theda Hovind, Katy Lapinski, Jane Kidder, and Annabelle Forster. Most of all, we are indebted to all our students, who have made the teaching of composition such a joy. We thank them for their insights and for their willingness to engage with problems, discuss ideas, and, as they compose and revise, share with us their frustrations and their triumphs. They have sustained our love of teaching and inspired us to write this book.

Finally, John Bean thanks his wife, Kit, also a professional composition teacher, whose dedication to her students as writers and individuals manifests the sustaining values of our unique profession. John also thanks his children, Matthew, Andrew, Stephen, and Sarah, who have grown to adulthood since he began writing textbooks and who continue to give him insights for writing assignments and contemporary issues. June Johnson thanks her husband, Kenneth Bube, a mathematics professor and geophysics consultant, for his insights into the fascinating intersections between learning to think mathematically and the critical thinking and development of writing knowledge and skills in composition. Finally, June also thanks her daughter, Jane Ellen, whose college coursework in the interdisciplinary field of environmental studies and graduate work in landscape architecture has highlighted the importance of deep learning, rhetorical knowledge, and versatile writing.

JOHN C. BEAN
JUNE JOHNSON

Part I
A Rhetoric for Writers

This image is a photograph of a kinetic sculpture by Billie Grace Lynn. The sculpture won the 2011 grand prize at the West Collection, headquartered in Oaks, Pennsylvania. This electric/hybrid motorcycle, which is made from cow bones, a bicycle frame, and a motor, is fully rideable. Lynn has also built a larger version of the Mad Cow on a motorcycle frame designed to run on waste vegetable oil, and she has taken the motorcycle on a cross-country tour. This activist sculpture is intended to draw people into conversation about the consumption of meat, the health of our bodies, and the sustainability of our lifestyles. What questions does this sculpture raise for you? How might a sculpture like this make an "argument" about the environment?

Mad Cow Motorcycle by Billie Grace Lynn

Chapter 1

Posing Problems: The Demands of College Writing, Reading, and Critical Thinking

---

Learning Objectives

1.1 Understand subject-matter problems as the starting point of academic writing.

1.2 Read rhetorically.

1.3 See the "big picture" about college writing and reading in order to promote transfer of learning.

It seems to me, then, that the way to help people become better writers is not to tell them that they must first learn the rules of grammar, that they must develop a four-part outline, that they must consult the experts and collect all the useful information. These things may have their place. But none of them is as crucial as having a good, interesting question.

—*Rodney Kilcup, historian*

What abilities and skills do the professionals and global citizens of the twenty-first century need? According to Harvard educator Tony Wagner, among the most important competencies are the ability to think critically and solve problems, to communicate effectively both orally and in writing, to assess and analyze information, and to exercise curiosity and imagination.[1] One recent study

---

[1]Tony Wagner, *The Global Achievement Gap: Why Even Our Best Schools Don't Teach the New Survival Skills Our Children Need—and What We Can Do about It* (New York: Basic Books, 2008): 14–15, 34–41.

showed that college graduates in business or professional life spend, on average, 44 percent of their time writing, including (most commonly) letters, memos, short reports, instructional materials, and professional articles and essays. With an eye to your future, this textbook seeks to cultivate the reading, critical thinking, and writing skills that you need to succeed in college and your career. However, because no writing course can teach you everything you need to know about writing, the key to your success is to become the kind of learner who knows *how to learn.* Particularly, you need to understand key principles about writing and reading so that you can transfer the skills you acquire in first-year composition to new writing situations.

In Part I of this book, we introduce some of these important big-picture principles. Specifically, we want you to see problem posing as the heart of college-level writing and reading. As we show throughout this textbook, writers pose two sorts of problems: *subject-matter problems* (for example, What can the United States do to reduce gun violence?) and *rhetorical problems* (for example, Who are my readers? What are their current views about gun violence? What form and style should I use?).

Psychologists who study critical and creative thinking see problem solving as a productive and positive activity. Indeed, humans pose and solve problems all the time and often take great pleasure in doing so. According to one psychologist, "Critical thinkers are actively engaged with life. . . . They appreciate creativity, they are innovators, and they exude a sense that life is full of possibilities."[2] In this chapter, we explain the demands of college writing and reading and provide strategies for developing these skills. The payoff will be a big-picture overview that will help you transfer what you learn in this course to your other courses, your major, and your career.

Concept 1.1: Subject-matter problems are the heart of college writing.

1.1   Understand subject-matter problems as the starting point of academic writing.

From your previous schooling, you are probably familiar with the term **thesis statement**, which is the main point a writer wants to make. However, you may not have thought much about the question that lies behind the thesis. A paper's thesis statement is actually the writer's proposed answer to the question or problem that the writer is trying to solve, and it is this question that has motivated the writer's thinking. Experienced writers immerse themselves in subject-matter questions in pursuit of answers or solutions. They write to share their proposed solutions with readers who share their interests.

---

[2]Stephen D. Brookfield, *Developing Critical Thinkers: Challenging Adults to Explore Alternative Ways of Thinking and Acting* (San Francisco: Jossey-Bass, 1987): 5. Academic writers regularly document their quotations and sources. In this text, sources are documented either on the page or in the Credits section at the end of the text.

Shared Problems Unite Writers and Readers

For college professors, "a good, interesting question" is at the heart of good writing (see the quotation by historian Rodney Kilcup at the beginning of this chapter). College professors want students to become gripped by problems because they themselves are gripped by problems. For example, at a workshop for new faculty members, we asked participants to write a brief description of the question or problem that motivated their Ph.D. dissertation or a recent conference paper or article. Here is how a sociology professor responded:

> As a sociologist, I study the ways in which human behaviors that are often assumed to be biological are powerfully shaped by culture. The question of nature versus nurture is particularly relevant to the sexual behavior of adolescents. In a recent research project, I investigated how heterosexual adolescent males talk about sex. That teenage boys talk a lot about sex is a truism of popular culture (witness *Beavis & Butthead* or *American Pie*). But what do we actually know about that talk? What are some of the variations in the ways boys decide what is important or right for them when it comes to sex? How do boys talk about girls? Do they express a desire for loving relationships with a girl or do they see girls as objects to be conquered? Are there ways of talking about girls and sex that are more or less acceptable to other boys? This research question is significant because the results might show the extent to which male sexual desire is socially constructed. Although popular culture sees teenage boys driven by "raging hormones," perhaps there are social components of male sexual behavior that need to be better understood.

As you progress through college, you will find yourself increasingly engaged with the kinds of questions that motivate your professors. Around college campuses, you'll find clusters of professors and students asking questions about all manners of problems ranging from the effect of reforestation projects on soil erosion in Nicaragua to the changing portrayal of race and gender in American films. At the center of all these communities of writers and readers is an interest in common questions and the search for better or different answers. Writers write because they have a new, surprising, or challenging response to a question. Readers read because they share the writer's interest in the problem and want to deepen their understanding.

So where do these problems come from and how can you learn to pose them? The problems that college professors value might be different from what you at first think. Beginning college students typically imagine that a question has a right answer. Students ask questions about a subject because they are puzzled by confusing parts of a textbook, a lecture, or an assigned reading. They hope their professors will explain the confusing material clearly. Their purpose in asking these questions is to eliminate misunderstandings, not to open up inquiry and debate.

College Learning as Both Knowledge-Getting and Knowledge-Making

The difference between questions with right answers and questions that promote inquiry point to two different dimensions of college-level learning:

knowledge-getting versus **knowledge-making**. By *knowledge-getting*, we mean the acquisition of the new knowledge taught in every course you take. Every day you learn new facts, ideas, concepts, theories, and methods associated with the disciplines you are studying. Knowledge-getting entails transfer of knowledge from experts to new learners via textbooks, lectures, and homework activities. To do well in college generally and on exams specifically, you do need to do well in knowledge-getting.

College-level writing assignments, however, often focus on *knowledge-making* rather than knowledge-getting. They ask you to apply what you have learned to new problems—that is, to subject-matter problems that may not have an agreed-upon answer. Such assignments ask you to make your own contribution to a conversation—to discover or invent something new to say, to add your voice to a discussion, to make new knowledge.

The questions or problems that motivate college-level writing often resist a single right answer. They ask instead for a claim that you must support with analysis or argument. By **argument** we mean the use of reasons and evidence to support your claim combined with a fair-minded examination of alternative claims and counterevidence. Your argument is aimed at an audience interested in your question but perhaps skeptical of your claim. College writing assignments thus require a high degree of critical thinking. They are part of the knowledge-making dimension of learning. They help you extend, solidify, and deepen what you have learned through knowledge-getting.

Posing a Knowledge-Making Question

Although knowledge-getting questions are important, college writing assignments usually focus on unknowns or invite multiple points of view. So how do new college students become engaged with questions that require them to make knowledge rather than simply acquire it? We offer two approaches.

Sometimes you become engaged with a question that others are already debating—an existing question that is already "out there" in ongoing public dialog. Some of these are "big questions" that have sparked conversations for years or even ages: Do humans have free will? What is the best form of government? How did the universe get created? Why do good people have to suffer? Thousands of narrower subject-matter questions are being discussed by communities all the time—in classroom debates, discussion threads on blogs, and in the pages of scholarly journals or newspapers. As you advance in your major, you'll be drawn into disciplinary problems that may be new to you but not to your professors. In such cases, a problem that is already "out there" initiates your search for a possible answer and invites you to join the conversation.

Sometimes, though, you initiate a conversation by posing a problem fresh from your own brain. For example, you find a problem whenever you see something puzzling in the natural world, note curious or unexplained features in a cultural phenomenon or artifact, or discover conflicts or contradictions within your own way of looking at the world.

Table 1.1 summarizes some of the ways that writers can become gripped by a knowledge-making problem.

Table 1.1 How Writers Become Gripped by a Problem

Occasion That Leads to Your Posing a Problem	Examples	Your Interior Mental State
The problem is already "out there." *(You enter a conversation already in progress.)*		
You encounter others arguing about a problem, and you don't know where you stand.	Our class discussion has left me uncertain about whether health care should be rationed. My classmate Trevor thinks that Atticus Finch in *To Kill a Mockingbird* is not a good father, but I can't decide whether I agree with him.	• You are equally persuaded by different views or dissatisfied with all the views. • Part of you thinks X but another part thinks Y (you feel divided).
Your gut instinct tells you that someone else is wrong, but you haven't fully investigated the issue (your instinct may be wrong).	This article's proposal for reducing gun violence seems to misunderstand why people want guns in the first place. Shanita says that we should build more nuclear power plants to combat global warming, but I say nuclear power is too dangerous.	• Your skepticism or intuition pushes against someone else's view. • Your system of values leads you to views that differ from someone else's views. • NOTE: You aren't gripped by a problem until you have seen the possible strengths of other views and the possible weaknesses of your own. You must go beyond simply having an opinion.
Someone gives you a question that you can't yet answer or a problem that leaves you baffled.	Your boss asks you whether the company should enact the proposed marketing plan. Your history professor asks you, "To what extent does Frederick Jackson Turner's frontier hypothesis reflect a Eurocentric worldview?"	• You feel overwhelmed with unknowns. • You feel that you can't begin to answer until you do more exploration and research. • You may be able to propose a few possible answers, but you aren't yet satisfied with them.
You pose the problem yourself. *(You initiate the conversation.)*		
You see something puzzling in a natural or cultural phenomenon.	You note that women's fashion magazines have few ads for computers and begin wondering how you could market computers in these magazines. You notice that your little brother and his friends in middle school use Instagram as their social media of choice (rather than Facebook, Twitter, e-mail, or direct text messaging).You wonder why.	• You begin puzzling about something that other people don't notice. • Your mind plays with possible explanations or new approaches. • You begin testing possible solutions or answers. (Often you want to talk to someone—to start a conversation about the problem.)
You see something unexpected, puzzling, or unexplained in a poem, painting, or other human artifact.	Why is the person in this advertisement walking two dogs rather than just one? My classmates believe that Hamlet loves Ophelia, but how do you explain the nunnery scene where he treats her like a whore?	• You can't see why the maker/designer/artist made a particular choice. • You notice that one part of this artifact seems unexpected or incongruous. • You begin trying to explain what is puzzling and playing with possible answers.
You identify something inconsistent or contradictory in your own view of the world.	I agree with this writer's argument against consumerism, but I really want a large plasma TV. Is consumerism really bad? Am I a materialist?	• You feel unsettled by your own inconsistent views or values. • You probe more deeply into your own identity and place in the world.

In each of these cases, the problem starts to spark critical thinking. We examine the process of critical thinking in more detail when we discuss "wallowing in complexity" in the next chapter.

For Writing and Discussion
Finding a Problem

1. *Background:* Figure 1.1 shows a surrealist painting, *Portrait de Famille* (1954), by American painter, artist, and writer Dorothea Tanning (1910–2012). Surrealism was an early twentieth-century artistic movement that featured surprising, strange, and often disturbing contrasts, arresting symbolism, and a blending of reality and the painter's subconscious dreams. These features make interpretation of surrealist art particularly open to speculation. What is surprising or strange about this painting? What questions does a close look at this painting inspire you to ask?

2. *Task:* Spend several minutes writing one or more questions that emerge from your examination of this painting. The best questions will lead to a genuine conversation among your classmates, who will likely offer differing viewpoints and hypotheses. These questions will therefore be knowledge-making questions that you have to answer by conducting your own analysis and forming your own conclusions.

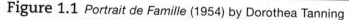

Figure 1.1 *Portrait de Famille* (1954) by Dorothea Tanning

We will return to this painting in Chapter 2 during our discussion of *analysis*.

Concept 1.2: College writers must learn to read rhetorically.

1.2   Read rhetorically.

So far we have shown how college writers must bring their own critical thinking to bear on subject-matter problems. But writing in college also makes special demands on you as a reader.

The Demands of College Reading

Many new college students are overwhelmed by the amount and complexity of their reading assignments. Many of these assignments require you to read textbooks, which are the main vehicles for the knowledge-getting dimension of college learning. Although textbooks can be challenging to read (particularly textbooks in the social or physical sciences), they are written specifically for the purpose of transmitting knowledge to new learners.

But college students are also asked to read material that is very different from textbooks—for example, historical documents, Platonic dialogs, Supreme Court decisions, scholarly journal articles, reports of scientific experiments, and a host of magazine articles, newspapers, opinion pieces, blogs, Web materials, zines, and so forth. These non-textbook readings immerse you in the knowledge-making rather than knowledge-getting side of college.

To add to the challenge, many college writing assignments are text based. By *text based*, we mean that the writing assignment asks students to analyze a reading. (These reading-based assignments ask you to approach a written text in the same analytical way we asked you to approach Dorothea Tanning's *Portrait de Famille*.) These non-textbook readings can be particularly difficult because you as student aren't the intended audience. Instead, you are an outsider. Because you are an outsider, you can expect to be confused by unfamiliar vocabulary, by references to background knowledge that you don't have, and by unfamiliar conventions of style and format.

Reading Rhetorically: Using the Reading Strategies of Experts

When you are asked to analyze a reading for a text-based writing assignment, your strategy for reading textbooks—reading to extract information—often doesn't work well. Your goal isn't to take an exam on this reading but rather to enter into conversation with it. To do so, you must learn to read these pieces rhetorically. When we say that readers read *rhetorically*, we mean that they try to reconstruct the text's original context—its place and date of publication, its original intended audience, its author's original purpose—and analyze how the piece intends to influence those original readers. Rhetorical readers also analyze whether the text works persuasively for them, and they think critically about whether to accede to or challenge the text's intentions. When giving a text-based assignment, college instructors expect you to engage with the reading, think critically about it, analyze it, and respond to it in a way that adds your voice to a conversation—in other words, that makes new knowledge.

Table 1.2 Differences between Novice and Expert Readers

Inexperienced Readers (Novice) [Weak or Minimal Rhetorical Reading]	Experienced Readers (Expert) [Strong Rhetorical Reading]
• Seek to extract information from a text (see reading as knowledge-getting)	• Go beyond extracting meaning from a text to bring critical thinking to bear on that meaning (view reading as knowledge-making)
• Approach a text's message as content to be learned	• Approach a text's message as content to be analyzed, evaluated, and perhaps argued with
• Approach a text's data and concepts as neutral facts or non-controversial ideas or theories	• Approach a text's data as selected and shaped by the writer's biases and purposes and open to evaluation and judgment
• Neglect to consider the author as a real person with a point of view, passion, and personal reason for writing; may think of readings as written by nobody	• Use textual clues and research to identify the author and determine the author's intended audience and purpose
• View the text primarily as a container of information	• View the text as trying to bring about some change in the reader's view of something; determine how much to agree or disagree with the author's view; see themselves in conversation with author
• Frequently highlight important material with a yellow marker	• Frequently take marginal notes that show the reader interacting with the writer
• Read all texts from beginning to end at the same speed	• Match reading speed to the situation and reader's purpose—sometimes skim, sometimes read with close care, sometimes read sections out of order
• Read text only once (often hoping the instructor will explain the reading in class)	• Take personal responsibility for understanding the reading; recognize that complex texts need to be read multiple times; hold confusing passages in mental suspension, hoping that later parts of the reading will clarify earlier parts

Table 1.2 summarizes the differences between the typical reading strategies of new college students and the expert reading strategies that instructors hope students will learn as soon as possible. These reading strategies are explained in more detail in Chapter 6, "Reading Rhetorically," which explains how rhetorical readers both "listen" to a text (by summarizing it) and then join its conversation through their own analysis and critical thinking.

Concept 1.3: Seeing the "big picture" about college writing and reading promotes transfer of learning.

1.3   See the "big picture" about college writing and reading in order to promote transfer of learning.

So far, this chapter has tried to give you a "big picture" view of college writing and reading. As part of this big picture we have shown how authentic subject-matter problems are the heart of academic writing, how writers are expected to make knowledge rather just get knowledge, and how academic writing depends on rhetorical reading. Learning to think about writing and reading in this big-picture way produces the kind of deep learning that promotes transfer of your learning to your other courses, your major, and your career. In this final section of the chapter, we explain what we mean by *deep learning* and *transfer*.[3]

How Deep Learning Requires Both Knowledge-Getting and Knowledge-Making

Experts in teaching and learning have distinguished between surface learning and deep learning. Surface learning occurs when learners focus primarily on knowledge-getting, often directing their efforts toward performing well on exams. Unfortunately, knowledge gained through surface learning may be quickly forgotten, and it often doesn't transfer to other contexts. In contrast, **deep learning** occurs when students focus on underlying principles, make connections among concepts, and see patterns that link parts to a whole. Table 1.3 is a summary of the main differences between surface learning and deep learning.

Let's explore these distinctions further. Suppose that an exam question in an introductory psychology course asks students to demonstrate an understanding of operant conditioning.[4] Students might be able to do so adequately by relying primarily on their memory of textbook or lecture definitions and examples. But a paper assignment might ask students to move beyond surface learning toward

Table 1.3 Differences Between Surface Learning and Deep Learning

Surface Learning	Deep Learning
• Surface learning focuses primarily on knowledge-getting.	• Deep learning is an important part of knowledge-making.
• Surface learners tend to learn course material as unconnected bits of knowledge; they focus on memorizing facts, definitions, or routine procedures.	• Deep learning focuses on underlying principles, making connections among concepts, and seeing patterns that link parts to a whole.
• Surface learning may lead to good performance on exams but often is not retained for long.	• Deep learning is active in that students try to fit individual pieces of learning into a big picture.
• Surface learning does not lead to big-picture connections between courses and different areas of knowledge. Example: Surface learners often don't see how concepts learned in a sociology course might connect to concepts or ideas from an economics course or a history course.	• Deep learning involves applying knowledge of new disciplinary problems by making claims and arguments rather than expressing single right answers.
	• Deep learning combines knowledge-getting with knowledge-making.
	• Deep learners don't just *learn* a discipline. They *do* the discipline. Instead of simply studying history or economics, they are guided to think like historians or economists.

[3]Our ideas in this section are influenced by recent research in the scholarship of teaching and learning and in writing studies. We are particularly indebted to the following works: John D. Bransford, James W. Pelligrino, and M. Suzanne Donovan, eds. *How People Learn: Brain, Mind, Experience, and School, Expanded Edition* (Washington D.C. National Academic Press, 2000); Willingham, Daniel T. *Why Students Don't Like School: A Cognitive Scientist Answers Questions about How the Mind Works and What It Means for the Classroom* (San Francisco, Jossey-Bass, 2009); Linda Adler-Kassner and Elizabeth Wardle, *Naming What We Know: Threshold Concepts of Writing Studies* (Logan, Utah State University, 2015); and Kathleen Blake Yancey, Liane Robertson, and Kara Taczak, *Writing Across Contexts: Transfer, Composition, and Sites of Writing*, (Logan, Utah, Utah State University Press, 2014).

[4]Operant conditioning is a method of behavior modification that uses rewards and punishments to induce an organism toward one behavior or away from another behavior.

deep learning by applying this knowledge to a new problem. For example, the writing assignment might ask them to argue whether operant conditioning would be a good strategy for improving the behavior of an unruly child in a fourth-grade class, perhaps as an alternative to giving the child Ritalin (a drug often prescribed to children diagnosed with attention deficit-hyperactivity disorder, or ADHD). To write an effective paper, students would have to analyze both the strengths and the costs of this approach to modifying a child's behavior. They would have to see that there is something at stake.

Through this kind of critical thinking, students are more likely to retain the concept of "operant conditioning" for a longer time and to see its value in settings other than an end-of-term exam. The deep learning induced by this writing assignment may also change the way operant conditioning is stored in long-term memory. Brain research suggests that learners who combine knowledge-getting with knowledge-making have more elaborated neural structures in their brains so that the concept "operant conditioning" is stored in more areas of the brain. In our example, operant conditioning might get stored with other concepts from the psychology course but also stored with parenting, with fourth-grade classrooms, and with behavioral problems in children. Having to make an argument about operant conditioning in a new context helps promote deep learning while also developing writing skills.

Knowledge-Making, Transfer, and the Big Picture about Academic Writing

According to cognitive psychologists, the ways of thinking that promote deep learning—looking for patterns and underlying principles—also promote transfer of learning into new contexts. Here is an example of a big-picture concept that can be transferred from your writing course to other disciplines. In most academic writing, a writer's thesis adds something new to a conversation. This transferable concept can be encapsulated in the following template:

"Other people say (believe, argue) X, but I am going to say (show, argue) Y."[5]

There are many variations on this template, but the key idea is that your claim or thesis pushes against someone else's thesis and thus brings something new to the reader. You don't have to oppose or refute what other people say. You could qualify other people's position, contribute new ways to support their position, or simply analyze and evaluate their position. In all these cases, the tension between your view and other views helps clarify what is new or surprising in your argument. This tension also helps you show the significance of your argument. There is something is at stake in this conversation, some reason that you want to add your voice.

Given this background, you can now see why rhetorical reading is so crucial to college writing. It is through reading that the writer uncovers what other people have believed, argued, or said (the conversation surrounding a problem). Writers might also use readings as a source of evidence for their own claims (as

---

[5]Adapted from David Bartholomae, "Inventing the University," *When Writers Can't Write: Studies in Writer's Block and Other Composing Process Problems*, Ed. Mike Rose (New York, Guilford Press, 1985): 273–285.

in a research paper), or they might derive the motivating problem from something puzzling in a reading, as when literary critics argue about *Hamlet*, economists disagree about a new policy paper from the federal bank, or historians disagree about the intention and influence of an historical document.

Understanding these big-picture ideas helps you transfer your knowledge from one course to another. We don't mean, of course, that everything you learn in this course can be directly transferred to your other courses. Your first-year composition course will not teach you how to write like a scientist or a lawyer. It will not teach you how to write a psychology literature review, an anthropological ethnography, or a marketing report for business. However, it will give you big-picture concepts that help you approach new writing situations and meet the challenges of writing in other disciplines. Each of the numbered concepts in Part I of this text, as well as each of the numbered skills in Parts III and IV, are intended to be understood as transferable concepts or skills—part of the big picture of college writing.

We invite you to apply these transferable concepts and skills to the other courses you are taking this term and to future courses on your academic journey. This course will teach you about generalized academic writing, while advanced courses in your major will introduce you to your field's specialized ways of writing and thinking. What professors across disciplines value are the questioning, analyzing, and arguing skills that this course will help you develop. You will emerge from this course as a better reader, a stronger critical thinker, and a clearer and more persuasive writer, able to meet the demands of many different academic writing situations.

Besides the pragmatic benefits of college and career success, learning to write well can bring you the personal pleasure of a richer mental life. As we have explained in this chapter, writing is closely allied to thinking and to the innate satisfaction you take in exercising your curiosity, creativity, and problem-solving ability. Writing connects you to others and helps you discover and express ideas that you would otherwise never think or say. Unlike speaking, writing gives you time to think deeply about an idea. Because you can revise writing, it lets you pursue a problem in stages, with each new draft reflecting a deeper, clearer, or more complex level of thought. In other words, writing isn't just a way to express thought; it is a way to do the thinking itself. The act of writing stimulates, challenges, and stretches your mental powers and, when you do it well, is profoundly satisfying.

Chapter Summary

This chapter introduced three big-picture concepts about college writing:

Concept 1.1   Subject-matter problems are the heart of college writing. The starting point of college writing is a subject-matter problem that interests both the writer and the reader. Writers write because they have something new, surprising, or challenging to say in response to that problem. When

they make their own claims about the problem, they are making knowledge rather than simply getting knowledge. Writers can engage questions or problems that are already "out there," or they can pose their own questions.

Concept 1.2   College writers must learn to read rhetorically. College students are assigned difficult readings ranging from textbooks to scholarly journal articles to primary source readings. Textbooks, which are written specifically for students, transmit knowledge from experts to new learners and are primarily concerned with knowledge-getting. Other readings, which require knowledge-making, are not written for students and must be read rhetorically. Rhetorical readers try to reconstruct a reading's original context (purpose and intended audience) and analyze how a text works persuasively.

Concept 1.3 **Seeing the big picture about college writing promotes transfer of**

learning. The big picture in any discipline focuses on high-level organizing principles rather than low-level details. Deep learning occurs when thinkers apply new learning to new subject-matter problems rather than simply study for an exam. Deep learners see themselves as agents who can use knowledge to solve problems rather than as passive memorizers. This approach promotes transfer of learning to new contexts. The big picture of academic writing shows that a writer's claim emerges from a context of what others have said.

Brief Writing Project

An Introductory Learning and Writing Reflection

For this assignment, choose one of the following options. Each asks you to think about yourself as a learner and writer in light of the concepts presented in this chapter. Using the guiding questions, write a two-page double-spaced letter to your instructor in which you share some insights about your own learning and writing experiences. Try to connect your insights to the ideas about college-level reading and writing discussed in this chapter.

Option 1

Describe a situation from your past schooling in which you practiced the habits of problem posing and deep learning in a specific assignment or project. How did you pose your problem? How did you combine knowledge-getting and knowledge-making in your work? How did you go beyond surface learning to analyze, evaluate, or make an argument? How do you think this learning experience will be useful to you in college?

Option 2

Describe the types of writing you have done most frequently in and outside of school (personal essay, literary analysis essay, book report, position paper, argument, lab report, wiki contribution, short story, creative nonfiction, journalistic writing, blog, online discussion board, text messaging, personal letter, business letter, PowerPoint presentation, and so forth). Select several of these types of writing and explain what you enjoyed about this writing and what you found difficult. How would you describe your writing process in doing this writing? Finally, thinking about the discussion of problem posing, expert reading, and deep learning in this chapter, speculate about how the writing you will do in college and in your career will be different from and more demanding than your previous writing.

The purpose of this assignment is to encourage personal reflection about your past learning and writing experiences as you look ahead to college writing. Research on the transfer of knowledge has shown the value of students taking an inventory of their prior learning experiences in preparation for new learning. Applied to a writing course, this research suggests that you articulate what you have learned about writing so far in your previous schooling and life experiences and then anticipate the new skills and knowledge you will need for success in your college writing course, your major, and your career.

Chapter 2
Exploring Problems: Making Claims

Learning Objectives

2.1 "Wallow in complexity" in order to determine your thesis.

2.2 Use exploratory strategies to generate and deepen ideas.

2.3 Write a strong thesis statement that surprises readers with something new or challenging.

2.4 Support your thesis with organized points and related details.

> **"In management, people don't merely 'write papers,' they solve problems," said [business professor A. Kimbrough Sherman]. . . . He explained that he wanted to construct situations where students would have to "wallow in complexity" and work their way out, as managers must.**
>
> —*A. Kimbrough Sherman, Management Professor,* *Quoted by Barbara E. Walvoord and Lucille P. McCarthy*

In the previous chapter we explained that subject-matter problems are the heart of college writing. This chapter focuses on how writers explore these problems and arrive at claims.[1] We show you how experienced writers often "wallow in complexity" in their search for a claim; how they use exploratory writing to stimulate and deepen their thinking; how they construct thesis statements that bring something new, surprising, or challenging to the reader; and how they make their arguments using points and subpoints supported by details.

---

[1] In this text we use the words *claim* and *thesis statement* interchangeably. In courses across the curriculum, instructors typically use one or the other of these terms. Other synonyms for *thesis statement* include *proposition, main point,* or *thesis sentence.*

Concept 2.1: To determine their thesis, writers must often "wallow in complexity."

2.1   "Wallow in complexity" in order to determine your thesis.

The starting point of academic writing is a good, interesting question. Such questions are "knowledge-making" questions that activate your own critical thinking. They focus on unknowns or uncertainties* and invite inquirers into a problem-solving conversation that might advance knowledge or improve our world in some way. Our way of thinking about problems is motivated by the South American educator Paulo Freire, who wanted his students (often poor, illiterate villagers) to become *problematizers* instead of memorizers. Freire opposed what he called "the banking method" of education, in which students deposit knowledge in their memory banks and then make withdrawals during exams. The banking method, Freire believed, left villagers passive and helpless to improve their situations. Using the banking method, students who are learning to read and write might learn the word *water* through drill-and-skill workbook sentences such as, "The water is in the well." With Freire's problematizing method, students might learn the word *water* by asking, "Why is the water dirty and who is responsible?" Freire believed that good questions have stakes and that answering them can make a difference in the world.

Learning to Wallow in Complexity

This focus on important problems explains why college professors want students to go beyond simply understanding course concepts as taught in textbooks and lectures. Such comprehension is important, but it is only a starting point. As management professor A. Kimbrough Sherman explains in the epigraph to this chapter, college instructors expect students to wrestle with problems by applying the concepts, data, and thought processes they learn in a course to new situations. As Sherman puts it, students must learn to "wallow in complexity" and work their way out. To put it another way, college professors want students to "earn" their thesis. (Earning a thesis is very different from simply stating an opinion, which might not be deeply examined at all.)

Because college professors value complex thinking, they often phrase essay exam questions or writing assignments as open-ended problems that can be answered in more than one way. They are looking not for the right answer, but for well-supported arguments that acknowledge alternative views. A C paper and an A paper may have the same "answer" (identical thesis statements), but the C writer may have waded only ankle deep into the mud of complexity, whereas the A writer wallowed in it and worked a way out.

What skills are required for successful wallowing? Specialists in critical thinking have identified the following:

CRITICAL THINKING SKILLS NEEDED FOR "WALLOWING IN COMPLEXITY"

- The ability to pose problematic questions
- The ability to analyze a problem in all its dimensions—to define its key terms, determine its causes, understand its history, appreciate its human dimension and its connection to one's own personal experience, and appreciate what makes it problematic or complex
- The ability (and determination) to find, gather, and interpret facts, data, and other information relevant to the problem (often involving library, Internet, or field research)
- The ability to imagine alternative solutions to the problem, to see different ways in which the question might be answered and different perspectives for viewing it
- The ability to analyze competing approaches and answers, to construct arguments for and against alternatives, and to choose the best solution in light of values, objectives, and other criteria that you determine and articulate
- The ability to write an effective argument justifying your choice while acknowledging counterarguments

We discuss and develop these skills throughout this text.

Seeing Each Academic Discipline as a Field of Inquiry and Argument

In addition to general thinking abilities, critical thinking requires what psychologists call "domain-specific" skills. Each academic discipline has its own characteristic ways of approaching knowledge and its own specialized habits of mind. The questions asked by psychologists differ from those asked by historians or anthropologists; the evidence and assumptions used to support arguments in literary analysis differ from those in philosophy or sociology. Here are some examples of how different disciplines might pose different questions about rap and hip-hop music:

- *Psychology:* To what extent do hip-hop lyrics increase misogynistic or homophobic attitudes in male listeners?
- *History:* What was the role of urban housing projects in the early development of hip-hop?
- *Sociology:* How does the level of an individual's appreciation for rap music vary by ethnicity, class, age, geographic region, and gender?
- *Rhetoric/Composition:* What images of urban life do the lyrics of rap songs portray?
- *Marketing and Management:* How did the white media turn a black, urban phenomenon into corporate profits?

- *Women's Studies:* What influence does hip-hop music have on the self-image of African-American women?
- *Global Studies:* How are other countries adapting hip-hop to their cultures?

As these questions suggest, when you study a new discipline, you must learn not only the knowledge that scholars in that discipline have acquired over the years, but also the processes they used to discover that knowledge. It is useful to think of each academic discipline as a network of conversations in which participants exchange information, respond to one another's questions, and express agreement and disagreement. As each discipline evolves and changes, its central questions evolve also, creating a fascinating, dynamic conversation that defines the discipline. Table 2.1 provides examples of questions that scholars have debated over the years as well as questions they are addressing today.

This big-picture overview of scholarly conversations across disciplines points again to the centrality of questions at the heart of college writing and to the importance of "wallowing in complexity" as you seek to find your own voice in the conversation. So how do you go about wallowing in complexity? The next section shows you some powerful exploratory strategies for doing so.

Table 2.1 Scholarly Questions in Different Disciplines

Field	Examples of Current Cutting-Edge Questions	Examples of Historical Controversies
Anatomy	What is the effect of a pregnant rat's alcohol ingestion on the development of fetal eye tissue?	In 1628, William Harvey produced a treatise arguing that the heart, through repeated contractions, causes blood to circulate through the body. His views were attacked by followers of the Greek physician Galen.
Literature	To what extent does the structure of a work of literature (for example, Conrad's *Heart of Darkness*) reflect the author's class and gender bias?	In the 1920s, a group of New Critics argued that the interpretation of a work of literature should be based on close examination of the work's imagery and form and that the writer's intentions and the reader's biases were not important. These views held sway in U.S. universities until the late 1960s, when they came increasingly under attack by deconstructionists and other postmodernists, who claimed that author intentions and reader's bias are important parts of the work's meaning.
Rhetoric/ Composition	How does hypertext structure and increased attention to visual images in Web-based writing affect writers' composing processes?	Prior to the 1970s, college writing courses in the United States were typically organized around the rhetorical modes (description, narration, exemplification, comparison and contrast, and so forth). This approach was criticized by the expressivist school associated with the British composition researcher James Britton. Since the 1980s, composition scholars have proposed various alternative strategies for designing and sequencing assignments.
Psychology	What are the underlying causes of gender identification along the continuum from female to intersex/transgender to male? To what extent is gender identification attributable to nature (genetics, body chemistry) versus nurture (social learning)?	In the early 1900s under the influence of Sigmund Freud, psychoanalytic psychologists began explaining human behavior in terms of unconscious drives and mental processes that stemmed from repressed childhood experiences. Later, psychoanalysts were opposed by behaviorists, who rejected the notion of the unconscious and explained behavior as responses to environmental stimuli.

Concept 2.2: Expert writers use exploratory strategies to generate and deepen their ideas.

2.2 Use exploratory strategies to generate and deepen ideas.

One of the important discoveries of research in rhetoric and composition is the extent to which experienced writers use writing as a strategy to generate and discover ideas. In other words, not all writing is intended as a final product for readers. The very act of writing—often without concern for audience, structure, or correctness—can stimulate the mind to produce ideas. Moreover, when you write down your thoughts, you'll have a record of your thinking on which you can draw later.

In this section we first describe four exploratory writing and talking strategies to stimulate thinking: freewriting, focused freewriting, idea mapping, and dialectic conversation. We then explain two idea-generating "games" that will broaden and deepen your thinking, often taking you out of your comfort zone: the "believing and doubting game" and the "analysis game."

Four Strategies for Exploratory Writing and Talking

When expert writers explain their thinking process, they often describe a repeated cycle of "writing" and "cooking" (or "incubating"). By *cooking* or *incubating* they mean letting their ideas sit in the heat of the subconscious while they do something else—go for a walk, nap, stare out the window, or take time off for recreation or other tasks. The more obviously active part of generating ideas is writing—not finished-product writing but writing simply to make thoughts visible. Experts write on the backs of envelopes or in a journal or in the margins of what they are reading or in a rapidly composed first draft. This writing is exploratory, done with faith that the actual movement of a pen on paper or hands on a keyboard somehow stimulates the brain. Here are four exploratory strategies.

FREEWRITING *Freewriting*, sometimes called *nonstop writing* or *silent, sustained writing*, asks you to record your thinking directly. To freewrite, put pen to paper (or sit at your computer screen, perhaps turning *off* the monitor so that you can't see what you are writing) and write rapidly, *nonstop*, for ten to fifteen minutes at a stretch. Don't worry about grammar, spelling, organization, transitions, or other features of edited writing. The object is to think of as many ideas as possible. Some freewriting looks like an unedited stream of free-flowing thoughts. Some is more organized and focused, although it lacks the logical connections and development that would make it suitable for an audience of strangers.

Many freewriters find that their initial reservoir of ideas runs out in three to five minutes. If this happens, force yourself to keep your fingers moving. If you can't think of anything to say, write, "Relax" over and over (or "This is stupid" or "I'm stuck") until new ideas emerge.

What do you write about? The answer varies according to your situation. Often you will freewrite in response to a question or problem posed by your instructor. Sometimes you will pose your own questions and use freewriting to explore possible answers or simply to generate ideas.

The following freewrite, by student writer Kent Ansen, formed the starting point for his later exploration of mandatory public service. It was written in response to a class discussion of service learning. We will return to Kent's story occasionally throughout this text.

KENT ANSEN'S INITIAL FREEWRITE

The class discussion of service learning was interesting. Hmmm. What do young people gain from community service? I gained a lot from my own volunteer activities in high school. They taught me about my neighbors and myself. Would it be a good idea for every American citizen to have some kind of public service experience? But that would make it mandatory. Interesting idea—mandatory community service program, sort of like the draft. Hmmm. What could it offer the country and young adults? The word that keeps catching my attention is "mandatory." The immediate connection that comes to mind is the military draft during the Vietnam War and all of the protests that went along with it. I think what really bothered people was that they didn't want to be forced to risk their lives for what they considered to be an unjust war. As a contemporary example, Israel requires a term of military service from its young citizens, although I am not sure of the particulars or of its level of support among young people and society at large. Mandatory *civil* service, on the other hand, would be controversial for different reasons. While the program would not ask people to risk their lives, it would still impose a requirement that significantly affects a person's life. I can hear the outcry already from those who oppose government involvement in citizens' choices and lives. I am not sure I disagree with them on this issue, particularly as I consider what I assume would be the high cost of a mandatory national service program and the major federal budget cuts that recently went into effect. On the other hand, when I think of how much money went into the Iraq War, I wonder why it at times seems less controversial to fund activities that tear communities apart rather than something like national service, which would probably make our communities a better place. I wonder [out of time]

Note how this freewrite rambles, moving associatively from one topic or question to the next. Freewrites often have this kind of loose, associative structure. The value of such freewrites is that they help writers discover areas of interest or rudimentary beginnings of ideas. When you read back over one of your freewrites, try to find places that seem worth pursuing. Freewriters call these places *hot spots, centers of interest, centers of gravity*, or simply *nuggets* or *seeds*. Because we believe this technique is of great value to writers, we suggest that you use it to generate ideas for class discussions and essays.

FOCUSED FREEWRITING   Freewriting, as we have just described it, can be quick and associational, like brainstorming aloud on paper. Focused freewriting, in contrast, is less associational and aimed more at developing a line of thought. You wrestle with a specific problem or question, trying to think and write your way into its complexity and multiple points of view. Because the writing is still informal, with the emphasis on your ideas and not on making your writing grammatically or stylistically polished, you don't have to worry about spelling, punctuation, grammar, or organizational structure. Your purpose is to deepen and extend your thinking on the problem. Some instructors will create prompts or give you specific questions to ponder, and they may call this kind of exploratory writing *focused freewriting*, *thought papers*, *learning log pieces*, *journal entries*, or *thinking pieces*.

IDEA MAPPING Another good technique for exploring ideas is *idea mapping*, a more visual method than freewriting. To make an idea map, draw a circle in the center of a page and write down your broad topic area (or a triggering question or your tentative thesis) inside the circle. Then record your ideas on branches and subbranches that extend out from the center circle. As long as you pursue one train of thought, keep recording your ideas on subbranches off the main branch. But as soon as that chain of ideas runs dry, go back and start a new branch.

Often your thoughts will jump back and forth between one branch and another. This technique will help you see them as part of an emerging design rather than as strings of unrelated ideas. Additionally, idea mapping establishes a sense of hierarchy in your ideas. If you enter an idea on a subbranch, you can see that you are more fully developing a previous idea. If you return to the hub and start a new branch, you can see that you are beginning a new train of thought.

An idea map usually records more ideas than a freewrite, but the ideas in an idea map are not as fully developed. Writers who practice both techniques report that they can vary the kinds of ideas they generate depending on which technique they choose. Figure 2.1 shows a student's idea map made while he was exploring issues related to the grading system.

DIALECTIC CONVERSATION Another effective way to explore the complexity of a topic is through dialectic discussions with others, whether in class, in the student union, late at night in a coffee shop, or online in blogs or discussion boards. Not all discussions are productive; some are too superficial and scattered, others too heated. Good ones are *dialectic*—that is, participants with differing views on a topic try to understand one another and resolve their differences by examining contradictions in each person's position.

The key to dialectic conversation is careful listening, which is made possible by an openness to other people's views. A dialectic discussion differs from a talk-show shouting match or a pro–con debate in which proponents of opposing positions, their views set in stone, attempt to win the argument. In a dialectic discussion, participants assume that each position has strengths and weaknesses and that even the strongest position contains inconsistencies, which should be exposed and examined. When dialectic conversation works well, participants scrutinize their own positions more critically and deeply, and they often alter their views. True dialectic conversation implies growth and change, not a hardening of positions.

Dialectic discussion can be particularly effective online through electronic discussion boards, chat rooms, blogs, and other digital sites for the informal exchange of ideas. If your goal is to generate ideas, your stance should be the exact opposite of the flamer's stance. A flamer's intention is to use brute rhetorical power (sometimes mindlessly obscene or mean, sometimes clever and humorous) to humiliate another writer and shut off further discussion. In contrast, the dialectician's goal is to listen respectfully to other ideas, to test new ways of thinking, to modify ideas in the face of other views, and to see as many sides of an issue as possible. If you take part in a discussion board to learn and

Figure 2.1 Idea Map on Problems with the Grading System

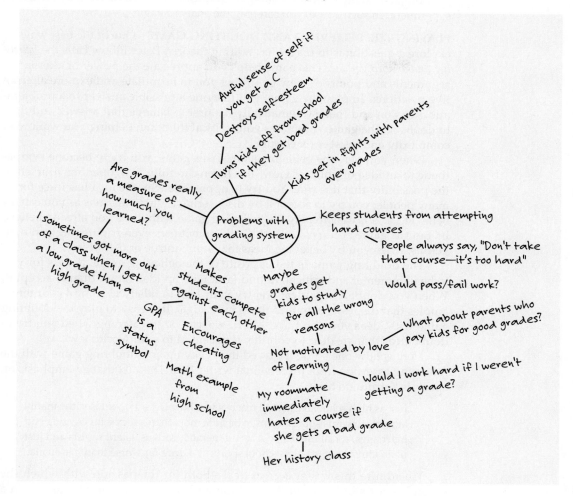

change, rather than to defend your own position and shut off other views, you will be surprised at how powerful this medium can be.

Two Heuristic Games for Generating, Extending, and Deepening Thought

A **heuristic** (from the Greek word for "find" or "discover") is an easy-to-remember, repeatable, gamelike strategy that helps you generate new ideas or discover new perspectives. This section explains two powerful heuristic games. The first is the *believing and doubting game*, which you can play whenever you are wrestling with a problem that is already "out there." When you play this game, you usually summarize one point of view and then systematically believe and then doubt that point of view. The second is the *analysis game*, which you can play whenever you have to find the problem yourself through your own observations. For example, you might be asked to analyze something—a photograph, painting, poem, short story, musical score, advertisement, sociological phenomenon, data set (from a table or graph), or the results from a laboratory experiment. In such a case, you can play the analysis game.

PLAYING THE BELIEVING AND DOUBTING GAME   One of the best ways to explore a question is to play what writing theorist Peter Elbow calls the *believing and doubting game*. This game helps you appreciate the power of alternative arguments and points of view by urging you to formulate and explore alternative positions. To play the game, you imagine a possible answer to a problematic question and then systematically try first to believe that answer and then to doubt it. The game stimulates your critical thinking, helping you wallow in complexity and resist early closure.

When you play the believing side of this game, you try to become sympathetic to an idea or point of view. You listen carefully to it, opening yourself to the possibility that it is true. You try to appreciate why the idea has force for so many people; you try to accept it by discovering as many reasons as you can for believing it. It is easy to play the believing game with ideas you already believe in, but the game becomes more difficult, sometimes even frightening and dangerous, when you try believing ideas that seem untrue or disturbing.

The doubting game is the opposite of the believing game. It calls for you to be judgmental and critical, to find fault with an idea rather than to accept it. When you doubt a new idea, you try your best to falsify it, to find counterexamples that disprove it, to find flaws in its logic. It is easy to play the doubting game with ideas you don't like, but it, too, can be threatening when you try to doubt ideas that are dear to your heart or central to your worldview.

Here is how one student played the believing and doubting game with the following assertion from professional writer Paul Theroux that an emphasis on sports is harmful to boys.

> Just as high school basketball teaches you how to be a poor loser, the manly attitude towards sports seems to be little more than a recipe for creating bad marriages, social misfits, moral degenerates, sadists, latent rapists and just plain louts. I regard high school sports as a drug far worse than marijuana.

We admire this writer a great deal—both for the passion with which she defends sports in her doubting section and for the courage of walking in a sports basher's shoes in the believing section. This exercise clearly engaged and stretched her thinking.

Believing and Doubting Paul Theroux's Negative View of Sports

Believe

1   Although I am a woman I have a hard time believing this because I was a high school basketball player and believe high school sports are *very* important. But here goes. I will try to believe this statement even though I hate it. Let's see. It would seem that I wouldn't have much first-hand experience with how society turns

(continued)

boys into men. I do see though that Theroux is right about some major problems. Through my observations, I've seen many young boys go through humiliating experiences with sports that have left them scarred. For example, a 7-year-old boy, Matt, isn't very athletic and when kids in our neighborhood choose teams, they usually choose girls before they choose Matt. I wonder if he sees himself as a loser and what this does to him? I have also experienced some first-hand adverse effects of society's methods of turning boys into men. In our family, my dad spent much of his time playing football, basketball, and baseball with my brother. I've loved sports since I was very young so I was eager to play. In order to play with them, I had to play like a boy. Being told you threw or played like a girl was the worst possible insult you could receive. The phrase, "be tough" was something I heard repeatedly while I was growing up. Whenever I got hurt, my dad would say, "Be tough." It didn't matter how badly I was hurt, I always heard the same message. Today, I think, I have a very, very difficult time opening up and letting people get to know me, because for so long I was taught to keep everything inside. Maybe sports does have some bad effects.

Doubt

2 I am glad I get to doubt this too because I have been really mad at all the sports bashing that has been going on in class. I think much of what Theroux says is just a crock. I know that the statement "sports builds character" is a cliché, but I really believe it. It seems to me that the people who lash out at sports clichés are those who never experienced these aspects of athletics and therefore don't understand them. No one can tell me that sports didn't contribute to some of my best and most meaningful friendships and growing experiences. I am convinced that I am a better person because through sports I have had to deal with failure, defeat, frustration, sacrificing individual desires for the benefit of the team, and so on. After my last high school basketball game when after many years of mind games, of hating my coach one minute and the next having deep respect for him, of big games lost on my mistakes, of hours spent alone in the gym, of wondering if the end justifies the means, my coach gave me a big pat on the back and told me how proud he was of me. Everything, all the pain, frustration, anxiety, fear, and sacrifice of the past years seemed so worthwhile. You might try to tell me that this story is hackneyed and trite, but I won't listen because it is a part of me, and something you will never be able to damage or take away. I think athletes share a special bond. They know what it is like to go through the physical pain of practice time and again. They understand the wide variety of emotions felt (but rarely expressed). They also know what a big role the friendships of teammates and coaches play in an athlete's life.

PLAYING THE ANALYSIS GAME   **Analysis** is a thinking strategy in which the thinker observes the whole, breaks the whole down into parts, and then examines the connections of the parts to one another and to the whole. If you are asked to

---

For Writing and Discussion
Using Exploratory Writing and Talking to Play the Believing and Doubting Game

Playing the believing and doubting game. On your own, play the believing/doubting game with one of the following controversial assertions or another assertion provided by your instructor. First spend at least five minutes believing the assertion. Then spend the same amount of time doubting the assertion.

(continued)

- Although hateful or mean comments about nearby individuals or groups are almost a daily occurrence on YikYak, high schools and colleges should not try to ban YikYak.
- It is always wrong to tell a lie.
- Athletes should be allowed to use steroids and other performance-enhancing drugs.

Dialectic conversation. Share ideas you discovered during this process with your classmates. Also share reflections on whether (for you) playing the believing side or the doubting side was more difficult and why. Which side was more helpful for extending your thinking?

analyze something (for example, write an analysis paper), the *analysis game* helps you find something new, interesting, or enlightening to say. Your job is to increase your readers' understanding or appreciation of the object being analyzed. At the root of the analysis game is an insight from philosopher Ludwig Wittgenstein: "Everything we see could be otherwise." The game urges you to *defamiliarize* the object you are analyzing—to see it new by imagining how key parts might have been something else. You can then ask why the part is the way it is.

You can play the analysis game with almost anything that can be observed. In some cases, you can observe something all at once (a painting, a photograph, a short poem, a data table, a print ad, a spider web). At other times, the object to be analyzed has to be observed through time (a video, a film, a short story, a magazine article, the spider's process while making a web). For this introduction to the analysis game, we will focus on analyzing a painting. More examples occur throughout this textbook. When you analyze a human-made artifact (such as a painting, a poem, or a piece of architecture), you often raise questions about the artist's intentions, about the impact of the artwork on the observer, or about the artifact's theme or meaning. When you analyze a natural or cultural object/phenomenon in the sciences or social sciences (such as lab results or observations of gendered behavior in a classroom), you often ask questions about function, evolutionary or cultural origins, or future implications but not (unless you are thinking theologically or philosophically) about purpose or meaning.

We will first present an overview of the steps in the analysis game. We will then illustrate it with an analysis of a painting.

STEPS IN THE ANALYSIS GAME

- **Dwell with the object by observing it carefully and then describing it (or summarizing it) for someone else.** Look at the whole; then look at each part. Consider the relationship of each part to other parts and to the whole. Open yourself to the object. Listen to it. Notice everything down to the smallest details. Don't judge. Don't interpret. Your goal at this stage is to write a description of the object for someone who hasn't seen it. If you are analyzing a reading or a short story, your goal would be to write a summary or a plot summary. If you are analyzing a data table, you would demonstrate knowledge of what the table shows, its units of measure, the meanings of its labels, and so forth.
- **Start the analysis by identifying patterns or disruptions in the pattern and noting puzzles.** Note repetitions, contrasts, or oppositions. What patterns or parts are emphasized? What fits or doesn't fit? What parts meet or don't meet your expectations? What associations are triggered by various parts? Are there patterns or oppositions in these

associations? Begin making notes on what is unusual or puzzling. In a poem, what words or images get repeated or form contrasts? In a data table, what stories are being told through different patterns observed in rows and columns?

- **For selected parts, ask why the part is this way rather than some other way**. Apply to your object Wittgenstein's observation that "everything we see could be otherwise." This process makes the familiar unfamiliar or unstable. For human-made artifacts, begin speculating why the maker made this choice rather than some other choice. Why is the tree in this poem a willow rather than a maple? In analyzing a natural phenomenon, imagine how nature might have been different. Why does this planet orbit in an ellipse rather than a circle?

- **Pose one or two key questions that could serve as the starting point of your analysis.** Posing a question is the heart of your own knowledge-making process.

- **Use freewriting, idea mapping, or dialectic conversation to explore possible answers to your question**. You are now looking for meanings, explanations, interpretations, and larger understandings. You are adding your voice to the conversation. You are wallowing in complexity.

Let's now illustrate the analysis game using a student writer's attempt to analyze Dorothea Tanning's surrealist painting *Portrait de Famille* reproduced at the end of Concept 1.1. We'll use excerpts from the student's exploratory writing so that you can see the stages of her thinking as she worked through the steps of the analysis game.

A Student's Exploratory Writing For Each Step in the Analysis Game

Step 1: Dwell with the object by observing it carefully and then describing it for someone else.	Tanning's painting shows a dinner table on which sit a serving dish, a basket of bread, and other objects, but no silverware or glasses. The right side of the table is not shown. At the left side sits a young woman with shoulder-length blonde hair. She sits up straight with her hands on her lap. Sitting on the far side of the table is a man drawn to a proportion perhaps three times larger than the woman. He dominates the far side of the table. He wears a brown suit and a yellow tie. The top of his head is cut off above the eyes so that his round glasses draw the viewer's attention. At the front side of the table stands what appears to be a maid or cook wearing an apron. Her hair is tied up in a knot. She appears to be giving a treat to a furry poodle-like dog that is sitting up as if taught a trick. Both the dog and the maid are drawn to proportions much smaller than the woman sitting at the table. The maid seems to be about the same height as the table. The dog seems to be large compared to the maid but small compared to the sitting woman.
Step 2: Start the analysis by identifying patterns or disruptions in the pattern and noting puzzles.	The reader expects a portrait of a family, but the proportions are all distorted with a huge male figure and diminutive maid. The man is apparently the father figure in the portrait but there doesn't seem to be any mother. (Do we imagine her seated at the cut off end of the table?) The seated woman seems to be a daughter since she is considerably younger than the father. Why does the artist not put the father's forehead in the frame? Why the emphasis on the glasses? Also why is the maid/cook giving a treat to the dog instead of facing forward as part of the family portrait? Why does the artist draw her so small? [This exploration continues . . .]

Step 3: For selected parts, ask why the part is this way rather than some other way.	Tanning could have drawn the father without glasses or she could have made the lens in the glasses less mirror-like so that we could see the father's eyes. What is she trying to do with the glasses? I don't think she likes the father, but he doesn't look mean. She could have drawn a more threatening father who seemed mean or abusive. However, she makes him seem ordinary middle class—boring with a brown suit. If he isn't mean and is just ordinary, what makes him seem ominous? I still think it has something to do with the glasses.
	Why did she frame the portrait so that the right side of the table is missing? She could have included the whole table and drawn in a mother figure. Why is the mother figure missing?
	She could have had the maid/cook normal sized and serving the dinner. Why is she drawn small and why is she giving a treat to the dog?
	It might be typical to include a dog in a family portrait. But why does she have the dog doing a sit up trick? Why did she choose a poodle-like dog instead of lab or a retriever?
Step 4: Pose one or two key questions that could serve as the starting point of your analysis.	The question that most intrigues me is this: What is the effect of the father's glasses, which seem to dominate the painting?
	A related question is this: Why is the maid tiny and why is she shown interacting with the dog rather than the family?
Step 5: Use freewriting, idea mapping, or dialectic conversation to explore possible answers to your question.	OK here goes my freewrite. I think this painting tries to show how the male perspective dominates the artist's world. The father doesn't seem mean or abusive, just very ordinary middle class with his brown suit. His brain also isn't emphasized since the top of his head is cut out of the frame. It is the glasses that dominate, suggesting that the man sees everything and what he sees gets to be counted as most important. Apparently what he sees or feels is that women are trivial. The mother doesn't even have to be in the picture and the maid seems to be less important than the dog. Perhaps the woman sitting in the chair is Tanning, the artist, and she remembers her family as dominated by a patriarchal male perspective. The father looms large while the mother is absent and the maid is trivialized and shown as someone in a serving role. If Tanning had painted a realistic family portrait, she would have drawn the family as it appears in actuality. In that case, she wouldn't have been able to express what it felt like to grow up in that family. [The freewrite continues . .]

For Writing and Discussion
Using Exploratory Writing and Talking to Play the Analysis Game

Playing the analysis game. On your own or in small groups, play the analysis game to analyze *Mad Cow Motorcycle* by Billie Grace Lynn (at the beginning of Part 1) or some other image or artifact provided by your instructor. Follow each step of the game.

Dialectic conversation. Share ideas you discovered during this process with your classmates.

Concept 2.3: A strong thesis statement surprises readers with something new or challenging.

2.3   Write a strong thesis statement that surprises readers with something new or challenging.

The strategies for exploring ideas that we offered in the previous section can prepare you to move from posing problems to proposing solutions. Your answer to your subject-matter question becomes your **thesis statement**. In this section we show that a good thesis surprises its readers either by bringing something new to the reader or by pushing against other possible ways to answer the writer's question.

A strong thesis usually contains an element of uncertainty, risk, or challenge. A strong thesis implies a naysayer who could disagree with you. According to composition theorist Peter Elbow, a thesis has "got to stick its neck out, not just hedge or wander. [It is] something that can be quarreled with." Elbow's sticking-its-neck-out metaphor is a good one, but we prefer to say that a strong thesis *surprises* the reader with a new, unexpected, different, or challenging view of the writer's topic. By *surprise*, we intend to connote, first of all, the thesis statement's freshness or newness for the reader. Many kinds of closed-form prose don't have a sharply contestable thesis of the sticking-its-neck-out kind highlighted by Elbow. For example, a geology report may provide readers with desired information about rock strata in an exposed cliff, or a Web page for diabetics may explain how to coordinate meals and insulin injections during a plane trip across time zones. In these cases, the information is surprising because it brings something new and significant to intended readers.

In other kinds of thesis-governed prose, especially academic or civic prose addressing a problematic question or a disputed issue, surprise requires an argumentative, risky, or contestable thesis. In these cases also, surprise is not inherent in the material itself but rather in the mind of the targeted reader; it comes from the way the thesis brings the reader something new or challenging.

In this section, we present two ways of creating a surprising thesis: (1) trying to change your reader's view of your subject; and (2) giving your thesis tension.

Trying to Change Your Reader's View of Your Subject

To change your reader's view of your subject, you must first imagine how the reader would view the subject *before* reading your essay. Then you can articulate how you aim to change that view. A useful exercise is to write out the "before" and "after" views of your imagined readers:

Before reading my essay, my readers think this way about my topic:

_____

_____

_____

After reading my essay, my readers will think this different way about my topic:

_____

_____

You can change your reader's view of a subject in several ways.*

1. *You can enlarge your reader's view.* Writing that enlarges a view is primarily informational. It provides new ideas and data to a reader's store of

---

* Our discussion of how writing changes a reader's view of the world is indebted to Richard Young, Alton Becker, and Kenneth Pike, *Rhetoric: Discovery and Change* (New York: Harcourt Brace & Company, 1971).

knowledge about the subject. For example, suppose you are interested in the problem of storing nuclear waste (a highly controversial issue in the United States) and decide to investigate how France stores radioactive waste from its nuclear power plants. You could report your researched findings on this problem in an informative paper. ("Before reading my paper, readers would be uncertain how France stores nuclear waste. After reading my paper, my readers would understand the French methods, possibly helping them better understand our options in the United States.")

2. *You can clarify your reader's view of something that was previously fuzzy, tentative, or uncertain.* Writing of this kind often explains, analyzes, or interprets. You do this kind of writing when you analyze a short story, a painting, an historical document, a set of economic data, or other puzzling phenomena or when you speculate on the cause, consequence, purpose, or function of something. Suppose you are analyzing the persuasive strategies used by various clothing ads. You are intrigued by a jeans ad that you "read" differently from your classmates. ("Before reading my paper, my readers will think that this jeans ad reveals a liberated woman, but after reading my paper they will see that the ad reinforces traditional gender stereotypes.")

3. *You can restructure readers' whole view of a subject.* Such essays persuade readers to change their mind or urge them to action. For example, in a letter to the editor of a local newspaper, a civil engineer wants to change his readers' views about wind power. ("Before reading my letter, readers will believe that wind-generated electricity can solve our energy crisis, but after reading my letter, they will see that the hope of wind power is a pipe dream.") (You can read his letter to the editor in Concept 3.1.)

Surprise, then, is the measure of change an essay brings about in a reader. Of course, to bring about such change requires more than just a surprising thesis; the essay itself must persuade the reader that the thesis is both sound and novel.

Giving Your Thesis Tension through "Surprising Reversal"

Another element of a surprising thesis is tension. By *tension* we mean the reader's sensation of being pulled away from familiar ideas toward new, unfamiliar ones. A strategy for creating this tension—a strategy we call *surprising reversal*—is to contrast your surprising answer to a question with your targeted audience's common answer, creating tension between your own thesis and one or more alternative views. Its basic template is as follows:

> "Many people believe X (common view), but I am going to show Y (new, surprising view)."

The concept of surprising reversal spurs the writer to go beyond the commonplace to change the reader's view of a topic.

One of the best ways to employ this strategy is to begin your thesis statement with an "although" clause that summarizes the reader's "before" view or the counterclaim that your essay opposes; the main clause states the surprising view or position that your essay will support. You may choose to omit the *although* clause from your actual essay, but formulating it first will help you achieve focus and surprise in your thesis. The following examples illustrate the kinds of tension we have been discussing and show why tension is a key requirement for a good thesis.

Question 1	What effect has the cell phone had on our culture?
Thesis without Tension	The invention of the cell phone has brought many advantages to our culture.
Thesis with Tension	Although the cell phone has brought many advantages to our culture, it may also have contributed to an increase in risky behavior among boaters and hikers.
Question 2	Do reservations serve a useful role in contemporary Native American culture?
Thesis without Tension	Reservations have good points and bad points.
Thesis with Tension	Although my friend Wilson Real Bird believes that reservations are necessary for Native Americans to preserve their heritage, the continuation of reservations actually degrades Native American culture.

In the first example, the thesis without tension (cell phones have brought advantages to our culture) is a truism with which everyone would agree and hence lacks surprise. The thesis with tension places this truism (the reader's "before" view) in an *although* clause and goes on to make a surprising or contestable assertion. The idea that the cell phone contributes to risky behavior among outdoor enthusiasts alters our initial, complacent view of the cell phone and gives us new ideas to think about.

In the second example, the thesis without tension may not at first seem tensionless because the writer sets up an opposition between good and bad points. But *almost anything* has good and bad points, so the opposition is not meaningful, and the thesis offers no element of surprise. Substitute virtually any other social institution (marriage, the postal service, the military, prisons), and the statement that it has good and bad points would be equally true. The thesis with tension, in contrast, is risky. It commits the writer to argue that reservations have degraded Native American culture and to oppose the counterthesis that reservations are needed to *preserve* Native American culture. The reader now feels genuine tension between two opposing views.

Tension, then, is a component of surprise. The writer's goal is to surprise the reader in some way, thereby bringing about some kind of change in the reader's view. As you are wallowing in complexity about your subject-matter problem, try the strategies in Strategies Chart 2.1 for bringing something new, surprising, or challenging to your targeted readers.

Strategies Chart 2.1 Strategies for Creating a Thesis with Tension or Surprise

How You Became Gripped with a Problem	Example of a Problem	Your Strategy while You "Wallow in Complexity"	Possible Thesis with Tension or Surprise
	The problem is already "out there."		
	(You enter a conversation already in progress.)		
You don't know where you stand on an issue.	Should health care be rationed?	Look at all sides of the issue, including all the available data, to determine where you stand based on your own examined values.	Although rationing health care at first seems inhumane, it may be the only ethical way to provide affordable health care to all citizens.
You do know where you stand on an issue but your position hasn't yet been "earned." [*You need to move from an opinion to an earned thesis.*]	Shanita says that we should build more nuclear power plants to combat global warming, but I say nuclear power is too dangerous.	Research the strengths of the opposing views and the weaknesses of your own view. (*Note: You may change your mind.*)	Although nuclear power poses danger from storage of waste or possible meltdown, the benefits of reducing greenhouse gases and cutting coal pollution outweigh the dangers.
Someone gives you a question that you can't yet answer.	Your boss asks you whether the company should enact the proposed marketing plan.	Do the research, critical thinking, and analysis needed to propose the "best solution" to the boss's question.	The marketing team's proposal, despite its creative advertising plan, is too risky to undertake at this time.
	You pose the problem yourself.		
	(You initiate the conversation.)		
You see something puzzling in a natural phenomenon or a cultural activity or artifact.	Why does Tanning give the father figure such noticeable glasses while cutting off the top of his head?	Through critical thinking and further analysis of the whole painting, try to figure out a plausible answer to your question.	Although Tanning does not make the father figure look mean or abusive, he is nevertheless threatening because his male vision of the world, symbolized by his glasses, dominates the painting.
You discover something inconsistent or contradictory in your own view of the world.	I agree with this writer's argument against consumerism, but I really want a large plasma TV. Is consumerism really bad? Am I a materialist?	Reflect on your own values and beliefs; try to achieve a consistent stand with regard to enduring social or ethical issues.	Although this writer makes me consider the potential shallowness of my desire for a huge plasma TV, I don't think I'm necessarily a materialist.

For Writing and Discussion
Developing Thesis Statements out of Questions

Writers can't create thesis statements on the spot because a thesis grows out of a writer's extended intellectual struggle with a problem. However, in response to a question one can often propose a hypothetical claim and treat it as a tentative thesis statement for testing. This exercise asks you to try this approach—formulate a surprising thesis statement that you could then test further through more exploration. We provide three possible questions for exploration. Your instructor might give you a different question. In formulating your claim, also imagine a targeted audience that would find your claim new, challenging, or otherwise surprising. Finally, speculate on the kinds of evidence you would need to support your thesis.

1. What can an individual do, if anything, to combat climate change? (Note: Your thesis will have no tension or surprise if you only state the obvious—that is, take the bus or change light bulbs.)

2. What should the federal government do, if anything, to help reduce the number of mass shootings in the United States?

3. What might be done, if anything, to combat the high cost of college?

Here is an example:

Problematic question: What can cities do to prevent traffic congestion?

One possible thesis: Although many people think that little can be done to get people out of their beloved cars, new light-rail systems in many cities have attracted former car commuters and alleviated traffic problems.

Intended audience: Residents of cities concerned about traffic congestion but skeptical about light rail

Kinds of evidence needed to support thesis: Examples of cities with successful light-rail systems; evidence that many riders switched from driving cars; evidence that the light-rail system alleviated traffic problems

Concept 2.4: A thesis is supported with organized points and related details.

2.4   Support your thesis with organized points and related details.

A surprising thesis is only one aspect of an effective essay. An essay must also persuade the reader that the thesis is believable as well as surprising. Although tabloid newspapers have shocking headlines ("Dolphin Grows Human Arms"), skepticism quickly replaces surprise when you look inside and find the article's claims unsupported. A strong thesis, then, must both surprise the reader *and* be supported with convincing points and details.

In fact, the details are the flesh and muscle of writing and comprise most of the sentences. In thesis-governed prose, these details are connected clearly to points, and the points are stated first. In this section, we explain this principle more fully.

How Points Convert Information to Meaning

Points are generalizations that assert a meaning. When details are clearly related to a point, the point gives meaning to the details, and the details give force and validity to the point. Details constitute the evidence, data, facts, examples, and subarguments that develop a point and make it convincing. By themselves, details are simply information—mere data without meaning.

In the following example, you can see for yourself the difference between information and meaning. Here is a list of information:

- Male chimpanzees win dominance by brawling
- To terrorize rival troops, they kill females and infants.

- The level of aggression among monkeys can be manipulated by adjusting their testosterone levels.
- Among humans, preliminary research suggests that male fetuses are more active in the uterus than female fetuses.
- Little boys play more aggressively than little girls despite parental efforts to teach gentleness to boys and aggression to girls.

To make meaning out of this list of information, the writer needs to state a point—the idea, generalization, or claim—that this information supports. Once the point is stated, a meaningful unit (a point accompanied by relevant details) springs into being:

> *In almost all species on Earth, males are more aggressive than females.* Male chimpanzees win dominance by brawling; to terrorize rival troops, they kill females and infants. Researchers have shown that the level of aggression among monkeys can be manipulated by adjusting their testosterone levels. Among humans, preliminary research suggests that male fetuses are more active in the uterus than female fetuses. Also, little boys play more aggressively than little girls despite parental efforts to teach gentleness to boys and aggression to girls.

Once the writer states this point, readers can see that the writer is taking the side of biology rather than culture to explain differences in gendered behavior. The writer now uses details as evidence to support this contestable point.

To appreciate the reader's need for a logical connection between points and particulars, note how readers would get lost if, in the preceding example, the writer included a particular that seemed unrelated to the point ("Males also tend to be taller and heavier than women"—a factual statement, but what does it have to do with aggression?) or if, without explanation, the writer added a particular that seemed to contradict the point ("Fathers play more roughly with baby boys than with baby girls"—another fact observed by sociologists, but one that points to culture rather than biology as a determiner of aggression).

Obviously, reasonable people seek some kind of coordination between points and details, some sort of weaving back and forth between them. Writing teachers use a number of nearly synonymous terms for expressing this paired relationship: *points/details, generalizations/specifics, claims/evidence, ideas/data, meaning/support.*

How Removing Details Creates a Summary

What we have shown, then, is that skilled writers weave back and forth between generalizations and specifics. The generalizations form a network of higher-level and lower-level points that develop the thesis; the details (specifics) support each of the points and subpoints in turn. In thesis-driven prose, the network of points is easily discernible because points are clearly highlighted with transitions, and main points are placed prominently at the start of paragraphs.

If you remove most of the details from an essay, leaving only the network of points, you will have written a summary or abstract of the essay. The ability to write summaries is an essential skill for college-level writing. We explain how to write summaries in Chapter 6.

Using Your Understanding of Points and Details When You Revise

The lesson to learn here is that in thesis-governed prose, writers regularly place a **point sentence** in front of detail sentences. When a writer begins with a point, readers interpret the ensuing details not as random data but as *evidence* in support of that point. The writer depends on the details to make the point credible and persuasive.

This insight may help you understand two of the most common kinds of marginal comments that readers (or teachers) place on writers' early drafts. If your draft has a string of sentences giving data or information unconnected to any stated point, your reader is likely to write in the margin, "What's your point here?" or "Why are you telling me this information?" or "How does this information relate to your thesis?" Conversely, if your draft tries to make a point that isn't developed with details, your reader is likely to write marginal comments such as "Evidence?" or "Development?" or "Could you give an example?" or "More specifics needed."

Don't be put off by these requests; they are a gift. It is common in first drafts for main points to be unstated, buried, or otherwise disconnected from their details and for supporting information to be scattered confusingly throughout the draft or missing entirely. Having to write point sentences obliges you to wrestle with your intended meaning: Just what am I trying to say here? How can I nutshell that in a point? Likewise, having to support your points with details causes you to wrestle with the content and shape of your argument: What details will make this point convincing? What further research do I need to do to find these specifics?

Chapter Summary

This chapter has introduced four concepts that comprise important critical thinking strategies for exploring problems and developing claims.

Concept 2.1   To determine their thesis, writers must often "wallow in complexity." Academic writing is initiated by a subject-matter question that forces thinkers to explore the problem's complexity before arriving at a thesis. To earn their thesis (rather than simply state an unearned opinion) writers must wallow in complexity.

Concept 2.2   Expert writers use exploratory strategies to generate and deepen their ideas. Besides letting ideas cook in their subconscious, experienced writers use exploratory writing to generate and deepen ideas. These strategies include freewriting, focused freewriting, idea mapping, and dialectic talk, as well as two heuristic games—the believing and doubting game and the analysis game.

Concept 2.3   A strong thesis surprises readers with something new or challenging. A good thesis tries to change the reader's view of the subject and often creates tension by pushing against alternative views.

Concept 2.4   A thesis is supported with organized points and related details. Points are generalizations that assert a meaning. These meanings are fleshed out with details. Working together, points with related details form meaningful units that support a thesis.

Brief Writing Project

Playing the Believing and Doubting Game

The For Writing and Discussion exercise in Concept 2.2 asks you to play the believing and doubting game as a freewriting exercise. Because this game is so helpful for developing critical thinking skills and learning to wallow in complexity, we repeat it here as a brief writing assignment.

Part 1. The Game. Play the believing and doubting game with one of the assertions listed here (or with another assertion provided by your instructor). Include at least one full paragraph or page (ask your instructor about length) believing the assertion, and then an equivalent stretch of prose doubting the assertion. When you believe an assertion, you agree, support, illustrate, extend, and apply the idea. When you doubt an assertion, you question, challenge, rebut, and offer counterreasons and counterexamples to the assertion. Try to include both points and details, general statements and specifics to probe your points and make your writing meaningful.

1. Grades are an effective means of motivating students to do their best work.

2. Facebook or other social media provide a good way to make new friends.

3. In recent years, advertising has made enormous gains in portraying women as strong, independent, and intelligent.

4. If there is only one kidney available for transplant and two sick persons need it, one in her thirties and one in her sixties, the kidney should go to the younger person.

5. The United States should require women as well as men to register for the draft.

Part 2. Reflection. Write a reflective paragraph in which you assess the extent to which the believing and doubting game extended or stretched your thinking. Answer these questions:

1. What was difficult about this writing activity?

2. To what extent did it make you take an unfamiliar or uncomfortable stance?

3. How can believing and doubting help you wallow in complexity?

Chapter 3
Thinking Critically About Rhetorical Problems

Learning Objectives

3.1 Explain how the features of good writing vary depending on the rhetorical context.

3.2 Make decisions about your writing based on genre, audience, and purpose.

3.3 Think rhetorically about the interactive Web environment with shifting audiences, purposes, genres, and authorial roles.

In the previous chapter, we showed you how an academic writer becomes engaged with a subject-matter problem, wrestles with it through analysis and critical thinking, and asserts a contestable thesis that surprises the reader with something new or thought-provoking. For example, the student writer contemplating Dorothea Tanning's painting *Portrait de Famille* formulated subject-matter problems like the following:

- Why did Tanning distort the relative sizes of the family members? Why does the father's portrait cut off his forehead and emphasize his glasses?

- Why did she include a dog in the painting? Why did she choose this breed of dog sitting in this posture? Why is the maid facing the dog?

In this chapter, we show how this student writer must also address *rhetorical problems*. For example, before she can write an analysis of Tanning's painting, she must address questions related to genre, audience, and purpose:

- **What is my genre?** Am I supposed to write an academic essay with a thesis statement or something more like museum notes to appear alongside the painting? Would it be appropriate to include my own feelings about this painting?

- **Who is my audience?** Am I writing to my teacher, my classmates, or someone else? Do I assume that my readers have already seen Tanning's painting? Are they already interested in the questions I am posing? Are they art majors who know technical terms or are they "beginners" without much experience with art criticism?

- **What is my purpose (besides getting a good grade)?** What change do I want to bring about in the way my audience initially understands this painting?

In this chapter we explore the kinds of rhetorical problems a writer must address. If you are unsure of what "rhetorical" means, we explain this term in detail in Concept 3.2.

Concept 3.1: The features of good writing vary depending on rhetorical context.

3.1 Explain how the features of good writing vary depending on the rhetorical context.

So far we have said that writers must address two types of problems: subject-matter problems and rhetorical problems. Rhetorical problems, as we will see, influence the writer's decisions about content, organization, and style. They often loom as large for writers as the subject-matter problems that drive their writing in the first place.

In this section, we focus on a rhetorical problem of particular interest to new college writers: Are there universal "rules" for good writing? In our experience, many student writers come to college guided by writing rules they learned in high school: "Never use 'I' in an academic paper." "Have a thesis statement." "Use good transitions." "Put a topic sentence in every paragraph." But are these really good rules to follow? To explore your own answer to this question, try your hand at the following thought exercise.

A Thought Exercise: Two Pieces of Good Writing That Follow Different "Rules"

Read the following short pieces of nonfiction prose. The first is a letter to the editor written by a professional civil engineer in response to a newspaper editorial arguing for the development of wind-generated electricity. The second is the beginning of a short essay entitled "Listen to the Lizards," originally published in *World Literature Today*. It was written by the American-born freelance writer and novelist, Kris Saknussemm, who lived for many years in Australia. After reading the two samples carefully, proceed to the discussion questions that follow.

David Rockwood
A Letter to the Editor

Your editorial on November 16, "Get Bullish on Wind Power," is based on fantasy rather than fact. There are several basic reasons why wind-generated power can in no way serve as a reasonable major alternative to other electrical energy supply alternatives for the Pacific Northwest power system.

First and foremost, wind power is unreliable. Electric power generation is evaluated not only on the amount of energy provided, but also on its ability to meet system peak load requirements on an hourly, daily, and weekly basis. In other words, an effective power system would have to provide enough electricity to meet peak demands in a situation when the wind energy would be unavailable—either in no-wind situations or in severe blizzard conditions, which would shut down the wind generators. Because wind power cannot be relied on at times of peak needs, it would have to be backed up by other power-generation resources at great expense and duplication of facilities.

Secondly, there are major unsolved problems involved in the design of wind-generation facilities, particularly for those located in rugged mountain areas. Ice storms, in particular, can cause sudden dynamic problems for the rotating blades and mechanisms, which could well result in breakdown or failure of the generators. Furthermore, the design of the facilities to meet the stresses imposed by high winds in these remote mountain regions, on the order of 125 miles per hour, would indeed escalate the costs.

Thirdly, the environmental impact of constructing wind-generation facilities amounting to 28 percent of the region's electrical supply system (as proposed in your editorial) would be tremendous. The Northwest Electrical Power system presently has a capacity of about 37,000 megawatts of hydro power and 10,300 megawatts of thermal, for a total of about 48,000 megawatts. Meeting 28 percent of this capacity by wind-power generators would, most optimistically, require about 13,400 wind towers, each with about 1,000 kilowatt (one megawatt) generating capacity. These towers, some 100 to 200 feet high, would have to be located in the mountains of Oregon and Washington. These would encompass hundreds of square miles of pristine mountain area, which, together with interconnecting transmission facilities, control works, and roads, would indeed have major adverse environmental impacts on the region.

There are many other lesser problems of control and maintenance of such a system. Let it be said that, from my experience and knowledge as a professional engineer, the use of wind power as a major resource in the Pacific Northwest power system is strictly a pipe dream.

Kris Saknussemm

Listen to the Lizards

Many years ago now, during a period of acute depression (the first time I began to consider that I might have some kind of metabolic imbalance), I had what amounted to a quiet but fairly total breakdown in full sunshine on a glorious autumn day at Albert Park Lake in Melbourne.

I was sitting by myself on a bench watching some sailing lessons, people jogging past, dogs chasing Frisbees—and I suddenly and unexpectedly burst into slow, hysterical weeping, for a reason I had not a clue about. I felt as if I were dead and watching myself through a filter. A complete and pervasive sense of isolation, alienation, disassociation, and final loss.

Then I very clearly heard a voice (of the kind that no one else could), which was disturbing and also deeply inspiring. It said, "Who are you to feel so alone?"

When I heard it, I looked down at my feet and saw this remarkable assemblage of ants. They were channeling and swarming through a smear of melting strawberry ice cream, and the patterns they formed

(continued)

were like a cross between a living mandala and the outline of some unknown machine. It was organic, it was mechanical—it was dynamic in some way that was both utterly foreign and familiar. It met every single criterion for my definition of art, and I watched in hypnotized fascination for two healing hours.

Ever since that afternoon, I've taken special note of my nonhuman neighbors wherever I've found myself. I had a fifteen-year relationship with a female dingo that was every bit as intense as my marriage. I count a big galumphy mastiff as my best personal friend of all time.

And whenever I travel, the creature spirits come to me. Dejected, exhausted, perspiring in the vapid heat of the most concrete and life-abandoned parking lot you could possibly imagine in Phoenix, Arizona, a brilliant green hummingbird came down to keep me company. It held tight in a perfect, frenzied stillness directly in front of me for more than two minutes. Then it showed me what real subtlety of movement in the world is all about—an object lesson in dance, the martial arts, and aerodynamics in one single, flowing meditation. It was a true flicker of pure animation in the midst of paved, soul-annihilating Western lostness that I will never forget.

A mandala is a Hindu spiritual and religious symbol.

For Writing and Discussion
Comparing Two Types of Writing

Working as a whole class or in small groups, share your answers to the following questions:

1. What are the main differences between the two types of writing?
2. Create a metaphor, simile, or analogy that best sums up your feelings about the most important differences between Rockwood's and Saknussemm's writing: "Rockwood's writing is like . . . , but Saknussemm's writing is like. . . ."
3. Explain why your metaphors are apt. How do your metaphors help clarify or illuminate the differences between the two pieces of writing?

Figure 3.1 A Continuum of Essay Types: Closed to Open Forms

Closed Forms

Top-down thesis-based prose
- thesis explicitly stated in introduction
- all parts of essay linked clearly to thesis
- body paragraphs develop thesis
- body paragraphs have topic sentences
- structure forecasted

Delayed-thesis prose
- thesis appears near end
- text reads as a mystery
- reader held in suspense

Distinctions Between Closed and Open Forms of Writing

Here now is our own brief analysis of the differences between these two pieces. David Rockwood's letter and Kris Saknussemm's essay are both examples of nonfiction prose. But as these examples illustrate, nonfiction prose can vary enormously in form and style. When we give this exercise to our students, they have no trouble articulating the differences between the two pieces of writing. Rockwood's piece has an explicit thesis statement, unified and coherent paragraphs with topic sentences, evidence to support each topic sentence, and strong transitions between each paragraph. Saknussemm's piece, in contrast, seems to ignore these rules; it is more artistic, more creative, more like a story. (Among our students, one group said that Rockwood's piece is like riding a train toward a clear destination while Saknussemm's piece is like floating down a river not knowing what's around the bend.) One way to label these differences is to say that Rockwood's piece is thesis based, whereas Saknussemm's piece is narrative based. But another way to distinguish between them is to place them on a continuum from closed-form prose to open-form prose (Figure 3.1).

CLOSED-FORM PROSE   Rockwood's letter illustrates tightly **closed-form prose** (far left on the continuum), which we can define as writing with a hierarchical structure of points and details in support of an explicit thesis. It is characterized by unified and coherent paragraphs, topic sentences, transitions between sentences and paragraphs, and forecasting of the whole before presentation of the parts. Once Rockwood states his thesis ("Wind-generated power isn't a reasonable alternative energy source in the Pacific Northwest"), he sets up the expectation that he will support his thesis with reasons and evidence. The thesis forecasts where he is going.

We say that this form is "closed" because it doesn't allow any digressions or structural surprises. Because its structure is predictable, its success depends entirely on the quality of its ideas, which must bring something new to readers or challenge them with something contestable. Closed-form prose is what most college professors expect from their students on most occasions. Likewise, it is

Open Forms

Thesis-seeking prose
- essay organized around a question rather than a thesis
- essay explores the problem or question, looking at it in many ways
- writer may or may not arrive at thesis

Theme-based narrative
- often organized chronologically or has storylike elements
- often used to heighten or deepen a problem, or show its human significance
- often has an implicit theme rather than a thesis
- often violates rules of closed-form prose by using literary techniques

often the most effective form of writing in professional and business settings. (Note that the five-paragraph essay, common in many high schools, is a by-the-numbers approach for teaching closed-form prose.)

OPEN-FORM PROSE   In contrast, Saknussemm's "Listen to the Lizards" falls toward the right end of the closed-to-open continuum. **Open-form prose** resists reduction to a single, summarizable thesis. It is characterized by narrative or storylike structure, sometimes with abrupt gaps without transitions, and it uses various literary techniques to make the prose memorable and powerful. Open-form prose unfolds and invites readers to infer connections and meaning. Although Saknussemm sees his "nonhuman neighbors" as an antidote to his depression, it is not quite clear what he finds comforting or healing. The ants seem to combine spirit and machine to create a work of art. Although the mastiff may be a typical kind of animal companion as pet, the ants and the hummingbird don't fit this category, nor probably does the dingo. Moreover, the title suggests that as this piece continues, it will involve lizards.

The main organizing principle of Saknussemm's piece, like that of most open-form prose, is a story or narrative—in this case the story of Saknussemm's becoming suddenly depressed, weeping, hearing a voice, and then being comforted by ants and later by a hummingbird. (A flashback also mentions the comfort of the dingo and the mastiff—with a strange and seemingly alienated reference to his wife.) Rather than announce a thesis and support it with reasons and evidence, Saknussemm lets his point emerge suggestively from his story and his language.

Open-form essays still have a focus, but the focus is more like a theme in fiction than like a thesis in argument. Readers may argue over its meaning in the same way that they argue over the meaning of a film or poem or novel. Consider also the extent to which Saknussemm violates the rules for closed-form prose. Instead of using hierarchically arranged points, Saknussemm jumps from one scene to another, setting up contrasts without transitions. The ants, which comfort him, are contrasted with people and Frisbee-chasing dogs, which don't comfort him. The hummingbird is contrasted with the hot Phoenix parking lot, a symbol of Western "lostness." Unlike paragraphs in closed-form prose, which typically begin with topic sentences and are developed with supporting details and impeccable grammar, the paragraphs in Saknussemm's piece do not follow these rules; paragraph 3, for example, has only two sentences, and paragraph 2 ends with a sentence fragment. These features of open-form prose often characterize personal essays, articles in popular magazines, exploratory or reflective writing, or character profiles that tell stories of a person's life. Open-form prose usually has an artistic or aesthetic appeal, and many examples are classified as literary nonfiction or creative nonfiction.

Flexibility of "Rules" along the Continuum

As you can see from the continuum in Figure 3.1, essays can fall anywhere along the scale. Not all thesis-with-support writing has to be top-down, stating its thesis explicitly in the introduction. In some cases writers choose to delay the thesis, creating a more exploratory, open-ended, "let's think through this together" feeling before finally stating the main point late in the essay. In some cases writers explore a problem without *ever* finding a satisfactory thesis, creating an essay that seeks a thesis rather than supporting one. Because exploratory essays are aimed at deepening the reader's engagement with a question and resisting easy answers, they often include digressions, speculations, conjectures, multiple perspectives, and occasional invitations to the reader to help solve the problem. When writers reach the far right-hand position on the continuum, they no longer state an explicit thesis. Instead, like fiction writers, they embed their points in plot, character, imagery, and dialogue, leaving their readers to *infer* a theme from the text.

Where to Place Your Writing along the Continuum

Clearly, essays at opposite ends of this continuum operate in different ways, possess different features, and obey different rules. Because each position on the continuum has its appropriate uses, the writer's challenge is to determine which sort of writing is most appropriate in a given situation. Most (but not all) college papers and much professional writing are written in closed form. Thus if you were writing a business proposal, a legal brief, or an academic paper for a scholarly audience, you would typically choose a closed-form structure, and your finished product would include elements such as the following:

- An explicit thesis in the introduction
- Forecasting of structure
- Cohesive and unified paragraphs with topic sentences
- Clear transitions between sentences and between parts
- No digressions

But if you were writing, say, to express your conflicted relationship with a parent, your first discovery of evil, or your life-changing encounter with a stranger, you would probably rely on well-crafted scenes, dialogues, and narratives, moving toward the open end of the continuum and violating one or more of these closed-form conventions.

What is important to see is that having a thesis statement, topic sentences, and good transitions is not a mark of "good writing" but simply a mark of "closed-form" writing. What makes closed-form writing good is the quality of its ideas. In contrast, powerful open-form writing often ignores closed-form rules. It's not that open-form prose doesn't have rules; it's that the rules are different, just as the rules for jazz are different from the rules for a classical sonata. The rhetorical context determines whether the writer uses a closed-form strategy, an open-form strategy, or something in between.

For Writing and Discussion
Thinking Personally about Closed and Open Forms

Do you and your classmates most enjoy writing prose at the closed or open end of the continuum? Recall a favorite piece of writing that you have done in the past. Jot down a brief description of the kind of writing this was (a personal-experience essay, a piece of workplace writing, a research paper, a blog post, a persuasive argument) and explain why you liked it. Where would you place this piece of writing on the closed-to-open continuum? Are you at your best in closed-form writing that calls for an explicit thesis statement and logical support? Or are you at your best in more open, creative, and personal forms? Share your preferences with your classmates.

Concept 3.2: Writers' decisions are shaped by genre, audience, and purpose.

3.2 Make decisions about your writing based on genre, audience, and purpose.

In the previous section we explained how the features of good writing vary according to rhetorical context. In this section, we examine in more detail what we mean by both *rhetoric* and *rhetorical context.*

What Is Rhetoric?

At the broadest level, **rhetoric** is the study of how human beings use language and other symbols to influence the attitudes, beliefs, and actions of others. One prominent twentieth-century rhetorician, Kenneth Burke, calls rhetoric "a symbolic means of inducing cooperation in beings that by nature respond to symbols." To understand what Burke means by "symbols," consider the difference in flirting behavior between peacocks and humans. When male peacocks flirt, they spread their fantastic tail feathers, do mating dances, and screech weirdly to attract females, but the whole process is governed by instinct. Peacocks don't have to make symbolic choices. They don't have to decide whether to buy the hipster tail feathers advertised in *Rolling Stone* or the Hugo Boss designer feathers displayed in a Neiman Marcus catalog. Unlike peacocks, flirting humans must make dozens of symbolic choices, all of which convey meanings to audiences. Consider the different flirting messages humans send to one another by their choice of clothes and accessories, their hairstyle, their opening moves in a conversation, or the content of their playlists. Rhetoricians study, among other things, how these symbols arise within a given culture and how they influence others.

In a narrower sense, rhetoric is the art of making messages persuasive. Perhaps the most famous definition of rhetoric comes from the Greek philosopher Aristotle, who defined rhetoric as "the ability to see, in any particular case, all the available means of persuasion." Effective speakers or writers begin by trying to understand their audience's values and beliefs and the kinds of arguments that different audience members might make about a given issue ("all the available means of persuasion"). If we imagine the interaction of several speakers, each proposing different points of view and each analyzing and appreciating others' viewpoints, we can see how mutual understanding might emerge. The study of rhetoric can therefore help humans construct more functional and productive communities.

At an operational level, writers "think rhetorically" whenever they are consciously aware of writing within a genre to an audience for a purpose. Let's look more closely at each of these terms—genre, audience, and purpose—in turn.

How Writers Think about Genre

The term **genre** refers to categories of writing that follow certain conventions of style, structure, approach to subject matter, and document design. Table 3.1 shows different kinds of genres.

Table 3.1 Examples of Genres

Personal Writing	Academic Writing	Popular Culture	Public Affairs, Civic Writing	Professional Writing	Literature
Letter	Scholarly article	Article for magazines such as *Seventeen*, *Ebony*, or *Vibe*	Letter to the editor	Cover letter for a job application	Short story
Diary/journal	Research paper		Newspaper editorial	Résumé	Novel
Memoir	Scientific report	Advertisement	Op-ed piece	Business memo	Graphic novel
Blog	Abstract or summary	Hip-hop lyrics	Advocacy Web site	Legal brief	Play
Text message		Fan Web sites	Political blog	Brochure	Sonnet
E-mail	Book review	Bumper sticker	Magazine article on civic issue	Technical manual	Epic poem
Facebook profile	Essay exam	Review of books, films, plays, music		Instruction booklet	Literary podcast
Personal essay	Annotated bibliography		Tweet	Proposal	
Literacy narrative	Textual analysis	Tweet		Report	
Status update				Press release	
Tweet					

The concept of genre creates strong reader expectations, placing specific demands on writers. Genres are social practices that arise out of particular social needs and conditions. How you write any given report, bumper sticker, memo, or academic article is influenced by the structure and style of hundreds of previous reports, bumper stickers, memos, or academic articles written before yours. Writers must always try to meet the reader expectations created by genre. If you wanted to write a *Reader's Digest* article, for example, you would have to use the conventions that appeal to its older, conservative readers: simple language, strong reliance on anecdotal evidence in arguments, high level of human interest, and choice of subject matter that reinforces the conservative values of individualism, self-discipline, and family. If you wanted to write for *Seventeen* or *Rolling Stone*, however, you would need to use quite different conventions concerning subject matter, style, and document design. Likewise, the conventions for writing for the Web (blogs, podcasts, Web pages) differ significantly from writing for print.

To illustrate the relationship of a writer to a genre, we sometimes draw an analogy with clothing. In any culture, humans create genres of clothing. For example, Americans recognize the genres of hipster, goth, preppy, country/western, blue-collar, business casual, cocktail party, and so forth. The genre of "country/western" attire typically includes blue jeans, big belt buckles, western-style boots (but not English riding boots), and cowboy hats. The conventions of this genre preexist your decision to look country/western. Within this genre, you could express your own tastes by the quality and design of leather tooling on your cowboy boots, but not by your wearing Birkenstock sandals. So, by analogy, if you are writing a business memo or an experimental report in scientific style, you are constrained by the conventions of each genre. The concept of genre raises intriguing and sometimes unsettling questions about the relationship between the creative self and social conventions.

How Writers Think about Audience

In addition to knowing the conventions of their chosen or assigned genre, writers must also ask questions about their **audience**. What you know about your readers—their initial views about your subject matter, their level of expertise, their reasons for reading, their values and beliefs—affects many of the choices you make as a writer.

In assessing your audience, you must first determine who that audience is—a single reader (for example, your boss), a select group (a scholarship committee; readers of a particular blog), or a general audience. If you imagine a general audience, you need to make some initial assumptions about their views, values, and current attitude toward your subject. Doing so creates an "implied audience," giving you a stable rather than a moving target so that you can make decisions about your own writing. You can use the strategies in Strategies Chart 3.1 to analyze your audience.

To appreciate the importance of audience, consider how a change in audience can affect the content of an argument. One example can be found in arguments to support an initiative to use tax dollars to fund a new baseball stadium in a major American city. Arguments aimed at baseball fans appealed to the fans' love of the game and to the improved fan amenities in the new park (more comfortable seats, better sight lines, bigger restrooms, more food options, and so forth). But arguments aimed at voters not interested in baseball took a different tack. These arguments appealed to civic values, stressing that the stadium would bring new tax revenues to the city, clean up a run-down area, revitalize local businesses, or stimulate tourism. The writers' purpose remained the same—to persuade taxpayers to fund the stadium—but the content of the argument changed in response to a different target audience.

For college papers, students may think that they are writing to an audience of one—the teacher. But because teachers often know more about the subject matter than the student writer (making it hard for the student to bring something new to the reader), teachers often ask students to address their fellow classmates or some

Strategies Chart 3.1 Strategies for Analyzing Audience

Questions to Ask about Your Audience	Reasons for Asking the Question
How busy are my readers?	• Helps you decide on length, document design, and methods of organization (see Concept 3.1 on open versus closed forms). • In workplace writing, busy readers usually appreciate tightly organized prose with headings that allow for skimming.
What are my readers' motives for reading?	• If the reader has requested the document, he or she will probably already be interested in what you say. • In most cases, you need to hook your readers' interest and keep them engaged.
What is my relationship with my readers?	• Helps you decide on a formal or informal style • Helps you select tone—polite and serious or loose and slangy
What do my readers already know about my topic? Do my readers have more or less expertise than I have, or about the same level of expertise?	• Helps you determine what will be old/familiar information for your audience versus new/unfamiliar information • Helps you decide how much background and context to include • Helps you decide to use or avoid jargon and specialized knowledge
How interested are my readers in my topic? Do my readers already care about it?	• Helps you decide how to write the introduction • Helps you determine how to make the problem you address interesting and significant to your reader
What will be my readers' attitudes toward my thesis? Do my readers share my beliefs and values? Will they be skeptical of my argument or even threatened by it?	• Helps you make numerous decisions about tone, structure, reference to alternative views, and use of evidence • Helps you decide on the persona and tone you want to project

other real or hypothetical audience. They may ask you to blog for a Web audience, to write to civic leaders for a community service project, or to imagine writing for a particular newspaper, magazine, or journal. As an alternative, they may create case assignments with built-in audiences (for example, "You are an accountant in the firm of Numbers and Fudge; one day you receive a letter from . . ."). If your instructor does not specify an audience, you can generally assume an audience of student peers who have approximately the same level of knowledge and expertise in the field as you do, who need to be drawn into the question you address, and who want to discover something new and engaging in your argument.

How Writers Think about Purpose

At a specific level, your **purpose** is to bring something new or contestable to your reader. At a more general level, your purpose can be expressed as a rhetorical aim. Let's look at each in turn.

PURPOSE AS A DESIRE TO BRING SOMETHING NEW OR CONTESTABLE TO YOUR READER   One powerful way to think about purpose is to articulate how you want to change your reader's view of your subject. Your statement of purpose focuses on what is new or controversial (contestable—capable of being contested) in your paper. For most essays, you can write a one-sentence, nutshell statement about your purpose.

> My purpose is to give my readers a vivid picture of my difficult struggle with Graves' disease. [What's new: a vivid account of what Graves' disease is and how one person struggled with it.]
>
> My purpose is to explain how Thoreau's view of nature differs in important ways from that of contemporary environmentalists. [What's new: a possibly controversial way of thinking about the difference between Thoreau and contemporary environmentalists.]
>
> My purpose is to persuade the general public to ban the sale of assault weapons. [What's new: a contestable argument that some would say violates the Second Amendment.]

This view of purpose was developed more fully in Chapter 2, where we showed that an effective thesis statement tries to bring about some change in the reader's view of the subject (Concept 2.2). Writers of closed-form prose often place explicit purpose statements in their introductions along with their thesis. In most other forms of writing, the writer uses a behind-the-scenes purpose statement to achieve focus and direction but seldom states the purpose explicitly.

PURPOSE AS RHETORICAL AIM   It is also possible to think of purpose more broadly by using the concept of **rhetorical aim**, which describes the effect the writer hopes to have upon the audience. Articulating your rhetorical aim can help you clarify your relationship to your audience and identify typical ways that a piece of writing might be structured and developed. The writing projects in Part 2 of this textbook are based on six different rhetorical aims: to express, to explore, to inform, to analyze/ synthesize, to persuade, and to reflect. Table 3.2 provides an overview of each of these rhetorical aims and summarizes how different aims typically use different approaches to subject matter, how the writer's task and relationship to readers differ according to aim, and how a chosen aim affects the writing's genre and its position on the spectrum from open to closed forms.

Table 3.2 Purpose as Rhetorical Aim

Rhetorical Aim	Focus of Writing	Relationship to Audience	Forms and Genres
Express or share (Chapter 7) May also include an artistic aim (Chapter 19)	Your own life, personal experiences, reflections	You share aspects of your life; you invite readers to walk in your shoes, to experience your insights.	**Form:** Has many open-form features **Sample genres:** journal, blog, personal Web site, or online profile; personal essays or literacy narratives, often with artistic features
Explore or inquire (Chapter 8)	A significant subject-matter problem that puzzles you	You take readers on your own intellectual journey by showing your inquiry process (raising questions, seeking evidence, considering alternative views).	**Form:** Follows open form in being narrative based; is thesis seeking rather than thesis supporting **Sample genres:** freewriting; research logs; articles and books focused on process of discovery
Inform or explain (Chapter 9)	Factual knowledge addressing a reader's need or curiosity	You provide knowledge that your readers need or want, or you arouse curiosity and provide new, surprising information. You expect readers to trust your authority.	**Form:** Usually has a closed-form structure **Sample genres:** encyclopedia articles; instruction booklets; sales reports; technical reports; informative magazine articles; informative Web sites
Analyze, synthesize, or interpret (Chapters 10–13)	Complex subject matter that you can break down into parts and put together in new ways for greater understanding	Using critical thinking and possibly research, you challenge readers with a new way of understanding your subject. Skeptical readers expect you to support your thesis with good particulars.	**Form:** Typically has a closed-form structure **Sample genres:** scholarly articles; experimental reports; many kinds of college research papers; public-affairs magazine articles; many kinds of blogs
Persuade (Chapters 14–16)	Subject-matter questions that invite differing points of view or have controversial answers	You try to convince readers, who may not share your values and beliefs, to accept your stance on an issue by providing good reasons and evidence and attending to alternative views.	**Form:** Usually closed form, but may employ many open-form features for persuasive effect **Sample genres:** letters to the editor; op-ed pieces; posts on a blog site; advocacy pieces in public-affairs magazines; advocacy Web sites; researched academic arguments
Reflect (Chapter 26)	Subject matter closely connected to your interests and experience; often involves self-evaluation of an experience	Writing for yourself as well as for a reader, you seek to find personal meaning and value in an experience or course of study. You assume a sympathetic and interested reader.	**Form:** Anywhere on the closed-to-open-form continuum **Sample genres:** memoirs; workplace self-evaluations; introductory letter for a portfolio; personal essays looking back on an experience

For Writing and Discussion
Thinking about Genre, Audience, and Purpose

Suppose that you are a political science major researching Second Amendment rights. Suppose further that you generally support the right to own hunting rifles and handguns but that your research has led you to oppose ownership of assault weapons and high-capacity ammo clips. Through your research, you have gathered different "means of persuasion" for your position—statistical data, sociological studies of gun violence, political studies of Second Amendment controversies, comparison data with other countries, and anecdotal stories (published in newspapers or on the Web) from witnesses or surviving victims of massacre shootings. You are ready to start writing. How would your piece of writing be different under the following conditions related to genre, audience, and purpose?

1. You are an intern for your district's member of the U.S. House of Representatives. She asks you to write a well-documented argument recommending the position she should take on gun-control issues.

2. You are an active citizen seriously worried about gun violence. You decide to start a blog devoted to building up public anger against easy access to assault weapons. You now need to write and post your first blog.

3. You are invited by your local newspaper to write an op-ed column on gun control. You have 500 words to make your best case.

4. You've read an argument opposing a ban on assault weapons and high-capacity ammo magazines on a blog sponsored by the National Rifle Association. You want to post a counterargument on this blog site—but you want to be taken seriously, not flamed.

5. You seek a broader public for your anti-assault weapon campaign. You decide to send a Twitter tweet as well as create a bumper sticker.

Concept 3.3: Online environments are rhetorically interactive with shifting audiences, purposes, genres, and authorial roles.

3.3   Think rhetorically about the interactive Web environment with shifting audiences, purposes, genres, and authorial roles.

The rhetorical concepts of genre, audience, and purpose become more complex when one moves from print to online environments. To appreciate the difference between a print and an online environment, consider the difference between a print version of a news story and the same newspaper's online version. Here is the headline from a recent front-page print story in a city newspaper: **"INTRUDER TERRIFIES STUDENTS."** According to the print story, a man wearing a trench coat and eating an ice cream cone entered a classroom at a local university and "frightened students with his bizarre behavior," which caused students to suspect he might be a shooter. According to the newspaper, campus security was slow to respond; meanwhile, students were terrified as they watched the man "talking incoherently and turn[ing] over tables and other classroom furniture." Once campus security arrived, the man was arrested and booked into the county jail. (He was unarmed.)

The print story portrays terrified students imagining a potentially armed gunman ready to open fire. But how accurate was the story? In the newspaper's online version, the same story was accompanied by posted comments from students who were in the classroom at the time. Many of these posts contradicted the newspaper's story, saying that the intruder was odd but not threatening, that campus security arrived within one minute of being called, and that students, rather than fleeing the classroom in terror, lingered out of curiosity. One commenter said that the intruder seemed to be enjoying his ice cream cone. Another said that he couldn't have possibly tipped over tables because the classroom furniture was fixed to the floor. Whereas the print version portrayed the incident as frightening and dangerous, the posts portrayed it collectively as a bizarre but harmless encounter with a possibly mentally ill street person.

Within a day, more than a hundred posts contributed to the story. The ensuing discussion thread evolved from concerns about what happened in the classroom to a larger conversation about the best way to respond to threats. One respondent said it was lucky that no one in the class carried a concealed weapon because an armed student might have killed the intruder (or accidentally shot a classmate), turning a harmless incident into a tragedy. The discussion thread was then dominated by heated exchanges over the advisability of laws allowing concealed carry on college campuses.

Our point in recounting this episode is that the Web creates an interactive participatory news environment very unlike that of traditional print newspapers and news magazines. Because Web readers are often Web writers, content published online can receive reader responses within minutes. These responses in turn can alter the way readers read the original content so that the "message" itself begins to evolve. This participatory environment has many implications for reading online communication rhetorically.

Shifting and Evolving Rhetorical Contexts Online

We can see the rhetorical implications of an online environment if we consider how an online environment destabilizes the concepts of audience, writer, and message.

SHIFTING AUDIENCES   When you write something online (an e-mail, a tweet, a Facebook post), whom do you picture as your audience? In some cases, you might think you can identify your readers precisely. For example, if you send an e-mail to someone, you assume that person is your audience. But sometimes recipients forward e-mails without your knowledge or consent, or sometimes, to your great embarrassment, you might hit "reply all" when you intended to hit "reply." Moreover, e-mails are always stored somewhere on servers and may be leaked by a whistleblower or read by attorneys who subpoena them in legal proceedings. Likewise, you might believe your Facebook audience is limited to "friends" only. However, unless you set your privacy codes very narrowly, one of your friends can "like" or "share" one of your posts, sending it to a whole new network of that person's friends. One of your posts or pictures may well be viewed by hundreds of strangers, including your boss or your teacher. (And we know, of course, that "friends" on a Facebook site are often not really friends at all, and sometimes not even acquaintances.)

Variability of audiences occurs in different ways if you write a blog, upload a video to YouTube, or create your own Web site. In such cases, you cast your net into a sea of potential readers, probably hoping for a large audience. Although a given post can sometimes go viral by spreading exponentially through social media, often you are thankful for a small readership that you hope will grow. Sometimes your post may be read by audiences that you didn't intend to target—people who disagree with you, for example—and these people may forward your work to a largely hostile audience. Other times, online communities work to shut off outside readers by creating "insider" discussion threads that reinforce insider views and make outsiders feel unwelcome. Sometimes, in fact, members of these communities will flame an outsider who posts unwittingly on a thread. The community thus tries to stabilize its audience through self-policing, but in the process often limits a real exchange of communication across differences. Wise online writers, we believe, will in most cases try to enlarge their audiences rather than limit them. This desire to reach more readers puts the burden on the writer to use the appeals that draw in readers rather than shut them out.

SHIFTING WRITERS   Just as the Web environment destabilizes our conception of "audience," so can it destabilize the concept of "writer." Online environments often blur the concept of the single, authoritative writer by creating texts written by communities. Through wikis, for example, writers who may not even know one another can build collaborative texts that cannot be identified with any individual writer. Although wiki writers don't produce texts in quite the way that bees build a hive, the text seems to emerge collaboratively without a controlling lead author. Similarly, discussion threads on blog sites can blur the individual writer. Although an originating blogger may have a strong individual identity, the responses posted by readers bring other voices to the original blogger's message, creating a larger and more complex "co-created" message. We saw this phenomenon in our example of the news story about the ice-cream-cone-eating classroom intruder: That story's "truth content" was not controlled by the original author (the news reporter) but by the collective weight of all readers who posted responses to the story. Finally, the concept of the writer is blurred by the anonymity created by the use of pseudonyms or avatars, which often make it difficult to identify texts with the actual human author.

EVOLVING MESSAGES   Very few pieces of content published on the Web are stable or permanent. Items appear and quickly disappear. An author can post a story or article on a Web site, make corrections or revisions, and then quickly repost the altered version. (This impermanence explains why academic conventions for citing and documenting sources sometimes require you to indicate the date on which you viewed the site.) Also, readers often don't read Web texts linearly from beginning to end in the stabilizing way they read print-based text. Rather, they are apt to click on embedded hyperlinks, jumping from text to text. Thus a message will be perceived differently by different readers according to their pathway through it. Messages evolve in still another way within threaded discussion sites where the reader's view of the subject is gradually modified by the cumulative impact of all the posts. Moreover, even an individual writer's view might evolve as the discussion continues. A writer who expresses one view early on in a thread may express a quite different view later.

For Writing and Discussion
How Do You Read and Write on the Web?

In small groups or as a whole class, share how you currently use the Web for reading and writing. When you are online, what do you typically view or read? Do you use social media? How? Do you post photos on Flickr? Have

(continued)

you ever uploaded a video on YouTube? Have you ever tweeted? Do you use e-mail? (If so, how do you use it differently from the way you text message on a phone?) Have you ever blogged? Created a Web site? Created a multimodal text? Have you ever responded to a blog or otherwise posted on a discussion thread? Have you ever written an online review? Have you ever contributed to a wiki? Your goal here is to share the various ways that you and members of your class read and write on the Web.

Maintaining Appropriate Online Privacy

As we have suggested, the Internet goes on forever. Therefore, it is important that writers are careful about the personal information they bring into the cyber universe. What writers publish in their early teens may come back to haunt them as they pursue careers later in life. Even the youngest writers must remember that the persona they cultivate in their earliest online publications will continue to exist online for decades to come. One good strategy is to follow the Parent/ Boss/Teacher Rule. Before posting something online, ask yourself, "Is this something I would want my parent/boss/teacher to see?" If the answer is no, there's a good chance it might pose problems for you later.

That said, we also want to emphasize that sharing online is not a bad thing. Quite the contrary, the willingness of ordinary people to share information and perspectives online has made the Internet a powerful tool for democracy. Individuals feel less isolated when they can interact with interested readers. When you are willing to share your views and knowledge online—honestly but carefully—you contribute to increased democratic interaction around the globe. This kind of sharing ranges from the most mundane Facebook posts to more sophisticated participation in blog sites devoted to political or social issues. Online chat rooms can blossom into fully formed support groups that help people overcome adversities and promote justice.

Creating an Ethical Online Persona

Online ethics partly involves the ethical use of sources that you find on the internet (see Skill 23.4 on using sources ethically and avoiding plagiarism). However, it also includes the way you present yourself online—your own *persona*. Sometimes the anonymity of the Web (especially if we compose under a pseudonym or an avatar) can bring out our dark sides, leading to mean-spirited flaming, to name-calling, or even to cyber-bullying. In many cases, it may not be our dark selves that emerge, but simply our impolite or nonrespectful selves. For example, we may create offensive stereotypes of our opponents on an issue—stereotypes that may play well on a Web site that attracts mostly like-minded people, but that may be deeply offensive to readers you weren't anticipating. Thus, given the instantaneous and global nature of the Web, writers can easily publish something online they might later regret. Because writing online is not usually restrained by editorial oversight, authors must become their own editors—not only for thought-intensive blog posts but also for the most hastily composed tweet, status update, or e-mail.

In our view, it is not okay to write something offensive or abusive online. The democratic potential of the Web depends on our promoting communication across differences rather than shutting people off into their own self-selected portion of the Web. You can be an agent for change simply by creating an

Figure 3.2 Problematic Online Personae

online persona who listens to others respectfully and advances conversations with politeness, kindness, and integrity. (For what we might call "problematic personae," see the cartoon in Figure 3.2.)

Another problem associated with online personas is sometimes humorously called "multiple personality disorder." If you compose regularly on the Web, you will find it all too easy to move in and out of "multiple personalities." Writers may take on a different persona for each different writing situation—a persona for their Facebook presence, a different persona for writing product reviews, a still different persona for blogging or for posting comments on someone else's blog. However, we suggest that it is good for new Web writers to avoid this disorder. Writers will be taken more seriously in the long run if they build toward an overall body of work characterized by a consistent, respectful, and sustainable persona.

Chapter Summary

This chapter has introduced three useful concepts connected to the demands of college writing.

Concept 3.1   The features of good writing vary according to rhetorical

context.   Good writing can vary along a continuum from closed to open forms. Closed-form prose has an explicit thesis statement, unified and coherent paragraphs with topic sentences, and good transitions. Closed-form prose is "good" only if its ideas bring something new or challenging to the reader. At the other end of the continuum, open-form prose often uses narrative techniques such as storytelling, evocative language, surprising contrasts, and other features that violate the conventions of closed-form prose.

Concept 3.2   Writers' decisions are shaped by genre, audience, and purpose.   Writers attend to genre by thinking about the conventions of content, structure, and style associated with the kind of document they are writing. To think about audience, they analyze how much their readers already know about (and care about) their subject and assess their readers' values, beliefs, and assumptions. To articulate purpose, writers focus on what is new or contestable in their intended work or, at a more general level, consider their rhetorical aim.

Concept 3.3   Online environments are rhetorically interactive with shifting audiences, purposes, genres, and authorial roles.   Online communication frequently destabilizes the concepts of audience, writer, and message. Audiences for online texts can shift rapidly because a reader can forward messages to new readers or post a message to a new site. The "writer" of an online text can be blurred through communally produced wiki texts or through the anonymity of pseudonyms and avatars. Online messages are ephemeral, frequently revised, and nuanced through the cumulative effect of posted reader responses. Finally, participating in online environments requires readers to maintain appropriate privacy and to develop an ethical online persona.

Brief Writing Project

Two Messages for Different Purposes, Audiences, and Genres

The purpose of this brief write-to-learn assignment is to let you experience firsthand how rhetorical context influences a writer's choices. The whole assignment, which has three parts, should not be more than two double-spaced pages long.

1. *A Text Message to a Friend.* Write a cell phone text message to a friend using the abbreviations, capitalization, and punctuation style typically used for text messages. Explain that you are going to miss Friday's social event (movie, pizza night, dance, party) because you are flying home to see your sister's new twin babies. Ask your friend about another time for a get-together. (Make up details as you need them.)

2. *An E-Mail Message to a Professor.* Compose an e-mail message to your professor explaining that you are going to miss Friday's field trip because you are flying home to see your sister's new twin babies. You are asking how you can make up for this missed field trip. (Use the same details as in item 1.) Create a subject line appropriate for this new context.

3. *Reflection on the Two Messages.* Using Items 1 and 2 as examples, explain to someone who has not read Chapter 3 of this text why a difference in your rhetorical context caused you to make different choices in these two messages. In your explanation, use the terms "purpose," "audience," and "genre." Your goal is to teach your audience the meanings of these terms.

Chapter 4
How Messages Persuade

Learning Objectives

4.1 Analyze how messages persuade through their angle of vision.

4.2 Analyze how messages persuade through appeals to *logos, ethos,* and *pathos*.

4.3 Analyze how messages persuade through the writer's style and voice.

A way of seeing is also a way of not seeing.

—*Kenneth Burke, Rhetorician*

The goal of this chapter is to help you analyze the rhetorical strategies that make messages persuasive. When you understand how messages achieve their effects, you will be better prepared to analyze and evaluate them and to decide whether to resist or accede to their arguments. You'll also be better prepared to use these rhetorical strategies effectively and ethically in your own writing.

Concept 4.1: Messages persuade through their angle of vision.

4.1 Analyze how messages persuade through their angle of vision.

One way that messages persuade is through their **angle of vision**, which causes a reader to see a subject from one perspective only—the writer's. Writers create an angle of vision through strategies such as the following:

- Stating point of view directly
- Selecting some details while omitting others
- Choosing words or figures of speech with intended connotations
- Creating emphasis or deemphasis through sentence structure and organization

The writer's angle of vision—which might also be called a lens, a filter, a perspective, or a point of view—is persuasive because it controls what the reader "sees." Unless readers are rhetorically savvy, they can lose awareness that they are seeing the writer's subject matter through a lens that both reveals and conceals.

A classic illustration of angle of vision is the following thought exercise:

Thought Exercise on Angle of Vision

Suppose you attended a fun party on Saturday night. (You get to choose what constitutes "fun" for you.) Now imagine that two people ask what you did on Saturday night. Person A is a close friend who missed the party. Person B is your parent. How would your descriptions of Saturday night differ?

Clearly there isn't just one way to describe this party. Your description will be influenced by your purpose and audience. You will have to decide:

- What image of myself should I project? (For your friend you might construct yourself as a party animal; for your parent, as a more detached observer.)
- How much emphasis do I give the party? (You might describe the party in detail for your friend while mentioning it only in passing to your parent, emphasizing instead all the homework you did over the weekend.)
- What details should I include or leave out? (Does my parent really need to know that the neighbors called the police?)
- What words should I choose? (The slang you use with your friend might not be appropriate for your parent.)

You'll note that our comments about your rhetorical choices reflect common assumptions about friends and parents. You might actually have a party-loving parent and a geeky friend, in which case you would alter your party descriptions accordingly. In any case, you are in rhetorical control. You choose what your audience "sees" and how they see it.

Recognizing the Angle of Vision in a Text

This thought exercise illustrates a key insight of rhetoric: There is always more than one way to tell a story, and no single way of telling it constitutes the whole truth. By saying that a writer writes from an angle of vision, we mean that the writer cannot take a godlike stance that allows a universal, unfiltered, totally unbiased or objective way of knowing. Rather, the writer looks at the subject from a certain location, or, to use another metaphor, the writer uses a lens that colors or filters the topic in a certain way. The angle of vision, lens, or filter determines what part of a topic gets seen and what remains unseen, what gets included or excluded, what gets emphasized or deemphasized, and so forth. It even determines what words get chosen—for example, whether the writer says "fetus" or "baby," "plutocrat" or "job creator," or "terrorist" or "freedom fighter."

What influences a writer's angle of vision in a piece of writing? The angle of vision a writer adopts is influenced by the rhetorical context—particularly the writer's purpose and targeted audience. Sometimes the writer consciously adopts an angle of vision. For example, a sales manager may adopt a positive angle of vision to promote a company's product, while a candidate for city council might focus on the negative aspects of her opponent's record. But the writer's angle of vision can also reflect his or her own authentic values and beliefs (including the writer's place of origin, ethnicity, profession, gender, sexual orientation, religious affiliation, and political views). Whether a writer is writing from an assumed role and/or from genuine conviction and personal stance, the angle of vision will shape what readers see.

As an illustration of angle of vision, consider the cartoon in Figure 4.1, which shows different ways that stakeholders "see" sweatshops. For each stakeholder, some aspects of sweatshops surge into view, while other aspects remain unseen or invisible. An alert reader needs to be aware that none of these stakeholders can portray sweatshops in a completely "true" way. Stockholders and corporate leaders emphasize reduced labor costs, enhanced corporate profits, and retirement portfolios while deemphasizing (or omitting entirely) the working conditions in sweatshops or the plight of U.S. workers whose jobs have been outsourced

Figure 4.1 Different Angles of Vision on "Sweatshops"

to developing countries. Consumers enjoy abundant low-cost goods made possible by sweatshops and may not even think about where or how the products are made. Opponents of sweatshops focus on the miserable conditions and low wages faced by sweatshop workers, the use of child labor, and the "obscene" profits of corporations. Meanwhile, as the U.S. union worker laments the loss of jobs in the United States, workers in developing countries and their children may welcome sweatshops as a source of income superior to the other harsh alternatives such as scavenging in dumps or prostitution. The multiple angles of vision show how complex the issue of sweatshops is. In fact, most issues are equally complex, and any one view of the issue is controlled by the writer's angle of vision.

To get a feel for how a writer creates an angle of vision, complete the following U. R. Riddle activity, which invites you to write a letter of recommendation for a student.

For Writing and Discussion
U. R. Riddle Letter

Background: Suppose that you are a management professor who regularly writes letters of recommendation for former students. One day you receive a letter from a local bank requesting a confidential evaluation of a former student, Uriah Rudy Riddle (U. R. Riddle), who has applied for a job as a management trainee. The bank wants your assessment of Riddle's intelligence, aptitude, dependability, and ability to work with people. You haven't seen U. R. for several years, but you remember him well. Here are the facts and impressions you recall about Riddle:

- Very temperamental student, seemed moody, something of a loner
- Long hair and very sloppy dress—seemed like a misplaced street person; often twitchy and hyperactive
- Absolutely brilliant mind; took lots of liberal arts courses and applied them to business
- Wrote a term paper relating different management styles to modern theories of psychology—the best undergraduate paper you ever received. You gave it an A+ and remember learning a lot from it yourself.
- Had a strong command of language—the paper was very well written
- Good at mathematics; could easily handle all the statistical aspects of the course
- Frequently missed class and once told you that your class was boring
- Didn't show up for the midterm. When he returned to class later, he said only that he had been out of town. You let him make up the midterm, and he got an A.
- Didn't participate in a group project required for your course. He said the other students in his group were idiots.
- You thought at the time that Riddle didn't have a chance of making it in the business world because he had no talent for getting along with people.
- Other professors held similar views of Riddle—brilliant, but rather strange and hard to like; an odd duck.

You are in a dilemma because you want to give Riddle a chance (he's still young and may have had a personality transformation of some sort), but you also don't want to damage your own professional reputation by falsifying your true impressions.

(continued)

Individual task: Working individually for ten minutes or so, compose a brief letter of recommendation assessing Riddle; use details from the list to support your assessment. Role-play that you have decided to take a gamble with Riddle and give him a chance at this career. Write as strong a recommendation as possible while remaining honest. (To make this exercise more complex, your instructor might ask half the class to role-play a negative angle of vision in which you want to warn the bank against hiring Riddle without hiding his strengths or good points.)

Task for group or whole-class discussion: Working in small groups or as a whole class, share your letters. Then pick representative examples ranging from the most positive to the least positive and discuss how the letters achieve their different rhetorical effects. If your intent is to support Riddle, to what extent does honesty compel you to mention some or all of your negative memories? Is it possible to mention negative items without emphasizing them? How?

Analyzing Angle of Vision

Just as there is more than one way to describe the party you went to on Saturday night or to write about sweatshops, there is more than one way to write a letter of recommendation for U. R. Riddle. The writer's angle of vision determines what is "seen" or "not seen" in a given piece of writing—what gets slanted in a positive or negative direction, what gets highlighted, what gets thrown into the shadows. As rhetorician Kenneth Burke claims in the epigraph for the chapter, "A way of seeing is also a way of not seeing." Note how the writer controls what the reader "sees." As Riddle's former professor, you might in your mind's eye see Riddle as long-haired and sloppy, but if you don't mention these details in your letter, they remain unseen to the reader. Note too that your own terms "long-haired and sloppy" interpret Riddle's appearance through the lens of your own characteristic way of seeing—a way that perhaps values business attire and clean-cut tidiness.

In an effective piece of writing, the author's angle of vision often works so subtly that unsuspecting readers—unless they learn to think rhetorically—will be drawn into the writer's spell and believe that the writer's prose conveys the whole picture of its subject rather than a limited picture filtered through the screen of the writer's perspective.

CONTRASTING ANGLES OF VISION IN TWO TEXTS   Consider the differences in what gets seen in the following two descriptions of the Arctic National Wildlife Refuge in Alaska (the ANWR), where proponents of oil exploration are locked in a fierce battle with anti-exploration conservationists. The first passage is from a pro-exploration advocacy group called Arctic Power. The second is from the website (defenders.org) of conservation advocates, "Defenders of Wildlife."

HOW ANGLE OF VISION PERSUADES   To understand more clearly how angle of vision persuades, you can analyze the language strategies at work. Some strategies that writers employ consciously or unconsciously are described in Strategies Chart 4.1.

Arctic Power's Description of the ANWR

On the coastal plain [of the ANWR], the Arctic winter lasts for 9 months. It is dark continuously for 56 days in midwinter. Temperatures with the wind chill can reach –110 degrees F. It's not pristine. There are villages, roads, houses, schools, and military installations. It's not a unique Arctic ecosystem. The coastal plain is only a small fraction of the 88,000 square miles that make up the North Slope. The same tundra environment and wildlife can be found throughout the circumpolar Arctic regions. The 1002 Area [the legal term for the plot of coastal plain being contested] is flat. That's why they call it a plain. [. . .]

    Some groups want to make the 1002 Area a wilderness. But a vote for wilderness is a vote against American jobs.

Defenders of Wildlife's Description of the ANWR

At more than 19 million acres, the Arctic National Wildlife Refuge is the crown jewel of the National Wildlife Refuge System. It is also one of the last intact landscapes in America, and home to 37 species of land mammals, eight marine mammals, 42 fish species, and more than 200 migratory bird species. Established in 1960 to protect its extraordinary wildlife, wilderness, and recreational qualities, the Arctic Refuge is a place where natural processes remain mostly uninfluenced by humans.

    But for all its unique beauty and importance for wildlife, the Arctic Refuge is under assault. The oil industry and its political allies continue to launch attacks to open this national treasure to destructive oil drilling, while climate change threatens to disrupt its habitats faster than wildlife can adapt. Defenders of Wildlife is committed to protecting the Arctic Refuge and the wildlife that calls this remarkable place home.

Strategies Chart 4.1   Strategies for Constructing an Angle of Vision

Strategy	ANWR Example	U. R. Riddle Example
State your intention directly.	• In the preceding excerpts, some passages directly state Arctic Power's (AP) pro-drilling stance and Defender of Wildlife's (DW) anti-drilling stance.	• You might say "Riddle would make an excellent manager" or "Riddle doesn't have the personality to be a bank manager."
Select details that support your intentions; omit or deemphasize others.	• The AP writer "sees" the cold, barren darkness of the ANWR; DW sees "exquisite beauty." • AP "sees" the people who live on the coastal plain and makes the animals invisible; DW "sees" the wildlife species and makes the people invisible. • AP "sees" jobs created by drilling; DW "sees" the ecosystem destroyed by drilling.	• A positive view of Riddle would select and emphasize Riddle's good traits and deemphasize or omit his bad ones. • A negative view would take the opposite tack.

Strategy	ANWR Example	U. R. Riddle Example
Choose words that frame your subject in the desired way or have desired connotations.	• AP frames the ANWR as the dreary "1002 Area"; DW frames it as "one of the last intact landscapes in America" and as a remarkable "home."	• "Riddle is an independent thinker who doesn't follow the crowd" (frames him positively in a value system that favors individualism). • "Riddle is a loner who thinks egocentrically" (frames him negatively in a value system favoring consensus and social skills). • You could say, "Riddle is forthright" or "Riddle is rude"—positive versus negative connotations.
Use figurative language (metaphors, similes, and analogies) that conveys your intended effect.	• AP avoids figurative language, claiming objective presentation of facts; AP uses the positive metaphor "crown jewel."	• To suggest that Riddle has outgrown his alienating behavior, you could say, "Riddle is a social late bloomer." • To recommend against hiring Riddle while still being positive, you could say, "Riddle's independent spirit would feel caged in by the routine of a bank."
Use sentence structure to emphasize and deemphasize your ideas. (*Emphasize an idea by placing it at the end of a long sentence, in a short sentence, or in a main clause.*)	• AP uses short sentences to emphasize main points: "It's not pristine." "It's not a unique ecosystem." "That's why they call it a plain." • DW uses longer sentences that place main points in main clauses at the end of the sentence.	Consider the difference between the following: • "Although Riddle had problems relating to other students, he is a brilliant thinker." • "Although Riddle is a brilliant thinker, he had problems relating to other students in the class."

Concept 4.2: Messages persuade through appeals to logos, ethos, and pathos.

4.2 Analyze how messages persuade through appeals to *logos, ethos,* and *pathos.*

Another way to think about the persuasive power of texts is to examine the strategies writers or speakers use to sway their audiences toward a certain position on an issue. To win people's consideration of their ideas, writers or speakers can appeal to what the classical philosopher Aristotle called *logos, ethos,* and *pathos.* Developing the habit of examining how these appeals function in texts and being able to employ these appeals in your own writing will enhance your ability to read and write rhetorically. Let's look briefly at each:

- **Logos *is the appeal to reason.*** It refers to the quality of the message itself— to its internal consistency, to its clarity in asserting a thesis or point, and to the soundness of its reasons and evidence used to support the point.

- **Ethos *is the appeal to the character of the speaker/writer.*** It refers to the speaker/writer's trustworthiness and credibility. One can often increase one's *ethos* in a message by being knowledgeable about the issue, by appearing thoughtful and fair, by listening well, and by respecting alternative points of view. A writer's accuracy and thoroughness in crediting sources and professionalism in caring about the format, grammar, and neat appearance of a document are part of the appeal to *ethos.*

Figure 4.2 Rhetorical Triangle

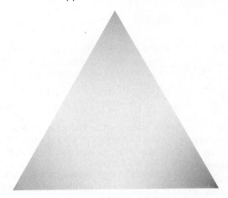

Message

Logos: *How can I make my ideas internally consistent and logical? How can I find the best reasons and support them with the best evidence?*

Audience

Pathos: *How can I make the readers open to my message? How can I best engage my readers' emotions and imaginations? How can I appeal to my readers' values and interests?*

Writer or Speaker

Ethos: *How can I present myself effectively? How can I enhance my credibility and trustworthiness?*

- **Pathos *is the appeal to the sympathies, values, beliefs, and emotions of the audience.* Appeals to *pathos* can be made in many ways. *Pathos* can often be enhanced through evocative visual images, which are frequently used in Web sites, posters, and magazine or newspaper articles. In written texts, the same effects can be created through vivid examples and details, connotative language, and empathy with the audience's beliefs and values.

A fuller discussion of these classical appeals appears in Chapter 14, "Writing a Classical Argument."

To see how these three appeals are interrelated, you can visualize a triangle with points labeled *Message, Audience,* and *Writer* or *Speaker.* Rhetoricians study how effective communicators consider all three points of this rhetorical triangle. (See Figure 4.2.)

We encourage you to ask questions about the appeals to *logos, ethos,* and *pathos* every time you examine a text. Here are some questions you might ask:

- Does the writer appeal effectively to *logos* through use of reasons and evidence?

- Does the writer appeal effectively to *ethos* by seeming credible, honest, and willing to listen to alternative views? Or do you distrust the writer in some way or dislike the writer's tone and voice?

- Does the writer use *pathos* effectively by drawing you into the subject, making you care about it, and feel what is at stake? Or does the writer rely too heavily on emotional words or heart-wringing examples?

Later chapters in this textbook will help you use these appeals competently in your own writing as well as analyze these appeals in others' messages.

Concept 4.3: Messages persuade through a writer's style and voice.

4.3   Analyze how messages persuade through the writer's style and voice.

So far we have shown how messages persuade through angle of vision and appeals to *logos, ethos,* and *pathos.* In this section we explain the persuasive power of style and voice, which are themselves factors in the creation of a message's angle of vision and contribute to its logical, ethical, or emotional appeals.

Understanding Factors That Affect Style

Style refers to analyzable features of language that work together to create different effects. As Figure 4.3 shows, style is composed of four factors:

- *Ways of shaping sentences,* such as length or complexity of sentence structure
- *Word choice,* such as abstract versus concrete or formal versus colloquial
- *Voice, or persona,* which refers to the reader's impression of the writer as projected from the page: expert versus layperson, scholarly voice versus popular voice, formal voice versus everyday voice

Figure 4.3 Ingredients of Style

Ways of shaping sentences	Types of words	Voice or persona	Tone
Long/short Simple/complex Many modifiers/few modifiers Normal word order/frequent inversions or interruptions Mostly main clauses/many embedded phrases and subordinate clauses	Abstract/concrete Formal/colloquial Unusual/ordinary Specialized/general Metaphorical/literal Scientific/literary	Expert/layperson Scholar/student Outsider/insider Political liberal/conservative Neutral observer/active participant	Intimate/distant Personal/impersonal Angry/calm Browbeating/sharing Informative/entertaining Humorous/serious Ironic/literal Passionately involved/aloof

- *Tone,* which refers to the writer's attitude toward the subject matter or toward the reader, such as cold or warm, humorous or serious, detached or passionate, straightforward or satirical

The style you adopt depends on your genre, audience, and purpose. Consider, for example, the style differences in two articles about the animated sitcom *South Park.* The first passage comes from an academic journal in which the author analyzes how race is portrayed in *South Park.* The second passage is from a popular magazine, where the author argues that despite *South Park*'s vulgarity, the sitcom has a redeeming social value.

Passage From Scholarly Journal

In these cartoons, multiplicity encodes a set of nonwhite identities to be appropriated and commodified by whiteness. In the cartoon world, obscene humor and satire mediate this commodification. The whiteness that appropriates typically does so by virtue of its mobile positioning between and through imagined boundaries contrarily shown as impassible to black characters or agents marked as black. Let me briefly turn to an appropriately confusing example of such a character in *South Park*'s scatological hero extraordinaire, Eric Cartman . . . . Eric Cartman's yen for breaking into Black English and interactions with black identities also fashion him an appropriator. However, Cartman's voice and persona may be seen as only an avatar, one layer of textual identity for creator Trey Parker, who may be regarded in one sense as a "blackvoice" performer.*(continued)*

—*Michael A. Chaney, "Representations of Race and Place in Static Shock, King of the Hill, and South Park"*

Passage From a Popular Blog

You can work overtime to protect your children's sweetness and innocence, or you can launch your pre-teens on the road to early cynicism by encouraging them to watch *South Park.* Consider the lessons that *South Park* teaches to its four protagonists, sensitive Kyle, A-student Stan, silent (and always one-step-away-from-death) Kenny, and obnoxious Cartman: Your teachers aren't very smart, and they come into the classroom with their own warped agendas. Your parents, and adults in general, are ignorant, pretentious, or downright moronic. The people running your country (and every other country) are power hungry, insane, and at least a little perverted. The people you consider your closest friends may not be friends at all, but simply a group of individuals with whom you are placed in an involuntary social net, whether a classroom, a town, or an office. While it's easy to be offended by *South Park*'s bitter and biting satire of American (and world) culture, there's no denying the elements of truth at its core. Education is inherently political; many adults are no more mature than most children; politicians, by virtue of their chosen profession, are by definition flawed (often desperately flawed) individuals. As the show's creators, Trey Parker and Matt Stone, prove in every episode, the most embittered cynics are the most disappointed idealists.

—Gareth Loken, *Teach Your Children Well*

For Writing and Discussion
Analyzing Differences in Style

Working in small groups or as a whole class, analyze the style differences of these two samples.

1. How would you describe differences in the length and complexity of sentences, in the level of vocabulary, and in the degree of formality?

2. How do the differences in style create different voices, personas, and tones?

3. Based on clues from style and genre, who is the intended audience of each piece? What is the writer's purpose? How does each writer hope to surprise the intended audience with something new, challenging, or valuable?

4. How are the differences in content and style influenced by differences in purpose, audience, and genre?

Ways to Make Your Style More Powerful

Your stylistic choices can enhance your appeals to *logos* (for example, by emphasizing main ideas), to *pathos* (by using words that evoke emotional responses and trigger associations), and to *ethos* (by creating an appropriate and effective voice). In the rest of this section we show how these strategies can make your own style more effective.

CONSTRUCT SENTENCES TO EMPHASIZE MAIN IDEAS   Experienced writers craft sentences that emphasize main ideas. For example, you can highlight an idea by placing it in a main clause rather than a subordinate clause or by placing it in a short sentence surrounded by longer sentences. We illustrated this phenomenon in our discussion of the U. R. Riddle exercise on angle of vision earlier in this chapter, where variations in sentence structure created different emphases on Riddle's good or bad points:

> Although Riddle is a brilliant thinker, he had problems relating to other students in my class. (Emphasizes Riddle's personal shortcomings)
> Although Riddle had problems relating to other students in my class, he is a brilliant thinker. (Emphasizes Riddle's intelligence)

Neither of these effects would have been possible had the writer simply strung together two simple sentences:

> Riddle had problems relating to other students in my class. He is also a brilliant thinker.

In this version, both points about Riddle are equally emphasized, leaving the reader uncertain about the writer's main point. If you string together a long sequence of short sentences—or simply join them with words like *and, or, so,* or *but*—you create a choppy effect that fails to distinguish between more important and less important material. Consider the example in Table 4.1.

WHERE APPROPRIATE, WRITE LOW ON THE LADDER OF ABSTRACTION
In previous writing courses, you might have been told to use concrete, specific

Table 4.1 Sentence Structure for Emphasis

Every Idea Equally Emphasized	Main Ideas Emphasized	Comment
I am a student at Sycamore College, and I live in Watkins Hall, and I am enclosing a proposal that concerns a problem with dorm life. There is too much drinking, so nondrinking students don't have an alcohol-free place to go, and so the university should create an alcohol-free dorm, and it should strictly enforce this no-alcohol policy.	As a Sycamore College student living in Watkins Hall, I am enclosing a proposal to improve dorm life. Because there is too much drinking on campus, there is no place for nondrinking students to go. I propose that the university create an alcohol-free dorm and strictly enforce the no-alcohol policy.	In the left-column version, every idea gets equal weight because every idea is in a main clause. In the middle-column version, subordinate ideas are tucked into phrases or subordinate clauses and the main ideas (the problem and the proposed solution) are placed in main clauses for emphasis.

language or to "show, not tell." Our advice in this section follows the same spirit: to write as low on the ladder of abstraction as your context allows.

We use the metaphor of a ladder to show how words can vary along a continuum from the abstract ("harm the environment") to the more specific and concrete ("poison freshwater trout with toxic sludge"). As a general rule, details that are low on the ladder of abstraction have a particular kind of rhetorical power: They appeal to *logos* by providing specific factual data as evidence or they appeal to *pathos* by triggering vivid images with emotional associations. As an illustration, consider Figure 4.4, which depicts a ladder of abstraction descending from abstract terms at the top toward more specific ones at the bottom.

Choosing words low on the ladder of abstraction is particularly effective for descriptive writing, where your goal is to create a vivid mental image for readers—hence the maxim "Show, don't tell." *Tell* words interpret a scene or

Figure 4.4 Ladder of Abstraction

Level on Ladder	Clothing Example	Charity Example	Global Agriculture Example	Gendered Play Examples
High level: abstract or general	Footwear	Love your neighbor	Traditional Crops grown in India versus commerical crops	Sam exhibited gendered play behavior.
Middle level	Flip flops	Help/feed the poor	Crops grown in India by traditional farmers versus genetically engineered crops.	Sam played with trucks and fire engines.
Low level: specific or concrete	Purple platform flip-flops with rhinestones	Chop vegetables for the Friday night soup kitchen dinner on 3rd Avenue	In Northern India, traditional mandua and jhangora versus genetically modified soy beans	Sam gleefully smashed his toy Tonka fire engine into the coffee table.

tell readers what to feel about a scene without describing it. ("The food smells wonderful and the people have happy faces.") In contrast, *show* words describe a scene through sensory details. ("The tantalizing smell of grilled hamburgers and buttered corn on the cob wafts from tailgate party barbecues, where men in their cookout aprons wield forks and spatulas and drink Budweisers.") The description evokes the desired effect without requiring the writer to interpret it overtly.

Of course, not all writing needs to be this low on the ladder of abstraction. Our advice, rather, is this: The supporting details for a paper should come from as low on the ladder as your context allows. Even the most abstract kind of prose will move up and down between several rungs on the ladder. In closed-form prose, writers need to make choices about the level of specificity that will be most effective based on their genre, audience, and purpose. Note the differences in the levels of abstraction in the following passages:

PASSAGE 1: FAIRLY HIGH ON LADDER OF ABSTRACTION

Although lightning produces the most deaths and injuries of all weather-related accidents, the rate of danger varies considerably from state to state. Florida has twice as many deaths and injuries from lightning strikes as any other state. Hawaii and Alaska have the fewest.

Point sentence

Details relatively high on ladder of abstraction

—*Passage from a general interest informative article on weather-related accidents*

PASSAGE 2: LOWER ON LADDER OF ABSTRACTION

Florida has twice as many deaths and injuries from lightning strikes as any other state, with many of these casualties occurring on the open spaces of golf courses. Florida golfers should carefully note the signals of dangerous weather conditions such as darkening skies, a sudden drop in temperature, an increase in wind, flashes of light and claps of thunder, and the sensation of an electric charge on one's hair or body. In the event of an electric storm, golfers should run into a forest, get under a shelter, get into a car, or assume the safest body position. To avoid being the tallest object in an area, if caught in open areas, golfers should find a low spot, spread out, and crouch into a curled position with feet together to create minimal body contact with the ground.

Point sentence

Details at middle level on ladder

Details at lower level on ladder

—*Passage from a safety article aimed at Florida golfers*

Both of these passages are effective for their audience and purpose. The first passage might be compared to a distant shot with a camera, giving an overview of lightning deaths in the United States, while the second zooms in for a more detailed look at a specific case, Florida golf courses. Sometimes, low-on-the-ladder particulars consist of statistics or quotations rather than sensory details. For example, civil engineer David Rockwood (see Concept 3.1) uses low-on-the-ladder numerical data about the size and number of wind towers to convince

For Writing and Discussion
Choosing Details for Different Levels on the Ladder of Abstraction

The following exercise will help you appreciate how details can be chosen at different levels of abstraction to serve different purposes and audiences. Working in small groups or as a whole class, invent details at appropriate positions on the ladder of abstraction for each of the following point sentences.

1. *Yesterday's game was a major disappointment.* You are writing an e-mail message to a friend who is a fan (of baseball, football, basketball, another sport) and missed the game; use mid-level details to explain what was disappointing.

2. *Although the game stank, there were some great moments.* Switch to low-on-the-ladder specific details to describe one of these "great moments."

3. *Advertising in women's fashion magazines creates a distorted and unhealthy view of beauty.* You are writing an analysis for a college course on popular culture; use high-to-mid-level details to give a one-paragraph overview of several ways these ads create an unhealthy view of beauty.

4. *One recent ad, in particular, conveys an especially destructive message about beauty.* Choose a particular ad and describe it with low-on-the-ladder, very specific details.

readers that wind generation of electricity entails environmental damage. Your rhetorical decisions about level of abstraction are important because too much high-on-the-scale writing can become dull for readers, while too much low-on-the-scale writing can seem overwhelming or pointless.

CREATE A VOICE MATCHED TO YOUR GENRE, AUDIENCE, AND PURPOSE College students often wonder what voice is appropriate for college papers. For most college assignments, we recommend that you approximate your natural speaking voice to give your writing a conversational academic style. By "conversational," we mean a voice that strives to be plain and clear while retaining the engaging quality of a person who is enthusiastic about the subject. Of course, as you become an expert in a discipline, you may need to move toward a more scholarly voice. For example, the prose in an academic journal article can be extremely dense with technical terms and complex sentence structure, but expert readers in that field understand and expect this voice.

Students sometimes try to imitate a dense academic style before they have achieved the disciplinary expertise to make the style sound natural. The result can seem pretentious or phony. At the other extreme, students sometimes adopt an overly informal or street slang voice that doesn't fit an academic context. Writing with clarity and directness within your natural range usually creates the most effective and powerful voice. Consider the differences in the examples shown in Table 4.2.

Although the conversational academic voice is appropriate for most college papers, especially those written for lower-division courses, many professors construct assignments asking you to adopt different voices and different styles. It is thus important to understand the professor's assignment and to adopt the style and voice appropriate for the assigned rhetorical situation.

Table 4.2 Levels of Formality in Voice

Overly Academic Voice	Conversational Academic Voice	Overly Informal Voice
As people advance in age, they experience time-dependent alterations in their ability to adapt to environmental change. However, much prior research on the aging process has failed to differentiate between detrimental changes caused by an organism's aging process itself and detrimental changes caused by a disease process that is often associated with aging.	As people get older, they are less able to adapt to changes in their environment. Research on aging, however, hasn't always distinguished between loss of function caused by aging itself and loss caused by diseases common among older people.	Old folks don't adapt well to changes in their environments. Some scientists who studied the cane and walker crowd found out that it was hard to tell the difference between bad stuff caused by age versus bad stuff caused by disease.

Chapter Summary

In this chapter we looked briefly at rhetorical theory in order to explain the persuasive power of both verbal and visual texts.

Concept 4.1 **Messages persuade through their angle of vision.** Any text necessarily looks at its subject from a perspective—an angle of vision—that selects and emphasizes some details while omitting or minimizing others. You can analyze writers' angle of vision by considering their direct statements of intention, their selection of details, their word choice, their figures of speech, and their manipulation of sentence structure to control emphasis.

Concept 4.2 **Messages persuade through appeals to *logos*, *ethos*, and *pathos*.**

Logos refers to the power of the writer's reasons and evidence; *pathos* to the way the writer connects to the reader's sympathies, emotions, values, and beliefs; and *ethos* to the way the writer portrays himself or herself as trustworthy and credible.

Concept 4.3 **Messages persuade through a writer's style and voice.** Stylistic features such as sentence structure, word choice, voice, and tone work together to create different rhetorical effects. An effective style highlights key ideas, moves down the ladder of abstraction for details, and establishes an appropriate voice.

Brief Writing Project

Two Contrasting Descriptions of the Same Scene

This brief writing project is a write-to-learn task that will help you appreciate how writers construct an angle of vision (see Concept 4.1) through selection of low-on-the-ladder details, word choice, and other means.

Adopt two different purposes for describing the same scene to an audience of your imagining. Use these contrasting purposes to create contrasting angles of vision. Your purpose in the first description is to convey a favorable impression of the scene, making it appear pleasing or attractive. Your purpose in the second description is to convey a negative or unfavorable impression, making the scene appear unpleasant or unattractive. Here is the catch: Both descriptions must contain only factual details and must describe exactly the same scene from the same location at the same time. It's not fair, in other words, to describe the scene in sunny weather and then in the rain or otherwise to alter factual details. Each description should be one paragraph long (approximately 125–175 words).

Your goal in these short passages is to create different rhetorical effects through the angle of vision you want to convey in your descriptions.

Once you have chosen your scene, you'll need to observe and take notes in preparation for writing the focused descriptions of the scene. You need to compose descriptions that are rich in sensory detail (low on the ladder of abstraction)—sights, sounds, smells, textures, tastes—all contributing to a dominant impression that gives the description focus.

You can train yourself to notice sensory details by creating a two-column sensory chart and noting details that appeal to each of the senses. Then try describing them, first positively (left column) and then negatively (right column). One student, observing a scene in a local tavern, made these notes in her sensory chart:

Positive Description	Negative Description
Taste	
salted and buttered popcorn	salty, greasy popcorn
frosty pitchers of beer	half-drunk pitchers of stale, warm beer
big bowls of salted-in-the-shell peanuts on the tables	mess of peanut shells and discarded pretzel wrappers on tables and floor
Sound	
hum of students laughing and chatting	din of high-pitched giggles and various obnoxious frat guys shouting at one another
the jukebox playing oldies but goodies from the early Beatles	jukebox blaring out-of-date music

Student Example

We conclude with a student example of this assignment.

Description 1—Positive Effect

Light rain gently drops into the puddles that have formed along the curb as I look out my apartment window at the corner of 14th and East John. Pedestrians layered in sweaters, raincoats, and scarves and guarded with shiny rubber boots and colorful umbrellas sip their steaming hot triple-tall lattes. Some share smiles and pleasant exchanges as they hurry down the street, hastening to work where it is warm and dry. Others, smelling the aroma of French roast espresso coming from the coffee bar next to the bus stop, listen for the familiar rumbling sound that will mean the 56 bus has arrived. Radiant orange, yellow, and red leaves blanket the sidewalk in the areas next to the maple trees that line the road. Along the curb a mother holds the hand of her toddler, dressed like a miniature tugboat captain in yellow raincoat and pants, who splashes happily in a puddle.

Description 2—Negative Effect

A solemn grayness hangs in the air, as I peer out the window of my apartment at the corner of 14th and East John. A steady drizzle of rain leaves boot-drenching puddles for pedestrians to avoid. Bundled in rubber boots, sweaters, coats, and rain-soaked scarves, commuters clutch Styrofoam cups of coffee as a defense against the biting cold. They lift their heads every so often to take a small sip of caffeine, but look sleep-swollen nevertheless. Pedestrians hurry past one another, moving quickly to get away from the dismal weather, the dull grayness. Some nod a brief hello to a familiar face, but most clutch their overcoats and tread grimly on, looking to avoid puddles or spray from passing cars. Others stand at the bus stop, hunched over, waiting in the drab early morning for the smell of diesel that means the 56 bus has arrived. Along the curb an impatient mother jerks the hand of a toddler to keep him from stomping in an oil-streaked puddle.

Chapter 5
Thinking Critically About Document Design, Visual Rhetoric, and Multimodal Messages

Learning Objectives

5.1 Analyze the rhetorical effects of document design and make appropriate document design choices.

5.2 Analyze the rhetorical use of images.

5.3 Analyze the rhetorical use of words, images, and sounds in multimodal texts.

In the last chapter we explained how verbal messages persuade through the writer's angle of vision; the writer's appeals to *logos, ethos,* and *pathos*; and the writer's style and voice. In this chapter we turn to visual rhetoric—particularly the rhetorical power of document design, images, and multimodal compositions that mix words, images, and sounds.

Concept 5.1: Document design has a persuasive effect on audiences.

5.1 **Analyze the rhetorical effects of document design and make appropriate document design choices.**

Document design, which refers to the format of a text on the page, can have a surprising rhetorical impact on a reader. The "look" of a document can signal to readers its purpose, its genre, its intended audience, and its writer's *ethos*. Writers need to distinguish between document design appropriate for keyboarded manuscripts and document design for camera-ready published works.

Document Design for Manuscripts and Papers

As a college student, you will usually be producing manuscript (keyboarded pages of typed text held together with a staple or folder, or submitted electronically) rather than a publication-ready document. Your document design choices mainly concern margins, font style and size, line spacing, and use of headers or footers. Generally these choices are dictated by the style guidelines of an academic discipline (for example, the guidelines of the American Psychological Association, or APA, for psychology papers) or by the conventions established in a business or professional setting. If you deviate from the expected document design, you risk appearing careless or simply unaware of academic or professional conventions. Attention to the design of your manuscripts thus signals your membership in an academic or professional community. An inappropriately formatted or sloppy paper can hurt your *ethos* and may send a message that you are unprofessional.

Document Design for Published Work

In contrast to manuscripts, published works require many more decisions about document design. Today's writers often use desktop-publishing software to produce camera-ready or Web-ready documents that have a professional visual appeal. What follows are some of the elements that must be considered.

TYPE   Type comes in different typeface styles, or **fonts,** which are commonly grouped in three font families:

1. **Serif fonts** have tiny extensions (called serifs) on the letters, which make them easier to read in long documents. This book is set in a serif font.
2. **Sans serif fonts** lack the extensions on the letters and are good for labels, headings, and short documents. This is an example of a sentence set in a sans serif font.
3. **Specialty fonts,** often used for decorative effect, include script fonts and special symbols. *This is an example of a sentence set in a specialty font.*

Fonts also come in different sizes and can be formatted with boldface, italics, underlining, or shading.

   In published documents, font use varies by genre. Scholarly print publications usually employ conservative typography: a consistently sized, plain, highly readable serif font with san serif variationsmainly reserved for titles and headings. Popular magazines, on the other hand, use fonts playfully and artistically; they vary font styles and sizes to attract readers' attention and to make articles look pleasingly decorative on the page. Although the body text of articles is usually the same font throughout, the opening page often uses a variety of fonts and sizes. Font variations may highlight key ideas for readers who are reading casually or rapidly. You may have noticed that this book uses **boldfaced words** to call attention to key terms.

SPACE AND LAYOUT **Layout** refers to how the text is formatted on the page. Layout includes the following elements:

- Page size, margin size, proportion of text to white space
- Arrangement of text on the page (single or multiple columns, spaces between paragraphs)
- Use of justification (alignment of text with the left or right margins or both margins)
- Placement of titles, use of headings and subheadings, and spacing before and after headings
- Use of numbered or bulleted lists or of boxes and sidebars to highlight ideas or break text into visual units

Academic and scholarly publications often use simple, highly functional document layouts. Most scholarly print journals use single or double columns of text that are justified at both margins to create a regular, even look. The layout of scholarly journals strikes a balance between maximizing the amount of text that fits on a page and ensuring readability.

In contrast, text layout in popular magazines and Web sites is usually more varied and playful, with text often wrapped around charts, sidebars, photographs, or drawings. While readability is important, so is visual appeal and entertainment: Readers must enjoy looking at the pages. For example, many popular print magazines try to blur the distinction between content and advertising so that ads become part of the visual appeal. This is why a magazine's table of contents is often buried a dozen or more pages into the magazine. The publisher wants to coax readers to think of the ads as part of the content. In contrast, the table of contents for academic print journals is often on the front cover.

COLOR Colors make powerful appeals, even affecting moods. Whereas manuscripts are printed entirely in black ink, published documents often use color to identify and set off main ideas or important information. Color-tinted boxes can indicate special features or allow different but related articles to appear on the same page. You will no doubt notice the use of color ink, tables, and boxes in this book. Ask yourself: Why has each of these elements been designed the way it appears?

GRAPHICS AND IMAGES **Graphics** include visual displays of information such as tables, line graphs, bar graphs, pie charts, maps, cartoons, illustrations, and photos. In scientific articles many of the important findings may be displayed in complex, technical graphs and tables. Sources of information for these graphics are usually prominently stated, with key variables clearly labeled. In the humanities and social sciences, content-rich photos and drawings also tend to be vital parts of an article, perhaps even the key subject of the analysis. In contrast, popular publications typically use less complex graphics, often designed to make a point (for example, a colorful pie chart or a dramatic graph). They often use many drawings or photos to create appeals to *pathos* and enhance interest.

For Writing And Discussion
Analyzing Rhetorical Effect

Your instructor will bring to class a variety of published documents—scholarly articles, popular magazine articles, newspapers, pamphlets, and so forth. Identify differences in design from document to document and analyze the rhetorical effects of those differences. In each case, how is document design related to genre? How does it contribute to the document's effectiveness?

Concept 5.2: Images have persuasive effects that can be analyzed rhetorically.

5.2 Analyze the rhetorical use of images.

Just as you can think rhetorically about texts, you can think rhetorically about photographs, drawings, and other images as well as cultural artifacts such as clothing.

The persuasive power of images can shape our impressions and understanding of events. Take, for instance, the heart-breaking photograph in summer 2015 of a drowned Syrian child washed up on a beach—a photograph that shocked audiences worldwide to care about refugees fleeing the Syrian civil war. As another example, consider the iconic photograph taken from an orbiting satellite of the jewel-like blue earth suspended in black space—a photograph that has inspired millions of people to care for our fragile earthly home.

Images and Appeals to *Logos*, *Ethos*, and *Pathos*

What gives these images their persuasive power? For one thing, viewers understand them at a glance. They condense an argument into a memorable scene or symbol that taps deeply into our emotions and values. Images also persuade by appealing to *logos*, *ethos*, and *pathos*. They make implicit arguments (*logos*) while also appealing to our values and emotions (*pathos*) and causing us to respond favorably or unfavorably to the artist or photographer (*ethos*). Like verbal texts, images have an angle of vision that controls what viewers see. (Note that "angle of vision" is itself a visual metaphor.) Through camera location, framing, filtering/lighting, and Photoshop techniques such as cropping, brushing, and blurring, the photographer steers us toward a particular view of the subject, influencing us to forget, at least momentarily, that there are other ways of seeing the same subject. For example, any college view book has photographs of the campus selected, cropped, and framed to make the campus look attractive, vigorous, and diverse. It is easy to imagine photographs taken from the same locations that would give a quite different impression of the campus.

Not only do photographs, paintings, and drawings have rhetorical power, but so do the images projected by many of our consumer choices. Consider the rhetorical thinking that goes into our choice of clothes. We choose our clothes not only to keep ourselves covered and warm but also to project visually our identification with certain social groups and subcultures. For example, if you want to be identified as a hipster, a geek, a NASCAR fan, or a junior partner in a corporate law firm, you know how to select clothes and accessories that convey that identification through visual cues. The way you dress is a code that communicates where you fit (or how you want to be perceived as fitting) within a class and social structure. Fashion ads consciously play on clothing codes to make consumers aware of the identifications that are signaled by different styles and brands. Our point, from a rhetorical perspective, is that in making a consumer choice, many people are concerned not only with the quality or cost of the item itself but also with its rhetorical symbolism. (Chapter 10 deals in depth with the rhetoric analysis of images, explaining how visual elements work together to create a persuasive effect.)

Images: Open to Interpretation

Although images can have powerful rhetorical effects, these effects may be less controllable and more audience dependent than those of verbal texts. Consider, for example, the photo in Figure 5.1 of a vast iceberg. This photo resembles those taken by environmental photographer James Balog for his Extreme Ice Survey, which documents the recent rapid melting of glaciers around the world. (Balog's work is featured in the award-winning documentary *Chasing Ice.*) In this photo, the iceberg towers above the water and glistens in the sun. When these photographs are used in the climate change debate, the intention is to document the

For a photo of melting glaciers that takes a clear stance in the climate change debate, see the image that introduces Part 3 of this text, which makes different appeals to *logos*, *ethos*, and *pathos*.

Figure 5.1 Floating Iceberg

rapid melting of Arctic and Antarctic ice—as shown by the size of the iceberg and the vast expanse of water in which it is floating. Viewers familiar with the context of shrinking glaciers and spectacular icebergs breaking off the glaciers will interpret the *logos* of this photo as evidence ofglobal warming, which in a matter of years is shrinking glaciers that took tens of thousands of years to form. In contrast, other viewers might find that the striking aesthetic beauty of this image distracts them from the global warming message. For them, the photographer's angle of vision and use of visual techniques have created a work of art that undermines its ability to convey scientific information in support of the idea that global climate change has reached crisis proportions. Interpreted in this way, the photo could be seen to use *pathos* to attract viewers to the magnificent, strange beauty of this part of the world, perhaps as a potential part of a travel brochure for Greenland or the northern Canadian territory of Nunavut. Because many images are open to different interpretations, writers of texts that include images should anticipate viewers' possible alternative interpretations and consider the importance of contextualizing images.

For further discussion of how to use words to guide viewers' interpretation of images, see Skill 20.2.

For Writing and Discussion
Analyzing Images

The following exercise asks you to think about the rhetorical effects of different images of wolves and particularly about how they can create implicit arguments in the public controversy about hunting wolves in western states. Ranchers and hunters argue that wolves are too numerous and aggressive in hunting livestock and game. The ranchers and hunters have lobbied state governments for hunting permits to kill hundreds of wolves. In contrast, animal rights groups, environmental organizations, and the Ojibwe/Anishinaabe and Sioux tribes have lobbied against these hunting permits, arguing that wolf populations sustain a natural ecological system in which wolves help keep deer and other wild animal populations in balance.

Analyzing the Photos. As you imagine the use of the images in Figures 5.2 to 5.5, explore the rhetorical effects of each image, noting how the effect may differ from viewer to viewer. In each photograph, on what details has the photographer chosen to focus? How do the details and angle of vision contribute to the dominant impression of wolves conveyed by the whole photograph? How does the photograph affect you emotionally? How does it shape your attitude toward wolves? How would you describe these images in terms of their emotional appeal and their favorable or unfavorable portrayalof wolves?

Using the Photos. Now imagine that you are creating a flyer for each of the following audiences and purposes. Which photo or photos would help you make the most compelling argument (consider *logos, ethos,* and *pathos*) for each group and purpose? Explain your rationale.

A. An organization consisting of hunters and ranchers has commissioned you to create a flyer that seeks to make the public more tolerant of hunting wolves now that the gray wolf has been taken off the Endangered Species list.

B. As part of its goal to protest the reinstated wolf-hunting permits, an environmental organization has asked you to create a flyer for the general public that seeks to generate appreciation for gray wolves' role in western ecosystems and to spark sympathy for wolves.

(continued)

Figure 5.2 Wolf in a Field of Grass

Figure 5.3 Four Wolves in Winter

Figure 5.4 Wolves with Deer Carcass

Figure 5.5 Wolf with Rabbit

Concept 5.3: Composers of multimodal texts use words, images, and sounds rhetorically to move an audience.

5.3   Analyze the rhetorical use of words, images, and sounds in multimodal texts.

In this concluding section of the chapter we expand our discussion of visual rhetoric to include a range of **multimodal texts**, by which we mean texts that supplement words with another mode of communication such as still images, moving images, or sounds. The word *multimodal* combines the concepts of "multi" (more than one) and "modality" (a channel, medium, or mode of communication). Multimodal texts can be either "stills" that combine words with images (a poster, a PowerPoint slide, a print advertisement) or texts in motion that combine video with voice, printed text, music, or other sounds (TV advertisements, advocacy videos, instructional YouTube videos).

The use of multimodal texts has increased dramatically in the digital age. Online technology allows full-color images, videos, animations, and sounds as well as text with embedded hyperlinks. The resulting interactive Web environment differs substantially from print text that you read in a linear fashion from left to right, top to bottom, beginning to end. Readers on the Web typically jump from page to page, influenced by multisensory stimuli urging them to pause on an image, scan a verbal text, or click on a link. In fact, research suggests that Internet surfers view a Web page for only a second or two before they move on to something else. Effective Web communicators have to use multimodal texts effectively to hook audiences quickly and keep them engaged. It is one thing to post on YouTube a funny video of leaping cats; it is quite another thing to compose a purposeful multimodal text that effectively uses rhetorical principles to move an audience.

Multimodal "Stills": Hook Audiences with Images and Take-Away Headlines

To appreciate the power of multimodal texts, let's begin with stills that combine images with words. As we explained in Concept 5.2, an effective image condenses an argument into a memorable scene or symbol that makes an impact at a glance and taps deeply into our emotions and values. But images by themselves usually need accompanying words to focus the image's point. Because many images have open-ended or multiple, ambiguous interpretations, designers of multimodal texts often use words to crystallize the intended meaning, thereby shaping the audience's response. A successful multimodal text thus combines an image with some kind of highlighted text (headline) that nutshells the text's take-away point. These nutshell headlines are the multimodal equivalent of a thesis statement or paragraph topic sentence in purely verbal text.

Consider as an example a classic World War II poster (Figure 5.6) alerting soldiers in jungle warfare to the dangers of unsafe drinking water. The poster shows a soldier, a canteen cup in his hand and a look of horror on his face, peering into a pond in search of drinking water. The poster's message is conveyed visually by the reflection of the soldier's face transfigured into a skull—a powerful appeal to *pathos*. But the same message is also conveyed textually through the words: "BEWARE . . . Drink Only Approved Water. Never give a germ a break!" The words, which appeal primarily to *logos*, serve as a nutshell for the whole argument, making the poster's message unmistakably clear.

But note how the words themselves also register visually through the effect of layout and font size. In the top half of the poster, the large-font, all-caps "BEWARE" seems to shout a warning to the soldier. In the bottom half of the poster, the text next to the skull—"Drink only approved water"—uses a smaller font and calm sentence to convey the poster's take-away message. Finally, the words along the poster's bottom border ("Never Give a Germ a Break!") in still a different font offer a causal explanation of why the water might kill you. Although the images alone convey the message at a glance, the poster's full punch comes from our registering the argument in both the visual and verbal parts of our brains.

Figure 5.6 World War II Poster

Multimodal Videos: Use Camera Strategies and Language to Make Narrative Arguments

Today anyone equipped with a smartphone or digital camera can make simple multimodal videos that can be edited with easy-to-learn software programs. Many students are therefore trying their hand at this powerful new genre. Although it is beyond the scope of this text to discuss the technology of video making, we can introduce you to the rhetorical thinking that underlies an effective multimodal video.

An effective video calls for a full range of visual analysis. A video can be paused at any moment to freeze single frames, each of which can be analyzed rhetorically as a still image using the strategies we just illustrated in the WWII poster. In the "play" mode, however, videos add the dimension of motion (narration, movement through time) as well as the power of sound (dialogue, background sounds, music, voice-over) to achieve desired effects. The trick is to make the visual and verbal language tell the same story.

A multimodal video makes its narrative impact along two channels, a visual and a verbal. First, a video's message is told in words through voice-overs, dialogue, or printed text overlaid on the screen. But the message is also conveyed through the visual grammar deployed through camera placement and technique. Teachers of video production say that beginning camera users tend to photograph the action from one camera position only— usually a distance or mid-distance shot—that requires minimal editing. In contrast, experienced videographers shoot from several positions and purposely use cutting and splicing techniques to narrate the action through the perspective of different camera positions. They choose each position for a rhetorical purpose in order to emphasize some parts of the action and deemphasize others. Their goal is to *design* or *compose* a video sequence that has a narrative arc and shape. Film specialists compose a sequence of shots by thinking about framing and camera position. They use wide-angle shots to establish the context; medium close-ups to show specific actions; and closeups—either relaxed or extreme—to show emotion on faces. They also create a narrative arc through different kinds of shots:

For more detailed discussion of visual analysis, see Chapter 10 ("Analyzing Images"). For a fuller discussion of multimodal compositions, see Chapter 20 ("Strategies for Composing Multimodal Texts").

- *Establishing shots* set the narrative in a context by showing location and setting (often wide-angle shots).
- *Reaction shots* show a close-up, often of a face, to reveal a character's emotional reaction.
- *Point-of-view shots* look at a scene through the eyes of one of the characters.

These three kinds of camera positions are illustrated in Figure 5.7, which shows still frames from a student video promoting urban gardens. The video

Figure 5.7 Urban Gardener Video

Establishing shot (wide-angle shot)

Point-of-view shot

Reaction shot (relaxed close-up shot)

features an urban gardener gathering eggs from her backyard chicken coop. The first image is a wide-angle establishing shot showing the chicken coop, some chickens, and the woman lifting the coop door to retrieve the day's eggs. Next we see a point-of-view shot (looking through the woman's eyes) of the eggs up close, including the woman's hand grasping one of the eggs. Finally, we see a relaxedclose-up reaction shot showing the woman's smiling face expressing happiness for the eggs and gratitude toward her hens. These different camera positions create a brief narrative arc of the urban gardener's anticipation of and satisfaction at getting eggs from her free-range backyard chickens.

For Writing And Discussion
Analyzing a Video Sequence

Watch and then analyze a short video assigned by your instructor or chosen by yourself. The video should use different camera positions as well as sounds for rhetorical effect.

1. *Analyzing editing choices.* After playing the whole clip several times, pause the video at each of the edits where the camera position shifts. Consider the following questions: How does the videographer use establishing, point-of-view, and reaction shots to achieve a desired effect on viewers? What is the rhetorical purpose of each camera position? What is emphasized in each camera position? How does the sequence create a thematic point or meaning?

2. *Analyzing still frames.* Pause the video on several frames that can be analyzed rhetorically like a photograph. How is the scene framed? How is it lighted or filtered? What is the camera angle and distance? What is the subject matter of the scene? If the scene contains people, what is the rhetorical effect of the characters' clothing and accessories, hairstyle, gestures, poses, and positioning? How would you analyze the scene in terms of gender, social class, or implied values?

3. *Analyzing sound.* Finally, play the clip again, this time paying attention to sounds. If the video includes music, what is the effect of the musical choices? If the clip has a voice-over, what is the effect of the choices about gender, vocal register, accent, pacing, and so forth? What sounds are emphasized in the video? What sounds might have been filtered out?

Chapter Summary

In this chapter we focused on visual rhetoric to analyze the power of document design, images, and multimodal texts.

Concept 5.1   Document design has a persuasive effect on audiences. Principles for document design differ depending on whether you are producing manuscript or desktop-published work. In producing manuscripts, expert writers follow the guidelines of their academic or professional communities, thereby signaling insider status. Design features for published documents include font sizes and styles, layout and spacing, use of color, and use of graphics or images. Academic articles generally adopt a conservative design while more popular genres approach design playfully and artistically.

Concept 5.2   **Images have persuasive effects that can be analyzed rhetorically.** Like verbal texts, images have an angle of vision created by the way the image is framed and by the perspective from which it is viewed. Images also make implicit arguments (*logos*), appeal to the viewer's emotions and values (*pathos*), and suggest the creator's character and trustworthiness (*ethos*). One can also analyze consumer choices (clothing, jewelry, cars) rhetorically because such choices make implicit arguments about the consumer's desired identity.

Concept 5.3   **Composers of multimodal texts use words, images, and sounds rhetorically to move an audience.** Multimodal texts can be either stills or texts in motion. Effective stills combine the emotional impact of images with verbal headlines that drive home the message's take-away point. Effective videos typically combine moving images with language (voice-overs, printed text), music, and other sounds. The visual channel of an effective video often uses camera angle and position (for example, establishing shots, point-of-view shots, and reaction shots) to achieve a visual grammar that tells a story.

Brief Writing Project

Description and Reflection on Your Creation of a Multimodal Composition

Recollect a multimodal text that you have created either for a class or for personal reasons. Your creation could have involved any combination of two or more media such as verbal text, still images, video, and sound. This brief assignment asks you to describe your creation and reflect on it.

1. *Part 1.* Describe the multimodal text that you created—for example, a poster or brochure, a research report that incorporated graphs and images, a podcast, a video, a slideshow set to music, a Facebook page, and so forth. Describe your multimodal creation. What was its core message? What was its rhetorical context—your purpose and your audience? What were you trying to accomplish with this multimodal text?

2. *Part 2.* Reflect on why you designed it the way you did and on the responses that you received. Particularly explain the challenges of creating this text and the effect you wanted this text to have on your audience. Think about the concepts in this chapter and explain which ones particularly relate to the challenges you faced and the degree of success you had with this text.

Part II
Writing Projects

This poster, sponsored by the Ad Council and StopBullying.gov, is part of an ongoing campaign to curtail bullying among young people. The ad is aimed at parents, urging them to encourage their children to be active in opposing bullying. Although the ad's creators chose to use lettering—not an image—to illustrate bullying, the poster has both visual and verbal rhetorical effects. It makes strong appeals to *pathos* in its use of shocking abusive language and disturbing lettering style. Note how the blurry presentation of the type makes a visual statement about both perception and psychological damage. It reinforces the idea that not everyone is aware of bullying and suggests that bullying dims the personhood of victims. Together with the line about parents' unawareness of the hostility present in their kids' environment, this ad presents a powerful message to parents.

Chapter 6
Reading Rhetorically: The Writer as Strong Reader

Learning Objectives

6.1 Apply strategies for reading texts rhetorically.

6.2 Apply analytical skills, including does/says analysis, to see a text's structure and to separate points from details.

6.3 Write effective summaries of texts.

6.4 Understand the different types of strong response writing.

6.5 Write strong responses to texts by analyzing their rhetorical strategies and engaging their ideas.

Understanding rhetorical reading

6.1 Apply strategies for reading texts rhetorically.

Many new college students are surprised by the amount, range, and difficulty of their college reading requirements. Every day they are challenged by reading assignments ranging from scholarly articles on complex subject matter to primary sources such as Plato's dialogues or Darwin's *Voyage of the Beagle*. To add to the challenge, many college writing assignments are text based—that is, instructors ask students to write critical essays provoked by their understanding and analysis of, and critical response to, one or more readings.

College-level reading often requires students to read as "outsiders." Many of these readings were written for occasions, purposes, and audiences that students may not know or understand. You must recreate these contexts through close reading, critical thinking, analysis, and sometimes research. Rather than reading to extract information for an exam, you must read rhetorically to join a conversation. To read *rhetorically* means to note how audience, purpose, occasion, and genre shape a text. Readers read rhetorically when they are aware of a text's intended effect on the reader. Strong rhetorical readers analyze how the parts of a text work together persuasively, and they think critically about whether to accede to or challenge the text's intentions. To read rhetorically, you need to practice the reading strategies of experts summarized in Table 1.2 in Chapter 1.

This chapter explains general strategies for reading texts rhetorically— filling the gaps caused by your outsider status and reading both with and against the grain. It then shows you how to observe and "listen" to a reading by writing a summary. Finally it shows you how to analyze the reading, critique it, and write your own strong response. The **summary**, and various kinds of **strong response essays**, are among the most common academic genres based on readings. In most cases, a strong response essay includes a summary of the text to which the writer is responding. This chapter will help you become a more powerful reader of academic texts, prepared to write with deeper understanding, and to take part in the conversations provoked by the readings.

As a first step, read the article that we will use throughout the chapter.

A Sample Reading for Analysis

The rest of this chapter uses the following reading to illustrate the strategies of rhetorical reading. It is an article from *The New York Times* by Canadian writer Stephen Marche, who holds a doctorate in early modern drama. He is known as a novelist and journalist whose work has appeared in *The Atlantic, Esquire, The Globe and Mail,* and *The Toronto Star,* among others. Read the article and respond to the questions that follow. As you read, you may note sections that are challenging or that contain concepts you are not familiar with. Take note of these challenging concepts and words, but keep reading.

Stephen Marche
The Epidemic of Facelessness

1   A part-time delivery driver named Peter Nunn was recently sentenced to 18 weeks in a British prison for tweeting and retweeting violent messages to Stella Creasy, a member of Parliament. He never saw his victim but the consequences of his virtual crime were real enough. In a statement, Ms. Creasy described fears for her physical safety, going so far as to install a panic button in her home. Mr. Nunn has been physically separated from the rest of society for posting abusive words on a social media site.

2   The fact that the case ended up in court is rare; the viciousness it represents is not. Everyone in the digital space is, at one point or another, exposed to online monstrosity, one of the consequences of the uniquely contemporary condition of facelessness.

3   Every month brings fresh figuration to the sprawling, shifting Hieronymus Bosch canvas of faceless 21st-century contempt. Faceless contempt is not merely topical. It is increasingly the defining trait of topicality itself. Every day online provides its measure of empty outrage.

4   When the police come to the doors of the young men and women who send notes telling strangers that they want to rape them, they and their parents are almost always shocked, genuinely surprised

(Continued)

that anyone would take what they said seriously, that anyone would take anything said online seriously. There is a vast dissonance between virtual communication and an actual police officer at the door. It is a dissonance we are all running up against more and more, the dissonance between the world of faces and the world without faces. And the world without faces is coming to dominate.

5   Recently Dick Costolo, chief executive of Twitter, lamented his company's failures to deal with the trolls that infested it: "I'm frankly ashamed of how poorly we've dealt with this issue during my tenure as CEO," he said in a leaked memo. It's commendable of him to admit the torrents of abuse, but it's also no mere technical error on the part of Twitter; faceless rage is inherent to its technology.

6   It's not Twitter's fault that human beings use it. But the faceless communication social media creates, the linked distances between people, both provokes and mitigates the inherent capacity for monstrosity.

7   The Gyges effect, the well-noted disinhibition created by communications over the distances of the Internet, in which all speech and image are muted and at arm's reach, produces an inevitable reaction—the desire for impact at any cost, the desire to reach through the screen, to make somebody feel something, anything. A simple comment can so easily be ignored. Rape threat? Not so much. Or, as Mr. Nunn so succinctly put it on Twitter: "If you can't threaten to rape a celebrity, what is the point in having them?"

8   The challenge of our moment is that the face has been at the root of justice and ethics for 2,000 years. The right to face an accuser is one of the very first principles of the law, described in the "confrontation clause" of the Sixth Amendment of the United States Constitution, but reaching back through English common law to ancient Rome. In Roman courts no man could be sentenced to death without first seeing his accuser. The precondition of any trial, of any attempt to reconcile competing claims, is that the victim and the accused look each other in the face.

9   For the great French-Jewish philosopher Emmanuel Levinas, the encounter with another's face was the origin of identity—the reality of the other preceding the formation of the self. The face is the substance, not just the reflection, of the infinity of another person. And from the infinity of the face comes the sense of inevitable obligation, the possibility of discourse, the origin of the ethical impulse.

10   The connection between the face and ethical behavior is one of the exceedingly rare instances in which French phenomenology and contemporary neuroscience coincide in their conclusions. A 2009 study by Marco Iacoboni, a neuroscientist at the Ahmanson-Lovelace Brain Mapping Center at the University of California, Los Angeles, explained the connection: "Through imitation and mimicry, we are able to feel what other people feel. By being able to feel what other people feel, we are also able to respond compassionately to other people's emotional states." The face is the key to the sense of intersubjectivity, linking mimicry and empathy through mirror neurons—the brain mechanism that creates imitation even in nonhuman primates.

11   The connection goes the other way, too. Inability to see a face is, in the most direct way, inability to recognize shared humanity with another. In a metastudy of antisocial populations, the inability to sense the emotions on other people's faces was a key correlation. There is "a consistent, robust link between antisocial behavior and impaired recognition of fearful facial affect. Relative to comparison groups, antisocial populations showed significant impairments in recognizing fearful, sad and surprised expressions." A recent study in the *Journal of Vision* showed that babies between the ages of 4 months and 6 months recognized human faces at the same level as grown adults, an ability which they did not possess for other objects.

12   Without a face, the self can form only with the rejection of all otherness, with a generalized, all-purpose contempt—a contempt that is so vacuous because it is so vague, and so ferocious because

it is so vacuous. A world stripped of faces is a world stripped, not merely of ethics, but of the biological and cultural foundations of ethics.

13   For the great existentialist Martin Heidegger, the spirit of homelessness defined the 20th century, a disconnected drifting in a world of groundless artificiality. The spirit of facelessness is coming to define the 21st. Facelessness is not a trend; it is a social phase we are entering that we have not yet figured out how to navigate.

14   As exchange and communication come at a remove, the flight back to the face takes on new urgency. Google recently reported that on Android alone, which has more than a billion active users, people take 93 million selfies a day. The selfie has become not a single act but a continuous process of self-portraiture. On the phones that are so much of our lives, no individual self-image is adequate; instead a rapid progression of self-images mimics the changeability and the variety of real human presence.

15   Emojis are an explicit attempt to replicate the emotional context that facial expression provides. Intriguingly, emojis express emotion, often negative emotions, but you cannot troll with them. You cannot send a message of faceless contempt with icons of faces. The mere desire to imitate a face humanizes.

16   But all these attempts to provide a digital face run counter to the main current of our era's essential facelessness. The volume of digital threats appears to be too large for police forces to adequately deal with. But cases of trolls' following through on their online threat of murder and rape are extremely rare. The closest most trolling comes to actual violence is "swatting," or sending ambulances or SWAT teams to an enemy's house. Again, neither victim nor perpetrator sees the other.

17   What do we do with the trolls? It is one of the questions of the age. There are those who argue that we have a social responsibility to confront them. Mary Beard, the British historian, not only confronted a troll who sent her misogynistic messages, she befriended him and ended up writing him letters of reference. One young video game reviewer, Alanah Pearce, sent Facebook messages to the mothers of young boys who had sent her rape threats. These stories have the flavor of the heroic, a resistance to an assumed condition: giving face to the faceless.

18   The more established wisdom about trolls, at this point, is to disengage. Obviously, in many cases, actual crimes are being committed, crimes that demand confrontation, by victims and by law enforcement officials, but in everyday digital life engaging with the trolls "is like trying to drown a vampire with your own blood," as the comedian Andy Richter put it. Ironically, the Anonymous collective, a pioneer of facelessness, has offered more or less the same advice.

19   Rule 14 of their "Rules of the Internet" is, "Do not argue with trolls—it means that they win.

20   Rule 19 is, "The more you hate it the stronger it gets."

21   Ultimately, neither solution—confrontation or avoidance—satisfies. Even if confrontation were the correct strategy, those who are hounded by trolls do not have the time to confront them. To leave the faceless to their facelessness is also unacceptable—why should they own the digital space simply because of the anonymity of their cruelty?

22   There is a third way, distinct from confrontation or avoidance: compassion. The original trolls, Scandinavian monsters who haunted the Vikings, inhabited graveyards or mountains, which is why adventurers would always run into them on the road or at night. They were dull. They possessed monstrous force but only a dim sense of the reality of others. They were mystical nature-forces that lived in the distant, dark places between human habitations. The problem of contemporary trolls is a subset of a larger crisis, which is itself a consequence of the transformation of our modes of communication. Trolls breed under the shadows of the bridges we build.

(Continued)

23   In a world without faces, compassion is a practice that requires discipline, even imagination. Social media seems so easy; the whole point of its pleasure is its sense of casual familiarity. But we need a new art of conversation for the new conversations we are having—and the first rule of that art must be to remember that we are talking to human beings: "Never say anything online that you wouldn't say to somebody's face." But also: "Don't listen to what people wouldn't say to your face."

24   The neurological research demonstrates that empathy, far from being an artificial construct of civilization, is integral to our biology. And when biological intersubjectivity disappears, when the face is removed from life, empathy and compassion can no longer be taken for granted.

25   The new facelessness hides the humanity of monsters and of victims both. Behind the angry tangles of wires, the question is, how do we see their faces again?

For Writing and Discussion
Your Initial Response to "The Epidemic of Facelessness"

Working individually, freewrite your responses to the following questions. Then share ideas in small groups or as a whole class.

1. What is your initial reaction to Marche's article?

2. Where did you experience difficulties in reading the article? What slowed you down, caused you to reread, or left you confused?

The full meaning and significance of *rhetorical context* is explained in Chapters 3 and 4.

Filling Gaps Caused by Your "Outsider" Status

Many students find the Marche essay moderately difficult to understand on first reading. Much of this difficulty stems from students' not being the target audience for the text. Here are four reasons why you might find Marche's article challenging, along with suggested strategies for filling in the gaps:

- **Unfamiliar rhetorical context.** Because college students aren't the intended audience for the reading, you have to figure out to whom the author was originally writing and why. Knowing an author's audience, purpose, and occasion may clarify confusing parts of a text. For example, Stephen Marche's article was published in the *New York Times Magazine*, which attracts a liberal, well-educated audience. Marche assumes that his audience has encountered Internet trolls, is disturbed by them, and doesn't know how to deal with them. His purpose is to persuade readers to understand the problem of anonymous verbal violence on the Internet in terms of the problem of "facelessness," and to suggest ways for making the Internet a kinder space for communication. A text's internal clues can sometimes help you fill in the rhetorical context, but often you may need to do outside research. Often a quick Web search of the author or the reading's title will provide needed context.

- **Unfamiliar genre.** Recall that *genre* refers to the different writing formats and styles that are used in certain situations. Each genre makes different demands on readers. In college you will encounter a wide range of genres, such as magazine articles, books, blogs, instruction manuals, scholarly articles, scientific reports, historical documents, newspaper editorials, and op-ed pieces. Marche's genre is what we might call a "public intellectual magazine article." It doesn't look or feel anything like a textbook, a newspaper editorial, or a Wikipedia article. With practice you will learn what to expect when you encounter different genres. As an outsider, just being aware that different genres make different demands on readers helps you know the questions to ask.

- **Unfamiliar vocabulary.** Many college-level readings contain unfamiliar or technical words or terminology. Stephen Marche's article, for example, uses the terms *phenomenology*, *metastudy*, and *intersubjectivity*. Be prepared for unfamiliar words by keeping a dictionary at hand (or keeping an online dictionary bookmarked on your Internet browser). However, some terms carry specialized meanings that evoke a whole history of conversation and debate that cannot be summarized in a simple dictionary entry. Good examples are *postmodernism, string theory, supply-side economics,* and *cultural materialism.* You will not fully understand these terms until you enter and take part in the disciplinary conversations that gave rise to them. You often just have to live for a while with this uncertainty.

Genre is explained in Concept 3.2.

- **Lack of background knowledge.** Writers necessarily make assumptions about what their readers already know. For example, Marche refers to the existentialist Martin Heidegger and the philosopher Emmanuel Levinas and to the Dutch painter Hieronymus Bosch. He also draws on readers' assumed knowledge of popular culture (tweeting and retweeting, selfies, emojis, trolls) and of intellectual culture (the Gyges effect, mirror neurons, and English common law). The more you possess this background knowledge, the more easily you will comprehend Marche's argument. You need to recognize where lack of background knowledge creates obstacles to understanding and develop research strategies for filling in gaps. In the Internet age, we are fortunate to have the almost instantaneous ability to fill in background gaps with a simple Web search.

For Writing and Discussion
Appreciating the Importance of Background Knowledge

The importance of background knowledge becomes readily apparent any time you read articles from outside your familiar communities. Readings from unfamiliar cultures, earlier historical periods, or special-interest communities often assume background knowledge that you don't have. Consider the following passage, spoken by water activist Maude Barlow in a speech to the United Nations. What cultural knowledge or background knowledge of ecology and environmental engineering would you need to have in order to reach a full understanding of this passage?

Finally, watersheds must be protected from plunder and we must revitalize wounded water systems with widespread watershed restoration programs. Simply put, we must leave enough water in aquifers, rivers and lakes for their ecological health. This must be the priority: the precautionary principle of ecosystem protection must take precedence over commercial demands on these waters. This means that we will have to abandon the "hard path" of large-scale technology - dams, diversion and desalination - in favor of the "soft path" of conservation, rainwater and storm water harvesting, recycling, alternative energy

(Continued)

use, municipal infrastructure investment and local, sustainable food production. Living in and with nature instead of over nature is our path to a water sustainable future.

As a crucial next step, nature must be seen as having inherent rights beyond its use to us. Most Western law has viewed natural resources as the property of humans. We need new laws to regulate human behavior in order to protect the integrity of the Earth and all species on it, from our wanton exploitation. Rivers have rights to flow to the sea.

We, none of us, can live on a dry planet. Let us celebrate moving waters on this first United Nations International Mother Earth Day.

— Maude Barlow*

Working in small groups or as a class, identify words and passages in this text that depend on background information or knowledge about water management for complete comprehension.

---

* From "Notes for U.N. Panel International Mother Earth," by Maude Barlow. Barlow gave this speech to the General Assembly of the United Nations on April 22 (Earth Day), 2009. Used with permission.

Reading with the Grain and against the Grain

Rhetorical readers read texts both with the grain and against the grain. When you read *with the grain* of a text, you see the world through its author's perspective, open yourself to the author's argument, apply the text's insights to new contexts, and connect its ideas to your own experiences and personal knowledge. When you read *against the grain* of a text, you resist it by questioning its points, raising doubts, analyzing the limits of its perspective, or even refuting its argument. Reading with and against the grain is analogous to the believing and doubting game we introduced in Concept 2.1. Both strategies enable skilled readers to interact strongly with texts.

When you read with the grain of a text, you withhold all judgment of a text. You practice what psychologist Carl Rogers calls *empathic listening*, in which you try to see the world through the author's eyes, role-playing as much as possible the author's intended readers by adopting their beliefs and values and acquiring their background knowledge. Reading with the grain is the main strategy you use when you summarize a text, but it also comes into play when you develop a strong response. When making with-the-grain points, you support the author's thesis with your own arguments and examples, or you apply or extend the author's argument in new ways.

When you read against the grain of a text, you question and perhaps even rebut the author's ideas. You are a resistant reader who asks questions, pushes back, and reads the text in ways unforeseen by the author. You note what the author has left out or covered weakly. Reading against the grain is a key part of creating a strong response. When you make against-the-grain points, you challenge the author's reasoning, sources, examples, or choices of language. You present alternative lines of reasoning, deny the writer's values, or raise points or specific data that the writer has omitted. Strategies Chart 6.1 offers strategies for thinking with the grain and against the grain, along with particular occasions when each is helpful.

Strategies Chart 6.1 Strategies for Reading with and against the Grain

Reading with the Grain	Reading against the Grain
• Listen to the text, follow the author's reasoning, and withhold judgment. • Try to see the subject and the world from the author's perspective. • Add further support to the author's thesis with your own points and examples. • Apply the author's argument in new ways.	• Challenge, question, and resist the author's ideas. • Point out what the author has left out or overlooked; note what the author has *not* said. • Identify what assumptions, ideas, or facts seem unsupported or inaccurate. • Rebut the author's ideas with counterreasoning and counterexamples.
Occasions When Most Useful	**Occasions When Most Useful**
Writing Summaries: In writing summaries, you listen to a text without judgment to identify the main ideas. **Writing Analysis and Synthesis Essays:** In writing analyses, you seek to understand a text to determine points to elaborate on and discuss. In synthesizing ideas from sources, you determine what ideas to adopt and build on. **Writing Arguments:** In writing arguments, you inhabit an author's viewpoint to deepen your understanding of an issue and to understand alternative views so you can represent them fairly.	**Writing Analysis, Critique, Strong Response, and Synthesis Essays:** In writing an initial strong response, you determine the ways in which your beliefs, values, and views might be different from the author's. In writing analyses, you identify limitations in the author's view. In synthesizing, you determine which ideas to reject, replace, or go beyond. **Writing Arguments:** In writing arguments, you develop refutations and rebuttals to the author's views.

Strong rhetorical readers develop their ability to read in both ways—with the grain and against the grain. Practicing this skill often requires emotional and psychic energy: If you agree with a text's ideas it can be challenging to read it against the grain. Likewise, if you disagree with a text's ideas, it can be challenging to read it with the grain. Some readers prefer to separate these approaches by first reading a text with the grain and then rereading it against the grain. Throughout the rest of this chapter, we show you different ways to apply these strategies in your reading and writing.

Understanding summary writing

6.2 Apply analytical skills, including does/says analysis, to see a text's structure and to separate points from details.

A **summary** is a condensed version of a text that extracts and presents main ideas in a way that does justice to the author's intentions. As fairly and objectively as possible, a summary states the main ideas of a longer text, such as an article or a book. Although the words *summary* and *abstract* are often used interchangeably, the term **abstract** is most often used for a stand-alone summary printed in conference programs or at the head of a published article in a scholarly journal. Often, however, summaries do not stand alone. Writer A may summarize Writer B's argument and insert that summary into Writer A's text. When you incorporate a summary of another person's argument into your own argument, you must distinguish your ideas from the other writer's ideas by using **attributive tags** (sometimes called **signal tags**). We explain these terms later in this chapter.

Usefulness of Summaries

Summary writing fosters a close engagement between you and the text. A good summary indicates that you have "listened" to another writer's argument and demonstrates your understanding of it. Because it forces you to distinguish between main and subordinate points and details, summary writing is a valuable tool for improving your reading comprehension. Summary writing is also useful in other ways. For example, summaries at the beginning of articles, in prefaces to books, and on book jackets help readers determine if they want to read the article or book. Engineers and business executives place "executive summaries" at the beginning of major reports. In the "literature review" section of scientific papers, summaries of previous research are used to point to knowledge gaps that the present researchers will try to fill. Finally, writing summaries is a particularly important part of college research writing, which often requires you to present condensed views of other writers' arguments, either in support of your own view or as alternative views that you are analyzing, refuting, or otherwise responding to. As students have noted later in their academic careers, summary writing is a useful, transferable skill.

The Process of Writing a Summary

The process of summary writing closely follows the first step of the "analysis game" described in Concept 2.1. As explained in Chapter 2, Step One asks you to slow down, to look at the whole of what you are analyzing, and then to look at each part—considering the relationship of each part to other parts and to the whole. It also asks you to distinguish main ideas from supporting details, the essential points from the layers of examples and discussion. Finally, the analysis game asks you to look individually at each paragraph, trying to understand both its function and content. The best way to do so is to read each paragraph carefully and then articulate what the paragraph does (its function within the reading as a whole) and what the paragraph says (its content). We call this process a *does/says analysis*. Here are the steps for writing a summary.

REREAD THE ARTICLE CAREFULLY   As you prepare to write your summary, read the article again fairly quickly for general meaning. If you get confused, keep going; later parts of the text might clarify earlier parts. As much as possible fill in the gaps caused by your "outsider" status: look up difficult vocabulary words, research needed background knowledge, and reconstruct the author's original purpose, audience, occasion, and genre. Then reread the text slowly, trying to dwell with the text, engaging its ideas.

DO A DOES/SAYS ANALYSIS   Now focus carefully on each paragraph. As you read, write gist statements in the margins for each paragraph. A *gist statement* is a brief indication of a paragraph's function in the text or a brief summary of its content. Sometimes it is helpful to categorize gist statements into "what it does" statements and "what it says" statements.* A *what it does* statement specifies the paragraph's function—for example, "summarizes an opposing view," "introduces another reason," "presents a supporting example," "provides statistical data in support of a point," and so on. A *what it says* statement summarizes the

---

*For our treatment of "what it does" and "what it says" statements, we are indebted to Kenneth A. Bruffee, A Short Course in Writing, 2nd ed. (Cambridge, MA: Winthrop, 1980).

paragraph's content in your own words. The *what it says* statement is the paragraph's main point, in contrast to its supporting ideas, examples, and details.

After you have made marginal gist statements, return again to the text paragraph by paragraph and write out complete *does* and *says* sentences for each paragraph. (You can shorten this process once you become skilled at writing summaries.) Here are student writer Scott Lindquist's *does* and *says* statements for selected paragraphs of Stephen Marche's "The Epidemic of Facelessness":

Paragraph 1:

Does: Provides an anecdote to engage readers' interest in the problem of trolls.

Says: A truck driver in Britain has been jailed for online harassment of a member of parliament.

Paragraph 2:

Does: Introduces online harassment as a pervasive problem.

Says: Everyone witnesses or experiences unprosecuted abuse online because the Internet is a "faceless" environment.

Paragraph 4:

Does: Elaborates further on the problem to underscore its seriousness and prevalence.

Says: Although trolls are often surprised when their victims take them seriously and call the police, individuals are beginning to be held more accountable for their behavior online.

Paragraph 5:

Does: Cites an expert to further develop the enormity of the problem.

Says: Powerful Internet company CEOs like Dick Costolo are unable to prevent online abuse from happening in social media platforms like Twitter because facelessness is a part of the online experience, and facelessness invites people to behave less ethically.

Paragraph 6:

Does: Presents the article's thesis.

Says: The fact that people are "faceless" online and aren't physically present to one another both encourages abusive communication and lessens its effects.

Paragraph 8:

Does: Provides historical support for Marche's argument about the importance of face-to-face communication in promoting law and morality.

Says: A precondition of law and morality is that the victim and the accused must see each other face-to-face.

Paragraph 10:

Does: Uses a scientific study to show the importance of face-to-face interaction.

Says: According to neuroscientist Marco Iacoboni, we develop compassion by experiencing what others feel through the mimicking responses of "mirror neurons" in our brains.

For Writing and Discussion
Completing a Does/Says Analysis of Marche's Article

Working individually, compose does/says statements for paragraphs 11–25 of Marche's article. Then compare your statements with those of classmates.

LOCATE THE ARTICLE'S MAIN DIVISIONS OR PARTS   In longer closed-form articles, writers often forecast the shape of their essays in their introductions or use their conclusions to sum up main points. For example, Marche's article uses some forecasting and transitional statements to direct readers through its parts and main points. Using his *does/says* statements as a guide, student writer Scott Lindquist (whose summary of and strong response to this article are featured in the rest of this chapter) decided that Marche's article divides into the following main chunks:

- An introductory section (paragraphs 1–6) sets up the problem of trolls who spew anonymous online contempt and ends with a thesis that even companies like Twitter can't curb "trolling" because faceless communication inhibits peoples' abilities to empathize with one another.

- A section (paragraphs 7–13) draws on philosophers and contemporary research to support the argument that face-to-face interaction helps people communicate ethically and compassionately.

- A section (paragraphs 14–16) analyzes selfies and emojis as inadequate attempts to include faces in online communications to provide more emotional context for Internet users.

- A section (paragraphs 17–21) details possible responses to trolls:
  - Five paragraphs (17–21) show the inadequacy of confrontation and avoidance.
  - Another paragraph (22) says that we can respond to trolls with compassion by drawing parallels between the trolls of Scandinavian myth who lived in "dark places between human habitations" and the Internet trolls who exist today as a consequence of their faceless online environments.
  - A transitional paragraph (23) calls for a "new art of conversation" that promotes compassion: "Never say anything online that you wouldn't say to somebody's face," and "Don't listen to what people wouldn't say to your face."

- A concluding section (paragraphs 24–25) reemphasizes the importance of faces for empathy and compassion.

Instead of listing its sections, you might prefer to make an outline or tree diagram of the article showing its main parts. In trying to identify the main sections of an article, it sometimes helps to formulate the question that you think a paragraph or sequence of paragraphs is answering. If you think of chunks of the text as answers to a logical progression of questions, you can often follow the main ideas more easily. Some of the main questions that Marche's article responds to are the following:

- How serious has the problem of online trolling become?
- How has lack of face-to-face contact on the Internet contributed to the problem of trolling?
- What is the psychological connection between seeing faces and feeling empathy?
- How should we respond to trolls?

WRITE A DRAFT OF YOUR SUMMARY   Once you have determined the main points and grasped the structure of the article you are summarizing, combine and condense your *says* statements into clear sentences that capture the article's main ideas. Although summaries range in length, they typically are between 150 and 250 words. These shortened versions of your *says* statements will make up most of your summary, although you might use an occasional *does* statement to show organization. For example, you might say, "[Author's name] makes four main points in this article . . . . The article concludes with a call to action . . . . "

REVISE YOUR SUMMARY   When you revise, ask yourself whether the author would accept your summary as an accurate, fair representation of his or her ideas. Determine if you have relied too heavily on quotations or have wandered too far away from the author's ideas. Also, make sure every sentence of your summary is sharp and clear.

Example Summaries of "The Epidemic of Facelessness"

Here are two examples of summaries written by student writer Scott Lindquist. The first is a stand-alone abstract that summarizes the article in the original author's voice. The second is a summary intended to be inserted into Scott's own strong-response essay. The first sentence of a summary typically presents the main idea or thesis of the entire article.

STAND-ALONE ABSTRACT FOR "THE EPIDEMIC OF FACELESSNESS"

The Internet's lack of face-to-face interaction reduces people's personal connection and empathy and contributes to hate speech online. Anonymous trolls frequently post hateful messages on social media without ever seeing their victims' fearful faces. Research from philosophy and neuroscience show the importance of face-to-face interaction for promoting human kindness and morality. In fact, the face has been at the root of justice and ethics for 2,000 years. The new phenomenon of selfies and emojis suggest our desire to bring faces into online communication. When people in online environments can't see the effects of their words on people's faces, they are more prone to develop a generalized, all-purpose contempt without regard for the consequences. Possible ways to respond to hate messages include confronting or ignoring trolls. But a better way is to cultivate compassion. In mythology, trolls are natureforces who inhabit dark places. To affirm the humanity of trolls, we need a new art of Internet communication that promotes the kind of courtesy and sensitivity associated with face-to-face interactions. When the face disappears from human communication, we lose empathy and compassion, thereby hiding the humanity of monsters and victims both. [189 words]

SUMMARY OF "THE EPIDEMIC OF FACELESSNESS" INTENDED FOR INCLUSION IN THE STUDENT WRITER'S OWN ESSAY

Identification of the article, journal, and author First sentence expresses the main idea of the whole article	In "The Epidemic of Facelessness" published in the *New York Times Magazine*, journalist Stephen Marche argues that the Internet's lack of face-to-face interaction reduces people's personal connection and empathy and contributes to hate speech online. Marche presents examples of anonymous trolls posting hateful messages on social media without ever seeing their victims' fearful faces. Drawing on research from philosophy and neuroscience, Marche shows the importance of face-to-face interaction for promoting human kindness and
Attributive tags. Note that in-text citations do not have page numbers because the Work Cited is from a Web source	mortality. He asserts that "the face has been at the root of justice and ethics for 2,000 years." According to Marche, people empathize with one another through facial expressions. He suggests that the new phenomenon of selfies and emojis shows our desire to bring faces into online communication. He argues that when people in online environments can't see the effects of their words on people's faces,
Includes short quotations from article MLA documentation style.	they are more prone to develop a "generalized, all-purpose contempt" without regard for the consequences. After considering possible ways to respond to trolls, including confronting or ignoring them, Marche proposes an approach that cultivates compassion. He notes the mythical origins of trolls as "nature-forces" who inhabit dark places and suggests that a "new art of communication" can affirm the humanity of trolls and promote the kind of courtesy and sensitivity associated with face-to-face interactions. Marche concludes that when the face disappears from human communication, we lose empathy and compassion, thereby hiding the "humanity of monsters and victims both." [240 words]
Bibliographic citation for Marche's article using MLS style. In a formal paper, the "Works Cited" list begins on a new page at the end of the paper.	**Work Cited** Marche, Stephen. "The Epidemic of Facelessness." *The New York Times*, 14 Feb. 2015, www.nytimes.com/2015/02/15/opinion/sunday/the-epidemic-of-facelessness.html?_r=0.

Note the various ways in which the second summary differs from the abstract. In the second summary, Scott needs to signal that he is summarizing Marche's ideas, not presenting his own. To signal this distinction, Scott uses the following strategies:

- Introduces the summary with contextual information giving the author's name, the article's title, and the original place of publication

- Uses **attributive tags** (also called **signal phrases**) such as "Marche proposes" or "according to Marche"

- Puts quotation marks around any passages that use Marche's original wording
- Cites the article and page numbers using an appropriate documentation style.

Scott's use of attributive tags, quotation marks, and citations makes it easy to tell that he is summarizing Marche's ideas rather than presenting his own. Note too the writer's ability to remain neutral and objective and not to impose his own views.

To avoid interjecting your own opinions in a summary, you need to choose your verbs in attributive tags carefully. Consider the difference between "Smith argues" and "Smith rants" or between "Brown asserts" and "Brown leaps to the conclusion that . . . . " In each pair, the second verb moves beyond neutrality and reveals the writer's judgment of the author's ideas. The following list presents the criteria for incorporating a summary effectively into your own prose.

CRITERIA FOR AN EFFECTIVE SUMMARY INCORPORATED INTO YOUR OWN PROSE

- Represents the original article accurately and fairly
- Is direct and concise, using words economically
- Remains objective and neutral, not revealing your own ideas on the subject, but rather only the original author's points
- Gives the original article balanced and proportional coverage
- Uses the writer's own words to express the original author's ideas
- Distinguishes the summary writer's ideas from the original author's ideas by using attributive tags (such as "according to Marche" or "Marche argues that")
- Uses quotations sparingly, if at all, to present the original author's key terms or to convey the flavor of the original
- Is unified and coherent (usually one paragraph)
- Cites and documents the text the writer is summarizing and any quotations used according to an appropriate documentation system

For Writing and Discussion
Evaluating Summaries

This exercise asks you to use the "Criteria for an Effective Summary Incorporated into Your Own Prose" to analyze two summaries of the same article from the business magazine *The Economist*. The first summary will help you understand the substance of the article. What features make this first summary highly effective? Where specifically does this summary meet the criteria? In contrast, which criteria does the second summary fail to meet? What suggestions do you have for revising it?

(Continued)

Summary 1: Effective Summary of *The Economist* Article

The staff-written article "From Horseless to Driverless: If Autonomous Vehicles Rule the World," from *The Economist* asserts that driverless cars will transform not only future driving but also many industries as well as work and life. Similar to the take-over of the car from horse-drawn carriages, driverless cars will eventually not resemble cars at all and will have their own far-reaching consequences. According to this article, self-driving cars will follow the pattern of car-sharing systems and fleet-ownership models, reducing the need for vehicles and the number of vehicles on the road. As a consequence, the car insurance business, the car parts industry, and the occupations of truck and taxi driving will all be profoundly affected. In contrast, the strongest benefit of self-driving cars, the article claims, will be increased road safety with the removal of "human error" such as accident-causing alcohol, speeding, and distraction. In addition, because self-driving vehicles can be directed, road capacity will increase in efficiency and flow, and groups of people such as children, the blind, and the elderly will have greater access to transportation. While this article admits that self-driving cars will raise ethical questions about the programs that govern them and liabilities in case of collisions, it concludes that people in the future will look back on cars, those "icons of personal freedom," in amusement, marveling at that "illusory freedom" we once associated with them while we accepted the high costs and the high rate of accidents. (242 words)

Work Cited

"From Horseless to Driverless: If Autonomous Vehicles Rule the World." *The Economist,* 1 Aug. 2015, worldif. economist.com/article/11/what-if-autonomous-vehicles-rule-the-world-from-horseless-to-driverless.

Summary 2

The Economist's article "From Horseless to Driverless: If Autonomous Vehicles Rule the World," paints a disturbing picture of the rapid societal changes that driverless cars will bring about as self-driving technology takes over the market. Making comparisons with the transition from horse-drawn carriages to "horseless carriages," the article asserts that vehicles of the future will be increasingly dissimilar from cars in appearance and will profoundly change urban living: "The spread of driver-assistance technology will be gradual over the next few years, but then the emergence of fully autonomous vehicles could suddenly make existing cars look as outmoded as steam engines and landline telephones."

This thinly supported causal argument emphasizes the connection between the future of self-driving cars and the growth of car-sharing systems, contending that both undermine car ownership, lead to more efficient use of the road, and result in fewer urban vehicles and lower costs for travelers. *The Economist* admits that driverless cars will especially damage the car insurance and car parts businesses and will deprive truck drivers and taxi drivers of jobs.

Yet this article raves about the benefits. Less traffic and more controlled traffic patterns, reduced need for parking, more transportation options for children, the blind, and the elderly, and most of all, increased safety will be the greatest advantages of driverless cars. The article explains that currently, human error accounts for a majority of the accidents. Drunk driving, speeding, and distraction are problems that driverless cars will avoid. The article speculates that "some places will probably ban ordinary cars on safety grounds."

However, while exaggerating the bright future of driverless cars, this article barely acknowledges the ethical complexities of them. It touches only briefly on the liabilities of the programmable systems that will determine lives if collisions do occur.

The article concludes by celebrating driverless cars as a more sensible and realistic approach to transportation. How foolish the danger, high cost, and illusory independence of cars will look in hindsight, it claims. (242 words)

Work Cited

"From Horseless to Driverless: If Autonomous Vehicles Rule the World." *The Economist,* 1 Aug. 2015, worldif. economist.com/article/11/what-if-autonomous-vehicles-rule-the-world-from-horseless-to-driverless.

Writing an abstract or summary

6.3 Write effective summaries of texts.

See Concept 2.2 for a discussion of surprising thesis statements.

> **Writing Project**: Write a summary of an article assigned by your instructor for an audience who has not read the article. Your instructor will specify a length and assign either a stand-alone abstract or a summary to be inserted into your own essay. If the latter, use attributive tags and provide an introductory context. Follow all the criteria for a successful summary, and use MLA documentation style, including a Works Cited entry for the article that you are summarizing.

Generating Ideas, Drafting, and Revising

To write a summary of your assigned reading, we recommend that you read it first for general understanding. Then, in the spirit of listening, we recommend that you follow the process described in the previous section:

- Reread the article carefully, filling in gaps concerning rhetorical context, genre, vocabulary, and needed background knowledge.
- Do a paragraph by paragraph "does/says" analysis, distinguishing main points from supporting points and details.
- Locate the article's main divisions or parts.
- Draft the summary, trying to condense the whole into an accurate presentation of the article's main ideas.
- Revise the draft for clarity, for required length, for accuracy and completeness, and for fairness to the author's ideas.

Questions for Peer Review

In addition to the generic peer review questions explained in Skill 17.4, ask your peer reviewers to address these questions. Questions 2, 3, and 6 apply to all abstracts/summaries. Questions 1, 4, and 5 apply to a reading summary intended to be inserted in the writer's own essay.

1. To what extent do the opening sentences provide needed contextual information and express the overall thesis of the text? What information could be added or more clearly stated?

2. How would you evaluate the writer's representation and coverage of the text's main ideas in terms of accuracy, balance, and proportion? What ideas have been omitted or overemphasized?

3. Has the writer treated the article fairly and neutrally? If judgments have crept in, where could the writer revise?

4. How could the summary use attributive tags more effectively to keep the focus on the original author's ideas?

5. Has the writer used quotations sparingly and cited them accurately? Has the writer translated points into his or her own words? Has the writer included a Works Cited?

6. Where might the writer's choice of words and phrasing of sentences be revised to improve the summary's clarity, conciseness, and coherence?

Understanding strong response writing

6.4   Understand the different types of strong response writing.

As explained in the previous section, the academic genre of the summary involves "listening" to a text in order to understand its ideas and convey its points to your readers. Many college writing assignments also ask you to analyze a text by writing a *strong response*, in which you examine how a piece is written and join the text's conversation. In writing a strong response, you practice the concluding steps of the analysis game described in Concept 2.1. You apply your own critical thinking to the text, looking for patterns or disruptions of patterns, asking why the author made a particular choice, and posing questions that you need to answer for yourself as a "knowledge maker." In a strong response, you draw your own conclusions, make interpretations, and evaluate the rhetorical effectiveness of readings and their ideas.

Strong response is an umbrella term for many ways you can speak back to a text. In this section we explain four different genres of strong response writing:

- Rhetorical critique (also called a *rhetorical analysis*)
- Ideas critique
- Reflection
- Blended version of all three of these

Strong Response as Rhetorical Critique or Analysis

A strong response as **rhetorical critique** analyzes a text's rhetorical strategies and evaluates how effectively the author achieves his or her intended goals. In Chapter 4, "How Messages Persuade," we explain the rhetorical strategies of angle of vision; appeals to *logos, ethos*, and *pathos*; and the rhetorical effects of different stylistic choices. A rhetorical critique or analysis evaluates how effectively a given text uses these strategies to achieve its goals.

When writing a rhetorical critique, you discuss how a text is constructed, what rhetorical strategies it employs, and how effectively it appeals to *logos, ethos*, and *pathos*. In other words, you closely analyze the text itself, giving it the same close attention that an art critic gives a painting, a football coach gives a game video, or a biologist gives a cell. A rhetorical critique enlists the close observations you have made about this text and assesses how well the details of the text work together to achieve its purpose. It moves from observation to interpretation. Based on your carefully built understanding of this text, how well does it work as a piece of writing? The focus you choose can be with the grain, noting the effectiveness of the text's rhetorical strategies, or against the grain, discussing what is ineffective or problematic about these strategies. Or an analysis might point out both the strengths and weaknesses of the text's rhetorical strategies.

For example, suppose that you are writing a rhetorical critique of an article from a conservative business journal advocating the construction of West Coast coal train terminals for shipping American coal to China and other markets. You might analyze the article's rhetorical strategies by asking these questions:

- How is the argument shaped to appeal to a conservative, business-oriented audience?
- How has the writer's angle of vision influenced the selection of evidence for his or her argument?
- How does the writer make himself or herself seem credible to this audience?

You would also evaluate the *logos* of the argument:

- How sound is the logic of the argument?
- Is the evidence accurate and current?
- What are the underlying assumptions and beliefs on which the argument is based?

Rhetorical critiques are usually closed-form, thesis-driven essays. The essay has a thesis that captures the writer's overall assessment of the text and maps out the specific points that the writer will develop in the analysis. When you are writing a rhetorical critique, your goal is to find a few rhetorical points that you find particularly intriguing, important, or disturbing to discuss and probe. Typically, your analysis zeroes in on some key features that you find noteworthy. Strategies Chart 6.2 lists the questions you can ask about a text to construct a rhetorical critique.

Strategies Chart 6.2 Question-Asking Strategies for Writing a Rhetorical Critique

Ask Questions about Any of the Following:	Examples
Audience and purpose: • Who is the intended audience? • What is the writer's purpose? • How well does the text suit its particular audience and purpose?	Determine Stephen Marche's audience (well-educated readers of *The New York Times* who are interested in Internet civility and the problem of trolls). Identify the change of views that Marche hopes to bring about in his readers. Analyze how well Marche's references to philosophy or his explanations of Internet jargon suit his purpose and audience.
Influence of genre on the shape of the text: • How has the genre affected the author's style, structure, and use of evidence?	Analyze how the genre of the feature editorial for a highbrow magazine accounts for the length, structure, and depth of Marche's argument. Examine Marche's combination of loosely structured paragraphs and his inclusion of recent events and popular culture as a feature of this magazine's investigation of contemporary issues. How might the reading experiences of someone reading this article online differ from someone reading it in print?
Author's style: • How do the author's language choices and sentence length and complexity contribute to the text's impact?	Examine how Marche's repetition of his key words "face" and "facelessness" and his use of negative words such as "viciousness" and "monstrosity" contribute to the article's effect.
Appeal to *logos*, the logic of the argument: • How well has the author created a reasonable, logically structured argument?	Analyze how Marche's use of logical points and supporting details support his claim and make his claim persuasive.

(continued)

Ask Questions about Any of the Following:	Examples
Use of evidence: • How reputable, relevant, current, sufficient, and representative is the evidence?	Analyze the persuasive effect of Marche's references from art history, psychology, neuroscience, history, and philosophy. Research one or two references that you didn't first understand and determine how well they support his main claim.
Appeal to *ethos* and the credibility of the author: • How well does the author persuade readers that he or she is knowledgeable, reliable, credible, and trustworthy?	Analyze Marche's methods for appearing knowledgeable, reliable, credible, and trustworthy. Examine the impression of Marche's authority. Examine the extent to which Marche speaks to your experience of the facelessness of the Internet.
Appeal to *pathos*: • How well does the writer appeal to readers' emotions, sympathies, and values?	Consider how the anecdote with which Marche begins his article and the others he interweaves throughout the piece give presence to the problems created by Internet trolls. Examine what effect his use of loaded negative words ("epidemic," "viciousness," "outrage," "faceless rage," "monstrosity," and others) and mention of rape threats on the Internet has on your response to his argument.
Author's angle of vision: • How much does the author's angle of vision or interpretive filter dominate the text, influencing what is emphasized or omitted?	How would you describe Marche's angle of vision? Analyze how this angle of vision shapes his perspective on abusive Internet communication and his suggested solutions.

For a rhetorical critique, you would probably not choose all of these questions but would instead select three or four to highlight. A with-the-grain rhetorical critique would focus on what you see as the strengths of the author's rhetorical strategies whereas an against-the-grain rhetorical critique would emphasize weaknesses. In either case, your goals are (1) to make insightful observations about how a text works rhetorically and (2) to support your points with examples and short quotations from the text so that readers will be inclined to see the text your way.

Strong Response as Ideas Critique

A second kind of strong response, the **ideas critique**, focuses on the ideas at stake in the text. Rather than treat the text as an artifact to analyze rhetorically (as in a rhetorical critique), you treat it as a voice in a conversation—one perspective on an issue or one solution to a problem or question. Your strong response also examines how the author's ideas mesh or conflict with your own. Based on your own critical thinking, personal experiences, and research, to what extent do you agree or disagree with the writer's thesis? From your perspective, what ideas does this text contribute to the public conversation on its subject? A with-the-grain reading of a text would support all or some of the text's ideas while supplying additional evidence or extending the argument, perhaps applying it in a new context. An against-the-grain reading would challenge the writer's ideas, point out flaws and holes in the writer's thinking, and provide counterexamples and rebuttals.

As an example, let's return to the article from the conservative business journal on building coal train terminals to ship U.S. coal to China and other markets. For an ideas critique, you would give your own views on the continued mining, transport, and export of coal to support or challenge the writer's views, to raise new questions, and to add your voice to the coal industry conversation:

• You might supply additional reasons and evidence for mining and exporting coal.

- You might oppose coal trains on the basis of their poor safety records or oppose shipping coal to China on the basis of coal's role in climate change.
- You might propose some kind of synthesis or middle ground, where you favor a gradual phasing out of the coal industry with heightened safety regulations for the transport of coal.

When you write an ideas critique you are thus joining an important conversation about the text's subject matter. Because much academic and professional writing focuses on finding the best solution to complex problems, idea critiques are common. Usually this genre requires closed-form, thesis-governed prose. Strategies Chart 6.3 suggests questions you can ask about a text to enter into its conversation of ideas.

Critiques of ideas appear in many contexts where writers search for the best solutions to problems, and this kind of thinking is essential for academic research. In writing research papers, writers typically follow the template "This other writer has argued A, but I am going to argue B." Often the writer's own view (labeled "B") results from his or her wrestling with other points of view.

Strong Response as Reflection

A third kind of strong response is often called a *reflection* or a *reflection paper*. (An instructor might say, for example, "Read Stephen Marche's article on online verbal abuse and write a reflection about it.") Generally, a **reflection** is an introspective genre. It invites you to connect the reading to your personal experiences, beliefs, and values. In a reflection paper, the instructor is particularly interested in how the reading has affected you personally—what

Strategies Chart 6.3 Question-Asking Strategies for Writing an Ideas Critique

Questions to Ask	Examples
Where do I agree with this author? (with the grain)	Consider how you might amplify or extend Marche's ideas. Build on his ideas by discussing examples where you or acquaintances have experienced or encountered the abusive language of trolls. Show how these experiences have influenced your views on the seriousness of the problem.
What new insights has this text given me? (with the grain)	Explore Marche's emphasis on the need for civility and empathy and his effort to draw attention to society's so-far ineffectual response to trolling.
Where do I disagree with this author? (against the grain)	Challenge Marche's assumptions about the magnitude of the problem. Challenge his idea that seeing people's faces encourages empathy. Challenge his proposed solution that following some golden rules for communication can improve civility online.
What points has the author overlooked or omitted? (against the grain)	Recognize that Marche overlooks the rudeness, meanness, and prejudice in offline, face-to-face communication. Consider that Marche chooses not to mention rape culture, the huge racial divide, and hostility against different groups of people due to prejudice based on ethnicity, religion, gender, and sexuality.
What new questions or problems has the text raised? (with or against the grain)	Explain how Marche minimizes the Internet's positive effect on communication. Consider how the Internet has united as well as divided people. Consider what, if any, steps have been successful in reducing trolling on the Internet.
What are the limitations or consequences of this text? (with or against the grain)	Consider ways that Marche excludes some of his readers even while reaching out to others. Consider how Marche's identity as a Canadian, a Ph.D. in early modern drama, a novelist, and a well-known journalist influences his views on the use of the Internet. Consider what new ideas he brings to his readers.

memories it has triggered, what personal experiences it relates to, what values and beliefs it has challenged, what dilemmas it poses, and so forth. A **reflection paper** is often more exploratory, open ended, musing, and tentative than a rhetorical critique or an ideas critique, which is usually closed form and thesis governed.

To illustrate, let's consider how you might write a reflection in response to the article in the conservative business journal on coal trains and coal exports. One approach might be to build a reflection around a personal conflict in values by exploring how the reading creates a personal dilemma:

- You might write about your experiences working for environmental causes, musing about the environmental damage you have observed firsthand and your concern for the environmental effects of the continued use of coal for energy.
- At the same time, you might reflect on the extent to which your own life depends on cheap energy and your awareness of the need for jobs in communities that would be affected by the new terminals for coal export.

In short, you want both environmental preservation and the benefits of economic growth. Another quite different approach might be to reflect on how this article connects to discussions you are having in your other courses—say, the economic cost of individuals' and companies' going green. Strategies Chart 6.4 provides some strategies you can use to generate ideas for a reflective strong response.

As you can tell from the questions in Strategies Chart 6.4, a reflective strong response highlights your personal experiences and beliefs in conversation with the text. Whereas a rhetorical critique analyzes the way the text works rhetorically and an ideas critique takes a stance on the ideas at stake in the text, a reflective response focuses on the personal dimension of reading the text. Reflections call for a degree of self-disclosure or self-exploration that would be largely absent from the other kinds of strong responses.

Strategies Chart 6.4 Question-Asking Strategies for Writing a Reflective Strong Response

Questions to Ask	Examples
What personal memories or experiences does this text trigger?	Explore how Marche's opening anecdote affected you. How have your own experience with online trolls influenced your attitude toward online anonymity? When have you sent positive or negative messages to others online?
What personal values or beliefs does this text reinforce or challenge?	Explore the extent to which you agree with Marche that seeing other peoples' faces is more likely to compel us toward ethical behavior. Have you had any experiences online in which empathy played a significant role in your exchange with another user?
What questions, dilemmas, or problems does this text raise for me?	Explore the more implicit arguments that Marche makes, such as the connections between face-to-face encounters and empathy or ethics. Does Marche in any way overestimate the role of faces in how people choose whether to behave ethically or not? Can you think of empathetic groups that have formed because of the Internet?
What new insights, ideas, or thoughts of my own have been stimulated by this text?	Consider Marche's statement that "everyone in digital space is at one point or another exposed to online monstrosity"—an experience Marche likens to a Hieronymus Bosch canvas. Do an Internet search to find Bosch's *Garden of Earthly Delights*. To what extent does Marche's view of the Internet match your own? What work of art might serve as a metaphor for your vision?

Strong Response as a Blend

The boundaries among the rhetorical critique, ideas critique, and reflection overlap, and a strong response could easily blend features of each. In deciding how to respond strongly to a text, you often don't have to confine yourself to a pure genre but can mix and match different kinds of responses. You can analyze and critique a text's rhetorical strategies, show how the text challenges your personal values and beliefs, and also develop your own stance on the text's ideas. In writing a blended response, you can emphasize what is most important to you while not limiting yourself to only one approach.

Writing a summary/strong response essay

6.5 **Write strong responses to texts by analyzing their rhetorical strategies and engaging their ideas.**

> **Writing Project:** In response to a text assigned by your instructor, write a summary/strong response essay that incorporates a 150- to 250-word summary of the article. In your strong response to that reading, speak back to its author from your own critical thinking, personal experience, values, and, perhaps, further reading or research. Unless your instructor assigns a specific kind of strong response (rhetorical critique, ideas critique, or reflection), write a blended response in which you are free to consider the author's rhetorical strategies, your own agreement or disagreement with the author's ideas, and your personal response to the text. Think of your response as your analysis of how the text tries to influence its readers rhetorically and how your wrestling with the text has expanded and deepened your thinking about its ideas. As you work with ideas from the text, remember to use attributive tags, quotation marks for any quoted passages, and MLA documentation to distinguish your own points about the text from the author's ideas and language.

The student example near the end of this chapter, by student writer Scott Lindquist, is a blended strong response that includes both a rhetorical critique of the article and some of his own views. He analyzes Marche's article rhetorically by pointing out both the persuasive features of the argument and the limiting dominance of Marche's perspective. He praises some of Marche's points, but he also reads Marche against the grain by suggesting how Marche's word choice and fixation on the face as the key to human empathy prevents him from developing ideas that might seem more compelling to some readers.

Exploring Ideas for Your Strong Response

Earlier in the chapter we presented the kinds of strong responses you may be asked to write in college. Your goal now is to figure out what kind of strong response you will be writing and what you want to say. Your first step, of course, is to read your assigned text closely and with the grain, listening to the text so well that you can write a summary of its argument.

After you have written your summary, which demonstrates your full understanding of the text, you are ready to write a strong response. Because your essay cannot discuss every feature of the text or every idea the text has evoked, you will want to focus on a small number of points that enable you to bring readers a new, enlarged, or deepened understanding of the text. You may decide to write a primarily with-the-grain response, praising, building on, or applying the text to a new context, or a primarily against-the-grain response, challenging, questioning, and refuting the text. If your strong response primarily praises or agrees with the text, you must be sure to identify its successful features and to extend the text by applying the ideas rather than simply make your essay one long summary of the article. If your strong response primarily criticizes and disagrees with the text, you must be fair and accurate in your criticisms.

Articulating Your Own Purpose for Reading

Although you usually read a text because you are interested in the author's ideas, you might occasionally read a text for a purpose quite different from what the author intended. For example, you might read the writings of nineteenth-century scientists not to join their conversation but to analyze their assumptions about nature (or women, or God, or race, or capitalism). Or suppose that you read a political speech to analyze the politician's metaphors rather than to engage his or her ideas. (These metaphors might reveal implicit values or beliefs.) Likewise you might read a *National Geographic* article not out of interest in its subject matter but out of a desire to uncover its political bias. Understanding your own purpose will help you read deeply both with and against the grain.

Strategies Chart 6.5 provides some specific rereading strategies that will stimulate ideas for your strong response. It is followed by an example of Scott Lindquist's marginal response notes to Marche's article (Figure 6.1).

Strategies Chart 6.5 Active Reading Strategies for Moving from Observation/Analysis to Interpretation

Strategies	What to Do	Comments
Take notes.	Make extensive marginal notes while rereading, observing important details, recording both with-the-grain and against-the-grain responses.	Writing a strong response requires a deep engagement with texts. For example, in Figure 6.1, observe how Scott Lindquist's notes express his close observations and incorporate with-the-grain and against-the-grain responses. Note how he is truly talking back to and interacting with Marche's text.
Identify "hot spots" in the text.	Mark all hot spots with marginal notes. These could be passages of tension, contradiction, or ambiguity. They could be passages that stand out for you personally. After you've finished reading, find these hot spots and freewrite your responses to them in a reading journal.	By "hot spot" we mean a quotation or passage that particularly catches your attention. You may notice it because you agree or disagree with it or because it triggers memories or other associations. Perhaps the hot spot strikes you as thought provoking. Perhaps it raises a problem or is confusing yet suggestive.
Ask questions.	Write several questions that the text caused you to think about. Then explore your responses to those questions through freewriting, which may trigger more questions.	Almost all texts trigger questions as you read. A good way to begin formulating a strong response is to note these questions.

Strategies	What to Do	Comments
Look for patterns.	Note patterns of language, including repetition of words and ideas, and speculate about their significance.	Patterns indicate emphasis and call for interpretation. Identify what patterns in the text stand out for you, what importance you assign them, and how they affect you rhetorically. For example, in Figure 6.1, Scott Lindquist responds that Marche's use of dramatic language, especially at the end of paragraphs, builds intensity.
Articulate your difference from the intended audience.	Decide who the writer's intended audience is. If you differ significantly from this audience, use this difference to question the author's underlying assumptions, values, and beliefs.	Your gender, age, class, ethnicity, sexual orientation, political and religious beliefs, interests, values, and so forth may cause you to see the author's ideas from a very different perspective. For instance, if you are an ethical vegan reading an article supporting the meat-packing industry or if you are a first-generation immigrant reading an op-ed piece proposing tighter restrictions on immigration, you may feel excluded from, even alienated by, the article. Identify what values and beliefs you would have to hold to accept the author's argument.

Figure 6.1 Scott Lindquist's Marginal Response Notes

"The Epidemic of Facelessness" by Stephen Marche
The New York Times

A part-time delivery driver named Peter Nunn was recently sentenced to 18 weeks in a British prison for tweeting and retweeting violent messages to Stella Creasy, a member of Parliament. He never saw his victim but the consequences of his virtual crime were real enough. In a statement, Ms. Creasy described fears for her physical safety, going so far as to install a panic button in her home. Mr. Nunn has been physically separated from the rest of society for posting abusive words on a social media site.

> *Opening anecdote grabs readers' attention with appeals to pathos.*

The fact that the case ended up in court is rare; the viciousness it represents is not. Everyone in the digital space is, at one point or another, exposed to online monstrosity, one of the consequences of the uniquely contemporary condition of facelessness.

> *Dramatic language*

Every month brings fresh figuration to the sprawling, shifting Hieronymus Bosch canvas of faceless 21st-century contempt. Faceless contempt is not merely topical. It is increasingly the defining trait of topicality itself. Every day online provides its measure of empty outrage.

> *Need to look up this artist*
>
> *An interesting phrase—key words?*

When the police come to the doors of the young men and women who send notes telling strangers that they want to rape them, they and their parents are almost always shocked, genuinely surprised that anyone would take what they said seriously, that anyone would take anything said online seriously. There is a vast dissonance between virtual communication and an actual police officer at the door. It is a dissonance we are all running up against more and more, the dissonance between the world of faces and the world without faces. And the world without faces is coming to dominate.

> *Begins Marche's mention of rape*
>
> *There seems to be important tension here*

Recently Dick Costolo, chief executive of Twitter, lamented his company's failures to deal with the trolls that infested it: "I'm frankly ashamed of how poorly we've dealt with this issue during my tenure as CEO," he said in a leaked memo. It's commendable of him to admit the torrents of abuse, but it's also no mere technical error on the part of Twitter; faceless rage is inherent to its technology.

> *Effective authority to cite*
>
> *One of Marche's main points*

It's not Twitter's fault that human beings use it. But the faceless communication social media creates, the linked distances between people, both provokes and mitigates the inherent capacity for monstrosity.

> *Continuing the pattern of ending on powerful words to construct a serious and concerned tone*

The Gyges effect, the well-noted disinhibition created by communications over the distances of the Internet, in which all speech and image are muted and at arm's reach, produces an inevitable reaction—the desire for impact at any cost, the desire to reach through the screen, to make somebody feel something, anything. A simple comment can so easily be ignored. Rape threat? Not so much. Or, as Mr. Nunn so succinctly put it on Twitter: "If you can't threaten to rape a celebrity, what is the point in having them?"

> *Need to look this is up, too.*
>
> *Two mentions of rape threats in this paragraph*

The challenge of our moment is that the face has been at the root of justice and ethics for 2,000 years. The right to face an accuser is one of the very first principles of the law, described in the "confrontation clause" of the Sixth Amendment of the United States Constitution, but reaching back through English common law to ancient Rome. In Roman courts no man could be sentenced to death without first seeing his accuser. The precondition of any trial, of any attempt to reconcile competing claims, is that the victim and the accused look each other in the face.

> *Is this the most effective quotation for Marche to use? Is he just trying to shock readers?*
>
> *One of Marche's main assumptions*

Writing a Thesis for a Strong Response Essay

A thesis for a strong response essay should present a succinct statement of the overall new perspective on a text that you want to bring to your readers. You might choose a high-level thesis that sketches in broad terms your main view of the text. Or you might choose a lower-level thesis that maps out the points that you want to develop and discuss. In all cases, your thesis should include some element of risk and controversy. It should surprise your readers with something new or challenging. Your thesis might focus entirely on with-the-grain points or entirely on against-the-grain points, but most likely it will include some of both. You should, however, avoid tensionless thesis statements such as "This article has both good and bad points."

See Concept 2.2 for a discussion of surprising thesis statements.

Table 6.1 shows examples of some thesis statements that students have written for strong responses in our classes. The lefthand column gives the question the assignment posed. The middle column shows the thesis statement as a high-level thesis, and the righthand column gives a version of the thesis written lower on the ladder of abstraction, mapping out the essay's

Table 6.1 Examples of Thesis Statements for Summary/Strong Response Essays

Question or Problem Addressed	High-Level Thesis	Low-Level Mapping Thesis
Will citizens interested in the water scarcity problems of cities find Charles Fishman's chapter "Dolphins in the Desert" from his book *The Big Thirst* an important contribution to the current controversies over water management?	In this chapter, Fishman successfully handles his risky pro-growth, pro-business views and constructs a credible, well-supported argument for water management.	Although Fishman's pro-business growth perspective may seem risky and narrow, this chapter successfully reaches out to an audience who might dismiss the environmental importance of water conservation. Fishman also creates strong appeals to *logos* and *ethos* through his use of numerical facts, memorable examples, and the contrasting case studies of Las Vegas and Atlanta.
What influence does Stephen Marche's article "The Epidemic of Facelessness" have on your understanding of the connection of Internet facelessness to the meanness of trolls?	Stephen Marche's article fails to persuade me that facelessness is the root cause of Internet meanness.	Stephen Marche puts too much emphasis on fanning anxieties about the Internet, on the connection between the face and empathy, and on the facelessness of the Internet to persuade me to accept his view of the cause of meanness on the Internet.
How well does Thoreau's chapter "Where I Lived, and What I Lived For" from *Walden* speak to American society in the twenty-first century?	Although Thoreau offers a poetic argument in favor of nature's power of spiritual renewal, his writing fails to connect with contemporary readers in other significant ways.	Although the images and figures of speech that Thoreau uses in his chapter "Where I Lived, and What I Lived For" effectively support his argument for the spiritually renewing power of nature, I disagree with his antitechnology stance and his extreme emphasis on isolation as a means to self-discovery.
How well does activist Annie Leonard in her article "How to Be a More Mindful Consumer" from *YES! Magazine* persuade general readers to move beyond "ethical consumerism" to push for democratic change?	While Annie Leonard's article "How to Be a More Mindful Consumer" successfully rallies the activist readers of *YES! Magazine*, it risks alienating general readers.	While *YES! Magazine* readers will respond to Leonard's urgent call to work politically against "stuff inequality," Leonard's critical tone, extreme examples, and demand for deep commitment will most likely offend general readers.

For Writing and Discussion
Examining Thesis Statements for Strong Response Essays

Working individually or in groups, identify the points in each of the thesis statements in Table 6.1 and briefly state them. Think in terms of the ideas you are expecting the writers to develop in the body of the essay. As a follow-up to this exercise, you might share your own thesis statements for your strong response essays. How clearly does each thesis statement lay out points that the writer will probe? As a group, discuss what new, important perspectives each thesis statement promises to bring to readers and how each thesis suits a rhetorical critique, ideas critique, or some combination of these.

points. Note that each thesis includes some attention to the rhetorical strategies of the text.

Shaping, Drafting, and Revising

Figure 6.2 shows a possible framework for a summary/response essay. Most strong response essays call for a short contextualizing introduction to set

Figure 6.2 Framework for a Summary/Strong Response Essay

Introduction (usually one paragraph)	• Introduces the topic/problem/question that the article (or book, chapter, or piece) addresses • Conveys the writer's investment in the author's topic • Identifies the rhetorical context of the article and its question, the author of the article, and the author's title and purpose
Summary (one paragraph)	• Summarizes the article, chapter, or book, giving a balanced, accurate, concise, and neutral presentation of its main points
Thesis statement (forms its own paragraph or comes at the end of the summary)	• Establishes the writer's stance on the author's text (the new perspective the writer wants to bring readers) as the focus of the essay • Perhaps presents the two or more rhetorical or ideas points that the writer will analyze and discuss in the body of the essay • Often maps out the analysis and critique to follow, giving readers a clear sense of the essay's direction and scope
Body section 1 (one or more paragraphs)	• Develops the first rhetorical or ideas point with examples from the text • Explains and discusses this point in a thorough critique with the writer's own perspective (and perhaps knowledge and personal experience, for an ideas critique)
Body section 2 (one or more paragraphs)	• Develops the second rhetorical or ideas point with examples from the text • Explains and discusses this point in a thorough critique with the writer's own perspective (and perhaps knowledge and personal experience, for an ideas critique)
Body section 3, 4, etc., on additional rhetorical or ideas points (one or more paragraphs per main point)	• Continues the critique and analysis by explaining writer's ideas with examples and elaboration until all points in the thesis statement are fleshed out
Conclusion (usually a short paragraph)	• Might briefly recap the writer's points, but summarizes these ideas only if the essay is long and complex • Wraps up the critique and analysis to leave readers thinking about both the author's piece and the writer's strong response
Work Cited	• Gives an appropriate citation in MLA format for the text discussed in the paper and any other sources mentioned in the essay (often only one source to list)

up your analysis. In the essay at the end of this section, student writer Scott Lindquist begins by establishing his and his readers' personal connection to the article and then raises the question that Marche will address: What conditions of online environments encourage abusive communication? Student writer Stephanie Malinowski (in the reading at the end of this chapter) uses a similar strategy. She begins by tapping into her readers' experiences with outsourcing. Then she poses the question that Thomas Friedman addresses in his op-ed piece: Should Americans support or question the outsourcing of jobs?

Both student writers introduce the question addressed by the article they are critiquing, and both include a short summary of the article that gives readers a foundation for the critique. They go on to present the points of the article that they will address in their strong responses. Both Scott's and Stephanie's thesis statements express their own stance on the articles and indicate several points that readers will expect to see developed and explained in the body of their essays.

- In a closed-form, thesis-driven strong response, readers will expect the points to follow the order in which they are presented in the thesis.
- If your strong response is primarily a rhetorical critique, your evidence will come mainly from the text you are analyzing.
- If your strong response is primarily an ideas critique, your evidence is likely to come from personal knowledge of the issue or from further reading or research.
- If your strong response is primarily reflective, much of your evidence will be based on your own personal experiences and inner thoughts.

A blended response can combine points from any of these perspectives.

Each point in your thesis calls for a lively discussion, combining general statements and specifics that will encourage readers to see this text your way. Just as you do in your summary, you must use attributive tags to distinguish between the author's ideas and your own points and responses. In addition, you must document all ideas taken from other sources and place all borrowed language in quotation marks or block indentations according to MLA format and include a Works Cited in MLA format. Most strong response essays have short conclusions—just enough commentary to bring closure to the essay. In a summary/strong response essay, you may want to work on the summary separately before you incorporate it into your whole essay.

Example of a Student Strong Response Essay as a Blend

We show you here Scott Lindquist's summary/strong response essay. It is a blend that interweaves rhetorical critique, ideas critique, and personal reflection. Note that the essay begins by conveying Scott's investment in Internet behavior. It then summarizes Marche's article. Following the summary, Scott states his thesis, followed by his strong response, which contains both rhetorical points and points engaging Marche's ideas.

Scott Lindquist (Student)

Is "Facelessness" the Real Cause of Online Trolling?
A Response to Stephen Marche

On a bad day, it can feel as though trolls are everywhere on the Internet. Scroll to any comment section of any Website and, if the moderators haven't already deleted them, you'll encounter several trolls: people who send abusive messages online. And okay, I'll say it: I've trolled someone online before; I've also been trolled. I'm willing to bet many people have experienced both sides of Internet abuse. The question of what compelled me and people like me who are ordinarily well-meaning human beings to say abusive things online that we might not say in person is a question for which Stephen Marche believes he has an answer in his *New York Times* article, "The Epidemic of Facelessness."

In "The Epidemic of Facelessness" Stephen Marche argues that the Internet's lack of face-to-face interaction reduces people's personal connection and empathy and contributes to hate speech online. Drawing on research from across different disciplines, Marche asserts, "the face has been at the root of justice and ethics for 2,000 years." According to Marche, people empathize with one another through facial expressions. Citing the prevalence of rape threats online, Marche argues that when people in online environments can't see the effects of their words on people's faces, they are more prone to develop a "generalized, all-purpose contempt" without regard for the consequences. After considering possible ways to respond to trolling, Marche proposes guidelines for reducing trolling by cultivating the kind of courtesy and sensitivity associated with face-to-face interactions. Marche concludes that when the face disappears from human communication, we lose empathy and compassion, thereby hiding the "humanity of monsters and victims both."

Readers may be attracted to the currency of Marche's argument, which contributes fascinating researched insights on empathy; however, they may also object, as I do, to his exploitive emotional appeals, narrow and unrealistic perspective on online communication, and inadequate solutions for creating more empathetic spaces online.

Marche's analysis is timely given the volume of our Internet communication today. I appreciate that Marche treats trolling as a serious issue. As Internet bullying and teen suicide continue to be important issues in schools, "empty outrage" on the Internet and the emotional effects of trolling on victims should be a topic of public discussion, a process Marche's article helps. Through offering one possible reason for why trolling has become so commonplace—faceless exchanges--Marche opens space for other people to respond to his reasoning with their own ideas, thereby expanding our understanding of trolling and the communication of empathy on the Internet.

Along with the timeliness of his ideas, Marche's research compellingly constructs an explanation for why trolling persists on the Internet—what he calls the "epidemic of facelessness." Marche's synthesis of knowledge from many different disciplines speaks well to his educated, intellectual *New York Times* readers and contributes to the *logos* of his argument. He opens his article with an anecdote of a recent court case in which the defendant was sentenced for "tweeting and retweeting violent messages," a reference that immediately grounds his argument

Academic Title
Introduces the topic/problem and shows the writer's investment

Identifies Marche's article and his purpose

Summary of Marche's article

No page reference is included because the article was located on the Web

Thesis statement focused on both rhetorical points and ideas critique

With-the-grain ideas critique point: timeliness and usefulness of Marche's article

With-the-grain rhetorical critique point, praising Marche's use of sources for his audience

(Continued)

Writer uses relevant examples from Marche's article to support his point

with the authority of judicial knowledge and the relevance of 21st century media. Following this reference, Marche describes the Internet as a "Hieronymus Bosch canvas of faceless 21st-century contempt." This reference to the 15th century Dutch artist (I had to look up this reference!), known for his nightmarish and gruesome paintings, vividly illustrates how Marche sees the current digital climate. Marche continues to cite studies in communications, such as "the Gyges effect," a theory that anonymity and invisibility on the Internet embolden people to violent or hateful speech. These studies, along with quotations from scholars in neuroscience, phenomenology and philosophy, give substance and authority to his editorial. By supporting his claim about facelessness and animosity with multidisciplinary theories and evidence, Marche gives rhetorical power to his argument.

Transition to against-the-grain rhetorical points: problems with narrow angle of vision and ineffective emotional appeals

Examples of these rhetorical weaknesses in the article

Despite these strengths, however, Marche chooses to intensify readers' alarm through emotional appeals while his focus on facelessness as a primary cause of trolling prevents him from seeing wider problems in our culture and gives him a narrow view of on-line communication. His use of anxiety-producing words associated with trolling—"viciousness," "monstrosity," and "empty outrage"— appeal to *pathos* but weaken the *logos* of his argument. The main example of emotionally loaded language begins in the article's opening paragraph where Marche employs an anecdote about a rape threat to hook readers' attention to his claim about online "faceless contempt." Then as the article proceeds other anecdotes of rape threats follow. In fact, Marche mentions the word "rape" five times. Readers may feel as I do that he uses rape examples primarily for shock effect, but this rhetorical move weakens his argument that "facelessness" is a primary explanation of vicious trolling. Perhaps the frequency of rape threats in trolling messages is not caused by facelessness but by the underlying social problems of misogyny, sexism, and the oppression of women. Marche's exclusive focus on Internet facelessness and his omission of closely related systemic social problems reveal his narrow angle of vision. By focusing on "faceless contempt" as *the* reason for why people send digital rape threats, he seems to ignore the fact that sexual assault and violence against women continue to be serious, relevant offline issues that don't go away when people look at each other face to face.

Writer presents an against-the-grain ideas critique point: what Marche has overlooked and left out

Marche's limited perspective also shows in his omission of examples of racism, homophobia, transphobia, ableism, and other forms of discrimination. Through his assertion that "the face has been at the root of justice and ethics for 2,000 years," Marche misses that face-to-face contact has not historically mitigated racism and abuse. As current civil rights movements like Black Lives Matter have made clear, faces alone aren't enough to create empathy between individuals. Although Marche's intent is to promote empathy in online communication, his argument about online facelessness may alienate scores of readers who regularly experience systemic injustices face to face.

Another against-the-grain ideas critique point about empathy on the Internet

Marche also overlooks a key reality of the Internet itself: that some faceless communications on the Internet actually foster empathy. One example is how hashtags on Twitter function as ways for people to empathize with one another around ideas and events. For example, in November, 2015, after the ISIS bombings in Paris, the hashtag \#PrayforParis trended worldwide. People on Twitter, the only digital community Marche mentions (and describes as "infested" with trolls), came together to grieve as a community for a city traumatized by violence. After the bombings, Twitter was a hub for empathy on the Internet for those experiencing grief. The Internet has in fact transformed how we experience grief and has helped people empathize with those who might otherwise feel isolated by the grieving process. As another example, when a person passes away, family members of the deceased person often convert that person's Facebook account into a digital memorial where friends and family post memories and condolences. In addition, for many marginalized subcultures, the Internet serves as a forum for thousands to empathize with one another, as in the example of AVEN, the Asexuality Visibility and Education Network.

Furthermore, Marche misses another reality of the Internet: the abundance of spaces on the Internet populated by photos and videos of people's faces. Where do Facebook, Instagram, Skype, and Snapchat figure into his argument? Marche dismisses selfies as a "continuous process of self-portraiture" that "mimics the changeability and the variety of real human presence"; however, sharing images of one's face online can be a means to elicit empathy from other people. I think of people posting images of themselves when they are feeling sad, lonely, or otherwise disconnected from community, or conversely, feeling happy, excited, or proud and want to share their emotions and experiences. Selfies are not always mere "self-portraiture"; they can be a popular and authentic way of communicating empathy and connection.

Finally, having alarmed readers about "an epidemic of facelessness," Marche offers unsatisfactory solutions to the problem of "faceless contempt." His code of conduct for Internet users includes two principles: "Never say anything to anybody that you wouldn't say to their face" and "Don't listen to what people wouldn't say to your face." Marche wants to spare us from the emotional wounds inflicted by trolls. However, these vague principles lack substance. People differ in what they would say to a person's face; some people would say hateful things face to face as well as offline, and this principle seems to legitimize such face-to-face meanness. For white racists who direct racial slurs toward people of color and for men who catcall women, this guideline will do little to erase the contempt Marche associates with online trolling. The second guideline also doesn't address the deeper societal problems. Rather than asking people to presume what someone would or wouldn't say to their faces, Marche should encourage people to communicate empathetically both online and in personal face-to-face encounters.

Ultimately, Marche's treatment of trolling remains superficial. Although I believe Marche's article furthers important conversations about empathy on the Internet, his emphasis on "facelessness" so dominates his view that he neglects to mention that a lack of empathy is a deep societal problem, not simply an Internet problem. Trolling has its roots in society's deep-seated racism, misogyny, and other prejudices—problems that won't be resolved online until they are resolved also in personal face-to-face encounters. We need further dialogue about how to encourage more empathetic communication in all forms.

Work Cited

Marche, Stephen. "The Epidemic of Facelessness." *The New York Times*, 14 Feb. 2015, www.nytimes.com/2015/02/15/opinion/sunday/the-epidemic-of-facelessness.html?_r=0.

Writer supplies counter-examples of empathetic communication on the Internet

Additional against-the-grain ideas critique point: the Internet is not completely faceless

Writer supplies counter-reasoning and examples

Final against-the-grain point, both rhetorical and ideas critique commenting on the inadequacy of Marche's solutions

Short concluding paragraph to wrap up the writer's stance on this article

Citation of work cited in the essay using MLA format

Questions for Peer Review

In addition to the generic peer review questions listed in Skill 17.4, ask your peer reviewers to address these questions:

1. How appealingly do the title and introduction of the essay set up the topic of critique, convey the writer's interest, and lay a foundation for the summary of the article and the writer's thesis?

2. How could the writer's thesis statement be clearer in presenting a focused stance and perhaps several points about the text's rhetorical strategies and ideas?

3. How could the body of the strong response follow the thesis more closely?

4. Where do you, the reader, need more clarification or support for the writer's points? How could the writer develop with-the-grain or against-the-grain points more appropriately?

5. Where could the writer work on the effectiveness of attributive tags, quotations, and documentation?

Multimodal or Online Assignment Options

1. **Summary/Strong Response to a Blog Post** Identify a blogger with a reputation for substantial, serious, in-depth analysis or commentary. Select a recent post from your chosen blogger (recent enough that the Comments feature for this post is still open). Write a summary/strong response critique of your chosen post, and post your critique to the Comments section of the blog, adapting your response to the conventions of responses on this site. Although all respondents will have read the original blog, a short summary of its argument will help frame your own response. Your goal is to contribute significantly to the conversation initiated by the blogger's original post.

2. **Online Book Review** Write a summary/strong response critique of a book and publish it as an online book review for a site such as Amazon or Goodreads. Typically, online customer reviews are likely to be much shorter than an academic essay, so you need to plan the points you want to highlight. Your job is not to give away all the plot details but rather to relay well-informed praise or criticism of features of the book. Writers contributing to these public online forums should be aware of their ethical responsibility. Customer reviews are a powerful marketing tool that can boost or hurt authors' sales and success. Take this responsibility seriously: Consider your *ethos* as a careful, insightful reader and insightful critic and make your review lively, interesting, and fair.

Reading

Our reading for this chapter is a summary/strong response essay by student writer Stephanie Malinowski in response to Thomas L. Friedman's op-ed piece "30 Little Turtles," which you can access in *The New York Times* archives. Malinowski's essay follows primarily a rhetorical critique strategy for the strong response.

Stephanie Malinowski (Student)

Questioning Thomas L. Friedman's Optimism in "30 Little Turtles"

1   You are struggling to fix a problem that arises when you are downloading new computer software on to your computer. You're about to give up on the whole thing when an idea hits you: call the software company itself to ask for assistance. Should you be surprised when the person who answers the phone to help you is based in India? Should Americans support or question outsourcing?

2   In "30 Little Turtles," an op-ed piece that appeared in the *New York Times* on February 29, 2004, journalist and foreign affairs columnist Thomas L. Friedman argues that outsourcing call center jobs from the Western world to India is transforming the lives of Indian workers and benefiting geopolitics. Friedman supports his argument by detailing his experience visiting a call center in India. He claims that the Indians working to serve Canadian and American markets are happy with how their work has improved their lives. Friedman points out that the working Indian women feel liberated now that they are making a decent wage and can afford such things as a college education. He describes Indian workers' view of their jobs, using words such as "self-confidence" and "independence." At the end of his article, Friedman states that he doesn't favor Indian employment over American employment but that outsourced jobs in countries like India or Pakistan create both prosperity and global security. Although Friedman's article clearly conveys to its audience how some Indian workers are benefiting from outsourcing, his argument relies heavily on personal experience and generalizations. I also think his condescending attitude hurts his argument, and he concludes his article too abruptly, leaving readers with questions.

3   Friedman succeeds in portraying the positive side of outsourcing to his *New York Times* readers who may be questioning the rationale for outsourcing. Friedman interviews the recipients of American jobs to see outsourcing from their perspective and enlightens Americans trying to understand how outsourcing is benefiting workers in other countries. Friedman's opening is vivid and captures the readers' interest by detailing his experience inside an Indian call center. He quotes the Indian workers expressing the joys of working for American and Canadian people. These workers testify to the financial and personal gains these jobs have brought. One woman says that she feels good about her job and herself "when

people come to you with a problem and you can solve it." The article is so full of optimism that the reader can't help but empathize with the Indians and feel happy that outsourcing has transformed their lives. Through these emotional appeals, Friedman succeeds in making readers who may have big reservations about outsourcing think about the human dimension of outsourcing.

4   However, Friedman also makes large generalizations based on his few personal experiences, lessening the credibility of his article. The first sentence of the article reads, "Indians are so hospitable." So are *all* Indians "so hospitable"? Friedman seems to make this generalization about national character based on the fact that he was applauded by a room full of Indians after reading a tongue twister paragraph in a perfect Canadian accent. I can see why Friedman appreciates his warm reception, but "feel good" moments can hardly provide evidence for the soundness of global economic policies. Friedman generalizes further about what he sees and hears in the call center room. He talks about the Indian employees in these terms: "All of them seem to have gained self-confidence and self-worth." From this single observation, Friedman makes the assumption that almost every Indian working an outsourced job must be gaining, and that the overall experience has done wonders for their lives. However, other articles that I have read have mentioned that call center work is basically a dead-end job and that $200 a month is not a big salary. Later in his conclusion, Friedman states, "[W]e make not only a more prosperous world, but a safer world for our own 20-year-olds." Can this conclusion be drawn from one visit to a call center where Indians expressed gratitude for their outsourcing work?

5   An even bigger problem with Friedman's article is the condescending way in which he describes the Indian workers. I think he portrays the culture as being incompetent before the American and Canadian outsourced jobs came to improve their accents and their lives. One statement that conveys condescension is this remark: "Watching these incredibly enthusiastic young Indians preparing for their call center jobs—earnestly trying to soften their t's and roll their r's—is an uplifting experience . . . ." This passage reminds me of the delight and pride of parents witnessing their children's growth milestones. Friedman is casting the accent neutralization of the Indian workers as overcoming a barrier in order to reach success. Friedman's condescending tone is apparent again when he restates the words of one American caller to an Indian worker, "They say you people are really good at what you do. I am glad I reached an Indian." I see Friedman's reason for including this quote; he wants the reader to know that Indian workers are being valued for their work. However, the words that the American uses, which Friedman deliberately chooses to include in his article, "you people," suggest that Indians are a whole other kind of people different from American workers in their skills. Friedman's condescension also appears when he says that these are "low-wage, low-prestige jobs." This remark is full of problems because it puts down the Indians taking the jobs and the Americans who have lost them, and it misrepresents the outsourcing scene that now includes many highly skilled prestigious jobs.

6   I also think that Friedman weakens his article by concluding abruptly and introducing new ideas to readers that leave them with unanswered questions. Friedman asks the reader, "What am I saying here? That it's more important for young

Indians to have jobs than Americans?" This point seems like a relevant question to investigate, but its weakness is that Friedman never even mentions any place in his article the loss that American workers are experiencing. At the end of the article, readers are left with questions. For example, the last sentence reads, "we make not only a more prosperous world, but a safer world for our own 20-year-olds." Although Friedman is implying that outsourcing improves our relationships with other countries and enhances our national safety, nowhere in the article does he substantiate this claim. He seems to have thrown this statement into the conclusion just to end the article on a happy note.

7   Giving a human face to outsourcing is a good idea; however, Friedman does not support his main argument well, and this article comes across as a simplistic, unexplored view of outsourcing. I and other readers are left needing to look for answers to serious questions about outsourcing elsewhere.

Work Cited

Friedman, Thomas L. "30 Little Turtles." *The New York Times*, 29 Feb. 2004, www.nytimes.com/2004/02/29/opinion/30-little-turtles.html.

THINKING CRITICALLY

About "Questioning Thomas L. Friedman's Optimism in '30 Little Turtles'"

1. What rhetorical points has Stephanie Malinowski chosen to analyze in her strong response essay?
2. What examples and quotations from Friedman's article work particularly well as support for her points? Where might she have included more support?
3. Where does Stephanie use attributive tags effectively?
4. What view of Friedman's article does Stephanie want you to have after reading her critique?

Chapter 7
Writing an Autobiographical Narrative

Learning Objectives

7.1 Explain and use open-form strategies for autobiographical writing.

7.2 Explain the special features of a literacy narrative.

7.3 Compose an effective autobiographical essay or literacy narrative.

Understanding autobiographical narrative

7.1 Explain and use open-form strategies for autobiographical writing.

This chapter asks you to write an autobiographical narrative about something significant in your life. Employing the rhetorical aim of "writing to express or share," autobiographical narrative can help you explore, deepen, and complicate your perceptions of the world. The writing projects for this chapter address two genres of narrative writing: (1) an **autobiographical narrative** on any significant event or moment in your life, and (2) a **literacy narrative** centered on your experience with language, reading, writing, school, teachers, or education.

Good autobiographical narrative does not depend on having an exciting life with highly dramatic moments. On the contrary, some of the most memorable autobiographical and literacy narratives relate ordinary experiences in a way that reveals the writer's new ways of understanding that serve to deepen, darken, or expand the reader's(and writer's) view of the world.

Autobiographical Tension: The Opposition of Contraries

Autobiographical narrative follows the principles of open-form rather than closed-form prose. Rather than state the significance of your narrative up front in a thesis statement, you let it unfold in storylike fashion. This narrative structure places autobiographical writing at the open end of the closed-to-open-form continuum, making it more like a nonfiction "story" than a traditional academic essay. Consequently, on several occasions in this chapter, we refer to Chapter 19, "Strategies for Writing Open-Form Prose."

Even though autobiographical narrative typically doesn't state a thesis, it shares with closed-form prose the posing of a problem—that is, the perception of conflicts or tensions that the writer tries to address or resolve in some way. In effective narration, the problem usually takes the form of **contraries**. By this term we mean oppositions, clashes, or tensions between two or more characters in the story, between the narrator and external forces in the culture, or between two or more parts of the narrator's divided self in which the narrator confronts competing values, expectations, or worldviews.

Here are three kinds of contraries that frequently form the plots of autobiographical narratives:

1. **Old self versus new self.** The writer perceives changes in himself or herself as a result of some transforming or breakthrough moment or event.

2. **Old view of person X versus new view of person X.** The writer's perception of a person (favorite uncle, childhood hero, scary teacher) changes as a result of some revealing moment; the change in the narrator's perception of person X also indicates growth in the narrator's self-perception.

3. **Old values versus new values that threaten, challenge, or otherwise disrupt the old values.** The writer confronts an outsider (or a new, unfamiliar situation such as a class or a learning task) that challenges his or her worldview, or the writer undergoes a crisis that creates a conflict in values.

The contraries in a story can often be summed up in statements like these:

> My teacher thought I was sullen and defiant, but she didn't know that I was afraid to read or why. (Writer reveals the real self that lies beneath the false self perceived by others.)

> Although I broke all Miller King's football records after he lost his arm in a motorcycle accident, I realized that he was a better person than I was. (Writer's old view of Person X yields to a new view—see "Phantom Limb Pain" later in this chapter.)

> The school that I had dreamed of attending turned into a nightmarish prison. (The writer's old view of the school is transformed through experience into a more insightful new view.)

An open-form narrative without contraries or tension is like a closed-form piece without a surprising thesis. It is the reader's experience of tension leading to resolution that distinguishes an effective narrative from an "and then" essay that rambles on like a diary, telling what happened in chronological order without a point. To illustrate the difference between "*and then* chronology" and an effective narrative, you can read our discussion of "The Stolen Watch" in Skill 19.1. It is a good example of what *not* to do for this assignment, especially when contrasted with "No Cats in America" at the end of this chapter.

Like the risky thesis statement in closed-form writing, the opposition of contraries functions as an organizing principle, helping the writer determine how to arrange scenes or decide what to include or exclude. The narrative's tension is typically resolved when the narrator experiences a moment of recognition or insight, experiences a loss or a triumph, or otherwise changes status. Usually the writer does not explain this resolution in an expository paragraph; rather, the writer reveals it implicitly in a scene that might be called a "moment of revelation." The moment of revelation in a story might be a gesture, a remark, a smile, a new piece of clothing, or a way of walking or shaking a hand—any narrative element that signals a new or changed perspective. Thus, when you search for a significant experience for your autobiographical narrative, think of *significant* not as "unusual" or "exciting" but rather as "revealing" or "conveying new and unexpected meaning or insight."

For Writing and Discussion
Imagining a Moment of Revelation

Try inventing a short scene in which a gesture, smile, or brief action reverses one character's feelings about, or understanding of, another character.

1. You thought that Maria had led a sheltered life until _____.

2. You thought Mr. Watson was a racist until _____.

3. Marco (Jillian) seemed the perfect date until _____.

Here is an example:

My dad seemed unforgivingly angry at me until he suddenly smiled, turned my baseball cap backward on my head, and held up his open palm for a high five. "Girl, if you don't change your ways, you're going to be as big a high school screw-up as your old man was."

Individual Task: Choose one or two of these hypothetical scenarios and fill out the "until" clause by imaging a scene with a revelatory moment. Use specific "show don't tell" words that are low on the ladder of abstraction.

Group Task: Share your brief imagined story with classmates. Your goal is to begin seeing how a scene in an open-form narrative can convey implicit meanings that would have to be made explicit in closed-form prose.

How Literary Elements Work Together in Autobiographical Narratives

The basic elements of a literary narrative that work together to create a story are plot, character, dialogue, setting, and theme.

THE IMPORTANCE OF PLOT   By **plot** we mean the basic action of the story, including the selection and sequencing of scenes and events. Often stories don't open with the earliest chronological moment; they may start *in medias res* ("in the middle of things") at a moment of crisis and then flash backward to fill in earlier details that explain the origins of the crisis. Your plot determines what you choose to include in your story, where you place it, and the amount of detail you choose to devote to each scene (that is, your **pacing**).

Plots typically unfold in the following stages: (a) an arresting opening scene; (b) the introduction of characters and the filling in of background; (c) the building of tension or conflict through oppositions embedded in a series of events or scenes; (d) the climax or pivotal moment when the tension or conflict comes to a head; and (e) reflection on the events of the plot and their meaning.

To help you recognize story-worthy events in your own life, consider the following list of pivotal moments that have figured in many autobiographical narratives:

- Moments of enlightenment or coming to knowledge
- Passages from one realm to another: from innocence to experience, from outsider to insider or vice versa, from novice to expert, from what you once were to what you now are
- Confrontation with the unknown or struggle against an external or societal pressure
- Problems maintaining relationships without compromising your own growth or denying your own needs
- Problems accepting limitations and necessities
- Contrasts between common wisdom and your own unique knowledge or experience

THE IMPORTANCE OF CHARACTER AND DIALOGUE   Who might be the characters in your autobiographical story? The answer depends on the nature of the tension that moves your story forward. Characters who contribute significantly to that tension or who clearly represent some aspect of that tension belong in your story. Whatever the source of tension in a story, a writer typically chooses characters who exemplify the narrator's fears and desires or who forward or frustrate the narrator's growth in a significant way.

Sometimes writers develop characters not through description and sensory detail but through dialogue. Particularly if a story involves conflict between people, dialogue is a powerful means of letting the reader experience that conflict directly. The following piece of dialogue, taken from African-American writer Richard Wright's classic autobiography *Black Boy,* demonstrates how a skilled writer can let dialogue tell the story, without resorting to analysis and abstraction. In the following scene, young Wright approaches a librarian in an attempt to get a book by Baltimore author and journalist H. L. Mencken from a whites-only public library. He has forged a note and borrowed a library card from a sympathetic white coworker and is pretending to borrow the book in his coworker's name.

> "What do you want, boy?"
>
> As though I did not possess the power of speech, I stepped forward and simply handed her the forged note, not parting my lips.
>
> "What books by Mencken does he want?" she asked.
>
> "I don't know ma'am," I said avoiding her eyes.
>
> "Who gave you this card?"
>
> "Mr. Falk," I said.
>
> "Where is he?"
>
> "He's at work, at the M— Optical Company," I said. "I've been in here for him before."
>
> "I remember," the woman said. "But he never wrote notes like this."
>
> Oh, God, she's suspicious. Perhaps she would not let me have the books? If she had turned her back at that moment, I would have ducked out the door and never gone back. Then I thought of a bold idea.
>
> "You can call him up, ma'am," I said, my heart pounding.
>
> "You're not using these books are you?" she asked pointedly.

"Oh no ma'am. I can't read."

"I don't know what he wants by Mencken," she said under her breath.

I knew I had won; she was thinking of other things and the race question had gone out of her mind.

—Richard Wright, *Black Boy*

It's one thing to hear *about* racial prejudice and discrimination; it's another thing to *hear* it directly through dialogue such as this. In just one hundred or so words of conversation, Wright communicates the anguish and humiliation of being a "black boy" in the United States in the 1920s.

Another way to develop a character is to present a sequence of moments or scenes that reveal a variety of behaviors and moods. Imagine taking several photographs of your character to represent his or her complexity and variety and then arranging them in a collage.

THE IMPORTANCE OF SETTING   Your choice of setting depends on how much a description of place will help readers understand the conflict or tension that drives the story. When you write about yourself, what you notice in the external world often reflects your inner world. In some moods you are apt to notice the expansive lawn, beautiful flowers, and swimming ducks in the city park; in other moods you might note the litter of paper cups, the blight on the roses, and the scum on the duck pond. The setting typically relates thematically to the other elements of a story. In "No Cats in America?", for example, the author contrasts his parents' parties in the Philippines, replete with music and dancing, firecrackers, a mahjong gambling room, and exotic food and drink such as homemade mango juice and coconut milk, with the American school lunchroom where he opened his Tupperware lunchbox filled with fish and bagoong. The contrast of these settings, especially when the author's American classmates laugh at his lunch, embodies the story's tension.

THE IMPORTANCE OF THEME   The word **theme** is difficult to define. Like thesis statements, themes organize the other elements of the essay. But in autobiographical narratives a theme is seldom stated explicitly and is never supported with reasons and factual evidence. Readers ponder—even argue about—themes, and often different readers are affected very differently by the same theme. Some literary critics view theme as simply a different way of thinking about plot. To use a phrase from critic Northrop Frye, a plot is "what happened" in a story, whereas the theme is "what happens" over and over again in this story and others like it. To illustrate this distinction, we summarize student writer Patrick José's autobiographical narrative "No Cats in America?", one of the essays in the Readings section of this chapter, from a plot perspective and from a theme perspective:

Plot Perspective It's the story of a Filipino boy who emigrates with his family from the Philippines to the United States when he is in the eighth grade. On the first day of school, he is humiliated when classmates snicker at the lunch his mother packed for him. Feeling more and more alienated each day, he eventually proclaims, "I hate being Filipino!"

Theme Perspective It's the story of how personal identity is threatened when people are suddenly removed from their own cultures and immersed into new ones that don't understand or respect difference. The story reveals the psychic damage of cultural dislocation.

As you can see, the thematic summary goes beyond the events of the story to point toward the larger significance of those events. Although you may choose not to state your theme directly for your readers, you need to understand that theme to organize your story. This understanding usually precedes and guides your decisions about what events and characters to include, what details and dialogue to use, and what elements of setting to describe. But sometimes you need to reverse the process and start out with events and characters that, for whatever reason, force themselves on you, and then figure out your theme after you've written for a while. In other words, theme may be something you discover as you write.

The special features of literacy narratives

7.2   Explain the special features of a literacy narrative.

A literacy narrative is a subset of autobiographical narrative: It uses the elements of a story to recount a writer's personal experience with language in all its forms—reading and writing, acquiring a second language, being an insider or outsider based on literacy level and cultural context—or with learning how to learn in general through experiences inside and outside of school. The academic and public fascination with literacy narratives has grown out of—and contributed to—contemporary discussions about cultural diversity in the United States and the connections between literacy and cultural power.

Literacy narratives are a frequently encountered and important genre. For example, one of the most famous literacy narratives is by Frederick Douglass, the ex-slave and abolitionist leader who describes learning to read and write as the key to his liberation from slavery. Another well-known literacy narrative is by Zitkala-Ša (Gertrude Bonnin), a Native American woman who exposes the forceful assimilation tactics employed by missionary schools to separate Native American children from their tribes in the late nineteenth and early twentieth centuries. Perhaps the most famous literacy narrative was written by Helen Keller, who recounts the moments when an understanding of language broke through the isolation created by her blindness and deafness. More recently, literacy narratives by immigrants from many cultures have explored the role of education in thwarting or encouraging their integration into American society.

Writing a literacy narrative in college classes can help students explore their adjustment to college, link their earlier learning experiences to the literacy demands of college courses, and take ownership of their education. Thinking about your own literacy experiences compels you to ponder your educational path and your own ideas about the purpose of education. In contemplating the way that ethnic, economic, gender, class, and regional considerations have shaped your own learning to read and write, you will experience the pleasure of self-discovery and cultural insight.

Literacy narratives resemble other autobiographical narratives in their open-form structure and their inclusion of some or all of these literary features: a plot built on tension and presented as well-sequenced scenes, vivid descriptions of settings, well-drawn characters, dialogue, and theme. Like other autobiographical narratives, literacy narratives rely on vivid, concrete language to make settings and dramatic moments come alive for readers. However, these two types of narratives differ in several important ways:

DISTINCTIVE FEATURES OF LITERACY NARRATIVES

- A focus on a writer's experience with language, reading, writing, schooling, teachers, or some other important aspect of education
- A focus on bringing an insight about the significance of learning, language, reading, or writing to readers through an implied theme (although this theme might be explicitly stated, most likely at the end of the narrative)
- A focus on engaging readers and connecting them to an understanding of the writer's educational/learning experience, prompting them to think about their own educational experiences and larger questions about the purpose and value of education

For Writing and Discussion
Analyzing Features of Literacy Narratives

Read the following passages that depict key moments in two students' literacy experiences, and answer the questions about them that direct your attention to specific features.

EXCERPT FROM MEGAN LACY'S LITERACY NARRATIVE

. . . I was placed in the remedial reading group. Our books had red plastic covers while the other kids had books with yellow covers that looked gold to me. When it was reading time, the rest of the red group and I congregated around a rectangular wood table where Mrs. Hinckley would direct each of us to read a passage from the story aloud. The first time this happened, my stomach dropped. Even the remedial kids were sounding out the words, but I had no idea what those symbols on the page meant.

When my turn came, I muttered meekly, "I can't. . . . "

"Don't say 'can't' in my classroom!" Mrs. Hinckley snapped. Then, more gently, she said, "Just sound it out. . . . "

I did as she recommended and could hardly believe what was happening. I was reading. I felt superhuman with such a power. After that moment, I read to my mom every night. . . .

EXCERPT FROM JEFFREY CAIN'S LITERACY NARRATIVE

In the Walla Walla Public Library, I remember the tomato soup colored carpet, the bad oil paintings of pioneers fording the Columbia River, the musty smell, the oak card catalog with brass knobs, the position of the clock when I first read Jerzy Kosinski's *The Painted Bird*.

"Just read it," my sister-in-law said. "I know you don't read much fiction, but just read this one," she pleaded.

Reluctantly, at first, I turned the pages. But each word covertly seduced me; slowly the odyssey of the dark-skinned gypsy affected my spirit like an exotic opiate, until Lehki's painted bird lay pecked to death on the ground. The image haunted my conscience for days. During some of my more restless nights, I was chased like the characters by Nazis through the Black Forest.

Who was this Kosinski? Why did his book affect me this way? How and why did he write like this? Did all writers write like Kosinski?

The novel incited a series of questions that forced me to begin writing notes and summarizing my thoughts. I began a reading journal and my development as a writer shadowed my habits as a reader. . . .

1. What literacy experiences have Megan and Jeffrey chosen to focus on?
2. How do Megan and Jeffrey use the narrative elements of plot, dialogue, setting, and concrete, specific language to involve their readers in their experiences?
3. Based on these excerpts, how would you articulate the theme of each piece?
4. What educational memories of your own do these excerpts trigger?

Writing an autobiographical or literacy narrative

7.3   Compose an effective autobiographical essay or literacy narrative.

Writing Project:

Option 1: Autobiographical Narrative
Write a narrative essay about something significant in your life using the literary strategies of plot, dialogue, character, and setting. Develop your story through the use of contraries, creating tension that moves the story forward and gives it significance. Use specific details and develop contraries that create tension and lead to a resolution or moment of revelation.

Option 2: Literacy Narrative
Write a narrative essay that focuses on your experiences with language, reading, writing, or education. You could explore positive or negative experiences in learning to read or write, breakthrough moments in your development as a literate person, or some educational experiences that have shaped your identity as a person or student. Incorporate the literary elements of plot, character, dialogue, setting, theme, and descriptive language in the telling of your story. Think of your task as finding new significance for yourself in these experiences and sharing your discoveries with your readers in ways that hold their interest and bring them new understanding.

   Both these options call for a "story," which follows the principles of open-form prose. In conjunction with this assignment, we recommend that you read Chapter 19, which will provide additional help with this assignment.

Generating and Exploring Ideas

As you generate and explore ideas, your goal is to develop a plot—a significant moment or insight arising out of the opposition between two ideas—that you can develop with the storytelling strategies of open-form prose. If you are still searching for ideas, the following questions might help:

QUESTIONS FOR AN AUTOBIOGRAPHICAL NARRATIVE

- **Questions arising from your achievement of a new status** (winning/losing a competition, passing/failing an important test, making/not making the team). If you failed, what did you learn from it or how did it shape you? If you succeeded, did the new status turn out to be as important as you had expected it to be?

- **Questions arising from challenges to your normal assumptions about life or from your failure to fit or fulfill others' expectations of you** (encounter with persons from a different culture or social class; your discovery that you have stereotyped someone or have been stereotyped; your difficulty in living up to someone's expectations of you)

- **Questions arising from conflicts of values or failure to live up to values** (a time when a person who mattered to you rejected you or let you down, or a time when you rejected or let down someone who cared for you; a time when you were irresponsible or violated a principle or law and thereby caused others pain—for example, shoplifting, leaving work early, or being drunk; a time when you were criticized unjustly or given a punishment you didn't deserve)

ADDITIONAL QUESTIONS FOR A LITERACY NARRATIVE

- **Questions about adjusting to college or educational challenges** (unexpected problems with reading and writing encountered in college, or earlier in middle school or high school; discovery of holes or weaknesses in your education; educational issues related to your "difference"—ethnic, class, physical/mental, sexual orientation—from the norm)

- **Questions about your experiences with language** (issues arising from learning a second language; from being bilingual; from speaking a nonstandard dialect; from having a speech or hearing impairment or a learning disability; from preferring math or art or athletics or video games to reading and writing)

- **Questions about influential (or inhibiting) teachers or mentors** (influence of people who have helped or hindered your literacy development; people who have changed your view of yourself as a reader or writer)

- **Questions about literacy and social status or citizenship** (issues connected to literacy and cultural power or economic success; the role of education in preparing you for local, national, or global citizenship)

Shaping, Drafting, and Revising Your Narrative

Once you've identified an event about which you'd like to write, you need to develop ways to show readers what makes that event particularly storyworthy. In thinking about the event, consider the questions in Strategies Chart 7.1.

When stuck, writers often work their way into a narrative by describing in detail a vividly recalled scene, person, or object. You may not be able to include all the descriptive material, but in the act of writing exhaustively about this one element, the rest of the story may begin to unfold for you, and forgotten items and incidents may resurface. In the course of describing scenes and characters,

Strategies Chart 7.1 Question-Asking Strategies to Help Shape and Draft Your Narrative

Element of the Narrative	Questions to Ask
How to Start	• What are the major contraries or tensions in this story? • What events and scenes portraying these contraries might you include in your narrative? • What insights or meaning do you think your story suggests? How would you articulate the theme of your narrative? • How might you begin your narrative?
How to Think about and Develop Characters and Setting	• What characters are important in this story? • How will you portray them—through description, action, dialogue, or some combination of these? • What settings or scenes can you recreate for readers? • What particulars or physical details will make the setting, characters, and conflicts vivid and memorable?
How to Think about and Develop the Plot	• How might you arrange the scenes in your story? • What would be the climax, the pivotal moment of decision or insight?
How to Conclude Your Narrative	• What resolution can you bring to the tensions and conflicts in your story? • How can you convey the significance of your story? What will make it something readers can relate to? • How can the ending of your narrative leave readers thinking about larger human issues and concerns?

you will probably also begin reflecting on the significance of what you are saying. Try freewriting answers to such questions as "Why is this important?" and "What am I trying to do here?" Then continue with your rough draft. Remember that it is the storyteller's job to put readers into the story by providing enough detail and context for the readers to see why the event is significant. Later, testing your narrative out on other readers can give you valuable feedback about your effectiveness in grabbing and holding their interest and conveying an insight. Plan to write several drafts of your narrative.

QUESTIONS FOR PEER REVIEW

In addition to the generic peer review questions explained in Skill 17.4, ask your peer reviewers to address these questions:

1. How could the title and opening paragraphs more effectively hook readers' interest and prepare them for the story to follow?

2. How might the writer improve the tension, structure, or pacing of the scenes?

3. How could the writer improve the connections between scenes or use a different organization (such as a collage of scenes or flashbacks) to enhance the clarity or drama of the narrative?

4. Where might the writer provide more information about characters or describe them more fully?

5. Where might the writer use dialogue more effectively to reveal character?

6. How might the writer make the setting more vivid and connected to the action and significance of the story?

7. What insight or revelation do you get from this story? How could the narrative's thematic significance be made more memorable or powerful?

8. Where do you find examples of specific language? Where could the writer use more concrete language?

Multimodal or Online Options

1. **Personal Narrative as Podcast** Tell your personal narrative or literacy narrative orally as a story suitable for radio or other oral settings. Produce a podcast and consider posting it online.

2. **Personal Narrative as Video Photo Essay** If your narrative lends itself to a visual telling, you can combine voice with images in a video photo essay. Tell your story orally through voice-over, but illustrate your narrative with photographs or drawings connected to your story. These might be actual photographs of the events depicted in your narrative or new photographs that you have taken or found (or drawings that you make) that enhance your story. Consider posting your video photo essay online. If you have not created these images yourself, be sure to acknowledge and identify their creators in an appropriate credit list.

3. **Personal Essay in Graphic Novel Format** If you have interest in drawing, consider transforming your personal narrative or literacy narrative into the style and format of a graphic novel. The drawings can add a powerful visual dimension to your narrative.

For advice on producing multimedia compositions, see Chapter 20.

Readings

Our first reading is by Kris Saknussemm, a poet and fiction writer. He is the author of the dystopian, futuristic novel *Zanesville* (2005) and the contemporary novel *Reverend America* (2011). His poems and short stories have appeared in literary magazines around the country, including *The Boston Review, New Letters, The Antioch Review,* and *ZYZZYVA.* This selection is taken from his autobiographical work in progress.

Kris Saknussemm
Phantom Limb Pain

1   When I was thirteen my sole purpose was to shed my baby fat and become the star halfback on our football team. That meant beating out Miller King, the best athlete at my school. He was my neighbor and that mythic kid we all know—the one who's forever better than we are—the person we want to be.

2   Football practice started in September and all summer long I worked out. I ordered a set of barbells that came with complimentary brochures with titles like "How to Develop a He-Man Voice." Every morning before sunrise I lumbered around our neighborhood wearing ankle weights loaded with sand. I taught myself how to do Marine push-ups and carried my football everywhere so I'd learn not to fumble. But that wasn't enough. I performed a ceremony. During a full moon, I burned my favorite NFL trading cards and an Aurora model of the great quarterback Johnny Unitas in the walnut orchard behind our house, where Miller and I'd gotten into a fight when we were seven and I'd burst into tears before he even hit me.

3   Two days after my ceremony, Miller snuck out on his older brother's Suzuki and was struck by a car. He lost his right arm, just below the elbow. I went to see him the day after football practice started—after he'd come back from the hospital. He looked pale and surprised, but he didn't cry. It was hard to look at the stump of limb where his arm had been, so I kept glancing around his room. We only lived about 200 feet away, and yet I'd never been inside his house before. It had never occurred to me that he would also have on his wall a poster of Raquel Welch from *One Million Years B.C.*

4   I went on to break all his records that year. Miller watched the home games from the bench, wearing his jersey with the sleeve pinned shut. We went 10–1 and I was named MVP, but I was haunted by crazy dreams in which I was somehow responsible for the accident—that I'd found the mangled limb when it could've been sewn back on—and kept it in an aquarium full of vodka under my bed.

5   One afternoon several months later, toward the end of basketball season, I was crossing the field to go home and I saw Miller stuck going over the Cyclone fence—which wasn't hard to climb if you had both arms. I guess he'd gotten tired of walking around and hoped no one was looking. Or maybe it was a matter of pride. I'm sure I was the last person in the world he wanted to see—to have to accept assistance from. But even that challenge he accepted. I helped ease him

down the fence, one diamond-shaped hole at a time. When we were finally safe on the other side, he said to me, "You know, I didn't tell you this during the season, but you did all right. Thanks for filling in for me."

6   We walked home together, not saying much. But together. Back to our houses 200 feet apart. His words freed me from my bad dreams. I thought to myself, how many things I hadn't told him. How even without an arm he was more of a leader. Damaged but not diminished, he was still ahead of me. I was right to have admired him. I grew bigger and a little more real from that day on.

THINKING CRITICALLY
About "Phantom Limb Pain"

Perhaps the first thing the reader realizes about Saknussemm's narrative is that the climactic event—one boy helping another climb down a Cyclone fence—is a small action; however, it has a big psychological and emotional meaning for the narrator. The events leading to this moment have prepared us to understand the writer's revelation of his new relationship to his rival. Saknussemm's last paragraph comments on the preceding narrative, making connections and pulling out threads of meaning.

1. Saknussemm chooses to leave a lot unsaid, depending on his readers to fill in the gaps. Why do you suppose that he had never been inside Miller King's house before? Why does he feel "somehow responsible for the accident"? What details does Saknussemm use to sketch in Miller's admirable traits?

2. What examples can you find in this narrative of what Chapter 19 calls revelatory words, memory-soaked words, and other concrete words low on the ladder of abstraction? Where does Saknussemm use words that *show* what is happening in the narrative instead of simply telling readers?

3. In closed-form prose, writers seldom use sentence fragments. In open-form prose, however, writers frequently use fragments for special effects. Note the two fragments in Saknussemm's final paragraph: "But together. Back to our houses 200 feet apart." Why does Saknussemm use these fragments? What is their rhetorical effect?

See Skill 19.2 for a discussion of concrete language including revelatory words and memory-soaked words. See Concept 4.3 for a discussion of *show* words and *tell* words.

For a different approach to narrative, consider student writer Patrick José's "No Cats in America?". Unlike Saknussemm's narrative, José's includes plentiful description. Note also how José creates tension through contrasts in his narrative: between an ideal image of America and a factual image, between life in the Philippines and life in California.

Patrick José (student)

No Cats in America?

1   "There are no cats in America." I remember growing up watching *An American Tail* with my sisters and cousins. Ever since I first saw that movie, I had always wanted to move to America. That one song, "There Are No Cats in America," in which the Mousekewitz family is singing with other immigrating mice, had the most profound effect on me. These were Russian mice going to America to find a better life—a life without cats. At first, I thought America really had no cats. Later, I learned that they meant that America was without any problems at all. I was taught about the American Dream with its promise of happiness and equality. If you wanted a better life, then you better pack up all your belongings and move to America.

2   However, I loved living in the Philippines. My family used to throw the best parties in Angeles City. For a great party, you need some delicious food. Of course there would be lechon, adobo, pancit, sinigang, lumpia, and rice. We eat rice for breakfast, lunch, and dinner, and rice even makes some of the best desserts. (My mom's bibingka and puto are perfect!) And you mustn't forget the drinks. San Miguel and Coke are usually sufficient. But we also had homemade mango juice and coconut milk. And a party wouldn't be a party without entertainment, right? So in one room, we had the gambling room. It's usually outside the house. Everybody would be smoking and drinking while playing mahjong. And sometimes, others would play pepito or pusoy dos. Music and dancing is always a must. And when there are firecrackers, better watch out because the children would go crazy with them.

3   Then one day, a mixed feeling came over me. My dad told us that he had gotten a job . . . in California. In the span of two months, we had moved to America, found a small apartment, and located a small private Catholic school for the kids. We did not know many people in California that first summer. We only had ourselves to depend on. We would go on car trips, go to the beach, cook, play games. In August, I thought we were living the American Dream.

4   But at the end of summer, school began. I was in the eighth grade. I had my book bag on one shoulder, stuffed with notebooks, folder paper, calculators, a ruler, a pencil box, and my lunch. I still can remember what I had for lunch on the first day of school—rice and tilapia and, in a small container, a mixture of vinegar, tomatoes, and bagoong. My mom placed everything in a big Tupperware box, knowing I eat a lot.

5   When I walked into the classroom, everyone became quiet and looked at me. I was the only Filipino in that room. Everyone was white. We began the day by introducing ourselves. When it got to my turn, I was really nervous. English was one of the courses that I took in the Philippines, and I thought I was pretty proficient at it. But when I first opened my mouth, everyone began to laugh. The teacher told everyone to hush. I sat down, smiling faintly, not understanding what was so funny. I knew English, and yet I was laughed at. But it had nothing to do with the language. It was my accent.

6   Some students tried to be nice, especially during lunch. But it didn't last long. I was so hungry for my lunch. I followed a group of students to the cafeteria and sat down at an empty table. Some girls joined me. I didn't really talk to them, but they

asked if they could join me. As I opened my Tupperware, I saw their heads turn away. They didn't like the smell of fish and bagoong. The girls left and moved to another table of girls. From the corner of my eye I saw them looking and laughing at me. I tried to ignore it, concentrating on eating my lunch as I heard them laugh. In the Philippines, the only way to fish and rice is with your hands. But that was in the Philippines. My manners were primitive here in America. I was embarrassed at the smell, was embarrassed at the way I ate, was embarrassed to be me.

7   When I got home, I lied to my parents. I told them school was great and that I was excited to go back. But deep down, I wanted to go back to the Philippines. When lunch came the next day, I was hungry. In my hand was my lunch. Five feet away was the trash. I stood up, taking my lunch in my hands. Slowly, I walked my way towards the trashcan, opened the lid, and watched as my lunch filled the trashcan. Again, I told my parents I enjoyed school.

8   When my grades began to suffer, the teacher called my parents and scheduled an appointment. The next day, my parents came to the classroom, and when they started talking to the teacher I heard laughter in the background. It humiliated me to have my classmates hear my parents talk.

9   That night, my parents and I had a private discussion. They asked why I lied to them. I told them everything, including my humiliation. They told me not to worry about it, but I pleaded for us to return to the Philippines. My parents said no. "Living here will provide a better future for you and your sisters," they said. Then the unexpected came. I didn't know what I was thinking. I yelled to them with so much anger, "I hate being Filipino!" Silence filled the room. Teardrops rolled down my cheeks. My parents were shocked, and so was I.

10   I went to my room and cried. I didn't mean what I said. But I was tired of the humiliation. Lying on my bed, with my eyes closed, my mind began to wander. I found myself in the boat with the Mousekewitz family singing, "There are no cats in America." If only they knew how wrong they were.

THINKING CRITICALLY

About "No Cats in America?"

Patrick José lets the reader infer his essay's significance from the details of the narrative and from their connection to the framing story of the fictional mice and cats.

1. How do the settings help you understand José's theme at different points in the narrative?
2. What would you say is the narrative's climax or pivotal moment?
3. José's title, first paragraph, and last paragraph are about a children's movie that features the Mousekewitzes' song proclaiming that there are no cats in America. How does the "no cats" image function both as part of the underlying tension of this narrative and as a symbolic vehicle for conveying the theme of José's essay? What insight has José achieved at the end?
4. During a rough-draft workshop, José asked his peer reviewers whether he should retain his description of parties in the Philippines, which he thought was perhaps unconnected to the rest of the narrative. His classmates urged him to keep those details. Do you agree with their advice? Why?
5. For Filipinos and Filipinas, the specific names of foods and party games would be rich examples of memory-soaked words. For other readers, however, these names are foreign and strange. Do you agree with José's decision to use these specific ethnic names? Why or why not?

   Our final reading, a literacy narrative, is by student writer Stephanie Whipple.

See Skill 19.2 for a discussion of the power of memory-soaked words.

Stephanie Whipple (student)

One Great Book

1   When first asked to remember my earliest experiences with reading, I thought of my favorite books as a young teen, and I was excited to explore how they shaped the person that I am today. However, upon trying to remember the very first books that I ever read as a child, some quite negative and frankly painful memories were brought to the surface.

2   When I was a little girl living in Memphis, Tennessee, I was a well-behaved bright child who never had trouble learning at a good pace or working with other children. In what I am guessing was my first grade class I remember being so excited when I found out that that year I was going to learn to read. My entire life, my mother and both of my older sisters have all loved reading. I was so excited to be able to read with them and join the big girls' conversations about the books that they were reading.

3   My very first vivid memory of reading was in the playroom of our house in Memphis. I was sitting with my father reading *The Poky Little Puppy* with him, and my younger brother, who had just started kindergarten, was playing with his Nerf gun.

4   "Okay, Steph. Start with this word." My dad points to the first word on the page.

5   "Ff . . . i . . . fi—"

6   "Five!" My little brother pops his little freckled face over my shoulder.

7   "Stevie, Steph and I are reading this first. You can read it after her," says my father turning to me. "Go ahead, Steph."

8   "Five . . . li . . . lit—"

9   "Little puppies!" yells Stevie from right behind me.

10   I turn away from the book, discouraged.

11   "Stephen!" says our father sternly. "Let Stephanie read. She knows the words; she just has to think about it for a little while. Go play over there and we will read a book when she is done." My Dad turns to me and smiles.

12   "Five little puppies . . . d . . . dug . . . a . . . h . . . h—"

13   "A hole under the fence!" My brother is behind me again, and I cannot believe that he is smarter than I am. He is only in kindergarten. You're not even supposed to start learning words until the first grade! I drop *The Poky Little Puppy* and run to my mommy, telling myself that reading is stupid, and I don't want to learn how anymore. Drawing and doing other arts and crafts are much more fun anyway, and Stevie can't even draw a bunny!

14   I was by no means a slow learner; Steve was just an exceptionally fast learner when it came to reading. He knew how to read whole chapter books before any of his peers could even read *The Poky Little Puppy*. However, the fact that my little brother could read better than I could made me feel stupid and I lost all of my previous enthusiasm about books.

15   Both of my parents desperately tried to get me to like reading. They were always sure to separate my brother and me when they were helping me with my

reading, but I had shut down. My mom always tried to read to me before bed, but I told her that I hated books. Instead I wanted her to make up stories and tell them to me, or tell me stories about when she was a little girl. I had made up my mind that I hated reading. If I didn't like it, I wouldn't have to be good at it. So, I did just as much reading as my teacher and my parents forced me to do, but that was it. When my brother was reading every word of *Calvin and Hobbes* comics and needing no help from my father, I was coloring Calvin's hair pink and turning Hobbes into a purple tiger with big black sunglasses on.

16   I continued to dislike reading for years. As I got older, I never finished any of the chapter books that I was required to read for school, and I certainly never read the other books that my mother was constantly trying to get me to read. I remember her telling me, "If you just find one book that you really love, you will love reading forever. I promise." My response was always, "Mom, reading is boring. I'm not a nerd." I wanted to spend my spare time playing with my friends and making friendship bracelets, not reading *A Wrinkle in Time* like my dorky little brother.

17   My parents have since told me that my not liking to read broke their hearts. My dad felt like it was his fault for reading with me around my brother. They did not know what to do, and they were convinced that I would go through my entire life without ever enjoying a good book.

18   One rainy summer day when I was about fourteen years old, however, all of this changed. My family and I were at our mountain house in the Poconos and the weather was too bad to go out on the boat or play outside, so I was bored. I approached my mom to ask her to play a game with me while she was sitting on our screened-in porch reading. She told me that she bought me a book that she loved when she was my age, and suggested that she read some of it to me just to see if I might like it. I don't know if it was out of utter boredom, being worn down by my mom constantly nagging me to read, or just out of really wanting to spend time with my mother, but I agreed. The book was about a little girl named Francie who was extremely poor and lived in a city that I was completely unfamiliar with, but I still related to her. I loved Francie, and after my mom finished reading the first chapter to me and left to go to the store, I continued reading the book and didn't put it down until it was time for dinner. I loved reading! When I was not reading, I was thinking about Francie and hoping that everything would turn out all right for her. The book had opened up a whole new world for me in which a family could be so poor and have almost none of the things that I was accustomed to, but still be happy and full of love and warmth and hope. I spent the whole week reading my book and discussing it with my mom and sisters.

19   I do not remember the next good book or even the next five good books that my mother gave me and I enthusiastically poured myself into. However, to this day whenever anyone mentions *A Tree Grows in Brooklyn*, or I see the movie on TV, or I read about another character named Frances or Francie, I get a warm feeling in my heart, and I thank God for my mother and her persistence. Without my mom, and without that one great book, I might not be the person and the reader that I am today. If anyone ever tells me that they do not like reading, I smile and tell them, "If you just find one book that you really love, you will love reading forever. I promise."

THINKING CRITICALLY

About "One Great Book"

1. In this literacy narrative, how does Stephanie Whipple create tension and establish the main conflicts?

2. In her desire to engage readers with her characters and setting, Stephanie chooses to use the present tense rather than the past tense for her early scene about reading. Do you find this choice effective? (It violates the normal rules about needless shifting of tense.) How else does she try to engage readers in her characters and setting?

3. This piece leads up to a moment of breakthrough and new insight about the significance of reading. How does Stephanie use story elements rather than straight exposition to convey the transformation in her attitude toward literature?

4. In much of this narrative, Stephanie includes words that are specific and descriptive—that is, low on the ladder of abstraction. What passages are vivid and memorable?

5. This piece is fairly straightforward, yet it points to some deeper themes about learning. What new understanding about children and reading does Stephanie want readers to grasp?

Chapter 8
Writing an Exploratory Essay or Annotated Bibliography

Learning Objectives

8.1 Use dialectic thinking to dwell with a problem and resist closure.

8.2 Find relevant sources and take double-entry notes.

8.3 Pose a significant and problematic research question and narrate your search for a thesis in an exploratory essay.

8.4 Summarize and critique your research sources in an annotated bibliography.

Understanding exploratory writing as dwelling with a problem

8.1 Use dialectic thinking to dwell with a problem and resist closure.

In earlier chapters, we explained how writers wrestle with subject-matter problems. During exploration, experienced writers often redefine their problem, discover new ideas, and alter or even reverse their initial thesis. In contrast, inexperienced writers often truncate this process, closing off the period of exploratory thinking. Asserting a thesis too soon can prevent writers from acknowledging an issue's complexity, whereas dwelling with a question invites writers to contemplate multiple perspectives, entertain new ideas, and let their thinking evolve. In this chapter, we introduce two genres of writing built on exploratory thinking:

- An **exploratory essay** narrates a writer's thinking process while doing research. The essay recounts your attempt to examine your question's complexity, explore alternatives, and arrive at a solution or answer. Because an exploration often requires research, you may need to consult Part 4, "A Rhetorical Guide to Research."

- An **annotated bibliography** summarizes and briefly critiques the research sources a writer used while exploring a problem. It encourages exploration and inquiry, provides a "tracing" of your work, and creates a guide for others interested in your research problem.

Even though academic readers usually expect thesis-driven arguments, both exploratory essays and annotated bibliographies are common. Exploratory essays exist in embryo in scholars' research or lab notebooks. For students, both the exploratory essay and the annotated bibliography serve as an intermediate stage in the research process. Student Kent Ansen's exploratory paper and annotated bibliography in this chapter are products of the exploratory phase of his research about mandatory public service, which later resulted in a researched argument. You can compare his exploratory essay and his annotated bibliography at the end of this chapter with his final thesis-driven argument at the end of Chapter 16.

Multiple Perspectives: Keeping the Question Open

The essential strategy for exploratory thinking and writing is to keep a problem alive by considering multiple solutions or points of view. The thinker identifies a problem, considers a possible solution or point of view, explores its strengths and weaknesses, and then moves on to consider another possible solution or viewpoint. The thinker resists closure—that is, resists settling too soon on a thesis.

To appreciate this process, complete the following thought exercise. Read the following two essays written for a freshman placement examination in composition at the University of Pittsburgh. The essays were written in response to this assignment:

> Describe a time when you did something you felt to be creative. Then, on the basis of the incident you have described, go on to draw some general conclusions about "creativity."

One of these essays received a much higher score than the other. Which essay scored higher?

ESSAY A

I am very interested in music, and I try to be creative in my interpretation of music. While in high school, I was a member of a jazz ensemble. The members of the ensemble were given chances to improvise and be creative in various songs. I feel that this was a great experience for me, as well as the other members. I was proud to know that I could use my imagination and feelings to create music other than what was written.

Creativity to me means being free to express yourself in a way that is unique to you, not having to conform to certain rules and guidelines. Music is only one of the many areas in which people are given opportunities to show their creativity. Sculpting, carving, building, art, and acting are just a few more areas where people can show their creativity.

Through my music I conveyed feelings and thoughts which were important to me. Music was my means of showing creativity. In whatever form creativity takes, whether it be music, art, or science, it is an important aspect of our lives because it enables us to be individuals.

ESSAY B

Throughout my life, I have been interested in and intrigued by music. My mother has often told me of the times, before I went to school, when I would "conduct" the orchestra on her records. I continued to listen to music and eventually started to play the guitar and the clarinet. Finally, at about the age of twelve, I started to sit down and to try to write songs. Even though my instrumental skills were far from my own high standards, I would spend much of my spare time during the day with a guitar around my neck, trying to produce a piece of music.

Each of these sessions, as I remember them, had a rather set format. I would sit in my bedroom, strumming different combinations of the five or six chords I could play, until I heard a series which sounded particularly good to me. After this, I set the music to a suitable rhythm (usually dependent on my mood at the time), and ran through the tune until I could play it fairly easily. Only after this section was complete did I go on to writing lyrics, which generally followed along the lines of the current popular songs on the radio.

At the time of the writing, I felt that my songs were, in themselves, an original creation of my own; that is, I, alone, made them. However, I now see that, in this sense of the word, I was not creative. The songs themselves seem to be an oversimplified form of the music I listened to at the time.

In a more fitting sense, however, I *was* being creative. Since I did not purposely copy my favorite songs, I was, effectively, originating my songs from my own "process of creativity." To achieve my goal, I needed what a composer would call "inspiration" for my piece. In this case the inspiration was the current hit on the radio. Perhaps, with my present point of view, I feel that I used too much "inspiration" in my songs, but, at the time, I did not.

Creativity, therefore, is a process which, in my case, involved a certain series of "small creations" if you like. As well, it is something the appreciation of which varies with one's point of view, that point of view being set by the person's experience, tastes, and personal view of creativity. The less experienced tend to allow for less originality, while the more experienced demand real originality to classify something a "creation." Either way, a term as abstract as this is perfectly correct, and open to interpretation.

For Writing and Discussion
Which Essay Scored Higher?

Individual task: Using freewriting, analyze the major differences between Essay A and Essay B. What might cause college professors to rate one essay higher than the other?

Group or whole-class discussion: Share your ideas and see if you reach consensus.

College professors tend to score Essay B higher. Why? The fundamental difference between Essay A and Essay B is that Writer B treats the concept of "creativity" as a true problem. Note that Writer A is satisfied with his or her initial definition:

> Creativity to me means being free to express yourself in a way that is unique to you, not having to conform to certain rules and guidelines.

Writer B, however, is *not* satisfied with his or her first answer and uses the essay to think through the problem. This writer remembers an early creative experience—composing songs as a twelve-year-old:

> At the time of the writing, I felt that my songs were, in themselves, an original creation of my own; that is, I, alone, made them. However, I now see that, in this sense of the word, I was not creative. The songs themselves seem to be an oversimplified form of the music I listened to at the time.

This writer distinguishes between two points of view: "On the one hand, I used to think x, but now, in retrospect, I think y." This move forces the writer to go beyond the initial answer to think of alternatives.

The key to effective exploratory writing is to create a tension between alternative views. When you start out, you might not know where your thinking process will end up. At the outset you might not have formulated an opposing, countering, or alternative view. Using a statement such as "I used to think . . . , but now I think" or "Part of me thinks this . . . , but another part thinks that . . . " forces you to find something additional to say. Writing then becomes a process of inquiry and discovery.

Dialectic Thinking: Playing Ideas against One Another

Writer B's dissatisfaction with the initial answer initiates a **dialectic** process that plays one idea against another, creating a tension that generates ideas. In contrast, Writer A offers no alternative to his or her definition of creativity. This writer presents no specific illustrations of creative activity (such as the specific details in Essay B about strumming the guitar) but presents merely space-filling abstractions ("Sculpting, carving, building, art, and acting are just a few more areas where people can show their creativity"). Writer B scores a higher grade, not because the essay creates a brilliant (or even particularly clear) explanation of creativity; rather, the writer is rewarded for thinking about the problem dialectically.

We use the term *dialectic* to mean a thinking process often associated with the German philosopher Hegel, who said that each thesis ("My act was creative") gives rise to an antithesis ("My act was not creative") and that the clash of these opposing perspectives leads thinkers to develop a synthesis that incorporates some features of both theses ("My act was a series of 'small creations'"). You initiate dialectic thinking any time you play Elbow's believing and doubting game (see Concept 2.2) or use other strategies to place alternative possibilities side by side.

Writer B uses a dialectic thinking strategy that we might characterize as follows:

1. Sees the assigned question as a genuine problem worth puzzling over

2. Considers alternative views and plays them against each other

For Writing and Discussion
Keeping a Problem Open

1. Working individually, read each of the following questions and write out the first plausible answer that comes to your mind.

   - Why on average are males more attracted to video games than females? Are these games harmful to males?

   - Have online social networks such as Facebook improved or harmed the lives of participants? Why?
   - The most popular magazines sold on college campuses are women's fashion and lifestyle magazines such as *Glamour, Elle*, and *Cosmopolitan*. Why do women buy these magazines? Are these magazines harmful?

2. As a whole class, take a poll to determine the most common first-response answers for each of the questions. Then explore other possible answers and points of view. The goal of your class discussion is to propose and explore answers that go against the grain of or beyond the common answers. Try to push deeply into each question so that it becomes more complex and interesting than it may at first seem.

3. How would you use library and Internet research to deepen your exploration of these questions? Specifically, what keywords might you use in a database search? What databases would you use? (See Skill 21.4)

---

3. Looks at specific examples and illustrations

4. Continues the thinking process in search of some sort of resolution or synthesis of the alternative views

5. Incorporates the stages of this dialectic process into the essay

These same dialectic thinking habits can be extended to research writing, where the researcher's goals are to find alternative points of view on the research question, to read sources rhetorically, to consider all the relevant evidence, to search for a resolution or synthesis of alternative views, and to use critical thinking to arrive at a thesis.

Finding sources and taking double-entry research notes

8.2   **Find relevant sources and take double-entry notes.**

Most exploratory essays require outside research. The assignments for this chapter therefore work in harmony with Part 4, "A Rhetorical Guide to Research," which explains how to use library databases to find sources, how to incorporate sources into your own arguments, how to cite and document your sources, and how to avoid plagiarism. One advantage of writing an exploratory paper or an annotated bibliography is the particular way these assignments develop your skill at taking meaningful research notes.

Whereas novice researchers often avoid taking notes and instead create a pile of photocopied or downloaded-and-printed articles, experienced researchers use note taking to promote strong rhetorical reading. We recommend *double-entry notes* in which you use one column for taking notes on a source and another column for recording your own thinking about the source. When you have finished taking notes in the first column, write a *strong response* to the source in the second column, explaining how the source advanced your thinking, raised questions, or pulled you in one direction or another.

What follows is Kent Ansen's double-entry research notes for one of the articles he used in his exploratory essay. When you read both his exploratory essay in this chapter and his final researched argument in Chapter 16, you'll be able to see how he used this article at a crucial place in his research.

Kent's Double-Entry Research Log Entry for the Opinion Piece in the *Chronicle of Philanthropy*

Date of entry so you can reconstruct chronological order ───▶ February 8

Rosenman, Mark. "A Call for National Service." *The Chronicle of Philanthropy*, 18 Oct. 2007, philanthropy.com/article/A-Call-for-National-Service/165721.

Bibliographic citation following assigned format, in this case MLA

Rhetorical notation about genre, purpose, audience ───▶ Editorial in the journalistic style in the opinion section of a magazine for "the nonprofit world"

Reading Notes	Strong Response Notes
Reading notes in column 1 on content of the source ───▶ —Begins with the current political discussions about national service as voluntary or compulsory. Expresses Rosenman's view that compulsory national service might be good for citizen participation in public policy. Identifies a problem *Include full quotations if you won't keep a copy of the full source* ───▶ that as tax and fee payers only "we are reduced to little more than consumers of government services, to being government's customers."	—*Rosenman's point is a good one, but I think as voters and campaigners for candidates we also have a role as citizens. This quotation could be useful.*
—Argues that people have to own their government and get in there and do work.	
Strong response notes in column 2 show reactions to the source —Says that "[m]andatory national service would change the relationship of people to their government and vice versa" and would lead to greater accountability required of leaders.	—*This point makes sense and is a compelling moral argument. Makes me think of how a volunteer army keeps us from having the kind of stakes in our government's decisions as we did when we had a military draft.*
—Moves into a section on the urgency of citizen involvement in deteriorating conditions, loss of economic status for poor and middle class, money spent on wars, and so forth.	—*I wish Rosenman could have offered more examples and maybe some statistics.*
—Mentions low voter turnout.	—*Could give more details.*

—Develops the reasons supporting his main claim by discussing his points: people would make a connection between policies and their effects; observing "constituencies poorly served by government" would increase people's involvement in government; service would connect Americans across typical barriers "by race, class, ethnicity, religion, geography, perhaps even age."

—Rosenman then briefly discusses the practical dimensions of his view—how to make a mandatory national service plan work. He mentions two-year service, stipends or salary, and credit toward education. He says that schools should make service an important part of the curriculum to build character and citizens . . . .

—He acknowledges that any employees who might have their jobs taken by community-service workers should be given new opportunities, maybe training the service workers. [Kent's research log continued to cover the whole article.]

—This thinking is useful in presenting one angle on my question. In my volunteer work I often saw how government service could be improved—made me want to do something.

—I am glad he devotes some space to practical considerations. However, I wonder if I would have found my high school volunteering as effective if the school made me do it?

—Good idea to confront this objection to mandatory public service.

Part of Kent's strong response summary:

Very useful article, not scholarly but clear in the argument it asserts. I will use this source to represent the liberal perspective on mandatory public service. Rosenman is a public service professor at Union Institute and University and clearly has a strong background in this issue. This article provides a broad-strokes approach and overview of the pro–national service position. I will want to give more depth to this view and also examine arguments against it.

Writing an exploratory essay

8.3   Pose a significant and problematic research question and narrate your search for a thesis in an exploratory essay.

Writing Project: Choose a question, problem, or issue that genuinely perplexes you. At the beginning of your essay, explain why you are interested in this problem, why you think it is significant, and why you have been unable to reach a satisfactory answer. Then write a first-person, chronologically organized narrative account of your thinking process as you investigate your question through research, talking with others, and doing your own reflective thinking. Your goal is to examine your question, problem, or issue from a variety of perspectives, assessing the strengths and weaknesses of different positions and points of view. Your goal is not to answer your question but to report on the process of wrestling with it.

This assignment asks you to dwell on a problem—and not necessarily to solve that problem. Your problem may shift and evolve as your thinking progresses. What matters is that you actively engage with your problem and demonstrate why it is problematic.

Posing Your Initial Problem

In essence, the *subject matter* of your exploratory essay is the process of your generating and exploring ideas. (See Concept 1.1 on how to pose a significant question.) If your instructor hasn't assigned a specific problem to be investigated, then your first step is to choose one that currently perplexes you. Perhaps a question is problematic for you because you haven't yet had a chance to study it (Should the United States turn to nuclear power for generating electricity?). Maybe the available data seem conflicting or inconclusive (Do social media make us lonely?). Or, possibly, the problem or issue draws you into an uncomfortable conflict of values (Should we legalize the sale of human organs for transplant?).

The key to this assignment is to choose a question, problem, or issue *that truly perplexes you*. Here are several exercises to help you think of ideas for this essay:

- Make a list of issues or problems that both interest and perplex you within the range of subjects specified by your instructor. Then choose two or three and freewrite about them for five minutes or so. Use as your model Kent Ansen's freewrite (in Concept 2.2), which marked the origin of his exploratory paper for this chapter. Share your questions and your freewrites with friends and classmates because doing so often stimulates further thinking and discovery.

- A particularly valuable kind of problem to explore for this assignment is a current public controversy. Often such issues involve disagreements about facts and values that merit open-ended exploration. This assignment invites you to explore and clarify where you stand on such public issues as police tactics, immigration, health care reform, energy policies, government responses to terrorism, and so forth. Make a list of currently debated public controversies that you would like to explore. Share your list with classmates and friends.

Formulating a Starting Point

After you've chosen a problem, you are ready to write a first draft of your introduction, in which you identify your chosen problem and show why you are interested in it, why you find it perplexing, and why it is significant. You might start out with a sharp, clearly focused question (Should the United States build a wall between the United States and Mexico?). Often, however, formulating a focused question will turn out to be part of the *process* of writing the paper. Instead of a single, focused question, you might start with a whole cluster of related questions swimming in your head. That's fine, too, because you can still explain why you are interested in this cluster of questions.

The goal of your introduction is to hook your reader's interest in your chosen problem. Often the best way to do so is to show why you yourself became interested in it. For example, Kent Ansen opens his exploratory essay (reproduced at the end of this chapter) by recalling his experience with volunteer work and his discussion with older friends who are questioning their majors and their futures. He then introduces the questions he wants to investigate—how could mandatory public service benefit the country and young people, and should it be required for all citizens?

Finding Sources and Taking Double-Entry Notes

After you have formulated your initial problem, you are ready to start your research. You will need to use library and Internet resources to find articles that will immerse you in multiple perspectives. (See Skills 21.3 and 22.1.) As you take notes, use the "double-entry" method explained earlier in this chapter. The double-entry method encourages you to read your sources rhetorically and to think dialectically about multiple points of view.

Drafting and Revising

Exploratory essays can be composed in two ways—the "real-time strategy" and the "retrospective strategy," summarized in Strategies Chart 8.1.

As you draft and revise, pay particular attention to the following:

- **Show how you chose sources with purpose rather than randomly.** As you transition from one source to the next, help your reader see your thought processes. Note the following examples of bridging passages that reveal the writer's purposeful selection of sources:

   At this point, I decided I should investigate more thoroughly the drawbacks of mandatory national service, so I turned to an online *Time* article that was a direct response to Stengel: Michael Kinsley's "National Service? Puh-lease" (from Kent Ansen's essay, paragraph 7).

   After reading Friedman's views of how globalization was changing lives in India and China, I realized that I needed to *talk* to some students from these countries, so I grabbed my backpack and headed to the International Student Center.

- **Give your draft both open-form and closed-form features.** Because your exploratory paper is a narrative, it follows an unfolding, open-form structure. Many of your paragraphs should open with chronological transitions such as "I *started* by reading," "*Early the next morning*, I headed for the library to . . . ," "On the *next* day, I decided," or "*After* finishing . . . I *next* looked at . . . ." At the same time, your summaries of your sources and your strong responses to them should be framed within closed-form structures with topic sentences and logical transitions: "This article, in raising objections to genetic screening of embryos, began changing my views about new advances in reproductive technology. Whereas before I felt . . . , now I feel . . . ."

- **Show yourself wrestling with ideas.** Readers want to see how your research stimulates your own thinking. Throughout, your paper should show you

Strategies Chart 8.1 Strategies for Composing an Exploratory Essay

Strategies	Advantages
Real-time strategy. Compose the body of the essay during the actual process of researching and thinking.	Yields genuine immediacy—like a sequence of letters or e-mails sent home during a journey.
Retrospective strategy. Look back over your completed research notes and then compose the body of the essay.	Allows for more selection and shaping of details and yields a more artistically designed essay.

responding strongly to your sources. Here is a good example from Kent's paper on mandatory public service.

> However, Rosenman did not offer any concrete evidence in support of his claims. Instead, his philosophical approach helped me understand some of the moral arguments—essentially, that public service can make us better people who live in better communities—but these arguments would not convince people who value small government and dislike government intrusion on personal freedom. I was particularly drawn to the idea that national service would make people feel more invested in their government. I wondered if I could locate any evidence showing that community service led people to become more personally involved in working on our country's problems.

Although you might feel that sentences that show your mind talking its way through your research will sound too informal, they actually work well in exploratory essays to create interest and capture your critical thinking.

Typical Structure of an Exploratory Essay

Your exploratory essay records the history of your researching and thinking process (what you read or whom you talked to, how you responded, how your thinking evolved). Along the way you can make your narrative more colorful and grounded by including your strategies for tracking down sources, your conversations with friends, your late-night trips to a coffee shop, and so forth. What you will quickly discover about this exploratory assignment is that it forces you to do the research. Unless you conduct your research in a timely fashion, you won't have any research process to write about. Figure 8.1 shows the typical structure of an exploratory essay.

QUESTIONS FOR PEER REVIEW

In addition to the generic peer review questions explained in Skill 17.4, ask your peer reviewers to address these questions:

1. In the introduction, how has the writer tried to show that the problem is interesting, significant, and problematic? How could the writer engage you more fully with the initial problem?

2. How does the writer provide cues that his or her purpose is to explore a question rather than argue a thesis? How might the opening section of the draft be improved?

3. Is the body of the paper organized chronologically so that you can see the development of the writer's thinking? Where does the writer provide chronological transitions?

4. Part of an exploratory essay involves summarizing the argument of each new research source. Where in this draft is a summary of a source particularly clear and well developed? Where are summary passages undeveloped, unclear, or too long? How could these passages be improved?

5. Another part of an exploratory paper involves the writer's strong response to each source. Where in this draft is there evidence of the writer's own critical thinking and questioning? Where are the writer's ideas

Figure 8.1 Framework for an Exploratory Essay

Introduction (one or more paragraphs)	• Establishes that your question is complex, problematic, and significant • Shows why you are interested in it • Presents relevant background You can begin with your question or build up to it, using it to end your introductory section.
Body section 1 on first source	• Introduces your first source and shows why you started with it • Provides rhetorical context and information about the source • Summarizes the source's content and argument • Offers your strong response to this source, frequently including both with-the-grain and against-the-grain points • Talks about what this source contributes to your understanding of your question: What did you learn? What value does this source have for you? What is missing from this source that you want to consider? Where do you want to go from here?
Body section 2 on second source	• Repeats the process with a new source selected to advance the inquiry • Explains why you selected this source (to find an alternative view, pursue subquestions, find more data, and so forth) • Summarizes the source's argument • Provides a strong response • Shows how your cumulative reading of sources is shaping your thinking or leading to more questions
Body sections 3, 4, 5, etc., on additional sources	• Continues the process
Conclusion	• Wraps up your intellectual journey and explains where you are now in your thinking and how your understanding of your problem has changed • Presents your current answer to your question based on all that you have read and learned so far, or explains why you still can't answer your question, or explains what further research you might do
Works Cited or References list	• Includes a complete list of citations in MLA or APA format, depending on your assignment

particularly strong and effective? Where are the writer's own ideas undeveloped, unclear, or weak?

6. Has the writer done enough research to explore the problem? How would you describe the range and variety of sources that the writer has consulted? Where does the writer acknowledge how the sources shape his or her perspective on the subject? What additional ideas or perspectives do you think the writer should consider?

Writing an annotated bibliography

8.4   **Summarize and critique your research sources in an annotated bibliography.**

Writing Project: Create an annotated bibliography that lists the research sources you used for your exploratory project. Because annotated bibliographies can vary in the number, length, and kinds of entries, follow guidelines provided by your instructor. Some instructors may also require a critical preface that explains your research question and provides details about how you selected the bibliographic sources.

What Is an Annotated Bibliography?

A **bibliography** is an alphabetized list of sources on a given topic, providing readers with the names of authors, titles, and publication details for each source. Unlike a plain list of sources, an **annotated bibliography** also includes the writer's "annotation" or commentary on each source. These annotations can be either *summary-only* or *evaluative*.

- A **summary-only annotation** provides a capsule of the source's contents without any additional comments from the bibliography's author.
- An **evaluative annotation** adds the author's critique or assessment of the work, including comments about the source's rhetorical context, its particular strengths or weaknesses, and its usefulness or value.

Whichever type is used, the length of the annotation is a function of its audience and purpose. Brief annotations comprise only a few sentences (one standard approach—to be described later—uses three sentences) while longer annotations can be up to 150 words. Brief annotations are most common when the annotated bibliography has numerous entries. Longer annotation allow for fuller summaries and more detailed analyses. They are often more helpful for readers but can make an annotated bibliography too long if there are many sources.

Annotated bibliographies serve several important functions. First, writing an annotated bibliography engages researchers in exploratory thinking by requiring that they read sources rhetorically like experts, entering critically into scholarly conversations. Annotated bibliographies can also be valuable time-saving tools for new researchers in a field. By providing overview information about potential sources, they help new researchers determine whether a particular source might be useful for their own purposes. Think of source annotations as analogous to short movie reviews that help you select your next film. (What's this movie about? How good is it?) Additionally, annotated bibliographies can establish the writer's *ethos* by showing the depth, breadth, and competence of the writer's research. A good annotated bibliography proves that you have read and thought about your sources.

Features of Annotated Bibliography Entries

Each entry has two main parts, the bibliographic citation and the annotation. The **bibliographic citation** should follow the conventions of your assigned documentation style such as the Modern Language Association (MLA) or the American Psychological Association (APA).

An **evaluative annotation** (the most common kind) typically includes three elements.

- **Rhetorical information.** This includes the source's rhetorical context, particularly its genre and (if not implied by the genre) its purpose and audience. Is this source a scholarly article? An op-ed piece? A blog? What is the author's purpose and who is the intended audience? Are any political biases present?

- **A summary of the source's content.** In some cases, the entry simply lists what is covered in the source. When possible, however, you should summarize the source's actual argument. (Note: In a *summary-only* annotation, this summary is the only element included.)

- **Your evaluation of the source.** What are the source's particular strengths or weaknesses? How useful is the source for specific purposes? How might you use the source for your research project? (Or, if the annotated bibliography comes at the end of the project, how did you use the source?)

It is possible to write a **three-sentence evaluative annotation** in which your cover each element in one sentence.

Examples of Annotation Entries

Here are examples of different kinds of annotations based on Kent Ansen's research notes for one of his sources:

SUMMARY-ONLY ANNOTATION

Rosenman, Mark. "A Call for National Service." *The Chronicle of Philanthropy*, 18 Oct. 2007, philanthropy.com/article/A-Call-for-National-Service/165721.

Rosenman argues that compulsory national service would engage Americans directly with the urgent problems facing our nation, shifting Americans from being passive consumers of government services to active stakeholders who demand accountability from elected officials. He suggests that compulsory service would promote empathy for the poor and marginalized, create awareness of the real-world impacts of public policy, and inspire a sense of shared responsibility for the results. He also provides some practical considerations for how to make compulsory service work.

EVALUATIVE ANNOTATION

Rosenman, Mark. "A Call for National Service." *The Chronicle of Philanthropy*, 18 Oct. 2007, philanthropy.com/article/A-Call-for-National-Service/165721.

The article is a call to action directed at nonprofit leaders, urging them to build bipartisan support for compulsory national service and providing tips on how to make their proposals effective. It was published in the opinion section of the *Chronicle of Philanthropy*, which provides news and information to influence philanthropic professionals who likely already support an expansion of national service. The author argues that compulsory national service would engage Americans directly with the urgent problems facing the nation, shifting a disengaged and passive public to an active, engaged citizenry capable of holding the government accountable for its results. The article provides a good overview of the basic arguments and assumptions that support mandatory service and is helpful in understanding how people who already believe in national service think about its value and impact. However, its claims lack specific evidence and therefore read mostly as assumptions, which weakens the persuasive power of the piece and its usefulness as backing for the call for national service.

THREE-SENTENCE EVALUATIVE ANNOTATION

Rosenman, Mark. "A Call for National Service." *The Chronicle of Philanthropy*, 18 Oct. 2007, philanthropy.com/article/A-Call-for-National-Service/165721.

This persuasive argument aims to help nonprofit leaders make an effective public-policy case for compulsory national service. Rosenman argues that by connecting Americans with real-world problems and the people negatively affected by them, compulsory service would create active, responsive citizens who hold government accountable for results. This source provides some good general suggestions for how to make compulsory national service work and asserts many of the common arguments in support of it, although its claims are mostly assumptions unsupported by evidence.

Writing a Critical Preface for Your Annotated Bibliography

Scholars who publish annotated bibliographies typically introduce them with a critical preface that explains the scope and purpose of the bibliography. When you write a critical preface for your own annotated bibliography, you have a chance to highlight your critical thinking and show the purposeful way that you conducted your research. Typically the critical preface includes the following information:

- A contextual overview that shows the purpose of the annotated bibliography and suggests its value and significance for the reader
- The research question posed by the author
- The dates during which the bibliography was compiled
- An overview of the number of items in the bibliography and the kinds of material included

A student example of an annotated bibliography with a critical preface is found in the Readings section of this chapter.

Shaping, Drafting, and Revising

The key to producing a good annotated bibliography is to take good research notes as you read. Compare the various versions of the previous annotations with Kent Ansen's research notes. Before composing your annotated bibliography, make sure that you understand your instructor's preferences for the number of entries required and for the length and kinds of annotations. Arrange the bibliography in alphabetical order as you would in a "Works Cited" (MLA format) or "References" (APA format) list.

The specific skills needed for an annotated bibliography are taught in various places in this text. If you are having problems with aspects of an annotated bibliography, you can find further instruction as follows.

Problems with	Where to Find Help
Formatting the citations	Refer to Skill 24.3 for MLA style, and Skill 24.4 for APA style.
Describing the rhetorical context and genre	Review to Skill 22.1, and reread Concept 3.2.
Writing a summary	Read the sections of Chapter 6 on summary writing; read also Skill 23.2.
Writing an evaluation	Use the strategies for strong response in Chapter 6, and also Skills 22.1–22.3.

Questions for Peer Review

The following questions are based on the assumption that your instructor requires evaluative annotations and a critical preface. Adjust the questions to fit a different assignment.

CRITICAL PREFACE

1. Where does the writer explain the following: The purpose and significance of the bibliography? The research question that motivated the research? The dates of the research? The kinds of sources included?

2. How could the critical preface be improved?

BIBLIOGRAPHIC CITATIONS

3. Does each citation follow MLA or APA conventions? Pay particular attention to the formatting of sources downloaded from a licensed database or from the Web.

4. Are the sources arranged alphabetically?

ANNOTATIONS

5. Where does each annotation include the following: Information about genre or rhetorical context? A capsule summary of the source's contents? An evaluative comment?

6. Identify any places where the annotations are confusing or unclear or where the writer could include more information.

7. How could one or more of the annotations be improved?

Multimodal or Online Assignment Options
Speech With Visual Aids (Flip Chart, Powerpoint, Prezi)

Deliver your exploratory paper as a formal speech supported with visual aids. You can imagine an occasion for a short speech in which the audience is interested in your exploratory process while you wrestled with an interesting and engaging problem. If you use PowerPoint or Prezi slides to illustrate your exploration, you can include slides showing how you found sources (screen shots of search results or database abstracts). If you used any online sources such as blogs or videos, you might use hyperlinks to show these to your audience also. Pay equal attention to the construction and delivery of your speech and to the multimodal design of the visual aids. Your goal is to reproduce for your audience the narrative of your thinking process, particularly the moments that advanced or complicated your thinking.

Readings

Our first reading is an exploratory essay by student writer Kent Ansen on mandatory public service for young adults. After completing the exploratory essay, Kent continued his research, writing a proposal argument on the benefits of instigating mandatory public service. Kent's final argument is our sample MLA student research paper that appears in Chapter 16.

Kent Ansen (Student)

Should the United States Establish Mandatory Public Service for Young Adults?

1   During high school, I volunteered at an after-school tutoring program in a poor neighborhood near my school. My guidance counselor stressed the importance of volunteer work in strong college applications, which was my primary motivation for volunteering. The more I volunteered, though, the more I began to see evidence of the two-way benefits of volunteer work. The program I volunteered with connected community members to a number of resources, such as food and healthcare benefits, and organized community cleanups and neighborhood celebrations. At the same time, I diversified my résumé and had memorable experiences that gave me a different view of the community I lived in and people who were struggling with issues like poverty and hunger.

2   This experience was in the back of my mind during some recent conversations I had with friends who are college seniors. As they make plans for their lives after graduation, some of them are questioning the value of their majors as they face the competitive job market. Others are not sure what they want to do, even after four years of focused study in a particular field. I have heard a lot of buzz about volunteer programs like AmeriCorps and Jesuit Volunteer Corps, which place volunteers in needy communities for a year in exchange for a living stipend and the opportunity to gain work experience. In fact, the tutoring program I volunteered with was run by an AmeriCorps team. This type of volunteer work seems like a valuable opportunity for our generation, often referred to as the "Lost Generation" because of our struggles to settle on career paths and find direction, find jobs at all, and achieve stability in our lives. I have even heard of proposals to bring back the draft, not necessarily for military service but for national service on a broader scale. While mandatory public service would probably be controversial, it might benefit the country and youth in numerous ways. Pondering what I could gain from a mandatory year working on a national service project, I decided to pose the following question for this exploratory paper: Should the United States require a year of national service for all its young adults?

3   To begin, I wanted to familiarize myself with current national service programs in the United States. First, I wanted to have a good grasp of the range of work that AmeriCorps workers do, so I consulted the AmeriCorps website. According to this site, team-based projects focus on service in five areas: "natural and other disasters, infrastructure improvement, environmental stewardship and conservation, energy conservation, and urban and rural

development" ("AmeriCorps"). Another part of the site spelled out this work even more concretely, explaining that participants can "tutor and mentor disadvantaged youth, fight illiteracy, improve health services, build affordable housing, teach computer skills, clean parks and streams, manage or operate after-school programs, and help communities respond to disasters . . . ." AmeriCorps also supports the work of nonprofit organizations such as Habitat for Humanity and the Red Cross.

4   I then did several Google searches using search terms such as "national public service," "mandatory public service," and "AmeriCorps." These searches gave me a quick overview of the issues. The first lead I followed in depth was an article from a fact-checking website run by the Annenberg Corporation, which explained a proposed bill in the House and the Senate aimed at expanding national service (Robertson). Called the GIVE Act ("Generations Invigorating Volunteerism and Education"), this bill expands national service organizations like AmeriCorps and funds increased participation to include 250,000 volunteers in the near future. Currently, 75,000 people participate in national service programs, so the GIVE Act represents a drastic increase in participation. Notably, the GIVE Act is not a bill for mandatory national service. It seems heavily reliant on expanding the current AmeriCorps program, which places volunteers in a variety of different volunteer settings in nonprofit and public agencies in exchange for a living stipend and an education award to pay for student loans or future educational opportunities. The GIVE Act helped me understand the scale of our current national service system. I was encouraged that the GIVE Act has strong bipartisan support. It suggests that there is public support for an expansion of national service.

5   To understand what an expanded national service program would look like, I wanted to find out if anyone had ever proposed a model. From my notes on my original Google searches, I found a 2007 article from *Time* entitled "A Time to Serve" (Stengel), which I then located in print in our library. Stengel describes a ten-point plan for creating universal national service, including a cabinet-level Department of National Service and the government purchase of a "baby bond" for each American baby. This bond would mature to around $19,000 by the time the baby reached young adulthood. This money could then be accessed if the person committed to a year of national service. The plan also includes ideas for a rapid response corps for disasters like Hurricane Katrina and for creating a national service academy. In addition to offering practical suggestions about how a national service program would work, Stengel argues that "a republic, to survive, [needs] not only the consent of the governed but also their active participation," asserting that "free societies do not stay free without the involvement of their citizens."

6   This article made me confident that mandatory national public service was feasible, but I also began to realize why many people might object to mandatory service. It is one thing to recruit more young adults to volunteer for public service. It is another thing to require them to do so through a draft-like process. But then I noted that this article does not actually advocate *mandatory* national service. Instead it's calling for the "compelling idea that devoting a year or more to national

service, whether military or civilian, should become a countrywide rite of passage" or a socially perpetuated norm, not a government-mandated one. It seems like a nation powered by a socially conscious momentum rather than a national service law would inspire more pride in and ownership of the service experience. Yet, would the people who might most benefit from doing public service actually volunteer if they weren't compelled to serve? For these people, national service could be incredibly transformative, but they might miss out on these opportunities if service were optional.

7   At this point, I decided I should investigate more thoroughly the drawbacks of mandatory national service, so I turned to an online *Time* article that was a direct response to Stengel: Michael Kinsley's "National Service? Puh-lease." (I Googled Michael Kinsley and discovered that he is a widely known conservative writer.) Kinsley uses a sarcastic tone to raise several problems with a mandatory national service plan or voluntary plans with strong incentives to participate. He argues that Stengel's proposal for a $19,000 bond that a person could access after completing a year of service would appeal to poor people more than rich people. In effect, the rich would simply buy their way out of public service. He also notes the hypocrisy of using social pressure and government incentives to encourage participation and then calling it "volunteerism." He sees Stengel's proposal as an infringement on personal freedom and on free markets. Arguing that people are willing to do any job for the right amount of money, Kinsley wonders why we would force someone to work for drastically less than a traditional employee would be paid when there is already a supply of workers in the market willing to do the same job for reasonable pay. Instead of making someone happy by providing a decently paying job, Stengel's proposal would put poor people out of work and force volunteers to work unhappily at minimum wage. For me, Kinsley's most powerful point was a reference to George Orwell's novel *1984*, which he uses to paint a picture of people forced into doing jobs that they would otherwise not take. Kinsley is also worried that volunteer work would be "make-work," meaning bureaucrats would spend time finding trivial ways to keep all the volunteers busy.

8   While I think Kinsley vastly underestimates the value of community service, I do understand his concern that forcing people to volunteer could undermine its impact. For me, though, a larger problem is putting volunteers to work on projects that require a lot of care when the volunteers themselves may not feel the intrinsic motivations and empathy required to deliver good service because they were forced into the role rather than choosing it for themselves. His article made me consider exactly how our democracy and the market do and should work together to create a socially optimal reality. I agree that mandating service is problematic in a country that values freedom, but I also agree that many young Americans seem to take our democracy for granted. I understand Kinsley's point that mandatory service would interfere with market solutions to problems. Yet my understanding of government is that it exists to provide goods and services that the market fails to provide on its own. If the market is failing poor people, why should we rely on it to provide the solutions? Again, the conflict seems to come back to values, in

this case the disagreements between those who value market solutions and those who value government intervention.

9   I decided I needed to pursue the perspective of someone who values government intervention and found Mark Rosenman's 2007 article "A Call for National Service." Rosenman's main argument is that military or civilian national service "may be invaluable for getting Americans more involved in their government and more concerned about influencing public policy." He argues that through this direct service, citizens become more involved in government-provided services and "would more likely demand accountability from their elected leaders." Rosenman is concerned that we have become citizens whose only responsibility to government is to pay taxes and user fees, which makes us customers who passively take from government without investing effort to maintain and manage our democracy. Becoming more involved through national service will help restore citizens to being "owners" of government.

10   Overall, I found Rosenman's argument compelling, even though it did not help me resolve the conflict between those who value market solutions and those who value government intervention. His thoughts on active versus passive citizens echoed some of the points raised by "A Time to Serve" and got me excited about the idea of using national service to reinvigorate our levels of public engagement. However, Rosenman did not offer any concrete evidence in support of his claims. Instead, his philosophical approach helped me understand some of the moral arguments—essentially, that public service can make us better people who live in better communities—but these arguments would not convince people who value small government and dislike government intrusion on personal freedom. I was particularly drawn to the idea that national service would make people feel more invested in their government. I wondered if I could locate any evidence showing that community service led people to become more personally involved in working on our country's problems.

11   At this point, I realized it would be helpful to gain the perspectives of young adults who had volunteered for public service. I decided to look more closely at the experiences of young adults who had worked for AmeriCorps ("AmeriCorps Reviews"). Several alumni noted the learning opportunities offered by AmeriCorps such as better understanding of the kinds of problems experienced by vulnerable populations and the difficulty of getting help. Several alumni noted how AmeriCorps provided opportunities for professional development and gave them work skills and leadership experiences that would transfer to future careers. Others noted how inspired they were by the people they worked with, both clients and coworkers.

12   These testimonials highlighted how impactful a year of service can be for individuals professionally and socially. I became convinced again that community service nurtures personal growth and civic engagement. Through helping others, AmeriCorps members are also able to help themselves—some even note they gain so much more than they give. This seemed like direct evidence of the two-way benefits I had experienced as a volunteer in high school and highlighted the potential value of service opportunities in light of the challenges young adults are facing today. However, I reminded myself that these testimonials did not constitute a random

sample of AmeriCorps volunteers and didn't provide evidence that every volunteer (much less somebody forced to serve) would experience the same benefits.

13   The testimonials highlighted the anecdotal evidence of the benefits of national service. However, I wanted to find out whether there were any empirical studies that showed these benefits. On the Web I found a report titled "Serving Country and Community: A Longitudinal Study of Service in AmeriCorps" (Jastrzab et al.). The study examines the impacts on participants' civic engagement, education, employment and life skills by surveying members upon entering and completing a term of service, including some follow-up three years after enrollment in AmeriCorps. This study found that participation in AmeriCorps had positive impacts on civic engagement and employment outcomes. In comparison to a control group not enrolled in service, alumni across AmeriCorps programs demonstrated statistically significant gains in basic work skills. Additionally, civic engagement behavior and attitudes were positively affected. Participation in AmeriCorps led to higher community-based activism and to a greater belief that communities could identify and solve problems. This study seemed to corroborate the AmeriCorps testimonials, providing evidence of the benefits of national service in terms of greater civic engagement.

14   Looking back over my research, I think the rewards of national service to individual volunteers and the communities they serve are clear. However, I continue to worry about the feasibility of making national service a mandatory program. As I end this exploratory paper, I still have some more research and thinking to do before I am ready to start my proposal argument. I am leaning in the direction of supporting mandatory public service. I am convinced that such service will benefit America's communities and also help the "Lost Generation" find themselves through learning more about our country's problems and developing valuable job skills. But the clincher for me—if I go in the direction I am leaning—is that mandatory public service would get Americans more involved in their government.

Works Cited

"AmeriCorps." *Corporation for National & Community Service*, www.nationalservice.gov/programs/americorps. Accessed 8 Apr. 2016.

"AmeriCorps Reviews." *Indeed*, www.indeed.com/cmp/Americorps/reviews. Accessed 8 Apr. 2016.

Jastrzab, JoAnn, et al. "Serving Country and Community: A Longitudinal Study of Service in AmeriCorps." *Corporation for National and Community Service*, Dec. 2004, updated Aug. 2006, www.nationalservice.gov/pdf/06_1223_longstudy_report.pdf.

Kinsley, Michael. "National Service? Puh-lease." *Time*, 30 Aug. 2007, content.time.com/time/specials/2007/article/0,28804,1657256_1657317_1658698,00.html.

Robertson, Lori. "Mandatory Public Service." *FactCheck.org*, 31 Mar. 2009, updated 21 Apr. 2009, www.factcheck.org/2009/03/mandatory-public-service.

Rosenman, Mark. "A Call for National Service." *The Chronicle of Philanthropy*, 18 Oct. 2007, philanthropy.com/article/A-Call-for-National-Service/165721.

Stengel, Richard. "A Time to Serve." *Time*, 30 Aug. 2007, content.time.com/time/specials/2007/article/0,28804,1657256_1657317,00.html.

THINKING CRITICALLY

About "Should the United States Establish Mandatory Public Service for Young Adults?"

1. How does Kent show that his personal experience contributed to his interest in his chosen question?

2. Earlier in this chapter, we suggested ways to organize and strengthen an exploratory essay. Where do you see Kent including the following features: (a) A blend of open-form narrative strategies with closed-form focusing sentences? (b) A purposeful selection of sources? (c) A consideration of the rhetorical context of his sources—that is, an awareness of the kinds of sources he is using and how the genre of the source influences its content? (d) Reflective/critical thinking that shows his strong response to his sources? (e) His dialectical thinking and critical evaluation of his sources?

3. Trace the evolution of Kent's ideas in this paper. How does his thinking change?

4. Read Kent's argument in favor of mandatory public service for young adults in his proposal argument at the end of Chapter 16. What new research did he do for his final argument? How do you see the exploratory paper contributing to Kent's argument in the final paper? How do differences in purpose (exploration versus persuasion) lead to different structures for the two papers?

5. What are the strengths and weaknesses of Kent's exploration of mandatory public service?

Our next reading is an excerpt from Kent's annotated bibliography based on the same research he did for his exploratory paper. We have used Kent's research for both examples so that you can compare an exploratory paper with an annotated bibliography. His original annotated bibliography contained six entries. We have printed three of these, along with his critical preface. Additionally, the evaluative annotated bibliography entry for the Rosenman article is shown earlier in this chapter.

Kent Ansen (student)

Should the United States Establish Mandatory Public Service for Young Adults?

An Annotated Bibliography

Critical Preface

Today, national service programs like AmeriCorps seem to be gaining the attention of young adults who are facing a hostile job market and are unsure about their futures. I have also noticed some proposals to create a kind of draft that would extend beyond military service to require terms of civil service from young adults, putting them to work on projects that help alleviate problems like hunger and poverty. These plans are always controversial, especially in America, where we value freedom of choice. With this research project, I set out to explore the following questions: Should the United States require a year of national service from all its young adults? How would a plan of this scale be feasible? These questions are particularly important during a time of scarce resources, Congressional budget battles, growing social and economic divisions among our citizens, and general public mistrust of government. The country seems to be reevaluating the optimal level of citizen involvement in public life and where we should invest public resources.

I conducted this research over several days in early April 2016. My research included a variety of sources: a scholarly research study, two articles from a popular newsmagazine, an article from an online non-profit-sector journal, two webpages that provided program overviews and background information, a fact-checking website, and a nonprofit webpage of testimonials from national service participants. This research helped me better understand our current system of national service opportunities and see how this system could be expanded. The testimonials and the scholarly research study by Jastrzab et al. also highlighted the impacts national service has on individual participants. Several of these sources (particularly Rosenman and Kinsley) illuminated the different values, beliefs, and assumptions that drive disagreements about mandatory national service. Ultimately, these sources convinced me that our nation and young adults could greatly benefit from expanding national service, although I remain concerned about the feasibility of implementing a mandatory plan.

Annotated Bibliography

Jastrzab, JoAnn, et al. "Serving Country and Community: A Longitudinal Study of Service in AmeriCorps." *Corporation for National and Community Service*, Dec. 2004, updated Aug. 2006, www.nationalservice.gov/pdf/06_1223_longstudy_report.pdf.

This scholarly research report examines the impacts of AmeriCorps participation on participants' attitudes and behavior related to civic engagement, education, employment, and life skills. The findings of the study were mixed. Surveys of participants initially and up to three years after enrolling in AmeriCorps revealed generally positive gains, particularly in measures of civic engagement, but the findings were not always statistically significant and revealed no impacts in educational outcomes. This study is helpful in providing statistically significant data on the positive impacts AmeriCorps participation can have on participants' future attitudes and behavior and provides some evidence of an important claim that national service increases lifelong civic engagement. However, it does not identify the impacts of mandatory service, because AmeriCorps enrollment is voluntary.

Kinsley, Michael. "National Service? Puh-lease." *Time*, 30 Aug. 2007, content.time.com/time/specials/2007/article/0,28804,1657256_1657317_1658698,00.html.

This op-ed written by a popular conservative writer offers a direct response to and critique of Stengel's proposal for universal national service. Kinsley scornfully addresses the Baby Boomer generation Stengel represents, chastising its attempts to force national service on young people from the safety of retirement. He opposes universal service on the following grounds: (1) service cannot be both universal and voluntary, which jeopardizes freedom of choice and undermines the virtue of volunteerism, (2) capitalism and our system of voting and taxation, when functioning well, properly respond to social needs, and (3) there is not enough work to go around, so a universal corps would end up doing unimportant work. This article provides a clear, well-reasoned conservative perspective on the problems with mandatory national service.

Stengel, Richard. "A Time to Serve." *Time*, 30 Aug. 2007, content.time.com/time/specials/2007/article/0,28804,1657256_1657317,00.html.

This article from a popular news magazine argues that the next president and the United States more broadly should take action to make national service a central part of American culture because a healthy republic requires not only the consent but the active participation of its citizens. It outlines a 10-point plan for how to institute universal national service by expanding the existing network of opportunities (like AmeriCorps) and creating new corps in education, health, environmental work, and disaster response. The article proposes using baby bonds that mature during young adulthood and increasing private investment to pay for the expansion. The proposal and 10-point plan are particularly valuable in illustrating how to make service work on a universal scale while simultaneously emphasizing why voluntary service motivated by a shared culture is superior to a mandatory plan.

THINKING CRITICALLY

About "Should the United States Establish Mandatory Public Service for Young Adults? An Annotated Bibliography"

1. Explain how Kent includes the three common elements of an evaluative annotation (genre/rhetorical context, summary of content, evaluation) in each of his annotations.

2. Compare Kent's annotated bibliography with his exploratory essay, noting differences between the way each source is described in the bibliography versus the essay. What insights do you get from the exploratory essay that are missing from the bibliography? What information about the sources comes through more clearly in the bibliography than in the essay?

3. How might Kent use information and points in this annotated bibliography in his researched argument?

Chapter 9
Writing an Informative (and Surprising) Essay or Report

Learning Objectives

9.1 Describe and explain two categories of informative writing.

9.2 Write an informative report that meets reader expectations for report writing.

9.3 Write a "surprising-reversal" essay that uses new information to change readers' initial understanding of a subject.

Overview to informative writing

9.1 Describe and explain two categories of informative writing.

As a reader, you regularly encounter writing with an informative aim, ranging from the instruction booklet for a new coffee maker to a Wikipedia article on Jimi Hendrix. Informative documents include instruction manuals, encyclopedias, cookbooks, and business reports as well as informative magazine and Web articles. In some informative prose, visual representations of information can be more important than the prose itself.

In informative writing, the writer is assumed to have more expertise than the reader on a given subject. The writer's aim is to enlarge the reader's view of the subject by bringing new information to the reader. The writer's information can come from a variety of sources:

- From the writer's preexisting expertise in a subject

- From the writer's personal experiences

- From field research such as observations, interviews, and questionnaires

- From library or Internet research

A useful way to begin thinking about informative writing is to place it in two categories according to the reader's motivation for reading.

- In the first category, readers are motivated by an **immediate need for information** or by **curiosity about a subject.** For example, if you need to set the clock on your new microwave, you consult the instruction manual. If you were curious about the impact of the Harlem Renaissance in the1920s, you might consult an historical encyclopedia or do a Web search looking for authoritative sources. In your professional life, your boss might need information on competitors' marketing strategies for a product and ask you to do the research and write a report. Informative writing in this category does not necessarily contain a governing thesis statement. Documents are organized effectively, of course, but they often follow a chronological order, a step-by-step order, or a topic-by-topic order. The writer provides factual information about a subject without necessarily shaping the information to support a thesis.

- The second category of informative writing is aimed at readers **who may not be initially interested in the subject matter.** The writer's purpose is to change someone's understanding of a subject by bringing to readers new, unanticipated, or surprising information. Such writing often asserts and supports a thesis. Because readers may not be initially motivated by a need to know or by curiosity, the writer's first task is to hook readers' interest and motivate their desire to continue reading. An excellent strategy for creating this motivation is the technique of "surprising reversal," which we explain later.

The assignment options for this chapter represent two common genres of informative writing: the informative report aimed at curious or "need-to-know" readers and the surprising-reversal essay aimed at readers whom the writer sees as possessing wrong or incomplete information about a topic and who could be enlightened by new, surprising information.

Writing an informative report

9.2 **Write an informative report that meets reader expectations for report writing.**

> **Writing Project:** Write a short informative report based on data you have gathered from observations, interviews, questionnaires, and/or library/ Internet research. Your report should respond to one of the following scenarios or to a scenario provided by your instructor:
>
> - Your boss runs a chain of health-food stores that sell high-nutrition smoothies. Because sales have been flat, she wants to create an advertising campaign to attract more customers to her smoothie bars. She has heard that the boutique coffee drinks sold at coffee shops such as Starbucks are actually high in calories and fat. She has asked you to research the nutritional information on coffee drinks. She would also like you to compare the fat/calorie content of various coffee drinks to that of cheeseburgers, fries, and milkshakes sold at fast-food restaurants. She's hoping that the information you provide will help her launch a campaign to lure customers from coffee shops to her smoothie bars. Write your

report in the form of a memorandum to your boss, providing the requested information in a closed-form, crisply presented style.

- You are doing a service-learning project for a health maintenance organization (HMO). Your manager is worried about hearing loss in young people, possibly caused by listening to loud music through earbuds. Your manager asks you to write a short informative article, suitable for publication in the HMO's newsletter, that reports on research on hearing loss due to earbuds. Write your report for a general audience who read the HMO newsletter for helpful health information.

- You are a freelance writer who writes short (500–600 word) informative pieces in "easy reading" style for a popular magazine or Web site. Write such a piece on a topic of your choice related to science, technology, popular culture, education, or some other subject.

Features of an Informative Report

Although the term *report* can have numerous meanings, we define a **report** as any document that presents the results of a fact-finding or data-gathering investigation. Sometimes report writers limit themselves to presenting newly discovered information. Other times they go further, analyzing or interpreting the information to explain its implications and significance or to uncover patterns of cause and effect.

Reports are among the most common genres that you will read and write as a workplace professional. Often managers have to prepare periodic reports to supervisors on sales, operations, expenses, or team productivity. Equally important are solicited reports, usually assigned by supervisors to individuals or task forces, requesting individuals to investigate a problem, gather crucial information, and report the results.

The text of a report should be concise, with a closed-form structure often broken into sections marked by headings. Individual points might be bulleted. Numeric data are usually displayed in graphs or tables. Long reports usually include a cover page and a table of contents and often begin with an *executive summary* that condenses the main findings into a paragraph.

How you write the introduction to a report depends on the audience you are addressing. In some cases, a report is solicited (say, by a supervisor); it is aimed at a specific reader who is already interested in the information and is waiting for you to provide it. In this case, the report is often written as a memorandum. Instead of a title, short reports usually have an informative *subject line* that identifies the report's topic and purpose. The introduction typically creates a brief context for the report, states its purpose, and maps its structure. Elise Berentson's fact-finding report about Planned Parenthood at the end of this chapter is an example of a solicited report.

In other cases a report is aimed at general readers and published in, say, a popular magazine. In such cases, you must arouse your readers' interest and provide necessary background, just as you would do in most closed-form introductions. Kirsten Smock's essay "Understanding Jihad: Is Islam a Violent Religion?" at the end of this chapter is a student example of an informative report written for a magazine audience. Note how Smock desktop-published her essay in a two-column format to make it look like a magazine article. To increase the impact of her essay, she also used the surprising-reversal strategy, which we explain later in this chapter.

Typical Structure of an Informative Report

Although there is no one correct way to organize an informative report, such reports typically have the structure shown in Figure 9.1. Elise Berentson's report on Planned Parenthood follows this framework for a solicited report. It is designed as a business memorandum with "To," "From," and "Subject" lines. The subject line serves as the title. At the beginning of the report, Elise references her supervisor's original e-mail request, explains how she did the research, and forecasts the report's structure. The same framework guides Kirsten Smock's "magazine article" on the meaning of jihad, but with significant differences in document design and style to appeal to general audiences. Kirsten creates a title that announces her research question, begins with an attention-grabber to hook the reader's interest, and strives for a popular "easy reading" style throughout.

Generating Ideas, Drafting, and Revising

Because most of the ideas in an informative report come from research, your initial goal is to use effective research strategies to find the needed information. If your report draws on library/Internet research, consult Part 4 of this textbook. If your report draws on field research such as personal observation, interviews, and questionnaires, consult Chapter 12 on gathering and analyzing data. For displaying numerical information in graphs or tables, consult Skill 18.9. As you draft your report, consider the typical structure outlined in Figure 9.1. As you edit, try to achieve a clear, concise style that allows a busy audience to read quickly. Adapt your style to your audience and genre.

Questions for Peer Review

In addition to the generic peer review questions explained in Skill 17.4, ask your peer reviewers to address these questions:

1. If the report is solicited, does the document have a professional appearance (memo format, pleasing use of white space, appropriate use of headings)?

Figure 9.1 Framework for an Informative Report

Title	• For a report addressed to a general audience, an interest-grabbing title • For a solicited report, an informative subject line
Introduction (one to several paragraphs)	• For general audiences, provides background and context and arouses interest • For a solicited report, refers to the request, explains the purpose of the report, and maps its structure
Body section 1 (brief)	• Explains your research process and the sources of your data
Body section 2 (major)	• Provides the information in a logical sequence • Uses closed-form organizational strategies • Displays numeric data in graphs or tables referenced in the text
Conclusion	• Suggests the significance of the information provided

Do the subject line and opening overview passage effectively explain the report's occasion, purpose, and structure?

2. If the report is aimed at a general audience, does it follow the manuscript style and document design specified by the instructor? Do the title and introduction provide context and motivate reader interest?

3. Does the writer explain how the research was conducted?

4. Is the report clear, concise, and well organized? How might the presentation of the information be improved?

5. If the report uses graphics, are the graphics referenced in the text? Are they clear, with appropriate titles and labels? How might they be improved?

Writing an informative essay using the surprising-reversal strategy

9.3 Write a "surprising-reversal" essay that uses new information to change readers' initial understanding of a subject.

> **Writing Project:** Using personal experience, field research, and/or library/ Internet research, write an informative magazine article using a surprising-reversal strategy in a tone and style suitable for general readers. Your task is to arouse your readers' curiosity by posing an interesting question, summarizing a common or expected answer to the question, and then providing new, surprising information that counters or "reverses" the common view. You imagine readers who hold a mistaken or overly narrow view of your topic; your purpose is to give them a new, surprising view.

Another commonly encountered genre is an informative essay that gives readers unexpected or surprising information that they hadn't been seeking. Because readers are assumed not to be looking for this information—perhaps they are casually surfing the Web or browsing through the pages of a magazine—the writer's rhetorical challenge is to arouse the reader's curiosity and then surprise readers with something unexpected or new.

Features of the Surprising-Reversal Strategy

To write an informative essay using the surprising-reversal strategy, the writer tries to hook the reader's interest in a question, presents what is a common or popular answer to that question, and then provides a new surprising answer. The surprising-reversal strategy uses the pattern for a "surprising thesis," explained in Concept 2.2, where the writer's thesis pushes against a counterthesis: "Whereas this other person says X, I say Y." This structure automatically creates a thesis with tension focused on a question or problem. Because of its power to hook and sustain readers, surprising-reversal essays can be found in many publications, ranging from easy-reading magazines to scholarly journals. In the rest of this section, we present some examples of the surprising-reversal pattern and then explain in more detail what we mean by "surprise."

EXAMPLES OF THE SURPRISING-REVERSAL STRATEGY A short example of the surprising-reversal strategy is Kirsten Smock's essay at the end of this chapter asking whether Islam is a violent religion. She summarizes the common view among many Americans that Islam is waging a holy war (jihad) against the West, but then she provides her own counteranswer that redefines *jihad*, showing that Islam worldwide doesn't condone violence. Another example is Shannon King's research paper on hydrogen cars (at end of this chapter). We discuss it in more detail later.

The surprising-reversal effect can also be created visually, as illustrated in the multimodal "high heels" poster shown in Figure 9.2. From a distance, the poster evokes the common view of high heels as stylish and fashionable. But the poster presents surprising counterinformation showing that high heels are dangerous. Every aspect of this poster supports the thesis highlighted in the top left corner: "**Heel to Toe**: Wearing high heels for an extended period can cause feet and leg problems." The image of the leg in high heels makes a visual appeal to the common view that high heels enhance feminine beauty; only when they get closer to the poster and note its text do they realize that the poster offers unexpected information.

Figure 9.2 Informative Poster

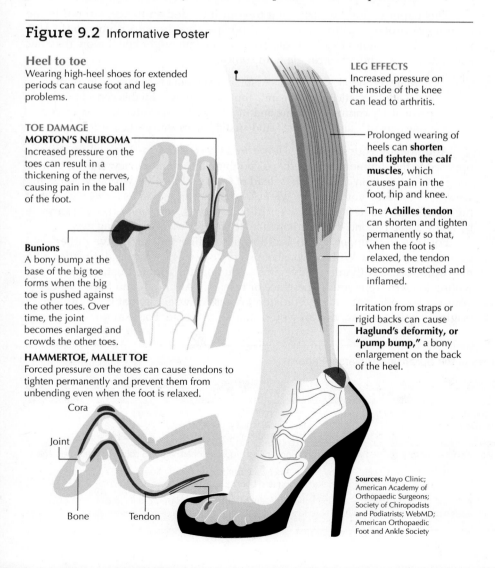

Heel to toe
Wearing high-heel shoes for extended periods can cause foot and leg problems.

TOE DAMAGE
MORTON'S NEUROMA
Increased pressure on the toes can result in a thickening of the nerves, causing pain in the ball of the foot.

Bunions
A bony bump at the base of the big toe forms when the big toe is pushed against the other toes. Over time, the joint becomes enlarged and crowds the other toes.

HAMMERTOE, MALLET TOE
Forced pressure on the toes can cause tendons to tighten permanently and prevent them from unbending even when the foot is relaxed.

Cora

Joint

Bone   Tendon

LEG EFFECTS
Increased pressure on the inside of the knee can lead to arthritis.

Prolonged wearing of heels can **shorten and tighten the calf muscles**, which causes pain in the foot, hip and knee.

The **Achilles tendon** can shorten and tighten permanently so that, when the foot is relaxed, the tendon becomes stretched and inflamed.

Irritation from straps or rigid backs can cause **Haglund's deformity, or "pump bump,"** a bony enlargement on the back of the heel.

Sources: Mayo Clinic; American Academy of Orthopaedic Surgeons; Society of Chiropodists and Podiatrists; WebMD; American Orthopaedic Foot and Ankle Society

Table 9.1 provides some more examples of this pattern from student essays.

"SURPRISE" AS A RELATIVE TERM   When using the surprising-reversal strategy, keep in mind that *surprise* is a relative term based on the relationship between you and your intended audience. You don't have to surprise everyone in the world, just those who hold a mistaken or narrow view of your topic. The key is to imagine an audience less informed about your topic than you are. For example, suppose that you have just completed an introductory economics course. You are less informed about economics than your professor, but more informed about economics than persons who have never taken an econ class. You might therefore bring surprising information to the less-informed audience:

> The average airplane traveler thinks that the widely varying ticket pricing for the same flight is chaotic and silly, but I can show how this pricing scheme makes perfect sense economically. [written for the "average airplane traveler," who hasn't taken an economics course]

This paper would be surprising to your intended audience, but not to the economics professor. From a different perspective, however, you could also write about economics to your professor because you might know more than her about, say, how students struggle with some concepts:

> Many economics professors assume that students can easily learn the concept of "elasticity of demand," but I can show why this concept was particularly confusing for me and my classmates. [written to economics professors who aren't aware of student difficulties with particular concepts]

Additionally, your surprising view doesn't necessarily have to be diametrically opposed to the common view. Perhaps you think the common view is *incomplete* or *insufficient* rather than *dead wrong*. Instead of saying, "View X is wrong, whereas my view, Y, is correct," you can say, "View X is correct and good as far as it goes, but my view, Y, adds a new perspective." In other words, you can also create surprise by going a step beyond the common view to show readers something new.

For this assignment, try to avoid issues calling for persuasive rather than informative writing. With persuasive prose, you imagine a resistant reader who may argue back. With informative prose, you imagine a more trusting reader, one willing to learn from your experience or research. Although you hope to enlarge your reader's view of a topic, you aren't necessarily saying that your audience's original view is wrong, nor are you initiating a debate. For example, suppose a

Table 9.1 Examples of the Surprising-Reversal Pattern

Commonly Held, Narrow, or Inaccurate View	New, Surprising Information
Pit bulls are aggressive and dangerous pets that responsible pet lovers should avoid.	The bad reputation of pit bulls is based on wrong information; in kind households, pit bulls can be gentle and loving pets.
Athletes' use of performance-enhancing drugs leads to dangerous health consequences in later life.	When taken and used under a doctor's supervision, performance-enhancing drugs are often safe and cause no future damage.
Native Americans used to live in simple harmony with the earth.	Many Native Americans used to "control" nature by setting fire to forests to make farming and hunting easier.
Having fathers present in the delivery room helps the mother relax and have an easier birth.	Having fathers present in delivery rooms may reduce the amount of oxytocin produced by the mother and lead to more caesarean sections.

writer wants to develop the following claim: "Many of my friends think that having an alcoholic mother would be the worst thing that could happen to you, but I will show that my mother's disease forced our family closer together." In this case the writer isn't arguing that alcoholic mothers are good or that everyone should have an alcoholic mother. Rather, the writer is simply offering readers a new, unexpected, and expanded view of what it might be like to have an alcoholic mother.

Typical Structure of a Surprising-Reversal Essay

Figure 9.3 shows the typical structure of an informative essay using the surprising-reversal strategy. Note that this structure has a delayed thesis that isn't stated until after you have explained your audience's common, expected answer to your opening question. This delayed thesis creates an open-form feel that readers often find engaging. Both Kirsten Smock's essay on jihad and Shannon King's research paper on hydrogen cars use variations on this surprising-reversal structure.

Generating Ideas, Drafting, and Revising

Depending on your instructor's wishes, your surprising-reversal essay can draw either on personal experience or on research. As you research a topic, you will soon learn more about your topic than most members of the general public. Ask yourself, "What has surprised me about my research so far? What do I now know that might surprise others?" Your answers to these questions can suggest possible approaches to your paper. For example, Shannon King began her research believing that fuel-cell technology produced totally pollution-free energy. She didn't realize that one needs to burn fossil fuels in order to produce the hydrogen. She decided that if this information surprised her, it would surprise others also.

You can also develop a surprising-reversal informative essay based on personal experience. The following "For Writing and Discussion" exercise will help you generate ideas.

Once you have your first draft on paper, the goal is to make it work better, first for yourself and then for your readers. If you discovered ideas as you wrote, you may need to do some major restructuring. Check to see that the question you are addressing is clear and make sure that you distinguish between your audience's common view and your own surprising view. Apply the strategies for global revision explained in Chapter 17.

Figure 9.3 Framework for an Informative Essay Using the Surprising-Reversal Strategy

Introduction (one to several paragraphs)	• Engages readers' interest in the writer's question • Provides background and context
Body section 1 (brief)	• Explains the common or popular answer to the writer's question
Body section 2 (major)	• Provides a delayed thesis—the writer's surprising answer to the question • Supports the thesis with information from personal experience or research • Displays numeric data in graphs or tables referenced in the text
Conclusion	• Suggests the significance of the writer's new perspective on the question

For Writing and Discussion
Generating Ideas Based on Personal Experience

Individual task: Think of several examples of topic areas or activities in which you have more expertise than somebody else. Use the following templates:

> I know more about X [topic area] than [specific person or persons]. OR I have more experience with X [activity] than [specific person or persons].

For example, you might say, "I know more about [computer games/gospel music/causes of hunger] than [my roommate/my high school friends/my parents]." Or "I have had more experience with [knitting/skateboarding/doing yoga] than [most of my classmates]." For each of your examples, use freewriting to search for ways that outsiders have misconceptions or misunderstandings about your expertise area. Your surprising-reversal essay could then correct this misperception.

Task for small groups: Assign a group recorder to make a two-column list, with the left column titled "Mistaken or Narrow View of X" and the right column titled "Groupmate's Surprising View." Using the surprising-reversal strategy, brainstorm ideas for essay topics until every group member has generated at least one entry for the righthand column. Table 9.2 provides several examples.

Once you have settled on a topic area for your essay, you can refine your thinking by answering the following five questions. For each question, we speculate about what King might have written if she had used the same questions to help her get started on her essay.

1. **What question does your essay address?** King might have asked, "Will hydrogen fuel-cell automobiles solve our nation's energy and pollution crises?"

2. **What is the common, expected, or popular answer to this question held by your imagined audience?** King might have said, "Most people believe that hydrogen fuel-cell cars will solve our country's pollution and energy crises."

3. **What examples and details support your audience's view?** Expand on these views by developing them with supporting examples and details. King might have noted her research examples praising fuel-cell technology, such as Mercedes Benz experimental fuel-cell cars or money being poured into fuel-cell research by Japan or the European Union.

4. **What is your own surprising view?** King might have said, "Although hydrogen fuel-cell cars are pollution free, getting the hydrogen in the first place requires burning fossil fuels."

5. **What examples and details support this view? Why do you hold this view? Why should a reader believe you?** Writing rapidly, spell out the evidence that supports your point. King would have done a freewrite about her research discoveries that hydrogen has to be recovered from carbon-based fossils or from electrolysis of water—all of which means continued use of pollution-causing fossil fuels.

After you finish exploring your responses to these five trigger questions, you will be well on your way to composing a first draft of your article. Now finish writing your draft fairly rapidly without worrying about perfection.

Table 9.2 Examples of the Surprising-Reversal Pattern Developed by Groupmates

Mistaken or Narrow View of X	Groupmate's Surprising View
Being an offensive lineman in football is a no-brain, repetitive job requiring size and strength, but only enough intelligence and athletic ability to push people out of the way.	Jeff can show that being an offensive lineman is a complex job that requires mental smarts as well as size, strength, and athletic ability.
Pawnshops are disreputable places.	Samantha's uncle owns a pawnshop that is a wholesome family business that serves an important social function.
To most straight people, *Frankenstein* is a monster movie about science gone amuck.	Cody can show how *Frankenstein* holds a special and quite different meaning for the gay community.

Questions for Peer Review

In addition to the generic peer review questions explained in Skill 17.4, ask your peer reviewers to address these questions:

1. What question does the paper address? How effective is the paper at hooking the reader's interest in the question?

2. Where does the writer explain the common or popular view of the topic? Do you agree that this is the common view? How does the writer develop or support this view? What additional supporting examples, illustrations, or details might make the common view more vivid or compelling?

3. What is the writer's surprising view? Were you surprised? What details does the writer use to develop the surprising view? What additional supporting examples, illustrations, or details might help make the surprising view more vivid and compelling?

4. Is the draft clear and easy to follow? Is the draft interesting? How might the writer improve the style, clarity, or interest level of the draft?

5. If the draft includes graphics, are they effective? Do the words and the visuals tell the same story? Are the visuals properly titled and labeled? How might the use of visuals be improved?

Multimodal or Online Assignment Options

1. **Informative Poster** Along the lines of the poster in Figure 9.2, make a poster that conveys new or surprising information about a popular or unpopular activity, consumer item, or phenomenon such as a food, a diet plan, an exercise, a sport, or a fad. Make your poster visually interesting, clear, and useful. Give credit to any sources that you use.

   For advice on producing multimodal compositions, see Chapter 20

2. **An Informative Video** Create a short video informing new students about some aspect of your college or university that you think students would benefit from knowing and that you believe your college or university does not adequately explain from students' perspective. Possible examples include the following: how to use the Writing Center; how to start an intramural team; how to get help with your computer; how to prepare for finals; how to dispute a grade. Make your video visually interesting and useful. If you use excerpts from interviews keep them short, focused, and lively. Your purpose is to helpfully inform other students.

3. **Pechakucha 20/20** Presentation Pick an area of knowledge in which you are an insider with more expertise than most of your classmates (growing tomatoes, beekeeping, backpacking, playing the flute, babysitting, shooting free throws, baking pies, repairing bicycles, playing video games, knowing the best coffee houses). Create an informative pechakucha presentation that shares with audiences some of your insider knowledge. A pechakucha presentation gives you twenty images, each projected on a screen for twenty seconds (see Chapter 20 for more details). You'll need to time your informative speech to fit the rhythm of your slide show.

Readings

Our first reading, by student writer Elise Berentson, is an example of a solicited informative report. Elise role-played being a student intern for the staff director for a U.S. Representative. For this assignment, Elise responded to the following e-mail request from her supervisor, Wanda Manning.

Supervisor's E-Mail Request

Subject Line: Information on Planned Parenthood

Good morning, Elise.

Representative Hurtado is trying to determine what position she should take on the recent brouhaha over Planned Parenthood, which has been accused of profiting from the sale of embryonic tissues to scientists for research. Conservatives are pushing to end federal funding for Planned Parenthood. Representative Hurtado is seeking more information about Planned Parenthood. I need you to do some Web research to provide some background for me. I don't want you to take a position on Planned Parenthood. I just need more contextual information. Please send me a short report that expands my current knowledge about PP. Is it primarily an abortion clinic? What other services does PP provide? If it is defunded by the feds, could it still survive? Are there alternatives for its current clients?
I need your report ASAP.
Best regards,
Wanda

Elise's Report

To: Wanda Manning, Staff Director

From: Elise Berentson, Student Intern

Subject: Requested Information on Planned Parenthood

This report responds to your email request on September 8 for information about Planned Parenthood (PP). The information is derived from the national PP Website and from the 2013 PP Annual Report that can be downloaded from the Web in PDF format. I also used several other reputable Websites (I can provide a bibliography). I have organized the report to match the questions you asked in your email.

Is Planned Parenthood primarily an abortion clinic? What other services does PP provide?

Although Planned Parenthood clinics provide abortion services, their centers are not primarily abortion clinics. In 2013 abortion services consisted of 3% of the total services provided at PP health centers. According to their Website, PP clinics seek to provide comprehensive reproductive healthcare for both men and women.

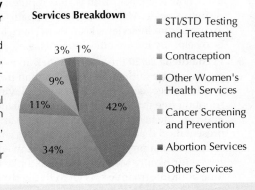

Services Breakdown

- ■ STI/STD Testing and Treatment
- ■ Contraception
- ■ Other Women's Health Services
- ■ Cancer Screening and Prevention
- ■ Abortion Services
- ■ Other Services

3% 1%
9%
11%
34%
42%

Other services provided by the non-profit include STI/STD testing and treatment, contraception, cervical and breast cancer screenings, pregnancy testing, prenatal services, family practice services, and adoption referrals. For a breakdown of services, see chart.

If the federal government defunds Planned Parenthood, would it still be able to survive?

In 2013 the federal government provided $528 million to PP in the form of grants and reimbursements for services provided to Medicaid patients. This level of federal funding consisted of 41 percent of PP's total revenue of $1.1 billion. If the federal government cut off these funds, PP would lose nearly half of its revenue source, making it difficult, perhaps even impossible, to keep its nearly 700 health clinics open.

Government proponents of defunding PP cite the group's ability to fund-raise as a reason that the non-profit does not need federal funding. In 2013, private donations and fundraising equaled $391 million, or 30 percent of PP's total revenue. To cover the lost 41 percent from federal funding, annual private contributions would need to more than double. It is not known whether the doubling of private contributions is possible.

Are there alternatives to Planned Parenthood?

If PP clinics closed their doors, 2.7 million patients would be displaced from their current health provider. There are conflicting beliefs about whether these patients would be able to find a new place to receive health care.

House Republicans believe these patients would be able to receive care at one of the other 13,000 community health centers within the United States, which provide the same services as PP. Opponents of PP calculate that the other 13,000 federally funded clinics would be able to cover the displaced patients by seeing one new patient every other day.

Supporters of PP, however, believe that these centers do not have the capacity to take on all 2.7 million PP patients. A report from the Congressional Budget Office estimates that 5 to 25 percent of displaced patients would lose access to care, citing loss of care to 390,000 patients as the likely outcome. These current patients would lose care either because existing clinics would not be able to take on new patients or because the patients have to travel too far to find another clinic.

If you need further elaboration or have further questions, I should be able to do the next round of research quickly.

THINKING CRITICALLY
About "Information on Planned Parenthoodt"

1. How effectively do you think Elise's report meets Wanda Manning's request for information? Would Wanda Manning be satisfied with this report?
2. Suppose that Elise maintained her own blog and wanted to present the information in this report to a general audience interested in the Planned Parenthood controversy. How would she need to rewrite the introduction? Explain the reasons for any changes she would need to make.
3. Pretending you are Elise, write the introduction (and new title) she would need for a blog post.

Our second reading, by student writer Kirsten Smock, uses the surprising-reversal strategy to make her informative research engaging and meaningful to general readers. It is formatted to look like a popular magazine article. When she submitted the "magazine article" to her instructor, she also submitted an annotated bibliography that documents her sources. We have not reprinted the bibliography.

Kirsten Smock

Understanding Jihad: Is Islam a Violent Religion?

I vividly remember watching the news coverage in my third-grade classroom on the morning of September 11, 2001. Eight-year-old me couldn't comprehend who would hijack planes and send them crashing into the Twin Towers. My impressionable self came to believe what the popular media claimed: Islam was a violent religion waging a jihad, or holy war, against the United States. This popular view was expressed by President Bush in a speech to the American people. "We are the targets of enemies who boast they want to kill—kill all Americans, kill all Jews, and kill all Christians . . . WE wage a war to save civilization itself." The ideology that Islam is a violent religion clouds our view of American Muslims as well. However, when I visited an Islamic mosque many years later, I was welcomed with kindness, not hate—the Muslims I met were not acting like the enemy my childhood had painted them to be. This unexpected interaction led me to ask whether Islam actually condones violence. Is it waging a jihad against non-believers?

In order to clarify my understanding of jihad, I turned to Qur'anic texts directly, as well as to interpretations of their meaning by Islamic scholars. Although in the United States the term *jihad* is often translated as "holy war," the term itself literally translates to a "struggle" or a "striving." While many Americans mistakenly believe that jihad indicates an outward struggle against non-believers, jihad instead represents the internal struggle required to maintain difficult tenets of the faith, including prayer five times daily.

The non-violent nature of Islamic jihad is seen in the Qur'an Sura 22:77-78, which reads, "You who believe! Bow and prostrate yourselves, and serve your Lord, and do good, so that you may prosper. And struggle [jihad] for God with the struggling due Him." According to Islamic scholar John Kaltner, this passage illuminates the internal struggle Islam requires of individuals to stay true to their faith in order to better themselves and to be closer to Allah.

This view of Islamic jihad as an internal struggle rather than a holy war is supported by a Pew research poll conducted in 2013. This poll shows that in most countries where Muslims are the religious majority, more than 75 percent believe that Islam rarely or never justifies violent acts, such as suicide bombings. These statistics support the idea that Islam is not an inherently violent religion. (See the graph below. Percentages not totaling 100 indicate that not all participants answered the question.)

Although the majority of Muslims do not believe that Islam condones violence, the notion that Muslims are to be feared is still rampant in the United States. Critics of Islam often cite extremist groups such as the Taliban or ISIS, which use violence to achieve their goals, as indicative of the religion as a whole. It is important to keep in mind, however, that just as we wouldn't claim that certain highly intolerant Christian groups—such as the homophobic Westboro Baptist Church—are representative of all Christianity, the violent tendencies promoted by extremist Muslim groups are not representative of Islam.

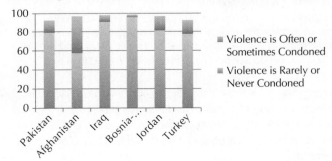

Percentage of Muslims Who Believe Islam Condones Violence

THINKING CRITICALLY

About "Understanding Jihad: Is Islam a Violent Religion?"

1. Students can appreciate the concept of genre more fully if they occasionally desktop-publish a manuscript to look like a magazine article, a poster, or a brochure rather than a standard double-spaced academic paper. How does document design help signal the document's genre? To what extent has Kirsten made this article sound like a popular magazine article as well as look like one?

2. Kirsten's instructor asked students to attach an annotated bibliography to their desktop-published magazine articles. Why do most magazine articles not include academic-style documentation? What causes most readers to trust the information provided in magazines? Should they trust this information? Why or why not?

3. Kirsten uses the surprising-reversal strategy to increase the impact and significance of her information. How does Kirsten try to grab her readers' attention? Where does she state the common or popular view? What is her own surprising view? How effectively does she support her view?

Our last reading, by student writer Shannon King, is a short academic research paper using the surprising-reversal strategy. Shannon's paper uses research information to enlarge her readers' understanding of hydrogen fuel-cell vehicles by showing that hydrogen fuel is not as pollution-free as the general public believes.

Shannon King (student)
How Clean and Green Are Hydrogen Fuel-Cell Cars?

1   The United States is embroiled in a controversy over energy and pollution. We are rapidly increasing the percentage of greenhouse gases in our atmosphere. Only a decade ago, one energy expert, Paul Roberts, believed, as did many others, that serious oil shortages would start occurring by 2015, when the world's demand for oil would outstrip the world's capacity for further oil production. Such oil shortage would itself force us to move to a low-carbon economy. However, oil suppliers have avoided shortages by using fracking to extract less-accessible oil found in shale, tar sands, or deep ocean floors. As a result, oil and natural gas again seem abundant. Unfortunately, this abundance causes even more pollution, greenhouse gases, and environmental destruction. With signs of climate change emerging faster than anticipated, the need to reduce carbon emissions has spurred efforts to limit the burning of fossil fuels, especially in the cars we drive.

2   One hopeful way of addressing fossil-fuel use is to develop hydrogen fuel-cell cars. According to Karim Nice and Jonathan Strickland, the authors of the fuel-cell pages on the *HowStuffWorks* Web site, a fuel cell is "an electrochemical energy conversion device that converts hydrogen and oxygen into water, producing electricity and heat in the process." A hydrogen-fueled car is therefore an electric car, powered by an electric motor. The car's electricity is generated by a stack of fuel cells that act like a battery. In the hydrogen fuel cell, the chemicals that produce the electricity are hydrogen from the car's pressurized fuel tank, oxygen from the air, and special catalysts inside the fuel cell. The fuel cell releases no pollutants or greenhouse gases. The only waste product is pure water.

3   To what extent will these pollution-free fuel cells be our energy salvation? Are they really clean and green? Many people think so. The development of hydrogen fuel cells has caused much excitement. I know people who say we don't need to worry about running out of oil because cars of the future will run on water. For example, Mercedes-Benz spokesman Ray Burke described the use of Mercedes fuel-cell vehicles at the U.S. Tennis Open, praising Mercedes-Benz's commitment to "exploring new ways of innovative eco mobility" ("Mercedes-Benz"). Many national governments are also pursuing the dream of hydrogen fuel-cell vehicles that will not spout out carbon emissions. Recently, Japan has opted to try out fuel cells in both homes and vehicles (Jean), while the European Union is subsidizing research into fuel cells, budgeting almost a billion euros over six years (De Colvenaer and Castel).

4   But what I discovered in my research is that hydrogen is not as green as most people think. Although hydrogen fuel cells appear to be an environmentally

friendly alternative to fossil fuels, the processes for producing hydrogen actually require the use of fossil fuels. The problem is that pure hydrogen doesn't occur naturally on earth. It has to be separated out from chemical compounds containing hydrogen, and that process requires other forms of energy. What I discovered is that there are only two major ways to produce hydrogen. The first is to produce it from fossil fuels by unlocking the hydrogen that is bonded to the carbon in coal, oil, or natural gas. The second is to produce it from water through electrolysis, but the power required for electrolysis would also come mainly from burning fossil fuels. These problems make hydrogen fuel-cell cars look less clean and green than they first appear.

5   One approach to creating hydrogen from fossil fuels is to use natural gas. According to Matthew L. Wald, writing in a *New York Times* article, natural gas is converted to hydrogen in a process called "steam reforming." Natural gas (made of hydrogen and carbon atoms) is mixed with steam (which contains hydrogen and oxygen atoms) to cause a chemical reaction that produces pure hydrogen. But it also produces carbon dioxide, which contributes to global warming. According to Wald, if fuel-cell cars used hydrogen from steam reforming, they would emit 145 grams of global warming gases per mile compared to the 374 grams an ordinary gas-powered car would emit. The good news is that using hydrogen power would cut carbon emissions by more than half. The bad news is that these cars would still contribute to global warming and consume natural gas. Moreover, Wald suggests that the natural gas supply is limited and that natural gas has many better, more efficient uses than being converted to hydrogen.

6   The next likely source of hydrogen is to produce it directly from water using an electrolyzer. Wald explains that the electrolyzer uses an electrical current to break down water molecules into hydrogen and oxygen atoms. Creating hydrogen through electrolysis sounds like a good idea because its only waste product is oxygen. But the hazardous environmental impact is not in the electrolysis reaction, but in the need to generate electricity to run the electrolyzer. Wald claims that if the electricity to run the electrolyzer came from a typical coal-fired electrical plant, the carbon dioxide emissions for a fuel-cell car would be 17 percent worse than for today's gasoline-powered cars. One solution would be to run the electrolyzer with wind-generated or nuclear-powered electricity. But wind power would be able to produce only a small fraction of what would be needed, and nuclear power brings with it a whole new set of problems, including disposal of nuclear waste.

7   Another nonpolluting energy source is solar energy, which scientists from the United States and Switzerland have used in a solar reactor to create the hydrogen for fuel cells ("Advantages"). However, Donald Anthrop, professor emeritus in environmental studies at San Jose State University, argues that solar—the clean energy solution to hydrogen fuel production—is impractical. He claims that to supply the amount of hydrogen fuel needed for California's goal of 80 percent fuel-cell vehicles, solar panels would cover about 1.2 million acres of land—a space far larger than Yosemite National Park. Another way of seeing the power requirements for hydrogen-fuel production, according to Anthrop, is to picture the power as equal to one-third of the total nuclear energy produced in the United States.

8   Although there seem to be various methods of producing hydrogen, the current sources being considered do not fulfill the claim that hydrogen fuel-cell technology will end the use of fossil fuels or eliminate greenhouse gases. The problem is not with the fuel cells themselves but with the processes needed to produce hydrogen fuel. I am not arguing that research and development should be abandoned, and I hope some day that the hydrogen economy will take off. But what I have discovered in my research is that hydrogen power is not as clean and green as I thought.

Works Cited

"Advantages of Solar Energy." *Conserve Energy Future*, www.conserve-energy-future.com/Advantages_SolarEnergy.php. Accessed 8 Apr. 2016.

Anthrop, Donald F. "Faulty Engineering Driving Air Board's Hydrogen Hypothesis." *Contra Costa Times*, 8 Apr. 2012, p. A15.

"Mercedes-Benz of Long Beach Confirm, Mercedes-Benz Is Leading the USTA's Green Mission at 2010 US Open." *WebWire,* 1 Sept. 2010, www.webwire.com/ViewPressRel.asp?aId=122313.

De Colvenaer, Bert, and Claire Castel. "The Fuel Cells and Hydrogen Joint Undertaking (FCH JU) in Europe." *International Journal of Low-Carbon Technologies*, vol. 7, no. 1, 2012, pp. 5–7.

Jean, Grace V. "Hydrogen Fuel Cells to Power Homes, Vehicles in Japan." *National Defense*, vol. 93, no. 657, 2008, p. 54.

Nice, Karim, and Jonathan Strickland. "How Fuel Cells Work." *HowStuffWorks.com*, auto.howstuffworks.com/fuel-efficiency/alternative-fuels/fuel-cell.htm. Accessed 8 Apr. 2016.

Roberts, Paul. "Running Out of Oil—and Time." *Los Angeles Times*, 7 Mar. 2004, articles.latimes.com/2004/mar/07/opinion/op-roberts7.

Wald, Matthew L. "Will Hydrogen Clear the Air? Maybe Not, Some Say." *The New York Times*, 12 Nov. 2003, p. C1.

THINKING CRITICALLY

About "How Clean and Green Are Hydrogen Fuel-Cell Cars?"

1. Explain Shannon King's use of the surprising-reversal strategy. What question does she pose? What is the common answer? What is her surprising answer? How effectively does she use research data to support her surprising answer?

2. The line between information and persuasion is often blurred. Some might argue that Shannon's essay has a persuasive aim that argues against hydrogen fuel-cell cars rather than an informative aim that simply presents surprising information about hydrogen production. To what extent do you agree with our classification of Shannon's aim as primarily informative rather than persuasive? Can it be both?

Chapter 10
Writing an Image Analysis Essay

Learning Objectives

10.1 Analyze documentary and news photographs with attention to their compositional features, angle of vision, cultural contexts, and technical strategies for persuasion.

10.2 Analyze paintings with attention to their compositional features, artistic technique, historical context, and cultural messages or meaning.

10.3 Analyze print ads and advocacy posters with attention to their compositional features, their integrated use of images and words, and their persuasive appeals to a targeted audience.

10.4 Write a comparative analysis of two visual texts.

This chapter asks you to think about three major kinds of communication through images—documentary or news photographs, paintings, and advertisements or posters—to increase your visual literacy skills. By **visual literacy**, we mean your awareness of the importance of visual communication and your ability to interpret or make meaning out of images by examining their context and visual features. We focus on the ways that images influence our conceptual and emotional understanding of a phenomenon and the ways that they validate, reveal, and construct the world.

This chapter invites you to analyze images in order to understand their rhetorical and experiential effects. To **analyze** means to divide the whole into its parts, examine these parts carefully, look at the relationships among them, and then use this understanding of the parts to better understand the whole. As explained in Concepts 1.1 and 2.2, when you analyze an object or phenomenon you closely observe its details, features, and patterns in order to raise interpretive questions to which you provide tentative answers, supported by points and details derived from your own close examination.

The ability to analyze visual texts rhetorically is important because we are surrounded by glamorous and disturbing images from photojournalism, the Internet, billboards, newspapers, television, and magazines—images that, as one critic has stated, "have designs on us," yet we may not fully understand how they affect us.

Analyzing documentary and news photographs

10.1 Analyze documentary and news photographs with attention to their compositional features, angle of vision, cultural contexts, and technical strategies for persuasion.

Documentary and news photos are aimed at shaping the way we think and feel about an event or cultural/historical phenomenon. For example, think of the persuasive effects of photos of melting glaciers, of ancient historic sites in the Middle East reduced to crumbled ruins by ISIS attacks, or of smiling politicians standing in front of American flags with arms raised in victory. Sometimes photos become lodged in the cultural consciousness, achieving iconic status. Consider the newspaper photos, TV news footage, or Internet videos of the billowing clouds of smoke and ash from the collapsing World Trade Center towers on September 11, 2001. Figures 10.1, 10.2, and 10.3 present three well-known documentary images of this event, taken from three different camera positions and at three slightly different moments as the event unfolded.

Although all three photos convey the severity of the terrorist attack, each has a different impact. Figure 10.1 records the event shortly before the north tower collapsed and just after the south tower was struck by the second plane, marked in the photo by the red flames. The sheer magnitude and horror of the moment-by-moment action unfolding before our eyes evoked shock, anger, and feelings of helplessness in Americans.

Figure 10.1 Terrorist Attack on the World Trade Center

Figure 10.2 World Trade Center Attack as a Close-up

Figure 10.3 Firefighters in the World Trade Center Wreckage

In contrast to the first image, which was taken from a distance below the towers, Figure 10.2 focuses in closely on the south tower, capturing the immensity of the explosion and fire after the plane struck this tower. It seems to bring viewers dangerously close to the billowing, towering clouds of smoke, which suggest the apocalyptic explosion and implosion of a contemporary city. The destruction pictured here is too massive to be an ordinary event such as a fire in a major building, and yet the streams of ash and smoke don't reveal exactly what is happening.

Another well-publicized view of this event is that of the firefighters on the ground amidst debris and dust, seen in Figure 10.3. Here the firefighters, risking their lives while trying to rescue the people in the towers, have come to symbolize the self-sacrifice, courage, and also vulnerability of the human effort in the face of such colossal destruction. This image also suggests the terror and suspense of a science-fiction-like conflict. All three photos, while memorializing the same event and trying to capture the incomprehensibility of this colossal attack, have different specific subjects, angles of vision, and emotional and psychological effects.

The rest of this section introduces you to the ways that photographers think about their use of the camera and the effects they are trying to achieve.

Angle of Vision and Credibility of Photographs

Although the word *documentary* is associated with an objective, transparent, unmediated glimpse of reality, the relationship of documentary photography to its subject matter has always been complex. Historians are now reassessing early documentary photographs, exploring the class and race agendas of the photographers in the scenes chosen, the photographers' stance toward them, and the wording of the narratives accompanying the photographs. In other words, despite a photograph's appearance of capturing a moment of reality (whose reality?), its effect is always influenced by the photographer's rhetorical angle of vision conveyed through the framing and focusing power of the camera. Perhaps now more than ever, we are aware that the photographer's purpose and techniques shape the reality that viewers see. (Think of the multiple cameras tracking a football game and replaying a touchdown from different angles, often creating very different impressions of a particular play.)

The photographer's power to shape reality is enhanced by the various strategies for making "unnatural" photographs seem "natural" or "real." For example, photographs can be manipulated or falsified in the following ways:

- Staging images (scenes that appear spontaneous but are really posed)
- Altering images (airbrushing, reshaping body parts)
- Selecting images or parts of images (cropping photographs so that only certain parts are shown)
- Mislabeling images (writing a caption that misrepresents the image)
- Constructing images (putting the head of one person on the body of another)

Research has revealed that many famous photographs were tampered with. As early as the Civil War, composite photos of generals were created by combining heads, bodies, and scenery and inserting figures into scenes. Today this manipulation is also enhanced by the versatile capabilities of photo editing software, which enables even amateur photographers to edit photos for effect. The potential for altering images gives us additional reasons for considering the photographer's active role and for investigating the credibility and purpose behind images when we analyze photographs.

How to Analyze a Documentary Photograph

Photographs are always created and interpreted within a social, political, and historical context—the original context in which the photograph was made and viewed and your own context as a current viewer and interpreter. At play are the assumptions, values, and cultural knowledge of the photographer, the original viewers, and the later viewers. Also important are the sites in which the photograph is viewed—whether in an original news story, a museum, an upscale art exhibit, an expensive coffee-table book, a documentary film, an Internet site, or a textbook. These sites invite us to respond in different ways. For example, one site may call us to social action or deepen our understanding of an event, while another aims to elicit artistic appreciation or to underscore cultural differences.

EXAMINING THE RHETORICAL CONTEXTS OF A PHOTO   A first step in analyzing a documentary photograph is to consider its various rhetorical contexts. Strategies Chart 10.1 will help you ask illuminating questions.

EXAMINING THE EFFECTS OF A PHOTO ON A VIEWER   In addition to considering rhetorical context, in analyzing photographs we need to explore how photographs achieve their effects—that is, how they move us emotionally or intellectually, how they imply arguments and cause us to see the subject in a certain way. An image might soothe us or repel us; it might evoke our sympathies, trigger our fears, or call forth a web of interconnected ideas, memories, and associations.

Analysis of photographs—and all images—begins with close observation and posing thoughtful questions. Before you begin a detailed analysis of a photograph, you will find it helpful to explore the photograph's immediate impact.

Recording Your First Responses to Photographs

- What features of this photograph stand out and attract your attention?
- What words come to mind when you view this photograph?
- What is the mood or overall feeling conveyed by the photo?
- Assuming that photographs "have designs on us," what is this photograph trying to get you to feel, think, do, or see?

Strategies Chart 10.2 will help you observe the features of a photograph and analyze how it achieves its persuasive effects.*

Strategies Chart 10.1 Strategies for Analyzing the Rhetorical Contexts of Documentary Photographs

Context	Questions to Ask
Photographer's purpose and context in making the photograph	• What was the photographer's original intention/purpose in making the image (to report an event, convey information, persuade viewers to think about the event or people a certain way)? • What was the original historical, cultural, social, and political context in which the photograph was taken?
Original context for displaying the photograph	• Where was the photograph originally viewed (news story, photo essay, scientific report, public exhibit, advocacy Web site)? • How does the original title or caption, if any, reflect the context and shape impressions of the image?
Cultural contexts for interpreting the photograph	• How does the photograph's appearance in a particular place influence your impression of it? • How does your own cultural context differ from that of original viewers? • What assumptions and values do you bring to the context?

---

* We are indebted to Terry Barrett, Professor Emeritus of Art Education at Ohio State University, for his formulation of questions, "Looking at Photographs, Description and Interpretation," and to Claire Garoutte, Associate Professor of Photography at Seattle University, for informing our discussion of context in analyzing documentary photographs.

Strategies Chart 10.2 Strategies for Analyzing the Persuasive Effects of Photographs and Other Images

What to Examine	Some Questions to Ask about Rhetorical Effect
Subject matter: People in portraits: Portraits can be formal or informal and can emphasize character or social role. The gaze of the human subjects can imply power through direct eye contact and deference or shyness through lack of eye contact.	Is the emphasis on identity, character, personality, or representative status (wife of wealthy merchant, political leader, soldier, etc.), or is the emphasis symbolic (an image of wisdom, daring, etc.)? What do details of clothing and setting (a room's furnishings, for example) reveal about historical period, economic status, national or ethnic identity?
Subject matter: People in scenes: Scenes can make a statement about everyday life or capture some aspect of a news event or crisis.	What is the relationship of the people to one another and the scene? Can you recreate the story behind the scene? Does the scene look natural/realistic or staged/aesthetically attractive?
Subject matter: Landscape or nature: Scenes can focus on nature or the environment as the dominant subject.	If the setting is outdoors, what are the features of the landscape: urban or rural, mountain or desert? What aspects of nature are shown? If people are in the image, what is the relationship between nature and the human figures? What vision of nature is the artist constructing—majestic, threatening, hospitable, tamed, orderly, wild?
Distance from subject: Close-ups tend to increase the intensity of the image and suggest the importance of the subject. Long shots tend to blend the subject into the environment.	Are viewers brought close to the subject or distanced from it? How does the distance from the subject contribute to the effect of the photo or painting?
Angle and orientation: The vantage point from which the photograph was taken and the positioning of the photographer to the subject determine the effect of images. Low angle makes the subject look larger. High angle makes the subject look smaller. A level angle implies equality. Front views tend to emphasize the persons in the image. Rear views often emphasize the scene or setting.	How does the angle influence what you see? Why do you think this angle was chosen? How would the photograph have changed if it had been taken from another angle?
Framing: Framing determines what is inside the image and what is closed off to viewers; it's a device to draw the attention of viewers.	How does the framing of the image direct your attention? What is included and what is excluded from the image? How does what the photo or painting allows you to see and know contribute to its effect? Why do you think this particular frame was chosen?
Light: The direction of the light determines the shadows and affects the contrasts, which can be subtle or strong. Lighting has different effects if it is natural or artificial, bright, soft, or harsh.	How does the light reveal details? What does the direction of the light contribute to the presence of shadows? How do these shadows affect the mood or feeling of the photo?
Focus: Focus refers to what is clearly in focus or in the foreground of the photo versus what is blurry. The range between the nearest and farthest thing in focus in the photo is referred to as the depth of field.	What parts of the image are clearly in focus? Are any parts out of focus? What effect do these choices have on viewers' impression of the image? How great is the depth of field and what effect does that have?
Scale, space, and shape: Size/scale and shape affect prominence and emphasis. Size and scale can be natural, minimized, or exaggerated. Use of space can be shallow, deep, or both. Both positive shapes and voids can draw viewers' attention.	How do the scale, space, and shape of objects direct viewers' attention and affect a feeling or mood? Are shapes geometric and angular or flowing and organic? Are shapes positive such as objects, or negative such as voids?
Use of repetition, variety, and balance: Repetition of elements can create order, wholeness, and unity. Variety can create interest. Balance can create unity and harmony.	What elements are repeated in this image? What variety is present, say, in shapes? Does the visual weight of the photo seem to be distributed evenly on the sides, top, and bottom? What roles do repetition, variety, and balance play in the impression created by the photo?

What to Examine	Some Questions to Ask about Rhetorical Effect
Line: Lines can be curved and flowing, straight, or disjointed and angular. Lines can be balanced/symmetrical, stable, and harmonious, or disjointed and agitated.	Does the use of line create structure and convey movement/action or calm/stasis? How does the use of line control how viewers look at the photo or painting?
Color: Choice of black and white can reflect the site of publication, the date of the photo, or an artistic choice. Colors can contribute to the realism and appeal; harmonious colors can be pleasing; clashing or harsh colors can be disturbing.	How many colors are used? What is the relationship of the colors? Which colors dominate? Are the colors warm and vibrant or cool, bright, or dull? How are light and dark used? How does the use of color direct viewers' attention and affect the impression of the image? What emotional response do these colors evoke?

Sample Analysis of a Documentary Photograph

To illustrate how a documentary photograph can work on the viewer's mind and heart, we show you our own analysis of a photo titled *The Fall of the Berlin Wall* (Figure 10.4), taken by photojournalist Peter Turnley in 1989. At the time, the Berlin Wall, which separated communist East Berlin from democratic West Berlin, symbolized the oppression of communism. In 1987 President Ronald Reagan appealed to Mikhail Gorbachev, president of the Union of Soviet Socialist Republics, saying in a famous speech, "Mr. Gorbachev, tear down this wall." When the border opened in November 1989, marking the end of communist rule in Eastern Europe, East Berliners flooded into West Berlin, sparking weeks of celebration. Peter Turnley is a world-famous American photojournalist whose photos of major world events have appeared on the covers of *Newsweek* as well as international magazines. This photograph appeared in a 1996 exhibit (and later a book) entitled *In Time of War and Peace* at the International Center of Photography in New York.

Figure 10.4 Fall of the Berlin Wall, 1989, by Peter Turnley

This documentary photograph of a celebratory scene following the opening of the Berlin Wall in 1989 uses elements of framing, orientation, focus, balance, and color to convey the dominant impression of a life-changing explosion of energy and emotion triggered by this significant event. This distance photo is divided into three horizontal bands—the sky, the wall, and the celebratory crowd—but the focal point is the yelling, triumphant German youth sitting astride the wall, wearing jeans, a studded belt, and a black jacket. The graffiti indicate that the photo was taken from the West Berlin side (East Berliners were not permitted to get close to the wall), and the light post between the two cranes was probably used to illuminate the no-person zone on the communist side.

Every aspect of the photograph suggests energy. In contrast with the mostly homogeneous sky, the wall and the crowd contain many diverse elements. The wall is heavily graffitied in many colors, and the crowd is composed of many people. The wall looks crowded, tattered, and dirty, something to be torn down rather than cleaned up. Most of the graffiti consist of tags, people's response to the ugly obstruction of the wall; West Berliners had no power to destroy the wall, but they could mark it up. The slightly blurred crowd of heads suggests that the people are in motion. At first it is hard to tell if they are angry protesters storming the wall or celebrators cheering on the German youth. The photograph captures this dual emotion—anger and joy—all at once.

At the center of the photograph is the German youth, whose dark jacket makes him stand out against the light blue sky. A few days earlier the wall had fenced him in (at that time, it would have been unthinkable even to approach the wall lest he be shot by border guards). Now he rides the wall like an American cowboy at a rodeo. He has conquered the wall. He has become transformed from prisoner to liberator. His cowboy gesture, reflecting European fascination with American cowboy movies, becomes the symbol of the ideological West, the land of freedom, now the wave of the future for these reunited countries. He holds in his hand a tool (a hammer or chisel?) used to chip away the wall symbolically, but the position of his arm and hand suggests a cowboy with a pistol.

What makes this photograph so powerful is the distance. Had Turnley used a telescopic lens to focus on the German youth up close, the photograph would have been about the youth himself, a personal story. But by placing the youth into a larger frame that includes the crowd, the long expanse of ugly wall, and the cranes and lamppost behind the wall, Turnley suggests both the enormous public and political nature of this event and the implications for individual lives. The youth appears to be the first of the energized crowd to demonstrate the conquering of the powerful barrier that had shaped so many German lives for almost three decades. Thus the composition of this photo packs many layers of meaning and symbolism into its depiction of this historic event.

For Writing and Discussion
Analyzing the Compositional Features and Rhetorical Effect of Photographs

The photographs shown in Figures 10.5 and 10.6 come from news coverage of the Syrian refugee crisis in the Middle East and Europe. According to Amnesty International, the UN High Commissioner for Refugees (UNHCR), and the World Bank, by 2016 nearly 5 million Syrians had fled violent conflict and instability in their country, with millions living precariously in refugee camps in Turkey, Lebanon, Jordan, Iraq, and Egypt. Thousands of these displaced people have risked the dangerous passage by small boats to Greece in hopes of resettling in European Union countries; however, closed borders have left thousands of people impoverished and stranded in crowded refugee camps. Photographs like these shown here have influenced world opinion and policies.

Analyze these news photographs using the questions in the list "Recording Your First Responses to Photographs" and the features and questions explained in Strategies Chart 10.2. Examine the features (lighting, angle and orientation, framing, and so forth) to explore the dominant impression conveyed by each photograph. Make notes that you can share with a group or your class.

Then, in groups or as a whole class, consider the rhetorical effect of these photographs by discussing your responses to these questions:

1. Which photograph would you use if you were designing a poster to appeal for donations to refugee camps? Explain.

2. Which photograph would you use to accompany an informational report on the urgency and complexity of the refugee crisis? Explain.

Figure 10.5 Syrian Refugees

Figure 10.6 Syrian Refugees at the European Border

Analyzing paintings

10.2 Analyze paintings with attention to their compositional features, artistic technique, historical context, and cultural messages or meaning.

When you are analyzing a painting, many of the strategies used for analyzing documentary photographs still apply. With paintings, you also look carefully at the subject matter (the setting, the people or objects in the setting, the arrangement in space, the clothing, the gaze of persons, the implied narrative story, and so forth). Likewise, you consider the painter's distance from the subject, the angle of orientation, the framing, and other features that paintings share with photographs. Additionally, your analysis of paintings will be enriched if you consider, as you did with documentary photographs, the context in which the painting was originally created and originally viewed as well as your own cultural context and place of viewing.

But painters—by means of their choice of paints, their brushstrokes, their artistic vision, and their methods of representation—often do something quite different from photographers. For example, they can paint mythological or imaginary subjects and can achieve nonrepresentational effects not associated with a camera, such as a medieval allegorical style or the striking distortions of Cubism. Also, the ways that historical periods and cultural traditions influence painters' choices of subject matter, medium, and style affect what viewers see and feel about paintings. Background on the artist and his or her culture, historical period, and style of paintings (for example, Baroque, Impressionism, Expressionism, and Cubism) can be found in sources such as the Oxford Art Online database. In analyzing paintings, art critics and historians often contrast paintings that have similar subject matter (for example, two portraits of a hero, two paintings of a biblical scene, two landscapes) but that create very different dominant impressions and effects on viewers.

How to Analyze a Painting

Just as with photographs, you should ground your interpretation of a painting in close observation. Many of the elements introduced in the Strategies Chart 10.2 for analyzing photographs can apply or be adapted to the analysis of paintings. In addition, you will want to use Strategies Chart 10.3 to examine the unique elements of the paintings you are analyzing.

Strategies Chart 10.3 Strategies for Analyzing the Unique Elements of Paintings

Elements to Analyze	Questions to Ask about Rhetorical Effect
Design and shape of the painting: The width to height, division into parts, and proportional relationship of parts influence the impression of the painting.	What is the viewer's impression of the shape of the painting and the relationship of its parts? How does line organize the painting? Is the painting organized along diagonal, horizontal, or vertical lines?
Medium, technique, and brushstrokes: The material with which the painting is made (for example, pen and ink, tempera/ water colors, charcoal, oil paints on paper or canvas) and the thickness and style of brushstrokes determine the artistic effect.	In what medium is the artist working? How does the medium contribute to the impression of the painting? Are brushstrokes sharp and distinct or thick, layered, or fused? Are they delicate and precise, or are they vigorous? What effect does the awareness or lack of awareness of brushstrokes have on the appearance of the painting?

Sample Analysis of a Painting

As an example of an analysis of a painting, we offer an interpretation of *Museum Security (Broadway Meltdown)*, a painting by Jean-Michel Basquiat (1960–1988), a young black Neo-Expressionist artist working in the 1980s. (See Figure 10.7, a photograph of the painting being viewed by a museum visitor.) Basquiat brought political urgency to the role of the individual in society and art. Of Puerto Rican and Haitian descent, Basquiat spoke three languages from an early age: English, Spanish, and French. His mother encouraged his artistic ability from the time Basquiat was young, regularly taking him to museums. Basquiat's family ties to Haiti and Puerto Rico, along with his experience as a black artist in New York, influenced his work, which frequently referenced Puerto Rican and Haitian politics. Although Basquiat died at age twenty-seven of a heroin overdose, he was prolific during his short life, working in many different mediums and collaborating with artists and musicians such as Andy Warhol, Keith Haring, and David Bowie.

In his 1983 piece *Museum Security (Broadway Meltdown)*, Basquiat brings into focus the tensions in an artist's relationship with money, property, and surveillance, drawing on his history with graffiti and his experience with art institutions. Basquiat first gained recognition as one-half of the street art duo SAMO, which spray-painted poetic, political, and surrealist tags in and around Lower Manhattan, attacking consumerism and the avant-garde art scene. After SAMO broke up, Basquiat began painting on canvas. Known for his focus on the individual and the artist as hero, Basquiat often painted single figures, emphasizing the head with hats or crowns, or simply painted isolated heads. He portrayed black men policed by and resisting white societal control.

Museum Security echoes Basquiat's graffiti past in a striking, dense piece, characterized by his usual flurry of text, codes, and symbols, which initially overwhelms viewers. The large, seven-foot square canvas is painted in acrylic and oil stick. It is covered with swathes of black and off-white paint and a patch of paper collage, which serve as the background for multicolored text and the occasional image. At the center, hemmed in by this text, is a face with bared teeth and angry eyebrows, drawn in multicolored lines, controlled by the surrounding text while

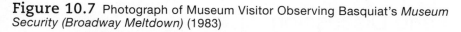

Figure 10.7 Photograph of Museum Visitor Observing Basquiat's *Museum Security (Broadway Meltdown)* (1983)

simultaneously bursting out of it. The painting at first feels busy. The few images in the piece are drawn in a flat style, but the variety of colors, repeated text, and street art techniques and aesthetics create depth. With the exception of bright, primary red, the colors are muted. Greens, tinged with blue, chalky pinks, and dull golden-yellows, contribute to the painting's distinctive texture.

As the viewer begins to focus on individual words, some of Basquiat's famous dichotomies—such as corporate conformity versus artistic expression, surveillance versus privacy, and control versus freedom—come into focus also. The collage of words, sometimes crossed out and rewritten, recalls Basquiat's work with SAMO and reads like an anticapitalist, anticolonialist litany: "sheriff," "law," "asbestos," "Hooverville" (a reference to Depression-era shantytown homelessness); "priceless art," "museum security," and the word "NEW" embedded in a comic-book drawing of an explosion. Another symbolic word, repeated several times, is "Papa Doc"—a reference to François Duvalier, President of Haiti from 1957 to 1971, who assumed the title "President for Life" and who represented totalitarian-style regimes and extreme political control over the public. This dictator had special significance for Basquiat because his paternal grandparents had been jailed under Duvalier's presidency, and Basquiat's father left Haiti when he was twenty. Basquiat includes references to currency as well, but in surprisingly small quantities—5 cents, 400 yen—drawing attention to disparities in wealth.

Through the painting's references to museums and museum security, Basquiat highlights questions related to public access to art. Historically, museums and art collectors have played their own complex role in colonialism, racism, and classism and have often neglected or excluded artists of color. Although Basquiat gained fame and respect among living artists during his short lifetime, he was frequently frustrated by institutional and structural exclusion. Mounted in a museum, *Museum Security* calls ironic attention to what counts as "museum-worthy." The painting's resemblance to street art makes it an agent of tension and rebellion that seems to mock the elitist values of the cultural space where it is exhibited. One of the great ironies of this painting is that on February 13, 2013, as reported by Bloomberg News, it was sold by Christie's auction house for approximately $14 million.

For Writing and Discussion
Contrasting the Compositional Features of Two Paintings

This exercise asks you to apply the ideas and questions presented in Strategies Chart 10.2 about analyzing photographs and Strategies Chart 10.3 on analyzing paintings to examine the painting *Reload* by contemporary Native American artist Natalie Ball, shown in Figure 10.8, and to compare and contrast it with Basquiat's painting in Figure 10.7. Natalie Ball, who holds a degree in Ethnic Studies and Indigenous Visual Arts from the University of Oregon and a Master in Maori Visual Arts from Massey University, New Zealand, works in painting, textiles, and figurative sculpture. She uses her art to speak to her complex ancestry—African-American, Anglo, and Native American (Modoc and Klamath tribes). In a 2012 interview for the *Contemporary North American Indigenous Blog*, she described her artwork as her "attempt at meshing historical narratives with counter memory, a type of political fantasy, to warrant suspicion as to what is the truth in order to challenge inconsistent and problematic historical narratives belonging to Native America." She painted *Reload* in 2007; the medium is acrylic and oil stick on canvas.

Working individually or in groups, analyze Ball's painting and then find some points of commonality or difference with Basquiat's painting. As you do your analysis, consider these questions: Why did Ball title her painting *Reload*? What view or feeling about life or about her world is she trying to convey? How is her vision similar to or different from Basquiat's? What ways of seeing or thinking are these paintings persuading you to adopt? How do these contemporary paintings by artists from underrepresented groups challenge dominant white culture and express alternative views?

Figure 10.8 Natalie Ball's *Reload* (2007)

Analyzing advertisements and advocacy posters

10.3 Analyze print ads and advocacy posters with attention to their compositional features, their integrated use of images and words, and their persuasive appeals to a targeted audience.

The images in advertisements are fascinating to analyze. Like other images, they employ the rhetorical strategies we described in the section on documentary photographs. Often, the ad's words (called the *copy*) also contribute to its rhetorical effect. Moreover, ads make a more direct and constant demand on us than do documentary photographs and paintings. Advertising, a multibillion-dollar global industry whose business is communicating across a wide range of media (the *media landscape*) to stimulate the purchase of products or services, comes to us in multiple forms: not just as slick, glamorous magazine ads, but also as direct mail, billboards, radio and television commercials, e-advertisements, bus ads, banners, pop-ups, and spam. Because of advertising's powerful role in shaping our culture and influencing our self-images, we have good reason to analyze the rhetorical strategies of advertisers. These same strategies can also be employed in advocacy posters urging public action for a cause.

Analyzing the Rhetorical Context of an Ad

Although in this section we focus primarily on print ads, it is important to recognize that most print ads are part of larger campaigns that play across the media landscape. Therefore, to analyze an ad, we need to think like an advertiser. Strategies Chart 10.4 will help you examine the rhetorical context of ads by prompting you to consider the behind-the-scenes decisions and negotiations that marketing professionals make when they are designing both individual ads and huge marketing campaigns.

Now that you have thought about the decisions and contexts that go into creating ads, the following exercise asks you to look at an ad from the inside out by creating your own.

Strategies Chart 10.4 Strategies for Analyzing the Rhetorical Context of Ads

Marketing Decisions	Questions to Ask about Rhetorical Context
Target audience: The specific audience identified for the product or service	Who is the target audience for this ad? More specifically, what gender, age, income level, ethnicity, and so forth are targeted? (For example, is the ad trying to reach low-budget or high-budget shoppers, steak eaters or vegans, skateboarders or geeks, the business community or parents?) What values, beliefs, and aspirations—assumed to be held by the targeted audience—does the advertiser appeal to?
Location in the media landscape: The variety of media where this ad appears; the positioning of the ad in various media	Is this ad a single ad or part of a larger marketing campaign? Does the ad appear in one media location only (magazines, newspapers, Internet pop-ups) or across the media landscape (also on billboards, on buses, as TV and radio commercials, wall posters in airports, T-shirts, coffee mugs, and other sites)? Is this a high-cost ad or a low-budget one? (A one-page ad in a nationally circulated magazine can cost $500,000 or more.) How does the positioning in the media landscape efficiently reach the target audience?
Goals of the ad: The goal could be to stimulate direct sales, develop long-term branding and image, or call forth a specific action	Is the goal of the ad to stimulate direct sales? ("Buy two, get one free.") Is the goal of the ad to build brand loyalty based on long-lasting relationships with consumers? (With *parity products*—products that are basically equal in quality among competitors—building brand loyalty is particularly important.) How do the advertisers and design teams try to conjure up a field of qualities, values, and imagery that consumers identify with? (For example, the goal is not just to buy Nikes but to become a Nike kind of person who identifies with the lifestyle and values in Nike ads.)
Use of "mirrors and windows" strategy: The psychological strategies used by product advertisers to motivate a target audience. The "mirrors" strategy urges targeted viewers to identify with a product by seeing their own self-image reflected in the ad. The "windows" strategy urges viewers to associate the product with their own dreams, hopes, fears, desires, and wishes for the future (often subconscious).	Is the strategy of mirrors and windows operating in this ad? How does the ad connect with the target audience's self-image so the audience says "I am part of the world reflected in this ad; I identify with this world" (mirror effect)? How does the ad provide a vision of the future, with promises of what ad viewers will become if they align with the brand (windows effect)? How does the ad promise to take consumers from their ordinary selves (mirror) to their aspirational selves (window)?

For Writing and Discussion
Designing an Ad Campaign

This exercise asks you to apply the marketing concepts in Strategies Chart 10.4 to designing your own ad. Imagine you are an advertising professional assigned to the Gloopers account. Gloopers is a seaweed (kelp)-based snack treat (a fiction, but pretend it is real) that is very popular under another name in Japan. It was introduced earlier in the American market and failed miserably—Americans said "Yuck! What sort of a treat is seaweed?" But now new laboratory evidence produces data showing that Gloopers provides crucial nutritional benefits for children and that it is a healthy alternative to junk food. Many snack food companies would kill for this scientific endorsement of their product's nutritional content, but this product is still made out of gunky seaweed. Working in groups or individually, develop a campaign for this product by working out your answers to the following questions:

- Who is your target audience? (Will you seek to appeal to parents as well as children?)
- What is your core message or campaign concept? (Think of a visual approach, including a mirror and window appeal, and perhaps a tagline slogan.)
- How could you use the mirrors and windows strategy?
- What is the best positioning in the media landscape for this campaign?
- How will you build a brand image and brand loyalty?

How to Analyze an Advertisement

In addition to thinking about the marketing decisions behind an ad, when you analyze a print ad you need to ask three overarching questions:

1. How does the ad draw in the target audience by helping them identify with the ad's problematic situation or story (mirror effect)?
2. How does the ad create a field of values, beliefs, and aspirations that serve as windows into a more fulfilled life?
3. How do the ad's images and words work together to create the desired persuasive effects?

For the images in an ad, all the strategies we have already described for documentary photographs and for paintings continue to apply—for example, angle of vision, framing, and so forth. (Review Strategies Charts 10.2. 10.3, and 10.4.) With many ads you also have to factor in the creative use of words—puns, connotations, and references to other ads or cultural artifacts. The words in an ad can interpret, comment on, reinforce, highlight, or otherwise shape readers' emotional and intellectual responses to the ad. In product ads that seek to build brand identity and loyalty, ad teams often create a tagline or slogan that conjures up a field of values that the target audience will identify with and that will be catchy enough to remember. In print ads, the use of type, space, and layout function as important visual elements. In our analysis, we must consider that in professionally created ads, every word, every punctuation mark, and every visual detail down to the props in the photograph or the placement of a model's hands are consciously chosen.

Strategies Chart 10.5 focuses on questions particularly relevant to print ads.

Strategies Chart 10.5 Strategies for Analyzing the Compositional Features of Print Ads

What to Do	Some Questions to Ask
Examine the settings, furnishings, and all other details.	• Is the room formal or informal; neat, lived-in, or messy? • How is the room furnished and decorated? • If the setting is outdoors, what are the features of the landscape: urban or rural, mountain or meadow? • Why are particular animals or birds included? (Think of the differences between using a crow, a hummingbird, or a parrot.)
Consider the social meaning of objects.	• What is the emotional effect of the objects in a den: for example, duck decoys and fishing rods versus computers and high-tech printers? • What is the social significance (class, economic status, lifestyle, values) of the objects in the ad? (Think of the meaning of a groomed poodle versus a mutt or a single rose versus a fuchsia in a pot.)
Consider the characters, roles, and actions.	• Who are these people and what are they doing? What story line could you construct behind the image? • Are the models regular-looking people, "beautiful people," or celebrities? • In product advertisements, are female models used instrumentally (depicted as mechanics working on cars or as consumers buying cars) or are they used decoratively (bikini-clad and lounging on the hood of the latest truck)?
Observe how models are dressed, posed, and accessorized.	• What are the models' facial expressions? • What are their hairstyles and what cultural and social significance do they have? • How well are they dressed and posed?
Observe the relationships among actors and among actors and objects.	• How does the position of the models signal importance and dominance? • Who is looking at whom? • Who is above or below, in the foreground or background?
Consider what social roles are being played out and what values appealed to.	• Are the gender roles traditional or nontraditional? • Are the relationships romantic, erotic, friendly, formal, uncertain? • What are the power relationships among characters?
Consider how document design functions and how the words and images work together.	• What features of document design (variations of font style and size, placement on the page, formal or playful lettering) stand out? • How much of the copy is devoted to product information or argument about superiority of the product or service? • How much of the copy helps create a field of values, beliefs, aspirations? • How do the words contribute to the "story" implied in the visual images? • What is the style of the language (for example, connotations, double entendres, puns)?

Sample Analysis of an Advertisement

Having explained strategies for analyzing the rhetorical context and compositional features of ads, we offer our own example of an ad analysis—for the advocacy ad shown in Figure 10.9. Because copyright law makes it difficult to use real ads in textbooks, we commissioned an ad team to create this ad for us, using the name of a fictitious organization, "Citizens for Reason." Our fictitious but very plausible ad focuses on the over-diagnosis of attention-deficit hyperactivity disorder (ADHD), a practice that classifies normal childhood behaviors as a problem to be treated medically.. The following sample analysis shows how close observation of an ad followed by analysis of its parts can yield an understanding of its persuasive strategies.

Figure 10.9

WHAT WOULD WE DO WITHOUT ADHD?

IT'S SUCH A CONVENIENT DIAGNOSIS. INATTENTION. DIFFICULTY FOCUSING. FIDGETING. MOOD SWINGS. TEMPER TANTRUMS. SOUNDS A LOT LIKE EVERYDAY CHILDHOOD, DOESN'T IT?

When did normal growing up become stigmatized into being a "condition," requiring serious psychoactive medication? Who benefits? Kids? Parents? Teachers? Hardly. You know who benefits. We used to worry about children discovering drugs on the playground. Now drugs are seen as a substitute for the playground. Is this any way to raise a generation?

CITIZENS FOR REASON

This striking advocacy ad criticizes the frequency of ADHD diagnoses. In its discussion of the target audience, media landscape, and goals for this ad, the ad team imagined a campaign aimed at families and parents, teachers and educators, and doctors and medical staff. The team envisioned the target audience encountering this ad in magazines to which families would subscribe or which they might find in waiting rooms in doctors' or school offices. Such magazines include *Parents*, *Parenting*, *Teach*, *Teaching PreK-8*, *Children's Health*, and *Kids Health & Wellbeing*. Also, variations on this ad might appear as billboards or posters. The goal of the campaign is to direct readers to Citizens for Reason and to cause adults in the target audience to reconsider the use of medication to control children's behavior.

When we analyze this ad, we note the dominance of the red, pink, orange, and yellow dragon and the size of the links in the chain link fence that separates the dragon from viewers. The image depicts an outdoor scene, a cropped photograph of a children's ride at an amusement park. The top half of the ad is occupied by the image and the bottom half features text. There are no people in this ad and noticeably no children, even though the ad is about children. The close-up, low-angle shot calls attention to the dragon, which is so big it fills almost the whole upper half of the ad, leaving room for only the hint of sky. The dragon's cartoon shape, its colors, and its size make it look both playful and somewhat disturbing. We can see one of the dragon's eyes, one of its horns, a hint of tooth, a hint of its tail, its gray belly, and one of its front feet with scaly claws. The bright colors signal the dragon's identity as a fantasy creature. The attraction of the dragon is complicated by the prominent chain link fence that stands between the viewers and the dragon, seeming to prevent access to the fun offered by the dragon. The red background for the bottom half of the ad containing the copy ties in well with the colorful dragon. The prominence of this primary red color—often associated with anger, passion, and violence—gives an air of something unmanageable to the big, humorous, playful dragon.

Why would the ad creators choose the concept of a fanciful amusement ride and a dragon, a creature of the imagination, for this ad that seeks to spur parents, educators, and medical staff to rethink the use of medication for active children? The words in the three bands of text in the lower half of the ad suggest the reasons for this choice. The largest type in white letters raises the pointed and provocative question "What would we do without ADHD?" The wording of this question suggests that the diagnosis ADHD serves a purpose. It benefits someone, and the "we" in the question is not children. The next layer of text in black answers the question with the words "convenient diagnosis" and lists the behaviors diagnosed as symptoms of ADHD: "inattention, fidgeting, mood swings, temper tantrums." But then the text offers a counterclaim: These behaviors are normal parts of childhood. The third chunk of text further drives home the ad's message that ADHD is frequently a misdiagnosis that is used to justify the prescription of medicine. The words in these sentences underscore the gulf between a child who is considered "normal" and a child who needs "serious psychoactive medication" and who is "stigmatized" with the label of a "condition."

Although the ad does not say it explicitly, it is directed against the pharmaceutical companies that make millions of dollars from the sale of medications while seducing parents into believing they are doing the right thing for their child. The final sentences accentuate this message and point out the negative changes that now govern parenting: "We used to worry about children discovering drugs on the playground. Now drugs are seen as a substitute for the playground." At this point it is clear why the dragon—representing outdoor fun and the playground—looks just ominous enough to be fenced off and why the color and the tone of the ad are disturbing. Citizens for Reason is asserting that our social values and judgments have become warped. A child's normal desires for play and normal rowdy behavior are now seen as abnormal. The ad calls the target audience to change the way that parents, under the influence of doctors and the pharmaceutical companies, are treating rambunctious children. These children need more understanding—someone to see the world through their eyes—and more play time, not quick fixes of medication.

We can now see how the ad makes ironic use of the mirrors and windows strategy. From the perspective of the medical community, the mirror is the rowdy child plagued by dragonlike emotions that pills can calm down, and the window is the safety of drugs that can build a fence between the child and the dragon. The parents' dream of a calm child can be achieved through purchase of medication. But from the ad-maker's perspective, the mirror is the medicated child barred from the energetic play represented by the dragon, and the window is the dismantling of the fence and the liberation of the child into the dragon's world of play. In this revised mirror-to-windows journey, the dragon only appears to be scary and dangerous. It is really a healthy playground.

Although this ad might have enhanced its *ethos* by citing facts and sources to validate its claims, the ad creators chose to work largely with appeals to *pathos* and with text statements and questions that build the *logos* of the case against medical treatment for ADHD. We think the ad is successful for its target audience because the impact of the bright colors, the memorable image, and the attention-grabbing text will continue to resonate in the minds of viewers and push them to consider *not* using medication to address their children's challenging behaviors.

For Writing and Discussion
Analyzing the Compositional Elements and Persuasive Effect of an Ad

Figure 10.10 is another mock ad for a new sound system product, Seeds from ClearVoyant. Use the compositional elements in Strategies Chart 10.5, as well as the other Strategies Charts in this chapter, to analyze this ad. Focus on these questions:

1. What is the story of the ad? Who are the characters? How would you describe their interaction?

2. What objects and details did the ad designers choose to include in this ad? Consider clothing, furniture, accessories, poses, and hairstyle. What is the social meaning of these objects and details? Consider what other choices the ad-designers could have made and then speculate why they made the decisions shown in the ad.

3. How does the copy contribute to the ad's persuasive effect? How do the ad-makers design the copy in terms of layout and use of type? Why did they make these choices?

4. Who is the target audience, and where in the media landscape might this ad appear?

5. Analyze the persuasive effects of this ad. How does it try to reach its target audience? How does it use the mirrors and windows strategy? What do you see as the main goals of this ad?

Figure 10.10

DO YOU KNOW WHERE YOUR PARENTS ARE?

SEEDS™
FROM CLEARVOYANT

They could be right in front of you, but they may not be paying attention. Because they're listening to "their kind of music" on the highest quality, smallest personal ear-in sound system in the world.

Seeds from ClearVoyant are so tiny, we're not even going to try to show them to you. You'll have to come into a Clear Store to see and hear them for yourself. Oh, and don't bother your parents for money. They're into the music – and maybe hipper than you.

Analyzing Posters

Posters share many similarities with product ads. They are often placed in highly visible locations where people will notice them (at a bus stop, in a shop window, posted on walls). The success of a poster comes from the way it focuses and encodes a complex meaning in a verbal-visual text, often using one or more striking images. Because one image must represent and transmit complex meaning, images in posters are often symbolic—for example, flags, homes, children at play, endangered animals, polluting smokestacks, beautiful landscapes, and so forth. Posters draw on these images to convey values shared with the target audience that the designers of the posters hope to activate. To accompany these images, posters often incorporate slogans or short memorable directives, and they blend the visual features of type size, font, and layout with the visual elements of color and images. (Strategies Charts 10.2, 10.4, and 10.5 are all useful in analyzing posters.) Posters are used elsewhere in this text to illustrate the power of images. (See the World War II "Beware the Water" poster in Concept 5.3, the "Black Lives Matter" poster in Figure 16.1, and the documentary film poster used in the Introduction to Part 4 of this text.)

A Sample Analysis of a Poster

Figure 10.11 is part of a poster series created by college students to combat what the poster-makers regard as casual, insensitive, racist attitudes toward other

Figure 10.11 Poster for Cultural Sensitivity

cultures. Racism manifests in many overt ways in our society, but also in more covert ways—for example, in the seemingly festive and playful costumes used on Halloween. There may be a fine line between cultural appropriation and cultural appreciation, but Halloween leads some people to make insensitive choices regarding their costumes. Every Halloween, some people choose costumes that are oversimplified, stereotypical, and wildly distorted representations of a culture that is not their own. Often, they do not understand why these costumes are hurtful to others.

The poster confronts this problem by using short, direct textual messages and contrasting images. The text at the top of the poster highlights the issue, recasting and reclaiming it for underrepresented and misrepresented cultures by stating, "We're a culture, not a costume." The poster delivers a strong directive, saying to viewers, "Don't behave like this." Notice how the word "not," repeated three times, underscores this message. The problem is illustrated by the poster's two images—a close-up photo of an Asian girl in a simple black T-shirt holding a picture of someone dressed in an elaborate geisha costume, complete with a black wig, white face paint, and long red nails. The photograph of the live person depicts her as sad and serious in contrast to the image in the drawing, which shows a woman posing as if she is acting. Together, the text and images convey the message that objectifying a culture for casual and shallow ends harms the people from that culture by reducing them to these exaggerated images. Contrasting the exaggerated costume with the individual it affects makes the poster's argument more quickly and more powerfully than would a lecture or essay on cultural appropriation. The person in a costume, the poster suggests, reduces a culture to a stagnant—often exaggerated—image, something that can be worn for a night for amusement and then discarded. However, the woman holding the picture deals with racism every day.

Ultimately, the poster hopes to discourage people from donning costumes that reduce people to stereotypes. However, it also aims to broaden awareness on a daily basis, rather than just on Halloween. This poster reminds us that making assumptions about individuals based on a culture is damaging and reductive, just like the costumes.

For Writing and Discussion
Analyzing the Compositional Elements and Persuasive Effect of a Poster

Using the strategies suggested throughout this chapter, analyze the poster in Figure 10.12. You might begin by doing an Internet search for Annie Leonard, an activist spokesperson for anticonsumerism, sustainability, and social justice. Then observe this poster closely. What is the background image? How do image and text work together? Examine the font and the layout. Consider the target audience and the message this poster wants this audience to understand and act on.

Figure 10.12 Poster by The Story of Stuff

Writing an image analysis essay

10.4 Write a comparative analysis of two visual texts.

Writing Project: Choose two documentary/news photographs, two paintings, or two advertisements to analyze in a closed-form essay. Your two visual texts should have enough in common to facilitate meaningful comparisons. Show these images in your essay (if you are analyzing videos, you'll need to show screen captures), but also describe your two visual texts in detail to highlight what you want viewers to see and to provide a foundation for your analysis. For this closed-form analysis, choose several key points of contrast as the focus. Your thesis statement should make a claim about key differences in the way that your chosen visual texts establish their purposes and achieve their persuasive effects.

Exploring and Generating Ideas for Your Analysis

For the subject of your analysis, your instructor may allow you to choose your own images or may provide them for you. If you choose your own, be sure to follow your instructor's guidelines. In choosing your visual texts, look for some important commonality that will enable you to concentrate on similarities and differences in your analysis:

- **Documentary or news photographs.** Analyze two photographs of an event from magazines with different political biases; two news photographs from articles addressing the same story from different angles of vision; or two images on Web sites presenting different perspectives on a recent controversial issue such as industrial farming, labeling genetically modified food, or transgender rights.
- **Paintings.** Find two paintings with similar subject matter but different dominant impressions or emotional impacts.
- **Print ads or television (YouTube) ads.** Look for two ads for the same product (for example, cars, perfume, watches, shampoo) that are aimed at different target audiences or that make appeals to noticeably different value systems.

No matter what type of visual texts you are using, we suggest that you generate ideas and material for your analysis by using the question-asking strategies presented earlier in this chapter's Strategies Charts.

To help you generate more ideas, go detail by detail through your images, asking how the rhetorical effect would be different if some detail were changed:

- How would this documentary photo have a different effect if the homeless man were lying on the sidewalk instead of leaning against the doorway?
- Why did the artist blur images in the background rather than make them more focused?
- What if the advertisers had decided the model should wear jogging shorts and a tank top instead of a bikini? What if the model were a person of color rather than white?

Shaping, Drafting, and Revising Your Analysis

Your closed-form essay should be fairly easy to organize at the big-picture level, but each part will require its own organic organization depending on the main points of your analysis. At the big-picture level, you can generally follow a structure like the one shown in Figure 10.13.

If you get stuck, we recommend that you write your rough draft rapidly, without worrying about gracefulness or correctness, merely trying to capture your initial ideas. Many people like to begin with the description of the two visual texts and then write the analysis before writing the introduction and conclusion. After you have written your draft, put it aside for a while before you begin revising.

Most experienced writers make global changes in their drafts when they revise, especially when they are doing analytical writing. The act of writing a rough draft generally leads to the discovery of more ideas. You may also realize that some of your original ideas aren't clearly developed or that the draft feels scattered or disorganized.

Figure 10.13 Framework for an Analysis of Two Visuals

Introduction	• Hooks readers' interest; • Gives background on the two visual texts you are analyzing; • Sets up the similarities; • Poses the question your paper will address; • Ends with initial mapping in the form of a purpose or thesis statement.
General description of your two visual texts (ads, photographs, paintings)	• Describes each visual text in turn.
Analysis of the two visual texts	• Analyzes and contrasts each text in turn, using the ideas you generated from your observations, question asking, and close examination.
Conclusion	• Returns to the big picture for a sense of closure; • Makes final comments about the significance of your analysis.

We recommend that you ask your classmates for a peer review of your draft early in the revising process to help you enhance the clarity and depth of your analysis.

Questions for Peer Review

In addition to the generic peer review questions listed in Skill 17.4, ask your peer reviewers to address these questions:

1. How well do the title, introduction, and thesis set up an academic analysis?

2. Where does the writer capture your interest and provide necessary background information? How might the writer more clearly pose the question to be addressed and map out the analysis?

3. Where could the writer describe the visual texts more clearly so that readers can "see" them?

4. How has the writer established the complexity of the texts and their commonalities and differences?

5. How well has the writer used the questions about angle of vision, artistic techniques, and compositional features presented in this chapter to achieve a detailed and insightful analysis of the texts? Where could the writer add more specific details about settings, props, posing of characters, facial expressions, styles of dress, story line, and so forth?

6. In what ways could the writer improve this analysis by clarifying, deepening, expanding, or reorganizing the analysis? How has the writer helped you understand something new about these two texts?

Multimodal or Online Assignment Options

For advice on preparing a podcast, see Skill 20.3.

1. **Museum Audioguide Podcast** Many art museums feature portable audioguide recordings that prompt viewers to pause in front of exhibits to hear an analysis of the painting or photograph. Assume that your chosen images (if you have selected two paintings or two documentary photographs) are exhibited side by side at a museum as part of a featured display. Create a podcast describing and analyzing the exhibits. You can assume that your audience will be looking at the exhibit as you talk.

For advice on preparing oral presentations with visual aids, see Skill 20.3.

2. **Lecture with Visual Aids** Assume that for a global business outreach program you have been invited to present an analysis of two ad campaigns for the same product or company as this product or company is marketed in different cultures. For example, how are Coca-Cola products advertised in China? How is McDonald's advertised in Central America? Prepare a lecture with PowerPoint or Prezi slides that you can record on video and upload to YouTube. Your slides can hone in on certain features of the ads as you talk.

Reading

Our reading is student Lydia Wheeler's analytical essay written for the writing project in this chapter. It analyzes two documentary photos focused on economic hardship and displacement. One photo, taken by photographer Stephen Crowley, accompanied a *New York Times* story about a mother and her daughters during the economic recession that began in 2008, which was caused by the collapse of the housing bubble in the United States. The subject, Isabel Bermudez, was subsisting on food stamps and unable to find a job; previously she had supported her daughters with a six-figure salary. Then the market collapsed and she lost her job. The second photo is a famous image taken in 1936 in Nipoma, California, during the Great Depression. The photo is part of the *Migrant Mother* series by photographer Dorothea Lange. Lydia decided to examine the original newspaper contexts for these photographs and to approach them as depictions of women's experiences of economic crisis.

Lydia Wheeler (student)

Two Photographs Capture Women's Economic Misery

1   During economic crises, the hardship of individuals is often presented to us as statistics and facts: number of bankruptcies, percentage of the population living below the poverty line, and foreclosures or unemployment rates. Although this numerical data can be shocking, it usually remains abstract and impersonal. In contrast, photographers such as Stephen Crowley and Dorothea Lange help us visualize the human suffering involved in the economic conditions, skillfully evoking the emotional, as well as the physical, reality of their subjects. Crowley's color photograph, first published January 2, 2010, in a *New York Times* article titled "Living on Nothing but Food Stamps," is captioned "Isabel Bermudez, who has two daughters and no cash income." Lange's black-and-white photograph was commissioned by the Resettlement Agency to document Americans living in the Great Depression; she originally captioned it *Destitute pea pickers in California; a 32 year old mother of seven children. February 1936.* However, in March of the same year, the *San Francisco Times* published Lange's photograph in an article demanding aid for workers like Florence Owens Thompson, the central subject of the picture. Once published, the photograph became famous and was nicknamed *Migrant Mother.* A close look at these two photos shows that through their skillful use of photographic elements such as focus, framing, orientation, and shape, Stephen Crowley and Dorothea Lange capture the unique emotional and physical realities of their subjects, eliciting compassion and admiration, respectively.

2   Stephen Crowley's photograph of a mother sitting in a room, perhaps the dining room of her house, and her young daughter standing and reaching out to comfort her sets up contrasts and tensions that underscore loss and convey grief. The accompanying article explains that Isabel Bermudez, whose income from real estate once amply supported her family, now has no income or prospect for employment and relies entirely on food stamps. A careful examination of Crowley's photograph implies this loss by hinting that Bermudez's wealth is insecure.

3   The framing, distance, and focus of Crowley's photograph emphasize this vanished wealth and the emotional pain. The image is a medium close up with its

human subjects to the side, surrounding them with empty space and hints of expensive furnishings. While part of the foreground is sharply focused, the background is blurry and unfocused. There is a suggestion that the room is spacious. Further, the high, decorative backs of the room's chairs, the repetitive design decorating the bookshelf on the frame's left, and the houseplant next to the bookshelf show that the room is well furnished, even luxurious. Bermudez and her daughter match their surroundings in being elegantly dressed. Bermudez looks across the room as if absorbed in her troubles; her daughter looks intently at her. Viewers' eyes are drawn to Bermudez's dark dress and her pearl necklace and earrings. However, the ostensible comfort of Bermudez and her surroundings starkly contrasts with her grief.

4   Crowley heightens this contrast and tension through the subjects' orientation and the space between them. The space between Bermudez and her daughter is one of the photograph's dominant features, but it contains only out-of-focus objects in the background. Neither figure is centered in the photo; neither looks at the camera. Consequently, the viewers' attention moves back and forth between them, creating a sense of uneasiness. The meaning of this photo is focused not on what Bermudez has but on what she has lost.

5   Crowley also evokes sympathy and compassion for his subjects with his choice of angle, scale, and detail. The photograph's level close up of Bermudez creates intensity, drawing viewers to look at her face. Viewers feel her vulnerability and powerlessness and realize that her losses in the economic crisis could be theirs The most striking bid for compassion is the tears streaming down Bermudez's well-made-up face. The contrast between her tidy appearance and the tear tracks on her face suggests overwhelming sadness. The poignancy of her apparent breakdown is heightened by her somber daughter's attempt to wipe away the tears on her mother's face. Crowley's decisions regarding *Isabel*'s composition create an image that makes disturbing appeals to pathos.

Isabel Bermudez, who has two daughters and no cash income, by Stephen Crowley

Destitute pea pickers in California; a 32 year old mother of seven children [*Migrant Mother*] by Dorothea Lange

6   In contrast to Crowley's photograph, Lange's *Migrant Mother*—through its content, focus, frame, rhythm, and angle—conveys long-standing poverty. Yet through this image of inescapable poverty pressing upon its subjects, it evokes admiration for this mother.

7   Lange's frame and focus generate much of the intensity of *Migrant Mother*. This photo is also a medium close up, but Lange's frame is tight with no open space. The lack of this openness cramps Lange's subjects and creates a claustrophobic feel intensified by the number of subjects shown—four to *Isabel*'s two. There is almost no background. The subjects filling the foreground are crowded and sharply focused. The contrast between crowded foreground and empty background exaggerates the former and adds a touch of loneliness to *Migrant*

Mother; this mother has no resources besides herself. Additionally, the subjects of *Migrant Mother* almost epitomize poverty: Their hair is messy and uncombed, their skin dirt-stained. Even their clothes are worn—from the hem of Thompson's frayed sleeve to the smudges on her baby's blanket, Lange's photograph shows that Thompson can barely afford functional items.

8   *Migrant Mother*'s circular lines also create a sense of sameness, stagnation, and hopelessness. Thompson's face draws viewers' eyes as the dominant feature, and Lange has ringed it with several arcs. The parentheses of her standing children's bodies, the angle of her baby in its blanket, and the arc of her dark hair form a ring that hems Thompson in and creates a circular path for the eyes of viewers. Seen with the obvious destitution of Lange's subjects, this repetition is threatening and grimly promises that it will be difficult, if not impossible, for this family to escape its poverty.

9   Like Crowley's *Isabel*, the impact of Lange's *Migrant Mother* derives from both the tragedy of her subjects' situation and their reactions. Lange uses angle and scale to generate sympathy and admiration for Thompson's strength. We see a slightly high angle highlighting the subjects' vulnerability, which Lange reinforces by the slender necks of Thompson's children and a glimpse of her brassiere. However, Lange then contrasts this vulnerability with Thompson's strength, fostering viewers' admiration rather than compassion. *Migrant Mother*'s scale, for example, exaggerates rather than diminishes Thompson's size: the photograph's frame focuses viewers' attention on the mother, who looks large, compared to her children. Additionally, Lange's subject literally supports the bodies of the children surrounding her. Unlike Bermudez, Thompson sits tall as a pillar of strength for her vulnerable children. Even her expression—worried but dry-eyed—fosters admiration and respect in viewers. By juxtaposing Thompson's vulnerability with her strength, Lange creates a photograph that conveys both its subjects' poverty and their stoicism in facing the Great Depression.

10   Lange and Crowley guide viewers' reactions to their photographs through careful control of the elements that influence our emotional responses to their work. Though they both show women in economic crises, these artists are able to convey the distinct realities of their subjects' situations and consequently send viewers away in different emotional states: one of compassion, one of admiration. The fame and veneration of Lange's *Migrant Mother* is a testament to her ability to evoke desired emotions. The photograph was exhibited at the Museum of Modern Art in 1941 and again in 1955, and was co-opted by countless movements since it was first published. Whether Crowley's *Isabel* will achieve similar fame for epitomizing this generation's economic crisis remains to be seen, but both photographs certainly succeed in delivering strong, lasting emotional statements.

THINKING CRITICALLY
About "Two Photographs Capture Women's Economic Misery"

1. What photographic elements has Lydia chosen to emphasize in her analysis of each of these photos?
2. What parts of Lydia's analysis help you see and understand these photos with greater insight? Do you agree with her choice of important elements and her analysis of their effects?
3. If you were analyzing these photos, what features would you choose to compare and emphasize?

Chapter 11
Writing a Literary Analysis Essay

Learning Objectives

11.1 Understand the difference between reading literally and reading literarily.

11.2 List and describe the elements of a literary text.

11.3 Practice the process for analyzing a short story.

11.4 Pose an interpretive question about a short story and write an analytical argument in response using textual detail for support.

Understanding literary analysis

11.1 **Understand the difference between reading literally and reading literarily.**

This chapter asks you to apply your skills of analysis to a short story by reading *literarily* rather than *literally*. When you read something **literally**, you attempt to reduce its meaning to one clear set of statements without ambiguity. When you read something **literarily**, you value ambiguity, perceive possible layers of meanings within the text, and enlist your imagination to fill in gaps and bring the story to life. To exercise your imagination fully, you must read closely and actively, connecting the dots created by the author's words into an imaginary movie in your mind.

To illustrate what we mean by reading literarily versus literally, consider the difference between a six-word declarative sentence and a six-word short story (allegedly by Ernest Hemingway)—widely regarded as one of our language's shortest stories:

Declarative sentence: Baby shoes are on sale tomorrow.

Short Story: For sale: Baby shoes. Never worn.

If you are like most readers, you processed these two examples differently. The declarative sentence simply states a fact that requires little imaginative energy from the reader. In contrast, the short story invites readers to slow down, to fill in gaps, to create their own mental images of a plot with characters. These six words, sequenced as three idea-bearing units or elements, invite readers to imagine a couple who were expecting a baby and, during the pregnancy, bought baby shoes in anticipation of happy days ahead. Then, before this anticipation could be fulfilled, they must have lost the baby. Now they are selling the shoes, perhaps trying to reach closure by wiping away the memories. The last two words of the story, "Never worn," produce the kind of layered multiple meanings characteristic of literature. On the one hand, "never worn" (or "never used") is simply the way people advertise a secondhand item that is actually new. On the other hand, the two words startle us with the realization that the baby didn't live, evoking our sadness that tiny feet never touched these tiny shoes. The story works only if we help make it work. In other words, we have to use our imaginations to read literarily rather than literally.

Critical elements of a literary text

11.2   List and describe the elements of a literary text.

The difference between closed-form and open-form prose is introduced in Concept 3.1. See also Chapter 18 on closed-form prose and Chapter 19 on open-form prose.

Short stories, along with novels and literary nonfiction (such as the autobiographical narrative explained in Chapter 7), belong to the category of open-form prose, which uses literary elements such as plot, character, setting, imagery, metaphor, and theme to create meaning in ways different from that of thesis-governed closed-form prose. To analyze a short story, you will need to be familiar with the critical elements that comprise a literary text.

Formal Elements

Stories involve sequences of narrative events that take place within time. The formal elements of a story are plot, character, and setting, which work together to create the story's theme. These formal elements occur in any kind of narrative prose, whether fiction or nonfiction. To analyze a short story, you need to explore the relationships among these formal elements, which we explain in detail in Chapter 7 on writing an autobiographical narrative. Rather than repeat the explanations here, we ask you to see the discussion of literary elements in Chapter 7, which are as relevant to short stories as they are to autobiographical narratives. Also in Chapter 7, read our analysis of Kris Saknussemm's "Phantom Limb Pain"

Tension and Resolution

The difference between an "and then" narrative and a story is explained in Chapter 19, Skill 19.1.

In a story, the chronological events are connected causally or thematically to create tension that is resolved through action, insight, or understanding. A story's plot (the actions of the characters within settings) is artistically designed to create and resolve tension in such a way that all the story's formal elements work together purposefully. A story thus differs from an "and then" narrative that simply recounts events chronologically without point or significance. When you analyze a short story, you'll need to identify the story's sources of tension and try to see how these tensions are resolved or left open. How tension gets resolved contributes to the story's theme—that is, to its meaning or significance. But the meaning of the story can't be summed up in a single statement. It has layers of meanings or, to use metaphors from music rather than space, various pitches or resonances that cause us to hear different combinations of sounds rather than single notes.

Ambiguity and Layered Meanings

Open-form prose often evokes ambiguity whereas closed-form prose usually tries to avoid it. Ambiguity allows us to hold in tension several different layers of meaning at once. The word "ambiguity" comes from the Latin words *ambi* meaning "both ways" and *agere* meaning "to lead or drive." Ambiguous words, metaphorically speaking, lead us two ways at once. Within an ambiguous word or phrase, two or more meanings may be echoing simultaneously.

Often ambiguities are sparked by figurative language such as similes or metaphors. If we say "A great football coach is a chess master," our minds are led in the direction of football and chess simultaneously. The sentence doesn't mean literally that great football coaches are great chess players, but it invites us to consider how football strategy and chess strategy share similar elements. Ambiguity or layered meanings can also be triggered by the internal context of a story. The following humorous example illustrates how context can cause words to go "two ways at once." Consider what happens to the apparently unambiguous phrase "Some people just need a pat on the back" when it is put in an unexpected context, as in the following example found on a T-shirt:

See Skill 19.4: "Tap the power of metaphors and other tropes."

Now the "pat on the back" must be read ironically not as an affectionate sign of support but as a shove down the stairs. The humor resides in the tension between two different ways of reading the same line. Similarly, in a story a simple statement such as "You look nice," could echo with different meanings depending on the context. We can imagine contexts in which a speaker might be genuinely sincere (you really do look nice), ironic (actually you look hideous), or awkwardly conflicted (you look tired and stressed out, but I'm trying to be kind).

Historical and Cultural Context

Literary texts have an historical and cultural context based on the time in which the story was written as well as the time period it depicts. The historical/cultural contexts create the societal conversations that the text grows out of, reflects, and contributes to. In a few moments we will ask you to read a short story titled "The Barbie Birthday," which obviously joins a cultural conversation about the role of Barbie dolls in socializing American girls into womanhood. The story's historical/cultural context is triggered both by the title of the story (our preexisting cultural knowledge tells us who Barbie is) and by the author's quotation from *The Barbie Chronicles*, which is a book devoted entirely to the cultural debate about Barbie. Based on this context, we expect the story to make its own contribution to this conversation.

A process for analyzing a short story

11.3 Practice the process for analyzing a short story.

When you analyze a short story, we recommend that you begin by rereading it carefully several times. The shorter the story, the more you can reread it, keeping in mind the critical elements of a literary text that we just described. We will illustrate the process of analyzing a short story with "The Barbie Birthday," which is an example of a very short story—often called *flash fiction*—which is becoming increasingly popular in the digital age. Flash fiction lovers have created a vigorous market for stories that can be read on a single computer screen or on a smartphone while waiting for a bus. Flash fiction stories contain all the elements of longer fiction—plot, character, setting, figurative language, and imagery—all working together to express a theme. The analytical skills you use in reading flash fiction can also be applied to longer fiction. We invite you now to read "The Barbie Birthday."

Alison Townsend
The Barbie Birthday

> Girls learn how to be women not from their dolls but from the women around them.
>
> Yona Zeldis McDonough, *The Barbie Chronicles*

The first gift my father's girlfriend gave me was the Barbie I wanted. Not the original—blond, ponytailed Barbie in her zebra-striped swimsuit and matching cat-eye shades—but a bubble-cut brunette, her hair a color the box described as "Titian," a brownish-orange I've never seen since. But I didn't care. My hair was brown too. And Barbie was Barbie, the same impossible body when you stripped off her suit, peeling it down over those breasts without nipples, then pulling it back up again. Which was the whole point, of course.

There must have been a cake. And ten candles. And singing. But what I remember is how my future stepmother stepped from the car and into the house, her auburn curls bouncing in the early May light, her suit of fuchsia wool blooming like some exotic flower, just that, then Barbie—whom I crept away with afterwards, stealing upstairs to play with her beneath a sunny window in what had been my parents' bedroom.

She likes me; she really likes me, I thought, recalling Shirley's smile when I opened the package. As I lifted the lid of Barbie's narrow, coffin-like box, she stared up at me, sloe-eyed, lids bruised blue, lashes caked thick with mascara, her mouth stuck in a pout both seductive and sullen. Alone, I turned her over and over in my hands, marveling at her stiff, shiny body—the torpedo breasts, the wasp waist, the tall-drink-of-water legs that didn't bend, and the feet on perpetual tiptoe, their arches crimped to fit her spike-heeled mules as she strutted across the sunny windowsill.

All Barbie had to do was glance back once and I followed, casting my lot with every girl on every block in America, signing on for life. She was who I wanted to be, though I couldn't have said then, anymore than I could have said that Barbie was sex without sex. I don't think my stepmother-to-be knew that either, just that she wanted to please me, the eldest daughter who remembered too much and who had been too shy to visit. My mother had been dead five months, both her breasts cut off like raw meat. But I yearned for the doll she'd forbidden, as if Barbie could tell me what everything meant—how to be a woman when I was a girl with no mother, how to dress and talk, how to thank Shirley for the hard, plastic body that warmed when I touched it, leading me back to the world.

For Writing and Discussion
Reading "The Barbie Birthday" Literarily

Working individually, explore your responses to the following questions. Then share ideas in small groups or as a whole class.

1. What does the story suggest or imply about the value of Barbie dolls or about the role of Barbie dolls for girls growing up?
2. What does it suggest or imply about the relationship of daughters to mothers or stepmothers?
3. The narrator calls the box that the Barbie comes in "coffin-like." What effect does this image have on your interpretation of the story?
4. What are some more puzzling questions that you might pose about this story?

Now that you have thought about the story, you can use the following process to help you deepen your analysis.

Write a Plot Summary

To read literarily, a good first task is simply to articulate what happens in the story at a literal level. An effective strategy is to write your own plot summary of the story. Later, when you analyze the story, you will be showing why the story itself is much richer and more complex than the plot summary alone. Here is our plot summary of "The Barbie Birthday."

The narrator recalls that on her tenth birthday her father's girlfriend, Shirley, gave her a Barbie doll. She particularly remembers the moment that Shirley stepped from her car into the house and met the narrator, apparently for the first time. The narrator loved every feature of this Barbie doll and played with it in her parents' bedroom. Near the end of the story we learn that the narrator's mother had been dead for five months. The mother had died of breast cancer and had forbidden her daughter to have a Barbie.

Pose Possible Interpretive Questions

The next step is to switch from reading literally to reading literarily, trying to figure out how all the elements of the story connect and contribute to the story's theme. That is, before you can fully and persuasively argue what you believe the story expresses or suggests at the thematic level, you must first explore the elements that the story uses to convey that theme. You are looking for puzzling elements of the story—parts or layers or resonances that don't at first seem to fit or that strike you as perhaps significant but you can't figure out why.

Because the thesis of academic prose typically addresses a problem, your first step is to identify an interpretive problem arising from the text. Strategies Chart 11.1 will guide you through the critical elements of literary analysis, helping you pose interpretive questions or problems. The last column shows our own problem-posing questions based on "The Barbie Birthday."

Strategies Chart 11.1 Strategies for Posing Questions about Formal Features of a Short Story

Formal Feature	Possible Questions to Ask	Illustrations from "The Barbie Birthday"
Character	Who are the main characters in the story? What are each character's values? Which characters are flat and which are round? Which characters change and which are static? What is the significance of any changes? Are any of the characters ambiguous or hard to figure out? If so, why?	How are Shirley's values different from the dead mother's values? How does the narrator change from her ten-year-old self to her adult self? How does the narrator's attitude toward Barbies change?
Plot	What puzzling things happen in the story? What tensions or conflicts develop? Are there any turning points? Do the events occur in chronological order, or is time sequence distorted and, if so, why? Does the action take place in one place, or is there movement from one location to another? Is this switch in locality significant (see also Setting)?	Why does Shirley give the girl a bubble cut brunette Barbie rather than a blond, pony-tailed Barbie? Why does the child worry whether Shirley "likes her"? Does the Barbie gift create a turning point in the narrator's life? Why do the events occur out of chronological order (we hear about the dead mother late in the story, not at the beginning)?
Point of view	Is the narration first person or third person? Is the narrator omniscient (knows the inner thoughts of all characters) or limited (knows the thoughts and actions of one character but sees other characters only through the eyes of the first character)? Is the narrator reliable, or is the narrator's (metaphorical) blindness or bias part of the narrative's plot? How does your awareness of point of view affect the way you read the narrative? With whom do readers sympathize?	The point of view is complex—an older, wiser, first-person narrator looks back on an event when she was ten. The narrator's point of view toward Barbies seems different from that of the ten-year-old. To what extent does the adult narrator still feel sympathy for her ten-year-old's view?
Setting	What are the physical characteristics of the setting? Are these used metaphorically? Do the settings shift as the narrative progresses? How does setting contribute to ambiguities, echoes, or resonances in the story? How does your awareness of time and place affect the way you read the narrative?	Almost all the description focuses on the Barbie rather than setting, but the setting might be important. Why does the main character play in her parents' bedroom rather than, say, her own bedroom?

Formal Feature	Possible Questions to Ask	Illustrations from "The Barbie Birthday"
Imagery, metaphor, and other figurative language	What are the dominant images in the story? What figures of speech occur in certain passages? What patterns do you find in the use of images, metaphors, or other figures of speech? What do you understand to be the purpose or meaning of these patterns?	Imagery, metaphors, and other figurative language often trigger resonances or layers of meaning. Why is the box Barbie comes in described as "coffin-like"? Why does the narrator choose "bruised blue" to describe Barbie's eyelids? What is the significance of the metaphor "warmed" in the last sentence? What is the significance of the difference between Barbie's "torpedo breasts" and the dead mother's breasts "cut off like raw meat"?
Language, tone, style	What is the significance of the author's language and style (sentence length, word choice, grammatical complexity, abstract versus concrete language)? Does the style change as the narrative progresses? Are different characters associated with differences in style/language? Is the style or tone ironic? Why?	The narrator as an adult seems to use words that would not have occurred to the ten-year-old—such as "torpedo breasts" or "breasts cut off like raw meat." What is suggested by the gap between the adult narrator's language and the language used by the child? Is the narrator ironic in saying that the Barbie led "me back into the world"?

Strategies for Posing Questions about the Contexts of a Short Story

Context	Possible Questions to Ask	Illustrations from "The Barbie Birthday"
Internal context	How does the relationship between characters or the timing of an event cause us to see ambiguities or "double meanings" in what characters say or think? How does context help us read between the lines at certain points?	A Barbie doll seems like an ordinary gift that many girls would receive on their tenth birthday. How does the context of this gift—given to the narrator by her future stepmother—have special significance? How does the context deepen our understanding of her concern whether Shirley "likes me"? Does the Barbie fill a void left by the dead mother?
Story's time period(s)	During what time period is the story set, and when was it written? What background knowledge about that time period is needed and relevant?	A Google search shows that Barbies were first marketed in 1959 and that some had bendable legs starting in 1965. The *Barbie Chronicles* was published in 1999. The narrator's adult time period is after 1999, but the ten-year-old's birthday may have occurred in the early 1960s.
Relevant cultural debates and anxieties	To what extent does the story participate in cultural debates occurring at the time of its publication? How does the narrative try to influence the readers' view of something? How does the narrative reflect cultural concerns and anxieties?	Why does the story open with a quotation from *The Barbie Chronicles*? What view of Barbie dolls does the story try to persuade us toward? Another relevant context is cultural anxiety about breast cancer or about stability of marriage. The father already seems to have replaced his wife with his new girlfriend, Shirley. But can Shirley replace the narrator's mother? Can the Barbie replace the mother?

Strategies for Putting It All Together: Posing Questions about Theme and Significance

	Possible Kinds of Questions to Ask	Illustrations from "The Barbie Birthday"
Tensions, conflicts	What are the chief tensions or conflicts in the story? What values or worldviews are in conflict? What cultural anxieties are reflected in the story? What cultural debates does the story join?	The chief tensions are between the contrasting views of Barbie dolls and contrasting role models for a young girl. What view of Barbie dolls emerges from this story? What view of mothers or of role models for girls emerges?

(continued)

	Possible Kinds of Questions to Ask	Illustrations from "The Barbie Birthday"
Resolution	To what extent are the tensions resolved? Does the story argue a position inside a cultural debate? Is there a single-view resolution or does the resolution try to hold in tension two or more contrasting views?	The ending of the story at first seems to resolve in favor of Barbies because the child's touch warms the plastic back into the child back into the world. But does the overall impact argue against Barbies? What is the story's final resolution of the tension?
Theme, significance	What does the story seem to be "about" in terms of ideas or of shared human issues, problems, or questions? Does the story make any arguments about good versus bad values, right versus wrong behavior, or meaningful versus trivial pursuits? What views of power or justice emerge from the story? To what extent does the title give us any hints about theme?	What is this story saying about womanhood and motherhood? Was it good or bad that Shirley gave the narrator a Barbie? What does the story say about death and loss and about the process of filling a spot left by an absent mother? What is the significance of the title, "The Barbie Birthday," which puts more emphasis on the Barbie than on the narrator?

Through Analysis, Determine Your Own Answers to Your Interpretive Questions

It is now time to wallow in complexity by further engaging your own critical thinking. Your goal is to work out some of your own answers to your interpretive questions. But recognize that you aren't looking for "right answers," just for plausible answers that you could support by reference to specific details in the text. One of the pleasures of literary analysis is the extent to which critics disagree about how to read a text. As in all academic writing, you will need to be aware of alternative interpretations and assume a skeptical audience who will read the story differently from the way you do.

Sample Analysis of "The Barbie Birthday"

To illustrate what a literary analysis might look like, we show you our own analysis of "The Barbie Birthday."

Alison Townsend's short story "The Barbie Birthday" tells the story of a young girl's pleasure over receiving a Barbie doll for her tenth birthday. The opening epigraph from *The Barbie Chronicles* draws attention to the cultural significance of Barbie and raises questions about the role Barbie dolls play in the life of young girls. Does the story reinforce a feminist rejection of Barbie for the way the Barbie culture objectifies women, as some readers might claim? Or does it treat Barbie more sympathetically? We argue that the tensions in this story between two views of Barbie are not fully resolved.

The major tension in this story is between two views of Barbie. One view is closely identified with the father's girlfriend, Shirley, who is the pro-Barbie woman. Through the Barbie birthday gift, Shirley initiates her relationship with this motherless ten-year-old girl. Shirley, the story suggests, resembles a Barbie doll in her fashionable appearance. Like the doll, Shirley has auburn hair similar to Barbie's "brownish-orange" hair. Shirley's outfit, as the narrator remembers it as she "stepped from the car" into the house, has the style and trendiness of the outfits made for Barbie. (And as all girls know, Barbie's fashionable wardrobe and endless accessories are her main attraction.)

The other view of Barbie comes from the girl's mother, who died five months previously of breast cancer and had forbidden her daughter to have one of these dolls. We wonder whether the mother had always objected to Barbies because of their materialism and sexual objectification of women, or whether her objection emerged during her battle with breast cancer when she lost all control of her own body and beauty, and therefore of her ability to guide her daughter through the Barbie stage of emerging womanhood. The story leaves this question unanswered; however, it is clear that the young girl, in gratefully accepting this present on her tenth birthday, "sign[s] on for life," to this culturally approved version of womanhood, along with "every girl on every block in America". The young girl eagerly receives the doll as a toy and as a guide to identity—"as if Barbie could tell me what everything meant—how to be a woman when I was a girl with no mother".

The tension between two views of Barbie also resides in the disconnect between the ten-year-old's thrill at getting a Barbie and the older narrator's interpretation of this incident from her adult perspective. The young girl's pleasure is twofold. The first pleasure comes from the doll itself. After opening the package, she is soon delighting in dressing and undressing her, which, as she says, "was the whole point, of course". She plays with Barbie, using the "sunny windowsill" in her parents' former bedroom as a stage for Barbie to "strut." She is resuming former play habits, and the familiar sunny spot seems comforting and pleasurable. An equally important pleasure, the story suggests, is the girl's realization that her father's girlfriend cares about her and will become a positive part of her life, filling the void left by the dead mother: *She likes me; she really likes me*, I thought, recalling Shirley's smile when I opened the package". Barbie represents both a cherished toy and a token of a new relationship that will be important for the young narrator in her loneliness over the loss of her mother.

However, interwoven with this positive view of Barbie are hints of death, darkness, and criticism. Whereas the ten-year-old loved her Barbie, the adult narrator, looking back, subtly associates the Barbie with a funeral and death: "As I lifted the lid of Barbie's narrow, coffin-like box, she stared up at me, sloe-eyed, lids bruised blue". The doll seems to have rigor mortis with its "stiff and shiny" body, its bruised eyelids, its mouth that was "stuck in a pout," and its "legs that didn't bend". The child in the moment of pleasure is unaware of the questions and meanings raised by the Barbie, as her happy play with Barbie indicates. However, the older narrator now links the Barbie image not with the bouncing, auburn-curled Shirley but with a bruised, sloe-eyed cadaver. The adjective "sloe-eyed" transfers to the doll the qualities of sloe, i.e., dark purple plums or blackthorn fruit with a sour taste. If the narrator as a young girl thinks Barbie can teach her "how to dress and talk" in a culturally sanctioned way, the older, wiser narrator perceives this toy as an unrealistic, warped, and dangerous image of womanhood: "feet on perpetual tiptoe," "the torpedo breasts [without nipples], the wasp waist". She also underscores the irony of an image of female beauty that had proved to be so fragile and destructible in the dying mother with her breasts "cut off like raw meat". The gift of this forbidden toy seems to accentuate the absence of the mother, who would have guided her daughter differently from the way that Shirley (and the dominant culture) did.

The story further asks readers to accept a degree of irresolution in this tension between Barbie as a wonderful toy and Barbie as an image of death. Although the older narrator sees the wisdom in the mother's prohibition of Barbie's false and shallow vision of womanhood, she acknowledges Barbie's value. This ambiguity is powerfully conveyed in the last lines of the story when she describes Barbie as "the hard plastic body that warmed when I touched it, leading me back to the world". The body is "hard" and "plastic"—lifeless and fake—and yet this Barbie plays a vital role in this girl's life. Pulling her out of her grief and reconnecting her to the present, the doll warms to her touch and revives her interest in life.

In its various powerful tensions, this story refuses simple answers about the value of Barbie dolls and their effects on young girl's budding womanhood. With its title—"The Barbie Birthday"—the story emphasizes both the culturally iconic doll and the girl's taking one more step toward assuming her grown-up identity. Ultimately, we argue that in its tensions and ambiguities, this story offers insight into the cultural confusion facing young girls as they grapple with distorted but appealing images of femininity represented by Barbie dolls and harsh realities facing women, including young mothers whose bodies and lives are destroyed by cancer.

Writing a literary analysis essay

11.4 Pose an interpretive question about a short story and write an analytical argument in response using textual detail for support.

> **Writing Project:** Pose an interpretive question about a short story and respond to it analytically, showing your readers where and how the text of the story supports your interpretation. Use the introduction of your essay to pose your interpretive question, showing how it is both problematic and significant. Your one-sentence summary answer to that question will serve as your thesis statement. Your task in this assignment is not to discover the right way to interpret the text, but to show why your analysis is plausible and can be supported by textual detail.

Although this assignment asks you to analyze an open-form short story, the essay you produce should be closed-form academic prose. Before you give your thesis, make clear what question you are putting to the text and why. It is this question that will engage your readers' interest and make them look forward to your analysis. Then, in the body of your paper, use your close reading of key scenes and passages to support your interpretation. You should be aware of alternative readings and imagine a skeptical audience. Without necessarily disputing the alternative interpretations, concentrate on showing your readers how you arrived at *your* interpretation and why you think that your interpretation can deepen your readers' appreciation of the story. A student example of an analytical essay written to this assignment is Michelle Eastman's analysis of "Forsythia" in the readings section of this chapter.

Generating and Exploring Ideas

We suggest that you follow the process that we explained in our own analysis of "The Barbie Birthday."

WRITE A PLOT SUMMARY   Begin by writing a summary of the plot. The act of simply saying what happens in the story can urge you to ponder the function of the material that makes the whole story richer and more complex than the plot summary itself.

See our summary of "The Barbie Birthday" earlier in this chapter.

POSE POSSIBLE INTERPRETIVE QUESTIONS   Return to Strategy Chart 11.1, which we used for posing possible questions about "The Barbie Birthday." In the third column of the chart we posed questions about the Barbie story. Use these as models for possible questions you can pose about the story that you are analyzing. As you pose questions, let your mind play with possible ways you might answer them. Especially rich are questions that also puzzle your classmates or that lead to disagreements during discussions. Your goal is to begin seeing how all parts of the story "connect."

Choosing Your Problematic Question and Exploring Your Answer

You're now ready to choose the question that will initiate your essay and to explore your answer. If you have posed a number of different questions about your story, identify the one that seems the most significant, interesting, and manageable to you, realizing that one of the principles of effective open-form prose is "connectedness"—that is, all the story's details, if read *literally*, contribute in some way to the story's theme and meaning.

Shaping, Drafting, and Revising

As you write your first draft, follow the general principles for composing and revising closed-form prose. Literary analysis is a form of academic argument that follows a problem-thesis pattern, as shown in the Framework for a Literary Analysis Essay (Figure 11.1).

After you have produced a good rough draft, let it sit for a while. Then try it out on readers, asking them to respond to the following questions for peer

Figure 11.1 Framework for a Literary Analysis Essay

Introduction (one to several paragraphs)	• Poses your question about the text • Shows why your question is interesting, problematic, and significant • Presents relevant background about the story • Presents your thesis statement—a one-sentence answer to your question
Body (several paragraphs)	• Develops and supports your thesis using textual details and quotations and argument • Summarizes and responds to alternative interpretations (if not done in the introduction)
Conclusion	• Returns to your question and suggests why your answer is significant • Addresses the larger implications of your interpretation

review. Based on their advice, begin revising your draft, making it as clear as possible for your readers. Remember to start with the big issues and major changes and then work your way down to the smaller issues and minor changes.

Questions for Peer Review

In addition to the generic peer review questions listed in Skill 17.4, ask your peer reviewers to address these questions:

INTRODUCTION

1. Does the title arouse interest and forecast the problem to be addressed? How might the author improve the title?

2. How effectively does the introduction capture your interest, explain the question to be addressed, and suggest why it is both problematic and significant?

3. Does the introduction conclude with the writer's thesis? Is the thesis surprising? How might the author improve the introduction?

ANALYSIS AND INTERPRETATION

1. How is the essay organized? Does the writer helpfully forecast the whole, place topic sentences at the head of paragraphs (points before supporting details), use transitions, and follow the old/new contract as explained in Chapter 17? How might the author improve or clarify the organization?

2. Where does the author quote from the story (or use paraphrase or other specific references to the text)? How is each of the author's points grounded in the text? Where does the author do a particularly good job of reading *literarily* through attention to plot, character, setting, figurative language, and so forth? What passages not cited might better support the argument? What recommendations do you have for improving the author's use of supporting details?

3. Where do you disagree with the author's analysis? What aspects of the story are left unexplained? What doesn't fit?

Multimodal or Online Assignment Options

1. **Post to an Online Flash Fiction Site** If you do a Web search for "flash fiction," you will find numerous sites, many of which have a "comments" function where you can post your own analysis of a selected short story. Your goal is to find a flash fiction piece that invites analysis, and then post a comment that goes beyond the typical "liked it" or "didn't like it" response. Use strategies from this chapter to advance readers' understanding of the story and deepen their appreciation. Such a post would typically be shorter than the analyses modeled in this chapter, but it should have enough depth to make an engaging contribution to the way readers experience the story.

2. **Podcast Reading** Choose a flash fiction story and do a podcast reading of it as you imagine the author might read it. Read the story expressively to make readers engage with the story and think about it. Then, using the strategies from this chapter to examine how the story achieves its effects, give a brief commentary about several of its important literary features.

Readings

Our first reading is "Forsythia" by Jacquelyn Kolozov. It was first published in 2006 in the literary magazine *Pisgah Review.* Kolozov is the author of several young adult novels.

Jacqueline Kolosov

Forsythia

1   Miranda pulls the old Chevy into the drive. A neat row of daffodils and grape iris border the front walk. Here, too, forsythia blooms, the spiraling branches like captured sunshine. Beyond, the house is white-washed brick.

2   When Grace Wickersham steps onto the porch, Miranda's hands instinctively curve around her swelling belly. "Please come in." Grace's voice is husky, nervous.

3   This is only the second time they've met.

4   Inside, Miranda takes in the room in one long sweep. In the corner, there is an overstuffed sofa covered with red poppies. On the sofa a big, gray dog lies drowsing.

5   Grace's husband, Matt, enters with a plate of cookies and three glasses of juice. Miranda smiles at the bright drink chock full of vitamins. Surely she is the reason why they're drinking orange juice at three o'clock in the afternoon.

6   Crumbs fall into their laps as they circle around the subject that has brought them together. How could she possibly tell them that at night she lies awake thinking about keeping him, for she's sure he is a boy? In bed, with the curtains drawn back, the sky becomes a magician's cape, and the edges of reality are softened.

7   Morning restores the sharp outlines. In the kitchen, her mother's face is a grid of gray planes, and she is wearing the catsup stained factory uniform that always smells of sweat and tomatoes.

8   "We have two extra bedrooms upstairs," Grace Wickersham says, her eyes meeting Miranda's. "The one beside ours will be the baby's room. The other is for guests."

9   "What Grace is trying to say is we'd like you to be our guest for the remainder of the pregnancy," Matt adds. "We'd like to help you in any way we can."

10   Miranda is reminded of the neat rows of daffodils, the forsythia, their delicate branches swaying in the breeze. "Thank you," she says, "but I live at home with my mother and my sister Kate."

11   "We didn't mean to imply—" Matt says, fiddling with the ice in his glass.

12   "Do you think I could see the baby's room?" Miranda asks.

13   "I'll wait down here," Matt says, as the two women move toward the staircase.

14   Grace opens the door.

15   It is everything a child's room should be. The walls are a warm, honey gold. There is a border of crayon-bright sunflowers and frogs running along the floor. A refinished crib sits beside the window; beside it, a rocker.

16   "I spent the past month getting the room ready," Grace says.

17   Miranda nods, unable to imagine how it would feel to be an expectant mother painting flowers and animals on the walls of a room in her own home, then sitting down in the rocker to admire her handiwork, a cup of tea warming her hands.

18   "Would you like to see the extra room?" Grace asks her then.

19   "All right."

20   Down the hallway, Grace opens another neatly painted door, and Miranda beholds a double bed, heaped with pillows. A single dresser holds a crystal vase filled with forsythia. White lace curtains adorn the windows. The room is exactly what Miranda would have chosen for herself.

21   "We thought it would be nice to get to know each other better," Grace tells her.

22   Miranda watches the play of sunlight in Grace's long auburn hair. She would like to take the silver-backed brush from the dresser and run it through Grace's hair. She would like to tell Grace that the baby's father is on a scholarship at the University of Michigan. He, too, comes from one of the factory towns, but he managed to get out. Miranda doesn't even know when she will see him again.

23   What she does know is she cannot move into this sunny room. If she were to enter into the inner spaces of this life, how would she ever find the strength to say goodbye?

24   On the drive back to Ipswich, Miranda listens to Bruce Springsteen sing about love and amusement parks. The song brings back the summer her father took her and her sister to a carnival. Miranda's front tooth was loose, and as they walked through the fairgrounds, she kept wiggling it with her tongue. She wanted to loosen it, but she didn't want it to fall out there. Miranda was afraid of losing that tooth, afraid of missing out on the tooth fairy's visit.

25   Miranda's father held her hand and Kate's. They passed the Ferris wheel with its Lifesaver-colored lights, the shooting gallery with its toys. Even with her small hand in his, Miranda hadn't felt secure.

26   Her father, a very tall man with rough, reddish whiskers, looked down. "What's the matter, little mouse?" he asked. "Aren't you having fun? You're supposed to be having fun."

27   After that, Miranda tried hard to have fun. She wanted to please her father. She wanted to show him that she was a good girl.

28   That next summer when the carnival returned, Miranda had already lost half a dozen more teeth. And that next summer, her father was already gone.

29   When Miranda told her mother that she was going to have a baby, her mother stayed silent for a long time, her hopes and fears interlaced as tightly as her hands. "I just don't want you to wind up like me," her mother said finally. "I want you to have more choices in your life."

30   Miranda understood what her mother was saying. Don't become a woman with a high school diploma, a job at the catsup factory, a mortgage on a ramshackle house, two daughters, and no husband.

31   *And yet*, Miranda thinks, *you did your best.*

32   Miranda nears the Ipswich exit and recalls the daffodils and the forsythia, the hopping frogs and sunflowers, the white wicker rocker, and understands—deep within herself, where her baby stirs—that, by giving up her child to them, she won't be doing her best for him, but she will be doing the best she can.

33   And this, she knows, *this* will have to be enough.

Our last reading is an analysis of "Forsythia" by student writer Michelle Eastman. This literary analysis essay was written for the assignment in this chapter.

Michelle Eastman (student)

Unconditional Love and the Function of the Rocking Chair in Kolosov's "Forsythia"

1   In Jacqueline Kolosov's short story "Forsythia," Miranda decides to give her baby up for adoption after thinking about the details of the adoptive family's home. An important feature in the home is the rocking chair in the baby's bedroom, first mentioned when Miranda notes that the bedroom with its rocker "is everything a child's room should be" (149). At the end of the story—as the final detail about the house—the rocker is described more fully as "white wicker" (151). What function does this rocking chair serve in the story? Miranda's repeated mention of the rocker suggests that is it more than simply a piece of furniture. I believe that the chair represents domestic security and suggests a mother's unconditional love for her child. But it also reminds Miranda of her status as an outsider and of the different direction her life is heading. The rocker is what allows her to realize that she cannot keep her baby. By giving the baby to Grace and Matt, Miranda hopes that her son will have the unconditional love that is missing from her own life.

2   At first, the rocker in the baby's room represents Miranda's awareness of how different her economic and social status is from that of Grace and Matt. Miranda is "unable to imagine how it would feel to be an expectant mother painting flowers and animals on the walls of a room in her own home, then sitting down in the rocker to admire her handiwork, a cup of tea warming her hands" (149). To be able to take that kind of time and care in preparing for a baby implies having the resources to do so, resources that Miranda lacks. Grace and her husband Matt live in a house that is carefully put together with its "neatly painted door[s]" for the upstairs bedrooms, the "warm honey gold" walls of the baby's room, the "double bed, heaped with pillows" in the guest room along with a vase of flowers and "[w]hite lace curtains"—all surrounded by "forsythia blooms . . . like captured sunshine" (149). There is even a "big gray dog . . . drowsing" on the sofa (148).

3   In contrast, Miranda lives in a "ramshackle" house and pictures her mother, whose face is like a "grid of gray planes," "wearing the catsup-stained factory uniform that always smells of sweat and tomatoes" (148). Like Miranda, her mother does not have a husband (he seems to have abandoned the family years before), so the mother has to support her children by herself with her limited factory worker's pay. Miranda has no clue about whether her boyfriend will be a part of her life, so like her mother she does not have someone to provide financial and parental support to her and her child. While Miranda does fantasize about keeping the child, a part of her also wants to escape her mother's fate.

4   The rocker thus represents the economic security and domestic stability of the Wickershams' middle-class, two-parent family. Miranda's own life is represented instead by the ups and downs of a Ferris wheel at a carnival. Prompted by the "Bruce Springsteen song about love and amusement parks," Miranda remembers a childhood visit to a carnival with her father (150). Miranda recalls how she was afraid of losing her tooth and how she did not feel "secure" holding her father's hand (150). Her insecurity stems from the notion that when her father asks what the problem is, he tells her that she "is supposed to be having fun," which Miranda

takes to mean that she must try "to have fun" to be "a good girl" in order "to please" him (150). Miranda's efforts to gain her father's approval show that she feels his love is conditional based on his approval of her behavior. A couple of years later, Miranda's father himself disappears from the family's life. Miranda's insecurity connects back to the Wickershams' invitation to live with them during the remainder of her pregnancy. Whatever love she would feel in the Wickersham household would also be conditional based on her ability to give them a baby. Her stay would be only temporary, and then she would disappear from the Wickershams' lives.

5   Although Miranda is unable to feel security and love in her own life, she still hopes that her baby might find unconditional love in the Wickershams' home. The interconnection between mother and child is represented by the "white wicker" rocker. The rocker represents the interconnection between mother and child because it would be a primary place where Grace would bond with her baby, rocking her child to sleep. A wicker rocker represents this interconnection metaphorically because wicker furniture is made of interwoven strands of wood. These strands create a whole piece of furniture much in the way that mother and child are interconnected. (Although the idea might seem far-fetched, perhaps Kolosov chooses the name "Wickersham" to connect with "wicker.") The white wicker rocking chair thus has two different meanings for Miranda. For her, the rocker represents temporary conditional love. But for the baby it represents the unconditional love promised by Grace and Matt.

6   The white wicker rocker helps us understand Miranda's final decision. If she keeps her baby, she will "wind up" like her mother, "a woman with a high school diploma, a job at the catsup factory, a mortgage on a ramshackle house, two daughters, and no husband" (151). But if she gives the baby to the Wickershams she might be able to free herself from her mother's fate while also giving a better life to the baby. She perhaps feels guilty that she is not giving her own unconditional love to her child. Maybe that is why she thinks she is not "doing her best" (151). But she is "doing [(courageously, I think)] the best she can" (151).

Work Cited

Kolosov, Jacqueline. "Forsythia." *Sudden Flash Youth: 65 Short-Short Stories*, edited by Christine Perkins-Hazuka et al., Persea Books, 2011, pp. 147-51.

THINKING CRITICALLY

About "Unconditional Love and the Function of the Rocking Chair in Kolosov's 'Forsythia'"

1. The assignment in this chapter asks for an essay that poses a problematic and significant interpretive question. Is Michelle Eastman successful in articulating a problematic question and demonstrating its importance in her understanding of the story? What other problematic questions might someone pose about "Forsythia"?

2. What is Eastman's thesis? Does her thesis adequately respond to the question? Does she supply enough details to support her analysis?

3. To what extent do you agree with Eastman's analysis of this story? Do you think the story portrays Grace and Matt as ideal adoptive parents who will love Miranda's baby unconditionally? Eastman believes that Miranda's decision to give up the baby for adoption is "courageous." Do you agree with her?

4. What do you think Eastman does especially well in this essay? What recommendations do you have for improving the essay?

Chapter 12
Writing a Scientific Research Report

Learning Objectives

12.1 Understand the format of a scientific research report and how it follows the logic of scientific thinking.

12.2 Pose a determinate research question.

12.3 Conduct and report your research using the scientific method.

12.4 Follow ethical standards when conducting research.

12.5 Present your findings in the form of an American Psychological Association (APA) research report.

Understanding how the structure of a scientific research report follows the logic of scientific thinking

12.1 Understand the format of a scientific research report and how it follows the logic of scientific thinking.

This chapter introduces you to scientific research reports that analyze empirical data—a common genre of scientific writing. By **empirical** data, we mean data that has been scientifically gathered and verified. If you major in the social or physical sciences or in related professional fields (engineering, business, education, nursing), you will encounter this genre on a regular basis. If you major in the arts or humanities, this chapter will familiarize you with ways that scientists and other professionals gather and interpret research data as they investigate empirical questions.

How the Structure of a Scientific Research Report Parallels the Process of Scientific Thinking

A framework chart for a typical research report is shown in Figure 12.1. Formatting conventions call for section headings so that readers can quickly find the sections labeled "Introduction," "Method," "Results," and "Discussion." The main sections of a research report follow the logic of the scientific method.

Figure 12.1 Framework for an Empirical Research Report*

(Title Page)	• For format of an APA title page and body of research report, see the student example of an APA research report at the end of this chapter • Gives title of paper and author's name; short version of title appears flush left, the page number in the upper right-hand corner on this and all subsequent pages
ABSTRACT	• Provides a 120-word or less summary of paper (research question, methods, major findings, significance of study)
INTRODUCTION	• Explains the problem to be investigated • Shows importance and significance of the problem • *Reviews previous studies examining the same problem (called a "literature review") and points to conflicts in these studies or to unknowns meriting further investigation* [†] • Poses the determinate research question(s) to be investigated • Presents the researcher's hypothesis
METHOD	• Describes how the study was done (enables future researchers to replicate the study exactly) • Often has subheadings such as "Participants," "Materials," and "Procedure" • Often provides operative definitions of key concepts in the problem/hypothesis
RESULTS	• Presents the researcher's findings or results • Often displays findings in figures, charts, or graphs as well as describes them in words • Usually does not present raw data or behind-the-scenes mathematics; data focus on composite results • *Presents statistical analysis of data to show confidence levels and other advanced statistical implications or meanings* [†]
DISCUSSION	• Presents the researcher's analysis of the results • Interprets and evaluates the collected data in terms of the original research question and hypothesis • Speculates on causes and consequences of the findings • Shows applications and practical or theoretical significance of the study • Usually includes a section pointing out limitations and possible flaws in the study and suggests directions for future research
REFERENCES	• Bibliographic listing of cited sources • For format of APA references, see Skill 23.4 and the "References" section at end of the student APA research report example in this chapter
APPENDICES	• Provides place to include questionnaires or other materials used in study

* Based on guidelines in *Publication Manual of the American Psychological Association*, 6th ed., Washington, DC: APA, 2010, pp. 21–59.

[†]*Italicized sections are not required for the writing projects in this chapter.*

INTRODUCTION (STAGE 1: POSING THE QUESTION) Scientists begin by posing a research question and formulating a **hypothesis**—that is, a hypothetical answer based on their initial theories, assumptions, hunches, and reasoning. The

"Introduction" section of the research report corresponds to this stage: It describes the research question, explains its significance, and reviews previous scientific research addressing the same or a similar question. (Note: The writing projects for this chapter do not ask you to do a literature review.) Typically, the introduction ends with the scientist's hypothesis predicting what the observed data will show.

METHOD (STAGE 2: COLLECTING DATA)   Scientists develop a method for collecting the data needed to confirm or disprove the hypothesis. The materials and methods used to conduct the research, along with definitions of any key terms, are described in detail in the "Method" section of the report. The Method section is like a recipe that allows future researchers to replicate the research process exactly. It also allows peer reviewers to look for possible flaws or holes in the research design.

RESULTS (STAGE 3: DETERMINING RESULTS)   Scientists examine the collected data carefully. The findings are reported in the "Results" section, usually displayed in tables or graphs as well as described verbally. To help determine the extent to which researchers can have confidence in the gathered data, expert researchers perform a variety of statistical tests that show, among other things, whether the results can be attributed simply to chance. (The writing projects for this chapter do not require statistical tests.)

DISCUSSION (STAGE 4: ANALYZING RESULTS)   Finally, scientists interpret and analyze their findings, drawing conclusions about what the findings mean and how the research advances knowledge. This stage of the scientific process corresponds to the "Discussion" section of the research report. Typically, the Discussion section also points to limitations and flaws in the research design and suggests directions for future research. The thesis statement for a scientific report typically comes at the beginning of the Discussion section. It states the extent to which the data confirm or do not confirm the initial hypothesis. Evidence in support of the thesis comes from the data reported in the preceding Results section.

OTHER SECTIONS   In addition to the four main sections, research reports often include an **abstract** of 120 words or less that summarizes the research problem, research design, results, and major implications of the study. The abstract allows readers to get a basic understanding of the research at a glance. At the end of the report, a "References" section lists bibliographic details about any cited sources. Finally, scientists can add, in the "Appendices" section, copies of questionnaires used, interview questions asked, or special calculations that might interest readers.

How Readers Typically Read a Research Report

Readers often don't read research reports in a linear fashion. The advantage of a well-marked structure is that readers can skim a report first and then, if interested, return to read skimmed parts carefully. Readers will typically skim the Introduction (often skipping over the literature review) to understand the problem under investigation and then turn directly to the Discussion, where the results are analyzed. Readers with special interest in the question and results can then return to read the whole report carefully. However, readers working in the same field may be particularly interested in the literature review (in the introduction) and the Methods section and thus read these parts first. Our point is that the conventional format of a research report allows readers to tailor their reading practices to their own interests.

We will now go back through the sections of a research report, explaining in more detail the thinking involved at each stage of the research process.

Posing a determinate research question

12.2   Pose a determinate research question.

Although scientists are inspired by big, open-ended questions (Is space expanding? What causes cancer?), when they conduct research they transform these speculative, indeterminate questions into narrow determinate questions. By *determinate*, we mean questions that can be answered either with yes/no or with a number, a range of numbers, or a percentage. The kinds of determinate questions that scientists typically ask can be placed in five categories in ascending order of complexity (Table 12.1).*

For Writing and Discussion
Generating Research Questions

This exercise encourages you to brainstorm ideas for a research question of your own. The goal here is not to settle on a research question but to get a feeling for the range of options you might choose for your own investigation.

Example: A group of first-year composition students decided to conduct a research project that would increase our understanding of college students' exercise habits. The following list shows how these students used the five categories in Table 12.1 to frame their questions.

CATEGORIES OF RESEARCH QUESTIONS APPLIED TO STUDY OF EXERCISE HABITS

1. *Existence Questions ("Does X exist in domain Y?"):* Does "yoga" appear as an exercise choice among the respondents to this questionnaire?
2. *Measurement Questions ("How large/small/fast/much/many/bright is X?"):* On average, how many hours per week do female (and male) college students devote to physical exercise? What percentage of females (and males) report five or more hours per week of physical exercise?
3. *Comparison Questions ("Is X greater/less than Y or different from Y?"):* Do more male college students than female college students report five or more hours per week of physical exercise?
4. *Correlation Questions ("If X varies, does Y vary?"):* Do students who report studying more than thirty hours per week exercise more than students who report studying fewer than thirty hours per week?
5. *Experimental Questions ("Does a variation in X cause a variation in Y?"):* Will an experimental group of students asked to keep an exercise log exercise more regularly than a control group of students who do not keep such a log?

Individual task: Spend ten minutes thinking of possible ideas for your own research project. Try using the five categories of questions to stimulate your thinking, but don't worry whether a question exactly fits one category or another. Remember to ask determinate questions that can be answered by yes/no or by a single number, percentage, or range of numbers.

Group task: Working in small groups or as a whole class, share your initial ideas, using your classmates' proposed research questions to stimulate more of your own thinking. Your goal is to generate a wide range of possible research questions you might like to investigate.

*Table source note: Table 12.1 is based on an unpublished paper by psychologist Robert Morasky, "Model of Empirical Research Question." Morasky's model was used for the section on "Asking Empirical Research Questions for Science" in John C. Bean and John D. Ramage, *Form and Surprise in Composition: Writing and Thinking Across the Curriculum* (New York: Macmillan, 1986), pp. 183–189.

Table 12.1 Asking Determinate Research Questions

Question Type	Explanation	Natural Science Example	Social Science Example*	Question That You Might Ask for This Chapter's Writing Project
1. *Existence Questions:* "Does X exist in domain Y?"	Researchers simply want to determine if a given phenomenon occurs or exists in a given domain	Do fragments of fungi exist in Precambrian sediments?	Do racial stereotypes exist in current world history textbooks?	Do advertisements for computers appear in women's fashion magazines?
2. *Measurement Questions:* "How large/small/fast/much/many/bright is X?"	Researchers want to measure the extent to which something occurs (percentages) or the degree or size of a phenomenon	How hot is the surface of Venus?	What percentage of homeless persons suffer from mental illness?	What percentage of children's birthday cards currently displayed at local stores contain gender stereotyping?
3. *Comparison Questions:* "Is X greater/less than Y or different from Y?"	Researchers want to study how two events, groups, or phenomena differ according to some measure	Is radiation from lo greater in volcanic areas than in non-volcanic areas?	Is the incidence of anorexia greater among middle-class women than among working-class women?	Do humanities majors report fewer study hours per week than nonhumanities majors?
4. *Correlation Questions:* "If X varies, does Y vary?"	Researchers determine whether differences in X are accompanied by corresponding differences in Y	Does the aggression level of male rats vary with testosterone levels in their blood?	Do students' evaluations of their teachers vary with the grades they expect to receive for the course?	Does students' satisfaction with university food services vary with their family size?
5. *Experimental Questions:* "Does a variation in X cause a variation in Y?"	Researchers move beyond correlations to try to determine the direct causes of a certain phenomenon	If male rats are forced into stress situations to compete for food, will the level of testosterone in their blood increase?	Will preschool children taken shopping after watching TV commercials for high-sugar cereals ask for such cereals at a higher rate than children in a control group who did not see the commercials?	Will persons shown a Monsanto ad promoting biotech corn reveal a more favorable attitude toward genetically modified foods than a control group not shown the ad?

* Direct experiments can be difficult to design and conduct in some of the social sciences. Also, experimental questions often raise ethical issues whenever experiments place human subjects in psychological stress, cause physical pain and suffering to laboratory animals, or otherwise bring harm to individuals. We discuss ethical issues in research later in this chapter.

Conducting and reporting your research using the scientific method

12.3 Conduct and report your research using the scientific method.

Once they have posed an empirical research question they must collect and analyze data and report their results in a scientific manner. The first stage is to collect data.

Collecting Data through Observation or Other Field Research Methods

Scientists collect data directly through observation in a lab or field setting, or indirectly through interviews or questionnaires.

OBSERVATION A common method of collecting data is direct observation of a phenomenon, whether in a lab (as when a chemist observes the contents of a test tube or a psychologist observes children's drawings after they have watched a violent cartoon) or in the field (as when an entomologist observes the distribution of butterfly cocoons in a transitional rural/urban area or a public health researcher observes restroom handwashing behavior). How scientists in any given field observe phenomena, how they record their observations, and how they develop and use specialized tools and technology are things you would study in advanced courses in a major. The key to successful observation is combining a clear sense of your purpose with advance preparation.

Here are examples of how two student research teams used observation to gather needed data:

- **Jasmine and Torval's empirical question:** On the route from Eliot Hall to Marcuse Commons, what percentage of male students versus female students violate the "Do Not Walk on the Grass" sign by taking a shortcut across the lawn rather than staying on the sidewalks? **Their research method:** They observed the lawn for one week during mornings between classes and counted the number of males and females who took a shortcut across the grass and also the numbers of males and females who followed the sidewalks.

- **Lauren, Charlie, and Tyler's empirical question**: Does *SpongeBob Square Pants* display more or less gender stereotyping than a Mickey Mouse cartoon? **Their research method:** The researchers watched the cartoons in one-minute segments and for each segment recorded the presence of behaviors that they categorized as stereotypical or nonstereotypical male behavior and stereotypical or nonstereotypical female behavior. (You can read their research report and their poster in the Readings section of this chapter.)

OTHER FIELD RESEARCH METHODS—QUESTIONNAIRES AND INTERVIEWS In addition to using direct observation to gather empirical data, researchers in the social sciences often use questionnaires or interviews. For example, a student research team that wanted to investigate differences in the exercise patterns of vegetarians versus non-vegetarians created a questionnaire that asked students to report how much exercise they got each week (the questions included exercise options such as walking, jogging, yoga, using the gym, playing sports, and so forth) and also a question about whether the respondent was a vegetarian/vegan. They also selected several respondents for in-depth interviews. (For help with designing questionnaires and conducting interviews, see Chapter 21 (Skill 21.5).)

For Writing and Discussion
Developing a Research Plan

Consider a question suitable for the writing project for this chapter. Working individually, articulate a possible determinate research question that you might investigate for your project—a question that can be answered either with a yes/no or with a single number, a range of numbers, or a percentage. Consider ways that you might use one of the research methods just discussed—observation, interviews, or questionnaires—to answer your question. Begin planning your research method. What procedures will you use for observations? What questions will you use for a questionnaire or for interviews? Then, working in small groups or as a whole class, share your brainstorming. Your goal is to develop the beginnings of a research plan. Help each other talk through the stages of a possible investigation.

Reporting Results in Both Words and Graphics

Once scientists have completed their research, they are ready to write the "Results" section of the report. Many research projects result in complex data that need to be analyzed statistically (what scientists often call "crunching the numbers") to tease out patterns of cause or correlation and to determine whether the patterns are "statistically significant"—a measure of the likelihood that these patterns could have occurred simply by chance. In almost all cases, the results are reported in both words and graphics (tables, charts, graphs, and so forth). Their purpose is (1) to help readers understand research findings both verbally and visually, and (2) to quickly see whether the data support or do not support the hypothesis.

For your own research project for this chapter, you are not expected to do a statistical analysis. Nevertheless, you should report your results in both words and graphics. For help in creating appropriate graphics for displaying your data, in labeling and referencing your graphics, and in making sure that your words and graphics tell the same story, see Skill 18.9, which explains how to create reader-effective tables, pie charts, line graphs, and bar graphs.

Analyzing Results in the Discussion Section

The "Discussion" section of a research report is devoted to the writer's analysis of the results. This section most resembles a thesis-governed essay addressing a problem. Think of the Discussion section as answering the following questions: Do these results confirm or disconfirm the initial hypothesis? How do these results advance our understanding? How are these results important or significant?

The Discussion section should open with a thesis statement that indicates whether the researcher's findings support or do not support the original hypothesis. Here is an example from a professional research report entitled "Marital Disruption and Depression in a Community Sample." Note how the thesis statement in the Discussion section connects to the research question and hypothesis in the Introduction:

PROFESSIONAL EXAMPLE OF RESEARCH QUESTION, HYPOTHESIS, AND THESIS STATEMENT

Research question (from Introduction): Researchers have long known that recently divorced persons tend to show high degrees of depression, but the direction of causation is unknown: Does divorce cause depression or does depression cause divorce?

Hypothesis (from Introduction): Marital disruption contributes to higher levels of depression in recently divorced persons.

Thesis statement (from Discussion): According to the results, marital disruption does in fact cause a significant increase in depression compared to pre-divorce levels within a period of three years after the divorce.

Although there are no formulas for the Discussion section of a research report, most reports contain the following four conventional features:

1. Identification of significant patterns in the data and speculation about causes
2. Implications and significance of the results
3. Limitations of the study
4. Suggestions for further research

Let's look at each in turn.

IDENTIFICATION OF SIGNIFICANT PATTERNS IN THE DATA AND SPECULATION ABOUT CAUSES   The first part of a Discussion section often points out patterns within the results that bear directly on the researcher's hypothesis. For example, in studying exercise habits of college students, you might find that, contrary to your hypothesis, women exercise more than men. Depending on other findings derived from your questionnaire, you might note additional patterns—for example, that persons claiming to be on a diet exercise more than those who don't or that persons who are regular runners tend to spend more time studying than do persons who play lots of pickup team sports.

The discovery of significant patterns leads naturally to speculation about causes. Understanding how a certain event or condition leads to other events or conditions contributes to our knowledge of the world and often has practical consequences for improving the world or our situation in it. As you contemplate questions raised by your research, consider the following ways that data may suggest causality:

- *Causality induced from a recurring pattern:* If numerous observations reveal a recurring pattern, you may be justified in inducing causality. For example, psychologists attempting to understand the causes of anorexia have discovered that many (but not all) anorexics come from perfectionist, highly work-oriented homes that emphasize duty and responsibility. This frequently recurring element is thus a suspected causal factor leading to anorexia.

- *Causality hypothesized from correlations:* **Correlation** is a statistical term indicating the probability that two events or phenomena will occur together. For example, various studies have shown a correlation between creativity and left-handedness. (The percentage of left-handed people within a sample of highly creative people is considerably higher than the percentage of left-handed people in the general population.) But does being left-handed cause a person to be more creative? Or does some other factor cause both left-handedness and creativity? The presence of this puzzling correlation leads scientists to speculate about the causes of creativity and to design further research that might pin down an answer.

- *Causality demonstrated through experimental control of variables:* In some cases, scientists try to resolve causal questions through direct experiment. By controlling variables and testing them one at a time, scientists can sometimes isolate causal factors quite precisely. For example, through experimentation, scientists now know that a particular bacterium causes typhoid fever and that particular antibiotics will kill that bacterium.

For Writing and Discussion
Analyzing Results

Working in small groups or as a whole class, speculate on possible explanations for each of the following phenomena:

1. White female teenagers are seven times more likely to smoke than African-American female teenagers (a finding based on several professional studies).

2. When polled about the "car of their dreams," 91 percent of students at an environmentally activist liberal arts college listed an SUV, luxury car, or high-performance sports car. Only 3 percent specifically mentioned a fuel-conserving vehicle such as a hybrid. (The researchers had hypothesized that more than half the respondents would list an electric or hybrid vehicle as the "dream car.")

IMPLICATIONS AND SIGNIFICANCE OF THE RESULTS   Another typical portion in the Discussion section focuses on the implications and significance of your research—the "So what?" question. What is important about this research? How does it advance our knowledge? What, if any, are its practical applications? For example, the discovery that white female teenagers smoke at a higher rate than African-American female teenagers could lead to speculation on ways to reduce teenage smoking among white females or offer clues into the psyches of white versus African-American women. (One theory proposed in the scientific literature is that white women are more obsessed with weight and body image than African-American women and see smoking as a way to suppress appetite.)

LIMITATIONS OF THE STUDY   Another common feature of the Discussion section is the researcher's skeptical analysis of his or her own research methods and data. It may seem counterintuitive that authors would explicitly point out problems with their own research, but this honesty is part of the scientific *ethos* aimed at advancing knowledge. By nature, scientists are skeptical and cautious. Typically, authors go out of their way to mention possible flaws and other limitations of their studies and to caution other scholars against overgeneralizing from their research. They might refer to problems in sample size or duration of the study, flaws in the research design that might contaminate results, possible differences between an experimental group and a control group, or lack of statistical confidence in the data.

SUGGESTIONS FOR FURTHER RESEARCH   At the conclusion of their Discussion sections, researchers often suggest avenues for future research. Typically they show how their own research raises new questions that could be fruitfully explored.

Following ethical standards

12.4 Follow ethical standards when conducting research.

When research involves human subjects, researchers must scrupulously adhere to ethical standards. History is filled with horrible cases of unethical research using human subjects. Among the most notorious are Nazi medical experiments on Jews in concentration camps and the Tuskegee syphilis study, in which four hundred low-income African-American males with syphilis were denied treatment—even though a cure for syphilis had been discovered—because the researchers wanted to continue studying the progress of the untreated disease.

To prevent the mistreatment of the people being studied, scientific bodies have established strict ethical guidelines for research using human subjects. Today, almost all colleges and universities have Institutional Review Boards that provide oversight for such research. In the case of your own research, for example, consider how certain items on a questionnaire might cause stress to a potential respondent or be considered an invasion of privacy. You probably wouldn't invade respondents' privacy by asking if they prefer a Mac to a PC, but it would be certainly invasive to ask if they have ever cheated on an exam or gotten drunk at a party. As a general rule, the research that you do for this chapter's writing project will not require oversight from your university's Institutional Review Board, but you should nevertheless adhere to the following guidelines:

- *Obtain informed consent*. Explain to potential respondents the purpose of your research, your methods for collecting data, and the way your data will be used. In the case of interviews, reach agreement on whether the respondent will be named or anonymous. Obtain direct permission for recording the session.

- *Explain that participation in your study is voluntary*. Do not apply any kind of personal or social pressure that would make it difficult for a respondent to say no.

- *In the case of questionnaires, explain that no respondent will be individually identified and that results will be reported as statistical aggregates*. If possible, ensure that all responses are anonymous (don't try to identify handwriting or otherwise match responses to an identified individual). If such anonymity is impossible (for example, you might be administering the survey by asking questions verbally), then assure the respondent that you will keep all answers confidential.

- *If any of your respondents are minors, check with your instructor because human-subject regulations are particularly strict in such instances*. Parents or guardians generally have to give consent for interviews with their children.

Writing a scientific research report

12.5 Present your findings in the form of an American Psychological Association (APA) research report.

> **Writing Project:** Write a scientific report in APA style that presents and analyzes your research findings in response to an empirical question about a phenomenon, behavior, or event. Your research can be based on direct observations, interviews, or questionnaires. Your report should have a title page and abstract, followed by the four main sections of a research report: Introduction, Method, Results, and Discussion. Also include a References page if you cite any sources. You do not need to include a review of previous research or perform a statistical analysis of data.

This assignment is a modified version of a standard empirical research report. Note that we have omitted advanced features that would be required of upper-division science majors, such as a statistical analysis of the data or a review of previous research.

An example of a student empirical research report written for this writing project is found at the end of this chapter. In the Introduction section of this report, the student researchers present a brief review of the literature based on readings about gender identity that the instructor had used in class. In most cases, your report will not be expected to have a similar section.

Generating Ideas for Your Research Report

In addition to the ideas presented earlier in this chapter, here are some suggestions for possible research projects:

- Using a questionnaire to gather evidence, investigate students' usage patterns or levels of satisfaction with some aspect of student services on your campus (for example, computer labs, campus security, student newspaper, recreational facilities in the student union, study skills workshops).

- Using direct observation, investigate the degree of gender stereotyping in randomly selected children's birthday cards from a local card store or supermarket. Or investigate adherence to road rules at a chosen intersection, testing variables such as car type, weather conditions, time of day, amount of traffic, and so forth.

- Using interviews or a questionnaire, investigate the way students spend their time during a typical week (for example, studying, watching television, playing video games, logging on to Facebook, playing recreational sports, working, and so forth). You might also try to determine whether there are differences in these patterns depending upon factors such as gender, major, GPA, ethnicity, career aspirations, job status, part-time/full-time student status, or commuter/residential.

Designing Your Empirical Study and Drafting the Introduction and Method Sections

To design your study, you'll need to begin with a determinate research question that can be answered with yes/no or with a number, a range of numbers, or percentage. Review Table 12.1 on asking a determinate research question.

We recommend that you write a draft of your Introduction and your Method section *before* you do the actual research. Drafting these sections first not only gets them out of the way but also helps you think through your whole research process. Drafting your Introduction helps you understand your purpose more clearly and serves to clarify your research question and hypothesis. Drafting the Method section helps you plan exactly the steps you will take to do the research. If your research uses a questionnaire, make sure you carefully design it, test it on a few volunteers, and revise it before you start distributing it. Many research projects are ruined when the researcher discovers that the questionnaire had ambiguous questions or didn't ask the right questions. (See Skill 21.5 for help with designing questionnaires.)

Doing the Research and Writing the Rest of the Report

Your next step is to do the research, record your raw numbers, and do the calculations needed for creating composite numbers that answer your research question. The following brief advice will help you draft the rest of the report.

- *Writing the Results section:* This section simply presents your results both in words and in graphics. Refer to Skill 18.9 for advice on how to reference graphs and tables.

- *Writing the Discussion section:* Novice science writers often have trouble determining what goes in the Results section versus the Discussion section. The Results section answers the question, "What are my findings?" In contrast, the Discussion section addresses the question, "What do my findings mean?" It is the place where you bring your own critical thinking to bear on your results, creating your own thesis and argument.

- *Writing the Abstract:* When you have finished your draft, write a summary (no more than 120 words) of your report. In a few sentences indicate the broad problem you were investigating and the narrower purpose of your research; state your research question and your hypothesis. Then briefly describe your methods. In the last half of the abstract, describe your results and the extent to which they support your hypothesis. Conclude by suggesting the significance and implications of your research.

Revising Your Report

Because a scientific report follows a conventional structure, you should check your draft against the framework chart in Figure 12.1. Make sure you have placed the right type of material in the appropriate section. Inside each section, revise for effective transitions, conciseness, and clarity. Getting feedback from peers can be very helpful.

Questions for Peer Review

In addition to the generic peer review questions listed in Skill 17.4, ask your peer reviewers to address these questions:

TITLE AND ABSTRACT

1. Can the title be improved to better focus the paper and pique reader interest?
2. Can the abstract be improved for accuracy, coverage, or clarity? Where does it state the research question and hypothesis? Briefly summarize the methods? Briefly state the results? Discuss the significance of the results?

INTRODUCTION

1. Where does the writer present the research question(s) and hypothesis(es)? Are these clear and focused?
2. Where does the writer suggest the importance or significance of the research question? What overall suggestions would you make to improve the introduction?

METHOD

1. Will the writer's method provide the data necessary to answer the research question?
2. If you had to replicate the writer's research, where might you have problems? How could the Method section be improved?

RESULTS

1. Are the writer's results clearly stated in both words and graphics? Are there any graphics that need more explanation?
2. Are the graphics well designed? What suggestions do you have for improving the titles, labels, legends, and overall design of graphics?

DISCUSSION

1. Where is the thesis statement that shows whether the research supports the hypothesis? Can you suggest ways to improve the thesis?
2. Where does the writer: (a) identify significant patterns in the data and speculate about possible causes? (b) show the significance and importance of the study? (c) describe the limitations of the study? (d) suggest ideas for future research or next steps? How might the Discussion section be improved?

Multimodal and online assignment options: *A scientific poster.*

Scientific Poster: Publish the results of your empirical research project as a scientific poster suitable for display at an undergraduate research conference. Your poster should combine visual and verbal elements to hook participants' interest in your project, show your research question and results, and provide a frame for further personal discussion of your research. Explanations of the scientific poster as a genre as well as instructions on how to produce one are shown in Chapter 20. An example of a student-produced poster is found in the Readings section of this chapter.

Readings

The following readings include a professional research report, a student research report in APA style, and a student example of a scientific poster. The first reading is a short empirical report published in the "Clinical and Program Notes" section of the peer-reviewed *Journal of American College Health*. You should be able to read this article easily, even though you may need to skip over the statistical analysis in the "Results" section. Because the article is short, the discussion section is labeled "Comment" rather than "Discussion." The References at the end of the article do not follow MLA or APA format; rather, they are reprinted as they originally appeared in the journal, which uses its own in-house style.

LeAnne M. Forquer, Ph.D.; Adrian E. Camden, B.S.; Krista M. Gabriau, B.S.; and C. Merle Johnson, Ph.D.*

Sleep Patterns of College Students at a Public University

Abstract. Objective: The authors' purpose in this study was to determine the sleep patterns of college students to identify problem areas and potential solutions. **Participants**: A total of 313 students returned completed surveys. **Methods:** A sleep survey was e-mailed to a random sample of students at a North Central university. Questions included individual sleep patterns, problems, and possible influencing factors. **Results**: Most students reported later bedtimes and rise times on weekends than they did on weekdays. More than 33% of the students took longer than 30 minutes to fall asleep, and 43% woke more than once nightly. More than 33% reported being tired during the day. The authors found no differences between freshmen, sophomores, juniors, seniors, and graduate students for time to fall asleep, number of night wakings, or total time slept each night. **Conclusions:** Many students have sleep problems that may interfere with daily performance, such as driving and academics. Circadian rhythm management, sleep hygiene, and white noise could ameliorate sleep difficulties.

Keywords: college students, night wakings, sleep, sleep aids, sleep deprivation

1   Adolescents and young adults, including college students, appear to be one of the most sleep-deprived groups in the United States.[1-3] Individuals in this age group require about 9 hours of sleep each night; however, most receive only 7 to 8 hours.[1] This sleep deprivation can have detrimental effects on performance, including driving[4] and academics.[5] According to Carskadon,[1] 55% of sleep-related accidents involve individuals younger than 25 years. In a survey by the American College Health Association[5] involving students from 33 universities across the United States, researchers examined the top impediments to academic performance. Both men (23%) and women (25%) rated sleep difficulties as the third most common impediment, after stress and illness such as colds, flu, or sore throats. In this study we examined college students' sleep patterns to identify problem areas and potential solutions.

* At the time of the study, all authors were with the Department of Psychology at Central Michigan University in Mount Pleasant.

Methods

Participants

2   Graduate and undergraduate students from a North Central university participated in an e-mail survey. We randomly selected these students from the approximately 20,000 currently enrolled. The Dean of Students approved the release of
their university-issued e-mail addresses by the Registrar's office. The university's
institutional review board approved this project.

Measures

3   To identify students' potential problem areas and factors influencing these
problems, we conducted a sleep survey that included questions from the Pittsburgh Sleep Quality Index[6] and the Sleep Hygiene Test.[7]

Procedure

4   We attached the survey to an e-mail that explained the study's purpose. We sent
this e-mail to the university-issued e-mail addresses of students randomly selected
to participate. All information was confidential; only a number identified participants.
Students who decided to participate were instructed to complete the attached
survey and return it via e-mail or campus mail. We sent all participants a reminder
2 weeks later with another copy of the survey. We conducted the study during the
beginning of the spring semester, when sleep deprivation should be lowest.

Results

5   We e-mailed surveys to 2,024 students; 44 of the surveys could not be delivered and 241 were completed. We e-mailed a second survey 2 weeks later, and
this time 43 could not be delivered and 72 more were completed. A total of 313
students returned completed surveys, although 23 more surveys were returned
without attachments. The sample of participating students was 62% female,
90% Caucasian, 93% unmarried, and 87% undergraduate; their mean age was
21.4 years ($SD = 4.3$). Most participants (90%) had roommates, including spouses
(7%). Demographics were representative of the university.

6   The survey asked the students about their typical sleep patterns (see Table
1). When asked about their typical sleeping situation, most participants reported
sleeping with roommates, although in separate beds. Bedtimes on weekends
were more than 1 hour later and rise times were more than 2 hours later; thus,
most participants slept more on weekend nights ($M = 8.6$ hours, $SD = 1.5$) than
they did on weekdays ($M = 7.2$ hours, $SD = 1.2$). Furthermore, women averaged
8 hours of sleep compared with 7.7 for men ($F[1, 312] = 5.27$, $p <.01$). Participants took an average of 25 minutes to fall asleep ($SD = 20$). An analysis of vari-
ance showed that women averaged 27.3 minutes to fall asleep, compared with
21.2 for men ($F[1, 312] = 6.93$, $p < .01$). We observed no sex differences in the
number of night wakings ($M = 1.7$, $SD = 1$), nor any class differences (freshmen
through graduate students) in the number of night wakings, time to fall asleep,
or hours of nightly sleep. The most common reasons for night wakings included
hearing noise from others (41%), going to the bathroom (40%), and being worried
about something (33%).

Table 1 Participants' Sleep Patterns

Pattern	Value
Typical sleeping situation (%)	
Roommate in different room	41
Share a room	31
Share a bed	16
Alone	12
Mean bedtime (am)	
Weekday	12:24
Weekend	1:54
Mean rise time (am)	
Weekday	8:12
Weekend	10:30
Why do you awaken during the night? (Check all that apply)	
Noise from others	41
Need to go to bathroom	40
Worried about something	33
Bad dreams	20
Pain	9
Muscle spasms	7
Do you typically use sound to help you sleep? (%)	
Yes	47
No	53
If yes, what type of sound do you use? (%)	
Fan	55
Music	34
Humidifier	22
Television	8
Sound machine	3
Do you use any other aids to help you sleep? (%)	
Yes	10
No	90
If yes, what aids do you use? (%)	
Medication	60
Reading	13
Relaxation exercises	13
Earplugs	7
Alcohol	3

Note. The standard deviations for mean bedtimes and mean rise times are as follows: bedtime. $SD = 1.4$ and $SD = 1.6$, respectively, weekday and weekend; rise time, $SD = 1.4$ and $SD = 2.0$, respectively, weekday and weekend.

7   When asked what a typical night's sleep consisted of, most participants answered that they slept all night (26%), had 1 waking (26%), or had 2–3 wakings (21%). The participants were also asked about sleep aids; half reported using sounds such as fans or music. Less common sleep aids included medication (6%). When asked how they felt during waking hours, 58% of participants reported being tired in the morning but okay once they got going. However, more than 33% reported that they started out energetic and then got tired or were tired all day.

Comment

8   College students reported later bedtimes and wake times on weekends than on weekdays. Of the participants, 33% took more than 30 minutes to fall asleep and 43% woke more than once a night. These data suggest sleep difficulties consistent with research of the National Sleep Foundation,[8] which reported that more than 40% of Americans have difficulty falling asleep or have night wakings.

9   Our results support American College Health Association[5] survey findings on college students' sleep difficulties, including long sleep latencies, short sleep time, and frequent night waking. Sleep problems may be worse than these self-reported responses, as students may give socially desirable answers such as not noting sexual encounters or alcohol abuse before bedtime. Thus, this survey may be limited by underreporting.

10   Improving sleep may enhance academic performance. Possible strategies include circadian rhythm management, sleep hygiene, and white noise.[1,9,10] The circadian rhythm is the 24-hour day–night cycle that influences quantity and quality of sleep.[9] The more stable and consistent this circadian rhythm, the better a person sleeps. This implies that individuals should go to bed and wake at the same time every day, including on weekends.[10] Clearly, students in this sample disrupted circadian rhythms when weekday sleep is compared with weekend sleep. Improvements in sleep hygiene—including limiting naps to less than 1 hour, using beds only for sleeping (no reading, TV, or homework), and making sure the bedroom is comfortable[9,10]—also promote sleep. White noise, which is continuous sound covering the entire range of human hearing from 20 to 20,000 Hertz (or approximations to white noise such as fans or humidifiers), also could improve sleep.[9,10] College students need to address sleep problems with better sleep management, which may improve academic performance and driving.

Note

For comments and further information, address correspondence to Dr LeAnne M. Forquer, Division of Counselor Education and Psychology, Delta State University, Box 3142, Cleveland, MS, USA 38733. (e-mail: lforquer@deltastate.edu).

References

1. Carskadon MA. *Adolescent Sleep Patterns: Biological, Social, and Psychological Influences*. New York: Cambridge University; 2002.

2. Pilcher JJ, Walters AS. How sleep deprivation affects psychological variables related to college students' cognitive performance. *J Am Coll Health*. 1997;46:121–126.

3. Tsai L, Li S. Sleep patterns in college students: gender and grade differences. *J Psychosom Res*. 2004;56:231–237.

4. Subramanian R. *Motor Vehicle Traffic Crashes as a Leading Cause of Death in the US, 2002.* http://nhtsa.gov/people/crash/LCOD/Index.htm. Accessed April 27, 2005.

5. American College Health Association. The American College Health Association–National College Health Assessment (ACHA–NCHA), spring 2003 reference group report. *J Am Coll Health.* 2005;53:199–210.

6. Buysse DJ, Reynolds CF, Monk TH, et al. The Pittsburgh Sleep Quality Index: a new instrument for psychiatric practice and research. *Psychiatry Res.* 1989;28:193–213.

7. *Sleep Hygiene Test–Abridged.* http://www.discoveryhealth.queendom.com/sleep_hygiene_abridged_access.html. Accessed September 22, 2004.

8. National Sleep Foundation. *The Basics of Sleep.* http://www.harvestmoonstudio.com/assets/SLEEP_HTML/pub_newsmaker.htm. Accessed September 28, 2005.

9. Breus M. *Sleep Dos and Don'ts: Sleep Hygiene Solutions for Better Sleep.* http://my.webmd.com/content/Article/62/71839.htm. Accessed June 2, 2005.

10. Dement WC. How To Sleep Well. http://www.stanford.edu/~dement/howto.html. Accessed June 2, 2005.

THINKING CRITICALLY
About "Sleep Patterns of College Students at a Public University"

1. The introduction to this article doesn't state its research question directly, even though a question is clearly implied. In your own words, what is the question these researchers are asking? How does the introduction try to show readers that the question is significant and worth researching?

2. The first paragraph of the Methods section states that the dean of students approved the release of e-mail addresses and that the institutional review board approved the project. Why do the researchers need to provide this information? Without an approval process, what unethical behaviors might arise from research like this?

3. The results of the survey (see Results section) are reported in two different ways: in linear prose and also in Table 1, where the Value column represents percentages of respondents. How does the material in the prose section differ from the material in Table 1? What is the authors' purpose in selecting the material emphasized in the prose section?

4. The last sentence of the introduction promises that this report will "identify problem areas and potential solutions." How does the Comment section fulfill this promise? What are the key sleep problems identified in the report? What are the potential solutions? Are you convinced? Would this report cause you to try changing your sleep behavior in any way?

Our second reading, which was written for this chapter's writing project, was jointly authored by a team of three students. We have reproduced it in manuscript format to illustrate the form and documentation style of the APA (American Psychological Association) system for research papers. For further explanation of APA style, see Skill 24.4.

Running head: GENDER STEREOTYPES   1

A Comparison of Gender Stereotypes in *SpongeBob SquarePants* and a 1930s

Mickey Mouse Cartoon

Lauren Campbell, Charlie Bourain, and Tyler Nishida

APA
Style

*Include
shortened
title and page
number on
each page.
On p. 1, include
"Running head"*

*Center
title and
authors.*

APA
STYLE

Brief abstract summarizes paper and appears on a separate page.

Abstract

Researchers in gender identity have continually argued whether gender differences are biological or social. Because television is a prime place for teaching children gender differences through socialization, we studied the extent of gender stereotyping in two 1930s Mickey Mouse cartoons and two recent *SpongeBob SquarePants* cartoons. We analyzed the cartoons in one-minute increments and recorded the number of gender stereotypical and gender-non-stereotypical actions in each increment. Our results confirmed our hypothesis that *SpongeBob SquarePants* would have fewer gender stereotypes than Mickey Mouse. This study is significant because it shows that in at least one contemporary cartoon males and females have a range of acceptable behaviors that go beyond traditional gender stereotypes.

A Comparison of Gender Stereotypes in *SpongeBob SquarePants*

and a 1930s Mickey Mouse Cartoon

Researchers in gender identity have long argued over the role of biology versus culture in causing gendered behavior. Pinker (2005) has argued that biology plays a more significant role in gender identity. In contrast, Barres (2006) has argued that culture plays the more significant role in gender identity. Proponents of socialization over biology have shown that cultural influences begin at a very young age. For example, Clearfield and Nelson (2006) show that mothers are more verbal and nurturing towards girls but are more focused on promoting independence and use more commands with boys.

Also of interest are the effects of media and popular culture on children and adults. A large part of a child's life is spent watching cartoons; therefore we believe it is important to find how much of a role gender stereotypes play in the media. In response to this question, we have examined data about gender stereotypes from two different kinds of children's cartoons. The first is a recent, somewhat controversial cartoon called *SpongeBob SquarePants*. The other is a popular 1930s Mickey Mouse cartoon.

The purpose of our study is to see if there is a difference in the extent of gender stereotypes between *SpongeBob SquarePants* and the earlier Mickey Mouse cartoon. We asked the following research question: To what extent has *SpongeBob SquarePants* rejected or reinforced gender stereotypes compared to the Mickey Mouse cartoon? Our hypothesis is that *SpongeBob SquarePants* will show fewer gender stereotypes than the older Mickey Mouse cartoon. We believe this because SpongeBob SquarePants has been attacked by some conservative religious groups as a gay character (Kirkpatrick, 2005). We hypothesize that this characterization comes from the cartoon's male characters' not exhibiting stereotypical male behaviors. In contrast, we believe that the older Mickey Mouse cartoon will show Mickey exhibiting stereotypical male behavior and Minnie stereotypical female behavior.

Methods

To analyze the cartoons, we developed four specific categories for coding the data: Stereotypical Female Action, Stereotypical Male Action, Non-Stereotypical Female Action, and Non-Stereotypical Male Action. For each category we developed certain criteria that can be viewed in Table 1.

We watched two episodes of each cartoon (obtained from the Internet) in one-minute intervals. After each minute, we stopped the cartoon and waited for each team member to record his or her analysis. We all watched the same episodes at the same time, but we recorded our data separately and later compiled the data after the last episode had been watched.

Here is a representative example of how we applied our coding scheme: In one one-minute segment from *SpongeBob SquarePants*, SpongeBob and his friend

Repeat title before body of paper.

Double-space all text.

Use italics for titles.

Center section headings in bold.

Reference tables in text.

APA STYLE

Table 1

Coding Criteria for Gender Stereotypes

Category	Criteria for Making Category Decision
Stereotypical Female Action	Female character behaves in a timid, submissive, or passive way; breaks into tears; shows caring, nurturing, empathic, or motherly behavior; dresses in stereotypical way (frilly clothes, dresses, feminine accessories)
Stereotypical Male Action	Male character behaves in an aggressive, fearless, or competitive way; is cocky or taunting; shows physical strength; dresses in stereotypical male way
Non-Stereotypical Female Action	Female character exhibits stereotypical male behavior
Non-Stereotypical Male Action	Male character exhibits stereotypical female behavior

Patrick decide to lift weights. While lifting weights, SpongeBob infuriates a body building fish who is much bigger and stronger than SpongeBob. SpongeBob runs away in fear while his friend Sandy (the female squirrel) stands up to the mean body building fish. She then makes sure SpongeBob is okay before she returns to lifting weights. We coded this example as containing a stereotypical male action (body building fish), a non-stereotypical male action (SpongeBob showing fear), a stereotypical female action (Sandy expressing concern for others), and non-stereotypical female actions (Sandy challenging the fish and also lifting weights).

Results

Reference figures in text.

Our results (see Figure 1) show that the Mickey Mouse cartoon had a higher percentage of stereotypical male and female actions than did *SpongeBob SquarePants*, which had an almost equal amount of non-stereotypical and stereotypical gendered actions.

As shown in Figure 1, female actions in *SpongeBob SquarePants* were 59% gender stereotypical and 40% gender non-stereotypical while in Mickey Mouse female actions were 84% gender stereotypical and only 16% gender non-stereotypical. Similarly, male actions in *SpongeBob SquarePants* were 48% gender stereotypical and 52% gender non-stereotypical, while in Mickey Mouse male actions were 87% gender stereotypical and 12% gender non-stereotypical.

Discussion

Our hypothesis that *SpongeBob SquarePants* will have fewer gender stereotypes than the Mickey Mouse cartoon was confirmed. The data show that overall

GENDER STEREOTYPES   5

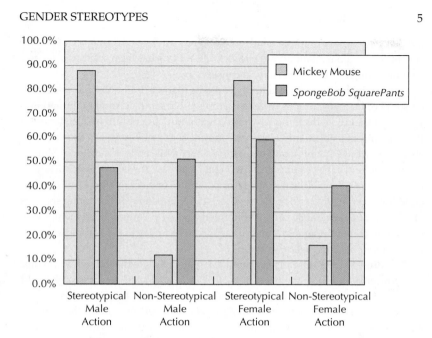

Figure 1 Stereotypical Behaviors by Gender in SpongeBob SquarePants and
Mickey Mouse.

SpongeBob SquarePants is the more gender-neutral cartoon, showing balance
between non-stereotypical and stereotypical actions, while Mickey Mouse showed
strong gender stereotypes.

    The study we have done is important because it shows that *SpongeBob
SquarePants* does not reveal gender stereotyping in the stereotypical ways
exhibited in the Mickey Mouse cartoon. In *SpongeBob SquarePants*, almost every
gender stereotypical action (like SpongeBob acting tough or macho) was followed
by a gender non-stereotypical action (like SpongeBob crying). This was not
the case for Mickey Mouse, where there were many more gender stereotypical
actions (for instance, Mickey Mouse rescuing Minnie Mouse) than gender non-
stereotypical actions (for instance, Mickey Mouse quivering in fear).

    The trends found in the *SpongeBob SquarePants* and Mickey Mouse cartoons
suggest to us that these cartoons reveal ways that society's view of gender is
evolving. In *SpongeBob SquarePants*, the greater variation and complexity of
behavior may reflect such cultural and social changes as women and mothers
in the workforce, stay-at-home dads raising the kids, shared household
responsibilities, women in the military, and nontraditional families. These recent
social and cultural changes have complicated our culture's views of gender,
and we speculate that it is these less-rigid gender restrictions that we glimpse in
SpongeBob SquarePants. However, there is still a cultural war going on over gender
roles in the media. Our class's discussion of advertising showed that the media in

the 21st century still promote gender stereotypes, and the continuation of these stereotypes could explain why *SpongeBob SquarePants* has been controversial and has come under attack from cultural conservatives.

A potential limitation of our study could be that we didn't observe enough episodes of the two cartoons to get a representative sample. Another limitation was our difficulty in deciding how to code continuous actions that lasted more than one minute. For example, in a one-minute segment, *SpongeBob SquarePants* characters would exhibit many different actions, while actions in Mickey Mouse would last longer. For example, there might be a chase scene in which Mickey exhibited the same male action for several minutes or a scene where Minnie cried for several minutes. Should we count the chase scene or the crying scene as one action or as several because it continued across one-minute increments? We decided to count the same continuous action as several actions. Making another choice might have changed our data.

For future studies, researchers could ask questions like the following: Do other modern cartoons follow the trend of *SpongeBob SquarePants*? New research could compare *SpongeBob SquarePants* with other recent cartoons like *The Justice League* or *Jimmy Neutron* to see if they follow *SpongeBob SquarePants'* gender-neutral tendencies. If we believe that gender stereotyping is harmful, further research on gender stereotypes in the media could help identify how to promote a more gender-neutral society in the future.

GENDER STEREOTYPES   7

                                References

Barres, B. A. (2006, July 13). Does gender matter? *Nature, 442,* 133–136.

Clearfield, M., & Nelson, N. (2006, January). Sex differences in mothers'
    speech and play behavior with 6-, 9-, and 14-month-old infants.
    Sex Roles, 54(1/2), 127–137.

Kirkpatrick, D. (2005, January 20). Conservatives pick soft target: A cartoon
    sponge. *The New York Times.* Retrieved from http://www.nytimes.com

Pinker, S. (2005, February 7). The science of difference. Sex ed. *The New Republic
    Online.* Retrieved from http://www.tnr.com

THINKING CRITICALLY

About "A Comparison of Gender Stereotypes in *SpongeBob SquarePants* and a 1930s Mickey Mouse Cartoon"

1. Explain how this paper follows the genre conventions for a scientific report.

2. To what extent do you think the authors' research design was effective? Are you persuaded that *SpongeBob SquarePants* has moved away from gender stereotypes?

3. This research project was part of a class unit on issues in gender identity that included the readings by Pinker, Barres, and Clearfield and Nelson referred to in the introduction. What does this brief review of the literature add to the paper?

4. The authors located the reference to Kirkpatrick on their own. How does the use of this source contribute to the paper?

5. How might the authors expand their speculations about causes of new approaches to gender in cartoons and their ideas about the significance of the study? How has this study inspired you to think about gender and cartoons?

   Our final reading is the poster created by the authors of the *SpongeBob SquarePants* paper for presentation at a poster session.

THINKING CRITICALLY

About "*SpongeBob SquarePants* Has Fewer Gender Stereotypes than Mickey Mouse"

1. To what extent does this poster present the same scientific content as the complete research report? If you attended a conference, would you rather listen to a fifteen-minute talk by the authors or view their poster and ask them questions? Why?

2. How does this poster employ the "sound-bite" principle by using minimal text connected to visual elements?

3. In what ways do you think this poster is effective? What questions would you want to ask the creators of this poster?

SpongeBob SquarePants Has Fewer Gender Stereotypes than Mickey Mouse

Lauren Campbell, Charlie Bourain, and Tyler Nishida

Introduction

Television cartoons may influence children's learning of gender stereotypes. Knowing how a contemporary cartoon portrays gender stereotypes would help us understand messages children receive.

Objective

We wanted to see if there is a difference in gender stereotypes between *SpongeBob SquarePants* and a 1930s Mickey Mouse cartoon.

Method

We analyzed cartoons in one-minute increments.

- *Stereotypical female* [timid, passive, tearful; caring, motherly; wearing frilly clothes, accessories]
- *Stereotypical male* [aggressive, fearless, competitive; cocky; showing physical strength; wearing typical male clothing]
- *Non-stereotypical female* [female exhibiting stereotypical male action]
- *Non-stereotypical male* [male exhibiting stereotypical female action]

Results

More Non-Stereotypical Behavior for Males and Females in SpongeBob

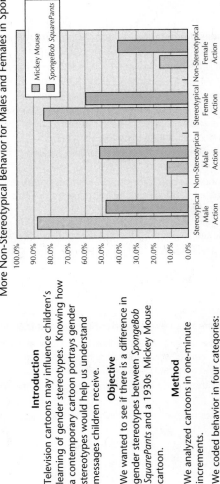

- *SpongeBob SquarePants* has almost equal ratio of stereotypical and non-stereotypical behaviors for both males and females (49%/51% for males; 59%/41% females)
- Mickey Mouse has mostly stereotypical behaviors (88%/12% for males; 84%/16% for females)

Discussion

SpongeBob SquarePants showed males and females engaged in wider range of behavior with fewer gender stereotypes than Mickey Mouse.

- *SpongeBob SquarePants* intermixed gender stereotypical action (SpongeBob acting tough, Sandy being nurturing) and non-stereotypical behavior (SpongeBob crying, Sandy rescuing SpongeBob)
- Mickey Mouse had mostly gender stereotypical actions (Mickey rescuing Minnie, who is in tears).

These differences may match changes in culture since 1930s (women's movement, working women, stay-at-home dads) and may explain why *SpongeBob SquarePants* has been attacked by cultural conservatives.

Chapter 13
Writing a Synthesis of Ideas Essay

Learning Objectives

13.1 Understand analysis and synthesis as a knowledge-making process.

13.2 Apply a sequence of thinking strategies for analyzing multiple texts and synthesizing their ideas to present a new perspective of your own.

13.3 Write a synthesis essay that includes a focused thesis, a summary and analysis of each text under discussion, and a synthesis that contributes your own ideas.

Many college courses require analysis and synthesis essays in which you explore connections and contradictions among groups of texts, bring your critical thinking to bear on the texts' ideas, and work your way to your own perspective. These thinking and writing moves involve wallowing in complexity (introduced in Chapter 2 and discussed further in Chapter 6) as you wrestle with problems and ideas in texts to discover something new to say in response to the texts' discussions. The series of critical thinking and writing strategies explained in this chapter will deepen your analysis and synthesis skills. You need first to formulate a synthesis question that invites a conversation among your chosen or assigned texts. You then need to summarize the texts accurately, analyze the main commonalities and disagreements among them, and, through your own critical thinking, arrive at your own perspective on the synthesis question.

Understanding analysis and synthesis as a knowledge-making process

13.1 Understand analysis and synthesis as a knowledge-making process.

Synthesis is a knowledge-making activity that starts with analysis and takes it further. (See Chapter 1 for an explanation of knowledge-making versus knowledge-getting.) It is a way of seeing and coming to terms with multiple perspectives and complexities. When you **analyze** something, you break it down into its parts to see the relationships among them. When you **synthesize**, you take one more step, putting parts together in some new fashion. The cognitive researcher Benjamin Bloom defined *synthesis* as the "putting together of constituent elements or parts to form a whole requiring original creative thinking" and considered it one of the highest levels of critical thinking. Recent educational theorists place synthesis at the top of the hierarchy of critical thinking skills, even relabeling it *creating*. This new label emphasizes the creative aspect of synthesis through which you arrive at your own revelations ("Aha!" moments) based on new ways of seeing something or on creating a new idea or product. In synthesizing, you extend and deepen what you have learned through analysis to construct your own interpretation and contribution to a conversation of texts.

We can also think of synthesis as a dialectical critical thinking process (as discussed in Chapter 2). Throughout this text, we have explained that college writing involves posing a significant question that often forces you to encounter clashing or contradictory ideas. Such conflicts intrigued the German philosopher Georg Hegel, who posited that thinking proceeds dialectically when a thesis clashes against an **antithesis,** leading the thinker to formulate a synthesis encompassing dimensions of both the original thesis and the antithesis. When you write to synthesize ideas, your thinking exemplifies this dialectical process. Through this process you arrive at new perspectives on texts and their ideas, enabling you to make your own contribution to a conversation.

Synthesis is an especially important component of academic research writing, where you must use synthesis to sift through the writings of others and arrive at your own contribution to a question. Synthesis, then, is the skill of wrestling with ideas from different sources and creatively forging a new whole out of potentially confusing parts. It is the principal way you enter into a conversation on a social, civic, or scholarly issue.

Two Common Kinds of Synthesis Essays

The synthesis assignments you encounter in college courses will take many different forms, but here is an explanation of two of the most common types.

ANALYZING TWO OR MORE TEXTS IN SEARCH OF YOUR SYNTHESIS PERSPECTIVE   In this form of synthesis, you are asked to read and analyze two or more texts, to summarize their key ideas, to examine points of agreement and disagreement, and to arrive at a synthesis that represents your own understanding and independent thinking. The following examples show typical synthesis assignments of this sort with both the synthesis questions and the texts provided in each case.

Texts to Be Analyzed	Possible Synthesis Questions
Environmental Studies Course	
A chapter from Gary Chamberlain's *Troubled Waters: Religion, Ethics, and the Global Water Crisis* (2008)	• Who owns our water? Should water be a human right or a commodity?
A chapter from Charles Fishman's *The Big Thirst: The Secret Life and Turbulent Future of Water* (2011)	• Who should have control of water sources and management—corporations or governments representing citizens?
Maude Barlow, "Address to the UN General Assembly on Need to Conserve Water" (2009)	• What are the best solutions to providing safe drinking water in water-stressed areas of the world?

Texts to Be Analyzed   Possible Synthesis Questions

Introductory Sociology Course on Global Culture

Samuel P. Huntington's article "The Clash of Civilizations?" *Foreign Affairs* (1993)

Helena Norberg-Hodge's *Ancient Futures: Learning from Ladakh* (1991)

Tony Karon, "What Soccer Means to the World" *Time* (2004)

- What power dynamics are at work when globalization begins to change a culture?
- Can cultural exchange be an instrument for promoting global understanding, cooperation, and peace?
- How does increased intercultural contact affect cultural diversity?

APPLYING ONE TEXT AS A CONCEPTUAL LENS TO INTERPRET ANOTHER TEXT   In this form of synthesis, you are asked to use one text as a conceptual lens through which to analyze another text and reach your own interpretation of that second text. In this version of synthesis writing, usually one text explains a theory, historical perspective, methodology, or larger concept, and you use that text to illuminate the patterns, implications, and meanings of another text. This form of synthesis, which is common across the disciplines, is usually assigned in advanced courses in your major after you have studied the discipline's theory and methods. Here are examples.

Texts to Be Analyzed   Possible Synthesis Questions

Literature Course

Michel Foucault, "The Means of Correct Training"

Marge Piercy, *Woman on the Edge of Time*

How do Foucault's ideas on modern forms of power and its techniques of discipline help readers understand a novel about a woman unjustly incarcerated and experimented on in a mental hospital?

Women's Studies Course

A theoretical article from the journal *Sex Roles*

The animated film *Frozen*

To what extent do the female characters in *Frozen* represent what feminist theorists call a "false" feminism?

The assignment for this chapter will focus on the first of these two kinds of synthesis essays.

Posing a Synthesis Question

As we have shown throughout this text, most academic and professional writing begins by posing a significant problem. A synthesis question, like a research question, is a particular kind of significant problem. It is an open-ended question that invites a variety of responses or points of view. The need to synthesize ideas usually begins when you pose a problem that sends you on an intellectual journey to investigate what others have said. Your goal is to uncover a conversation driven by this problem. You will analyze how other writers have addressed the problem and then bring them into conversation with one another, analyzing how they are similar and different. Eventually you synthesize their ideas into an informed, coherent view of your own—a view that draws on what others have said and adds something new to the conversation.

You can arrive at your synthesis question in different ways. Sometimes an instructor will give you the synthesis question along with the sources to use. At other times you might be given just the sources and asked to formulate your own synthesis question. Perhaps most commonly an instructor will ask you to pose your own synthesis question and then find your own sources. For example, Chapter 14 on classical argument includes two articles addressing the problem of gun violence in the United States. For a synthesis essay, you might be required to read those two articles and then pose the synthesis question that you want to address. Alternatively, you might pose your own synthesis question about gun violence and then find articles on your own. The two articles in Chapter 14 offer differing points of view relevant to a wide range of possible synthesis questions—for example:

- Does the Second Amendment allow any kind of government restrictions on gun ownership?
- What actions could be taken to reduce the frequency of mass murders?
- Would open carry make college campuses safer?
- Is requiring a license to own a gun analogous to requiring a license to drive a car?

For each of these questions, you would analyze how each of your sources might answer the synthesis question and how these answers would be similar to or different from one another. You then present your own answer to the question, drawing on ideas and evidence from the texts but also adding your own critical thinking and experience to the conversation.

Synthesis Writing as an Extension of Summary/ Strong Response Writing

A synthesis essay is an extension of the summary/strong response essay explained in Chapter 6. In writing a synthesis essay, you listen carefully to texts, analyze the relationship of their parts to the whole, and summarize them to determine their main points. You use both with-the-grain and against-the-grain thinking. You also conduct—at least informally in your exploratory stages—a critique of these texts' rhetorical features and ideas. This analysis builds the platform on which you create a synthesis of ideas based on your own independent thinking.

A synthesis essay differs from a summary/strong response essay in that a synthesis essay extends the process to more texts with the aim of bringing them into conversation with one another. A synthesis essay takes apart, makes sense of, assesses, and recombines the ideas into your own new vision of the subject. A synthesis essay most likely incorporates the following features:

TYPICAL FEATURES OF A SYNTHESIS ESSAY

- A synthesis question that shows your interest in the texts and presents this question as problematic and significant
- Short summaries of each text to give your readers a sense of the readings you are working with

- A thesis that indicates how you have analyzed and synthesized the readings to arrive at a new perspective

- Your analysis of key points in these texts, determined in part by the synthesis question

- Your new view, which combines ideas gathered from readings with your own independent ideas

The student example of a synthesis essay by Rosie Evans at the end of this chapter shows you how these parts are developed in a complete essay.

The thinking process for writing a synthesis essay

13.2 Apply a sequence of thinking strategies for analyzing multiple texts and synthesizing their ideas to present a new perspective of your own.

A synthesis essay involves summarizing, analyzing, and synthesizing. A productive way to move through these stages is to break your process into incremental thinking and exploratory writing steps that help you analyze the texts' ideas and discover your own new ideas. These steps and strategies will help you prepare for this chapter's writing project and for all other essays requiring analysis and synthesis.

In the following sections, we explain each of these thinking and writing steps in more detail, provide examples, and offer strategies for completing them. We also provide exercises to help you wrestle with the texts you will use for your own synthesis essay. Our examples come from the idea-generating strategies used by student writer Rosie Evans, whose final synthesis essay appears at the end of this chapter. Rosie's essay focuses on the phenomenon of "boomerang kids"—the trend among millennials to delay marriage, to put off deciding on a career, and sometimes to live with their parents while looking for a job or deciding their next step. Rosie chose to analyze and synthesize two articles that appeared in 2010, when the boomerang kids phenomenon first began to be recognized as a cultural puzzle.

- Robin Marantz Henig, "What Is It about 20-Somethings?" from the *New York Times Magazine*, August 18, 2010

- A blog post by ScammedHard! "What's Wrong with 20-Somethings?" posted on the Web on August 20, 2010

Rosie's summaries and exploratory pieces will familiarize you with the content of these two articles. (You can also look up the original sources on the Web.) Her essay asks and answers the question, "What are the causes of Generation Y's (the Millennials') delayed-adulthood and how should society respond?"

Summarizing Your Texts to Explore Their Ideas

The texts you are working with will most likely be magazine articles, op-ed pieces, blogs, scholarly articles, and/or book chapters. As a starting point for grappling

Instructions on how to write a summary are found in Chapter 6.

with each author's ideas, we recommend that you compose careful summaries of each text. As Chapter 6 explains, summary writing is a method of analysis that requires you to read texts closely, dwell with their ideas, and examine the relationship of the parts to the whole. Writing summaries prompts you to read each text with the grain, adopting each text's perspective and walking in each author's shoes. When you summarize a text, you try to achieve an accurate, thorough understanding of it by stating its main ideas in a tightly distilled format. It is often a good idea to create a paragraph-length summary of each reading to give you the space you need to cover the main ideas of the article or chapter. Later, for your essay itself, your instructor may give you a word limit for your summaries, asking you to shorten them to make more room in your essay for your analysis and synthesis.

Instructions on how to use attributive tags are found in Skill 23.3.

What follows are student Rosie Evans's summaries of the two readings she used in her synthesis essay. Notice how she uses attributive tags to show that she is representing the authors' ideas, not her own, and notice the neutral, non-judgmental approach she takes.

Rosie Evans's Summary of Robin Marantz Henig's Article

In her *New York Times Magazine* article "What Is It About 20-Somethings?" Robin Marantz Henig explores psychology professor Jeffrey Arnett's claim that twentysomethings are experiencing a new life stage called "emerging adulthood." For Arnett, this is a time for twentysomethings to explore their possibilities and identities, but this exploration also brings uncertainty, instability, and fear. He argues that these experiences are meaningful even though twentysomethings can seem lazy and directionless. Arnett thinks we should devote more resources to supporting them during this time. Henig links Arnett's claims to scientific findings that brains are not fully developed until the mid-twenties and suggests that Millennials' transition to adulthood may be limited because their brains haven't fully matured. She also wonders if changing cultural norms about traditional signs of adulthood, like marriage and financial independence, have removed pressure on twentysomething brains to assume adult functioning earlier in life. If brain development or emerging adulthood are really causing Millennials to delay adulthood, then Henig thinks some of our social institutions, like education and health care, should change to offer better support. She imagines expanding programs like AmeriCorps to help young people explore their interests and options before choosing a career. She acknowledges some drawbacks to providing more time for twentysomething to become self-supporting adults such as the drain on their parents' long-term financial security. Although she never firmly settles on a cause of Generation Y's delayed adulthood, she ultimately seems drawn to the idea of Arnett's emerging adults who use their twenties to become better-prepared adults.

Rosie Evans's Summary of Scammed Hard!'s Blog Post

In response to Henig, blogger Scammed Hard! argues in "What's Wrong with 20-Somethings?" that the economy is to blame for Generation Y's struggles. While agreeing that the brain is constantly changing, he characterizes Arnett's theory of emerging adulthood as a psychology professor's attempt to gain professional distinction by inventing a new theory. Referencing twentysomethings like Alexander the Great and Winston Churchill, he argues that our ancestors would not have achieved the success they did if emerging adulthood were a real life stage. Instead, he blames Baby Boomers for creating the conditions that killed the ambition and creativity of Generation Y. According to Scammed Hard!, the Boomers promoted the comfort of a middle-class lifestyle, encouraged dangerous levels of student debt, and then wrecked the economy. By setting high expectations and then limiting the possibility of meeting those expectations, they have destroyed this generation's incentives for hard work and sacrifice needed to succeed in America today. Scammed Hard! believes that although drifting through the twenties may provide Generation Y with a fun distraction, it does not prepare them with the skills and motivation to respond to our serious economic problems. Scammed Hard! notes that this reality endangers our shared welfare by failing to create a new generation of productive workers contributing to tax revenue. Most dangerous of all in the eyes of this blogger is characterizing Generation Y's shared strife as a positive new life stage, diverting attention from the urgent economic problems that drive this generation's reality.

For Writing and Discussion
Summarizing Your Texts

Begin by writing a 200–250-word summary of each of the texts you will use for your synthesis essay. Then confirm your decisions about main ideas by working in small groups or as a whole class to list the ideas that must be included in a summary of each piece for the summary to be accurate and complete. What points do you agree are secondary and can be left out?

Analyzing the Rhetorical Features of Your Texts

After you have summarized your texts, the next step is to analyze them rhetorically. Using the skills for rhetorical analysis taught in Chapters 4 and 6, analyze the way your texts handle purpose, audience, genre, angle of vision, evidence, and the use of appeals to *logos*, *ethos*, and *pathos*. Seek out background information on the author of a text and on the publication and genre (for instance, whether it's a scholarly book, journal, popular magazine, or a blog). Answering the following questions as you analyze each text will help you reach a deeper understanding of how the text conveys its ideas.

QUESTIONS TO ASK TO EXAMINE RHETORICAL FEATURES IN EACH TEXT

- Who is the author? To whom is the author writing and why? What is the motivating occasion?
- How do the publication and genre of the text influence the author's choices about structure and language?
- What angle of vision shapes the text and accounts for what is included, emphasized, and excluded?
- How logically developed and consistent is this text? Is the author's argument well supported with relevant evidence?
- How fair, reliable, knowledgeable, and authoritative does the author appear to be?

- How well does the author appeal to readers' emotions, imaginations, and values?
- Do you share the values of the author and his or her intended audience?

Rosie Evans's informal rhetorical analyses of her texts show her exploratory thinking.

Rosie Evans's Rhetorical Analysis of Henig's Article

Henig's article poses a set of related questions about Millennials and then tries to answer them by exploring psychological studies, neuroscience research, case studies, and survey data. The piece is written for a general audience; the readership of *The New York Times Magazine* is typically educated and liberal. However, the article is not directed at the Millennials themselves. Instead, it addresses their parents and society at large, who may feel responsible for causing and even solving the generation's problems. Henig aims to raise awareness about the twentysomething experience, explore the possible causes, and convince readers about the importance of the questions she raises and the solutions we choose. In my research, I discovered that the popularity of this article led Henig to write a book on the topic with her twentysomething daughter. I thought this suggested her investment in the topic as a mother witnessing her daughter or her daughter's friends adrift in their twenties.

Writer comments on the author's purpose.

Writer comments on the audience and publication.

Writer discusses the author's purpose.

Writer shares background information about the author.

Henig is a science writer, so she discusses the science and psychology of emerging adulthood in a balanced, reasoned way and uses survey data as evidence. For example, she explains a Purdue University survey that provides information about how much parents help their twentysomething children. Then, she uses the survey findings to suggest that the gap between the resources of low-income and high-income emerging adults probably grows during this time. Henig also carefully examines Arnett's claims and points out his contradictions. She questions how emerging adulthood could be a new life stage when not every twentysomething experiences it. She is concerned that Arnett uses one case study to represent all low-income Millennials and wants more evidence of their experiences. Henig's use of evidence and the problems she identifies with some of the information she finds help build trust with her readers.

Writer discusses the author's use of evidence.

However, what her article lacks is the voice of the twentysomethings themselves. The details of the twentysomething experience are revealed by academics' studies and experts' observations. When we finally meet a Millennial at the end of the article, her words and experiences are interpreted for us by her caregivers at a mental-health treatment facility. As the talking heads fret over the experiences of Generation Y, I wonder how the so-called emerging adults feel about all of this? In examining the Millennials' problems, I think Henig should have included them in the conversation.

Writer identifies gaps in the author's article, commenting on the limitations of the angle of vision and raising her own question.

Rosie Evans's Rhetorical Analysis of Scammed Hard!'s Blog Post

In contrast, Scammed Hard! is writing as a Millennial, and he is angry! In his post, he identifies as an "older (young) curmudgeon," and the tagline of his blog, "Sold down the river for a law school dream," hints that he is a disillusioned law student or graduate. He is

Writer identifies the angle of vision and tone of the blog author.

probably writing from the "scam blog" movement, a loose band of law school students and graduates who feel cheated by the high cost of school and the limited availability of jobs. The blog post reads as more of a stream-of-consciousness rant than a carefully-reasoned argument, but the writer's anger itself is convincing. You can feel his outrage at the economic realities crippling his generation and at Henig's willingness to consider a psychological explanation for their problems.

Writer shares her speculations about the author's background.

Posting anonymously on a blog, with its typical informal format, gives Scammed Hard! greater freedom of expression. For example, he uses sarcasm to show his disgust with Arnett and Henig, whom he calls "academic puffs and their pals at the *NYT*." But this sarcasm is also an example of his failure to build trust with his readers. Readers from the older generations whom he blames for the current state of affairs would probably be offended by his tone and aggression. He also sometimes treats Henig unfairly, assigning meaning to her work that I do not think she intended. He rarely supports his claims, and when he does, he uses underdeveloped anecdotes (like name-dropping Alexander the Great). The unbalanced nature of his work, combined with his sarcastic tone, is unlikely to convince readers who do not already agree with his views, no matter how large a role the economy plays in delaying adulthood for Millennials.

Writer discusses how the blog genre influences the depth and shape of this argument.

Writer points out the weaknesses of this blog post as persuasive writing and the blog author's limited audience appeal.

For Writing and Discussion
Analyzing the Rhetorical Strategies in Your Texts

Use the questions in the bulleted list titled "Questions to Ask to Examine Rhetorical Features in Each Text" (earlier in this chapter) to analyze the rhetorical features of your selected texts. You may choose to list the features as bullet points or write out paragraph descriptions. In small groups or as the whole class, discuss the features that you listed. Which particular features give you a deeper understanding of the texts?

Analyzing the Main Themes and Similarities and Differences in Your Texts' Ideas

After you understand how your texts work rhetorically, you are ready to analyze closely how each text addresses your synthesis question and to envision these texts in conversation. At this stage in your thinking, your main task is to identify main issues, ideas, or themes that surface in your texts. Then, from closely examining the ideas in each individual text, you can move to looking for similarities and differences among your texts. This process of thinking—using comparison and contrast—will help you clarify your understanding of each reading, but it will also help you see the texts in relationship to your synthesis question and in relationship to one another. As you consider each author's ideas, underlying values, and assumptions, think about how each text offers answers to your synthesis question and where these answers coincide and where they clash.

The following questions can guide your thinking and help you generate ideas for the analysis part of your synthesis essay.

QUESTIONS TO ASK TO HELP YOU EXPLORE SIMILARITIES AND DIFFERENCES IN YOUR TEXTS

- What dominant patterns of language and ideas (repetitions, emphases, tensions, and omissions) do you observe in each text?
- From these patterns you have observed, what main ideas or themes related to your synthesis question emerge in each text?
- What similarities and differences do you see in the way the authors choose to frame the issues they are writing about? How do their theses (either implied or stated) differ?
- What are the main similarities and differences in their angles of vision?
- What commonalities and intersections related to your synthesis question do you see in their ideas? What contradictions and clashes do you see in their ideas?
- What similarities and differences do you see in the authors' underlying values and assumptions?
- What overlap, if any, is there in these authors' examples and uses of terms?
- On the subject of your synthesis question, how would Author A respond to Author B?

In the following example of Rosie Evans's exploratory analysis of ideas in her texts, note how she has identified similarities among her texts. Note also how she begins to organize comparisons by points, to make analytical connections among them, and to push herself to think out exactly where these authors agree and differ.

Rosie Evans's Analysis of Similarities and Differences

Synthesis Question: What are the causes of the delayed-adulthood trends we see within Generation Y, and how should society respond?

SIMILARITIES BETWEEN THE TWO ARTICLES

- Both authors acknowledge that Generation Y's problems are not unique to their generation, and both use Baby Boomer experiences in the 60s and 70s as evidence.
- Despite the similarities between Generation Y and the Baby Boomers, both authors seem to think that Generation Y's problems are worse.
- Both authors find Arnett's theory limited by the fact that the emerging adult experience is more common among the privileged and therefore is not universal.
- Both authors accept the evidence that brains continue to develop into the mid- and late-twenties.

Differences between the Two Articles

Henig	Scammed Hard!
• Henig explores in-depth how psychology and brain science offer explanations for the Millennials' unsettled condition.	• Scammed Hard! does not accept psychological or neurological explanations and finds that these theories divert attention from the true causes.
• Henig believes the economy exacerbated trends already present in Millennials and would point to evidence of Generation Y's trends beginning before the Great Recession.	• Scammed Hard! believes the economy is the primary cause of the Millennials' drifting and blames the Baby Boomers for wrecking economic opportunity for Millennials.
• Henig suggests that if emerging adulthood is a new life stage, then social services should adapt to expand opportunities for Millennials to support themselves while simultaneously exploring their identities.	• Scammed Hard! implies that if the economy is the problem, then fixing it will address the Millennials' problems. He would be frustrated if resources were diverted from fixing the economy to encouraging Millennial self-exploration.
• Henig agrees with Arnett that Millennials may appear lazy and directionless and suggests that experiences in their twenties might help them make better choices later in life.	• Scammed Hard! thinks the Baby Boomers have ruined Millennials' work ethic with high expectations that reality cannot match. He seems to find Millennials lazy, but does not blame them.
• Henig finds evidence of parental support among both low-income and privileged Millennials, but also finds that privileged Millennials receive more benefits. These findings show how emerging adulthood, if it exists, is problematic because it widens the resource gap.	• Scammed Hard! believes that the lack of evidence of emerging adulthood in low-income Millennials falsifies Arnett's theory.

For Writing and Discussion
Generating Points about Themes, Shared Ideas, and Differences

Working on your own, identify main issues or themes in your assigned or chosen texts. Then explore the similarities and differences in their ideas. You may find that using bullets for your points helps you picture your points clearly, or you may want to write out your ideas in a draft form. Then, working in small groups or as a whole class, review the accuracy and importance of these similarities and differences. To deepen your analysis, discuss this question: How do each author's purposes, assumptions, and values account for the similarities and differences you have identified?

Generating Ideas of Your Own

One of your biggest challenges in writing a synthesis essay is to move beyond summary and analysis to synthesis. A successful synthesis essay incorporates ideas from your texts and yet represents your own independent, creative thinking, showing evidence of the dialectic process. As you synthesize ideas, you put ideas together in new combinations and you demonstrate how your analysis has informed and influenced the development of your own views. To move to synthesis, you need to think about how each text's differing perspectives have led you to new realizations that you want to contribute to the conversation. As you begin to formulate your synthesis, you will also need to reassert your personal/intellectual investment in the conversation. You will need to take ownership of the ideas and to emerge with a clearer sense of your own views. You may want to evaluate the texts to determine which has influenced your thinking the most and why. You may also want to consider which text—in your mind—makes the most significant contribution to the question you are exploring. The following questions can help you develop your own views.

QUESTIONS TO HELP YOU DEVELOP YOUR OWN VIEWS

- Do I have any knowledge from my personal experiences that is influencing my response to these texts?
- What do I agree with and disagree with in the texts I have analyzed?
- If I find one author's perspective more valid, accurate, interesting, or useful than another's, why do I feel this way?
- How have these texts changed my perception and understanding of an issue, question, or problem? (You might want to use these prompts: "I used to think _____, but now I think _____." "Although these texts have persuaded me that _____, I still have doubts about _____.")
- What is my current view on the synthesis question that connects my texts and that all my texts explore?
- Related to my synthesis question, what new, significant questions do these texts raise for me? What do I now see as the main controversies?
- How would I position myself in the texts' conversation?

To illustrate this step in writing a synthesis essay, we show you how Rosie Evans wrestled with the ideas in both texts and with her own experiences as she began to work out her position. You may find that some of these questions resonate more with you than others do, and you may choose to probe your responses to those particular questions.

Rosie Evans's Exploration of Her Personal Connections to Her Texts and the Synthesis Question

My older sister always seemed to succeed easily. She was high school valedictorian and mastered a long list of academic and leadership achievements in college. After she graduated, though, she seemed to drift. After several years of volunteer work and traveling, she returned home during the height of the Great Recession to live with our parents and work a retail job. My parents and other adults who expected success and greatness from her were baffled. I saw her frustration and even signs of depression as she worked a job she was overqualified for and struggled to afford health insurance while averaging 25 hours per week at $10 per hour. At the time, I felt sorry for her and suspected that she just didn't know what she was supposed to do without the structure of school and a clear definition of success to strive for. I sympathized with my parents, who were frustrated by her moping around the house and staying out late with friends while they footed her grocery bills and paid for her car insurance.

Writer chooses to explore the personal experience that led to her interest in the synthesis question.

Both Henig's and ScammedHard!'s articles caused me to consider other causes of my sister's struggles. I related to Scammed Hard!'s piece because I could hear my sister's voice in his angry exclamations. She definitely feels cheated by our parents, who raised us to believe if we studied hard and earned a Bachelor's degree, professionals would be begging us to work for them. It seems clear that the Great Recession changed the economic reality Millennials face once they graduate, perhaps permanently, and that they feel underprepared for the uncertain future. However, I had never considered that brain development had anything to do with it. Although I am not totally persuaded that "emerging adulthood" exists, Henig's article convinced me that the state of the economy alone cannot have caused Millennials' delayed adulthood. Like Henig, I wonder how changing cultural norms impact the pathways our brains choose for us. Henig at one point mentions that the Baby Boomer generation of "helicopter parents" might actually be pleased to be so needed by their children this late in life. Other articles I've skimmed offer deeper studies on the psychology of emerging adults, isolating variables like Millennials' relationships with their parents and their social support structures to understand their experiences as emerging adults. I wonder how much parents' willingness and capacity to help their children enables Millennials to postpone the traditional markers of adulthood? If my sister hadn't had the option to spend three years traveling and volunteer teaching and then return home to my parents' couch, would she have harnessed her talents and grown up earlier?

Writer shows how the texts have influenced her thinking.

She discusses her attraction to one of her text's ideas.

She discusses how the texts opened up new avenues of thought for her.

She shows how the texts have enlarged her view of the synthesis question and prompted her new questions

Taking Your Position in the Conversation: Your Synthesis

After you have generated your initial synthesis ideas—what perspectives you accept and reject, what new questions you have formulated, how your ideas have been modified and transformed through your analysis of your texts—you need to find a way to pull your ideas together. How do you want to enter the conversation of your synthesis question and your texts? What two or three main synthesis points would you like to develop? How will you respond to the ideas you have presented in your analysis and build on them in your own independent way? Your synthesis view should be the fruit of your intellectual work, a perspective that you have come to after analyzing the ideas of other authors and pondering those ideas reflectively and keenly. Here are some questions that can help you articulate the points that you want to develop in your essay.

QUESTIONS TO HELP YOU FORMULATE AND DEVELOP YOUR SYNTHESIS VIEWS

- What discoveries have I made after much thought?
- What are the most important insights I have gotten from these readings?
- What is my intellectual or personal investment with the synthesis question at this point?
- Where can I step out on my own, even take a risk, in my thinking about the ideas discussed in these texts?
- What new perspective do I want to share with my readers?

In the following passage, we show you Rosie Evans's step toward integrating her own ideas with ideas from her texts as she inserts her voice into the conversation about Millennials.

Rosie Evans's Exploration of Her Synthesis Points

I think both authors make strong cases for what they think is causing Millennials to delay adulthood, Scammed Hard! with his impassioned experiential case and Henig with her willingness to seek out and carefully examine evidence. They have convinced me that the unsettled state of Millennials is far too complex to have one isolated cause. Rather, it is the result of numerous factors: a shift in cultural expectations and parent-child relationships, economic realities created by the previous generation, and even twentysomethings' brains' responses to these changing circumstances. This high level of complexity is the very reason why identifying problems and agreeing on solutions are so difficult. What is the relationship between individuals and their parents? What role does the economic damage of decades of irresponsible policies play? How should social services respond to the increasingly accepted idea that young adults experience dramatic brain development? Rather than grapple with all these factors, I think many people fret over Millennials' mental health and argue over who deserves blame. Society at large seems guilty of the same inaction they see in the Millennials.

However, I don't think the Millennials are as inert as adults—and even these authors—seem to think they are. My sister worked very hard to survive on a retail salary while trying to navigate a home life she had left many years earlier. What she gave up on, though, was seeking out other opportunities, instead channeling her energy into surviving her immediate situation. When she faced the job market for a second time after earning a graduate degree, she submitted over fifty job applications, participated in multiple rounds of interviews for a total of eight positions, and was finally offered a part-time job she probably could have done without her graduate degree. She had gone from living a life where hard work led to success to a life where hard work led to a cycle of rejection and more hard work. Because of this, she feels powerless and trapped. How can we expect Millennials to stay motivated under such circumstances? It seems as though everyone needs to adjust their expectations, adults and Millennials alike.

Writer tentatively offers two main synthesis points.

First synthesis point: no simple or single cause of Millennials' problems.

Second synthesis point: writer speaks back to her texts: need to examine who Millennials really are and look at their individual experiences before generalizing about them.

These points incorporate writer's personal knowledge with ideas from the texts.

For Writing and Discussion
Generating and Developing Your Synthesis Points

In light of the ideas you have developed through your exploratory analysis of your texts, explore your own views of your synthesis question by freewriting in response to the "Questions to Help You Formulate and Develop Your Synthesis Views." What do you want to say in your own voice to show the connections you have made and the new insights you now have? What risky, surprising, or new views could you bring to your readers? Share your ideas with a writing partner or a group and explain why these points interest you.

Writing a synthesis essay

13.3 Write a synthesis essay that includes a focused thesis, a summary and analysis of each text under discussion, and a synthesis that contributes your own ideas.

Writing Project: Write a synthesis essay that meets the following criteria:

- Addresses a synthesis question that your instructor provides or that you formulate for yourself
- Summarizes and analyzes the views of at least two writers on this question (Your instructor might provide the texts or ask you to find your own as part of a research project.)
- Shows how you have wrestled with different perspectives on the question and have synthesized these ideas to arrive at your own new view of the question

---

Posing Your Synthesis Question

Posing your significant synthesis question is a key thinking move in writing a synthesis essay. Your instructor may give you a synthesis question, may ask you to pose your own synthesis question after a first reading of your assigned texts, or ask you to pose a synthesis question and find your own texts that speak to it. No matter what your exact starting point, articulating a synthesis question early on helps you zero in on a problem that invites alternative views and leads you to the texts that you will analyze and synthesize. Try to formulate a question that highlights important ideas in your readings, that has significance to you and others, and that will push you toward deep thinking about your texts. You can revise and refine your question as you proceed with your synthesis essay through the exploratory steps that we have just described.

Generating Ideas and Drafting

To generate ideas for your synthesis essay, do the sequence of thinking and exploratory writing strategies described earlier in this chapter. Your main project in drafting your synthesis essay is to move from the kernels of good ideas that you generated during exploratory writing to a focused, logically organized, and fully developed discussion of these ideas. Strategies Charts 13.1 and 13.2 provide strategies for developing the analysis and synthesis sections of your essay.

Writing a Thesis for a Synthesis Essay

In a synthesis essay, your thesis statement is particularly important, and it can be challenging to write. It sets up your readers' expectations, promising an illuminating view of the texts you have worked with. It should reflect earnest intellectual work, promise insights achieved through serious reflection, present your own original connection of ideas, and contain some element of risk and newness. Avoid bland, noncontestable thesis statements such as "These articles have both good and bad points."

Strategies Chart 13.1 Strategies for Shaping the Analytical Section of Your Essay

What to Consider in Planning the Analysis Section of Your Essay	Questions and Decisions
• Your analysis section, usually one-half to two-thirds of your essay, lays the foundation for your synthesis. • This section discusses several ways that your texts relate to your synthesis question.	• How many analytical points do you want to develop? • What are these points?
• Your analysis section should show that you have wallowed in the complexity of your texts. • It may include points about the rhetorical features of your texts (as in a rhetorical critique), and it may include points about the ideas (as in an ideas critique). • It should map out and explain a number of important similarities and differences in your texts.	Consider developing answers to these questions: • How do your texts frame the problem? How do they present different angles of vision? Where do they intersect in their perspectives and approaches? How do they argue and support their views with evidence? • How rhetorically effective are these texts? • What do the authors do to make their readers think?

Strategies Chart 13.2 Strategies for Shaping the Synthesis Section of Your Essay

What to Consider in Planning the Synthesis Section of Your Essay	Questions and Decisions
• Your essay should build to your synthesis section, typically one-third to one-half of your essay.	• How can you best show where the texts and their authors promote your own independent thinking? • What synthesis points do you want to explore and discuss?
• The synthesis section of your essay should show your informed, independent thinking. • It should show how you have worked your way to a new understanding and created your own view.	• What new insights have you developed through studying these texts? • What new perspectives have you gained through the contrast and/or clash of different ideas? • How much or how little have these texts changed your views and why?

You will probably want to work back and forth between formulating your thesis statement and drafting the analysis and synthesis sections of your essay. We recommend that you map out a rough thesis, draft your essay, and then revise and sharpen your thesis. For a synthesis essay, it is sometimes difficult to write a one-sentence, high-level thesis statement that encompasses both your analysis and your synthesis points. In such cases, you can write two lower-level, more specific thesis statements—one for your analysis section and one for your synthesis section—and simply join them together. What is important is that your thesis encapsulates your stance on these texts. It should concisely convey what views, informed by your analysis of the texts, you are adding to the conversation. By forecasting your main analysis and synthesis points, you create a map for your readers. The following examples use Rosie Evans's thesis statement to illustrate these different options.

LOW-LEVEL, TWO-SENTENCE THESIS

Although both authors identify the negative impacts of Generation Y's delayed adulthood and call for society's urgent attention and action, Henig highlights the positive opportunities while Scammed Hard! focuses on the economic dangers. Both articles helped me understand why it is complicated to identify causes and propose solutions and nurtured my conviction that any workable solution must offer Millennials an active role in crafting society's response.

HIGH-LEVEL, ONE-SENTENCE THESIS

Both Henig's more psychological approach to the problems of Millennials and Scammed Hard!'s economic critique and their suggestions for solutions have led me to examine more closely the causes of Millennials' problems and to endorse a more complex explanation and a solution that involves active participation of Millennials themselves.

Organizing and Revising a Synthesis Essay

The biggest organizational decisions you have to make in writing a synthesis essay are how much to summarize your texts and how to incorporate these summaries into your essay. Your decisions should be guided by your audience's familiarity with the texts you are discussing and the complexity of the points you are making. Two ways of organizing a synthesis essay are shown in Figure 13.1.

As you revise your synthesis essay, make sure that you have set up the synthesis question effectively. Then work on clarifying and developing your analytical points while striving for an engaging style. Also consider how to make your synthesis views more clearly reflect your own wrestling with the texts' ideas. Think about finding the most interesting ways to show how these texts have enlarged and deepened your own views.

Questions for Peer Review

In addition to the generic peer review questions explained in Skill 17.4, ask your peer reviewers to address these questions:

INTRODUCTION, SUMMARIES OF THE TEXTS, AND THESIS

1. What works well about the writer's presentation of the synthesis question that connects the texts under examination? How could the writer better show this question's significance and problematic nature?

2. Where could the writer's summaries of the texts be expanded, condensed, or clarified? Where would the summaries be better located in the essay to help readers?

3. How could the thesis be made more focused, risky, and clear in setting up the writer's analytical and synthesis points?

ANALYTICAL SECTION OF THE ESSAY

1. How could the writer's analytical points more clearly compare and contrast the authors' values, assumptions, angles of vision, or rhetorical strategies in addressing the synthesis question?

2. What further textual evidence could the writer add to develop these analytical points and make them more interesting or comprehensive?

SYNTHESIS SECTION OF THE ESSAY

1. How could the writer's synthesis points more clearly demonstrate the writer's thoughtful interaction with these texts?

2. What examples or other specifics could the writer include to develop these synthesis points more effectively?

3. How could the writer conclude this essay more effectively to leave readers with a new perspective on the texts and on the underlying question?

Figure 13.1 Two Frameworks for a Synthesis Essay

Framework 1

Introduction and summary of both texts (several paragraphs)	• Presents the synthesis question and hooks readers • Summarizes the texts (unless your instructor posits that readers have already read the texts, in which case you can omit the summaries or reduce them to one or two sentences each) • Presents your thesis, which maps out your main analytical and synthesis points (Your thesis might come at the end of the paragraphs with your summaries or in a mini-paragraph of its own.)
Analytical section	• Includes paragraphs discussing and developing your analytical points
Synthesis section	• Includes paragraphs discussing and developing your synthesis points
Concluding paragraph	• Reiterates the values and limitations of the texts you have analyzed • Pulls together your new insights • Leaves readers thinking about your views

Framework 2

Introduction	• Presents the synthesis question and hooks readers • Presents your thesis, which maps out your main analytical and synthesis points
Summary/analysis of first text	• Summarizes the first text • Analyzes the first text
Summary/analysis of second text	• Summarizes the second text • Analyzes the second text, perhaps with connections and differences with the first text
Synthesis section	• Develops several main synthesis points
Concluding paragraph	• Reiterates values and limitations of the texts you have analyzed • Pulls together your new insights • Leaves readers thinking about your views

Multimodal or Online Assignment Options

Online Discussion On a class discussion board, class blog, or wiki space, post your own summaries of several readings your class has done and then include your own synthesis of these readings, exploring several points of similarity and difference. Share your own perspective of the way these readings have shaped your thinking. You may also want to respond to the synthesis discussions that others have posted.

Reading

The reading for this chapter is Rosie Evans's final synthesis essay, which developed out of the exploratory writing and thinking steps described earlier.

Rosie Evans (student)

Boomerang Kids: What Are the Causes of Generation Y's Growing Pains?

My older sister always seemed to succeed easily—that is, until she graduated from college. She went from high school valedictorian and university academic leader to perpetual volunteer and wandering world traveler. When the economy collapsed during the Great Recession, she returned home to live with our parents and work a retail job, confounding the many adults who expected great accomplishments from her. As it turns out, my sister's experience is not isolated but rather represents the experience of a larger cohort, those born roughly between 1980 and 2000. This generation is delaying life choices that traditionally signaled adulthood—like marriage, parenthood, or establishing a career—choosing instead to travel and experiment with different jobs. Many from this generation end up returning to live at home and/or relying on their parents for financial support, putting stress on their family relationships and their own mental health. The numerous labels attached to this generation—Millennials, Generation Y, the Lost Generation, boomerang kids, the Peter Pan generation, emerging adults, accordion families—show that our society is struggling to name and define exactly what is happening and what to do about it. What are the causes of the delayed-adulthood trends we see within Generation Y and how should society respond?

One point of view I explored on this question is discussed in Robin Marantz Henig's 2010 *New York Times Magazine* article "What Is It About 20-Somethings?" Henig, a science writer, probes possible psychological and neurological explanations for Generation Y's delayed adulthood. She examines psychology professor Jeffrey Arnett's claim that twentysomethings are experiencing a new life stage called "emerging adulthood" in which they explore their possibilities and identities while also dealing with the instability, uncertainty, and fear that exploration brings. Rather than seeing Millennials as lazy and directionless, Arnett sees them as having meaningful experiences leading to better decisions about the kinds of lives they want to lead as adults. Henig links Arnett's claims to scientific findings that brains are not fully developed until the mid-twenties and suggests that immature brains might contribute to Millennials' delaying of adulthood. She also wonders if changing cultural norms about traditional signs of adulthood have removed pressure on twentysomething brains to achieve adult functioning earlier in life. If these claims are true, Henig suggests that our social institutions, like education and health care, should change to offer better support to Millennials as they transition to adulthood.

In response to Henig's article, blogger Scammed Hard! argues in his post "What's Wrong with 20-Somethings?" that the economy is to blame for Generation Y's struggles. While agreeing that the brain is constantly changing, he dismisses Arnett's theory of emerging adulthood as a bogus psychological theory designed to give its inventor

Opens with writer's investment and introduces the context for the issue, showing why it is problematic, and leads into the synthesis question.

States the synthesis question.

Introduces the first text and summarizes it.

Introduces the second text and summarizes it.

professional distinction. Instead, Scammed Hard! blames Generation Y's struggles on Baby Boomers' destruction of the economy combined with their promotion of dangerous levels of student debt and their encouragement of a comfortable middle-class lifestyle. By setting high expectations and then making those expectations impossible to fulfill, Boomers have destroyed Generation Y's incentives for hard work and sacrifice. Scammed Hard! believes that although drifting toward adulthood may provide Millennials with a fun distraction, it does not prepare them with the skills and motivation needed to find success in a destroyed economy.

Although both authors identify the negative impacts of Generation Y's delayed adulthood and call for society's urgent attention and action, Henig highlights the positive opportunities while Scammed Hard! focuses on the economic dangers. Both articles helped me understand why it is complicated to identify causes and propose solutions and nurtured my conviction that any workable solution must offer Millennials an active role in crafting society's response.

Both Henig and Scammed Hard! acknowledge that the current trends among Millennials are not unique to this generation (after all, the Baby Boomers themselves went through a hippie period). Nevertheless, they acknowledge that the problem of delayed adulthood is more widespread and troubling today. Using survey data, Henig compares the average age of marriage and the percentage of twentysomethings living at home in the 70s and today to show that delayed adulthood is more prevalent now. Scammed Hard! argues that even hippies eventually had to settle down and make productive contributions to society. Both authors worry about the long-term impacts to our society as Millennials take longer to reach adulthood and become innovative, industrious, taxpaying members of society.

While both authors accept the science on brain development, they disagree on the role it plays in causing the Millennials' problems. Henig uses the psychological research to suggest that it might be time for society to enact policies that enrich "the cognitive environment of people in their 20s" in order to better shape their brains for the demands of adulthood. As a science writer and parent of a Millennial, Henig constructs a balanced, reasoned discussion that builds trust with her readers—other parents and the larger society who may feel responsible for causing and solving the Millennials' problems. In contrast, Scammed Hard's refuses to "write off the problems my generation faces as merely 'normal stages of development.'" He thinks that focusing on a new "life stage" diverts attention from the urgent economic problems that drive this generation's reality and account for Millennials' anger, depression, and humiliating inability to support themselves. Writing as a Millennial from the "scam blog" movement, a loose band of law school students and graduates who feel cheated by the high cost of education and the limited availability of jobs, Scammed Hard! effectively employs his outrage to make a compelling argument for economic causes of Generation Y's problems. He believes that the Boomers' decision to outsource jobs, lend irresponsibly, and encourage student debt led to the catastrophic economic collapse that has limited Millennials' financial independence, whereas Henig thinks the economy has merely accelerated trends that already existed among Millennials before the Great Recession.

The differences in how each author views the causes of Generation Y's problems affect their proposed solutions. Henig thinks we should devote our resources to modifying and expanding social services that support Millennials of all income levels as their brains and identities develop. In contrast, Scammed Hard! urges Baby Boomers to fix the economy and calls on everyone to mobilize to create better incentives for hard work and innovation among the younger generation.

Henig's discussion of emerging adulthood raised some important questions for me. She mentions that the Boomer generation of "helicopter parents" might actually be pleased to be so involved in their children's lives. I wonder how much parents' willingness and capacity to help their children enable Millennials to delay adulthood. If my sister hadn't had the parent-subsidized option to spend three years volunteering and traveling and then return home to our parents' couch, would she have harnessed her talents and grown up earlier? And if mostly privileged Millennials are the ones choosing to delay adulthood, does it make sense to devote even more resources to this already well-supported group? Or should the social support systems be expanded to provide low-income Millennials similar opportunities for financial security and self-exploration?

After reading these articles, I am convinced that Generation Y's delayed adulthood is the result of many complex causes, not just one. These factors include shifts in cultural expectations for young adults, evolving parent-child relationships, collapse of the job market, and other economic realities created by the previous generation, and maybe also the effects of not-yet-mature twentysomething brains. The factors also likely reinforce one another, strengthening their collective impact. For example, perhaps Baby Boomer parents are subconsciously trying to cover up their guilt over the state of the economy by lifting their children's financial burdens. Also, because it is more culturally acceptable to marry later in life and medically possible to have kids during middle age, perhaps Millennials don't worry about a career because they do not yet need financial security for starting a family. Rather than tackle the complex causes of the problems, I sense that established adults find it easier to fret over Millennials' mental health and argue over who is to blame, making society at large guilty of the same inaction they accuse Millennials of.

However, when I think about my sister, I can't agree that Millennials are as inert as adults seem to think they are. What concerns me about the perspectives on Millennials is how often older generations view them as passive actors in their own lives. I think Millennials work a lot harder and more courageously than people realize and make active, intentional choices as best they can under the circumstances. Henig's piece, for all its measured evidence in its ten pages, fails to offer the authentic perspective of a Millennial voice. She should have talked to my sister, who worked very hard to survive on a retail salary while trying to navigate a home life she had left behind years earlier. However, as my sister devoted most of her energy to survival, she gave up on seeking other opportunities for herself. I think this happened because of her disappointment as she transitioned between life where hard work led to success and life where hard work led to a cycle of rejection and more hard work. When she faced the job market for a second time after earning a graduate degree, she submitted over fifty job applications, participated in multiple rounds of interviews for a total of eight positions, and was finally offered a part-time job she probably could have done without her graduate degree. This situation—certainly not unique among Millennials—made her feel powerless and trapped, because she wants to be making successful, valuable contributions to society.

Synthesis point discusses the writer's own view.

I believe a real solution to Millennials' problems must be multifaceted if it is going to significantly impact the numerous interrelated causes. But more importantly, an effective solution will be one that creates a partnership with Millennials, listens to *them*, and offers them an active role in the response. It is a challenge I think all of their experiences and self-reflection have prepared them for. And it will align with their desires to participate, rather than watch, as the economy, and maybe even adulthood, pass them by.

Conclusion with final connections.

Henig and Scammed Hard! offer differing perspectives on the causes and solutions to Generation Y's delayed adulthood. I encourage them, and anyone else who is serious about making changes to the systems and social structures that have created an America in which it is difficult to grow up, to begin by connecting with the Millennials themselves. They might find that Generation Y is full of ideas, creativity, and possibility waiting to be unleashed.

Works Cited

Complete citation of texts in MLA format.

Henig, Robin Marantz. "What Is It about 20-Somethings?" *The New York Times Magazine*, 18 Aug. 2010, www.nytimes.com/2010/08/22/magazine/22Adulthood-t.html?pagewanted=all&_r=0.

"What's Wrong with 20-Somethings?" *Scammed Hard!*, 20 Aug. 2010, scammedhard.blogspot.com/2010/08/whats-wrong-with-20-somethings.html.

Chapter 14
Writing a Classical Argument

Learning Objectives

14.1 Explain the theory and rhetorical principles underlying effective arguments.

14.2 Describe the stages through which many people travel in their growth as arguers.

14.3 Use your knowledge of the components of argument to create an effective argument plan.

14.4 Avoid logical fallacies in your arguments.

14.5 Write a classical argument that offers reasons and evidence in support of your position while also summarizing and responding to opposing views.

Understanding classical argument

14.1 Explain the theory and rhetorical principles underlying effective arguments.

On many occasions in your academic or civic life you will be asked to take a stand on an issue, to support your stand persuasively with reasons and evidence, and to respond ethically to opposing or alternative views. The need for argument arises whenever members of a community disagree about the best solution to a problem or the best answer to a question. Classical rhetoricians believed that the art of arguing is essential for good citizenship. If disputes can be resolved through exchange of perspectives, negotiation of differences, and flexible seeking of the best solutions to a problem, then nations won't have to resort to war or individuals to fist fights.

What Is Argument?

The ethical use of argument involves two principles: truth seeking and persuasion.

- *Truth seeking* is a diligent, open-minded, and responsible search for the best course of action or solution to a problem, taking into account all the available information and alternative points of view.

- *Persuasion* is the art of making a claim about an issue and justifying it with evidence that overcomes the audience's initial resistance and moves them toward your position. (By long-standing tradition, the thesis of an argument is often called its *claim*.)

These two principles of argument may seem at odds. Truth seeking asks us to relax our certainties and be willing to change our views, while persuasion asks us to be certain, to be committed to our claims, and to get others to change their views. We can overcome this paradox if we dispel two common misleading views of argument.

The most common misconception is that argument is a fight, as in "I just got into a horrible argument with my roommate." This view of argument as a shouting match in which you ridicule anyone who disagrees with you (popularized by radio and television talk shows and the Internet) entirely disregards argument as truth seeking. It also misrepresents argument as persuasion because it polarizes people rather than promoting understanding, new ways of seeing, and change.

The second misconception is that argument is a pro/con debate modeled after high school or college debate matches. Although debating can be an excellent way to develop critical thinking skills, it is not synonymous with argument. A debate is a two-sided contest with winners and losers. However, controversial issues involve many different points of view, not just two, and reducing an issue to pro/con positions oversimplifies the complexity of the disagreement. Instead of thinking of *both* sides of an issue, we need to think of *all* sides. Equally troublesome, a debate invites us to ask, "Who won the debate?" rather than "What is the best solution to the question that divides us?" The best solution might be a compromise between the two debaters or an undiscovered third position. Unlike an effective argument, a debate tends to privilege the confident extremes rather than the complex and muddled middle.

Thus the best way to understand argument is neither as a fight nor a debate, but rather as the deliberations of a committee representing a wide spectrum of community voices charged with finding the best solution to a problem. From this perspective, argument is both a *process* and a *product*. As a process, argument is an act of inquiry characterized by fact-finding, information gathering, and consideration of alternative points of view. As a product, it is someone's contribution to the conversation at any one moment—a turn taken in a conversation, a formal speech, or a written position paper such as the one you will write for this chapter.

The goal of argument as process is truth seeking; the goal of argument as product is persuasion. When members of a diverse committee are willing to argue persuasively for their respective points of view but are simultaneously willing to listen to other points of view and to change or modify their positions in light of new information or better arguments, then both components of argument are fully in play.

Truth-Seeking and Persuasion in Practice: A Thought Experiment

The following thought experiment, which asks you to think about the ethical treatment of animals, will help you experience argument as truth seeking and persuasion. References to this thought experiment will recur as the chapter progresses. Your initial position may reflect your personal *ideology*—that is, the network of basic values, beliefs, and assumptions that guide your view of the world. However, if you adopt an open-minded, truth-seeking attitude, your initial position may evolve as the argumentative conversation progresses. In fact, the conversation may even change some of your basic beliefs, because ideologies aren't set in stone and because many of us have unresolved allegiances to competing ideologies that may be logically inconsistent (for example, a belief in freedom of speech combined with a belief that hate speech should be banned). In this thought exercise we ask you to record your initial views and then to keep track of how your views may change during further reflection or ensuing class discussions.

THOUGHT EXPERIMENT

Situation: Starlings build nests in the attic of a family's house, gaining access to the attic through a torn vent screen. Soon the eggs hatch, and every morning at sunrise the family is awakened by the sound of birds squawking and wings beating against rafters as the starlings fly in and out of the house to feed the hatchlings. After losing considerable early morning sleep, the family repairs the screen. Unable to get in and out, the parent birds are unable to feed their young. The birds die within a day.

Question at issue: Was the family's action an instance of cruelty to animals (that is, was their decision to repair the screen ethically justifiable or not)?

For Writing and Discussion
Exploring the Starling Case

Individual Task

1. Freewrite your initial response to this question. Explain why you think the family's act was or was not ethical.

2. We initially framed this issue as an after-the-fact yes/no question: Is the family guilty of cruelty to animals? But we can also frame it as an open-ended, before-the-fact question: "What should the family do about the starlings in the attic?" Suppose you are a family member discussing the starlings at dinner, prior to the decision to fix the vent screen. Make a list of your family's other options and try to determine whether one of these options would have been better than fixing the vent screen. Why?

Small Groups or Whole Class

1. Share your individual responses to these questions and then try to reach a group consensus on the issues. Was fixing the screen an instance of cruelty to animals? What other alternatives, if any, might have been ethically preferable?

2. If class discussion caused some students' views to evolve or change, how did those views change and why?

Stages of development: your growth as an arguer

14.2 Describe the stages through which many people travel in their growth as arguers.

Having introduced you to argument as both process and product, we now turn to the details of effective argumentation. We begin by describing the typical stages that mark students' growth as arguers. While these stages may or may not describe your own development, they suggest the skills you should strive to acquire.

- *Stage 1: Argument as personal opinion.* When learning about argument for the first time, many students express strong personal opinions but have trouble justifying their opinions with reasons and evidence. They often create short, undeveloped, circular arguments that lack evidence and insult those who disagree. The following freewrite, written by a student first confronting the starling case, illustrates this stage:

  > The family shouldn't have killed the starlings because that is really wrong! I mean that act was disgusting. It makes me sick to think how so many people are just willing to kill something for no reason at all. How are these parents going to teach their children values if they just go out and kill little birds for no good reason?!! This whole family is what's wrong with America!

- This writer's opinion is passionate and heartfelt, but it provides neither reasons nor evidence why someone else should hold the same opinion.

- *Stage 2: Argument structured as claim supported by one or more reasons.* Stage 2 represents a quantum leap in argumentative skill because the writer can now produce a rational plan containing *point sentences* (the reasons) and *supporting details* (the evidence). The writer who produced the previous freewrite later developed this structure:

  The family's act constituted cruelty to animals

  - because the starlings were doing minimal harm.
  - because other options were available.
  - because the way they killed the birds caused needless suffering.

- *Stage 3: Increased attention to truth seeking.* In Stage 3, students become increasingly engaged with the complexity of the issue as they listen to their classmates' views, conduct research, and evaluate alternative perspectives and stances. They are often willing to change their positions when they see the power of other arguments.

- *Stage 4: Ability to articulate the unstated assumptions underlying the arguments.* Each reason in a writer's argument is based on an assumption, value, or belief (often unstated) that the audience must accept if the argument is to be persuasive. Often the writer needs to state these assumptions explicitly and support them. At Stage 4, students identify and analyze their own assumptions and those of their intended audiences. Students gain increased skill at accommodating alternative views through refutation (that is, disproving or pointing to weaknesses in a competing argument) or concession (that is, granting that a competing argument has some merit).

- *Stage 5: Ability to link an argument to the intended audience's values and beliefs.* At Stage 5, students are increasingly able to link their arguments to their audience's values and beliefs and to adapt structure and tone to their audience's resistance level. Students also appreciate how delayed-thesis arguments and other strategies can be more effective than closed-form arguments when addressing hostile audiences.

The rest of this chapter helps you progress through these stages.

Understanding the components of argument

14.3 Use your knowledge of the components of an argument to create an effective argument plan.

This section provides a compact but comprehensive overview of argumentation. It describes the components of argument and then explains how to use this knowledge to plan your argument effectively to appeal to your intended audience. Although you can read this section in one sitting, we recommend that you break your reading into subsections, going over the material slowly and applying its ideas to your own evolving argument in progress. If you let these explanations sink in gradually, you will appreciate their power in helping you become an effective, persuasive arguer.

Creating an Argument Frame: A Claim with Reasons

Somewhere in the writing process, whether early or late, you need to create a **frame** for your argument. This frame includes a clear question that focuses the argument, your claim, and one or more supporting reasons. Often you can attach your reasons (stated as *because* clauses) to your claim to provide a working thesis statement.

FINDING AN ARGUABLE ISSUE   At the heart of any argument is an **issue**, which we can define as a question that invites more than one reasonable answer and thus leads to perplexity or disagreement. This requirement excludes disagreements based on personal tastes, where no shared criteria can be developed ("Baseball is more fun than soccer"). It also excludes purely private questions because issues arise out of disagreements in *communities*.

Issue questions are often framed as yes/no choices, especially when they appear on ballots or in courtrooms. For example:

- Should concealed carry be allowed on college campuses?
- Should the federal government enact a carbon tax to fight climate change?
- Is this defendant guilty of armed robbery?

Just as frequently, issue questions can be framed openly, inviting many different possible answers. For example:

- What is the best federal policy for fighting global warming?
- Which government policies, if any, would reduce the frequency of mass shootings?

It is important to remember that framing an issue as a yes/no question does not mean that all points of view fall neatly into pro/con categories. Although citizens may be forced to vote yes or no on a proposed ballot initiative, they can support or oppose the initiative for a variety of reasons. Some may vote happily for the initiative, others vote for it only by holding their noses, and still others oppose it vehemently for a variety of reasons. To argue effectively, you need to appreciate the wide range of perspectives from which people approach the yes/no choice.

How you frame your question necessarily affects the scope and shape of your argument. In our thought experiment, we framed the starling question in two ways: (1) Was the family guilty of cruelty to animals? and (2) What should the family do about the starlings? Framed in the first way, your argument would have to develop criteria for "cruelty to animals" and then argue whether the family's actions met those criteria. Framed in the second way, your argument would focus on a solution to the problem, ranging from doing nothing (waiting for the birds to grow up and leave, then fixing the screen) to climbing into the attic and drowning the birds so that their deaths are quick and painless. Or you could word the question in a broader, more philosophical way: When are humans justified in killing animals? Or you could focus on a sub-issue: When can an animal be labeled a "pest"?

For Writing and Discussion
Identifying Arguable Issues

1. Working individually, make a list of several communities that you belong to and then identify one or more questions currently being contested within those communities. (If you have trouble identifying a question, check your local campus and city newspapers or an organizational newsletter; you'll quickly discover a wealth of contested issues.) Then share your list with classmates.
2. Pick two or three issues of particular interest to you, and try framing them in different ways: as broad or narrow questions, as open-ended or yes/no questions. Share several examples for class discussion.

STATING A CLAIM   Your **claim** is the position you take on the issue. It is your brief, one-sentence answer to your issue question. All of the following are claims:

The family was not ethically justified in killing the starlings.
The city should build skateboarding areas with ramps in all city parks.
The federal government should enact a carbon tax to fight climate change.

You will appreciate argument as truth seeking if you find that your claim evolves as you think more deeply about your issue and listen to alternative views. Be willing to rephrase, soften, refocus, or even reverse your claim as you progress through the writing process.

Articulating Reasons

Your claim, which is the position you take on an issue, needs to be supported by reasons and evidence. A **reason** (sometimes called a **premise**) is a subclaim that supports your main claim. In speaking or writing, a reason is usually linked to the claim with such connecting words as *because, therefore, so, consequently,* and *thus.* In planning your argument, a powerful strategy for developing reasons is to harness the grammatical power of the conjunction *because*; think of your reasons as *because* clauses attached to your claim. Formulating your reasons in this way allows you to create a thesis statement that breaks your argument into smaller parts, with each part devoted to one of the reasons.

For advice on how much of your supporting argument you should summarize in your thesis statement, see Skill 18.4 on effective introductions.

Suppose, for example, that you are examining the issue "Should the government legalize hard drugs such as heroin and cocaine?" Here are several different points of view on this issue, each expressed as a claim with *because* clauses:

ONE VIEW

Cocaine and heroin should be legalized

- because legalizing drugs will keep the government out of people's private lives.
- because keeping these drugs illegal has the same negative effects on our society that alcohol prohibition did in the 1920s.

ANOTHER VIEW

Cocaine and heroin should be legalized

- because taking drug sales out of the hands of drug dealers would reduce street violence.
- because decriminalization would cut down on prison overcrowding and free police to concentrate on dangerous crime rather than on finding drug dealers.
- because elimination of underworld profits would change the economic structure of the underclass and promote shifts to socially productive jobs and careers.

STILL ANOTHER VIEW

The government should not legalize heroin and cocaine

- because doing so will lead to an increase in drug users and addicts.
- because doing so will send the message that it is okay to use hard drugs.

Although the yes/no framing of this question seems to reduce the issue to a two-position debate, many different value systems are at work here. The first pro-legalization argument values maximum individual freedom. The second argument—although it too supports legalization—takes a community perspective, valuing the social benefits of eliminating the black market drug-dealing culture. Note, too, that individuals could oppose legalization for a variety of reasons.

For Writing and Discussion
Generating *Because* Clauses

Working in small groups or as a whole class, generate a list of reasons for and against one or more of the following yes/no claims. State your reasons as *because* clauses. Think of as many *because* clauses as possible by imagining a wide variety of perspectives on the issue.

1. The school year for grades 1 through 12 should be lengthened to eleven months.
2. The United States should institute a compulsory gun buyback program similar to what Australia has done.
3. The United States should adopt a single-payer, government-financed healthcare system like that of Canada.
4. Violent video games are a harmful influence on teenage boys. [or] Women's fashion and style magazines (such as *Glamour* or *Seventeen*) are harmful influences on teenage girls.
5. The minimum wage should be raised to $15 per hour.

Articulating Underlying Assumptions

So far, we have focused on the frame of an argument as a claim supported with one or more reasons. Shortly, we will proceed to the flesh and muscle of an argument, which is the evidence you use to support your reasons. But before turning to evidence, we need to look at another crucial part of an argument's frame: its **underlying assumptions**. Think of the underlying assumption as a general principle, rule, belief, or value that connects the reason to the claim. It answers your reader's question, "Why, if I accept your reason, should I accept your claim?"*.

WHAT DO WE MEAN BY AN UNDERLYING ASSUMPTION?   Every time you link a claim with a reason, you make a silent assumption that you may need to articulate and examine. Consider this argument:

> The family was justified in killing the starlings because starlings are pests.

To support this argument, the writer would first need to provide evidence that starlings are pests (examples of the damage they do and so forth). But the persuasiveness of the argument rests on the underlying assumption that it is okay to kill pests. If an audience doesn't agree with that assumption, then the argument flounders unless the writer articulates the assumption and defends it. The complete frame of the argument must therefore include the underlying assumption.

Claim: The family was justified in killing the starlings.

Reason: Because starlings are pests.

Underlying assumption: It is ethically justifiable to kill pests.

It is important to examine the underlying assumption that connects any reason to its claim *because you must determine whether your audience will accept that assumption. If your audience will not accept the assumption, you need to make it explicit and support it.*
Here are a few more examples of claims, reasons, and underlying assumptions:

Claim with reason: Students should be asked what pronoun they prefer because doing so would help society overcome binary gender stereotyping.

Underlying assumption: It is good to overcome binary gender stereotyping.

Claim with reason: The government should not legalize heroin and cocaine because doing so will lead to an increase in drug users.

---

* Our explanation of argument structure is influenced by the work of philosopher Stephen Toulmin, who viewed argument as a dynamic courtroom drama where opposing attorneys exchange arguments and cross-examinations before a judge and jury. Although we use Toulmin's strategies for analyzing an argument structure, we have chosen not to use his specialized terms, which include *warrant* (the underlying assumption connecting a reason to a claim), *grounds* (the evidence that supports the claim), *backing* (the evidence and subarguments that support the warrant), *conditions of rebuttal* (all the ways that skeptics could attack an argument or all the conditions under which the argument wouldn't hold), and *qualifier* (an indication of the claim's strength). However, your instructor may prefer to use these terms and in that case may provide you with more explanation and examples.

Underlying assumption: It is bad to increase the number of drug users.

Claim with reason: The family was guilty of cruelty to animals in the starling case because less drastic means of solving the problem were available.

Underlying assumption: A person should choose the least drastic means to solve a problem.

For Writing and Discussion
Identifying Underlying Assumptions

Identify the underlying assumptions in each of the following claims with reasons.

1. Cocaine and heroin should be legalized because legalizing drugs will keep the government out of people's private lives.

2. The government should raise gasoline taxes because the higher price would discourage people from driving gas-guzzling cars.

3. The government should not raise gasoline taxes because the higher gas prices would harm low-income people.

4. The government should not raise gasoline taxes because other means of fighting climate change would be more effective.

5. For-profit police practices (raising city or state income by aggressively writing tickets for traffic violations, burnt-out tail lights, and so forth) should be banned because these practices hurt people of color more than they hurt whites.

Using Evidence Effectively

Inside your arguments, each of your reasons (as well as any underlying assumptions that you decide to state explicitly and defend) needs to be supported either by sub-arguments or by evidence. By *evidence* we mean facts, examples, summaries of research articles, statistics, personal experiences, testimony, or other relevant data that will persuade your readers to accept your reasons.

Note that evidence always exists within a rhetorical context. As a writer you select and shape the evidence that best supports your position, knowing that skeptics may point to evidence that you did not select. Evidence is thus not the same as proof. Used ethically, evidence presents the best case for your claim without purporting to be the whole truth.

Evidence can sometimes come from personal experience, but in most cases it comes from your own field or library research. The following sections provide more information about the key types of evidence. *Note*: The examples in this section use the Modern Language Association (MLA) style for documenting sources. See Chapter 24 for full explanations of how to use both the MLA and APA (American Psychological Association) systems for citing and documenting sources.

FACTUAL DATA Factual data can provide persuasive support for your arguments. (Keep in mind that writers always select their facts through an angle of vision, so the use of facts doesn't stop skeptics from bringing in counterfacts.)

Here is how evolutionary biologist Olivia Judson used factual data to support her point that malaria-carrying mosquitoes cause unacceptable harm to human lives and the economy:

> Each year, malaria kills at least one million people and causes more than 300 million cases of acute illness. For children worldwide, it's one of the leading causes of death. The economic burden is significant too: Malaria costs Africa more than $12 billion in lost growth each year. In the United States, hundreds of millions of dollars are spent every year on mosquito control.

EXAMPLES   An example from personal experience can often be used to support a reason. Here is how student writer Ross Taylor used personal experience to argue that paintball is safe even though accidents can happen. (You can read his complete essay in the Readings section of this chapter.)

> I admit that paintball can be dangerous and that accidents do happen. I personally had a friend lose an eye after inadvertently shooting himself in the eye from a very close range. The fact of the matter is that he made a mistake by looking down the barrel of a loaded gun and the trigger malfunctioned. Had he been more careful or worn the proper equipment, he most likely would have been fine. During my first organized paintball experience I was hit in the goggles by a very powerful gun and felt no pain. The only discomfort came from having to clean all the paint off my goggles after the game. When played properly, paintball is an incredibly safe sport.

Besides specific examples like this, writers sometimes invent hypothetical examples, or *scenarios*, to illustrate an issue or speculate about the consequences of an event. (Of course, you must tell your reader that the example or scenario is hypothetical.)

SUMMARIES OF RESEARCH   Another common way to support an argument is to summarize research articles. Here is how a student writer, investigating whether menopausal women should use hormone replacement therapy to combat menopausal symptoms, used one of several research articles in her paper. The student began by summarizing research studies showing possible dangers of hormone replacement therapy. She then made the following argument:

> Another reason not to use hormone replacement therapy is that other means are available to ease such menopausal symptoms as hot flashes, irritability, mood changes, and sleep disturbance. One possible alternative treatment is acupuncture. One study (Cohen, Rousseau, and Carey) revealed that a randomly selected group of menopausal women receiving specially designed acupuncture treatment showed substantial decreases in menopausal symptoms as compared to a control group. What was particularly persuasive about this study was that both the experimental group and the control group received acupuncture, but the needle insertion sites for the experimental group were specifically targeted to relieve menopausal symptoms whereas the control group received acupuncture at sites used to promote general well-being. The researchers concluded that "acupuncture may be recommended as a safe and effective therapy for

reducing menopausal hot flushes as well as contributing to the reduction in sleep disruptions" (299).

STATISTICS   Another common form of evidence is statistics. Here is how one writer used statistics to argue that the federal government should raise fuel-efficiency standards placed on auto manufacturers:

> There is very little need for most Americans to drive huge SUVs. One recent survey found that 87 percent of four-wheel-drive SUV owners had never taken their SUVs off-road (Yacobucci) . . . . By raising fuel-efficiency standards, the government would force vehicle manufacturers to find a way to create more earth-friendly vehicles that would lower vehicle emissions and pollution. An article entitled "Update: What You Should Know Before Purchasing a New Vehicle" states that for every gallon of gasoline used by a vehicle, 20 to 28 pounds of carbon dioxide (CO_2) are released into the environment. This article further states that carbon dioxide emissions from automobiles are responsible for 20 percent of all carbon dioxide released into the atmosphere from human causes.

Just as writers select facts, examples, and research studies according to their angle of vision, so do they select and shape numerical data. In the previous example, the writer focuses on the environmental harm caused by vehicles, especially SUVs. But you must always read statistics rhetorically. For example, the same statistical "fact" can be framed in different ways. These two ways of using the same data provide a difference in focus and feel:

- "20 percent of human-caused CO_2 emissions come from automobiles." [puts automobiles in the foreground]
- "Although cars do cause some pollution, a full 80 percent of human-caused CO_2 emissions come from sources other than cars." [puts automobiles in the background]

TESTIMONY   Writers can also use expert testimony to bolster a case. The following passage from a student essay arguing in favor of therapeutic cloning uses testimony from a prominent physician and medical researcher. Part of the paragraph quotes this expert directly; another part paraphrases the expert's argument.

> As Dr. Gerald Fischbach, Executive Vice President for Health and Biomedical Sciences and Dean of Medicine at Columbia University, said in front of a United States Senate subcommittee: "New embryonic stem cell procedures could be vital in solving the persistent problem of a lack of genetically matched, qualified donors of organs and tissues that we face today." Fischbach goes on to say that this type of cloning could also lead to the discovery of cures for diseases such as ALS, Parkinson's disease, Alzheimer's disease, diabetes, heart disease, cancer, and possibly others.

Rather than provide direct research evidence that stem cell cloning might one day lead to cures for diseases, the writer draws on testimony from the dean of a prestigious medical school. Opponents of stem cell research might draw on other experts, selecting those who are skeptical of this claim.

SUB-ARGUMENTS   Sometimes writers support reasons not directly through data but through sequences of sub-arguments. Sometimes these sub-arguments develop a persuasive analogy, hypothesize about consequences, or simply advance the argument through a chain of connected points. In the following passage, taken from a philosophic article justifying torture under certain conditions, the author uses a sub-argument to support one of his main points—that a terrorist holding victims hostage has no rights:

> There is an important difference between terrorists and their victims that should mute talk of the terrorist's "rights." The terrorist's victims are at risk unintentionally, not having asked to be endangered. But the terrorist knowingly initiated his actions. Unlike his victims, he volunteered for the risks of his deed. By threatening to kill for profit or idealism, he renounces civilized standards, and he can have no complaint if civilization tries to thwart him by whatever means necessary.

Rather than using direct empirical evidence, the author supports his point with a sub-argument showing how terrorists differ from victims and thus relinquish their claim to rights.

Evaluating Evidence: The STAR Criteria

To make your arguments as persuasive as possible, apply to your evidence what rhetorician Richard Fulkerson calls the STAR criteria (**S**ufficiency, **T**ypicality, **A**ccuracy, and **R**elevance), as summarized in Table 14.1.

It is often difficult to create arguments in which all your evidence fully meets the STAR criteria. Sometimes you need to proceed on evidence that might not be typical, verifiable, or as up-to-date as you would like. In such cases, you

Table 14.1 The STAR Criteria for Evaluating Evidence

STAR Criteria	Implied Question	Comments
Sufficiency	Is there enough evidence?	If you don't provide enough evidence, skeptical audiences can dismiss your claim as a *hasty generalization*. To argue that marijuana is not a harmful drug, you would probably need more evidence than the results of one study or the testimony of a healthy pot smoker.
Typicality	Are the chosen data representative and typical?	If you choose extreme or rare-case examples, rather than typical and representative ones, your audience might accuse you of cherry-picking your data. Testimony from persons whose back pain was cured by yoga may not be enough to support the general claim that yoga is good for back pain.
Accuracy	Are the data accurate and up-to-date?	Providing recent, accurate data is essential for your own *ethos* as a writer. Data from 1998 on homelessness or inaccurately gathered data may be ineffective for a current policy argument.
Relevance	Are the data relevant to the claim?	Even though your evidence is accurate, up-to-date, and representative, it will be ineffective if it's not pertinent to the claim. For example, evidence that nuclear waste is dangerous is not relevant to the issue of whether it can be stored securely in Yucca Mountain.

Source: Richard Fulkerson, *Teaching the Argument in Writing,* Urbana: National Council of Teachers of English, 1996, pp. 44–53. In this section we are indebted to Fulkerson's discussion.

can often increase the effectiveness of your argument by qualifying your claim. Consider the difference between these two claims:

- *Strong claim:* Watching violent TV cartoons increases aggressive play behavior in boys.

- *Qualified claim:* Watching violent TV cartoons can increase aggressive play behavior in some boys.

To be made persuasive, the strong claim requires substantial evidence meeting the STAR criteria. In contrast, the qualified claim requires less rigorous evidence, perhaps only an example or two combined with the results of one scientific study.

As you gather evidence, consider also its source and the extent to which your audience will trust that source. While all data must be interpreted and hence are never completely impartial, careful readers are aware of how easily data can be skewed. Newspapers, magazines, blogs, and journals often have political biases and different levels of respectability. Generally, evidence from peer-reviewed scholarly journals is more highly regarded than evidence from secondhand sources. Particularly problematic is information gathered from Internet Web sites, which can vary widely in reliability and degree of bias.

See Skill 22.2 for advice on evaluating sources for reliability and bias. See Skill 22.3 for help on evaluating Web sites.

Addressing Objections and Counterarguments

Having looked at the frame of an argument (claim, reasons, and underlying assumptions) and at the kinds of evidence used to flesh out the frame, let's turn now to the important concern of anticipating and responding to objections and counterarguments. In this section, we provide an extended example of a student's anticipating and responding to a reader's objection. We then describe how you can use your argument frame to anticipate objections and respond to counterarguments, either through refutation or concession. Finally, we show how your active imagining of alternative views can lead you to qualify your claim.

ANTICIPATING OBJECTIONS: AN EXTENDED EXAMPLE   In our earlier discussions of the starling case, we saw how some readers might object to the argument "The family was justified in killing the starlings because starlings are pests." What disturbs these readers is the underlying assumption that it is okay to kill pests. Imagine an objecting reader saying something like this:

It is *not* okay to get annoyed with a living creature, label it a "pest," and then kill it. This whole use of the term *pest* suggests that humans have the right to dominate nature. We need to have more reverence for nature. The ease with which the family solved their problem by killing living things sets a bad example for children. The family could have waited until fall and then fixed the screen.

Imagining such an objection might lead a writer to modify his or her claim. But if the writer remains committed to that claim, then he or she must develop a response. In the following example in which a student writer argues that it is okay to kill the starlings, note (1) how the writer uses evidence to show that starlings are pests; (2) how he summarizes a possible objection to his underlying assumption that killing pests is morally justified; and (3) how he supports his assumption with further arguments.

STUDENT ARGUMENT DEFENDING REASON AND UNDERLYING ASSUMPTION

Claim with reason

Evidence that starlings are pests

The family was justified in killing the starlings because starlings are pests. Starlings are nonindigenous birds that drive out native species and multiply rapidly. When I searched "starlings pests" on Google, I discovered thousands of Web sites dealing with starlings as pests. Starlings, like other pests, create potential safety, health, and economic damage. As invasive nesters, starlings can damage attics by tearing up insulation, exposing electrical wires, and defecating on stored items. Starlings are hated by farmers and gardeners because huge flocks of them devour newly planted seeds in spring as well as fruits and berries at harvest. A flock of starlings can devastate a cherry orchard in a few days. Many of the Web site articles focused on ways to kill off starling populations. In killing the starlings, the family was protecting its own property and reducing the population of these pests.

Summary of a possible objection

Many readers might object to my argument, saying that humans should have a reverence for nature and not quickly try to kill off any creature they label a pest. Further, these readers might say that even if starlings are pests, the family could have waited until fall to repair the attic or found some other means of protecting their property without having to kill the baby starlings. I too would have waited until fall if the birds in the attic had been swallows or some other native species

Response to the objection

without starlings' destructiveness and propensity for unchecked population growth. But starlings should be compared to rats or mice. We set traps for rodents because we know the damage they cause when they nest in walls and attics and their potential for carrying diseases. We don't get sentimental trying to save the orphaned rat babies. In the same way, we are justified in eliminating starlings as soon as they begin infesting our houses.

In the preceding example, we see how the writer uses evidence to support his reason and then, anticipating readers' objection to his underlying assumption, summarizes that objection and provides a response to it. One might not be convinced by the argument, but the writer has done a good job of trying to support both his reason (starlings are pests) and his underlying assumption (it is morally justifiable to kill at least some pests).

USING YOUR ARGUMENT FRAME TO ANTICIPATE OBJECTIONS In the previous example, the student's arguing strategy was triggered by his anticipation of reader objections. Note that a skeptical audience can attack an argument by attacking either a writer's reasons or a writer's underlying assumptions. This knowledge allows writers to use their argument frame as a planning device to make the argument persuasive to its intended audience. A persuasive plan encourages writers to articulate their argument frame (claim, reason, and underlying assumption) and then to imagine what kinds of evidence or arguments could be used to support both the reason and the underlying assumption. Equally important, the plan encourages writers to anticipate counterarguments by imagining how skeptical readers might object to the writer's reason, underlying assumption, or both.

To use your argument frame for planning, simply make a chart with slots for each of these elements. Here is how another student writer planned an argument on the starling case:

CLAIM WITH REASON

The family showed cruelty to animals because the way they killed the birds caused needless suffering.

UNDERLYING ASSUMPTION

If it is necessary to kill an animal, then the killing should be done in the least painful way possible.

EVIDENCE TO SUPPORT REASON

First I've got to show how the way of killing the birds (starving them slowly) caused the birds to suffer. I've also got to show that this way of killing was needless because other means were available such as calling an exterminator who would remove the birds and either relocate them or kill them painlessly. If no other alternative was available, someone should have crawled into the attic and found a painless way to kill the birds.

EVIDENCE/ARGUMENTS TO SUPPORT UNDERLYING ASSUMPTIONS

I've got to convince readers it is wrong to make an animal suffer if you don't have to. Humans have a natural antipathy to needless suffering—our feeling of unease if we imagine cattle or chickens caused to suffer for our food rather than being cleanly and quickly killed. If a horse is incurably wounded, we put it to sleep rather than let it suffer. We are morally obligated to cause the least pain possible.

WAYS SKEPTICS MIGHT OBJECT

How could a reader object to my reason? A reader might say that the starlings didn't suffer much (baby birds don't feel pain). A reader might also object to my claim that other means were available: They might say there was no other way to kill the starlings. Poison may cause just as much suffering. Cost of exterminator is prohibitive.

How could a reader object to my underlying assumption? Perhaps the reader would say that my rule to cause the least pain possible does not apply to animal pests. In class, someone said that we shouldn't worry about the baby starlings any more than we would worry about killing baby rats. Laws of nature condemn millions of animals each year to death by starvation or by being eaten alive by other animals. Humans occasionally have to take their place within this tooth-and-claw natural system.

How many of the ideas from this plan would the writer use in her actual paper? That is a judgment call based on the writer's analysis of the audience. If this student's target audience includes classmates who think it is morally okay to kill pests by the most efficient means possible, then she should summarize her classmates' argument fairly and then try to convince them that humans are ethically obligated to rise above tooth-and-claw nature.

For Writing and Discussion
Creating Argument Frames for Planning

Working individually or in small groups, create plans for the following arguments. For each claim with reason: (a) imagine the kinds of evidence needed to support the reason, (b) identify the underlying assumption, (c) imagine a strategy for supporting the assumption, and (d) anticipate possible objections to the reason and to the assumption.

(Continued)

1. ***Claim with reason:*** Instead of buying a car, we should use car sharing (Car-To-Go or ZIPcar) because doing do so will save us money on car payments, maintenance, insurance, and parking. (Imagine this argument aimed at your significant other, who wants to buy a car.)

2. ***Claim with reason:*** Parents should not allow their children to play tackle football because the danger of concussive head injuries is too severe. Aim this argument at a teenager who wants to play high school football or at a parent who supports the teenager's wishes.

3. ***Claim with reason:*** Social networking sites are good for society because they help isolated or shy persons connect with other people. (Aim this argument at critics of social networking sites, particularly those who emphasize the superficiality of these sites and their potential for cyber-bullying or wasting time.)

Responding to Objections, Counterarguments, and Alternative Views

We have seen how a writer needs to anticipate alternative views that give rise to objections and counterarguments. One of the best ways to approach counterarguments is to summarize them fairly. Make your imagined reader's best case against your argument. By resisting the temptation to distort a counterargument, you demonstrate a willingness to consider the issue from all sides. Moreover, summarizing a counterargument reduces your reader's tendency to say, "Yes, but have you thought of . . . ?" After you have summarized an objection or counterargument fairly and charitably, you must then decide how to respond to it. Your two main choices are to rebut it or concede to it.

REBUTTING OPPOSING VIEWS   When rebutting or refuting an argument, you can question the argument's reasons and supporting evidence, the underlying assumptions, or both. In the following student example, the writer summarizes her classmates' objections to abstract art and then analyzes shortcomings in their argument.

> Some of my classmates object to abstract art because it apparently takes no technical drawing talent. They feel that historically artists turned to abstract art because they lacked the technical drafting skills exhibited by Remington, Russell, and Rockwell. Therefore these abstract artists created an art form that anyone was capable of and that was less time consuming, and then they paraded it as artistic progress. But I object to the notion that these artists turned to abstraction because they could not do representative drawing. Many abstract artists, such as Picasso, were excellent draftsmen, and their early pieces show very realistic drawing skill. As his work matured, Picasso became more abstract in order to increase the expressive quality of his work. *Guernica* was meant as a protest against the bombing of that city by the Germans. To express the terror and suffering of the victims more vividly, he distorted the figures and presented them in a black and white journalistic manner. If he had used representational images and color—which he had the skill to do—much of the emotional content would have been lost and the piece probably would not have caused the demand for justice that it did.

CONCEDING TO OPPOSING VIEWS In some cases, an alternative view can be very strong. If it is, don't hide that view from your readers. Rather, summarize it and concede to it.

Making concessions to opposing views is not necessarily a sign of weakness. In many cases, a concession simply acknowledges that the issue is complex and that your position is tentative. In turn, a concession can enhance a reader's respect for you and invite the reader to follow your example and weigh the strengths of your own argument charitably. Writers typically concede to opposing views with transitional expressions such as the following:

admittedly	I must admit that	I agree that	granted
even though	I concede that	while it is true that	

After conceding to an opposing view, you should shift to a different field of values where your position is strong and then argue for those values. For example, adversaries of drug legalization argue plausibly that legalizing drugs would increase the number of users and addicts. If you support legalization, here is how you might deal with this point without fatally damaging your own argument:

> Opponents of legalization claim—and rightly so—that legalization will lead to an increase in drug users and addicts. I wish this weren't so, but it is. Nevertheless, the other benefits of legalizing drugs—eliminating the black market, reducing street crime, and freeing up thousands of police from fighting the war on drugs—more than outweigh the social costs of increased drug use and addiction, especially if tax revenues from drug sales are invested in drug education and rehabilitation programs.

The writer concedes that legalization will increase addiction (one reason for opposing legalization) and that drug addiction is bad (the underlying assumption for that reason). But then the writer redeems the case for legalization by shifting the argument to another field of values (the benefits of eliminating the black market, reducing crime, and so forth).

QUALIFYING YOUR CLAIM The need to summarize and respond to alternative views lets the writer see an issue's complexity and appreciate that no one position has a monopoly on the truth. Consequently, writers often need to qualify their claims—that is, limit the scope or force of a claim to make it less sweeping and therefore less vulnerable.

Consider the difference between the sentences "After-school jobs are bad for teenagers" and "After-school jobs are often bad for teenagers." The first claim can be refuted by one counterexample of a teenager who benefited from an after-school job. Because the second claim admits exceptions, it is much harder to refute. Unless your argument is airtight, you will want to limit your claim with qualifiers such as the following:

perhaps	maybe
in many cases	generally
tentatively	sometimes
often	usually
probably	likely
May *or* might (*rather than* is)	

You can also qualify a claim with an opening *unless* clause ("*Unless* your apartment is well soundproofed, you should not buy such a powerful stereo system").

Seeking Audience-Based Reasons

Much of the advice that we have presented so far can be consolidated into a single principle: Seek "audience-based reasons." By **audience-based reasons**, we mean reasons that depend on underlying assumptions, values, or beliefs that your targeted audience already holds. In such cases, you won't need to state and defend your underlying assumptions because the audience already accepts them.

A good illustration comes from civil engineer David Rockwood's argument against wind power that we used in Chapter 3. Rockwood's targeted readers are environmentalists who have high hopes for wind-generated electricity. Rockwood's final reason opposing wind power is that constructing thousands of wind towers will damage the pristine mountain environment. To environmentalists, this reason is powerful because its underlying assumption ("Preserving the environment is good") appeals to their values.

When you plan your argument, seek audience-based reasons whenever possible. Suppose, for example, that you are advocating the legalization of heroin and cocaine. If you know that your audience is concerned about street crime, then you can argue that legalization of drugs will make the streets safer.

We should legalize drugs *because doing so will make our streets safer*: It will cut down radically on street criminals seeking drug money, and it will free up narcotics police to focus on other kinds of crime.	Audience-based reason: Underlying assumption is that making our streets safer is a good thing—a value the audience already holds.

For another group of readers—those concerned about improving the quality of life for young people in inner cities—you might argue that legalization of drugs will lead to better lives for people in poor neighborhoods.

We should legalize drugs *because doing so will improve the lives of inner-city youth* by eliminating the lure of drug trafficking that tempts so many inner-city youth into crime.	Audience-based reason: Underlying assumption is that it is good to improve the lives of inner-city youth.

If your audience is concerned about high taxes and government debt, you might say:

We should legalize drugs *because doing so will help us balance federal and state budgets*: It will decrease police and prison costs by decriminalizing narcotics; and it will eliminate the black market in drugs, allowing us to collect taxes on drug sales.	Audience-based reason: Underlying assumption is that it is a good thing to balance federal and state budgets.

In contrast, if you oppose legalizing drugs, you could appeal to those concerned about drug addiction and public health by using the following audience-based reason:

We should not legalize drugs *because doing so will increase the number of drug addicts and make drug use seem socially acceptable.*

Audience-based reason:

Underlying assumption is that increasing the number of drug addicts and making drugs socially acceptable are bad things.

In each case, you move people toward your position by connecting your argument to their beliefs and values.

Appealing to *Ethos* and *Pathos*

When the classical rhetoricians examined ways that orators could persuade listeners, they focused on three kinds of appeals: *logos*, the appeal to reason; *ethos*, the appeal to the speaker's character; and *pathos*, the appeal to the emotions and the sympathetic imagination. We introduced you to these appeals in Chapter 4, Concept 4.2, because they are important rhetorical considerations in any kind of writing. Understanding how arguments persuade through *logos, ethos*, and *pathos* is particularly helpful when your aim is persuasion. So far in this chapter we have focused on *logos*. In this section we examine *ethos* and *pathos*.

APPEALS TO *ETHOS* A powerful way to increase the persuasiveness of an argument is to gain your readers' trust. You appeal to *ethos* whenever you present yourself as credible and trustworthy. For most readers to accept your argument, they must perceive you as knowledgeable, trustworthy, and fair. In Strategies Chart 14.1, we suggest ways to enhance your argument's *ethos*.

Strategies Chart 14.1 Strategies for Enhancing Your Argument's *Ethos*

What to Do	Explanation
Be knowledgeable by doing your homework.	Your credibility is enhanced when readers are convinced that you know your subject thoroughly.
Use evidence responsibly.	If you cherry-pick your evidence, readers may perceive you as a propagandist rather than as a thoughtful arguer who recognizes complexity.
Be fair to alternative views.	If you scorn or misrepresent opposing views, you will win favor only with those who already agree with you. If you are a good listener to others, they will be more apt to listen to you.
Search for values and assumptions you can share with your audience.	You will build bridges toward skeptical readers, rather than alienate them, if you can highlight shared assumptions or values. Use audience-based reasons where possible.
Show that you care about your issue; show also why your readers should care about it.	By showing why the issue matters both to you and your readers, you portray yourself as a person of integrity rather than as someone playing an argumentative game.

Strategies Chart 14.2 Strategies for Enhancing Your Argument's *Pathos*

What to Do	Explanation	Example
Include storylike anecdotes.	Specific stories often create more emotional appeal than abstract statistics or generalizations.	In the political debate about how to combat terrorism, some conservatives told stories about young Muslims being radicalized via the Internet (promotes fear); in contrast, liberals told stories about Syrian families seeking refugee status, with focus on the plight of mothers and children (promotes empathy for outsiders).
Choose words with emotional or values-laden connotations.	Connotations of words often carry heavy emotional impact.	Opponents of Obamacare used language like "budget-busting," "socialist," and "death panels." Supporters used words like "life-saving coverage," "safety nets," and "the heartbreak of illness-caused bankruptcy."
Where appropriate, use vivid language low on the ladder of abstraction. (See Concept 4.3 for explanation of the ladder of abstraction.)	Specific words paint pictures that have emotional appeal.	"The homeless man is huddled over the sewer grate, his feet wrapped in newspapers. He blows on his hands, then tucks them under his armpits and lies down on the sidewalk with his shoulders over the grate, his bed for the night." [creates sympathy for the homeless] "Several ratty derelicts drinking wine from a shared sack caused shoppers to avoid going into the store." [creates sympathy for shoppers rather than the homeless]
If the genre permits, include visuals with emotional impact.	Photographs or other visuals, including dramatic graphs or charts, can have a strong emotional appeal.	Proponents of policies to combat climate change often include photographs of smoggy haze in Beijing, melting glaciers, or smoke-belching factories. Opponents often use graphs emphasizing the costs of these policies—higher gasoline taxes or a weakened economy.

APPEALS TO *PATHOS* Besides appealing to *logos* and *ethos*, you might also appeal to *pathos*. Sometimes *pathos* is interpreted narrowly as an appeal to the emotions and is therefore devalued on the grounds that arguments should be rational rather than emotional. Although appeals to *pathos* can sometimes be irrational and irrelevant ("If you don't give me at least a B in this course, I will lose my scholarship and break my ill grandmother's heart"), they can also arouse audience interest and deepen understanding of an argument's human dimensions. They are really appeals to the readers' underlying sympathies and values. Strategies Chart 14.2 suggests ways to increase *pathos* in your arguments.

A brief primer on informal fallacies

14.4 Avoid logical fallacies in your arguments.

We conclude our explanation of classical argument with a brief overview of the most common informal fallacies. *Informal fallacies* are instances of murky reasoning that can cloud an argument and lead to unsound conclusions. Because they can crop up unintentionally in anyone's writing, and because advertisers and hucksters often use them intentionally to deceive, it is a good idea to learn to recognize the most common fallacies.

Post Hoc, Ergo Propter Hoc ("After This, Therefore Because of This")

The ***post hoc, ergo propter hoc*** comes from the Latin meaning "after this, therefore because of this." This fallacy involves mistaking sequence for cause. The fact that one event happens before another event doesn't mean the first event caused the second. The connection may be coincidental, or some unknown third event may have caused both of these events.

Example   In New York City, the decline in the crime rate in the 1990s was caused by new police tactics.

Explanation: In the early 1990s, the crime rate indeed plummeted, but were new police tactics the cause? Many experts attributed the decline to other causes. To state that new police tactics caused the drop in crime is a *post hoc* fallacy without further argument.

Hasty Generalization

Closely related to the *post hoc* fallacy is the **hasty generalization**, which refers to claims based on insufficient or unrepresentative data. Generally, persuasive evidence should meet the STAR criteria that we explained earlier in this chapter. Because the amount of evidence needed in a given case can vary with the audience's degree of skepticism, it is difficult to draw an exact line between hasty generalizations and justified generalizations.

Examples   The news frequently carries stories about vicious pit bulls. Therefore all pit bills must be vicious.

This experimental drug has been demonstrated safe in numerous clinical trials [based on tests using adult subjects]. Therefore this drug is safe for children.

False Analogy

Arguers often use analogies to support a claim. (For example, "We should require gun-owners to register and license their guns in the same way that we require car owners to register and license their cars.") However, analogical arguments are tricky because there are usually significant differences between the two things being compared as well as similarities. (Opponents of gun control point to all the dissimilarities between owning a gun and owning a car—including the presence of the Second Amendment.) Although it is hard to draw an exact line between a false analogy and an acceptable one, charges of **false analogy** are frequent when skeptical opponents try to refute arguments based on analogies.

Examples   Legalizing prostitution will work in our state because it works in Nevada.

It's a mistake to force little Johnnie to take piano lessons because you can't turn a reluctant child into a musician any more than you can turn a tulip into a rose.

Either/Or Reasoning

The **either/or fallacy** occurs when a complex, multisided issue is reduced to two positions without acknowledging the possibility of other alternatives.

> Example   Either you are pro-choice on abortion or you are against the advancement of women in our culture.

Ad Hominem ("Against the Person")

When people can't find fault with an argument, they sometimes attack the arguer, substituting irrelevant assertions about that person's character for an analysis of the argument itself. An attack on a person rather than argument is an *ad hominem* **argument**.

> Example   We should discount Senator Jones's argument against subsidizing wind and solar power because she has huge holdings in oil stock.

Appeals to False Authority and Bandwagon Appeals

These fallacies offer as support the fact that a famous person supports it (**false authority**) or the fact that "many people" already support it (**bandwagon appeal**). Unless the supporters are themselves authorities in the field, their support is irrelevant.

> Examples   Buy Freeble oil because Joe Quarterback always uses it in his fleet of cars.
>
> How can social media be addictive when millions of people enjoy it and use it regularly?

Non Sequitur ("It Does Not Follow")

The *non sequitur* fallacy occurs when there is no evident connection between a claim and its reason. Sometimes a *non sequitur* can be repaired by filling in gaps in the reasoning; other times, the reasoning is simply fallacious.

> Example   I don't deserve a B for this course because I am a straight-A student.

Circular Reasoning

Circular reasoning occurs when you state your claim and then, usually after rewording it, you state it again as your reason.

> Example   Marijuana is injurious to your health because it harms your body.

Red Herring

The **red herring** fallacy refers to the practice of raising an unrelated or irrelevant point deliberately to throw an audience off-track. Politicians often employ this fallacy when they field questions from the public or press.

Example   You raise a good question about my support of companies' outsourcing
               jobs to find cheaper labor. Let me tell you about my admiration for the
               productivity of the American worker.

Slippery Slope

The **slippery slope** fallacy is based on the fear that one step in a direction we
don't like inevitably leads to the next step with no stopping place.

Example   If we allow embryonic stem cells to be used for medical research, we
               will open the door for full-scale reproductive cloning.

Writing a classical argument

**14.5   Write a classical argument that offers reasons and evidence in support
of your position while also summarizing and responding to opposing
views.**

> **Writing Project:** Write an argument that takes a stand on a controversial
> issue. Your introduction should present your issue, provide background,
> and state the claim you intend to support. In constructing your claim, strive
> to develop audience-based reasons. The body of your argument should
> summarize and respond to opposing views as well as present reasons and
> evidence in support of your own position. You will need to choose whether
> to summarize and refute opposing views before or after you have made your
> own case. Try to end your essay with your strongest arguments. Try also to
> include appeals to *pathos* and to create a positive, credible *ethos*.

We call this assignment a "classical" argument because it is patterned after the persuasive speeches of ancient Greek and Roman orators. A framework chart showing the generic structure of a classical argument is shown in Figure 14.1. Although
there are many other ways to persuade audiences, the classical approach is a particularly effective introduction to persuasive writing.

Generating and Exploring Ideas

The tasks that follow are intended to help you generate ideas for your argument. Our goal is to help you build up a storehouse of possible issues, explore
several of these possibilities, and then choose one for deeper exploration before
you write your initial draft.

FINDING AN ISSUE   If you are having trouble finding an arguable issue for
this writing project, consider the strategies in Strategies Chart 14.3.

Figure 14.1 Framework for a Classical Argument

INTRODUCTION	• Attention-grabber (often a memorable scene) • Explanation of issue and needed background • Writer's thesis (claim) • Forecasting passage
PRESENTATION OF WRITER'S POSITION	• Main body of essay • Presents and supports each reason in turn • Each reason is tied to a value or belief held by the audience
SUMMARY OF OPPOSING VIEWS	• Summary of views differing from writer's (should be fair and complete)
RESPONSE TO OPPOSING VIEWS	• Refutes or concedes to opposing views • Shows weaknesses in opposing views • May concede to some strengths
CONCLUSION	• Brings essay to closure • Often sums up argument • Leaves strong, lasting impression • Often calls for action or relates topic to a larger context of issues

Strategies Chart 14.3 Strategies for Finding an Arguable Issue

What to Do	Explanation
Make an inventory of various communities you belong to.	Communities can range from the local (family, dorm, campus) to the state, nation, and world.
Brainstorm contested issues in these communities.	Start off with a fairly large list and then zero in on the communities that are experiencing the most controversy now and that most enlist your personal interest, current knowledge level, and degree of engagement.
On a few of these issues, explore the causes of disagreement.	Ask these questions: What is at the heart of the disagreement? Disagreement about facts? About beliefs and values? About benefits versus costs?
Then explore your own point of view.	Ask: What is my position on the issue and why? What are alternative points of view? What is at stake?
Determine how much research you'll need to do.	If your issue requires research (check with your instructor), do a bibliographic search and enough skim reading to determine the kinds of arguments surrounding your issue, the kinds of evidence available, and the alternative views that people have taken.
Choose your issue and begin your research.	Your goal is to "wallow in complexity" in order to earn your thesis and create a knowledgeable *ethos*. Consider consulting sources that will provide background on your issue, sketch out the arguments on different sides, and offer useful evidence. Note: Some issues allow you to argue from personal experience (see Ross Taylor's argument on paintball, later in this chapter.) Again, check with your instructor.
Brainstorm claims and reasons on various sides of the issue.	State your own claim and possible *because* clause reasons in support of your claim. Do the same thing for one or more opposing or alternative claims.

CONDUCT AN IN-DEPTH EXPLORATION PRIOR TO DRAFTING   The following tasks are designed to help you explore your issue in depth. Most students take one or two hours to complete these tasks. The time investment will pay off because most of the ideas that you need for your rough draft will be on paper.

1. Write out the issue your argument will address. Try phrasing your issue in several different ways, perhaps as a yes/no question and as an open-ended question. Try making the question broader, then narrower. Finally, frame the question in the way that most appeals to you.

2. Now write out your tentative answer to the question. This will be your beginning thesis statement or claim. Put a box around this answer. Next, write out one or more different answers to your question. These will be alternative claims that a neutral audience might consider.

3. Why is this issue controversial? Is there insufficient evidence to resolve the issue, or is the evidence ambiguous or contradictory? Are definitions in dispute? Do the parties disagree about basic values, assumptions, or beliefs?

4. What personal interest do you have in this issue? How does the issue affect you? Why do you care about it? (Knowing why you care about it might help you get your audience to care about it.)

5. What reasons and evidence support your position on this issue? Freewrite everything that comes to mind that might help you support your case. This freewrite will eventually provide the bulk of your argument. For now, freewrite rapidly without worrying whether your argument makes sense. Just get ideas on paper.

6. Imagine all the counterarguments your audience might make. Summarize the main arguments against your position and then freewrite your response to each of the counterarguments. What are the flaws in the alternative points of view?

7. What kinds of appeals to *ethos* and *pathos* might you use to support your argument? How can you increase your audience's perception of your credibility and trustworthiness? How can you tie your argument to your audience's beliefs and values?

8. Why is this issue important? What are the broader implications and consequences? What other issues does it relate to? Thinking of possible answers to these questions may prove useful when you write your introduction or conclusion.

Shaping and Drafting

Once you have explored your ideas, create a plan. Here is a suggested procedure:

Begin your planning by analyzing your intended audience. You could imagine an audience deeply resistant to your views or a more neutral, undecided audience acting like a jury. In some cases, your audience might be a single person, as when you petition your department chair to waive a requirement in your major. At other times, your audience might be the general readership of a newspaper, church bulletin, or blog. When the audience is a general readership, you need to imagine from the start the kinds of readers you particularly want to sway. Here are some questions you can ask:

- *How much does your audience know or care about your issue?* Will you need to provide background? Will you need to convince the audience that your issue is important? Do you need to hook their interest? Your answers to these questions will particularly influence your introduction and conclusion.

- *What is your audience's current attitude toward your issue?* Are they deeply opposed to your position? If so, why? Are they neutral and undecided? If so, what other views will they be listening to?

- *How do your audience's values, assumptions, and beliefs differ from your own?* What aspects of your position will be threatening to your audience? Why? How does your position on the issue challenge your imagined reader's worldview or identity? What objections will your audience raise toward your argument? Your answers to these questions will help determine the content of your argument and alert you to a need to conduct extra research that will allow you to respond to audience objections.

- *What values, beliefs, or assumptions about the world do you and your audience share?* Despite your differences with your audience, where can you find common links? How might you use these links to build bridges to your audience?

Your next step is to plan an audience-based argument by seeking audience-based reasons or reasons whose underlying assumptions you can defend. Here is a process you can use:

1. Create a skeleton, tree diagram, outline, or flowchart for your argument by stating your reasons as one or more *because* clauses attached to your claim. Each *because* clause will become the head of a main section or *line of reasoning* in your argument.

2. Create an argument frame for each line of reasoning and use it to plan your argument strategy. If your audience accepts your underlying assumption, you can concentrate on supporting your reason with evidence. However, if your audience is apt to reject the underlying assumption for one of your lines of reasoning, then you'll need to state that assumption directly and argue for it. Try to anticipate audience objections by exploring ways that an audience might question either your reasons or your underlying assumptions.

3. Using the skeleton you created, finish developing an outline or tree diagram for your argument. Although the organization of each part of your argument will grow organically from its content, the main parts of your classical argument should match the framework chart in Figure 14.1.

This classical model can be modified in numerous ways. A question that often arises is where to summarize and respond to objections and counterarguments. Writers generally have three choices:

1. Handle opposing positions before you present your own argument. The rationale for this approach is that skeptical audiences may be more inclined to listen attentively to your argument if you have assured them that you understand their point of view.

2. Place this material after you have presented your argument. This approach is effective for neutral audiences who don't start off with strong opposing views, but you have to be sure to answer these views with your own counter-reasoning and examples. Otherwise, you weaken, or even give away, your argument.

3. Intersperse opposing views throughout your argument at appropriate moments.

Any of these possibilities, or a combination of all of them, can be effective.

Another question often asked is, "What is the best way to order one's reasons?" A general rule of thumb is to put your strongest reason last and your second-strongest reason first. The idea here is to start and end with your most powerful arguments. If you imagine a quite skeptical audience, build bridges to your audience by summarizing alternative views early in the paper and concede to those views that are especially strong. If your audience is neutral or undecided, you can summarize and respond to possible objections after you have presented your own case.

Revising

As you revise your argument, you need to attend both to the clarity of your writing (all the principles of closed-form prose described in Chapter 18) and to the persuasiveness of your argument. As always, peer reviews are valuable, and especially so in argumentation if you ask your peer reviewers to role-play an opposing audience.

Questions for Peer Review

In addition to the generic peer review questions explained in Skill 17.4, ask your peer reviewers to address these questions:

INTRODUCTION

1. How could the title be improved so that it announces the issue, reveals the writer's claim, or otherwise focuses your expectations and piques interest?

2. What strategies does the writer use to introduce the issue, engage your interest, and convince you that the issue is significant and problematic? What would add clarity and appeal?

3. How could the introduction more effectively forecast the argument and present the writer's claim? What would make the statement of the claim more focused, clear, or risky?

ARGUING FOR THE CLAIM

1. Consider the overall structure: What strategies does the writer use to make the structure of the paper clear and easy to follow? How could the structure of the argument be improved?

2. Consider the support for the reasons: Where could the writer provide better evidence or support for each line of reasoning? Look for the kinds of

evidence for each line of reasoning by noting the writer's use of facts, examples, statistics, testimony, or other evidence. Where could the writer supply more evidence or use existing evidence more effectively?

3. Consider the support for the underlying assumptions: For each line of reasoning, determine the assumptions that the audience needs to grant for the argument to be effective. Are there places where these assumptions need to be stated directly and supported with arguments? How could support for the assumptions be improved?

4. Consider the writer's summary of and response to alternative viewpoints: Where does the writer treat alternative views? Are there additional alternative views that the writer should consider? What strategies does the writer use to respond to alternative views? How could the writer's treatment of alternative views be improved?

CONCLUSION

1. How might the conclusion more effectively bring completeness or closure to the argument?

Multimodal and Online Assignment Options

For advice on producing multimedia compositions, see Chapter 20. For an example of a student speech with PowerPoint slides, see the readings in Chapter 16.

1. **Speech with Visual Aids (Flip Chart, PowerPoint, Prezi)** Deliver your classical argument as a formal speech supported with visual aids. You can imagine an occasion for a short speech limited to three to five minutes (modeled, say, after public hearings) or a longer presentation such as a TED talk. Pay equal attention to the construction and delivery of your speech and to the multimodal design of the visual aids.

2. **Persuasive Poster, Advocacy Ad, or Zine** Create a one-page poster, an advocacy ad, or a zine that captures your argument in a highly condensed verbal/visual form. Consider how you will use all the features of visual argument—type sizes and fonts, layout, color, and images and graphics—to grab your audience's attention and drive home your claim. (A sample zine is provided in the readings at the end of this chapter.)

3. **Video** Create a short video aimed at moving neutral or opposing audiences toward your point of view. Use the resources of music, voice, words, and images to reach audiences who might not be expected to read your print argument. Conversely, create a video aimed at increasing the enthusiasm of people who already support your position. Your goal is to call them to action in some way (change an environmentally damaging habit, donate funds, vote, participate in a rally or strike).

4. **T-shirt or Bumper Sticker as Part of a Campaign Plan** Imagine a full-fledged campaign advocating your position on an issue. Design a T-shirt or bumper sticker in support of your claim.

Readings

Our first reading, by student writer Ross Taylor, aims to increase appreciation of paintball as a healthy sport. An avid paintballer, Ross was frustrated by how many of his friends and acquaintances didn't appreciate paintball and had numerous misconceptions about it. The following argument is aimed at those who don't understand the sport or those who condemn it for being dangerous and violent.

Ross Taylor (student)

Paintball: Promoter of Violence or Healthy Fun?

1   Glancing out from behind some cover, I see an enemy soldier on the move. I level my gun and start pinching off rounds. Hearing the incoming fire, he turns and starts to fire, but it is far too late. His entire body flinches when I land two torso shots, and he falls when I hit his leg. I duck back satisfied with another good kill on my record. I pop up again, this time to scan for more enemy forces. Out of the corner of my eye I see some movement and turn to see two soldiers peeking out from behind a sewer pipe. I move to take cover again, but it's futile. I feel the hits come one by one hitting me three times in the chest and once on the right bicep before I fall behind the cover. I'm hit. It's all over—for me at least. The paintball battle rages on as I carefully leave the field to nurse my welts, which are already showing. Luckily, I watch my three remaining teammates trample the two enemy soldiers who shot me to win the game. This is paintball in all its splendor and glory.

2   Paintball is one of the most misunderstood and generally looked down upon recreational activities. People see it as rewarding violence and lacking the true characteristics of a healthy team sport like ultimate Frisbee, soccer, or pickup basketball. Largely the accusations directed at paintball are false because it is a positive recreational activity. Paintball is a fun, athletic, mentally challenging recreational activity that builds teamwork and releases tension.

3   Paintball was invented in the early 1980s as a casual activity for survival enthusiasts, but it has grown into a several hundred million dollar industry. It is, quite simply, an expanded version of tag. Players use a range of CO_2 powered guns that fire small biodegradable marbles of paint at approximately 250–300 feet per second. The result of a hit is a small splatter of oily paint and a nice dark bruise. Paintball is now played nationwide in indoor and outdoor arenas. Quite often variants are played such as "Capture the Flag" or "Assassination." In "Capture the Flag" the point is to retrieve the heavily guarded flag from the other team and return it to your base. The game of "Assassination" pits one team of "assassins" against the "secret service." The secret service men guard an unarmed player dubbed the "president." Their goal is get from point A to point B without the president's getting tagged. Contrary to popular belief, the games are highly officiated and organized. There is always a referee present. Barrel plugs are required until just before a game begins and must be reinserted as soon as the game ends. No hostages may be taken. A player catching another off guard at close range

must first give the player the opportunity to surrender. Most importantly there is no physical contact between players. Punching, pushing, or butt-ending with the gun is strictly prohibited. The result is an intense game that is relatively safe for all involved.

4   The activity of paintball is athletically challenging. There are numerous sprint and dives to avoid being hit. At the end of a game, typically lasting around 20 minutes, all the players are winded, sweaty, and ultimately exhilarated. The beginning of the game includes a mad dash for cover by both teams with heavy amounts of fire being exchanged. During the game, players execute numerous strategic moves to gain a tactical advantage, often including quick jumps, dives, rolls, and runs. While undercover, players crawl across broad stretches of playing field often still feeling their bruises from previous games. These physical feats culminate in an invigorating and physically challenging activity good for building muscles and coordination.

5   In addition to the athletic challenge, paintball provides strong mental challenge, mainly the need for constant strategizing. There are many strategic positioning methods. For example, the classic pincer move involves your team's outflanking an opponent from each side to eliminate his or her mobility and shelter. In the more sophisticated ladder technique, teammates take turns covering each other as the others move onward from cover to cover. Throughout the game, players' minds are constantly reeling as they calculate their positions and cover, their teammates' positions and cover, and their opponents' positions and strength. Finally, there is the strong competitive pull of the individual. It never fails to amaze me how much thought goes into one game.

6   Teamwork is also involved. Paintball takes a lot of cooperation. You need special hand signals to communicate with your teammates, and you have to coordinate, under rapidly changing situations, who is going to flank left or right, who is going to charge, and who is going to stay back to guard the flag station. The importance of teamwork in paintball explains why more and more businesses are taking their employees for a day of action with the intent of creating a closer knit and smooth-functioning workplace. The value of teamwork is highlighted on the Web site of a British Columbia facility, Action and Adventure Paintball, Ltd, which says that in paintball,

> as in any team sport, the team that communicates best usually wins. It's about thinking, not shooting. This is why Fortune 500 companies around the world take their employees to play paintball together.

> An advantage of paintball for building company team spirit is that paintball teams, unlike teams in many other recreational sports, can blend very skilled and totally unskilled players. Women like paintball as much as men, and the game is open to people of any size, body type, and strength level. Since a game usually takes no more than seven to ten minutes, teams can run a series of different games with different players to have lots of different match-ups. Also families like to play paintball together.

7   People who object to paintball criticize its danger and violence. The game's supposed danger gets mentioned a lot. The public seems to have received the impression that paintball guns are simply eye-removing hardware. It is true that paintball can lead to eye injuries. An article by medical writer Cheryl Guttman in a trade magazine for ophthalmologists warns that eye injuries from paintball are on the rise. But the fact is that Guttman's article says that only 102 cases of eye injuries from paintballs were reported from 1985 to 2000 and that 85 percent of those injured were not wearing the required safety goggles. This is not to say that accidents don't happen. I personally had a friend lose an eye after inadvertently shooting himself in the eye from a very close range. The fact of the matter is that he made a mistake by looking down the barrel of a loaded gun and the trigger malfunctioned. Had he been more careful or worn the proper equipment, he most likely would have been fine. During my first organized paintball experience I was hit in the goggles by a very powerful gun and felt no pain. The only discomfort came from having to clean all the paint off my goggles after the game. When played properly, paintball is an incredibly safe sport.

8   The most powerful argument against paintball is that it is inherently violent and thus unhealthy. Critics claim paintball is simply an accepted form of promoting violence against other people. I have anti-war friends who think that paintball glorifies war. Many new parents today try to keep their kids from playing cops and robbers and won't buy them toy guns. These people see paintball as an upgraded and more violent version of the same antisocial games they don't want their children to play. Some people also point to the connections between paintball and violent video games where participants get their fun from "killing" other people. They link paintball to all the other violent activities that they think lead to such things as gangs or school shootings. But there is no connection between school shootings and paintball. As seen in Michael Moore's *Bowling for Columbine,* the killers involved there went bowling before the massacre; they didn't practice their aim by playing paintball.

9   What I am trying to say is that, yes, paintball is violent to a degree. After all, its whole point is to "kill" each other with guns. But I object to paintball's being considered a promotion of violence. Rather, I feel that it is a healthy release of tension. From my own personal experience, when playing the game, the players aren't focused on hurting the other players; they are focused on winning the game. At the end of the day, players are not full of violent urges, but just the opposite. They want to celebrate together as a team, just as do softball or soccer teams after a game. Therefore I don't think paintball is an unhealthy activity for adults. (The only reason I wouldn't include children is because I believe the pain is too intense for them. I have seen some younger players cry after being shot.) Paintball is simply a game, a sport, that produces intense exhilaration and fun. Admittedly, paintball guns can be used in irresponsible manners. Recently there have been some drive-by paintballings, suggesting that paintball players are irresponsible and violent. However, the percentage of people who do this sort of prank is very small and those are the bad apples of the group. There will always be those who misuse equipment. For example, baseball bats have been used in atrocious beatings, but

that doesn't make baseball a violent sport. So despite the bad apples, paintball is still a worthwhile activity when properly practiced.

10   Athletic and mentally challenging, team-building and fun—the game of paint-ball seems perfectly legitimate to me. It is admittedly violent, but it is not the evil activity that critics portray. Injuries can occur, but usually only when the proper safety equipment is not being used and proper precautions are ignored. As a great recreational activity, paintball deserves the same respect as other sports. It is a great way to get physical exercise, make friends, and have fun.

THINKING CRITICALLY

About "Paintball: Promoter of Violence or Healthy Fun?"

1. Before reading this essay, what was your own view of paintball? To what extent, if at all, did this argument create for you a more positive view of paintball? What aspects of the argument did you find particularly effective or ineffective?

2. How effective are Ross's appeals to *ethos* in this argument? Does he create a persona that you find trustworthy and compelling? How does he do so or fail to do so?

3. How effective are Ross's appeals to *pathos*? How does he appeal to his readers' values, interests, and emotions in trying to make paintball seem like an exhilarating team sport? To what extent does he show empathy with readers when he summarizes objections to paintball?

4. How effective are Ross's appeals to *logos*? How effective are Ross's reasons and evidence in support of his claim? How effective are Ross's responses to opposing views?

5. What are the main strengths and weaknesses of Ross's argument?

Our next reading is an op-ed piece by law professor E. Gregory Wallace at the Campbell School of Law in Raleigh, North Carolina. It appeared in the Raleigh *News and Observer* on December 12, 2015, shortly after the nation was shocked by massacres in Colorado Springs and San Bernardino. This reading, along with the one following, addresses the controversy over gun violence and mass killings. Opponents of gun control argue that guns are needed for self-defense, that an armed citizenry will reduce crime, and that gun control takes away Second Amendment rights. Proponents of gun control point out that there are more guns in the United States than people. They worry about gang-related shootings, about arguments turned deadly, about armed individuals propelled by rage, and about accidental shootings, especially among children. The public controversy over gun violence takes many different forms with intersecting points of view.

Insisting on Gun-Control Laws that Don't Work, Then Registration, Then Confiscation

E. Gregory Wallace

1   The recent tragedies in Colorado Springs and San Bernardino have prompted more calls for gun control. But what controls? And will they work?

2   Gun-control advocates say we need universal background checks and bans on assault weapons and gun sales to those on the no-fly list. Unfortunately, these laws are not likely to stop terrorists or deranged persons determined to commit mass murder.

3   Both Colorado and California have universal background checks, which means they require a background check on every sale – retail or private. These checks did not stop the recent attacks. Yet President Obama, Hillary Clinton and other gun control advocates keep pushing such checks at the federal level.

4   Universal background checks cannot stop people who are dangerous but have no disqualifying records. The Umpqua College shooter apparently was seriously mentally ill but passed Oregon's strict universal background-check law.

5   Background checks also are subject to bureaucratic error. The Charleston church shooter should not have been allowed to purchase a gun because he had confessed to a drug charge, but his data were not entered correctly into the background-check database.

6   President Obama wants to ban "powerful" assault weapons. So-called assault rifles sold to civilians are not the same guns our military uses in war. They do not spray bullets with a single press of the trigger like a machine gun. They fire only one bullet each time the trigger is pulled, like every other ordinary civilian firearm. They shoot small-to-intermediate-sized bullets common to hunting rifles used to shoot rabbits or deer, but not big animals like elk or bears.

7   The features that define assault rifles – telescoping stocks, barrel shrouds, pistol grips and bayonet lugs – make the rifle look scarier but have nothing to do with the gun's rate of fire, ammo capacity or firepower.

8   The federal government banned assault weapons from 1994 to 2004, but the ban had little or no effect on gun violence. Laws in France and Belgium banned the fully-automatic rifles used in the recent terror attacks. The terrorists still got the weapons they wanted. The two rifles used in the California attack were sold in compliance with the state's strict assault weapons ban, but then illegally modified.

9   President Obama wants to block gun sales to those on the government's secretive no-fly list. This list contains names of persons merely suspected of being terrorists – those who may be too dangerous to fly but are too harmless to arrest. The list is notoriously inaccurate. One report says 77 employees of the Homeland Security department are on the no-fly list. There is no fair and expeditious process for innocent persons to clear their names from the list.

10   Using the no-fly list to keep people from exercising their Second Amendment right to arms is almost surely unconstitutional. The government cannot deny constitutional rights based on mere suspicion and speculation.

11   If these laws don't work, why do gun-control advocates insist on having them? By taking advantage of the public's ignorance about guns and gun laws, they create an illusion of security. That's why politicians like them.

12   But there's another reason. Many gun-control advocates don't like guns and don't want anyone having guns. Their endgame is not gun control, but gun confiscation. Obama has pointed to the mass confiscation of guns in Australia as a model for the United States – despite the fact that the Australian ban had no effect on firearm homicides. Current gun-control proposals are just intermediate steps toward registration, then confiscation.

13   Americans own over 300 million guns. Gun confiscation means taking away a huge number of guns from a huge number of gun owners. We tried something like that with Prohibition, and it didn't work out so well. And then, of course, there's that inconvenient Second Amendment that would need to be repealed.

14   If gun control is the proper response to terrorism and mass murder, then gun-control advocates should give up their security theater and confiscation fantasies. Specify what gun laws would have made a difference in these cases, and let's talk about them – nobody wants these tragedies to continue. But please stop wasting our time with gun controls that burden law-abiding citizens but do little or nothing to stop mass murderers.

THINKING CRITICALLY

About "Insisting on Gun-Control Laws that Don't Work, Then Registration, Then Confiscation"

1. The first part of Wallace's argument proceeds by refutation. He says that the proposals put forward for limiting gun violence won't work. What are these proposals? Why does he believe that they won't work? What does he use for evidence?

2. What is Wallace's point when he argues that the "endgame" of gun control advocates is "not gun control but confiscation"? How does he make this case?

3. How persuasive is Wallace's argument to you? How effectively does Wallace appeal to *logos, ethos,* and *pathos*? How might readers disagree on what they interpret as strong appeals versus informal fallacies in Wallace's argument?

4. If you were going to write a strong response to Wallace's argument—either with the grain or against the grain—what further research would you do? What would you say?

Our next reading is also an op-ed piece. Its authors, Ralph Fascitelli and Jordan Royer, are longtime board members of Washington Ceasefire, a 32-year-old nonprofit organization dedicated to reducing gun violence. It was published in *The Seattle Times* on October 11, 2015.

Three Ways to Dramatically Cut Gun Violence
Ralph Fascitelli and Jordan Royer

1   Gun violence is like cancer: It comes in many different varieties and there is no single panacea to eliminate it.

2   But as businessmen with a combined 20 years on the front lines of this battle, we believe we can cut America's 32,000 annual death toll in half in 10 years with a three-pronged approach.

Public-health education:

3   About one-third of all homes in America possess a handgun and there is no better predictive metric to reducing gun violence. Those states that have the highest percentage of handgun ownership also have the highest percentage of gun violence, and vice versa. Research by David Hemenway of Harvard has shown that you are 22 times more likely to kill a family member or a friend versus an intruder with a gun in the home, and five times more likely to have a suicide.

4   A recent national poll by Washington CeaseFire of 508 homeowners shows that 70 percent of respondents either didn't know these statistics or didn't believe them. We envision an extensive public-health campaign on the same scale as the successful smoking campaign 50 years ago, aimed at getting the facts out on home gun ownership.

5   The effort would also encourage safe storage of handguns as well as a discussion among neighbors of which homes possess firearms. That's especially important since our own research shows only 12 percent of parents currently ask their neighbors, though there are an estimated 2 million homes in this country with unlocked guns and children under 18.

6   We believe, over a 10-year span, it's reasonable based on other public-health efforts to see a 20 percent drop or more in in-home gun ownership and up to 5,000 or more lives saved annually from fewer suicides, child gun accidents and domestic violence.

Technology:

7   Technology has played a vital role in the 50 percent drop in auto deaths over the past 30 years. New smart gun technology featuring proven radio-frequency-identification technology and operable only by the authorized user can similarly reduce gun deaths as well. Encouragingly, recent research of 615 U.S. adults by the firm Penn Schoen Berland found that 54 percent of gun owners under the age of 45 would consider swapping their old gun for a smart gun.

8   It's reasonable to believe that smart guns could save up to 10,000 lives annually by reducing suicide deaths (approximately 9,500 Americans commit suicide every year with a firearm they do not own), as well as childhood accidents and fatalities involving stolen guns. Up to now, smart gun distribution has been stalled by a controversial New Jersey law as well as limited availability. Both issues are expected to be resolved in the coming year.

Common-sense legislation:

9   Gun laws are effective, but difficult to achieve in the current polarized political climate. There is reason to believe that common ground can be found, such as the agreement achieved in 2009 between Washington Ceasefire and the National Rifle Association on taking gun rights away from people suffering from mental illness who are committed to a care facility for 30 days or more. California has a new law that allows a family to take away gun rights for up to a year for a family member with known mental-health issues. Perhaps such legislation might have prevented several mass shootings, including those at Sandy Hook Elementary in Connecticut, Cafe Racer in Seattle, and more recently at Umpqua Community College in Oregon.

10   There is other legislation that has a reasonable chance of passage in many states, if not nationally, including a ban on high-capacity ammunition magazines and tougher requirements for concealed weapons permits.

11   Gun violence is like cancer, but it's a public-health disease that other modern societies have addressed. The American gun death rate is almost 20 times that of other nations. Our "Operation Ceasefire" offers what we believe is an effective mix of public education, technology and common-ground legislation. It respects the Second Amendment as well as the lives and safety of our children. We believe it represents a path forward that can leave future generations here in Washington and across America much safer.

THINKING CRITICALLY
About "Three Ways to Dramatically Cut Gun Violence"

1. The authors propose three ways to cut gun violence. Explain to someone who hasn't read this op-ed piece what these three ways are.
2. How do you think that E. Gregory Wallace (the author of the previous reading) would respond to Fascitelli and Royer's proposals? Do you agree with Fascitelli and Royer's claim that their proposals respect the Second Amendment?
3. How effective is this argument rhetorically? How do the authors try to create "audience-based reasons" that tie into the assumptions, beliefs, and values of pro-gun readers who are apt to oppose their views? Are they successful?
4. Create a concept for a poster that treats gun violence as a public-health issue. What would a public-health campaign against gun violence look like?

Our next reading is a zine. A *zine* (an abbreviation for *fanzine*) is a small, self-published pamphlet that usually includes both visuals and text. Frequently reproduced in quantities up to several hundred, they are often self-distributed at public locations connected to their messages, such as malls, festivals, rallies, and protests. Often, zines focus on controversial issues and have an activist purpose. They convey their creators' passionate concerns, raise awareness, and may call for change. For information on how to construct an eight-page zine from one piece of paper—folded and creased into eight panels, cut along the horizontal center crease of the panels in the middle, and then folded into a little pamphlet—consult the Internet. In the zine we show here, Theda Hovind, a student who worked in museum education for her summer job, seeks to change parents' views about how to make museum visits meaningful for children. This zine's audience also includes museum administrators and other museum goers. The dotted lines in the zine help you imagine which panels form a full page in this little pamphlet.

Theda Hovind (Student)

Exit Through the Gift Shop, or Entrance to Life-Long Learning?

Learning at Museums

THINKING CRITICALLY

About "Exit Through the Gift Shop, or Entrance to Life-Long Learning?"

1. As you imagine Theda's zine as a little pamphlet with the first panel as its cover page and the last panel (top right) as its back cover page, think about the argument Theda is making. What is the problem or issue that she is addressing?

2. What are her main claim and reasons?

3. What alternative views does this zine argument engage explicitly and implicitly? How does it answer them?

4. The genre of the zine does not allow much space for development of an argument with detailed evidence. However, how do the text and images work together in this zine to present an abbreviated version of support for the argument?

5. Theda chose to draw her own images to look like illustrations in a children's book. How well do the style and choice of the drawings and layout suit the purpose, audience, and message?

6. With this example of a zine argument in mind, what arguments and audiences could you imagine addressing in the multimodal genre of the zine?

Our last reading is by student writer Claire Giordano, who wrote this paper for an argument assignment like the one in this chapter. In challenging the national enthusiasm for the expansion of online courses, Claire Giordano draws on her research and her experience and knowledge as an environmental studies major.

Claire Giordano (student)

Virtual Promise: Why Online Courses Will Not Adequately Prepare Us for the Future

1   In 2012 more than 6.7 million students took at least one online course (Allen and Seaman). Proponents of online education hope that such courses will improve the current educational system, but this potential is undermined by the problems of reliance on technology. A 2013 Kaiser Family Foundation Survey found that children and teens spend more than 53 hours using digital media every week (Toppo). Educational programs that place more people behind more computers may not be the best way to improve education for the future, and we as a country seem to be at a critical decision-making point of whether to increase technology's role in our lives. At this historical moment, I, as an environmental studies major concerned about my education and the well-being of the environment around me, believe the costs and consequences of online education must be evaluated based on how well they prepare us for future engagement with the world. Although many people have great expectations for the possibilities of online courses, their negative repercussions ultimately outweigh the supposed benefits. Online courses are not the best way to educate students because these virtual classes are more expensive, promote inequality by requiring technology that is inaccessible to many of our fellow citizens, inhibit the full development of our critical thinking skills, and further entrench our reliance on technology.

2   The optimism surrounding online courses arises from the belief that they will make higher education less expensive and more accessible and thus alleviate education inequality. From this perspective, the opportunities, flexibility, and lower costs of online courses outweigh their potential drawbacks. For example, Dr. Hershey Friedman, a business professor at Brooklyn College, who is widely published on the use of technology and media in education, supports the expansion of online education. He states that online courses ease the financial burden on both the student and the university and provide flexible schedules, which allow students to engage in other activities.

3   However, while these ideas sound good, they have fundamental problems with cost and accreditation. For example, one of the most common arguments in favor of virtual courses cites the cost effectiveness. The problem with this claim, though, is that it oversimplifies the issue. There are currently many models for online education that students could choose, from Massive Open Online Courses (MOOCs) that don't provide credit to programs that do grant credit. Within this range of possibilities, the programs that offer accreditation are the only ones students could use in the job market and in reality do not save us substantial amounts of money. A study by Tamara Battaglino et al. found that the average per pupil cost to a university for a full online education ranges from $6,400 to $10,200, which translates into a higher cost to students that is in some cases close to the rates of a traditional education (4). With these figures in mind, I cannot see why we would advocate for a course of education that is not only unacceptable in most of the job market but that also does not substantially reduce costs to make the classes more accessible.

4   Proponents who mistakenly believe that online education is cheaper also believe that its widespread accessibility will alleviate education inequalities. Thomas Friedman, who is a Pulitzer Prize winning journalist for the *New York Times*, believes that online courses will reduce poverty by granting all citizens equal access to the best education possible. This hope for accessibility nurtures a vision of universities "as central informational hubs that offer learning and knowledge and skills for anyone around the globe willing to absorb them" (Lagos). This image is quite compelling, and I will admit that arguments like Friedman's are appealing, especially when I consider students in similar situations like that of my sister, who has recently been overwhelmed with health problems and has missed a semester of high school and is still struggling to catch up in her classes. For students like her, online courses could be a godsend, giving them equal access to material and classes otherwise inaccessible.

5   However, the problem with believing that online courses create equality is that credit-bearing courses are too expensive and require technology that is simply not available to everyone. Many people struggling with poverty are not computer and Web users. This fundamental inequality is illustrated by the FCC's Broadband Access Report, which found that 119 million Americans do not have access to broadband Internet as a result of poverty or deficient wireless infrastructure. This problem was especially pronounced in rural areas, where 25% lacked access (Brodkin). The implications of this exclusion are explained clearly by Cynthia L. Selfe, who is a Distinguished Professor of the Humanities at Ohio State University and the first female English teacher to receive the EDUCOM Medal for innovative computer use. She explains that the push for technological literacy by the government and businesses "disguises the fact that technology is not available to everyone in this country or to every student in our schools . . . and distracts our attention from the realization that, in America, technology supports social divisions along race, class, and gender" (xxi). In light of this statement, it is clear to me that online courses are not the solution to education inequality because they require technology that perpetuates social inequality—the very problem they strive to address.

6   Supporters also claim online courses are the best way to transform current educational practices. From this point of view, advocates like Hershey Friedman and Linda Weiser Friedman believe that online courses can produce deeper-level thinking because they appeal to different learning styles and enhance creativity by using "numerous teaching tools that include animations, videos, wikis, and virtual labs." According to this argument, online courses provide an atmosphere conducive to the development of critical thinking skills just as effectively as conventional courses do.

7   While I cannot deny that online courses employ innovative tools with the potential to engage students, the virtual nature of the classes simply cannot recreate the environment of intellectual and interpersonal challenge that is necessary for fully developing critical thinking skills. The importance of critical thinking has been emphasized by many people, from the great American philosopher John Dewey (Michael Roth) to current educational leaders like Tony Wagner. To people like Dewey and Wagner, critical thinking skills are a prerequisite for being an engaged

member of society. I would add that critical thinking is also crucial if we are going to creatively and successfully address the wicked problems that face our world, from poverty, to water shortages, to toxic environments, to global climate change.

8   In light of this importance, I believe that critical thinking skills are too vital to entrust to a purely virtual environment. The weaknesses of online courses in promoting critical thinking are highlighted by Rick Roth, who has worked as an academic adviser for over twenty-four years and taught at the University of Washington and Skidmore College. Roth argues that online education is in fact detrimental to the growth of our critical thinking skills. He states that virtual learning through online classes strips education of its context and interdisciplinary nature: "[B]y demanding answers every few minutes in the form of quizzes, . . . they can't provide enough reflective time or space for those all-important 'it all depends on what you mean by' realizations." Furthermore, he explains that online courses deprive us of the learning that occurs when we become stuck and have to use reason and creativity to find a solution. Roth believes that "profoundly challenging learning needs the oxygen of uncertainty and ambiguity" that arises from the challenges posed by our professors and peers. This direct interaction is critical to engaging with the world and simply cannot be facilitated in a virtual environment where the ability to respond with a right or wrong answer is reinforced through repetitive quizzes and evaluations. This impersonal and simplistic way of learning lacks the challenging interactions that develop our ability to reason, to think creatively, and to work collaboratively—important skills we need in order to address the social and environmental problems we face as a global community.

9   Finally, advocates of virtual learning claim that online courses prepare students for the future by developing technological proficiency, which is needed in most occupations and even in many job applications (Lagos). The problem with this point of view, however, is that it ignores the many other skills that we need to succeed in the world, and does not acknowledge the consequences of relying on technology. I am not saying that all technology is bad and should be abandoned, but that the modern reliance on computers and superfluous gadgets may be more detrimental than helpful. This concept is captured nicely by the Dutch social critic Michiel Schwarz, who believes that "technology has become our environment as well as our ideology . . . we no longer use technology, we live it" (qtd. in Glendinning 45). These views suggest that the proliferation of technology (including online courses) may have far reaching negative effects on our lives and the entire global community.

10   Additionally, the dependence on technology in virtual classes merely supports and further promotes, in the words of ecopsychologists Allen Kanner and Mary Gomes, "an almost religious belief among Americans in the ultimate good of all technological progress, through its claim that there is a product to solve each of life's problems" (84). From the perspective of Kanner and Gomes, however, these hopes are merely part of the larger misplaced faith in the power of technology to cure all of the world's social and environmental ills. This misguided faith in technology encourages misunderstanding of pressing environmental problems, something that especially troubles me because I believe we should devote our resources and brain power to collaboratively solving our problems *now* rather than

hoping that future generations will invent new technologies to solve the crises we are creating by living beyond the limits of our planet. Rather than blindly looking to future technology as a savior, we must act now to slow the environmental degradation while we still can.

11   Furthermore, attachment to technology not only affects our physical, social, and cultural futures, but also has huge repercussions for the health of the earth we depend on and must preserve for our own health as well as the well-being of future generations. Recent international research is finding that as the use of technology increases, we are slowly losing our ability to interact with the world through all of our senses because current technology overemphasizes visual information (Sewall 202). Thus, the rise of technology (such as online courses) means that we are interacting with the world through screens rather than enjoying the simple beauty and life that surround us, from the movement of clouds on a windy day to the smell of the first spring daffodil. This change also has direct impacts on our physical, mental, and emotional health, as Richard Louv explains in his work *Last Child in the Woods*. He cites studies that link a lack of play in nature with higher rates of ADHD, depression, and other mental disorders, especially pronounced in children. But these same patterns are also seen in adults in study after study (Louv 107-110). For everyone's health, we need nature. We must spend time outside, whether it is watching a sunset from a high-rise or helping kids plant seeds and get their hands dirty in rich soil. Online courses may help us become more technologically adept, but they will also keep us more isolated behind computer screens. This gain is not worth the cost of becoming further alienated from the endangered natural world and from other people who need our compassion and understanding.

12   While I admit that online courses have many strong advocates and some potential to make positive change in the world, these changes simply come at too high a price. Credit-bearing virtual courses are expensive and require a technology not everyone can access. They also create an environment devoid of the necessary challenges and interactions that foster complex critical thinking. The online courses also entrench our dangerous reliance on technology and perpetuate unsustainable attitudes about how we should interact with the natural world. Amidst the current intense societal pressure to develop and employ ever more technology in every aspect of life, we must decide whether this is a direction our education should also follow. At a time when the polar ice is melting at unprecedented rates, species are becoming extinct every day, and the very air we breathe is toxic from the pollution of industrialization, entrusting our education to technology is not the answer.

Works Cited

Allen, I. Elaine, and Jeff Seaman. "Changing Course: Ten Years of Tracking Online Education in the United States." Babson Research Group, 2013, www.onlinelearningsurvey.com/reports/changingcourse.pdf.

Brodkin, Jon. "119 Million Americans Lack Broadband Internet, FCC Reports." *ArsTechnica*, 21 Aug. 2012, arstechnica.com/business/2012/08/119-million-americans-lack-broadband-internet-fcc-reports.

Battaglino, Tamara Butler, et al. "The Costs of Online Learning: Creating Sound Policy for Digital Learning." Thomas B. Fordham Institute, Creating Sound

Policy for Digital Learning Series, 9 Jan. 2012, www.edexcellencemedia.net/publications/2012/20120110-the-costs-of-online-learning/20120110-the-costs-of-online-learning.pdf.

Friedman, Hershey H., and Linda Weiser Friedman. "Crises in Education: Online Learning as a Solution." *Creative Education*, vol. 2, no. 3, 2011, pp. 156-63.

Friedman, Thomas L. "Revolution Hits the Universities." *The New York Times*, 26 Jan. 2013, www.nytimes.com/2013/01/27/opinion/sunday/friedman-revolution-hits-the-universities.html?_r=0.

Glendinning, Chellis. "Technology, Trauma, and the Wild." *Ecopsychology: Restoring the Earth, Healing the Mind,* edited by Theodore Roszak, et al., Sierra Club Books, 1995, pp. 41-54.

Kanner, Allen D., and Mary E. Gomes. "The All-Consuming Self." *Ecopsychology: Restoring the Earth, Healing the Mind,* edited by Theodore Roszak, et al., Sierra Club Books, 1995, pp. 77-91.

Lagos, Taso. "Pro: Are Online Courses Good for Higher Education?" *The Seattle Times*, 18 Aug. 2012, www.seattletimes.com/opinion/pro-are-online-courses-good-for-higher-education.

Louv, Richard. *Last Child in the Woods: Saving Our Children from Nature-deficit Disorder.* Algonquin Books of Chapel Hill, 2006.

Roth, Michael S. "Learning as Freedom." *The New York Times*, 6 Sept. 2012, p. A23.

Roth, Rick. "Con: Online Learning Turns College into Assembly Line." *The Seattle Times*, 18 Aug. 2012, www.seattletimes.com/opinion/con-online-learning-turns-college-into-assembly-line.

Selfe, Cynthia L. *Technology and Literacy in the Twenty-First Century: The Importance of Paying Attention*. Southern Illinois UP, 1999.

Sewall, Laura. "The Skill of Ecological Perception." *Ecopsychology: Restoring the Earth, Healing the Mind*, edited by Theodore Roszak, et al., Sierra Club Books, 1995, pp. 201-15.

Toppo, Greg. "Kids' Electronic Media Use Jumps to 53 Hours a Week." *USA Today*, 20 Jan. 2010, usatoday30.usatoday.com/tech/news/2010-01-20-1Avideokids20_ST_N.htm.

Wagner, Tony. *The Global Achievement Gap: Why Even Our Best Schools Don't Teach the New Survival Skills Our Children Need – and What We Can Do About It.* Basic Books, 2008.

THINKING CRITICALLY

About "Virtual Promise: Why Online Courses Will Not Adequately Prepare Us for the Future"

1. What is Claire Giordano's main claim and what are her reasons for opposing online courses?

2. While some classical arguments group alternative views after the writer's development of the reasons, others structure the whole argument as a rebuttal with the writer's reasons in effect answering the opposing views. What choice has Claire made? Why do you think she chose to organize her argument this way? What alternative or opposing views does she address?

3. What audience do you think Claire is trying to reach with this argument? How well does she use appeals to *pathos* to connect with readers' values, beliefs, and emotions?

4. How effectively does Claire create appeals to *ethos* in this argument? Where does her evidence draw on her experience and knowledge as an environmental studies major?

5. How would you assess the appeals to *logos* in this argument? Consider the range, quality, and depth of her supporting evidence.

6. What do you see as the major strengths and weaknesses of this argument?

Chapter 15
Making an Evaluation

Learning Objectives

15.1 Explain the criteria-match structure and other rhetorical principles that underlie effective evaluation arguments.

15.2 Use a planning schema to develop a line of reasoning for an evaluation argument.

15.3 Understand and apply a step-by-step process for making an evaluation argument.

15.4 Write an evaluation argument for an audience of skeptical readers.

As a thinking human being, you are always doing evaluative thinking. What career choices best fit my interests and skills? What players should I draft for my fantasy sports league? Of these three apartments in my price range, which one should I rent? To stimulate evaluative thinking, you might also read reviews of restaurants, movies, or consumer products. Perhaps you have even written such reviews on Yelp, Angie's List, or Amazon. In college and during your career, you will often be the subject of evaluative reviews, as when a professor writes you a recommendation for graduate school or your supervisor writes your annual performance review.

Evaluation arguments are also common as academic assignments. According-ing to a study by Barbara Walvoord and Lucille McCarthy, college assignments often take the form of "good/better/best" evaluation questions. For example, a world history professor might ask you to rank several postcolonial rulers in Africa and to argue which governed most effectively and why. Or an engineering student might be asked to evaluate alternative design approaches for a given engineering problem.

The criteria-match structure of evaluation arguments

15.1 Explain the criteria-match structure and other rhetorical principles that underlie effective evaluation arguments.

Evaluations usually involve a two-step critical thinking process—sometimes called a **criteria-match process**. The first step in this process is to establish criteria; the second step is to show how well your subject matches these criteria. Thus if you are trying to decide what courses to take next term, you first determine the criteria you will apply, such as your interest in the subject, the instructor's reputation, the manageability of the workload, or the days and times that the class meets. Once you establish criteria, you then begin looking for the courses that best meet those criteria.

Here are several more examples:

- Which students should be awarded the prestigious presidential scholarship?

    Criteria task: What are the criteria for the presidential scholarship?

    Match task: Which of the candidates best meet the criteria?

- Is hospitalization a good treatment for anorexia?

    Criteria task: What are the criteria for a good treatment for anorexia?

    Match task: Does hospitalization meet these criteria?

- What is the best cell phone for an elderly relative who desires only to make and receive phone calls?

    Criteria task: What are the criteria for a good cell phone for this specific person? [Note: These criteria might be quite different from those you would select for yourself.]

    Match task: Which phone best meets the criteria?

The preceding examples show how evaluation claims require you to establish criteria and then to match the criteria to the thing being evaluated. Stakeholders can disagree about the criteria, the match, or both. For example, consider a couple deciding what used car to buy. They might initially disagree about the criteria. One partner might value low price and economy while the other partner values performance and a certain "cool" factor. Even if the couple finally agree on the criteria—let's say, (1) low cost, (2) reliability, and (3) sporty appearance—they might still disagree whether a specific car meets the criteria. In terms of cost, Car A may be initially cheaper than Car B but may be less economical to drive and need repairs more frequently. In this match argument, the couple would argue over whether Car A or Car B better meets the low-cost criterion.

For Writing and Discussion
Establishing and Applying Criteria

Whenever you evaluate something, you first need to establish criteria—that is, for any given class of items, you have to determine the qualities, traits, behaviors, or features that constitute excellence for members of that class.

(continued)

Then you need to match those criteria to the thing you are evaluating. The following exercise will help you practice thinking in this systematic, two-stage way:

1. Working individually, make a list of criteria that are important to you in choosing a career. These criteria will differ from person to person. Some people might place "high income" at the top of their list, while others might put "interesting," "being outdoors," or "time for family and leisure" at the top. Then rank your criteria from highest to lowest priority.

2. Share your criteria lists in small groups or as a whole class. Then write on the board two or three representative lists of criteria.

3. Finally, write several different careers on the board and match them to the lists of criteria. Possible careers to consider might include elementary school/high school teacher, lawyer, auto mechanic, computer programmer, engineer, event planner, small business owner, homemaker, social worker, police officer, and farmer/rancher.

4. When disagreements arise, try to identify whether they are disagreements about criteria or disagreements about the facets of a given career.

The Role of Purpose and Context in Determining Criteria

The criteria for any evaluation depend on the purpose of the thing being evaluated and on the particular context in which the evaluation is conducted. For example, the kind of cell phone desired by an elderly relative who wants only to make phone calls may be different from the kind of cell phone you would desire for yourself. You might prefer a high-end smartphone, but such a phone would be bewildering to your relative. Rather than a smartphone, you might recommend something like the following:

Uncle Pete, I recommend that you buy the Spiderman 500 flip-top phone

- Because this phone has a large-screen visual display for easy reading
- Because its large numeric keyboard has physical buttons for easy touch dialing
- Because it comes with a reliable, low-cost plan

Here your criteria are good visibility, easy dialing, reliability, and low cost. Having established those criteria, you believe that the Spiderman 500 flip-top best meets those criteria.

Let's look further at the role of both purpose and context in an evaluation. If you ask a professor for a recommendation, he or she will necessarily ask "recommendation for what?" (graduate school? Peace Corps volunteer? summer job in a national park? internship in a law office? scholarship?) The qualities of a successful law office intern differ substantially from those of a successful Peace Corps volunteer. The recommendation isn't about you in the abstract but about your qualifications for fulfilling the purposes of a certain class—for example, the class "law office intern" or "Peace Corps volunteer." Similarly, if you were evaluating a bicycle, you would need to ask, "a bicycle for what purpose?" (Urban commuting? Touring? Racing?)

Decisions about criteria are also affected by context. For example, consider a recent review of a city's soup kitchens appearing in a newspaper produced by homeless people. In most contexts, restaurant reviews focus on the quality of food. But in this review the highest criterion was the sense of dignity and love that the staff extended to homeless people.

For Writing and Discussion
Seeing How Criteria Vary with Purpose

1. Working in small groups or as a whole class, decide how you would evaluate a local restaurant for different purposes. How would you evaluate it as a place for gourmet dining? As a place for fast food or tavern food? As a place for a romantic date? As a place to study? As a place to congregate with friends before or after a game?

2. As a whole class or in small groups, discuss how this individual exercise helped you realize how criteria for excellence vary when you place the same item into different classes with different purposes.

Special Problems in Establishing Criteria

Establishing criteria for evaluation arguments often entails special problems that make it difficult to determine what values or standards to apply. Table 15.1 shows five typical kinds of problems and their solutions.

Table 15.1 Problems and Solutions in Establishing Criteria

Problem	Explanation	Solution
Different classes: Apples and oranges	You can't evaluate apples against oranges unless you try to evaluate them both as "fruit." (It is harder to establish criteria for a good fruit than it is to establish criteria for a good apple or a good orange.)	Place the thing to be evaluated in the smallest possible class. Compare one kind of apple against another kind. Even better, evaluate apples in the class "eating apples" or "pie apples" rather than apples in general. Compare Chris Paul to other basketball guards rather than to basketball players in general.
Competing standards: The ideal versus the doable/achievable	This problem is illustrated by the aphorism "Don't let the perfect be enemy to the good." Sometimes we have to evaluate something highly if it is "good enough" or "better than what we have now" rather than ideal.	Clarify whether you are using an ideal standard or the lesser standard of "achievable." In moving toward universal health care, many Americans wanted a single-payer system like Canada's—what they considered the ideal. But they still voted for Obamacare because it was achievable and "good enough." It made affordable health care available to many more Americans.
Competing measures: The ideal versus the commonplace or average	This problem overlaps with competing standards. Do you evaluate something using an ideal measure or a lower measure based on what is commonplace or average?	Clarify whether the measure you are using derives from an ideal or from what is commonplace or average. For example, fighting climate change by burning natural gas from fracking doesn't meet the ideal measure of no carbon emissions, but it is still better than burning oil or coal. In terms of carbon emissions, natural gas is a "good fuel" compared to coal but a "bad fuel" compared to the ideal of renewable energy. Your item might not measure up to the ideal, but it is ahead of the others in its class.

(continued)

Problem	Explanation	Solution
Seductive empirical measures: The power of numbers	We may be tempted to evaluate something based on traits that can be quantified—for example, grade point averages for scholarships; student evaluations for a teacher's tenure/promotion; five-year survival rates for best cancer treatments. Because numbers rank-order themselves, they can hold huge sway in evaluations.	Although numbers can be persuasive, they often don't measure the nonquantifiable things that we really value. Always ask what the numbers do *not* measure and seek ways to evaluate the traits that might be more important.
Tyranny of cost: Can we afford it?	Sometimes the things we evaluate highest simply cost too much. (Note: Cost may be measured by money, time, emotional stress, or other factors.)	You may have to eliminate the top choices in your evaluation because they cost too much. Recognize the inhibiting factor of cost from the start. You may need to evaluate only those items in your cost range.

Distinguishing Necessary, Sufficient, and Accidental Criteria

Another factor in establishing criteria is recognizing that some criteria are more important than others. Suppose you said, "I will be happy with any job as long as it puts food on my table and gives me time for my family." In this case the criteria "adequate income" and "time for family," taken together, are **sufficient**, meaning that once these criteria are met, the job being rated meets your standard for excellence. Suppose you said instead, "I am hard to please in my choice of a career, which must meet many criteria. But I definitely will reject any career that doesn't put enough food on my table or allow me time for my family." In this case the criteria of "adequate income" and "time for family" are **necessary but not sufficient**, meaning that these two criteria have to be met for a career to meet your standards, but that other criteria must be met also.

Besides necessary and sufficient criteria, there are **accidental** criteria, which are added bonuses but not essential. For example, you might say, "Although it's not essential, having a career that would allow me to be outside a lot would be nice." In this case "being outside" is an accidental criterion (nice but not required).

Using a planning schema to develop evaluation arguments

15.2 Use a planning schema to develop a line of reasoning for an evaluation argument.

In Chapter 14, we showed you how to use a planning schema to develop ideas for an argument. The schema encourages writers to articulate their argument frame (each reason along with its underlying assumption that links the reason back to the claim) and then to imagine what kinds of evidence could be used to support both the reason and the underlying assumption. Equally important, the schema encourages writers to anticipate counterarguments by imagining how skeptical readers might object to the writers' reasons, underlying assumptions, or both.

Let's say that you are the student member of a committee to select a professor for an outstanding teaching award. Several members of the committee want to give the award to Professor M. Mouse, a popular sociology professor at your institution. You are opposed. One of your reasons is that Professor Mouse's courses aren't rigorous. Here is how you could use a planning schema to develop this line of reasoning.

CLAIM WITH REASON

Professor Mouse does not deserve the teaching award because his courses aren't rigorous.

EVIDENCE TO SUPPORT THE REASON

I need to provide evidence that his courses aren't rigorous. From the dean's office records, I have discovered that 80 percent of his students get As or high Bs. A review of his syllabi shows that he requires little outside reading and only one short paper. He has a reputation in my residence hall of being fun and easy.

UNDERLYING ASSUMPTION (CRITERION)

Having rigorous academic standards is a necessary criterion for the university teaching award.

EVIDENCE/ARGUMENTS TO SUPPORT THE ASSUMPTION

I need to show why I think rigorous academic standards are necessary. Quality of teaching should be measured by the amount that students learn. Good teaching is more than a popularity contest. Good teachers draw high-level performance from their students and motivate them to put time and energy into learning. High standards lead to the development of skills that are demanded in society.

WAYS SKEPTICS MIGHT OBJECT

How could someone attack my reason and evidence? Might a person say that Mouse has high standards? Could someone show that students really earned the high grades? Are the students I talked to not representative? Could someone say that Mouse's workload and grading patterns meet or exceed the commonplace behavior of faculty in his department?

How could someone attack my underlying assumption? Could someone argue that rigorous academic standards aren't as important as other criteria—that this is an accidental not a necessary criterion? Could a person say that Mouse's goal—to inspire interest in sociology—is best achieved by not loading students down with too many papers and too much reading, which can appear to be busywork? (I'll need to refute this argument.) Could someone say that the purpose of giving the university teaching award is public relations and it is therefore important to recognize widely popular teachers who will be excellent speakers at banquets and other public forums?

Developing an evaluation argument: an extended example

15.3 Understand and apply a step-by-step process for making an evaluation argument.

Now that we have explored some potential difficulties in establishing and defending criteria for an evaluation, let's consider in more detail the process of making an evaluation argument.

The student examples in this section focus on the evaluation of a rock-and-roll museum in Seattle, Washington, called Experience Music Project (EMP). Designed by architect Frank Gehry (who is known for his creation of the Guggenheim Museum in Bilbao, Spain; the Aerospace Hall in Los Angeles; and other famous buildings around the world), EMP was sponsored by Microsoft cofounder Paul Allen as a tribute to rock singer Jimi Hendrix and to rock music itself.

In Figure 15.1, you can see this innovative structure, which sparked much controversy (is it a wonder or an eyesore?). Sharing some characteristics with the Rock and Roll Hall of Fame and Museum in Cleveland, Ohio, EMP features some permanent exhibits—the Hendrix Gallery, the Guitar Gallery (tracing the development of guitars from the 1500s to the electric guitars of today), Milestones (including displays from rhythm and blues to hip-hop and current rap artists), and Northwest Passage (focusing on popular music in Seattle, from jazz and rhythm and blues to heavy metal, punk, grunge, and the contemporary music scene). EMP also includes Sound Lab (where visitors can play instruments using interactive technology),On Stage (where visitors can pretend to be rock stars playing before a cheering crowd), traveling exhibits,

FIGURE 15.1 Experience Music Project, Seattle, Washington

and a retail store. (To see for yourself what EMP is and how it looks on the inside, you can go to its Web site.)

Let's now turn to the specific steps of making an evaluation argument.

Step 1: Determining the Class to Which X Belongs and the Purposes of That Class

When you conduct an evaluation argument, you must first assign your person/ object/phenomenon (the X you are evaluating) to a category or class and then determine the purposes of that class. Often people disagree about an evaluation because they disagree about the arguer's choice of category for the thing being evaluated. EMP, as students soon discovered, can be placed in several different categories, leading to different criteria for evaluation. Here are typical categories or classes proposed by students:

- A tourist attraction (for an audience of visitors to Seattle)
- A museum of popular music history (for people interested in the development of popular music as an art form)
- A rock-and-roll shrine (for rock fans who want to revere their favorite artists and feel like part of the rock scene for a day)

Clearly these categories or classes have different purposes. The purpose of a tourist attraction is to offer a unique, fun place to spend the day during a visit to Seattle. The purpose of a popular music museum is to teach about the history of its subject in an informative, interesting, and accessible way. The purpose of a rock-and-roll shrine is to honor famous rock stars, bring visitors into their lives and work, and let them experience the music scene.

Step 2: Determining and Weighting Criteria

The criteria for your evaluation are directly connected to the purposes of the class to which the item being evaluated belongs. The following lists show typical criteria chosen by different students for each of the categories/classes listed in Step 1:

A good *tourist attraction* should

- be entertaining and enjoyable.
- be affordable and worth the price, not simply out to gouge tourists' wallets.
- be unique—something tourists wouldn't find in another city.

A good *museum of popular music* should

- have a clear, well-organized layout that is easy to navigate.
- display objects of clear aesthetic or historical significance.
- teach the public by providing clear, meaningful information about the development of popular music forms.
- arouse interest in popular music as an art form and encourage the public's appreciation and involvement.

A good *rock-and-roll shrine* should

- take fans up close and personal into the lives of major artists.
- encourage fans to appreciate the complexity of rock and the skills of artists.
- help fans experience the rock scene and fantasize about being rock stars themselves.

In addition to identifying criteria, you should arrange them in order of importance so that you build to your most important criterion. In each of the preceding examples, students placed their most important criterion last.

Step 3: Determining the Extent to Which the Item Being Evaluated Meets Your Criteria

The third step in constructing an evaluation argument is to make your match argument: To what extent does the item being evaluated meet or not meet the criteria you have formulated? The following examples show how three students framed the match part of their evaluation arguments on EMP. Note how each student matches EMP to the specific criteria he or she selected.

Although the Experience Music Project has tourist-worthy uniqueness, it is a disappointing tourist attraction because

- its chaotic arrangement of exhibits reduces enjoyment by causing frustrating repetition of the same experiences.
- the headphones and heavy computerized MEGs (Museum Exhibit Guides) further reduce enjoyment by keeping everyone isolated, making companionship difficult.
- it's too expensive and commercial, leaving the tourist feeling ripped off.

Experience Music Project is a good museum of popular music history because

- it covers a range of popular music styles from jazz and blues to reggae, punk, grunge, and hip-hop.
- it provides interesting information on musicians, musical styles, and key moments in popular music history.
- it makes people excited about and interested in popular music and its history through the museum's interactive exhibits, its displays of instruments and rock memorabilia, and technologically advanced museum guide devices, which help visitors easily navigate the museum's layout.

For rock fans, Experience Music Project is a good rock-and-roll shrine because

- it gives illuminating insights into the lives and artistry of many rock musicians.
- it gives an in-depth look at some of the greats like Jimi Hendrix and helps fans really appreciate these musicians' talent.
- the "onstage" room lets fans fulfill a fantasy by pretending they are rock stars.

Step 4: Determining What Alternative Views You Must Respond to in Your Evaluation Argument

Finally, in constructing your evaluation argument you need to determine whether your intended audience is likely to object to (1) the category or class in which you have placed your object, (2) the criteria you have developed for assessing objects in that class, or (3) the degree to which your object meets the criteria you have chosen. You have numerous options for accommodating your audience's doubts or objections:

- If your proposed class is controversial, you might choose to justify it in your introduction.
- If your criteria might be controversial, you could address objections before you start the match part of your argument.
- If you think your match argument will raise doubts, you could intersperse alternative views throughout or treat them separately near the end of your argument.

In the Readings section of this chapter, we include a student writer's complete evaluation argument on the Experience Music Project.

For Writing and Discussion
Responding to Objections

Consider how student writer Katie Tiehen confronts and responds to alternative views. After reading this passage from her argument, answer the questions that follow:

> . . . Some may challenge my contention that EMP is an ineffective museum of rock history by arguing that a day spent at EMP is entertaining and fun. I'll be the first to admit that EMP is fun. From a rock-and-roll fan's perspective, EMP is nonstop entertainment, a musical paradise. I felt like a five-year-old on Christmas morning when I saw Eric Clapton's guitar, Jimi Hendrix's personal journals, and walls plastered in punk memorabilia. These items, coupled with video documentaries and hands-on activities, provided hours of enjoyment. Because of the fun factor, it's easy for people to jump to EMP's defense. However, it is not the entertainment value of EMP that I am questioning. There's no doubt that it is a fun and amusing place to visit. The problem arises when one tries to classify EMP as an historical museum, which should provide visitors with access to objects of lasting historical significance. Some entertainment is fine, but not to the point that it clouds the true purpose of the museum, as it does in EMP's case. After two visits, I still couldn't tell you where rock and roll originated, but I could tell you that the line to play the drums in Sound Lab is really long. Entertainment is the main purpose of EMP and it shouldn't be.

1. What objections to her argument does Katie anticipate?
2. How does Katie respond to alternative views?

Writing an evaluation argument

15.4 **Write an evaluation argument for an audience of skeptical readers.**

> **Writing Project:** Write an argument in which you use evaluative thinking to persuade your audience to see the value (or lack of value) of the person, place, thing, event, or phenomenon that you are evaluating. The introduction to your argument should hook your audience's interest in your evaluation question. The body of your argument should establish criteria for evaluating your chosen subject, and then show how your subject meets or does not meet those criteria. Depending on the degree of controversy surrounding your subject, follow the procedure for other arguments by summarizing alternative views and responding to them through either concession or refutation.

For this assignment you need to pose an evaluative question that is important to your audience and invites multiple views. In planning for this assignment, you may choose to evaluate a controversial person, event, thing, or phenomenon—something that engenders lively disagreement within a particular community. (For example: Is a caucus system a good method for choosing a political party's presidential candidate? Is raising the minimum wage a good way to combat poverty?) When your subject is controversial, you need to consider alternative evaluations and show why yours is better.

You may also choose to evaluate something that is not itself controversial. Your purpose might be to help a specific audience determine how to spend their time or money. For example, is taking an art gallery walk a good way for students to spend a Saturday afternoon in your city? Or you might consider writing your evaluation for a specific forum. For example, you might write a review for a parenting Web site evaluating whether the *Hunger Games* movies are good family films. Or you might write an editorial for your school newspaper explaining why tutoring with the local children's literacy project is a good experience for education majors.

Generating and Exploring Ideas

For your evaluation essay, you will try either to change your readers' assessment of a controversial person, event, thing, or phenomenon or to help your readers decide whether an event or thing is worth their time or money.

If you have not already chosen an evaluation issue, try thinking about evaluative questions within the various communities to which you belong:

Local civic community: evaluative questions about transportation, land use, historical monuments, current leaders, political bills or petitions, housing, parking policies, effectiveness of police

National civic community: evaluative questions about public education, environmental concerns, economic policies, responses to terrorism, Supreme Court decisions, foreign policies, political leaders

Your college or university community: evaluative questions about academic or sports programs, campus life programs, first-year or transfer student orientation, clubs, dorm life, campus facilities, financial-aid programs, campus security, parking, cultural programs

Your scholarly community or disciplinary community in your major: evaluative questions about internships, study-abroad programs, general-studies programs, course requirements, first-year studies, major curriculum, advising, course sequences, teaching methods, homework requirements, academic standards, recent books or articles, new theories in a field, library resources, laboratory facilities, Web site sources of primary documents or numerical data in a field

Culture and entertainment issues within your social or family communities: evaluative questions about restaurants, movies, plays, museums, TV shows, musicians, video games, entertainment Web sites, concerts, books, paintings, sports figures, buildings

Consumer issues within your social or family communities: evaluative questions about computer systems, CDs, cars, clothing brands, stores, products, e-commerce

Work communities: evaluative questions about supervisors or subordinates, office efficiency, customer relations, advertising and marketing, production or sales, record keeping and finance, personnel policies

Another good strategy for finding a topic is to think about a recent review or critique with which you disagree—a movie or restaurant review, a sportswriter's assessment of a team or player, an op-ed column or blog assessing a government official or proposed legislation. How would you evaluate this controversial subject differently?

Once you have chosen a possible controversial topic, use Strategies Chart 15.1 to help you explore and develop ideas for your evaluation argument.

Strategies Chart 15.1 Strategies for Developing an Evaluative Claim

Strategies	Questions to Ask and Steps to Follow
Place the item you will evaluate in the smallest and most meaningful category for your intended audience.	For the audience you have in mind, what is the smallest, most relevant class in which to place the thing being evaluated? For example, Is *Mad Max: Fury Road* a good action movie (rather than simply a good movie)? Or even more narrow, is *Mad Max: Fury Road* a good action movie for family viewing?
Determine the criteria you will use to make your evaluation meaningful and helpful to your audience.	What are the purposes of the class in which you have placed your subject? Use freewriting or idea mapping to explore the qualities a member of that class needs to have to achieve those purposes.
Think about the objections to your criteria your audience might raise.	How will you justify your criteria? What reasoning and evidence will you use?
Think about how you will weight or rank your criteria.	Which of your criteria are most important and why?
Evaluate your subject by matching it to each of your criteria.	Why does your subject match or not match each of the criteria? Freewrite to find examples and counterexamples.

Shaping, Drafting, and Revising

In drafting your evaluation argument, you have two key developmental and organizational questions to consider: (1) Will you have to defend your choice of criteria as well as complete the match part of your argument? (2) Where should you locate and respond to alternative views? Your answers to these questions will depend on your specific evaluation claim and on your audience. Although there are many ways to organize an evaluation argument, the framework chart in Figure 15.2 is a good place to start.

As you revise, think of ways that you can make your evaluation clearer and more useful for your audience. Consider ways to sharpen your criteria and build up the match part of your argument to make your evaluation more persuasive.

Questions for Peer Review

In addition to the generic peer review questions explained in Skill 17.4, ask your peer reviewers to address these questions:

INTRODUCTION

1. How well do the title and introduction capture your interest, provide needed background, identify the controversy, and show the importance of the subject?
2. How well has the writer established the evaluative question, the claim, and the criteria? How could these be improved?

THE CRITERIA-MATCH ARGUMENT

1. How fitting and persuasive is the writer's choice of criteria for evaluating this subject? How could the writer support or defend his or her criteria and the weighting of those criteria more clearly or persuasively?

Figure 15.2 Framework for an Evaluation Argument

Introduction	• Presents your issue • Shows why evaluating X is problematic or controversial • Presents your evaluation claim and your criteria
Argument	• States criterion 1 and defends it if necessary • Shows that X meets/does not meet criterion 1 • States criterion 2 and defends it if necessary • Shows that X meets/does not meet criterion 2 • Continues with additional criteria and match arguments
Treatment of alternative or opposing views	• Summarizes objections to your criteria or your match • Responds to these objections
Conclusion	• Sums up your evaluation

2. How does the writer support and develop the match part of the argument? What evidence helps readers see that the thing being evaluated meets or fails to meet each criterion? How could the writer improve the match argument?

3. Where does the writer summarize and address alternative views? How could this treatment of alternative views be improved?

Multimodal and Online Writing Project Options

1. **Online Evaluation** Write an online evaluation of a product, device, store, restaurant, book, film, agency, or something equivalent. Your evaluation should be suitable for posting on Yelp, Angie's List, Amazon, Goodreads, or some other Web site that posts user or consumer reviews. In your evaluation, make your criteria clear and relevant to your chosen audience and site. Use specific examples to show how your item under review measures up to your criteria. Try to make this evaluation useful to the audience you have in mind. Also appreciate that evaluative reviews have business consequences. Make sure that your evaluation is respectful, fair, and well supported.

2. **Speech with Visual Aids (Flip Chart, PowerPoint, Prezi)** Choose as your subject to be evaluated a proposed policy, action, candidate for office, or other situation or phenomenon that is open to civic debate. Deliver your evaluation argument as a formal speech supported by visual aids and limited to five minutes. Pay attention to the construction and delivery of your speech and to the multimodal design of your visual aids.

For advice on producing multimedia compositions, see Chapter 20. For an example of a student speech with PowerPoint slides, see the readings in Chapter 16.

Readings

The first reading is a student essay by Jackie Wyngaard evaluating the Experience Music Project in Seattle, Washington.

Jackie Wyngaard (student)

EMP: Music History or Music Trivia?

1   Along with other college students new to Seattle, I wanted to see what cultural opportunities the area offers. I especially wanted to see billionaire Paul Allen's controversial Experience Music Project (known as EMP), a huge, bizarre, shiny, multicolored structure that is supposed to resemble a smashed guitar. Brochures say that EMP celebrates the creativity of American popular music, but it has prompted heated discussions among architects, Seattle residents, museumgoers, and music lovers, who have questioned its commercialism and the real value of its exhibits. My sister recommended this museum to me because she knows I am a big music lover and a rock-and-roll fan. Also, as an active choir member since the sixth grade, I have always been intrigued by the history of music. I went to EMP expecting to learn more about music history from exhibits that showed a range of popular musical styles, that traced historical connections and influences, and that enjoyably conveyed useful information. However, as a museum of rock history, EMP is a disappointing failure.

2   EMP claims that it covers the history of rock and roll from its roots to the styles of today, but it fails at this task because it isolates musicians and styles without explaining historical progressions or cultural influences. For instance, the museum doesn't show how Elvis Presley's musical style was influenced by his predecessors like Chuck Berry and Muddy Waters. It doesn't show how early folk and blues influenced Bob Dylan's music. It doesn't show how early jazz paved the way for rock and roll. How are these isolated and separate EMP exhibits connected? How did rock and roll progress from the '50s "Let's Go to the Hop" beats to the laid-back guitar riffs of the '60s and '70s? How did '70s music become the heavy metal, head-banger rock of the '80s and '90s? How did these styles lead to rap? The exhibits show the existence of these different styles, but they don't help viewers understand the historical developments or historical context. While it is interesting to see a peace patch once owned by Janis Joplin, this exhibit does not explain either the social and political events of the time or Joplin's political views.

3   Another fault of EMP is that it omits many influential groups and musicians, particularly women. For example, there is no display about the Beatles, the Rolling Stones, Led Zeppelin, or the Doors. The exhibits also exclude many major female artists who made substantial contributions to popular music. I found nothing about Joan Baez, Ella Fitzgerald, Aretha Franklin, Carly Simon, or Joni Mitchell. I was also surprised that there were few women mentioned in the Northwest Passage exhibit. Weren't more women involved in the Seattle music scene? As a woman interested in music, I felt left out by EMP's overall neglect of women musicians.

4   Perhaps most frustrating about EMP is the way exhibits are explained through the awkward, difficult-to-use handheld computer called a Museum Exhibit Guide (MEG). The explanations are hard to access and then disappointing in their content. I wanted to hear a landmark song that an artist wrote or an interesting analysis of the artist's musical style. Instead, I listened to "how Elvis made the leather jacket famous" and other random trivia. The MEG also offers too many choices for each exhibit, like a Web page with a dozen links. But after all the time and effort, you learn nothing that increases your understanding or stimulates your thinking about music history. The MEGs themselves are very heavy, clunky, and inconvenient. If you don't point this gadget exactly at the activator, nothing happens. It took me a good ten minutes to figure out how to get the device to play information for me, and many of my classmates had to keep going back to the booth to get new batteries or other repairs. The museum would be much more effective if visitors had the option of just reading about the displays from plaques on the walls.

5   I know that many people will disagree with my assessment of EMP. They'll point to the fun of the interactive exhibits and the interesting collection of album covers, crushed velvet costumes, concert clips, famous guitars, and old jukeboxes. But a good museum has to be more than a display of artifacts and an array of hands-on activities. Pretending you're a rock star by performing on stage with instruments doesn't tell you how a certain style of music came about. Displaying trivial information about Elvis's leather jacket or Janis Joplin's feather boa doesn't help you appreciate the importance of their music. Devoting half an exhibit to punk rock without any analysis of that style doesn't teach you anything. In short, the museum displays frivolous trivia tidbits without educational substance.

6   Music lovers hoping for an educational experience about the rock-and-roll era of musical history will be disappointed by EMP. And this is without the additional insult of having to shell out $19.95 to get in the door. Speaking for serious music lovers and students of music history, I have to say that EMP is a failure.

THINKING CRITICALLY
About "EMP: Music History or Music Trivia?"

1. What strategies particularly appropriate for evaluation arguments does Jackie Wyngaard use in her introduction?
2. How has Jackie chosen to classify Experience Music Project? What criteria does she choose?
3. In the match part of her argument, what evidence does Jackie use to support her assessment of Experience Music Project?
4. What alternative views does Jackie acknowledge and where in her argument does she choose to treat them? Does she anticipate objections to her criteria or to the match part of her argument? What other objections might people raise to her argument?
5. What do you find persuasive about her arguments? How might this evaluation argument be improved?

Our second reading, by student writer Katy Lapinski, evaluates the Facebook page of PETA2, the youth organization for People for the Ethical Treatment of Animals.

Katy Lapinski (Student)

Is the PETA2 Facebook Page a Good Recruiting Platform for Vegetarianism?

1   When I first created a Facebook profile as a socially conscious high schooler, I expected to find my home page filled mostly with messages, photos, or blogs posted by friends. One day as I scrolled through these posts, I was shocked by the horrific image of a cow soaked with blood and pus from sores sticking inches out of its body. The assaulting image was posted by PETA2 (the youth organization under the umbrella of People for the Ethical Treatment of Animals); a friend had "liked" the organization, causing the image to appear on my home page. Despite being an animal rights activist who became vegetarian at the age of 13, I was appalled by the gruesome images of animal cruelty posted by PETA2. My own repulsion to the PETA2 Facebook page left me wondering whether the campaign is a good way to recruit teens to become vegetarians. My subsequent research has convinced me that the PETA2 Facebook page is not a good tool for promoting vegetarianism. Although the page is effective at recruiting teens to support animal rights, it does so unethically by over-emphasizing appeals to *pathos*, by oversimplifying the issues behind vegetarianism, and by demonizing people who consume any type of animal product.

2   PETA2 does seem to be effective at recruiting teens to become animal rights activists. Like all advocacy Websites, the PETA2 Facebook page aims to motivate its audience to action. It even tells its audience explicitly that its goal "is to arm you with all the info, literature, advice, and (most importantly) stickers you need to get active for animals" ("About"). On the day I started my new investigation I observed that nearly 1,400,000 people had shown their support by "liking" the page, and many of the posts had received thousands of "shares"–meaning supporters had reposted the information on their own page in an effort to recruit their friends. Viewers' comments on PETA2's posts are also a testament to the Webpage's effectiveness at motivating people to stop consuming animal products. For example, one viewer showed how PETA2 had motivated her to action by stating that "This [a video on cruel treatment of chickens] is why I am not eating chicken anymore" (Reguero). Another Facebook user was convinced by PETA2's video of a calf being shoved into a pen, stating "this is about one out of ten videos of yours [I']ve seen and [I']m really thinking of being a veg[e]tarian" ("How the Diary"). Clearly, the PETA2 Facebook page has achieved its goal of motivating many Facebook users to become active for animal rights.

3   Although I am a vegetarian and an animal rights activist–and thus a supporter of PETA2's message–I have reservations about the ethics of PETA2's methods. PETA2 overemphasizes *pathos* by relying on heart-wrenching photos, videos, and illustrated articles to persuade readers. These visuals, which are chosen for their extreme emotional impact, graphically depict animal torture involved in making products, some so extreme that PETA2 must warn viewers by forecasting their "graphic" nature. One such video shows ostriches being used for production of Prada handbags. The video shows ostriches forced into machines with only their

heads sticking out above a blood-soaked bin. In full view, a man slashes their necks with a knife, beheading them as blood gushes out and the ostrich flails in pain. The bodies are hung upside down, a torrential downpour of blood spewing from where their head once was, before they are skinned on a factory line. Even the most toughened viewers must feel repugnance. The video ends with the words "Will you help them?" flashing across the screen, leaving viewers feeling obligated to change their life choices and boycott such cruel companies ("How Animals"). This is only one example out of hundreds of equally grisly videos or photographs.

4   PETA2 also appeals to *pathos* from the other end of the spectrum by posting smile-inducing images of adorable animals that evoke a sense of awe and love. For example, one video shows a compilation of cute pigs, including a tiny, fuzzy piglet cuddling up in a person's arms and an adult pig lounging on a bed, smiling ear to ear ("These Piglets"). Viewers are drawn to these cute images that play on our instinctual urge to care for the young and that attribute human emotions to animals. These combinations of appalling and appealing photos and videos win teenagers to the animal rights cause, but by appealing almost entirely to *pathos* they don't encourage a balanced reflection on issues connected to humans' relationship to animals.

5   By appealing almost solely to *pathos*, the PETA2 Facebook page oversimplifies the issues addressed by the vegetarian cause. PETA2 could expand its animal rights message by using *logos*-centered appeals such as the health or environmental benefits of leading a meat-free lifestyle. The site so emphasizes emotional appeals that it rarely discusses the effect vegetarianism can have on reducing the risk of obesity, cardiovascular disease, high blood pressure, and even colorectal and prostate cancer (see, for example, Winston, 2009). The PETA2 Facebook page also posts comparatively little about how vegetarian diets promote sustainability by reducing water consumption, fossil energy consumption, and soil erosion (see the sustainability studies reviewed in Pimental and Pimental, 2003).

6   Perhaps PETA2 neglects the sustainability argument because it brings up a complex array of sustainable lifestyle choices other than strict vegetarianism. Many eco-conscious people still consume animal products; they simply choose more sustainable alternatives such as products from small, free-range, local farms rather than the notorious factory farms. These people are often proponents of animal welfare too, choosing to purchase goods from farms that adhere to cruelty-free methods. Yet the PETA2 Facebook page demonizes all people who consume animal products, posting pointed statements such as "Chickens need their wings, you don't!" in conjunction with an image of a bloody chicken in the process of being beheaded ("You Don't"). Although PETA2 motivates people to abstain from all animal products, these people are motivated out of shame rather than enlightened empowerment.

7   Although the PETA2 Facebook page successfully recruits teens to become vegetarian, it does so in an unethical manner. Supporters of PETA2 might say that my ethical objections are irrelevant: The purpose of PETA is to motivate young

people to action. The criterion that matters is the success rate at recruiting new animal activists. However, I argue that young people are more apt to sustain their commitment to animal welfare if they have a broader base of knowledge. People do not need to be shamed to promote animal rights. Rather than being assaulted with emotionally laden images, they need to be holistically informed of the various kinds of lifestyle choices that promote animal welfare as well as the various arguments for choosing vegetarianism. Unfortunately, the current PETA2 Facebook page does not provide this ethical approach to animal rights activism because it relies primarily on shocking and shaming its audience.

Works Cited

"About." *PETA2 Facebook*, www.facebook.com/peta2/info/?tab=page_info. Accessed 8 May 2016.

"How Animals Suffer for Prada." *PETA2 Facebook*, 27 Apr. 2016, www.facebook.com/peta2/videos/10154016088970560.

"How the Dairy Industry Hurts Babies." PETA2 Facebook, 6 Apr. 2016, www.facebook.com/peta2/videos/10153968944555560.

Pimentel, Daniel, and Pimentel, Marcia. "Sustainability of Meat-Based and Plant-Based Diets and the Environment." *The American Journal of Clinical Nutrition*, Sept. 2003, ajcn.nutrition.org/content/78/3/660S.full#.

Reguero, Janice. "Your Chicken Dinner in Reverse." *Facebook*, 3 May 2016, www.facebook.com/official.peta/videos/10154177367704586.

"These Piglets Have a Question for Bacon Lovers." *PETA2 Facebook*, 26 Feb. 2016, www.facebook.com/peta2/videos/10153852552555560.

"You Don't Need Chicken Wings!" *PETA2 Facebook*, 10 Apr. 2016, www.facebook.com/peta2/videos/10153978694555560.

Winston, Craig. "Health Effects of Vegan Diets." *The American Journal of Clinical Nutrition*, 11 Mar. 2009, doi:10.3945/ajcn.2009.26736N.

THINKING CRITICALLY
About "Is the PETA2 Facebook Page a Good Recruiting Platform for Vegetarianism?"

1. What criteria does Katy Lapinski use to evaluate the PETA2 Facebook page?
2. What evidence does the author use to make the "match" argument for each criterion? That is, what evidence does she use to show that the PETA2 campaign meets or does not meet each criterion? How effective do you find her evidence?
3. Where does the author anticipate objections to her evaluation? How successful is she in responding to these objections?
4. How persuasive do you find her argument? What recommendations would you make for improving the argument?

Chapter 16
Proposing a Solution

Learning Objectives

16.1 Describe the types of proposals, their common components, and their special challenges.

16.2 Apply the "three-strategy" approach (arguments from principle, from consequence, or from analogy/precedent) for justifying a proposal claim.

16.3 Use multimodal strategies to create effective proposal arguments.

16.4 Write a proposal argument that persuades your audience that a problem exists, proposes a solution, and justifies that solution.

Understanding proposal arguments

16.1 Describe the types of proposals, their common components, and their special challenges.

Proposal arguments call an audience to action. They make a claim that some action should to be taken. Sometimes referred to informally as *should arguments*, proposals are among the most common kinds of arguments that you will write or read.

Types of Proposals

Proposal arguments can be divided into two types. **Practical proposals** focus on local, practical problems and generally target a specific audience (usually the person with the power to act on the proposal). For example, Lucy Morsen's proposal at the end of this chapter advocates banning laptops and cell phones in classrooms. In the work world, many individuals and businesses generate new revenues by writing competitive proposals to solve a prospective client's practical problem.

Another kind of proposal, a **policy proposal**, addresses public policy issues with the aim of swaying public support toward the writer's proposed solution. Student writer Kent Ansen's proposal to institute mandatory public service for young adults illustrates a researched policy proposal (also included in this chapter).

The power of proposal arguments is often enhanced with images, which can appeal to both *logos* and *pathos*. In fact, proposal arguments sometimes take the form of multimodal texts such as **posters** or **advocacy advertisements** calling an audience to action. Additionally, proposal arguments can be delivered as **oral presentations**—for example, when a citizen presents a proposal at an open-mic public hearing.

Common Components of Proposal Arguments

All proposals have one feature in common—they offer a solution to a problem. For every proposed solution, there are always alternative solutions, including doing nothing. Your task therefore is to convince readers that the problem is worth solving, that your proposed solution will work, and that the benefits outweigh the costs. Accordingly, a proposal argument typically has three main components:

1. *Description of the problem.* You must first demonstrate that a significant problem exists. Your goal is to make the problem vivid and real for your readers. Who is affected by the problem? What are its causes? Why hasn't it been solved before? What are the negative consequences of not solving the problem?

2. *Proposal for a solution.* You must describe your solution with enough detail to show how it would work and what it would cost. If you don't have a solution, you may choose to generate a planning proposal calling for a committee to propose solutions at a later date.

3. *Justification.* Here you persuade your audience that your proposal should be enacted. Typically you show that the benefits of your proposal outweigh the costs. You also need to show why your proposed solution is better than alternative solutions. Point out why other possible approaches would not solve the problem, would provide fewer benefits, or would cost significantly more than your proposed solution.

In the following sections, we examine the challenges of proposal arguments and then show you a powerful strategy for developing the proposal's justification section.

For Writing and Discussion
Practicing the "Thinking Moves" of a Proposal Argument

Working individually: Identify and list several major problems facing students in your college or university. Then decide which problems are most important and rank them in order of importance.

Working in groups: Share your lists and decide on your group's number-one problem.

1. Use that problem to explore answers to the following questions. Be prepared to present answers to the class as a whole.
   a. Why is the problem a problem?
   b. For whom is the problem a problem?
   c. How will these people suffer if the problem is not solved? Give specific examples.
   d. Who has the power to solve the problem?
   e. Why hasn't the problem been solved up to this point?
   f. How can the problem be solved? Create a proposal for a solution.
   g. What are the probable benefits of acting on your proposal?
   h. What costs are associated with your proposal?

i. Who will bear these costs?
j. Why should this proposal be enacted?
k. What makes this proposal better than alternative proposals?
2. As a group, draft an outline for a proposal argument in which you:
a. Describe the problem and its significance.
b. Propose your solution to the problem.
c. Justify your proposal by showing how the benefits outweigh the costs.
3. Write the group's outline on the board and be prepared to present the group's argument orally to the class.

Special Challenges of Proposal Arguments

To get your readers to take action—the ultimate purpose of a proposal—you must overcome some challenges. Strategies Chart 16.1 lists the special difficulties people encounter when writing proposal arguments and offer strategies for overcoming them.

Strategies Chart 16.1 Strategies for Overcoming the Special Challenges of Proposal Arguments

Challenge	Explanation	What to Do
Giving the problem presence	To convince readers that a problem exists, you must make them *see* and *feel* the problem—that is, give the problem *presence*.	• Use anecdotes or examples of people suffering from the problem. • Provide startling facts or statistics to dramatize the problem. • Include a photograph or other image that conveys the problem. • Use other appeals to *pathos*.
Appealing to the interests and values of decision makers	A proposal that benefits one group often creates costs for others. Decision makers may not share the sufferers' perspective on a problem. Solving your problem may simply cause more problems for the decision maker.	• Show decision makers how acting on your proposal will benefit *them* directly. • Use audience-based reasons. • If appropriate, appeal to idealism and principle (do the right thing, even if it will cause temporary grief). • Show how benefits to the sufferers outweigh costs to others.
Overcoming inherent conservatism	People are inherently resistant to change, often willing to live with a flawed but bearable situation rather than risk change that could make the situation worse. "Better the devil you know than the one you don't know."	• Emphasize the seriousness of the problem (give it *presence*). • Stress the benefits of solving the problem. • Emphasize the lost potential in not acting. • Show that the risks are minimal. • Show that negative consequences are unlikely.
Predicting consequences	Often readers distrust the proposal writer's rosy scenario. They doubt that the predicted benefits will occur, or they fear negative consequences.	• Take care not to overpromise benefits. • Persuade readers that your predictions are realistic—show how the links in the chain lead directly from the solution to the benefits. • Cite cases where a similar proposal led to real benefits.
Evaluating consequences	Any solution that benefits one group may impose costs on another group. It is difficult to establish a common principle of measurement for weighing costs against benefits.	• In some cases, you can use money as measurement—the savings from this proposal will be more than the initial costs. • In other cases, emphasize that the benefits of increased happiness, less suffering, or saved time outweigh the initial dollar costs. • Emphasize the greatest good for the greatest number (more people will have benefits; fewer will bear costs). • Emphasize idealism and principle (this is the right thing to do despite the cost).

Strategies for justifying a proposal

16.2 Apply the "three-strategy" approach (arguments from principle, from consequence, or from analogy/precedent) for justifying a proposal claim.

The distinctions between proposals and other kinds of arguments invite particular kinds of support for proposals. Writers often develop support for their proposals by using the three-strategy approach, which focuses sequentially on principles, consequences, and precedents or analogies, as explained in Strategies Chart 16.2.

Each of these argumentation strategies was clearly evident in a public debate in Seattle, Washington, over a proposal to raise county sales taxes to build a new baseball stadium. Those favoring the stadium put forth arguments such as these:

> We should build the new stadium because preserving our national pastime for our children is important (*argument from principle*), because building the stadium will create new jobs and revitalize the adjacent Pioneer Square district (*argument from consequence*), and because building the stadium will have the same beneficial effects on the city that building Camden Yards had in Baltimore (*argument from precedent*).

Strategies Chart 16.2 Strategies for Developing a Justification Section

Strategies	What to Do	Templates and Comments	Examples
Argument from principle	Argue that an action should (should not) be taken because it is right (wrong) according to some value, assumption, principle, or belief you share with your audience.	We should (should not) do (this action) because (this action) is _____. Fill in the blank with a belief or value that the audience holds: *good, honest, fair*, and so on.	"We should create publicly financed jobs for poor people because doing so is both charitable and just."
Argument from consequence	Argue that an action should (should not) be taken because doing so will lead to consequences that you and your audience think are good (bad).	We should (should not) do (this action) because (this action) will lead to these good (bad) consequences: _____, _____, and _____. Use consequences that your audience will agree are good or bad, as needed.	"We should create publicly financed jobs for poor people because doing so will provide them with money for food and housing, promote a work ethic, and produce needed goods and services."
Argument from precedent or analogy	Argue that an action should (should not) be taken because doing so is similar to what was done in another case, which turned out well (badly).	We should (should not) do (this action) because doing (this action) is like _____, which turned out to be good (bad). Use precedents or analogies that are similar to your proposed action and that have good (bad) associations for your audience.	*Precedent:* "We should create publicly financed jobs for poor people because doing so will alleviate poverty just as a similar program has helped the poor in Upper Magnesia." *Analogy:* " . . . because doing so is like teaching the poor how to fish rather than giving them fish."

Those opposing the stadium created arguments using the same strategies:

> We should not build the stadium because it is wrong to subsidize rich owners and players with tax dollars (*argument from principle*), because building a stadium diverts tax money from more important concerns such as low-income housing (*argument from consequence*), and because Toronto's experience with Skydome shows that once the novelty of a new stadium wears off, attendance declines dramatically (*argument from precedent*).

For Writing and Discussion
Using Different Strategies to Develop Support

Working individually or in small groups, use the strategies of principle, consequence, and precedent/analogy to create *because* clauses that support (or oppose) the following proposals. Try to have at least one *because* clause for each of the strategies, but generate as many reasons as possible. Here is an example:

Claim	Spanking children should be made illegal.
Principle	Because it is wrong to cause bodily pain to children.
Consequence	Because it teaches children that it is okay to hit someone out of anger; because it causes children to obey rules out of fear rather than respect; because it can lead children to become abusive parents later in life.
Precedent/analogy	Because spanking a child is like throwing dishes or banging your fists against a wall—it relieves your anger but turns the child into an object.

1. The school year for grades K–12 should/should not be extended to eleven months.
2. Our city should/should not require all restaurants to post the calorie content of every menu item.
3. Federal law should/should not ban assault weapons and large ammunition clips.
4. Division 1 football and basketball players should/should not be paid as employees of the university.
5. The federal government should/should not enact a much higher tax on gasoline.

Multimodal proposal arguments

16.3 Use multimodal strategies to create effective proposal arguments.

Proposal arguments can be particularly powerful in multimodal forms. In non-motion or print formats, verbal text can be enhanced by photographs, drawings, graphs, or other images. Frequently we encounter multimodal proposal arguments in the form of posters or flyers, paid advertisements in newspapers or magazines, brochures, or Web pages in advocacy Web sites. Their creators know that the arguments must work fast to capture our attention, give presence to a problem, advocate a solution, and enlist our support. These multimodal proposals frequently use photographs, images, icons, or layout of words that are arresting or in some way memorable and that appeal to a reader's emotions and

Advice for creating effective multimodal arguments is provided in Chapter 20.

imagination. Such arguments can be enhanced further in digital environments where videos or podcasts can employ the narrative power of sound and motion. Multimodal arguments can also be presented orally as speeches, often supplemented with presentation slides in PowerPoint or Prezi.

As an example of visual advocacy, consider the BlackLivesMatter poster displayed in Figure 16.1. This poster represents the views of #BlackLivesMatter, a national organization created in 2012 after the acquittal of George Zimmerman for his shooting of Trayvon Martin, which was soon followed by other high-profile violence against Blacks, including a number of incidents in which young Black men were killed by the police. On their Web site, this organization declares that its purpose is to broaden "the conversation around state violence to include all the ways in which Black people are intentionally left powerless at the hands of the state."

This poster, arguing for a change in attitudes toward and treatment of Blacks, participates in a complex rhetorical context. In response to this organization's activism, some people have asserted that "All Lives Matter." but taking that perspective, according to this organization and this poster, denies the "concrete differences in context, experience, and oppression" of Blacks and reinforces anti-Black racism.

Note how this poster encapsulates this complex controversy in its use of lettering (all capitals), stark colors (black on a white background), and layout (tightly packed lines of words). The size and density of the lettering keep viewers focused on the words and the ideas they represent. The poster is a rebuttal argument that concedes the value of all lives but reinforces the organization's central points that "Black lives are deprived of our basic human rights and dignity" and that the value of Black lives needs to be affirmed through social, political, and judicial change. The size of the lettering draws special attention to "MATTER" and "APPARENT" to highlight how problems with perception, lack of knowledge, or indifference contribute to anti-Black racism. The thickness of the lettering and the density of the wording create the impression of impassioned insistence and urgency, an intensity that doesn't need images. The poster argues that denial of the problem or the claim that everyone is the same can no

Figure 16.1 BlackLivesMatter poster

longer cover up the pervasive racism against Blacks. #BlackLivesMatter, which began as a social media protest movement, has become a verbal-visual message on the streets with advocacy posters like this one.

For a multimodal argument that employs both text and image, consider the poster in Figure 5.6 in Chapter 5. This poster, "BEWARE . . . Drink Only Approved Water," produced by the United States War Department in 1944, employs a visual shock technique through its horrific image of a reflected skull to warn against drinking infected water.

Writing a proposal argument

16.4 Write a proposal argument that persuades your audience that a problem exists, proposes a solution, and justifies that solution.

> **Writing Project:** Call your audience's attention to a problem, propose a solution to that problem, and present a justification for your solution. You have two choices (or your instructor may limit you to just one): (a) create a practical proposal, with a letter of transmittal, proposing a nuts-and-bolts solution to a local problem; or (b) write a more general policy proposal, addressing a public issue, in the form of a research paper that might be an editorial for a state, local, or college newspaper. If you choose (b), your instructor might ask you to do research and model your proposal after a magazine or journal article.

Generating and Exploring Ideas

If you have trouble thinking of a proposal topic, try making an idea map of local problems you would like to see solved. Consider some of the following starting points.

FINDING A PROPOSAL ISSUE   Use the following idea-starters to brainstorm ideas for a proposal issue:

Problems at your university: parking, registration system, absence of recycling options, hours of cafeterias and eating facilities, too many activities on campus during the week, poor school spirit, problems with residence halls, availability of internships

Problems in your city or town: lack of bike paths, inadequate lighting, unattractive public parks or lack of public parks, zoning problems, inadequate support for public education, need for public transportation, conservation of water

Problems at your place of work: flow of customer traffic, inadequate staffing during peak times, unclear division of responsibilities, no policies for raises or training new employees, health care coverage, safety issues

Social problems and problems related to other aspects of your life: problems with credit card debt, need for financial literacy, physical fitness in the public schools, aid for victims of disasters, employment opportunities for college students, media consumption and awareness of current events

Another approach is to freewrite your response to these trigger statements:

I would really like to solve the problem of _____.

I believe that X should _____. (Substitute for X words such as *my instructor, the president, the school administration, Congress, my boss,* and so forth.)

Note that the problem you pose for this paper can be personal, but shouldn't be private; that is, others should be able to benefit from a solution to your personal problem. For example, your inability to find child care for your daughter is a private problem. But if you focus your proposal on how zoning laws discourage development of in-home day care—and propose a change in those zoning laws to permit more in-home day care centers—then your proposal will benefit others.

USING STOCK ISSUES OR "THREE-STRATEGIES" APPROACH TO EXPLORE YOUR PROBLEM   Once you have decided on a proposal issue, explore it by freewriting your responses to the following questions. These questions are often called **stock issues** because they represent generic, or stock, questions that apply to almost any kind of proposal.

1. Is there a problem here that has to be solved?
2. Will the proposed solution really solve this problem?
3. Can the problem be solved in a simpler way without disturbing the status quo?
4. Is the proposed solution practical enough that it really stands a chance of being implemented?
5. What will be the positive and negative consequences of the proposal?

Also try thinking of justifications for your solution by using the principles/consequences/precedents or analogies strategy described earlier in this chapter.

AVOIDING PRESUPPOSING YOUR SOLUTION IN YOUR PROBLEM STATEMENT   A common mistake of inexperienced proposal writers is to write problem statements that presuppose their solutions. As a restaurant server, suppose you notice that customers want coffee refills faster than servers can provide them. To solve this problem, you propose placing carafes of hot coffee at each table. When describing your problem, don't presuppose your solution: "The problem is that we don't have carafes of hot coffee at the tables." Rather, describe the problematic situation itself: annoyed customers clamoring for coffee and harassed servers trying to bring around refills. Only by giving presence to the original problem can you interest readers in your proposed solution, which readers will compare to other possible approaches (including doing nothing).

Here is another example:

Weak: The problem is that the Student Union doesn't stay open late enough at night.

Better: The problem is that students who study late at night don't have an attractive, convenient place to socialize or study; off-campus coffee houses are too far to walk to and often close at night; resident hall lounges aren't attractive or conducive to studying and are often noisy.

Figure 16.2 Framework of a Proposal Argument

Introduction	• Presents and describes a problem that needs solving, giving it presence • Gives background including previous attempts to solve the problem • Argues that the problem is solvable (optional)
Presentation of the proposed solution	• States the solution succinctly • Explains the specifics of the solution
Justification	• Persuades readers that the proposal should be implemented • Presents and develops Reasons 1, 2, and so forth (Reasons to support the proposed solution may be arguments from principle, consequence, and precedent or analogy)
Summary and rebuttal of opposing views	*Policy proposal:* • Presents opposing view(s) • Rebuts opposing view(s) *Practical proposal:* • Presents alternative solution(s) • Explains why alternative solution(s) are inferior
Conclusion	• Asks readers to act (sometimes incorporated into the last sentences of the final supporting reason)

Shaping, Drafting, and Revising

Figure 16.2 shows a typical organizational plan for a proposal argument.

After you have completed your first draft and begun to clarify your argument for yourself, you are ready to start making your argument clear and persuasive for your readers. Use the strategies for clear closed-form prose outlined in Chapter 18. At this stage, feedback from peer readers can be very helpful.

Questions for Peer Review

In addition to the generic peer review questions explained in Skill 17.4, ask your peer reviewers to address these questions:

INTRODUCTION AND STATEMENT OF PROBLEM

1. How could the title more effectively focus the paper and pique your interest?

2. Where does the writer convince you that a problem exists and that it is significant (worth solving) and solvable? Where does the writer give the problem presence? How could the writer improve the presentation of the problem?

PROPOSED SOLUTION

1. Does the writer's thesis clearly propose a solution to the problem? Could the thesis be made more precise?

2. Could the writer give you more details about the solution so that you can understand it and see how it works? How could the writer make the solution clearer?

JUSTIFICATION

1. In the justification section, how could the writer provide stronger reasons for acting on the proposal? Where could the reasons be better supported with more details and evidence? How could the reasons appeal more to the values and beliefs of the audience?

2. Can you help the writer think of additional justifying arguments (arguments from principle, from consequences, from precedent or analogy)? How else could the writer improve support for the proposal?

3. Where does the writer anticipate and address opposing views or alternative solutions? How does the writer convince you that the proposed solution is superior to alternative solutions?

4. Has the writer persuaded you that the benefits of this proposal will outweigh the costs? Who will pay the costs and who will get the benefits? What do you think the gut reaction of a typical decision maker would be to the writer's proposal?

5. Can you think of other, unforeseen costs that the writer should acknowledge and address? What unforeseen benefits could the writer mention?

6. How might the writer improve the structure and clarity of the argument?

Multimodal or Online Assignment Options

Advice on creating advocacy posters is found in Skill 20.3.

1. **Advocacy Ad or Poster** Create a one-page advocacy ad or poster that presents a controversial public problem and calls for action and support. Consider how you will use all the features of visual arguments—type sizes and fonts, layout, color, and images and graphics—to grab the attention of your audience, construct a compelling sketch of the problem, and inform your audience what course of action you want them to take. In this advocacy piece, you need to capture your proposal argument in a highly condensed form, while making it visually clear and memorable. Your instructor might ask you instead to create a longer brochure-length handout or a Web page.

Advice on giving oral presentations and designing presentation slides is provided in Skill 20.3.

2. **Proposal Speech with Visual Aids** Deliver a proposal argument as a prepared speech of approximately five to eight minutes supported with visual aids created on presentation software such as PowerPoint or Prezi. Your speech should present a problem, propose a solution, justify the solution with reasons and evidence, and defend it against objections or alternative solutions. As you deliver your speech, use appropriate visual aids to give presence to the problem, highlight points, provide memorable data or evidence, or otherwise enhance appeals to *logos, ethos,* and *pathos.* Although presentation software is commonly used in oral presentations, low-tech visual aids (for example, white boards or flip charts) can also be effective. Follow the guidelines provided by your instructor. As you contemplate this project, consider its three different components: creating the speech itself, designing the visuals, and delivering the speech.

Readings

Our first reading, by student writer Lucy Morsen, is a practical proposal entitled "A Proposal to Improve the Campus Learning Environment by Banning Laptops and Cell Phones from Class." Because practical proposals are aimed at a specific audience, they are often accompanied by a letter of transmittal that introduces the writer, sets the context, and summarizes the proposal. We reproduce here Lucy's transmittal letter followed by her proposal, in which she uses APA documentation guidelines. We also show you the appearance of her title page.

Professor Ralph Sorento
Chair, Faculty Senate
_____ UniversityStreet
City, State, Zip

Dear Professor Sorento:

1   Enclosed is a proposal that I hope you will present to the Faculty Senate. It asks the university to ban all laptops and cell phones from classes in consideration of those many students like myself whose educational experience is diminished by classmates who surf the Web or send text messages during lectures or class discussion. As I try to show in this proposal, the effect of laptops and cell phones in class is distracting to many students and may hurt the academic performance of students who think they can multitask without any negative effects. I use both personal experience and recent research reports on multitasking as support for my argument.

2   Banning laptops and cell phones from class would deepen students' engagement with course material and make for more lively and energetic class discussions. I argue that an outright campus ban would be more effective than leaving the decision up to individual instructors.

3   Thank you for considering my proposal. I am happy that this university has a Faculty Senate that welcomes ideas from students on how to make teaching and learning more effective.

Sincerely,

Lucy Morsen,

First-Year Student

A PROPOSAL TO IMPROVE THE CAMPUS LEARNING ENVIRONMENT BY BANNING LAPTOPS AND CELL PHONES FROM CLASS

Submitted to Professor Ralph Sorento

Chair of the Faculty Senate

Lucy Morsen

First-Year Student, Williamson Hall

If this were the actual proposal, it would begin on a new page following the cover page.

1 Although I am generally happy as a first-year student at this university, I wish to call the Faculty Senate's attention to a distracting problem: classmates' frequent use of laptops and cell phones during class. In many classes more than half the students have open laptops on their desks or are openly text-messaging on cell phones. Inevitably, laptop users multitask between taking notes and checking email, perusing Facebook, surfing the Web, looking at YouTube videos, playing a game, or working on an assignment for another class. (I have yet to see a student use his or her laptop solely for note-taking.) Even though I try to focus on class lectures and discussion, I find myself missing key points and ideas as my eyes are drawn to the animations and flashing colors on neighboring laptop screens. Other distractions come from the clicking of cell phone keypads—or the momentary vibration of a phone on a desktop—which can seem surprisingly loud in an otherwise quiet environment. When the person next to me continually picks up and sets down her phone to send and receive text messages, she not only distracts me from the lecture but also lets me know that she is not engaged in class, and seemingly has no interest in being so. My annoyance at my classmates and my frustration at not being able to focus undercut my enjoyment of class.

2 Given the extensive use of laptops and cell phones in class, I question the academic motivation of my classmates. As a student, I most enjoy classes when I and my classmates are actively interested and engaged in class lecture and discussion. Collective interest has a way of feeding on itself. I mean, we as students do not operate in isolation from one another, but instead we affect and influence one another in gross and subtle ways. Together with our professor we create a collective environment in the classroom, and just as we as individuals affect this collective environment, this collective environment influences us as individuals. The broad effects and consequences of this dynamic interplay should not be underestimated. Humans are highly social beings; we have the power to influence one another in both positive and negative ways. I believe that the distracting nature of laptops and cell phones is negatively affecting classroom environments. Any steps we can take collectively to help one another learn and succeed should be considered.

3 To address this problem, I propose a campus-wide ban on laptops and cell phones during class. I believe a campus-wide ban would be more effective than the more limited measures some institutions have adopted, such as blocking wireless access from classrooms or allowing each professor to choose whether or not to ban laptops in his or her classroom. Blocking wireless access does not address the problem of cell phones or non-Web-based laptop distractions (such as computer games or other class work). Leaving the decision up to professors creates an added difficulty for them. I can imagine that professors, fearing resentment and poor evaluations from their students, would be reluctant to enforce a ban in their classrooms, even if they feel it would improve the classroom experience.

4 A campus-wide ban, on the other hand, would be easy to enforce, and students would more easily establish new habits—namely, not using laptops and cell phones during class. Over time, this could become the new campus norm.

5 Although many students might at first object to a ban, the decision to ban all laptops and cell phones in class would bring benefits not only to distracted students like me but also to current users of laptops and cell phones as well as to professors.

6   For one thing, the banning of laptops and cell phones would improve the learning atmosphere of a classroom. These technologies simply create too many distractions for students, and the negative consequences of these distractions are significant enough to call for institutional intervention. While some of my classmates may begrudge the ban, I believe they would quickly get used to it and notice improvements in their own classroom interest and performance. Many of my classmates may actually welcome the ban because they—like myself—are aware of the negative distractions that laptops and cell phones create. In fact, an informal survey by a Georgetown University law professor who bans laptops in his classroom indicated that 70% of his students welcomed the ban (Cole, 2008).

7   Second, a ban might directly improve academic performance of current users of laptops and cell phones. A study at the University of Winona (Fried, 2008) found that laptop use in the classroom had a significant negative effect on class performance. In Fried's study, students who brought laptops to class received lower grades than their classmates who did not bring laptops to class. Moreover, those who brought laptops to class reported using their laptops for non-class purposes for nearly a quarter of class time.

8   Many of my classmates will likely argue that this study doesn't apply to them. They believe that they are skilled multitaskers who can continue to pay attention to a lecture while also engaging in these other activities. There is empirical evidence that they are in fact mistaken about their ability to multitask. A study by three Stanford University researchers found that persons who self-reported being heavy multitaskers were *more* easily distracted from a primary task than those who reported themselves as light multitaskers (Ophir, Nass, & Wagner, 2009). The researchers conducted this study in a lab by giving multitasking tasks to a group of self-identified heavy multitaskers and then to a group of light multitaskers. This study suggests that a person's own perception of how well he or she multitasks may not be reliable. Moreover, it suggests that large amounts of daily multitasking may actually decrease a person's ability to concentrate on a single task and to suppress irrelevant information.

9   A handful of students will likely argue that they use their laptops only for class-related purposes, and that an outright ban on laptops in the classroom would be unfair because they would be prohibited from using them for note-taking. However, I am skeptical of any claims that students make of using laptops only for class-related purposes. I personally have never seen any evidence of this, and research is indicating that multitasking is overwhelmingly the common norm among laptop users in the classroom. In a study by Benbunan-Fich and Truman (2009), student laptop use was monitored for 28 classroom sessions of 80 minutes (with students' permission). The researchers analyzed how often the students toggled between screens, and whether the screens were class-related or non-class-related. They found that 76% of the time students toggled between screens that were non-class-related. On average, students toggled between computer-based activities 37.5 times per 80-minute session. This research suggests that the temptations of non-class-related activities are simply too great for students *not* to engage in multitasking in class—it is just too easy to do a brief check of email or a quick Facebook scan with a swift click of a mouse.

10   University institutions may feel reluctant to propose a campus-wide ban on laptops and cell phones in the classroom for fear of seeming overly authoritative and unnecessarily limiting student freedom. After all, students might rightly claim that they have a

right to do whatever they want in the classroom as long as they aren't harming anyone else. (I have already shown that they actually are harming others.) While I believe that individual rights are an important concern—in general I believe that university institutions should allow for a great amount of autonomy for their students—I think that laptop use has too many negative consequences to be allowed simply in the name of student freedom. (Of course, a professor can always allow laptop use for students with special needs.)

11   For these reasons, I propose that a campus-wide ban on laptops and cell phones in the classroom should be considered. A campus-wide ban would help to create more positive, cohesive classroom experiences, and it would provide a reprieve for students from the myriad of distractions this modern technological age presents us. A campus-wide ban would be easier on professors to enforce, and it would help to establish a new (and improved) norm.

References

Benbunan-Fich, R., & Truman, G. E. (2009). Multitasking with laptops during meetings. *Communications of the ACM, 52*(2), 139–141. doi:10.1145/1461928.1461963

Cole, D. (2008, October 23). Why I ban laptops in my classroom [Web log post]. Retrieved from http://www.britannica.com/blogs/2008/10/why-i-ban-laptops-in-my-classroom

Fried, C. B. (2008). In-class laptop use and its effects on student learning. *Computers and Education, 50,* 906–914. Retrieved from www.elsevier.com

Ophir, E., Nass, C., & Wagner, A. D. (2009). Cognitive control in media multitaskers. *Proceedings of the National Academy of Sciences.* PNAS Early Edition. Retrieved from www.pnas.org

THINKING CRITICALLY

About "A Proposal to Improve the Campus Learning Environment by Banning Laptops and Cell Phones from Class"

1. What strategies does Lucy Morsen use to convince the Faculty Senate that a problem exists?
2. What strategies does Lucy employ to persuade the Faculty Senate that her proposal is worth enacting and that it is more effective than alternative solutions?
3. How does Lucy tie her proposal to the values and beliefs of her audience—college professors who are members of the Faculty Senate?
4. How effective is Lucy's use of research evidence to support her proposal?
5. If you were a faculty member, how effective would you find Lucy's proposal? How effective do you find it as a student? What are its chief strengths and weaknesses?

Our second reading, by student writer Sam Rothchild, illustrates a multimodal argument—a speech supported with visual aids. We have reproduced Sam's outline for his speech along with six of his PowerPoint slides. His final slide was a bibliography of the sources used in the speech and the slides. Note how Sam has constructed the slides as visual arguments to support specific points in the speech as opposed to using his slides to reproduce his speech outline. In Chapter 20 (Skill 20.3) , we offer advice on preparing and delivering speeches and creating presentation slides.

Sam Rothchild (Student)

Reward Work Not Wealth:

A Proposal to Increase Income Tax Rates for the Richest 1 Percent of Americans

Problem

1. Since 1980 the gap between rich and poor has increased enormously.
    a. Statistical evidence demonstrates the gap.
        (i) The rich have gotten richer.
        (ii) The poor have gotten poorer.
        (iii) The middle class are treading water.
    b. A primary cause of the income gap is the Bush-era tax cuts that benefited the rich more than the poor.
    c. Income gap leads to an unhealthy middle class and increased poverty, hurting all Americans.

Solution

2. The solution is to raise the income tax rates on the ultra-rich back to 1980 levels.

Reasons to Support this Proposal

3. A more progressive income tax structure promotes a more just society.
    a. Sales taxes and payroll taxes (Social Security, Medicare) take a high-percentage chunk out of low-income salaries and a tiny percentage out of high-income salaries.
    b. Progressive income tax balances the regressive effect of sales taxes and payroll taxes.
4. Reducing the gap between rich and poor creates a stronger middle class and reduces poverty.
5. Increasing tax rates on the very rich will not hurt the incentive to work or the entrepreneurial spirit.
6. The ultra-rich will still be ultra-rich.

Figure 16.3 Sam's Title Slide Using an Image for *Pathos*

Reward work not wealth
A proposal to increase income tax rates
for the richest 1% of Americans

Figure 16.4 Slide Using an Image for *Pathos*

Figure 16.5 First of a Two-Slide Sequence Using Images to Illustrate the Income Gap

Figure 16.6 Second Slide in Sequence, Designed by Sam to Dramatize Wealth

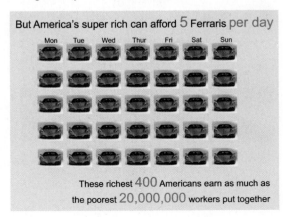

Figure 16.7 Slide with Point Title and Graphics for Evidence

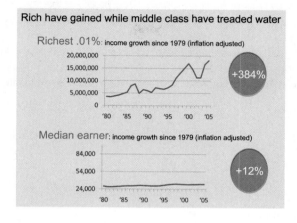

Figure 16.8 Another Slide with Point Title and Graphics for Evidence

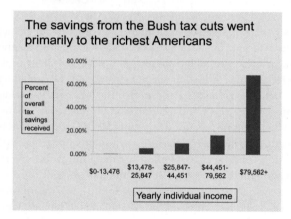

THINKING CRITICALLY

About "Reward Work Not Wealth: A Proposal to Increase Income Tax Rates for the Richest 1 Percent of Americans"

1. Although it is common to design PowerPoint slides using topics and bullets to reproduce the speaker's outline, many media specialists prefer the approach Sam uses here, in which the titles of slides are complete sentences that make a point. (See our explanation of "assertion/ evidence" slides in Chapter 20.) Sam's intention is to use the slide title to make a point and then use photographs, drawings, or graphics to support the point through immediate appeals to *logos* and *pathos*. How does each of Sam's slides make a point? How does the image on each slide support the point?

2. Sam was particularly proud of the way he constructed his two Ferrari slides. He wanted to create a startling way to show his audience the extreme wealth of the super-rich: "Not only can they afford a Ferrari. They can afford five Ferraris every day of the year!" Do you find these Ferrari slides effective? What other ways might he have shown visually the wealth of the super-rich?

3. Overall, how effective do you find Sam's argument? How effectively has he used slides to support his argument? What suggestions do you have either to improve his speech or improve his visual aids?

Our final reading is by student writer Kent Ansen, who proposes that the United States institute mandatory national service for young adults. Kent's process in producing this paper has been discussed in various places throughout the text. Particularly see Kent's original freewrite in Chapter 2, his exploratory paper and annotated bibliography in Chapter 8 and his "nutshell" and outline in Chapter 18. We present his proposal as an illustration of a student research paper written and formatted in MLA style. For a compete explanation of MLA style, see Chapter 24.

Put last name and page number in header on each page.

Place name, course information, and date on first page.

Center title.

Indent paragraphs ½ inch.

Use one-inch margins at top, bottom, and both sides.

Double-space all parts of the text (no single spacing anywhere).

Ansen 1

Kent Ansen
Professor Johnson
Writing Seminar
15 May 20XX

Engaging Young Adults to Meet America's Challenges:
A Proposal for Mandatory National Service

In high school, I volunteered at an afterschool program for elementary school students located in one of the poorest, most dangerous neighborhoods in town, known for high crime and gang activity. I spent a couple hours per week helping kids complete homework and crafts, reading stories, supervising field games, and serving snacks. The kids' snacks—usually a piece of fruit, some crackers, and a carton of milk—often filled in for dinner because there was no food for them at home. The program was run by a team of AmeriCorps members, who also ran a summer program so the kids had supervision, learning opportunities, and food during the long months of summer. In addition to providing tutoring and food, AmeriCorps connected students and their families to resources like clothing, healthcare, and school supplies. They partnered with Habitat for Humanity to repair dilapidated homes, haul trash to garbage pickup sites, and landscape overgrown yards. Over time, the AmeriCorps program gained so much trust and respect that its program expanded to other neighborhoods like this one, mobilizing an even greater number of volunteers and resources to fight poverty and injustice in our town.

The successes I witnessed in AmeriCorps suggest that volunteer programs can help address problems in our communities. But it is possible that they can also address problems faced by young people, whose job choices are limited by the slow economic recovery, the reduced number of entry-level jobs, and the crushing burden of student loans. A 2012 Pew Research study found that only 54 percent of Americans aged 18-24 were currently employed

Ansen 2

(the lowest rate since the government began tracking this data in 1948) and
that these young adults experienced the greatest drop in earnings of any
age group in the last four years ("Young, Underemployed and Optimistic").
Young Americans have been classified as a "Lost Generation" struggling to
overcome these obstacles and find the path to success and achievement.

Problems like these present us with a unique opportunity for creative
problem solving. I propose instituting a mandatory year of national service
for Americans ages 18-25. A mandatory service program would engage
today's underemployed Lost Generation in helping America's vulnerable
communities become stable, healthy, vibrant, and self-sufficient. It would help
our nation by promoting democracy through increased civic engagement.

What would this year of mandatory service look like? It would require
all citizens between the ages of 18 and 25 to spend a year in national service.
(Alternatively, persons could volunteer for military service.) Some students
might choose to serve immediately after high school as a gap year before
starting college or a job. Others might take a gap year during college or wait
until they graduate. Mandated national service could be built upon the model
of AmeriCorps. It would allow volunteers to choose placements in a variety of
nonprofit, public, faith-based, and educational organizations, including work
in schools and after-school programs, employment training organizations,
environmental restoration and stewardship, food banks, shelters, and
emergency response. It would pay minimum wage, provide health benefits,
defer student loan payments, and offer a financial incentive tuition award
at the end of service, which could also be taken as a cash stipend. (For an
example of how a national mandatory service program might be organized
and funded, see Stengel.)

Although there will be costs associated with mandatory public service,
these will be far outweighed by the benefits. First, a program of mandatory
national service would be an investment in communities by attacking poverty
and building social capital. A national service program would build on the
documented success of AmeriCorps, which in 2010 received $480 million in
donations and mobilized and managed 3.4 million volunteers (Corporation
for National and Community Service). By helping the poor become self-
sufficient, mandatory service could help reduce the needs for future
expenditures on poverty. According to an Urban Institute research study on
childhood poverty (Ratcliffe and McKernan 14), childhood poverty costs $550
billion annually. Whereas current poverty spending largely aims to provide
food, clothing, and housing for the poor, projects like AmeriCorps provide
people-to-people contact that can help address the root causes of poverty.
Particularly, service programs can help communities build social capital
to enhance their capacity to solve their own problems. Social capital is the
idea that the number of social connections within a community—things like

Parenthetical citation—for
full citation, see entry under
"Young . . ." in Works Cited.

An entry beginning with
"Stengel" appears in Works
Cited.

Ansen 3

civic participation, organizational membership, degree of trust in neighbors, educational achievement—determine its ability to solve shared problems. According to Lew Feldstein, a United Way director, communities with high social capital tend to have better outcomes in areas like crime, health, and education than do communities with low social capital. Expanding national service will increase people-to-people contact, creating more opportunities to form the connections that build social capital. In addition, expanded national service will benefit those who serve. Jastrzab et al. have noted that volunteer community service increases career skills. In a 2007 longitudinal study, the researchers found that AmeriCorps alumni experienced statistically significant gains in employment outcomes and job skills compared to peers not enrolled in AmeriCorps (Jastrzab et al. 45).

    Mandatory national service would also bring a second vital benefit to our country: It would increase the civic engagement of young people. When the United States eliminated the draft and moved to an all-volunteer army, it ended the specter of unwanted military service, but it also undermined citizens' sense of being stakeholders in America by allowing citizens to hire volunteers to fight their wars. This vital sense of personal investment in our nation—lost when the draft was eliminated—could be restored through mandatory national service, but in a context of helping our neighbor rather than fighting wars. Currently, low voter turnout and political apathy, especially among young people, suggests that our citizenry is disengaged from government ("2012 Voter Turnout"). According to Mark Rosenman, an applied researcher on anti-poverty programs and an opinion writer for the *Chronicle of Philanthropy,* Americans are becoming increasingly passive citizens whose "only obligation is to pay taxes, [reducing Americans to being] little more than consumers of government services, to being government's customers." To form a healthy democracy, Rosenman argues, citizens need to be "more directly and personally involved in working on the problems facing the country and the world." They need to be more "involved in their government and more concerned about public policy."

    For citizens to engage with government on the level advocated by Rosenman, they must first be able to identify community problems, feel a sense of responsibility for those problems, and be compelled to hold elected officials accountable for contributing to solutions. Currently, service in AmeriCorps builds these civic skills because volunteers experience first-hand the impact of government failure to serve specific constituencies. For some AmeriCorps teams, a civic engagement project is built into the service experience. Teams follow a six-module civic engagement curriculum in which they work together to identify community needs, prioritize a need, and develop and implement a corresponding service project. The 2007 AmeriCorps alumni study found statistically significant gains in markers of civic engagement among alumni, including increased community-based activism, increased confidence in the ability of communities to identify and

"45" indicates page number in pdf document.

Use italics for titles of books or Web sites.

Use brackets to indicate alteration of quotation to fit grammar of sentence.

solve problems, and increased connection to the community (Jastrzab et al. 45). These markers were present eight years after service was completed, evidence that the impact of mandatory national service will extend far beyond the service year to create a generation of responsive citizens and strengthen the foundation of our democracy.

Of course, there are many objections to mandatory national service. Some fear that mandating a year of national service would harm our democracy by limiting individual freedom. These critics cite the unpopular military draft during the Vietnam War as evidence of public hostility to mandatory service. However, I argue that the unpopularity of the draft reflected the unpopularity of the Vietnam War rather than an objection to serving one's country. Moreover, the personal sacrifice of risking one's life in war is far greater than the sacrifice required for a year of service work on our own soil. Furthermore, individuals will have a greater degree of choice in terms of where, when, and how they serve—choices that were not available during the draft. And while freedom is certainly a central American value, it does not mean that our freedom is without limits or that those limits are without benefits. By creating a national culture of service in this country, mandatory national service will engage young people in solving our communities' pressing problems, create bonds of friendship, and link youth to older citizens, thus creating a powerful cross-generational force of people working together.

One powerful critique of national service comes from Michael Kinsley, a consultant for the conservative think tank Heritage Foundation, in a *Time* magazine online article entitled "National Service? Puh-lease." Kinsley objects to government bureaucrats drawing on a huge labor pool of minimum-wage workers to create largely useless jobs that interfere with market forces and waste taxpayer money. Arguing that people are willing to do any job for a decent enough wage, Kinsley wonders why we would force conscripted laborers to work for minimum wage when there is already a supply of workers in the market willing to do the same job for reasonable pay. Kinsley uses George Orwell's novel *1984* to paint a picture of workers forced to do jobs that they would otherwise not take. Furthermore, Kinsley believes that most of these jobs would be "make-work" activities, meaning that bureaucrats would have to spend their time finding trivial ways to keep all the volunteers busy.

Kinsley's argument is provocative, but it fails to recognize the documented valuable work already provided by AmeriCorps—work that could be scaled up nationally without leading to "make-work" jobs. Kinsley fails to acknowledge that the kind of work provided by AmeriCorps does not compete with market forces. AmeriCorps jobs supplement the work of the nonprofit sector; they do not displace market-sector jobs such as garbage haulers or carpenters. The best response to Kinsley's fear of make-work jobs created by bureaucrats is to recognize that the organizational structures for a national service program are already in place through AmeriCorps.

Relying on AmeriCorps would ease the transition to mandatory national service by providing a foundational, established program from which to grow and model additional partnerships. An expansion of national service is already underway through 2009's Generations Invigorating Volunteerism and Education (GIVE) Act (Robertson). This legislation is intended to expand participation in national service from 75,000 to 250,000 and diversifies the focus of programs to include disaster relief, urban and rural development, infrastructure improvement, and energy conservation. Building on GIVE Act's public and congressional support could boost momentum for the transition to mandatory national service.

The point to emphasize, then, is that the money used to fund mandatory national service is money directly reinvested in our communities. Our country is currently facing numerous challenges: increasing inequality, expansive poverty, slow economic recovery, environmental and educational crises, and a disengaged citizenry. But we also have a remarkable opportunity to involve our young adults in meeting these challenges. By taking bold action to create a system of mandatory national service built on the AmeriCorps model, we have the chance to fulfill our potential as a nation.

Ansen 6

Works Cited

Corporation for National and Community Service. *AmeriCorps Works: AmeriCorps Impact Guide*, www.nationalservice.gov/sites/default/files/documents/2012_impact_guide_lowres_0.pdf. Accessed 10 Apr. 2016.

"2012 Voter Turnout." *Bipartisan Policy Center*, 8 Nov. 2012, bipartisanpolicy.org/library/2012-voter-turnout.

Feldstein, Lew. "The Importance of Strengthening Social Capital in Communities." United Way of King County, Guest Lecture, 18 Dec. 2012, Seattle, WA.

Jastrzab, JoAnn, et al. "Serving Country and Community: A Longitudinal Study of Service in AmeriCorps." *Corporation for National and Community Service*, Dec. 2004, updated Aug. 2006, www.nationalservice.gov/pdf/06_1223_longstudy_report.pdf.

Kinsley, Michael. "National Service? Puh-lease." *Time*, 30 Aug. 2007, content.time.com/time/specials/2007/article/0,28804,1657256_1657317_1658698,00.html.

Ratcliffe, Caroline E., and Signe-Mary McKernan. "Childhood Poverty and Its Lasting Consequence." *Urban Institute*, Low-Income Working Families, Paper 21, 20 Sept. 2012, www.urban.org/research/publication/child-poverty-and-its-lasting-consequence.

Robertson, Lori. "Mandatory Public Service." *FactCheck.org*, 31 Mar. 2009, updated 21 Apr. 2009, www.factcheck.org/2009/03/mandatory-public-service.

Rosenman, Mark. "A Call for National Service." *The Chronicle of Philanthropy*, 18 Oct. 2007, philanthropy.com/article/A-Call-for-National-Service/165721.

Stengel, Richard. "A Time to Serve." *Time*, 30 Aug. 2007, content.time.com/time/specials/2007/article/0,28804,1657256_1657317,00.html.

"Young, Underemployed and Optimistic." *Pew Research Center Social & Demographic Trends*, 9 Feb. 2012, www.pewsocialtrends.org/2012/02/09/young-underemployed-and-optimistic.

Start Works Cited on a new page.

List sources alphabetically by author's last name or by title if there is no named author.

Use hanging indentation. Indent each line after the first by ½ inch. Double space throughout.

Use day-month-year format for dates.

Use quotation marks for article titles.

Use italics for book, periodical, and Web site titles

THINKING CRITICALLY

About "Engaging Young Adults to Meet America's Challenges: A Proposal for Mandatory National Service"

1. Proposal arguments typically begin with the problem that the proposed solution is intended to address. How effectively does Ansen introduce the problems that mandatory national service might solve? What are these problems?

2. Where does Ansen present his solution to the problem? How effective is he at explaining the details of the solution and convincing the audience that the solution is doable?

3. Where does Ansen justify his solution by presenting reasons for enacting it? What are his primary reasons in favor of the proposal? Which of these reasons do you find particularly strong or particularly weak?

4. Where does Ansen summarize objections to his proposal? If you have objections to his proposal, are your reservations or doubts adequately summarized and addressed? Why or why not?

5. How effective is Ansen's attempt to rebut the objections?

6. Overall, how would you evaluate the logos of Ansen's argument? How effectively does he use reasons and evidence to move his audience toward his views? How effective are Ansen's appeals to ethos and pathos? Does he project a credible and trustworthy persona? To what extent does he connect his argument to the values or beliefs of his audience or otherwise appeal to their emotions?

Part III
A Guide to Composing and Revising

This recent photo depicts the receding Athabasca Glacier in Alberta, Canada, in the Canadian Rockies. A multimodel text, this photo uses words and image to convey its appeals to *logos*, *ethos*, and *pathos*. The sign informs visitors of the change in the glacier in the last 35 years. The visual impact of the photo with the people hiking up the mountain to get to the glacier, once much closer to the road, dramatically confirms the message of change and loss. You might contrast this photo with the image of the vast iceberg in Figure 5.1. Which photo do you think is more effective in conveying the extent and urgency of global warming?

Chapter 17
Writing as a Problem-Solving Process

Learning Objectives

17.1 Follow the experts' practice of using multiple drafts.

17.2 Revise globally as well as locally.

17.3 Develop ten expert habits to improve your writing processes.

17.4 Use peer reviews to help you think like an expert.

Throughout this text, we have emphasized writing as a critical thinking process requiring writers to "wallow in complexity." This opening chapter of Part 3 explains how experienced writers use multiple drafts to manage the complexities of writing.

Skill 17.1: Follow the experts' practice of using multiple drafts

17.1   Follow the experts' practice of using multiple drafts.

We begin this chapter with a close look at why expert writers use multiple drafts to move from an initial exploration of ideas to a finished product. As composition theorist Peter Elbow has asserted about the writing process, "meaning is not what you start out with" but "what you end up with." In the early stages of writing, experienced writers typically discover, deepen, and complicate their ideas before they can clarify them and arrange them effectively. Only in the last drafts will expert writers be in sufficient control of their ideas to shape them elegantly for readers.

What most distinguishes expert from novice writers is the experts' willingness to keep revising their work until they feel it is ready to go public. They typically work much harder at drafting and revising than do novice writers, taking more runs at their subject. Expert writers also make more substantial alterations in their drafts during revision—what we call "global" rather than "local" revision. This difference between expert and novice writers might seem counterintuitive. One might think that novices would need to revise more than experts. But decades of research on the writing process of experts reveal how extensively experts revise. The experienced writer crosses out pages and starts over while the inexperienced writer crosses out a word or two. The experienced writer feels cognitive overload while drafting, having to attend to many different levels and agendas at once. In contrast, the inexperienced writer seems to think only of replacing words or adding an occasional transition. Learning to revise extensively is thus a hallmark of a maturing writer.

Figure 17.1 shows how a first-year college student demonstrates expert writing behavior when she makes a substantial revision of an early draft. Note that she crosses out several sentences at the end of one paragraph, creates a new topic sentence for the next paragraph, and moves a detail sentence so that it follows the topic sentence.

Figure 17.1 A First-Year Student's Substantial Revisions

First Draft with Revisions

sticks of our favorite flavors in the bottom of the bag. ~~That discovery was, by far, the best discovery that could ever be made, week after week. So, as you can probably guess, my opinion of farmer's markets has always been very high as they were what fulfilled my sugar fix.~~

~~However, another important point can come out of that story. That point being about~~ the man who sold us our precious honey sticks. He was kind, patient, and genuinely happy to have our business. [In contrast to] ~~Not quite the same vibe that one would expect to get from~~ the supermarket employee who [often] doesn't ~~even really~~ know what isle you need in order to find the peanut butter. [Another] A huge selling point of farmer's markets, for me, is that you can go and talk to people who know about the food they are selling. It is so refreshing to go

Revised Draft

sticks of our favorite flavors in the bottom of the bag.

Another huge selling point of farmer's markets, for me, is that you can go and talk to people who know about the food they are selling. The man who sold us our [precious] honey sticks was kind, patient, and genuinely happy to have our business, in contrast to the supermarket employee who [often] doesn't ~~even really~~ know what aisle you need in order to find the peanut butter.

Why Expert Writers Revise So Extensively

Our emphasis on experts' substantial revision might have surprised you. If the experts are such good writers, why do they need multiple drafts? Why don't they get it right the first time? Our answer is simply this: Expert writers use multiple drafts to break a complex task into manageable subtasks. Let's look more closely at some of the functions that drafting and revising can perform for writers.

- *Multiple drafts help writers overcome the limits of short-term memory.* Cognitive psychologists have shown that working memory—often called short-term memory—has remarkably little storage space. You can picture short-term memory as a small tabletop surrounded by filing cabinets (long-term memory). As you write, you can place on your tabletop (working memory) only a few chunks of material at any given moment—a few sentences of a draft or several ideas in an outline. The remaining portions of your draft-in-progress fall off the table without getting stored in long-term memory. (Think of your horror when your computer eats your draft—proof that you can't rely on long-term memory to restore what you wrote.) Writing a draft captures and stores your ideas as your working memory develops them. When you reread these stored ideas, you can then see your evolving ideas whole, note problem areas, develop more ideas, see material that doesn't fit, recall additional information, and begin extending or improving the draft.

- *Multiple drafts help accommodate shifts and changes in the writer's ideas.* Early in the writing process, expert writers often are unsure of where their ideas are leading; they find that their ideas shift and evolve as their drafts progress. An expert writer's finished product often is radically different from the first draft—not simply in form and style but also in actual content.

- *Multiple drafts help writers clarify audience and purpose.* While thinking about their subject matter, experienced writers also ask questions about audience and purpose: What do my readers already know and believe about my subject? How am I trying to change their views? In the process of drafting and revising, the answers to these questions may evolve so that each new draft reflects a deeper or clearer understanding of audience and purpose.

- *Multiple drafts help writers improve structure and coherence for readers.* Whereas the ideas in early drafts often follow the order in which writers conceived them, later drafts are often restructured—sometimes radically—to meet readers' needs. Writing teachers sometimes call this transformation a movement from writer-based to reader-based prose.* The composing and revising skills taught in Chapter 18 will help you learn how to revise your drafts from a reader's perspective.

- *Multiple drafts let writers postpone worrying about correctness.* Late in the revision process, experienced writers turn their energy toward fixing errors and revising sentences for increased cohesion, conciseness, and clarity. Focusing on correctness too soon can shut down the creative process.

---

*The terms "writer-based prose" and "reader-based prose" come from Linda Flower, "Writer-Based Prose: A Cognitive Basis for Problems in Writing." *College English*, 1979, 41.1, 19–37.

An Expert's Writing Processes Are Recursive

Given this background on why expert writers revise, we can see that for experts, the writing process is *recursive* rather than linear. That is, writers continually cycle back to earlier stages as their thinking evolves. Sometimes writers develop a thesis statement early in the writing process. But just as frequently, they formulate a thesis during an "aha!" moment of discovery later in the process, perhaps after several drafts. ("So *this* is my point! Here is my argument in a nutshell!") Even very late in the process, while checking usage and punctuation, experienced writers are apt to think of new ideas, thus triggering more revision.

Skill 17.2: Revise globally as well as locally

17.2 Revise globally as well as locally.

To think like an expert writer, you need to appreciate the difference between global and local revision. You revise **locally** whenever you make changes to a text that affect only the one or two sentences that you are currently working on. In contrast, you revise **globally** when a change in one part of your draft drives changes in other parts of the draft. Global revision focuses on the big-picture concerns of ideas, structure, purpose, audience, and genre. It often involves substantial rewriting, even starting over in places with a newly conceived plan. For example, your revising part of the middle of your essay might cause you to rewrite the whole introduction or to change the tone or point of view throughout the essay.

Strategies Chart 17.1 provides some on-the-page strategies that you can adopt to practice the global and local revision strategies of experts.*

Strategies Chart 17.1 On-the-Page Strategies for Doing Global and Local Revision

Strategies to Use on the Page	Reasons
Throw out the whole draft and start again.	• Original draft helped writer discover ideas and see the whole territory. • New draft needs to be substantially refocused and restructured.
Cross out large chunks and rewrite from scratch.	• Original passage was unfocused; ideas have changed. • New sense of purpose or point meant that the whole passage needed reshaping. • Original passage was too confused or jumbled for mere editing.
Cut and paste; move parts around (then write new transitions, mapping statements, and topic sentences).	• Parts didn't follow in logical order. • Parts occurred in the order the writer thought of them rather than the order needed by readers. • Conclusion was clearer than introduction; part of conclusion had to be moved to introduction. • Revised thesis statement required different order for parts.

*We have chosen to say "on the page" rather than "on the screen" because global revision is often facilitated by a writer's working off double-spaced hard copy rather than a computer screen. We explain this advice later in the chapter.

Strategies to Use on the Page	Reasons
Add/revise topic sentences of paragraphs; insert transitions.	• Reader needs signposts to see how parts connect to previous parts and to the whole. • Revision of topic sentences often requires global revision of paragraphs.
Make insertions; add new material.	• Supporting particulars needed to be added: examples, facts, illustrations, statistics, other evidence (usually added to bodies of paragraphs). • New section was needed or more explanation was needed for a point. • Gaps in argument needed to be filled in.
Delete material.	• Material is no longer needed or is irrelevant. • Deleted material may have been good but went off on a tangent.
Recast sentences (cross out and rewrite portions; combine sentences; rephrase sentences; start sentences with a different grammatical structure).	• Passage violated old/new contract (see Skill 18.7). • Passage was wordy/choppy or lacked rhythm or voice. • Grammar was tangled, diction odd, or meaning confused. • Passage lost focus of topic sentence of paragraph.
Edit sentences to correct mistakes.	• Writer found comma splices, fragments, dangling modifiers, nonparallel constructions, or other problems of grammar and usage. • Writer found spelling errors, typos, repeated or omitted words.

For Writing and Discussion
Revising a Paragraph Globally

Choose an important paragraph in the body of a draft you are currently working on. Then answer these questions about that paragraph.

1. Why is this an important paragraph?
2. What is its main point?
3. Where is that main point stated?

Now—as an exercise only—write the main point at the top of a blank sheet of paper, put away your original draft, and, without looking at the original, write a new paragraph with the sole purpose of developing the point you wrote at the top of the page.

When you are finished, compare your new paragraph to the original. What have you learned that might help you revise your original?

Here are some typical responses of writers who have tried this exercise:

*   I recognized that my original paragraph was unfocused. I couldn't find a main point.
*   I recognized that my original paragraph was underdeveloped. I had a main point but not enough details supporting it.
*   I began to see that my draft was scattered and that I had too many short paragraphs.
*   I recognized that I was making a couple of different points in my original paragraph and that I needed to break it into separate paragraphs.
*   I recognized that I hadn't stated my main point (or that I had buried it in the middle of the paragraph).
*   I recognized that there was a big difference in style between my two versions and that I had to choose which version I liked better. (It's not always the "new" version!)

Skill 17.3: Develop ten expert habits to improve your writing processes

17.3 Develop ten expert habits to improve your writing processes.

Now that you understand why experts revise more extensively than novices and what they do on the page, we describe the habitual ways of thinking and acting that experts use when they write. Our hope is that this description will help you develop these same habits for yourself. Because one of the best ways to improve your writing process is to do what the experts do, we offer you the following ten habits of experienced writers, expressed as advice:

1. *Use exploratory writing and talking to discover and clarify ideas.* Don't let your first draft be the first occasion when you put your ideas into writing. Use exploratory strategies such as freewriting and idea mapping to generate ideas (see Concept 2.1). Also seek out opportunities to talk about your ideas with classmates or friends in order to clarify your own thinking and appreciate alternative points of view.

2. *Schedule your time.* Don't begin your paper the night before it is due. Plan sufficient time for exploration, drafting, revision, and editing. Recognize that your ideas will shift, branch out, and even turn around as you write. Allow some time off between writing the first draft and beginning revision. For many writers, revision takes considerably longer than writing the first draft. If your institution has a writing center, consider scheduling a visit.

3. *Discover what methods of drafting work best for you.* Some people compose rough drafts directly on the computer; others write longhand. Some make outlines first; others plunge directly into drafting and make outlines later. Some revise extensively on the computer as they are drafting; others plough ahead until they have a complete draft before they start revising. Some people sit at their desk for hours at a time; others need to get up and walk around every couple of minutes. Some people need a quiet room; others work best in a coffee shop. Discover the methods that work best for you.

4. *Think about audience and purpose from the start.* Early on, think about the effect you want your writing to have on readers. In formulating a thesis, look to change your readers' view of your subject. ("Before reading my paper, my readers will think X. But after reading my paper, my readers will think Y.")

5. *For the first draft, reduce your expectations.* Many novice writers get blocked by trying to make their first draft perfect. In contrast, expert writers expect the first draft to be an unreadable mess. (They often call it a "zero draft" or a "garbage draft" because they don't expect it to be good.) They use the first draft merely to get their ideas flowing, knowing they will revise later. If you get blocked, just keep writing. Get some ideas on paper.

6. *Revise on double- or triple-spaced hard copy.* Although many experienced writers revise on the screen without going through paper drafts, there are powerful advantages in printing occasional paper drafts. Research suggests that writers are more apt to make global changes in a draft if they work from hard copy because they can see more easily how the parts connect to the

whole. They can refer quickly to page two while revising page six without having to scroll back and forth. We suggest that you occasionally print out a double- or triple-spaced hard copy of your draft and then mark it up aggressively. (See again Figure 17.1, which shows how a first-year student learned the benefits of revising off hard copy.) When your draft gets too messy, keyboard your changes into your computer and begin another round of revision.

7. *As you revise, think increasingly about the needs of your readers.* Experts use first drafts to help them clarify their ideas for themselves but not necessarily for readers. In many respects, writers of first drafts are talking to themselves. Through global revision, however, writers gradually convert writer-based prose to reader-based prose. Writers begin to employ consciously the skills of reader-expectation theory that we explain in detail in Chapter 18.

8. *Exchange drafts with others.* Get other people's reactions to your work in exchange for your reactions to theirs. Experienced writers regularly seek critiques of their drafts from trusted readers. Later in this chapter we explain procedures for peer review of drafts.

9. *Save correctness for last.* To revise productively, concentrate first on the big questions: Do I have good ideas in this draft? Am I responding appropriately to the assignment? Are my ideas adequately organized and developed? Save questions about exact wording, grammar, mechanics, and documentation style for later. These concerns are important, but they cannot be efficiently attended to until after higher-order concerns are met. Your first goal is to create a thoughtful, richly developed draft.

10. *To meet deadlines and bring the process to a close, learn how to satisfice.* Our description of the writing process may seem formidable. Technically, it seems, you could go on revising forever. How can you ever know when to stop? There is no ready answer to that question, which is more a psychological problem than a technical problem. Expert writers have generally learned how to **satisfice**, a term coined by influential social scientist Herbert Simon from two root words, *suffice* and *satisfy*. It means to do the best job you can under the circumstances considering your time constraints, the pressures of other demands on you, and the difficulty of the task. Expert writers begin the writing process early and get as far as they can before their deadline looms. Then they let the deadline give them the energy for intensive revision. From lawyers preparing briefs for court to engineers developing design proposals, writers have used deadlines to help them put aside doubts and anxieties and to conclude their work, as every writer must. "Okay, it's not perfect, but it's the best I can do for now."

Skill 17.4: Use peer reviews to help you think like an expert

17.4 Use peer reviews to help you think like an expert.

One of the best ways to become a better reviser is to see your draft from a *reader*'s rather than a *writer*'s perspective. As a writer, you know what you mean; you are already inside your own head. But you need to see what your draft looks like to readers—that is, to people who are not inside your head.

For Writing and Discussion
Analyzing Your Own Writing Process

When you write, do you follow a process resembling the one we just described? Have you ever

- had a writing project grow out of your engagement with a problem or question?
- explored ideas by talking with others or by doing exploratory writing?
- made major changes to a draft because you changed your mind or otherwise discovered new ideas?
- revised a draft from a reader's perspective by consciously trying to imagine and respond to a reader's questions, confusions, and other reactions?
- road-tested a draft by trying it out on readers and then revising it as a result of what they told you?

Working in groups or as a whole class, share stories about previous writing experiences that match or do not match the description of experienced writers' processes. To the extent that your present process differs, what strategies of experienced writers might you like to try?

A good way to learn this skill is to practice reading your classmates' drafts and have them read yours. In this section we offer advice on how to respond candidly to your classmates' drafts and how to participate in peer reviews.

Becoming a Helpful Reader of Classmates' Drafts

When you respond to a writer's draft, learn to make *readerly* rather than *writerly* comments. For example, instead of saying, "Your draft is disorganized," say, "I got lost when . . . ." Instead of saying, "This paragraph needs a topic sentence," say, "I had trouble seeing the point of this paragraph." In other words, describe your mental experience in trying to understand the draft rather than use technical terms to point out problem areas or to identify errors.

When you help a writer with a draft, your goal is both to point out where the draft needs more work and to brainstorm with the writer possible ways to improve the draft. Begin by reading the draft all the way through at a normal reading speed. As you read, make mental notes to help focus your feedback. We recommend that you also mark passages that you find confusing. Write "G!" for "Good" next to parts that you like. Write "?" next to places where you want to ask questions.

After you have read the draft, use the advice in Strategies Chart 17.2 for making helpful responses, either in writing or in direct conversation with the writer.

Using a Generic Peer Review Guide

When participating in peer reviews, writers and reviewers often appreciate a list of guiding questions or checkpoints. What follows is a list of generic questions that can be used for peer-reviewing many different kinds of drafts. In each assignment chapter for Part 2 of this text, we provide additional peer review questions tailored specifically to that chapter's rhetorical aim and genres. For any given peer review session, your instructor may specify which generic or assignment-specific questions you are to use for the peer review.

Strategies Chart 17.2 Strategies for Responding Helpfully to a Classmate's Draft

Kinds of Problems Noted	Helpful Responses
If the ideas in the draft seem thin or undeveloped, or if the draft is too short	• Help the writer brainstorm for more ideas. • Help the writer add more examples, better details, more supporting data or arguments.
If you get confused or lost in some parts of the draft	• Show the writer where you got confused or miscued in reading the draft ("I started getting lost here because I couldn't see why you were giving me this information" or "I thought you were going to say X, but then you said Y"). • Have the writer talk through ideas to clear up confusing spots.

If you get confused or lost at the "big-picture" level	• Help the writer sharpen the thesis: suggest that the writer view the thesis as the answer to a controversial or problematic question; ask the writer to articulate the question that the thesis answers.
	• Help the writer create an outline, tree diagram, or flowchart (see Skill 18.3).
	• Help the writer clarify the focus by asking him or her to complete these statements about purpose:
	  • The purpose of this paper is _____.
	  • The purpose of this section (paragraph) is _____.
	  • Before reading my paper, my reader will think _____. But after reading my paper, my reader will think _____.

If you can understand the sentences but can't see the point	• Help the writer articulate the meaning by asking "So what?" questions, making the writer bring the point to the surface. ("I can understand what you are saying here but I don't quite understand why you are saying it. What do these details have to do with the topic sentence of the paragraph?" Or "What does this paragraph have to do with your thesis?") • Help the writer create transitions, new topic sentences, or other means of making points clear.
If you disagree with the ideas or think the writer has avoided alternative points of view	• Play devil's advocate to help the writer deepen and complicate ideas. • Show the writer specific places where you had queries or doubts.

Generic Peer Review Guide

For the writer

Give your peer reviewer two or three questions to address while responding to your draft. The questions can focus on some aspect of your draft that you are uncertain about, on one or more sections where you particularly seek help or advice, on some feature that you particularly like about your draft, or on some part you especially wrestled with.

For the reviewer

Basic overview: As you read at normal speed do the following:

• Mark a "?" next to any passages that you find confusing, that somehow slow down your reading, or that raise questions in your mind.
• Mark a "G" next to any passages where you think the writing is particularly good, strong, or interesting.

Going into more depth: Prior to discussion with the writer, complete the following tasks:

• Identify at least one place in the draft where you got confused. Note why you got confused, using readerly rather than writely comments.

- Identify one place in the draft where you think the ideas are thin or need more development. Make discussion notes.
- Identify one place where you might write "So what?" after the passage. These are places where you don't understand the significance or importance of the writer's points. These are also places where you can't see how certain sentences connect to a topic sentence or how certain paragraphs or sections connect to the thesis statement.
- Identify at least one place where you could play devil's advocate or otherwise object to the writer's ideas. Make notes on the objections or alternative views that you will raise with the writer.

Evaluating the writer' argument: Look at the draft's effectiveness from the perspective of the classical rhetorical appeals:

- *Logos:* How effectively does the writer use reasons and evidence to support his or her claim? How effectively does the writer use details, particulars, examples, and other means as evidence to support points? How logical are the points, and how clearly are they connected?
- *Ethos:* What image does the writer project? How effective is the tone? How trustworthy, reliable, knowledgeable, and fair does this writer seem?
- *Pathos:* How effectively does the writer engage the audience's interest? How effectively does the writer tie into the audience's beliefs and values? To what extent does the writer make the reader care about the topic?

Noting problems of grammar and editing: Mark problems in grammar, spelling, punctuation, documentation, or other issues of mechanics.

Summing up: Create a consolidated summary of your review:

- Sum up the strengths of the draft.
- Identify two or three main weaknesses or problem areas.
- Make two or three suggestions for revision.

For Writing and Discussion
Practicing a Peer Review

Background: In the following exercise, we invite you to practice a peer review by responding to a student's draft ("Should the University Carpet the Dorm Rooms?" below) or to another draft provided by your instructor. The "Carpets" assignment asked students to take a stand on a local campus issue. Imagine that you have exchanged drafts with this student and that your task is to help this student improve the draft through both global and local revision.

Individual task: Read the draft carefully following the instructions in the "Generic Peer Review Guide." Write out your responses to the bulleted items under "Going into more depth," "Evaluating the writer's argument," and "Summing up."

(continued)

Small group or whole class: Share your responses. Then turn to the following additional tasks:

1. With the instructor serving as a guide, practice explaining to the writer where or how you got confused while reading the draft. Readers often have difficulty explaining their reading experience to a writer. Let several class members role-play being the reader. Practice using language such as "I like the way this draft started because . . . ," "I got confused when . . . ," "I had to back up and reread when . . . ," "I saw your point here, but then I got lost again because . . . ." Writing theorist Peter Elbow calls such language a "movie of your mind."

2. Have several class members role-play being devil's advocates by arguing against the writer's thesis. Where are the ideas thin or weak?

Should The University Carpet The Dorm Rooms?

Tricia, a university student, came home exhausted from her work-study job. She took a blueberry pie from the refrigerator to satisfy her hunger and a tall glass of milk to quench her thirst. While trying to get comfortable on her bed, she tipped her snack over onto the floor. She cleaned the mess, but the blueberry and milk stains on her brand-new carpet could not be removed.

Tricia didn't realize how hard it was to clean up stains on a carpet. Luckily this was her own carpet.

A lot of students don't want carpets. Students constantly change rooms. The next person may not want carpet.

Some students say that since they pay to live on campus, the rooms should reflect a comfortable home atmosphere. Carpets will make the dorm more comfortable. The carpet will act as insulation and as a soundproofing system.

Paint stains cannot be removed from carpets. If the university carpets the rooms, the students will lose the privilege they have of painting their rooms any color. This would limit students' self-expression.

The carpets would be an institutional brown or gray. This would be ugly. With tile floors, the students can choose and purchase their own carpets to match their taste. You can't be an individual if you can't decorate your room to fit your personality.

According to Rachel Jones, Assistant Director of Housing Services, the cost will be $300 per room for the carpet and installation. Also the university will have to buy more vacuum cleaners. But will vacuum cleaners be all that is necessary to keep the carpets clean? We'll need shampoo machines too.

What about those stains that won't come off even with a shampoo machine? That's where the student will have to pay damage deposit costs.

There will be many stains on the carpet due to shaving cream fights, food fights, beverage parties, and smoking, all of which can damage the carpets.

Students don't take care of the dorms now. They don't follow the rules of maintaining their rooms. They drill holes into the walls, break mirrors, beds, and closet doors, and leave their food trays all over the floor.

If the university buys carpets our room rates will skyrocket. In conclusion, it is a bad idea for the university to buy carpets.

Participating in Peer Review Workshops

If you are willing to respond candidly to a classmate's draft—in a readerly rather than a writerly way—you will be a valuable participant in peer review workshops. In a typical workshop, classmates work in groups of two to six to respond to one another's rough drafts and offer suggestions for revisions. These workshops are most helpful when group members have developed sufficient levels of professionalism and trust to exchange candid responses. A frequent problem in peer review workshops is that classmates try so hard to avoid hurting each other's feelings that they provide vague, meaningless feedback. Saying, "Your paper's great. I really liked it. Maybe you could make it flow a little better" is much less helpful than saying, "Your issue about environmental pollution in the Antarctic is well defined in the first paragraph, but I got lost in the second paragraph when you began discussing penguin coloration."

RESPONSIBILITIES OF PEER REVIEWERS AND WRITERS Learning to respond conscientiously and carefully to others' work may be the single most important thing you can do to improve your own writing. When you review a classmate's draft, you are not acting as a teacher, but simply as a fresh reader. You can help the writer appreciate what it's like to encounter his or her text for the first time. Your primary responsibility is to articulate your understanding of what the writer's words say to you and to identify places where you get confused, where you need more details, where you have doubts or queries, and so on.

When you play the role of writer during a workshop session, your responsibilities parallel those of your peer reviewers. You need to provide a legible rough draft, preferably typed and double-spaced, that doesn't baffle the reader with hard-to-follow corrections and confusing pagination. Your instructor may ask you to bring copies of your draft for all group members. During the workshop, your primary responsibility is to *listen,* taking in how others respond to your draft without becoming defensive. Many instructors also ask writers to formulate two or three specific questions about their drafts—questions they particularly want their reviewers to address. These questions might focus on something writers particularly like about their drafts or on specific problem areas or concerns.

Responding to Peer Reviews

After you and your classmates have gone over one another's papers and walked through the responses, everyone should identify two or three things about his or her draft that particularly need work. Before you leave the session, you should have some notion about how you want to revise your paper.

You may get mixed or contradictory responses from different reviewers. One reviewer may praise a passage that another finds confusing or illogical. Conflicting advice is a frustrating fact of life for all writers, whether students or professionals. Such disagreements reveal how readers co-create a text with a writer: Each brings to the text a different background, set of values, and way of reading.

It is important to remember that you are in charge of your own writing. If several readers offer the same critique of a passage, then no matter how much you love that passage, you probably need to follow their advice. But when readers disagree, you have to make your own best judgment about whom to heed.

Once you have received advice from others, reread your draft again slowly and then develop a revision plan, allowing yourself time to make sweeping, global changes if needed. You also need to remember that you can never make your draft perfect. Plan when you will bring the process to a close so that you can turn in a finished product on time and get on with your other classes and your life.

Chapter 18
Strategies for Writing Closed-Form Prose

Learning Objectives

18.1 Satisfy reader expectations by linking new material to old material.

18.2 Convert loose structures into problem-thesis-support structures.

18.3 Nutshell your argument and visualize its structure.

18.4 Start and end with the "big picture" through effective titles, introductions, and conclusions.

18.5 Keep readers on track with effective topic sentences.

18.6 Guide readers with transitions and other signposts.

18.7 Make sentences cohere by following the old/new contract.

18.8 Learn four expert moves for organizing and developing ideas: the *for example* move, the *summary/however* move, the *division-into-parallel-parts* move, and the *comparison/contrast* move.

18.9 Present numerical data effectively through tables, graphs, and charts.

18.10 Use occasional open-form elements to achieve "voice" in closed-form prose.

This chapter gives nuts-and-bolts advice for writing effective closed-form prose. As explained in Part 1 of this text, c**losed-form prose** has an explicit thesis statement that is supported with points, subpoints, and details. Its features include unified and coherent paragraphs headed by topic sentences, good transitions between sentences and paragraphs, and forecasting of the whole before presentation of the parts. The strategies explained in this chapter are organized into ten self-contained lessons, each of which can be read comfortably in twenty minutes or less. The first lesson (Skill 18.1) provides a theoretical overview of the rest of the chapter. The remaining lessons can then be assigned and read in any order your instructor desires. Together these lessons will teach you transferable skills—useful in any academic discipline or professional setting—for producing clear, reader-friendly, and persuasive closed-form prose.

See Concept 3.1 for a detailed explanation of closed-form versus open-form prose.

Skill 18.1: Satisfy reader expectations by linking new material to old material

18.1 Satisfy reader expectations by linking new material to old material.

In this opening lesson, we ask you to imagine how readers make sense of a verbal text. Imagine for a moment that your readers have only so much *reader energy*, which they can use either to follow your ideas or to puzzle over confusing passages.* To follow your ideas, readers must see how each new sentence in your essay connects to what has come before. Specifically, they need to see two things:

1. How the current sentence connects to the immediately preceding sentences, and

2. How the current part or section they are reading connects to the whole.

If you continually signal this information to your readers, you will conserve their reader energy. They will stay focused on your meaning without having to puzzle over your structure.

The Principle of Old Before New

What makes closed-form prose "closed" is the way it consistently links a current sentence to previous sentences and a current part to the whole. It makes these links by adhering to the principle of old before new. Rhetoricians sometimes call this principle the **old/new contract**, which refers to the writer's obligation to help readers connect each new sentence or part to previous material. As readers read, they don't memorize your text as if they are memorizing a list of facts. Rather, they construct in their heads a big picture of your unfolding meaning, usually organized by points and subpoints. If a new sentence doesn't meaningfully connect to that big picture, it diverts the reader's energy from following your ideas into puzzling over your structure. "Whoa, you lost me on the turn," your reader might say. "I can't see how this sentence (or this part) relates to what you just said."

This principle of old before new is grounded in brain circuitry. Cognitive researchers have shown how humans must link new information to old information to form meaningful units. You can discover this linking pattern for yourself through the following thought exercise.

---

*For the useful term *reader energy*, we are indebted to George Gopen and Judith Swan, "The Science of Scientific Writing," *American Scientist* 78 (1990): 550–559. In addition, much of our discussion of writing in this chapter is indebted to the work of Joseph Williams, George Gopen, and Gregory Colomb. See especially Gregory G. Colomb and Joseph M. Williams, "Perceiving Structure in Professional Prose: A Multiply Determined Experience," in Lee Odell and Dixie Goswamie (eds.), *Writing in Nonacademic Settings* (New York: The Guilford Press, 1985), pp. 87–128.

THOUGHT EXERCISE: HOW THE BRAIN PROCESSES OLD AND NEW INFORMATION

Suppose you go into a new office building for a doctor's appointment and want to find the room number for your doctor's office. You go to the building directory. How would you like it to be organized? (Suppose your doctor's name is Hisako Ono.)

Arrangement A	Arrangement B
Room 1302 Randersoll, Kim	Chavez, Jose Room 1303
Room 1303 Chavez, Jose	Graff, Theresa Room 1306
Room 1304 Smith, William	Jones, Raquel Room 1307
Room 1305 Ono, Hisako	Ono, Hisako Room 1305
Room 1306 Graff, Theresa	Randersoll, Kim Room 1302
Room 1307 Jones, Raquel	Smith, William Room 1304

If you are like most people, you prefer Arrangement B. The old information that you already know is your doctor's name (Hisako Ono). The new information that you need to find is her room number. Because in English we read from left to right, you need to have her name on the left. You also need the names in alphabetical order so that you can quickly find "Ono." (Knowing the order of the alphabet is another piece of required "old information.") You can still find Dr. Ono's room number with Arrangement A, but it takes much more reader energy. (Imagine how long it would take if this building had 20 floors with, say, 30 rooms per floor.)

The principle of old before new is as important when we listen as when we read. Suppose you are a passenger on a flight into Chicago and need to transfer to a flight to Memphis. As you descend into Chicago, the flight attendant announces transfer gates. Which of the following formats is easier for you to process? Why?

Arrangement A		Arrangement B	
Atlanta	Gate C12	Gate C12	Atlanta
Dallas	Gate C25	Gate C25	Dallas
Memphis	Gate B20	Gate B20	Memphis
St. Louis	Gate D15	Gate D15	St. Louis

You probably prefer column A. In this case, the old or known information is our destination (Memphis), while the new or unknown information is the gate number—Gate B20. Announcement B causes us to expend more *listener energy* than does A because it forces us to hold each gate number in memory until we hear its corresponding city. The number of the gate is meaningless until it is linked to the crucial old information, "Memphis." Arrangement A allows us to relax until we hear the word "Memphis," while B forces us to concentrate intensely on each gate number until we find the meaningful one.

How the Principle of Old Before New Creates Unified and Coherent Paragraphs

This principle of old before new is crucial to our understanding of how readers find meaning in verbal texts. To keep readers on track, writers should begin their sentences with old information that hooks back to the previous material that the reader has already read. The last part of the sentence then contains the new information that drives the argument forward. When writers follow this principle, the result is tightly organized closed-form prose. Such prose is said to have both unity and coherence—two defining features of closed-form prose:

- **Unity** refers to the relationship between each part of an essay and the larger whole.
- **Coherence** refers to the relationship between adjacent sentences and paragraphs.

As an illustration of these terms, consider the differences in the following three passages, each of which begins with the same sentence about the father's role in childrearing. However, the first two of these passages thwart the principle of old before new while the third fulfills it.

PASSAGE 1: EXHIBITS NEITHER UNITY NOR COHERENCE

Recent research has given us much deeper—and more surprising—insights into the father's role in childrearing. My family is typical of the east side in that we never had much money. Their tongues became black and hung out of their mouths. The back-to-basics movement got a lot of press, fueled as it was by fears of growing illiteracy and cultural demise.

PASSAGE 2: EXHIBITS COHERENCE BUT NOT UNITY

Recent research has given us much deeper—and more surprising—insights into the father's role in childrearing. Childrearing is a complex process that is frequently investigated by psychologists. Psychologists have also investigated sleep patterns and dreams. When we are dreaming, psychologists have shown, we are often reviewing recent events in our lives.

PASSAGE 3: EXHIBITS BOTH UNITY AND COHERENCE

Recent research has given us much deeper—and more surprising—insights into the father's role in childrearing. It shows that in almost all of their interactions with children, fathers do things a little differently from mothers. What fathers do—their special parenting style—is not only highly complementary to what mothers do but is by all indications important in its own right. [The passage continues by showing the special ways that fathers contribute to childrearing.]

If you are like most readers, Passage 1 comically frustrates your reader energy because it is a string of random sentences without connections to any point. Passage 2 also frustrates your reader energy but in a more subtle way. If you aren't paying attention, Passage 2 may seem to make sense because each sentence is linked to the one before it. But the individual sentences don't develop a larger whole: The topics switch from a father's role in childrearing to psychology to sleep patterns to the function of dreams. This passage has coherence (links between sentences) but not unity (links to a larger point). In contrast, Passage 3 exhibits both coherence and unity. The passage is unified because it makes a consistent point—that fathers have an important role in childrearing. It is also coherent because the opening of sentences 2 and 3 include words that refer to previous information: The pronoun "it" in sentence 2 refers to "research" in sentence 1. In sentence 3 the word "fathers" links to "fathers" in both sentences 1 and 2. We'll have more to say about the old/new contract at the sentence level in Skill 18.7.

How the Principle of Old Before New Helps Readers Construct Meaning

The principle of old before new helps readers construct meaning from closed-form prose. When a text adheres to the principle of old before new, it forecasts what is coming (thereby setting up reader expectations) and then fulfills that forecast (satisfying those expectations). The clarity of the structure allows the reader to focus on and comprehend the writer's meaning.

Let's look at a how a reader processes a new text. When a reader starts reading a new essay, the reader has no specific expectations: Everything in the essay is new information. However, once the reader reads the title, the title becomes old information. If the title is effective, it forecasts what will be new in the essay, arousing the reader's anticipation of what will follow and propelling the reader's desire to continue reading. The first part of the introduction further arouses reader desire by explaining a problem or question or knowledge gap (tying backwards into the reader's interest in the question or problem), while the last part presents the thesis (what's new). Once read, the thesis then becomes old information. Because the thesis summarizes the essay's big picture, it leads readers to anticipate what is coming in the body of the essay. If the essay does what the thesis forecasts, the reader experiences the essay's structure as a gratifying sequence of anticipation and fulfillment.

As we will see throughout this chapter, the principle of old before new has important explanatory power for writers. As the mind reads a text from left to right or from top to bottom, it continually needs to link new material backwards to old material. At the level of the whole essay, this principle helps writers understand the following:

- Why writers need to lay out an essay's big picture before presenting the parts (Skill 18.3)
- Why writers need to place a topic sentence at the beginning of a paragraph (Skill 18.5)
- Why writers must craft effective transitions between sentences and between parts (Skill 18.6)
- Why writers need to begin sentences with old information and put the new information later in the sentence (Skill 18.7)

What readers need from a closed-form text, then, is an ability to predict what is coming as well as regular fulfillment of those predictions. The rest of this chapter gives you more specific advice on how to keep your reader on track throughout your essay.

Skill 18.2: Convert loose structures into problem-thesis-support structures

18.2 Convert loose structures into problem-thesis-support structures.

This lesson shows you how to convert loose structures into thesis-support structures that begin with a problem, assert a thesis, and then support that thesis with points and details. Because developing a structure of points and details requires wallowing in complexity, writers often retreat into simpler structures that avoid this kind of problem-thesis-support thinking. You can better understand thesis-based writing by contrasting it with writing that might seem thesis-based but isn't.

Avoiding "and Then" Writing (Avoiding Chronological Structure)

One way writers fail to produce a problem-thesis-support structure is to organize primarily by time, arranging sentences and paragraphs in a chronological sequence. Chronological structure, often called *narrative*, is the most common organizing principle of open-form prose, but effective open-form writers handle time artistically using literary techniques. In closed-form prose, chronological order is usually ineffective—it is a strategy for avoiding a thesis.

To a large degree, chronological order is the default mode we fall into when we aren't sure how to organize material. For example, if you were asked to analyze a character in a short story, you might slip into a plot summary instead. In much the same way, you might substitute historical chronology ("First A happened, then B happened . . . ") for historical analysis ("B happened because A happened . . . "); or you might give a chronological recounting of your research ("First I discovered A, then I discovered B . . . ") instead of organizing your material into an argument ("A's account of this phenomenon calls B's account into question because. . . . "). We call this kind of chronological structure "**and then**" **writing**, meaning the writer strings together one event after another through time.

The tendency toward *and then* writing is revealed in the following example from a student's essay on Shakespeare's *The Tempest*. This excerpt is from the introduction of the student's first draft.

> **PLOT SUMMARY—*AND THEN* WRITING**
>
> Prospero cares deeply for his daughter. In the middle of the play Prospero acts like a gruff father and makes Ferdinand carry logs in order to test his love for Miranda and Miranda's love for him. In the end, though, Prospero is a loving father who rejoices in his daughter's marriage to a good man.

Here the student seems simply to retell the play's plot without any apparent thesis. (The body of her rough draft primarily retold the same story in more detail.) However, during an office conference, the instructor discovered that the student regarded her sentence about Prospero's being a loving father as her thesis. In fact, the student had gotten in an argument with a classmate over whether Prospero was a good person or an evil one. The instructor helped her convert her draft into a thesis-support structure:

> **REVISED INTRODUCTION—THESIS-SUPPORT STRUCTURE**
>
> Many persons believe that Prospero is an evil person in the play. They claim that Prospero exhibits a harsh, destructive control over Miranda and also, like Faust, seeks superhuman knowledge through his magic. However, I contend that Prospero is a kind and loving father.

This revised version implies a problem (What kind of father is Prospero?), presents a view that the writer wishes to change (Prospero is harsh and hateful), and asserts a contestable thesis (Prospero is a loving father). The body of her paper can now be converted from plot summary to an argument with reasons and evidence supporting her claim that Prospero is loving.

Avoiding "All About" Writing (Avoiding Encyclopedic Structure)

Another kind of loose, thesis-less structure is **"all about" writing**, which covers a topic by presenting information organized by categories, like an encyclopedia. When the categories are clearly marked and the information within them is clearly presented, *all about* writing can be organized and interesting, but it doesn't make a thesis-based argument. The categories do not function as points and details in support of a thesis. Rather, like the shelving system in a library, the topic categories are simply ways of arranging information for convenient retrieval.

When students are assigned a research paper or a term paper, they might mistakenly imagine that the task calls for an *all about* report rather than an argument in response to a problem. To illustrate the differences between *all about* writing and *problem-thesis* writing, consider the case of two students choosing to write term papers on the subject of female police officers. One student imagines the task as an *all about* report; the other poses and investigates a problem related to female police officers and writes a thesis-based argument in response. The *all about* writer may produce an initial outline like the following:

    I. History of women in police roles

        A. Female police or soldiers in ancient times

        B. 19th century (Calamity Jane)

        C. 1900s–1960

        D. 1960–present

    II. How female police officers are selected and trained

   III. A typical day in the life of a female police officer

   IV. Achievements and acts of heroism of female police officers

    V. What the future holds for female police officers

This paper simply presents information about female police officers organized into categories. Several of the categories (particularly I, II, and III) invite chronological order (*and then* writing). Although the information reported in the paper might be interesting, it is riskless. The paper requires the writer simply to gather and report information without doing critical thinking in response to a problem.

In contrast, consider the case of a student, Lynnea, who wrote a research paper entitled "Women Police Officers: Should Size and Strength Be Criteria for Patrol Duty?" Her essay begins with a story reported to her by her boyfriend (a police officer) about being assigned to patrol duty with a new female officer, Connie Jones (not her real name), who is four feet ten inches tall and weighs ninety pounds. Here is the rest of the introduction to Lynnea's essay.

FROM LYNNEA'S INTRODUCTION

Connie Jones has just completed police academy training and has been assigned to patrol duty in _____. Because she is so small, she has to have a booster seat in her patrol car and has been given a special gun, since she can barely manage to pull the trigger of a standard police-issue .38 revolver. Although she passed the physical requirements at the academy, which involved speed and endurance running, sit-ups, and monkey bar tests, most of the officers in her department doubt her ability to perform competently as a patrol officer. But nevertheless she is on patrol because men and women receive equal assignments in most of today's police forces. But is this a good policy? Can a person who is significantly smaller and weaker than her peers make an effective patrol officer?

Lynnea examined all the evidence she could find—through library and field research (interviewing police officers)—and arrived at the following thesis: "Because concern for public safety overrides all other concerns, police departments should set stringent size and strength requirements for patrol officers, even if these criteria exclude many women." This thesis has plenty of tension because it sets limits on gender equity. Because Lynnea considers herself a feminist, it distressed her to advocate for public safety over women's rights. The resulting essay was engaging precisely because of the tension it creates and the controversy it engenders.

Avoiding Engfish Writing, or Structure That Doesn't Address a Real Problem

Unlike *and then* papers or *all about* papers, **engfish** papers have a thesis, but the thesis is a riskless truism that doesn't respond to a real problem with stakes.* The writer supports the thesis with predictable reasons—often structured as the three body paragraphs in a traditional five-paragraph essay. It is fill-in-the-blank writing: "The food service is bad for three reasons. First, it is bad because the food is not tasty. Blah, blah, blah about tasteless food. Second, it is bad because it is too expensive. Blah, blah, blah about the expense." And so on. The writer is on autopilot and is not contributing to a real conversation about a real question. (Perhaps in this case there would be a real question if the campus were engaged in a genuine argument about switching food services.) *Engfish* writing can therefore be well organized, but it brings no surprise to the reader, nor does it grow out of the writer's wallowing in complexity. In the end, *engfish* is bad not because what you say is *wrong*, but because what you say couldn't *possibly* be wrong. To avoid *engfish*, stay focused on the need to surprise your reader.

Skill 18.3: Nutshell your argument and visualize its structure

18.3 Nutshell your argument and visualize its structure.

The previous lesson showed you how to convert loose structures into problem-thesis-support structures organized by points and details. In this

---

*The term *engfish* was coined by the textbook writer Ken Macrorie to describe a fishy kind of canned prose that bright but bored students mechanically produce to please their teachers. See Ken Macrorie, *Telling Writing* (Rochelle Park, NJ: Hayden Press, 1970).

lesson, we provide tips for getting your points and details effectively focused and organized. Specifically, we'll show you the value of nutshelling your argument and then visualizing its structure. A chief take-away insight from this lesson is that points need to be stated as complete sentences rather than as topic phrases. A topic phrase by itself—let's say "peanut butter"—invites you to picture (in this case) a tasty substance but not to conceptualize a meaningful point within an argument. To make a point about peanut butter you need to add a predicate (verb): "Peanut butter is surprisingly nutritious." Now you have a point—one that you can support through details about the nutritional content of peanut butter. As we show later in this lesson, creating an effective outline for your paper helps you organize *meanings*, not topics, and meanings require complete sentences.

Making a List of "Chunks" and a Scratch Outline Early in the Writing Process

Early in the writing process, while you are still searching for meanings, you probably won't know how to organize your paper. But you may know that you have certain ideas, sections, parts, or "chunks" that you want to include somewhere in your paper. Although you don't yet know where they will go or how long they will be, just listing these chunks will help you get thinking about structure—like placing the pieces of a jigsaw puzzle onto a tabletop. Here is student writer Kent Ansen's list of chunks early in his process of writing a researched argument on mandatory public service for young adults.

Kent Ansen's final proposal argument is shown at the end of Chapter 16.

Kent's List of Chunks to Include

- Section on my own high school experience as a volunteer (perhaps in introduction)
- Rosenman's argument that national public service would make Americans feel more engaged with their country and be better citizens
- Kinsley's conservative argument against national public service (I'll need to summarize this and refute it)
- A section where I argue that mandatory public service would increase young people's civic engagement.

Once you make a list of chunks, you can begin thinking about which of them are high-level points and which are details in support of a point. Before writing a rough draft, many writers like to make a brief scratch outline to help with planning. Here is Kent's initial scratch outline.

Kent's Initial Scratch Outline

- Introduction
  - Attention grabber (my volunteer experience—show that it benefited me)
  - Problems with Lost Generation (maybe national service would help them)
  - Thesis—we should institute national public service
- Explain my idea, show what my plan would look like

- Show the benefits of public service
  - Would help alleviate poverty
  - Would encourage civic engagement among young people.
- Summarize Kinsley's opposition
- Try to refute Kinsley

To Achieve Focus, "Nutshell" Your Argument and Create a Working Thesis Statement

As you begin drafting, you will find your ideas gradually becoming clearer and more focused. At this point, doing the following nutshell exercise will ensure that your paper has a *problem-thesis* structure rather than an *and then* or *all about* structure. The six prompts in this exercise will help you focus on your argument's "big picture"—its main high-level point and purpose. We recommend that you write your responses to each prompt as a way of seeing the "whole" of your paper.

Often writers have to go through several drafts to figure out the point of certain sections. See Skills 17.1 and 17.2.

EXERCISE FOR NUTSHELLING YOUR ARGUMENT

1. What puzzle or problem initiated your thinking about X? _____

2. *Template: Many people think X, but I am going to argue Y.*

   Before reading my paper, my readers will think X: _____.
   But after reading my paper, my readers will think Y: _____.

3. The purpose of my paper is: _____.

4. My paper addresses the following question: _____.

5. My one-sentence summary answer to this question is this [my thesis statement]:
   _____.

6. A tentative title for my paper is: _____.

   Here are Kent Ansen's responses to these prompts:

1. I was initially puzzled about the value of volunteer work and then wondered if these same values would be obtained if national public service was made mandatory.

2. Before reading my paper, my readers will think that mandatory public service is a bad idea. But after reading my paper my readers will see the benefits of making public service mandatory for young adults.

3. The purpose of my paper is to show the benefits of mandatory public service for young adults.

4. Should the United States institute mandatory public service for young adults?

5. The United States should institute mandatory public service for young adults because such service would help fight poverty and promote civic engagement.

6. Engaging Young Adults to Meet America's Challenges: A Proposal for Mandatory National Service

Once you have nutshelled your argument, you are ready to create a working thesis statement that includes main supporting points. These supporting points help you visualize an emerging structure. Here is Kent's working thesis statement.

KENT'S WORKING THESIS STATEMENT

The United States should institute mandatory pubic service for young adults because such service would help impoverished neighborhoods and would promote democracy through increased civic engagement.

Visualize Your Structure

Once you have nutshelled your argument and created a working thesis statement, you can sketch your structure to show how points, subpoints, and details can be arranged hierarchically to support your thesis. We offer you three different ways to visualize your argument: a traditional outline, a verbal/visual tree diagram, or some other kind of visual flowchart that includes both words and images. Use whichever strategy best fits your way of thinking and perceiving.

An effective outline or diagram helps you organize *meanings*, not topics. Note that in the following examples, Kent uses *complete sentences* in the high-level slots in order to state meanings rather than identify topics. As we explained in our earlier peanut butter example ("Peanut butter is surprisingly nutritious"), points require both subjects and verbs. Any point—whether a thesis, a main point, or a subpoint—is an assertion that requires elaboration and supporting details. By using complete sentences rather than phrases in an outline, the writer is forced to articulate the point of each section of the emerging argument.

OUTLINES The most common way of visualizing structure is the traditional outline, which uses numbers and letters to indicate levels of points, subpoints, and details. If this traditional method works for you, we recommend that you use the outlining feature of your word processing program, which allows you to move and insert material and change heading levels with great flexibility. (You can also use bullets and other symbols rather than letters and numbers if you prefer.)

Figure 18.1 shows Kent's complete outline for his argument.

TREE DIAGRAMS A tree diagram displays a hierarchical structure visually, using horizontal and vertical space instead of letters and numbers. Figure 18.2 shows how selected points from Kent's argument could be displayed in a tree diagram. His thesis sits at the top of the tree. The main points of his argument appear as branches beneath his claim. Supporting evidence and arguments are subbranches beneath each main point. Unlike outlines, tree diagrams allow us to *see* the hierarchical relationship of points and details. When you develop a point with details, you move vertically down the tree. When you switch to a new point, you move horizontally to make a new branch. Our own teaching experience suggests that for many writers, this visual/spatial technique often produces fuller, more detailed, and more logical arguments than does a traditional outline.

Figure 18.1 Kent Ansen's Full-Sentence Outline

I. Introduction
  A. My high school volunteer project showed me the value of public service (attention grabber).
  B. Public service might also address problem of joblessness faced by young people.
  C. To solve these problems, I propose a mandatory year of national service for Americans ages 18-25 (thesis paragraph).

II. Mandatory public service would have certain benefits based on the model of AmeriCorps.

III. A mandatory program would invest in communities by attacking poverty and building social captial.
  A. National Public Service would fight poverty by helping the poor become self-sufficient.
    1. Data from Ratcliffe and McKernan show social costs of poverty.
    2. Public service provides people-to-people contact, which is better than simply providing money or food.
  B. Public service would build social capital within served communities while also increasing career opportunities for volunteers.

IV. Mandatory Public Service would make young people more engaged with our democracy.
  A. The ending of the draft following the Vietnam War undermined citizens' feeling of being stakeholders in the democracy.
    1. Young people have low voter turnout and are often apathetic about politics
    2. Roseman's research shows Americans are becoming increasingly "passive citizens."
  B. Mandatory public service would make young people stakeholders in democracy and increase their civic engagement (cite Jazrup).

V. Opponents of mandatory public service argue these jobs would be useless make-work tasks and would interfere with market forces (summarize Kinsley).

VI. But the example of AmeriCorps reveals the flaws in Kinsley's argument
  A. Rather than being makeshift, these jobs produce valuable civic benefits.
  B. These jobs don't interfere with markets because they do work that markets don't fund.
  C. The already proven benefits of AmeriCorps can be scaled up to meet a national need.

VII. The money used to fund mandatory national service is money directly reinvested in our communities (Conclusion).

YOUR OWN METHODS OF VISUALIZING STRUCTURE Many writers develop their own personal ways of visualizing structure. Some create flowcharts with big boxes to represent major parts of the paper and arrows and smaller boxes to show the various parts of the big box. Others use the branching methods of a tree diagram but arrange the parts as spokes on a wheel. Still others combine outlines and flow charts in visual ways that work for them. In all cases, the key to organizing meanings is to use complete sentences to state points.

Once you have sketched out an initial outline or structural diagram, you can use it to generate additional ideas. Use question marks on the outline or diagram to "hold open" spots for new points or supporting details. Think of your structural diagrams as evolving sketches rather than rigid blueprints. As your ideas grow and change, revise your outline or diagram, adding or removing points, consolidating and refocusing sections, moving parts around, or filling in details.

Figure 18.2 Tree Diagram of Selected Points from Kent Ansen's Argument

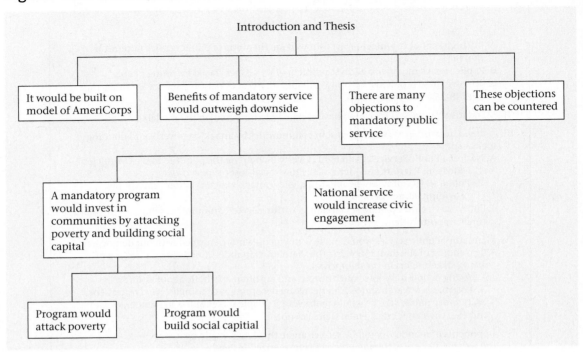

For Writing and Discussion
Nutshelling Your Ideas and Visualizing Your Structure

As you draft a paper, try out the ideas in Skill 18.3 for nutshelling your ideas and visualizing your structure. Then in small groups or as a whole class, share your nutshells and outlines or visual diagrams. What did you find helpful and why?

Skill 18.4: Start and end with the "big picture" through effective titles, introductions, and conclusions

18.4 Start and end with the "big picture" through effective titles, introductions, and conclusions.

In Skill 18.1, we explained that closed-form prose consistently follows the principle of old before new. What readers need from closed-form prose is an initial big-picture overview of what is coming as well as signals along the way that show how the parts connect to the whole. As we show in this section, writers lay out the big picture of their essay with their title and introduction and then often return to the big picture in the conclusion.

Creating Effective Titles

In accordance with the principle of old before new, a good title needs to have something old (a word or phrase that hooks into a reader's existing interests) and something new (a hint at what's coming). Here is an example of an effective title from a student essay in Chapter 13:

> "Boomerang Kids: What Are the Causes of Generation Y's Growing Pains?"

This title hooks into the interests of potential readers familiar with the phenomenon of boomerang kids and curious about their growing pains (old information). It also promises something new—the writer's ideas about the causes of the phenomenon (new information). Good titles, then, hook into readers' already existing interests while promising something new or challenging.

There are three basic approaches that academic writers take for composing a title, as shown in Strategies Chart 18.1.

Such titles might seem overly formal to you, but they indicate how much the reader of an academic article appreciates a preview of its big picture. Although the titles in popular magazines may be more informal, they often use these same strategies. Here are some titles or articles that appeared in popular magazines such as *Redbook* and *Forbes*:

"Is the Coffee Bar Trend About to Peak?" (question)

"A Man *Can* Take Maternity Leave—And Love It" (abbreviated thesis)

"Feed Your Face: Why Your Complexion Needs Vitamins" (two parts linked by colon)

Strategies Chart 18.1 Strategies for Writing Titles of Academic Papers

What to Do	Examples
State or imply the question that your essay addresses. (*Old information* is your audience's interest in the question. Implied *new information* is your answer to the question.)	• How Clean and Green Are Hydrogen Fuel Cell Cars? • The Impact of Cell Phones on Motor Vehicle Fatalities (*Implied question: What is the impact of . . . ?*)
State or imply, often in abbreviated form, your essay's thesis. (*Old information* is your audience's interest in the key words and concepts in your title; *new information* is your abbreviated thesis.)	• Reward Work, Not Wealth • How Foreign Aid Can Foster Democratization in Authoritarian Regimes (*Implied thesis: Foreign aid can foster democratization . . .*)
Use a two-part title separated by a colon: • On the left, arouse interest with a "mystery phrase" or key words from your essay's issue or problem. • On the right, forecast your thesis or purpose. (*Old information* is something in the mystery phrase or in key words on either side of the colon; *new information* is your thesis preview; mystery phrase serves as an attention-grabber.)	• Engaging Young Adults to Meet America's Challenges: A Proposal for Mandatory National Service • The Green Scam: How Volkswagen Bilked Eco-Conscious Consumers with Its Advertising for Diesel Cars

Composing a title for your essay can help you find your focus when you get bogged down in the middle of a draft. Thinking about your title forces you to *nutshell* your ideas by seeing your project's big picture. It causes you to reconsider your purpose and to think about what's old and what's new for your audience.

Writing Good Closed-Form Introductions

In Concept 2.3 we explained that in closed-form prose a writer's thesis statement is a tentative, contestable, and surprising answer to a question or problem that the writer shares with the reader. Before readers can understand or appreciate a writer's thesis, they must first know the problem or question that the thesis addresses. Typically a writer's thesis statement comes at the *end* of the introduction. What precedes the thesis is the writer's explanation of the problem that she is addressing or the conversation that she is joining. This problem-before-thesis structure is simply another example of placing old information before new information.

It follows, then, that a primary function of most closed-form introductions is to present the problem that you are addressing and to motivate your readers' interest in it. (If they aren't interested, they'll stop reading.) The length and complexity of the introduction depend on how much your readers already know and care about your problem. The less they know or care, the more your introduction needs to provide background and answer the "so what?" question that motivates caring. Once readers are on board with you about the problem being addressed and about why the problem matters, they are prepared for your thesis statement.

Just as effective titles present something old and something new, so do dynamic and powerful introductions. Old information is something your readers already know and find interesting before they start reading your essay. New information is the surprise of your argument, the unfamiliar material that you add to your readers' understanding.

Because the writer's thesis statement forecasts the new information that the paper will present, a thesis statement for a closed-form essay typically comes *at the end of the introduction.* What precedes the thesis is typically the problem or question that the thesis addresses—the old information that the reader needs in order to understand the conversation that the thesis joins. A typical closed-form introduction has the following shape:

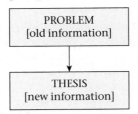

The function of an introduction is to capture the reader's interest in the first few sentences, to identify and explain the question or problem that the essay addresses, to provide any needed background information, and to present the thesis. You can leave out any of the first three elements if the reader is already hooked on your topic and already knows the question you are addressing. For example, in an essay exam you can usually start with your thesis statement because you can assume the instructor already knows the question and finds it interesting.

A TYPICAL CLOSED-FORM INTRODUCTION   In the following example of a closed-form introduction, note how the student writer begins with an attention-grabber to motivate the reader's interest (often not needed for academic subjects), identifies the problem to be addressed, and then states his thesis and provides a brief map of the parts.

PAINTBALL: PROMOTER OF VIOLENCE OR HEALTHY FUN?	Title forecasts controversy about value of paintball
Glancing out from behind some cover, I see an enemy soldier on the move. I level my gun and start pinching off rounds. Hearing the incoming fire, he turns and starts to fire, but it is far too late. His entire body flinches when I land two torso shots, and he falls when I hit his leg. I duck back satisfied with another good kill on my record. I pop up again, this time to see two soldiers peeking out from behind a sewer pipe. I move to take cover again, but it's futile. I'm hit. It's all over—for me at least. The paintball battle rages on as I carefully leave the field to nurse my welts, which are already showing. Luckily, I watch my three remaining teammates trample the two enemy soldiers who shot me to win the game. This is paintball in all its splendor and glory.	Attention-grabber (arouses reader interest in paintball. Such hooks are rare in scholarly writing)
Paintball is one of the most misunderstood and generally looked down upon recreational activities. People see it as rewarding violence and lacking the true characteristics of a healthy team sport like ultimate Frisbee, soccer, or pickup basketball. But these accusations against paintball are false.	Sets up problem by showing opposing view
Paintball is a fun, athletic, mentally challenging recreational activity that builds teamwork and releases tension.	Thesis statement that also forecasts main points of the argument.

TYPICAL ELEMENTS OF A CLOSED-FORM INTRODUCTION   Now that you understand the general principle of closed-form introductions, let's look more closely at its four typical features or elements:

1. *An opening attention-grabber.*   If you aren't sure that your reader is already interested in your problem, you can begin with an attention-grabber (what journalists call the *hook* or *lead*), which is typically a dramatic vignette, a startling fact or statistic, an arresting quotation, an interesting scene, or something else that taps into your reader's interests. Attention-grabbers are uncommon in academic prose (where you assume your reader will be initially engaged by the problem itself) but frequently used in popular prose.

2. *Explanation of the question to be investigated.*   If your reader already knows about the problem and cares about it, then you need only to summarize it. This problem or question is the starting point of your argument. If you aren't sure whether your audience fully understands the question or fully cares about it, then you need to explain it in more detail, showing why it is both problematic and significant.

3. *Background information, if needed.*   In order to understand the conversation you are joining, readers sometimes need background information such as a definition of key terms, a summary of events leading up to the problem,

factual details needed for explaining the context of the problem, and so forth. In academic papers, this background often includes a review of what other scholars have said about the problem.

4. *Writer's thesis, often accompanied with a blueprint statement or map.* The writer's thesis previews the kind of surprise or challenge that readers can expect in the essay. Because it sketches the big picture, this preview is initially new information (this is why it comes at the end of the introduction). Once stated, however, it becomes old information that readers will use to create a map for their journey through your argument.

To see the choice that Ansen actually made, see his paper in Chapter 16.

STRATEGIES FOR SKETCHING THE BIG PICTURE   The most succinct way to sketch the big picture is to state your thesis directly. But there are many options. Student writers often ask how detailed their thesis statements should be and whether it is permissible, sometimes, to delay revealing the thesis until the conclusion—an open-form move that gives papers a more exploratory, mystery-novel feel. It is useful, then, to outline briefly some of your choices as a writer (see Strategies Chart 18.2). To illustrate a writer's options for forecasting the

---

Strategies Chart 18.2 Strategies for Forecasting the Whole Paper

Options	What to Do	Example of What Ansen Could Have Done
Short thesis **(high-level thesis)**	State claim without summarizing your supporting argument or forecasting your structure.	The United States should institute a mandatory year of national service for Americans ages 18 to 25.
Detailed thesis **(low-level thesis)**	Summarize whole argument; may begin with an *although* clause that summarizes the view you are trying to change.	Despite arguments against the value of public service, the United States should institute mandatory public service for young adults because such service would help America's vulnerable communities become healthier and would promote democracy through increased civic engagement.
Purpose statement	State your purpose or intention without summarizing the argument. A purpose statement typically begins with a phrase such as "My purpose is to . . . " or "In the following paragraphs I wish to . . . "	My purpose is to show the benefits to American society of mandatory public service for young adults.
Blueprint or mapping statement	Describe the structure of your essay by announcing the number of main parts and describing the function or purpose of each one.	First I will explain how mandatory public service could be modeled on the present-day success of AmeriCorps. I will then show the benefits of mandatory public service. Finally, I will summarize the arguments against mandatory public service and respond to them.
Combination of elements	Include two or more of these elements. In long essays, academic writers sometimes have a purpose statement followed by a detailed thesis and blueprint statement.	[Kent's essay is not long enough nor complex enough to need an extensive overview that includes a purpose or blueprint statement along with a thesis.]

Options	What to Do	Example of What Ansen Could Have Done
Thesis question only *[Implies an exploratory or delayed thesis paper]*	State the question only, without initially implying your answer. This open-form strategy invites the reader to join the writer in a mutual search.	Although volunteer programs like AmeriCorps have been remarkably successful, I wonder if such programs would still work if people were coerced to participate. Would the benefits of a mandatory program outweigh the risks?

whole, we use Kent Ansen's researched proposal argument on mandatory public service.

Which of these options should a writer choose? There are no firm rules. How much you forecast in the introduction and where you reveal your thesis depend on your purpose, audience, and genre. The more you forecast, the clearer your argument is and the easier it is to read quickly. You minimize the demands on readers' time by giving them the gist of your argument in the introduction, making it easier to skim your essay if they don't have time for a thorough reading. On the other hand, readers sometimes find too much forecasting to be formulaic and boring. So some writers choose to include only what is needed for clarity. For short papers, readers usually don't need to have the complete supporting argument forecast in the introduction. In longer papers, however, or in especially complex papers, readers appreciate having the whole argument forecast at the outset. Academic writing in particular tends to favor explicit and often detailed forecasting.

For Writing and Discussion
Revising a Title and Introduction

Individual task: Choose an essay you are currently working on or have recently completed and examine your title and introduction. To what extent do your title and introduction follow the advice presented in this section? If you think the advice in this section might improve your title and introduction, revise as appropriate.

Group task: Working with a partner or in small groups, share the changes you made in your title or introduction and explain why you made the changes.

Writing Effective Conclusions

Conclusions can best be understood as complements to introductions. In both the introduction and the conclusion, writers are concerned with the essay as a whole more than with any given part. In a conclusion, the writer is particularly concerned with helping the reader move from the parts back to the big picture and understand the essay's importance or significance.

Because many writers find conclusions challenging to write, Strategies Chart 18.3 offers six strategies for ending an essay.

Strategies Chart 18.3 Strategies for Concluding an Essay

Strategies	What to Do	Comments
Simple summary **conclusion**	Recap what you have said.	This approach is useful in a long or complex essay or in an instructional text that focuses on concepts. However, in a short, easy-to-follow essay, a summary conclusion can be dull and even annoying to readers. A brief summary followed by a more artful concluding strategy can sometimes be effective.
Larger significance **conclusion**	Draw the reader's attention to the importance or the applications of your argument.	The conclusion is a good place to elaborate on the significance of your problem by showing how your proposed solution to a question leads to understanding a larger, more significant question or brings practical benefits to individuals or society. If you posed a question about values or about the interpretation of a confusing text or phenomenon, you might show how your argument could be applied to related questions, texts, or phenomena.
Proposal **conclusion**	Call for action.	Often used in analyses and arguments, a *proposal* conclusion states the action that needs to be taken and briefly explains its advantages over alternative actions or describes its beneficial consequences. If your paper analyzes the negative consequences of shifting from a graduated income tax to a flat-rate income tax, your conclusion may recommend an action such as modifying or opposing the flat tax.
	Call for future study.	A *call-for-future-study* conclusion indicates what else needs to be known or resolved before a proposal can be offered. Such conclusions are especially common in scientific writing.
Scenic or *anecdotal* **conclusion**	Use a scene or brief story to illustrate the theme without stating it explicitly.	Often used in popular writing, a scene or anecdote can help the reader experience the topic's emotional significance. For example, a paper favoring public housing for the homeless may end by describing an itinerant homeless person collecting bottles in a park.
Hook and return **conclusion**	Return to something mentioned at the beginning of the essay.	If the essay begins with a vivid illustration of a problem, the conclusion can return to the same scene or story but with some variation to indicate the essay's significance.
Delayed-thesis **conclusion**	State the thesis for the first time at the end of the essay.	This strategy is effective when you are writing about complex or divisive issues and you don't want to take a stand until you have presented all sides. The introduction of the essay merely states the problem, giving the essay an exploratory feel.

For Writing and Discussion
Writing Conclusions

Choose a paper you have written and write an alternative conclusion using one of the strategies discussed in this lesson. Then share your original and revised conclusions in groups. Have group members discuss which one they consider most effective and why.

Skill 18.5: Create effective topic sentences for paragraphs

See also Concept 2.3 on points and details.

18.5 Keep readers on track with effective topic sentences.

In our lesson on outlining (Skill 18.3) we suggested that you write complete sentences for the high-level slots of the outline in order to articulate the *meaning* of each section of your argument. In this lesson we show you how to place these points where readers expect them: near the beginning of the sections or paragraphs they govern.

When you place your point at the beginning of a paragraph, you again follow the principle of old before new. When you first state the point, it is the new information that the current paragraph or section will develop. Once you have stated it, it becomes old information that helps readers understand the meaning of the details that follow. If you withhold the point until later, the reader has to keep all the details in short-term memory until you finally reveal the point that the details are supposed to support.

Revising Paragraphs to Place Topic Sentences at the Beginning

Readers of closed-form prose need to have point sentences (usually called *topic sentences*) at the beginnings of paragraphs. However, writers of rough drafts often don't fulfill this need because, as we explained in Chapter 17, drafting is an exploratory process in which writers are often still searching for their points as they compose. Consequently, in their rough drafts writers often omit topic sentences entirely or place them at the ends of paragraphs, or they write topic sentences that misrepresent what the paragraphs actually say. During revision, then, you should check your body paragraphs carefully to be sure you have placed accurate topic sentences near the beginning.

What follow are examples of the kinds of revisions that writers typically make. We have annotated the examples to explain the changes the writer has made to make the paragraphs unified and clear. The first example is from a revision of the dorm room carpets essay we used in Chapter 17.

REVISION–TOPIC SENTENCE FIRST

Another reason for the university not to buy carpets is the cost.

ᴧAccording to Rachel Jones, Assistant Director of Housing Services, the initial purchase and installation of carpeting would cost $300 per room. Considering the number of rooms in the three residence halls, carpeting amounts to a substantial investment. Additionally, once the carpets are installed, the university would need to maintain them through the purchase of more vacuum cleaners and shampoo machines. This money would be better spent on other dorm improvements that would benefit more residents, such as expanded kitchen facilities and improved recreational space. ~~Thus carpets would be too expensive.~~

Topic sentence placed first

In the original draft, the writer states the point at the end of the paragraph. In his revision he states the point in an opening topic sentence that links back to the thesis statement, which promises "several reasons" that the university should not buy carpets for the dorms. The words "Another reason" thus link the topic sentence to the argument's big picture.

Revising Paragraphs for Unity

In addition to placing topic sentences at the heads of paragraphs, writers often need to revise topic sentences to better match what the paragraph actually says, or revise the paragraph to better match the topic sentence. Paragraphs have unity when all their sentences develop the point stated in the topic sentence. Paragraphs in rough drafts are often not unified because they reflect the writer's shifting, evolving, thinking-while-writing process. Consider the following paragraph from an early draft of an argument against euthanasia by student writer Dao Do. Her peer reviewer labeled it "confusing." What makes it confusing?

EARLY DRAFT–CONFUSING

First, euthanasia is wrong because no one has the right to take the life of another person. Some people say that euthanasia or suicide will end suffering and pain. But what proofs do they have for such a claim? Death is still mysterious to us; therefore, we do not know whether death will end suffering and pain or not. What seems to be the real claim is that death to those with illnesses will end *our* pain. Such pain involves worrying over them, paying their medical bills, and giving up so much of our time. Their deaths end our pain rather than theirs. And for that reason, euthanasia is a selfish act, for the outcome of euthanasia benefits us, the nonsufferers, more. Once the sufferers pass away, we can go back to our normal lives.

The paragraph opens with an apparent topic sentence: "Euthanasia is wrong because no one has the right to take the life of another person." But the rest of the paragraph doesn't focus on that point. Instead, it focuses on how euthanasia benefits the survivors more than the sick person. Dao had two choices: to revise the paragraph to fit the topic sentence or to revise the topic sentence to fit the paragraph. Here is her revision, which includes a different topic sentence and an additional sentence midparagraph to keep particulars focused on the opening point. Dao unifies this paragraph by keeping all its parts focused on her main point: "Euthanasia . . . benefits the survivors more than the sick person."

REVISION FOR UNITY

Revised topic sentence better forecasts focus of paragraph

Keeps focus on "sick person"

Concludes subpoint about sick person

Supports subpoint about how euthanasia benefits survivors

First, euthanasia is wrong because it benefits the survivors more than the sick person.

~~First, euthanasia is wrong because no one has the right to take the life of another person.~~ Some people say that euthanasia or suicide will end suffering *the sick person's* and pain. But what proofs do they have for such a claim? Death is still mysterious to us; therefore, we do not know whether death will end suffering and pain or not. *Moreover, modern painkillers can relieve most of the pain a sick person has to endure.* What seems to be the real claim is that death to those with illnesses will end *our* pain. Such pain involves worrying over them, paying their medical bills, and giving up so much of our time. Their deaths end our pain rather than theirs. And for that reason, euthanasia is a selfish act, for the outcome of euthanasia benefits us, the nonsufferers, more. Once the sufferers pass away, we can go back to our normal lives.

A paragraph may lack unity for a variety of reasons. It may shift to a new direction in the middle, or one or two sentences may simply be irrelevant to the point. The key is to make sure that all the sentences in the paragraph fulfill the reader's expectations based on the topic sentence.

Adding Details to Support Points

Just as writers of rough drafts often omit point sentences that give meaning to details, they also sometimes leave out the details needed to support a point. In such cases, the writer needs to add details such as facts, statistics, quotations, research summaries, examples, or further subpoints. Consider how adding particulars to the following draft paragraph strengthens a student writer's argument opposing the logging of old-growth forests.

DRAFT PARAGRAPH: DETAILS MISSING

One reason that it is not necessary to log old-growth forests is that the timber industry can supply the world's lumber needs without doing so. For example, we have plenty of new-growth forest from which timber can be taken (Sagoff 89). We could also reduce the number of trees used for paper products by using other materials besides wood for paper pulp. In light of the fact that we have plenty of trees and ways of reducing our wood demands, there is no need to harvest old-growth forests.

REVISED PARAGRAPH: DETAILS ADDED

One reason that it is not necessary to log old-growth forests is that the timber industry can supply the world's lumber needs without doing so. For example, we have plenty of new-growth forest from which timber can be taken as a result of major reforestation efforts all over the United States (Sagoff 89). In the Northwest, for instance, Oregon law requires every acre of timber harvested to be replanted. According to Robert Sedjo, a forestry expert, the world's demand for industrial wood could be met by a widely implemented tree farming system (qtd. in Sagoff 90). We could also reduce the number of trees used for paper products by using a promising new innovation called Kenaf, a fast-growing annual herb that is fifteen feet tall and is native to Africa. It has been used for making rope for many years, but recently it was found to work just as well for paper pulp. In light of the fact that we have plenty of trees and ways of reducing our wood demands, there is no need to harvest old-growth forests.

Added details support subpoint that we have plenty of new-growth forest

Added details support second subpoint that wood alternatives are available

For Writing and Discussion
Revising Paragraphs for Points-First Structure

Individual task: Bring to class a draft-in-progress for a closed-form essay. Pick out several paragraphs in the body of your essay and analyze them for "points-first" structure. For each paragraph, ask the following questions:

- Does my paragraph have a topic sentence near the beginning?
- If so, does my topic sentence accurately forecast what the paragraph says?
- Does my topic sentence link to my thesis statement or to a higher-order point that my paragraph develops?
- Does my paragraph have enough details to develop and support my topic sentence?

(continued)

Group task: Then exchange your draft with a partner and do a similar analysis of your partner's selected paragraphs. Discuss your analyses of each other's paragraphs and then help each other plan appropriate revision strategies. If time permits, revise your paragraphs and show your results to your partner. [Note: Sometimes you can revise simply by adding a topic sentence to a paragraph, rewording a topic sentence, or making other kinds of local revisions. At other times, you may need to cross out whole paragraphs and start over, rewriting from scratch after you rethink your ideas.]

Skill 18.6: Guide your reader with transitions and other signposts

18.6 Guide readers with transitions and other signposts.

As we have explained, when readers read closed-form prose, they expect each new sentence, paragraph, and section to link clearly to what they have already read. They need a well-marked trail with signposts signaling turns along the way. They also need resting spots at major junctions where they can review where they've been and survey what's coming. In this lesson, we show you how transition words and phrases as well as summary and forecasting passages can keep your readers securely on the trail.

Using Common Transition Words to Signal Relationships

Transitions are like signposts that signal where the road is turning and limit the possible directions that an unfolding argument might take. Consider how the use of "therefore" and "nevertheless" limits the range of possibilities in the following examples:

> While on vacation, Suzie caught the chicken pox. Therefore, _____.
>
> While on vacation, Suzie caught the chicken pox. Nevertheless, _____.

"Therefore" signals to the reader that what follows is a consequence. Most readers will imagine a sentence something like this:

> Therefore, she spent her vacation lying in bed itchy, feverish, and miserable.

In contrast, "nevertheless" signals an unexpected or denied consequence, so the reader might anticipate a sentence such as this:

> Nevertheless, she enjoyed her two weeks off, thanks to a couple of bottles of calamine lotion, some good books, and a big easy chair overlooking the ocean.

Table 18.1 provides a list of the most common transition words and phrases and what they signal to the reader.*

---

*Although all the words on the list serve as transitions or connectives, grammatically they are not all equivalent, nor are they all punctuated the same way.

Table 18.1 Common Transition Words and Phrases

Words or Phrases	What They Signal
first, second, third, next, finally, earlier, later, meanwhile, afterward	*sequence*—First we went to dinner; then we went to the movies.
that is, in other words, to put it another way, — (dash), : (colon)	*restatement*—He's so hypocritical that you can't trust a word he says. To put it another way, he's a complete phony.
rather, instead	*replacement*—We shouldn't use the money to buy opera tickets; rather, we should use it for a nice gift.
for example, for instance, a case in point	*example*—Mr. Carlyle is very generous. For example, he gave the janitors a special holiday gift.
because, since, for	*reason*—Taxes on cigarettes are unfair because they place a higher tax burden on the working class.
therefore, hence, so, consequently, thus, then, as a result, accordingly, as a consequence	*consequence*—I failed to turn in the essay; therefore I flunked the course.
still, nevertheless	*denied consequence*—The teacher always seemed grumpy in class; nevertheless, I really enjoyed the course.
although, even though, granted that (*with* still)	*concession*—Even though the teacher was always grumpy, I still enjoyed the course.
in comparison, likewise, similarly	*similarity*—Teaching engineering takes a lot of patience. Likewise, so does teaching accounting.
however, in contrast, conversely, on the other hand, but	*contrast*—I disliked my old backpack immensely; however, I really like this new one.
in addition, also, too, moreover, furthermore	*addition*—Today's cars are much safer than those of ten years ago. In addition, they get better gas mileage.
in brief, in sum, in conclusion, finally, to sum up, to conclude	*conclusion or summary*—In sum, the plan presented by Mary is the best choice.

For Writing and Discussion
Using Transitions

This exercise is designed to show you how transition words and phrases govern relationships between ideas. Working in groups or on your own, finish each of the following statements using ideas of your own invention. Make sure what you add fits the logic of the transition word.

1. Writing is difficult; therefore _____.
2. Writing is difficult; however, _____.
3. Writing is difficult because _____.
4. Writing is difficult. For example, _____.
5. Writing is difficult. To put it another way, _____.
6. Writing is difficult. Likewise, _____.
7. Although writing is difficult, _____.

In the following paragraph, various kinds of linking devices have been omitted. Fill in the blanks with words or phrases that would make the paragraph coherent. Clues are provided in brackets.

(continued)

Writing an essay is a difficult process for most people. _____ [contrast] the process can be made easier if you learn to practice three simple techniques. _____ [sequence] learn the technique of nonstop writing. When you are first trying to think of ideas for an essay, put your pen to your paper and write nonstop for ten or fifteen minutes without letting your pen leave the paper. Stay loose and free. Let your pen follow the waves of thought. Don't worry about grammar or spelling. _____ [concession] this technique won't work for everyone, it helps many people get a good cache of ideas to draw on. A _____ [sequence] technique is to write your rough draft rapidly without worrying about being perfect. Too many writers try to get their drafts right the first time. _____ [contrast] by learning to live with imperfection, you will save yourself headaches and a wastepaper basket full of crumpled paper. Think of your first rough draft as a path hacked out of the jungle—as part of an exploration, not as a completed highway. As a _____ [sequence] technique, try printing out a triple-spaced copy to allow space for revision. Many beginning writers don't leave enough space to revise. _____ [consequence] these writers never get in the habit of crossing out chunks of their rough draft and writing revisions in the blank spaces. After you have revised your rough draft until it is too messy to work from anymore, you can _____ [sequence] enter your changes into your word processor and print out a fresh draft, again setting your text on triple-space. The resulting blank space invites you to revise.

Writing Major Transitions between Parts

In long closed-form pieces, writers often put *resting places* between major parts—transitional passages that allow readers to shift their attention momentarily away from the matter at hand to get a sense of where they've been and where they're going. Often such passages sum up the preceding major section, refer back to the essay's thesis statement or opening blueprint plan, and then preview the next major section. Here are three typical examples:

So far I have looked at a number of techniques that can help people identify debilitating assumptions that block their self-growth. In the next section, I examine ways to question and overcome these assumptions.

Now that the difficulty of the problem is fully apparent, our next step is to examine some of the solutions that have been proposed.

These, then, are the major theories explaining why Hamlet delays. But let's see what happens to Hamlet if we ask the question in a slightly different way. In this next section, we shift our critical focus, looking not at Hamlet's actions, but at his language.

Signaling Major Transitions with Headings

In many genres, particularly scientific and technical reports, government documents, business proposals, textbooks, and long articles in magazines or scholarly journals, writers conventionally break up long stretches of text with headings and subheadings. Headings are often set in different type sizes and fonts, and they mark transition points between major parts and subparts of the argument.

Skill 18.7: Make sentences cohere by following the old/new contract

18.7 Make sentences cohere by following the old/new contract.

The previous skill focused on marking the reader's trail with transitions. This new skill, "Make sentences cohere by following the old/new contract," will enable you to build a trail of sentences without potholes or washed-out bridges.

The Old/New Contract in Sentences

When writing consecutive sentences in a paragraph, conserve "reader energy" by following the principle we introduced in Skill 18.1—the "old/new contract." Simply put, the old/new contract asks writers to begin sentences with words that link back to something old. The new information that advances the argument comes later in the sentence.

To understand the old/new contract more fully, try the following thought exercise. We'll show you two passages, both of which explain the old/new contract. One of them follows the principle it describes; the other violates it.

THOUGHT EXERCISE

Which of these passages follows the old/new contract?

VERSION 1

The old/new contract is another principle for writing clear closed-form prose. Beginning your sentences with something old—something that links to what has gone before—and then ending your sentences with new information that advances the argument is what the old/new contract asks writers to do. An effect called *coherence*, which is closely related to *unity*, is created by following this principle. Whereas the clear relationship between the topic sentence and the body of the paragraph is what *unity* refers to, the clear relationship between one sentence and the next is what *coherence* relates to.

VERSION 2

Another principle for writing clear closed-form prose is the old/new contract. The old/new contract asks writers to begin sentences with something old—something that links to what has gone before—and then to end sentences with new information that advances the argument. Following this principle creates an effect called *coherence*, which is closely related to unity. Whereas *unity* refers to the clear relationship between the body of a paragraph and its topic sentence, *coherence* refers to the clear relationship between one sentence and the next.

If you are like most readers, you have to concentrate much harder to understand Version 1 than Version 2 because Version 1 violates the old-before-new way that our minds normally process information. When a writer doesn't begin a sentence with old material, readers have to hold the new material in suspension until they have figured out how it connects to what has gone before. They can stay on the trail, but they have to keep jumping over the potholes between sentences.

To follow the old/new contract, place old information near the beginning of sentences in what we call the **topic position** and place new information that advances the argument in the predicate or **stress position** at the end of the sentence. We associate topics with the beginnings of sentences simply because in the standard English sentence, the topic (or subject) comes before the predicate—hence the notion of a "contract" by which we agree not to fool or frustrate our readers by breaking with the "normal" order of things. The contract says that the old, backward-linking material comes at the beginning of the sentence and that the new, argument-advancing material comes at the end.

For Writing and Discussion
Practicing the Old/New Contract

Here are two more passages, one that obeys the old/new contract and one that violates it. Working in small groups or as a whole class, reach consensus on which of these passages follows the old/new contract. Explain your reasoning by showing how the beginning of each sentence links to something old.

PASSAGE A

Play is an often-overlooked dimension of fathering. From the time a child is born until its adolescence, fathers emphasize caretaking less than play. Egalitarian feminists may be troubled by this, and spending more time in caretaking may be wise for fathers. There seems to be unusual significance in the father's style of play. Physical excitement and stimulation are likely to be part of it. With older children, more physical games and teamwork that require the competitive testing of physical and mental skills are also what it involves. Resemblance to an apprenticeship or teaching relationship is also a characteristic of fathers' play: Come on, let me show you how.

PASSAGE B

An often-overlooked dimension of fathering is play. From their children's birth through adolescence, fathers tend to emphasize play more than caretaking. This emphasis may be troubling to egalitarian feminists, and it would indeed be wise for most fathers to spend more time in caretaking. Yet the fathers' style of play seems to have unusual significance. It is likely to be both physically stimulating and exciting. With older children it involves more physical games and teamwork that require the competitive testing of physical and mental skills. It frequently resembles an apprenticeship or teaching relationship: Come on, let me show you how.

How to Make Links to the "Old"

To understand how to link to old information, you need to understand more fully what we mean by "old." In the context of sentence-level coherence, we mean everything in the text that the reader has read so far. Any upcoming sentence is new information, but once the reader has read it, it becomes old information. For example, when a reader is halfway through a text, everything previously read—the title, the introduction, half the body—is old information to which you can link to meet your readers' expectations for unity and coherence.

In making these backward links, writers have three targets:

1. They can link to a key word or concept in the immediately preceding sentence (creating coherence).

2. They can link to a key word or concept in a preceding point sentence (creating unity).

3. They can link to a preceding forecasting statement about structure (helping readers map their location in the text).

Writers have a number of textual strategies for making these links. In Figure 18.3 our annotations show how a professional writer links to old information within the first five or six words of each sentence. Strategies Chart 18.4 is a compendium of these strategies.

Figure 18.3 How a Professional Writer Follows the Old/New Contract

Recent research has given us much deeper—and more surprising—insights into the father's role in childrearing. It shows that in almost all of their interactions with children, fathers do things a little differently from mothers. What fathers do—their special parenting style—is not only highly complementary to what mothers do but is by all indications important in its own right.

For example, an often-overlooked dimension of fathering is play. From their children's birth through adolescence, fathers tend to emphasize play more than caretaking. This emphasis may be troubling to egalitarian feminists, and it would indeed be wise for most fathers to spend more time in caretaking.

Yet the fathers' style of play seems to have unusual significance. It is likely to be both physically stimulating and exciting. With older children it involves more physical games and teamwork that require the competitive testing of physical and mental skills. It frequently resembles an apprenticeship or teaching relationship: Come on, let me show you how.

Annotations (left):
- Refers to "fathers" in previous sentence
- Transition tells us new paragraph will be an example of previous concept
- Refers to "fathers"
- New information that becomes topic of this paragraph
- Repeats words "father" and "play" from the topic sentence of the preceding paragraph

Annotations (right):
- Refers to "research" in previous sentence
- Rephrases idea of "childrearing"
- Repeats "fathers" from previous sentence
- Rephrases concept in previous paragraph
- "points back to "emphasizes" in previous sentence."
- "It" refers to fathers' style of play

Strategies Chart 18.4 Strategies for Linking to the "Old"

What to Do	Example Shown in Figure 18.3
Repeat a key word from the preceding sentence or an earlier point sentence.	Note the number of sentences that open with "father," "father's," or "fathering." Note also the frequent repetitions of "play."
Use a pronoun to substitute for a key word.	In our example, the second sentence opens with the pronouns "It," referring to "research," and "their," referring to "fathers." The last three sentences open with the pronoun "It," referring to "father's style of play."
Summarize, rephrase, or restate earlier concepts.	In the second sentence, "interactions with children" restates the concept of childrearing. Similarly, the phrase "an often-overlooked dimension" sums up a concept implied in the preceding paragraph—that recent research reveals something significant and not widely known about a father's role in childrearing

(continued)

What to Do	Example Shown in Figure 18.3
Use a transition word such as *first* . . . , *second* . . . , *third* . . . , or *therefore* or *however* to cue the reader about the logical relationship between an upcoming sentence and the preceding ones.	Note how the second paragraph opens with "For example," indicating that the upcoming paragraph will illustrate the concept identified in the preceding paragraph.

These strategies give you a powerful way to check and revise your prose. Comb your drafts for gaps between sentences where you have violated the old/new contract. If the opening of a new sentence doesn't refer back to an earlier word, phrase, or concept, your readers could derail, so use what you have learned to repair the tracks.

Avoiding Ambiguous Use of "This" to Fulfill the Old/New Contract

Some writers try to fulfill the old/new contract by frequent use of the pronoun *this* to sum up a preceding concept. Occasionally such usage is acceptable or even effective. However, frequent use of *this* as a pronoun creates lazy and often ambiguous prose. Consider how our example passage might read if many of the explicit links were replaced by *this*:

LAZY USE OF *THIS* AS PRONOUN

Recent research has given us much deeper—and more surprising—insights into **this**. It shows that in doing **this**, fathers do things a little differently from mothers. **This** is not only highly complementary to what mothers do but is by all indications important in its own right.

For example, an often-overlooked dimension of **this** is play.

Perhaps this passage helps you see why we refer to *this* (used by itself as a pronoun) as "the lazy writer's all-purpose noun-slot filler."*

For Writing and Discussion
Applying the Old/New Contract to Your Own Draft

Individual task: Bring to class a draft-in-progress for a closed-form essay. On a selected page, examine the opening of each sentence. Place a vertical slash in front of any sentence that doesn't contain near the beginning some backward-looking element that links to old, familiar material. Then revise these sentences to follow the old/new contract.

Group task: Working with a partner, share the changes you each made on your drafts. Then on each other's pages, work together to identify the kinds of links made at the beginning of each sentence. (For example, does the opening of a sentence repeat a key word, use a pronoun to substitute for a key word, rephrase or restate an earlier concept, or use a transition word?)

---

*It's acceptable to use *this* as an adjective, as in "this usage"; we refer here only to *this* used by itself as a pronoun.

Skill 18.8: Learn four expert moves for organizing and developing ideas

18.8 Learn four expert moves for organizing and developing ideas: the *for example* move, the *summary/however* move, the *division-into-parallel-parts* move, and the *comparison/contrast* move.

Writers of closed-form prose often employ a conventional set of moves to organize parts of an essay. In using the term *moves*, we are making an analogy with the "set moves" or "set plays" in such sports as basketball, volleyball, and soccer. For example, a common set move in basketball is the "pick," in which an offensive player without the ball stands motionless in order to block the path of a defensive player who is guarding the dribbler. Similarly, certain organizational patterns in writing occur frequently enough to act as set plays for writers. These patterns set up expectations in the reader's mind about the shape of an upcoming stretch of prose, anything from a few sentences to a paragraph to a large block of paragraphs. As you will see, these moves also stimulate the invention of ideas. Next, we describe four of the most powerful set plays.*

The *For Example* Move

Perhaps the most common set play occurs when a writer makes an assertion and then illustrates it with one or more examples, often signaling the move explicitly with transitions such as *for example, for instance*, or *a case in point is.* . . . Here is how student writer Dao Do used the *for example* move to support her third reason for opposing euthanasia:

FOR EXAMPLE MOVE

My third objection to euthanasia is that it fails to see the value in suffering. Suffering is a part of life. We see the value of suffering only if we look deeply within our suffering. For example, I never thought my crippled uncle from Vietnam was a blessing to my grandmother until I talked to her. My mother's little brother was born prematurely. As a result of oxygen and nutrition deficiency, he was born crippled. His tiny arms and legs were twisted around his body, preventing him from any normal movements such as walking, picking up things, and lying down. He could only sit. Therefore, his world was very limited, for it consisted of his own room and the garden viewed through his window. Because of his disabilities, my grandmother had to wash him, feed him, and watch him constantly. It was hard, but she managed to care for him for forty-three years. He passed away after the death of my grandfather in 1982. Bringing this situation out of Vietnam and into Western society shows the difference between Vietnamese and Western views. In the West, my uncle might have been euthanized as a baby. Supporters of euthanasia would have said he wouldn't have any quality of life and that he would have

← Topic sentence

Transition signaling the move

Extended example supporting point

---

*You might find it helpful to follow the set plays we used to write this section. This last sentence is the opening move of a play we call "division into parallel parts." It sets up the expectation that we will develop four set plays in order. Watch for the way we chunk them and signal transitions between them.

been a great burden. But he was not a burden on my grandmother. She enjoyed taking care of him, and he was always her company after her other children got married and moved away. Neither one of them saw his defect as meaningless suffering because it brought them closer together.

This passage uses a single, extended example to support a point. You could also use several shorter examples or other kinds of illustrating evidence such as facts or statistics. In all cases the *for example* move creates a pattern of expectation and fulfillment. This pattern drives the invention of ideas in one of two ways: It urges the writer either to find examples to develop a generalization or to formulate a generalization that shows the point of an example.

For Writing and Discussion
Practicing the *For Example* Move

Working individually or in groups, develop a plan for supporting one or more of the following generalizations using the *for example* move:

1. Another objection to state sales taxes is that they are so annoying.
2. Although text messages are usually a good way to communicate with friends, sometimes they can cause you embarrassment.
3. Sometimes effective leaders are indecisive.

The *Summary/However* Move

The *summary/however* move occurs whenever a writer sums up another person's viewpoint in order to qualify or contradict it or to introduce an opposing view. Typically, writers use transition words such as *but, however, in contrast*, or *on the other hand* between the parts of this move. This move is particularly common in academic writing, which often contrasts the writer's new view with prevailing views. Here is how Dao uses a *summary/however* move in the introduction of her essay opposing euthanasia:

SUMMARY/HOWEVER MOVE

Issue over which there is disagreement

Summary of opposing viewpoint

Transition to writer's viewpoint

Statement of writer's view

Should euthanasia be legalized? My classmate Martha and her family think it should be. Martha's aunt was blind from diabetes. For three years she was constantly in and out of the hospital, but then her kidneys shut down and she became a victim of life support. After three months of suffering, she finally gave up. Martha believes this three-month period was unnecessary, for her aunt didn't have to go through all that suffering. If euthanasia were legalized, her family would have put her to sleep the minute her condition worsened. Then, she wouldn't have had to feel pain, and she would have died in peace and with dignity. However, despite Martha's strong argument for legalizing euthanasia, I find it wrong.

The first sentence of this introduction poses the question that the essay addresses. The main body of the paragraph summarizes Martha's opposing view on euthanasia, and the final sentence, introduced by the transition "However," presents Dao's thesis.

For Writing and Discussion
Practicing the *Summary/However* Move

For this exercise, assume that you favor development of wind-generated electricity. Use the *summary/however* move to acknowledge the view of civil engineer David Rockwood, whose letter opposing wind-generated electricity you read in Concept 3.1. Assume that you are writing the opening paragraph of your own essay. Follow the pattern of Dao's introduction: (a) begin with a one-sentence issue or question; (b) summarize Rockwood's view in approximately one hundred words; and (c) state your own view, using *however* or *in contrast* as a transition. Write out your paragraph on your own, or work in groups to write a consensus paragraph. Then share and critique your paragraphs.

The *Division-into-Parallel-Parts* Move

Among the most frequently encountered and powerful of the set plays is the *division-into-parallel-parts* move. To initiate the move, a writer begins with an umbrella sentence that forecasts the structure and creates a framework. ("Freud's theory differs from Jung's in three essential ways" or "The decline of the U.S. space program can be attributed to several factors.") Typical overview sentences either specify the number of parts that follow by using phrases such as "two ways," "three differences," or "five kinds," or they leave the number unspecified, using words such as *several, a few,* or *many.* Alternatively, the writer may ask a rhetorical question that implies the framework: "What are some main differences, then, between Freud's theory and Jung's? One difference is. . . . "

To signal transitions from one part to the next, writers use two kinds of signposts in tandem. The first is a series of transition words or bullets to introduce each of the parallel parts. Here are typical series of transition words and phrases:

First . . . Second . . . Third . . . Finally . . .

First . . . Another . . . Still another . . . Finally . . .

One . . . In addition . . . Furthermore . . . Also . . .

The second kind of signpost, usually used in conjunction with transitions, is an echolike repetition of the same grammatical structure to begin each parallel part.

> I learned several things from this course. First, *I learned that* [development]. Second, *I learned that* [development]. Finally, *I learned that* [development].

The *division-into-parallel-parts* move can be used within a single paragraph, or it can control larger stretches of text in which a dozen or more paragraphs may work together to complete a parallel series of parts. (For example, you are currently in the third part of a parallel series introduced earlier by the mapping sentence "Next, we describe four of the most powerful set plays.") Here is an example of a student paragraph organized by the *division-into-parallel-parts* move.

DIVISION-INTO-PARALLEL-PARTS MOVE

Mapping statement forecasts "move"

Transition to first parallel part

Transition to second parallel part

Transition to third parallel part

Final transition completes "move"

In this paper I will argue that political solutions to homelessness must take into account four categories of homeless people. A first category is persons who are out of work and seek new jobs. Persons in this category may have been recently laid off, unable to meet their rental payments, and forced temporarily to live out of a car or van. They might quickly leave the ranks of the homeless if they can find new jobs. A second category includes the physically disabled or mentally ill. Providing housing addresses only part of their problems since they also need medical care and medication. For many, finding or keeping a job might be impossible. A third category is the street alcoholic or drug addict. These persons need addiction treatment as well as clothing and shelter and will not become productive citizens until they become sober or drug free. The final category includes those who, like the old railroad "hobo," choose homelessness as a way of life.

Instead of transition words, writers can also use bullets followed by indented text:

Use of Bullets to Signal Parallel Parts

The Wolf Recovery Program is rigidly opposed by a vociferous group of ranchers who pose three main objections to increasing wolf populations:

- They perceive wolves as a threat to livestock. [development]
- They fear the wolves will attack humans. [development]
- They believe the government will not compensate ranchers for their loss of profits. [development]

For Writing and Discussion
Practicing the *Division-into-Parallel-Parts* Move

Working individually or in small groups, use the *division-into-parallel-parts* move to create, organize, and develop ideas to support one or more of the following point sentences.

1. To study for an exam effectively, a student should follow these [specify a number] steps.
2. Why do U.S. schoolchildren lag so far behind European and Asian children on standardized tests of mathematics and science? One possible cause is . . . [continue].
3. Constant dieting is unhealthy for several reasons.

The *Comparison/Contrast* Move

A common variation on the *division-into-parallel-parts* move is the *comparison/contrast* move. To compare or contrast two items, you must first decide on the points of comparison (or contrast). If you are contrasting the political views of two presidential candidates, you might choose to focus on four points of comparison: differences in their foreign policy, differences in economic policy, differences in social policy, and differences in judicial philosophy. You then have two choices for organizing the parts: the *side-by-side pattern,* in which you discuss all of candidate A's views and then all of candidate B's views; or the *back-and-forth pattern,* in which you discuss foreign policy, contrasting A's views with

Figure 18.4 Two Ways to Structure a Comparison or Contrast

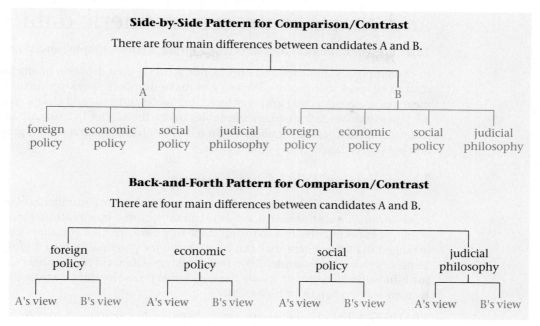

There are no cut-and-dried rules that dictate when to use the side-by-side pattern or the back-and-forth pattern. However, for lengthy comparisons, the *back-and-forth pattern* is often more effective because the reader doesn't have to store great amounts of information in memory. The *side-by-side pattern* requires readers to remember all the material about A when they get to B, and it is some-times difficult to keep all the points of comparison clearly in mind.

For Writing and Discussion
Practicing the *Comparison/Contrast* Move

Working individually or in groups, create tree diagrams for stretches of text based on one or more of the following point sentences, all of which call for the *comparison/contrast* move. Make at least one diagram follow the *back-and-forth pattern* and at least one diagram follow the *side-by-side pattern.*

1. To understand U.S. politics, an outsider needs to appreciate some basic differences between Republicans and Democrats.

2. Although they are obviously different on the surface, there are many similarities between the Boy Scouts and a street gang.

3. There are several important differences between a mountain bike and a road bike.

Skill 18.9: Use effective tables, graphs, and charts to present numeric data

18.9 Present numerical data effectively through tables, graphs, and charts.

In contemporary analyses and arguments, writers often draw on quantitative data to support their points. Writers can make numbers speak powerfully by means of reader-effective graphics including tables, graphs, and charts. Generally, quantitative data displayed in tables invite the reader to tease out many different stories that the numbers might tell. In contrast, line graphs, bar graphs, and pie charts focus vividly on one story.

How Tables Tell Many Stories

Data displayed in tables usually have their origins in raw numbers collected from surveys, questionnaires, organizational records, observational studies, scientific experiments, and so forth. These numbers are then consolidated and arranged in tables where they can be analyzed for potentially meaningful patterns. Consider, for example, Table 18.2, based on data from the National Center for Education Statistics. It shows the number of postsecondary degrees earned by men and women from 1970 to 2017.

READING A TABLE Tables are read in two directions: from top to bottom and from left to right. To read a table efficiently, begin with the title, *which always includes elements from both the vertical and horizontal dimensions of the table.* Note how this rule applies to Table 18.2.

- The table's horizontal dimension is indicated in the first part of the title: "Earned Degrees Conferred by Level and Sex." Reading horizontally, we see the names of the degrees (Bachelor's, Master's, First-professional, and Doctor's) with subcategories indicating total, males, and females.

- The table's vertical dimension is indicated in the second part of the title: "1970-2017." Reading vertically, we see the years between 1970 and 2017, many of which were selected in five-year intervals.

We are now prepared to read specific information from the table. In 1995-96, for example, 522,000 men and 642,000 women earned bachelor's degrees in colleges and universities in the United States. In that same year, 27,000 men and 18,000 women earned doctor's degrees.

DISCOVERING STORIES IN THE DATA When you peruse the table carefully, you will see interesting patterns begin to emerge. Among the stories the table tells are these:

- The percent of women receiving bachelor's degrees rose substantially between 1970 and 2017 (with a corresponding fall for men).

- This increased percentage of degrees given to women is more dramatic for bachelor's degrees than it is for doctoral degrees.

As we show in the next section, these two stories, which must be teased out of this table, can be told more dramatically with graphs. These stories are significant because they reflect major cultural changes in American society.

Table 18.2 Earned Degrees by Level and Sex, 1970–2017

[In thousands (477 represents 477,000)]

Year	Bachelor's			Master's			First-professional			Doctor's		
	Total	Males	Females	Total	Males	Females	Total	Males	Females	Total	Males	Females
1970-71	840	476	364	231	138	92	38	36	2	32	28	5
1975-76	926	505	421	312	167	145	63	53	10	34	26	8
1980-81	935	470	465	296	147	149	72	53	19	33	23	10
1985-86	988	486	502	289	144	145	74	49	25	34	22	12
1990-91	1,095	504	590	337	156	181	72	44	28	39	25	15
1995-96	1,165	522	642	406	179	227	77	45	32	45	27	18
2000-01	1,244	532	712	468	194	274	80	43	37	45	25	20
2005-06	1,485	631	855	594	238	356	88	44	44	56	29	27
2010-11	1,649	677	972	667	256	411	94	46	48	57	27	30
2015-16	1,747	704	1,043	753	282	471	103	48	54	65	29	36
2016-17 (projected)	1,764	707	1,057	774	287	487	105	49	56	67	30	37

Data from Degrees conferred by degree-granting institutions, by *level of degree and sex of student: Selected years, 1869—70 through 2016—17,* Table 258. U.S Department of Education, National Center for Education statistics.

Using a Graphic to Tell a Story

Whereas tables can embed many stories and invite detailed examination of the numbers, a graph or chart makes one selected story immediately visible.

LINE GRAPH   A line graph converts numerical data to a series of points on a grid and connects them to create flat, rising, or falling lines. The result gives us a picture of the relationship between the variables represented on the horizontal and vertical axes.

Suppose you wanted to tell the story of the increasing percentage of women receiving bachelor's degrees from 1970 to 2017 and the corresponding decrease in bachelor's degrees received by men. Using Table 18.2 you can calculate these percentages yourself and display them in a line graph as shown in Figure 18.5. To determine what a graph tells you, you need to clarify what's represented on the two axes. By convention, the horizontal axis of a graph contains the predictable, known variable that has no surprises, such as time or some other sequence—in this case, the years 1970 to 2017 in predictable chronological order. The vertical axis contains the unpredictable variable that tells the graph's story—in this case, the percent of degrees conferred on women and men in each year on the graph. The ascending line for women and the descending line for men tell the stories at a glance.

BAR GRAPH   Bar graphs use bars of varying lengths, extending either horizontally or vertically, to contrast two or more quantities. To make the story of women's progress in earning doctoral degrees particularly vivid, you could use a bar graph as shown in Figure 18.6. To read a bar graph, note carefully the title and the axes to see what is compared to what. Bars are typically distinguished from each other by use of different colors, shades, or patterns of cross-hatching. The special power of bar graphs is that they can help you make quick comparisons. Figure 18.6 tells you at a glance that in 1970-71, women received only 12 percent of doctoral degrees, but by 2015-16 they earned 55 percent of doctoral degrees.

PIE CHART   A pie chart, also called a circle graph, depicts the different percentages of a total (the pie) represented by variously sized slices. Suppose you

Figure 18.5 Percentage of Bachelor's Degrees Conferred on Males and Females: 1970–2017

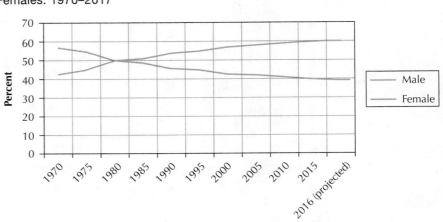

Figure 18.6 Percentage of Doctoral Degrees Conferred on Males and Females, 1970–71 and 2015–16

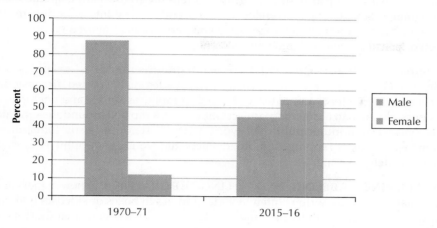

wanted to know the most popular undergraduate majors in American colleges and universities. These statistics, which are available in table format from the National Center for Education Statistics, can be quickly converted into a pie chart as shown in Figure 18.7. As you can see, a pie chart shows at a glance how the whole of something is divided into segments. In 2007, for example, 5 percent of graduating seniors majored in education while 22 percent majored in business. The effectiveness of pie charts diminishes as you add more slices. In most cases, you begin to confuse readers if you include more than five or six slices.

Figure 18.7 Distribution of Bachelor's Degrees by Majors, 2007

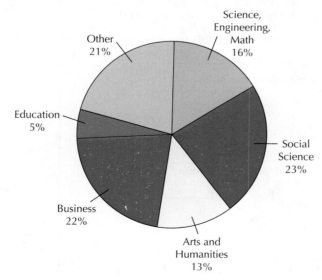

Incorporating a Graphic into Your Essay

Today, most word processing programs, often integrated with a spreadsheet program, easily allow you to create a graphic and insert it into your document. In some cases, your instructor may give you permission to make a graphic with pen or pencil and paste it into your document.

DESIGNING YOUR GRAPHIC   In academic manuscripts, graphics are designed conservatively without bells and whistles such as three-dimensional effects or special fonts and patterns. Keep the graphic as simple and uncluttered as possible. Also in academic manuscripts, do not wrap text around the graphic. In contrast, in popular published work, writers often use flashy fonts, three dimensions, text wrapping, and other effects that would undermine your *ethos* in an academic setting.

NUMBERING, LABELING, AND TITLING THE GRAPHIC   In newspapers and popular magazines, writers often include graphics in boxes or sidebars without specifically referring to them in the text. However, in academic manuscripts or scholarly works, graphics are always labeled, numbered, titled, and referred to in the text. Tables are listed as "Tables," while line graphs, bar graphs, pie charts, or any other kinds of drawings or photographs are labeled as "Figures." By convention, the title for tables goes above the table, while the title for figures goes below.

REFERENCING THE GRAPHIC IN YOUR TEXT   Academic and professional writers follow a referencing convention called *independent redundancy*. The graphic should be understandable without the text; the text should be understandable without the graphic. In other words, the text should tell in words the same story that the graphic displays visually. An example is shown in Figure 18.8.

Figure 18.8 Example of a Student Text with a Referenced Graph

In the decades following the 1960s feminist movement, women have made remarkable progress in higher education. As shown in Figure 1, in 1970-71 men earned 88 percent of all doctor's degrees granted in the United States. But by 2015-16, the number of women receiving doctor's degrees exceeded that of men. In 2017 women received 55 percent of doctor's degrees while men earned only 45 percent. These numbers suggest the substantial impact of the women's movement.

States point
References the graph
Tells same story as the graph

Figure 1: Percentage of Doctoral Degrees Conferred on Males and Females, 1970-71 and 2015-16

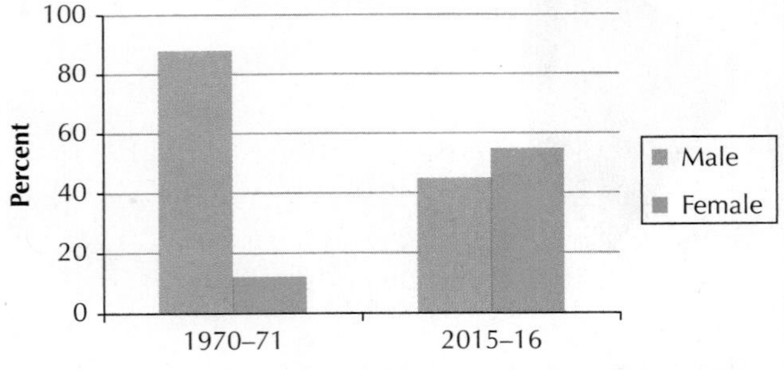

Skill 18.10: Use occasional open-form elements to create "voice" in closed-form prose

18.10 Use occasional open-form elements to achieve "voice" in closed-form prose.

So far we have been talking about tightly organized closed-form prose. Sometimes, however, writers wish to loosen closed-form prose by combining it with some features of open-form prose. If, for example, an academic wanted to share new developments in a field with a popular audience, he or she would be well advised to leaven his or her prose with some elements of open-form writing. For example, writers might use occasional humor or switch from strictly academic language into more popular language with jargon and occasional pop culture references.

Writers who publish regularly for popular audiences develop a vigorous, easy-reading style that differs from the style of much academic writing. The effect of this difference is illustrated by the results of a famous research study conducted by Michael Graves and Wayne Slater at the University of Michigan. For this study, teams of writers revised passages from a high school history textbook.* One team consisted of linguists and technical writers trained in producing closed-form texts using the strategies discussed earlier in this chapter (forecasting structure, putting points first, following the old/new contract, using transitions). A second team consisted of two *Time-Life* book editors.

Whereas the linguists aimed at making the passages clearer, the *Time-Life* writers were more concerned with making them livelier. The result? One hundred eleventh-grade students found the *Time-Life* editors' version both more comprehensible and more memorable. The problem with the original textbook wasn't lack of clarity but rather dryness. According to the researchers, the *Time-Life* editors did not limit themselves to making the passages lucid, well organized, coherent, and easy to read. Their revisions went beyond such matters and were intended to make the texts interesting, exciting, vivid, rich in human drama, and filled with colorful language.

To see how they achieved this effect, let's look at their revision. Here is a passage about the Vietnam War taken from the original history text:

ORIGINAL HISTORY TEXT

The most serious threat to world peace developed in Southeast Asia. Communist guerrillas threatened the independence of the countries carved out of French Indo-China by the Geneva conference of 1954. In South Vietnam, Communist guerrillas (the Viet Cong) were aided by forces from Communist North Vietnam in a struggle to overthrow the American-supported government. . . .

Shortly after the election of 1964, Communist gains prompted President Johnson to alter his policy concerning Vietnam. American military forces in

---

*The study involved three teams, but for purposes of simplification we limit our discussion to two.

Vietnam were increased from about 20,000 men in 1964 to more than 500,000 by 1968. Even so, North Vietnamese troops and supplies continued to pour into South Vietnam.

Here is the *Time-Life* editors' revision:

HISTORY PRESENTED IN POPULAR MAGAZINE STYLE

In the early 1960s the greatest threat to world peace was just a small splotch of color on Kennedy's map, one of the fledgling nations sculpted out of French Indo-China by the Geneva peacemakers of 1954. It was a country so tiny and remote that most Americans had never uttered its name: South Vietnam. . . .

Aided by Communist North Vietnam, the Viet Cong guerrillas were eroding the ground beneath South Vietnam's American-backed government. Village by village, road by road, these jungle-wise rebels were waging a war of ambush and mining: They darted out of tunnels to head off patrols, buried exploding booby traps beneath the mud floors of huts, and hid razor-sharp bamboo sticks in holes. . . .

No sooner had Johnson won the election than Communist gains prompted Johnson to go back on his campaign promise. The number of American soldiers in Vietnam skyrocketed from 20,000 in 1964 to more than 500,000 by 1968. But in spite of GI patrols, leech-infested jungles, swarms of buzzing insects, and flash floods that made men cling to trees to escape being washed away—North Vietnamese troops streamed southward without letup along the Ho Chi Minh Trail.

What can this revision teach you about invigorating closed-form prose? What specifically are the editors doing here?

First, notice that the revision is very low on the ladder of abstraction as explained in Concept 4.3. Instead of abstract words with no appeals to the senses, the revision is alive with sensory words and images ("South Vietnam" becomes a "small splotch of color on Kennedy's map"; "a struggle to overthrow the American-supported government" becomes "[They] buried exploding booby traps beneath the mud floors of huts, and hid razor-sharp bamboo sticks in holes").

Second, notice how much more dramatic the revision is. Actual scenes, including a vision of men clinging to trees to escape being washed away by flash floods, replace a chronological account of the war's general progress. According to the editors, such scenes, or "nuggets"—vivid events that encapsulate complex processes or principles—are the lifeblood of *Time-Life* prose.

Finally, notice how the revision tends to delay critical information for dramatic effect, moving information you would normally expect to find early on into a later position. In the first paragraph, the *Time-Life* writers talk about "the greatest threat to world peace" in the early 1960s for four lines before revealing the identity of that threat—South Vietnam.

For Writing and Discussion
Enlivening Closed-Form Prose with Open-Form Elements

Here is a passage from a student argument opposing women's serving on submarines. Working individually or in small groups, enliven this passage by using some of the techniques of the *Time-Life* writers.

Not only would it be very expensive to refit submarines for women personnel, but having women on submarines would hurt the morale of the sailors. In order for a crew to work effectively, they must have good morale or their discontent begins to show through in their performance. This is especially crucial on submarines, where if any problem occurs, it affects the safety of the whole ship. Women would hurt morale by creating sexual tension. Sexual tension can take many forms. One form is couples' working and living in a close space with all of the crew. When a problem occurs within the relationship, it could affect the morale of those directly involved and in the workplace. This would create an environment that is not conducive to good productivity. Tension would also occur if one of the women became pregnant or if there were complaints of sexual harassment. It would be easier to deal with these problems on a surface ship, but in the small confines of a submarine these problems would cause more trouble.

Chapter 19
Strategies for Writing Open-Form Prose

Learning Objectives

19.1 Make your narrative a story, not an *and then* chronology.

19.2 Evoke images and sensations by writing low on the ladder of abstraction.

19.3 Disrupt your reader's desire for direction and clarity.

19.4 Tap the power of metaphor and other tropes.

19.5 Expand your repertoire of styles.

See Concept 3.1 for a detailed explanation of closed-form versus open-form prose.

Although much of this book focuses on points-first, thesis-governed writing, we all share the desire at times to escape the demands of closed-form prose—to read and produce writing that stimulates the imagination and evokes sensations.

In this chapter, we shift our attention to **open-form prose**, which violates the conventions of closed-form prose to establish a different relationship with readers. Open-form prose is often characterized by its aesthetic or beautiful use of language—that is, language used to please and entertain. Because it is not organized as a sequence of points in support of a thesis, it depends on the specificity of words to create mental pictures and to appeal to readers' senses and emotions. In telling its stories, it uses the literary strategies of plot, characterization, setting, and theme to convey its meanings. It also demands imaginative effort from readers to fill in gaps, make connections, tolerate ambiguity, and apprehend a range of meanings and nuance. For all these reasons, open-form prose is often called *literary nonfiction* or *creative nonfiction*.

Of course, it should be remembered that writing exists on a continuum from closed to open forms and that many features of open-form prose can appear in primarily closed-form texts. In fact, many of the example essays in this book combine elements of both open and closed styles. Although at the extremes of the continuum, closed- and open-form writing are markedly different, the styles can be blended in pleasing combinations.

Our goal in this chapter is to give you some practical lessons on how to write effective open-form prose. But we need to acknowledge at the outset that, whereas closed-form prose is governed by a few widely accepted conventions, open-form prose plays freely with conventions in a variety of ways. Consequently, our discussion of open-form writing seeks more to introduce you to guiding principles than to treat open-form writing exhaustively.

Skill 19.1: Make your narrative a story, not an *and then* chronology

19.1 Make your narrative a story, not an *and then* chronology.

We have said that open-form prose is narrative based and uses the strategies of a story. In this first section we want you to think more deeply about the concept of a story—particularly how a story differs from an *and then* chronology. Both a story and an *and then* chronology depict events happening in time. But there are important differences between them. In the following thought exercise, we'd like you to try your own hand at articulating the differences between a story and an *and then* chronology.

THOUGHT EXERCISE ON *AND THEN* CHRONOLOGY VERSUS STORY

1. Read the student autobiographical narrative "No Cats in America?" by Patrick José at the end of Chapter 7.

2. Then read the following autobiographical narrative entitled "The Stolen Watch," which was submitted by a student as a draft for an assignment on narrative writing.

THE STOLEN WATCH

Last fall and winter I was living in Spokane with my brother, who during this time had a platonic girlfriend come over from Seattle and stay for a weekend. Her name was Karen, and we became interested in each other and I went over to see her at the first of the year. She then invited me to, supposedly, the biggest party of the year, called the Aristocrats' Ball. I said sure and made my way back to Seattle in February. It started out bad on Friday, the day my brother and I left Spokane. We left town an hour late, but what's new. Then my brother had to stop along the way and pick up some parts; we stayed there for an hour trying to find this guy. It all started out bad because we arrived in Seattle and I forgot to call Karen. We were staying at her brother's house and after we brought all our things in, we decided to go to a few bars. Later that night we ran into Karen in one of the bars, and needless to say she was not happy with me. When I got up the next morning I knew I should have stayed in Spokane, because I felt bad vibes. Karen made it over about an hour before the party. By the time we reached the party, which drove me crazy, she wound up with another guy, so her friends and I decided to go to a few bars. The next morning when I was packing, I could not find my watch and decided that someone had to have taken it. We decided that it had to have been the goon that Karen had wound up with the night before, because she was at her brother's house with him before she went home. So how was I going to get my watch back?

We decided the direct and honest approach to the problem would work out the best. We got in contact and confronted him. This turned out to be quite a chore. It turned out that he was visiting some of his family during that weekend and lived in Little Harbor, California. It turned out that Karen knew his half brother and got some information on him, which was not pretty. He had just been released by the army and was trained in a special forces unit, in the field of Martial Arts. He was a trained killer! This information did not help matters at all, but the next bit of information was just as bad if not worse. Believe it or not, he was up on charges of attempted murder and breaking and entering. In a way, it turned out lucky for me, because he was in enough trouble with the police and did not need any more. Karen got in contact with him and threatened him that I would bring him up on charges if he did not return the watch. His mother decided that he was in enough trouble and sent me the watch. I was astounded, it was still working and looked fine. The moral of the story is don't drive 400 miles to see a girl you hardly know, and whatever you do, don't leave your valuables out in the open.

1. How does your experience of reading "No Cats in America?" differ from your experience of reading "The Stolen Watch"? Try to articulate the different ways you reacted to the two pieces while in the process of reading them.

2. Based on the differences between these two pieces, how would you define a "story"? Begin by brainstorming all the ways that the two pieces differ. Then try to identify the essential differences that make one a "story" and the other an *and then* chronology.

Four Criteria for a Story

Now that you have tried to define a story for yourself, we would like to explain our own four criteria for a story: (1) depiction of events through time, (2) connectedness, (3) tension, and (4) resolution. If we combine these criteria into a sentence, it would read like this: A story depicts events that are connected causally or thematically to create a sense of tension that is resolved through action, insight, or understanding. These four criteria occurring together turn a chronology into a story. We will illustrate these criteria by referring to Kris Saknussemm's short autobiographical narrative "Phantom Limb Pain" at the end of Chapter 7.

DEPICTION OF EVENTS THROUGH TIME   The essence of storytelling is the depiction of events through time. Whereas thesis-based writing descends from problem to thesis to supporting reasons and evidence, stories unfold linearly, temporally, from event to event. You may start in the middle of the action and then jump backward and forward, but you always encounter some sequence of events happening in time. This temporal focus creates a sense of "onceness." Things that happen at a point in time happen only once, as the classic fairy-tale opening "Once upon a time" suggests. When you compose and revise a narrative, you want to try to capture the "onceness" of that experience. Saknussemm's essay contains several different depictions of events through time: the summer when he was thirteen lifting weights and trying to become stronger and more athletic than Miller King; the story of King's accident and the narrator's visit to King's house; the narrator's helping the one-armed King climb down from the Cyclone fence.

CONNECTEDNESS   The events of a story must also be connected, not merely spatially or sequentially, but causally or thematically. When discussing "The Stolen Watch" in the previous exercise, you might have asked yourselves, "What does all that stuff about forgetting to call Karen and stopping for parts, and so forth, have to do with the stolen watch? Is this story about the watch or about confronting a potential killer?" If so, you instinctively understood the concept of connectedness. Stories are more than just chronicles of events. Novelist E. M. Forster offered the simplest definition of a story when he rejected "The king dies and then the queen died," but accepted "The king died and then the queen died . . . of grief." The words "of grief" connect the two events to each other in a causal relationship, converting a series of events into a patterned, meaningfully related sequence of events. Likewise, we see that all the details in Saknussemm's essay contribute to the thematic intentions of the story. We hear about the narrator's "wearing ankle weights loaded with sand" (connected to his rivalry with Miller King) but not about other things that might have happened during his 13th summer, such as getting a new bike or going on a vacation. Rather than provide an "and then" narrative about his summer, Saknussemm selects only events connected to the rivalry theme.

TENSION OR CONFLICT   The third criterion for a story—tension or conflict—creates the anticipation and potential significance that keep the reader reading. In whodunit stories, the tension follows from attempts to identify the murderer or to prevent the murderer from doing in yet another victim. In many comic works, the tension is generated by confusion or misunderstanding that drives a wedge between people who would normally be close. Tension always involves contraries, such as those between one belief and another, between opposing values, between the individual and the environment or the social order, between where I am now and where I want to be or used to be. This plot tension in Saknussemm's essay is between himself and his rival Miller King, but the thematic tension is between Saknussemm's "old self" and his "new self."

RESOLUTION, RECOGNITION, OR RETROSPECTIVE INTERPRETATION   The final criterion for a story is the resolution or retrospective interpretation of events. The resolution may be stated explicitly or implied. Fables typically sum up the story's significance with an explicit moral at the end. In contrast, the interpretation of events in poetry is almost always implicit. In "Phantom Limb Pain," Saknussemm states part of the resolution explicitly: Despite losing his arm, Miller remains more of a leader than the narrator; the amputation has "damaged" King but not "diminished" him. But part of the resolution is also implicit. The narrator has moved from an "old self" to a "new self." He has grown in some way by being "freed from bad dreams," by becoming "a little more real." What exactly Saknussemm means is left to the reader to ponder.

The typical direction of a story, from singular event(s) to general conclusion, reverses the usual points-first direction of closed-form essays. Stories force readers to read inductively, gathering information and looking for a pattern that's confirmed or unconfirmed by the story's resolution. This resolution is the point *toward* which readers read. It often drives home the significance of the narrative. Typically, a reader's satisfaction or dissatisfaction with a story hinges on how well the resolution manages to explain or justify the events that precede it. Writers need to ask: How does my resolution grow out of my narrative and fit with the resolution the reader has been forming?

For Writing and Discussion
Identifying Criteria for Story

1. Working as a class or in small groups, return to Patrick José's essay "No Cats in America?" and explain how it qualifies as a story rather than an *and then* chronology. How does it meet all four of the criteria: depiction of events through time, connectedness, tension, and resolution?

2. Consider again "The Stolen Watch." It seems to meet the criterion of "depiction of events through time," but it is weak in connectedness, tension, and resolution. How could the writer revise the chronology to make it a story? Brainstorm several different ways that this potentially exciting early draft could be rewritten.

3. If you are working on your own open-form narrative, exchange drafts with a classmate. Discuss each other's draft in light of this lesson's focus on story. To what extent do your drafts exhibit the features of a story rather than those of an *and then* chronology? Working together, develop revision plans that might increase the story elements in your narratives.

Skill 19.2: Evoke images and sensations by writing low on the ladder of abstraction

19.2   Evoke images and sensations by writing low on the ladder of abstraction.

In Concept 4.3 we introduced the concept of *ladder of abstraction*, in which words can be arranged from the very abstract (living creatures, footwear) down to the very specific (our hen Lefty; my saltwater-stained Birkenstocks). In this lesson we show why and how open-form writers stay low on the ladder of abstraction through their use of concrete words, revelatory words, and memory-soaked words.

Concrete Words Evoke Images and Sensations

To appreciate the impact of specific, concrete language, look again at a passage from Kris Saknussemm's "Phantom Limb Pain."

> Every morning before sunrise I lumbered around our neighborhood wearing ankle weights loaded with sand. I taught myself how to do Marine push-ups and carried my football everywhere so I'd learn not to fumble.

Here is how that same passage might sound if rewritten higher on the ladder of abstraction:

> Each morning I did my exercises and practiced holding the football to prevent fumbling.

This version still makes the same narrative point about exercise, but it loses the power of concrete words to invoke images and sensations. The reader might imagine the narrator doing jumping jacks or spinning on a stationary bicycle. Instead we see ankle weights filled with sand and marine push-ups—all before sunrise. The lower you write on the ladder of abstraction, the more you tap into your readers' storehouse of particular memories and images.

The power of concrete words has been analyzed by writer John McPhee in a widely quoted and cited interview. When asked why he wrote the sentence "Old white oaks are rare because they had a tendency to become bowsprits, barrel staves, and queen-post trusses" instead of a more generic sentence, such as "Old white oaks are rare because they were used as lumber," he responded in a way that reveals his love of the particular:

> There isn't much life in [the alternative version of the sentence]. If you can find a specific, firm, and correct image, it's always going to be better than a generality, and hence I tend, for example, to put in trade names and company names and, in an instance like this, the names of wood products instead of a general term like "lumber." You'd say "Sony" instead of "tape recorder" if the context made it clear you meant to say tape recorder. It's not because you're on the take from Sony, it's because the image, at least to this writer or reader, strikes a clearer note.

Some readers might complain that the particulars "bowsprits, barrel staves, and queen-post trusses" don't help readers' understanding, as do particulars in closed-form prose, but instead give most readers a moment's pause. Today most barrel staves and bowsprits are made of metal, not oak, and few contemporary readers encounter them on a regular basis no matter what they're made of. Furthermore, few readers at any time could readily identify "queen-post trusses," a technical term from the building trade. Instead of smoothly completing the reader's understanding of a point, McPhee's particulars tend to arrest and even sidetrack, sending the reader in pursuit of a dictionary.

But if McPhee's examples momentarily puzzle, it's the sort of puzzlement that can lead to greater understanding. Precisely because they are exotic terms, these words arouse the reader's curiosity and imagination. "Exotic language is of value," says McPhee. "A queen-post truss is great just because of the sound of the words and what they call to mind. The 'queen,' the 'truss'—the ramifications in everything."

For McPhee, the fact that these words trip up the reader is a point in their favor. If McPhee had said that old white oaks are rare these days because they became parts of "ships, barrels, and roofs," no one would blink or notice. If you were to visualize the items, you'd probably call up some ready-made pictures that leave little trace in your mind. You also wouldn't hear the sounds of the words. (In this regard, notice McPhee's emphasis on images sounding "a clearer note.") Your forward progress toward the point would be unimpeded, but what would be lost? A new glimpse into a lost time when oak trees were used to make exotic items that today exist mostly in old books and memories.

Another quality also recommends words that readers trip over, words such as *bowsprit, barrel stave,* and *queen-post truss:* their power to persuade the reader to believe in the world being described. Tripping over things, whether they're made of steel or words, forces the reader to acknowledge their independence, the reality of a world outside the reader's own head. For this reason, writers of formula fiction—thrillers, westerns, romances, and the like—will load their texts with lots of little details and bits of technical information from the time and place they describe. Because their stories are otherwise implausible (e.g., the description of the Evil Empire's doomsday machine), they need all the help they can get from their details (the size of the toggle bolts used to keep the machine in place while it's blasting out intergalactic death rays) to convince readers that the story is real.

Using Revelatory Words and Memory-Soaked Words

As we have seen, concrete language, low on the ladder of abstraction, can evoke imaginative experiences for readers. Two particularly powerful kinds of concrete language are revelatory words and memory-soaked words. By *revelatory* words we mean specific details that reveal the social status, lifestyle, beliefs, and values of people. According to writer Tom Wolfe, carefully chosen details can reveal a person's *status life*—"the entire pattern of behavior and possessions through which people express their position in the world or what they think it is or hope it to be." Wolfe favors writing that records "everyday gestures, habits, manners, customs, styles of furniture, clothing, decoration, styles of traveling, eating, keeping house, modes of behaving toward children, servants, superiors, inferiors, peers, plus the various looks, glances, poses, styles of walking and other symbolic details that might exist within a scene." Thus subtle differences in a person's status life might be revealed in details about fast food (a Big Mac versus a Subway turkey wrap), body piercing (pierced ears versus pierced tongue), a watch (a Timex versus a Rolex), or music (Kenny Chesney versus Busta Rhymes).

Another way to create powerful concrete language is through *memory-soaked* words. Such words trigger a whole complex of ideas, emotions, and sensations in readers who share memories from a particular era. People who grew up in the 1950s, for example, might have deep associations with 45-rpm records, the *Ed Sullivan Show,* or the words "duck tail" or "tail fins." For Vietnam veterans, Nancy Sinatra's "These Boots Are Made for Walking" or the whirr of helicopter blades might evoke strong memories. Persons who grew up in the 1970s or 1980s might remember "Cookie Monster," "Pez dispensers," or 8-track tapes. Kris Saknussemn uses memory-soaked words from the 1960s when he mentions "an Aurora model of Johnny Unitas" and "a poster of Raquel Welch from *One Million Years B.C."* In recent years, our students have come up with these memory-soaked words from their own childhoods: Transformers, American Girl dolls, Harry Potter characters, Arkham series video games, Legoland, Wii Sports, Candy Crush Saga, *American Idol,* and The Sims.

For Writing and Discussion
Working Low on the Ladder of Abstraction

1. Working in small groups or as a class, try your own hand at using revelatory words to reveal status life. Create a list of specific details that you might associate with each of the following: middle school girls at a slumber party; friends at a tailgate party before a football game; the kitchen of an upscale urban apartment of a two-profession couple who subscribe to *Gourmet* magazine; the kitchen of a middle-class, middle-America family with three kids and a collection of *Good Housekeeping* magazines; the kitchen of an apartment shared by college students. (If you are describing kitchens, for example, consider the different *status life* signaled by ketchup versus stone-ground mustard or by an iceberg lettuce salad with ranch dressing versus an almond mandarin salad.)

2. Also try your hand at finding memory-soaked words. Make a list of specific words and names associated with your childhood that you now rarely hear or see. Share your list with others in your group and identify the items that have the strongest associations.

3. If you are working on your own open-form narrative, exchange drafts with a classmate and, working together, find specific examples where each of you has successfully used concrete, revelatory, or memory-soaked words. Then find passages that could be profitably revised by moving down a rung on the ladder of abstraction or by adding concrete details that follow the advice in this lesson.

Skill 19.3: Disrupt your reader's desire for direction and clarity

19.3 Disrupt your reader's desire for direction and clarity.

The philosopher Kenneth Burke speaks of form as "an arousing and fulfillment of desires." In closed-form prose, we can easily see this process at work: The writer previews what he or she is going to say, arousing the reader's desire to see the general outline fleshed out with specifics, and then fulfills that desire speedily through a presentation of pertinent points and particulars.

In more open-form prose, the fulfillment of desire follows a less straight-forward path. Writers offer fewer overviews and clues, leaving readers less sure of where they're headed; or writers mention an idea and then put it aside for a while as they pursue some other point whose relevance may seem tenuous to the reader. Rather than establish the direction or point of their prose, writers suspend that direction, waiting until later in the prose to show how the ideas are meaningfully related. In other words, the period of arousal is longer and more drawn out; the fulfillment of desire is delayed until the end, when the reader finally sees how the pieces fit together.

Open-form prose gives you the opportunity to overlay your narrative core with other patterns of ideas—to move associatively from idea to idea, to weave a complex pattern of meaning in which the complete picture emerges later. Often the way you achieve these surprising twists and turns of structure and meaning is by playing with the conventions of closed-form prose. For example, in the autobiographical narrative "No Cats in America?" Patrick José breaks the cardinal closed-form rule that titles should forecast the essay's thesis: If José's essay were closed form, it should be about some kind of surprising decline of cats in America. However, José's title is metaphoric, and the reader doesn't completely comprehend its significance until the last lines of the essay. This delaying of meaning—requiring the reader to help co-create the meaning—is typical of open-form prose. In this section we describe some of your open-form options for surprising your readers and delaying the fulfillment of their desires.

Disrupting Predictions and Making Odd Juxtapositions

Open-form writers frequently violate the principle of forecasting and mapping that we stressed in Chapter 18. They also make odd **juxtapositions** (that is, they place words, ideas, or scenes that don't seem to fit together side by side for comparison). Consider the following introduction to an essay:

PASSAGE WITH DISRUPTED PREDICTIONS AND ODD JUXTAPOSITIONS

Whose bones? What feathers?

I suppose their little bones have years ago been lost among the stones and winds of those high glacial pastures. I suppose their feathers blew eventually into the piles of tumbleweed beneath the straggling cattle fences and rotted there in the mountain snows, along with dead steers and all the other things that drift to an end in the corners of the wire. I do not quite know why I should be thinking of birds over the *New York Times* at breakfast, particularly the birds of my youth half a continent away. It is a funny thing what the brain will do with memories and how it will treasure them and finally bring them into odd juxtapositions with other things, as though it wanted to make a design, or get some meaning out of them, whether you want it or not, or even see it.
—Loren Eisley, "The Bird and the Machine"

Birds? What birds? What do birds have to do with how the brain works? Where is this writer going?

Note the sequence of ideas from bones to birds to breakfast over the *New York Times* to comments about the workings of the brain. In fact, in this essay it takes Eisley six full paragraphs in which he discusses mechanical inventions to return to the birds with the line: " . . . or those birds, I'll never forget those birds . . . . "

Throughout these paragraphs, what drives the reader forward is curiosity to discover the connections between the parts and to understand the meaning of the essay's title, "The Bird and the Machine." Actually, Eisley's comment about the brain's "odd juxtapositions" of memories with "other things, as though it wanted to make a design, or get some meaning out of them" could be a description of this open-form technique we've called *disrupting predictions and making odd juxtapositions*. Open-form writers can choose when odd juxtapositions are an appropriate strategy for inviting the reader to accompany the discovering, reflecting writer on a journey toward meaning.

Leaving Gaps

An important convention of closed-form prose is to avoid gaps. Closed-form prose follows the old/new contract, which specifies that the opening of every sentence should link in some way to what has gone before. Open-form prose often violates this convention, leaving *gaps* in the text, forcing the reader to puzzle over the connection between one part and the next.

The following passage clearly violates the old/new contract. This example recounts the writer's thoughts after startling a weasel in the woods and exchanging glances with it.

PASSAGE WITH INTENTIONAL GAPS

What goes on in [a weasel's brain] the rest of the time? What does a weasel think about? He won't say. His journal is tracks in clay, a spray of feathers, mouse blood and bone: uncollected, unconnected, loose-leaf, and blown.

I would like to learn, or remember, how to live. I come to Hollins Pond not so much to learn how to live as, frankly, to forget about it.

—Annie Dillard, "Living Like Weasels"

Gap caused by unexplained or unpredicted shift from weasel to philosophic musing

Dillard suddenly switches, without transition, from musing about the mental life of a weasel to asserting that she would like to learn how to live. What is the connection between her encounter with the weasel and her own search for how to live? Dillard's open-form techniques leave these gaps for readers to ponder and fill in, inviting us to participate in the process of arriving at meaning. Just as open-form writers can deliberately avoid predicting or mapping statements, they also have the liberty to leave gaps in a text when it suits their purpose.

For Writing and Discussion
Disrupting Reader Expectations

If you are currently working on an open-form narrative, exchange drafts with a classmate. Discuss in what way the strategies explained in this lesson might be appropriate for your purposes. Where might you currently "explain too much" and benefit by juxtaposing scenes without explanatory filler? Where might you use other strategies from this lesson?

Skill 19.4: Tap the power of metaphor and other tropes

19.4 Tap the power of metaphor and other tropes.

In situations where closed-form writers might value unambiguous, literal language, open-form writers might value metaphors or other tropes. The term **trope** is a synonym for figurative language. It comes from a Latin word meaning "turning" and refers to language situations where meanings turn suddenly in different directions, immersing the reader in ambiguity or a possible multiplicity of meanings. The word *ambiguous* comes from the Latin *ambi* meaning "both sides" (as in "ambidextrous") and *agere* meaning "to act" or "to go." So ambiguous words, by definition, go two ways. Whereas a closed-form writer might want a word to mean just one thing—to prevent confusion—open form writers often use words that turn two ways at once. In this brief section, we show you some of the power of figurative language.

When journalist Nicholas Tomalin describes a captured Vietnamese prisoner as young and slight, the reader understands him in a literal way, but when, a moment later, he compares the prisoner to "a tiny, fine-boned wild animal," the reader understands him in a different way. The reader understands not only what the subject looks like—his general physical attributes—but how that particular boy appears in that moment to those around him—fierce, frightened, trapped.

Figurative language abounds when literal words fail. Figurative language enables the writer to describe an unfamiliar thing in terms of different, more familiar things. The surprise of yoking two very unlike things evokes from the reader a perception, insight, or emotional experience that could not otherwise be communicated. The originality and vividness of the imaginative comparison frequently resonates with meaning for readers and sticks in their minds long afterward.

Consider the use of metaphors and similes in the following passage in which writer Isak Dinesen describes an experience that most of us have not had—seeing iguanas in the jungle and shooting one.

PASSAGE USING FIGURATIVE LANGUAGE

In the Reserve I have sometimes come upon the Iguana, the big lizards, as they were sunning themselves upon a flat stone in a riverbed. They are not pretty in shape, but nothing can be imagined more beautiful than their coloring. They shine like a heap of precious stones or like a pane cut out of an old church window. When, as you approach, they swish away, there is a flash of azure, green and purple over the stones, the color seems to be standing behind them in the air, like a comet's luminous tail.

Once I shot an Iguana. I thought that I should be able to make some pretty things from his skin. A strange thing happened then, that I have never afterwards forgotten. As I went up to him, where he was lying dead upon his stone, and actually while I was walking a few steps, he faded and grew pale, all color died out of him as in one long sigh, and by the time that I touched him he was gray and dull like a lump of concrete. It was the live impetuous blood pulsating within the animal, which had radiated out all that glow and splendor. Now that the flame was put out, and the soul had flown, the Iguana was as dead as a sandbag.

—Isak Dinesen, "The Iguana"

Similes heaped up

Simile

Metaphor of dying applied to color
Simile

Metaphor
Simile

At a literal level, this passage says simply that an iguana's colorful skin becomes instantly colorless when it dies. But Dinesen's tropes give a deeper, more wonderful, almost spiritual resonance to the phenomonon. The iguana's beautiful color (when alive) is like "precious stone" or "an old church window." Unlike color applied in a literal way like paint, the color of iguanas seems touched with cosmic mystery: It "seems to stand behind them in the air, like a comet's luminous tail." When iguanas die, they don't simply lose their color; they lose a kind of miraculous life principle. They become like an extinguished flame, inanimate, "dull like a lump of concrete," "dead as a sandbag." Dinesen's figurative language opens a multiplicity of meanings that transcend the literal meaning of the passage.

We can also see the possibility of multiple meanings and ambiguous turnings in Saknussemm's title "Phantom Limb Pain." At the literal level, "phantom limb pain" refers to the tingling and often painful sensations that amputees feel where their amputated limb used to be. From a literal perspective it should be Miller King who feels phantom limb pain. But as the narrative progresses, we begin to sense more and more that it is Saknussemm who feels phantom limb pain—metaphorically, of course. It was Saknussemm who "performed a ceremony" under the full moon that seemed to curse Miller King. It was Saknussemm who had his bad dreams. The double meaning of "phantom"—either "falsehood" or "imaginary spirit"—begins to transfer from King to Saknussemm, who seems to escape phantoms and become "more real" when the story resolves.

For Writing and Discussion
Using Figurative Language

1. Figurative language can fall flat when it takes the form of clichés ("I stood transfixed like a bump on a log") or mixed metaphors ("Exposed like a caterpillar on a leaf, he wolfed down his lunch before taking flight"). But when used effectively, figurative language adds powerfully compressed and meaningful images to a passage. Working individually or in small groups, find examples of figurative language in one or more of the example passages in this chapter or in Chapter 7. See if you can reach consensus on what makes a particular instance of figurative language effective or ineffective.

2. If you are currently working on an open-form narrative, exchange drafts with a classmate. See if you can find instances of figurative language in your current drafts and analyze their effectiveness. Perhaps you can also discover places where figurative language could be profitably added to the text.

Skill 19.5: Expand your repertoire of styles

19.5 Expand your repertoire of styles.

Style is a combination of sentence structure, word choice, and rhythm that allows writers to vary their emphasis and tone in a variety of ways. In this section, we show you how to expand your repertoire of styles through a classic method of teaching in which you try to imitate other writers' styles. This rhetorical practice—called "creative imitation"—has a long history beginning with the rhetoricians of classical Greece and Rome. When you do creative imitation, you examine a passage from an expert stylist and try to emulate it. You substitute your own subject matter, but you try to imitate the exact grammatical structures, lengths, and rhythms of the sentences, and the tones of the original passage. The long-range effect of creative imitation is to expand your stylistic choices; the more immediate effect is to increase your skill at analyzing a writer's style. Most practitioners find that creative imitation encourages surprising insights into their own subject matter (when seen through the lens of the original writer's style) as well as a new understanding of how a particular piece of writing creates its special effects.

You begin a creative imitation by asking these questions: What is distinctive about the sentences in this passage? How do choices about sentence length and complexity, kinds of words, figures of speech, and so forth create a writer's voice? After close examination of the passage, you then think of your own subject matter that could be appropriately adapted to this writer's style.

To help you understand creative imitation, we provide the following example. In this passage, the writer, Victoria Register-Freeman, is exploring how relations between young men and women today threaten to undo some of our culture's recent progress toward gender equality. In the section of her article that precedes this passage, Register-Freeman explains how she, as a single mother, taught her boys to cook, sew, do laundry, and "carry their weight domestically."

Register-Freeman Passage

Then came puberty and hunkhood. Over the last few years, the boys' domestic skills have atrophied because handmaidens have appeared en masse. The damsels have driven by, beeped, phoned and faxed. Some appeared so frequently outside the front door they began to remind me of the suction-footed Garfields spread-eagled on car windows. While the girls varied according to height, hair color and basic body type, they shared one characteristic. They were ever eager to help the guys out.

—Victoria Register-Freeman, "My Turn: Hunks and Handmaidens"

But then, as she explains in this passage, teenage girls undid her attempts at creating gender equality:

Register-Freeman's voice projects the image of a concerned mother and feminist social critic. Her tone includes a range of attitudes: serious, personal, factual, ironic, frustrated. Note how this passage begins and ends with short, clipped sentences. The second sentence states a problem that the next three sentences develop with various kinds of details. The third sentence includes a series of colorful verbs; the fourth uses a metaphor (the ever-present girls compared to Garfields on car windows). The fifth sentence builds to the point in the sixth sentence, which is delivered bluntly and simply.

Here is one writer's attempt at a creative imitation:

CREATIVE IMITATION OF REGISTER-FREEMAN

Then came prosperity and popularity. Over the last ten years, Seattle's special charms have faded because expansion has occurred too rapidly. Traffic has multiplied, thickened, amplified, and slowed. Traffic jams appeared so often on the freeways and arterials they began to remind me of ants swarming over spilled syrup. While the congestion varied according to time, seasons, and weather conditions, it had one dominant effect. It increasingly threatened to spoil the city's beauty.

For Writing and Discussion
Practicing Style through Creative Imitation

1. Do your own creative imitation of the passage by Register-Freeman.
2. Choose one or both of the following passages for creative imitation. Begin by jotting down all the specific observations you can make about the stylistic features of the passage. Then choose a topic that matches the topic of the original in its degree of lightness or seriousness and its depth. Explore your topic by presenting it using the sentence structures and kinds of words used in the original. Try to imitate the original phrase by phrase and sentence by sentence. You may find it helpful to use a dictionary and thesaurus.

    a. Africa is mystic; it is wild; it is a sweltering inferno; it is a photographer's paradise, a hunter's Valhalla, an escapist's Utopia. It is what you will, and it withstands all interpretations. It is the last vestige of a dead world or the cradle of a shiny new one. To a lot of people, as to myself, it is just "home." It is all of these things but one thing—it is never dull.

    —Beryl Markham, "Flying Elsewhere," *West with the Night*

    b. The disease was bubonic plague, present in two forms: one that infected the bloodstream, causing the buboes and internal bleeding, and was spread by contact; and a second, more virulent pneumonic type that infected the lungs and was spread by respiratory infection. The presence of both at once caused the high mortality and speed of contagion. So lethal was the disease that cases were known of persons going to bed well and dying before they woke, of doctors catching the illness at bedside and dying before the patient.

    —Barbara Tuchman, "This Is the End of the World," *A Distant Mirror*

Chapter 20
Strategies for Composing Multimodal Texts

Learning Objectives

20.1 Consider a range of multimodal options for accomplishing your rhetorical purpose.

20.2 Design multimodal texts so that each mode contributes its own strengths to the message.

20.3 Design multimodal texts in a variety of genres, including posters, speeches with visual aids, podcasts, and videos.

This chapter gives practical advice for composing multimodal texts. As we explained in Chapter 5, a **multimodal text** uses two or more "modalities" of communication by combining words, images, and sounds. Multimodal productions can be low tech (a speech with a flip chart for visual aids), medium tech (graphs or photographs embedded into a written text), or high tech (Web sites, videos, podcasts, desktop-published posters or brochures). It is beyond this text's scope to explain the technological aspects of digital productions. However, many digitally native students already possess technological know-how, and many institutions provide instruction and backup support for multimodal projects. Our purpose in this chapter is to offer rhetorical advice on how to make your multimodal texts as effective as possible for your targeted audience.

Skill 20.1: Consider a range of multimodal options for accomplishing your rhetorical purpose

20.1 Consider a range of multimodal options for accomplishing your rhetorical purpose.

One way to appreciate the power of multimedia texts is to imagine how a written text might be transformed or remixed to reach different audiences in different ways. Suppose, for example, that you have written an autobiographical narrative about your recovery from an accident when you were in the eighth grade. That essay might reach a wider audience if you transformed it into a podcast and posted a link to it on your Facebook page or blog. Perhaps you also have relevant and evocative photographs from this period. If you do, you can choose to create a video screencast combining your photographs with a voice-over narrative. You could enhance both the podcast and the screencast with music. Or, to take another example, suppose you have written an op-ed piece for your school's newspaper taking a stand on a controversial campus issue. You might widen the reach of your argument through a campaign that includes posters or brochures, a speech supported with PowerPoint or Prezi slides, and a batch of T-shirts emblazoned with your message in a verbal/visual design.

Of course, not all multimedia texts start off as written arguments. You might upload a funny video to YouTube purely for its entertainment value, or you might post on Flickr a slideshow, set to music, of beautiful photographs of flowers just for their aesthetic or inspirational appeal.

In all cases, when you design a multimodal text, you should think rhetorically about your audience and purpose. In Concept 3.2, we identified six common aims or purposes for written texts: to express, to explore, to inform, to analyze/synthesize, to persuade, and to reflect. Table 20.1 provides examples of multimodal texts designed for these aims. As the table suggests, designing effective multimodal texts requires both purposeful thinking and creative imagination. There is lots of room for trial and error (and fun) when you experiment with multimodal texts.

Table **20.1** Rhetorical Purposes and Multimodal Texts

Rhetorical Aim	Subject Matter/Focus of Writing	Possible Multimodal Forms
Express	You share aspects of your life; you invite your audience to walk in your shoes, to experience your insights.	Personal story narrated as a podcast or a video with images
Explore	You take your audience on your own intellectual journey by showing your inquiry process (raising questions, seeking evidence, considering alternative views).	A podcast or video that includes interviews with experts who progressively expand your thinking
Inform	You bring to your audience factual knowledge addressing a reader's need or curiosity.	An informative poster; a report with graphics; a collaborative wiki article; a how-to video
Analyze/ Synthesize	You provide your audience with deeper insights by breaking an artifact or phenomenon into parts and putting them together in new ways for greater understanding.	The text of a poem with marginal drawings that illustrate metaphors; an audioguide analyzing a museum exhibit
Persuade	You try to convince your audience, who may not share your values and beliefs, to accept your stance on an issue.	Advocacy poster, podcast, or video; persuasive speech with PowerPoint or Prezi slides
Reflect	You look back retrospectively on an experience or journey and bring to your audience your evaluation of its significance or meaning.	A collage of photographs, arranged in a way that represents retrospective thinking about value or meaning; same collage done as a pechakucha presentation*

*Pechakucha presentations are discussed later in this chapter.

Skill 20.2: Design multimodal texts so that each mode contributes its own strengths to the message

20.2 Design multimodal texts so that each mode contributes its own strengths to the message.

The main point of this lesson is intuitively simple: The various elements of a multimodal text should work together to send the same message. In a podcast, the music should match the content. In a poster, the words should reinforce the point of the images. In a PowerPoint presentation, the slide on the screen should match the speaker's current point and reinforce it through the visual channel. However, many PowerPoint users—perhaps inspired by the creative possibilities of the technology—produce slides that distract listeners, causing them to multitask. Either the slide has an image that doesn't match what the speaker is saying, or it has densely packed words that force the viewer to read the slide and listen to the speaker at the same time. "Hey," you want to shout at the speaker, "shut up a minute and let me figure out your slide." In the language of cognitive psychologists, the audience experiences *cognitive overload*—bombarded simultaneously by the speaker's message through the ears and by the slide's message through the eyes. If these are not in sync, the multimodal message fails.

This Design Principle at Work in Successful Multimodal Texts

Let's consider some examples of successful multimodal texts, starting with children's picture books. For many children, their first introduction to multimodal texts comes from being read to while snuggled in a parent's lap. As the child listens to the story of Peter Rabbit, he or she enjoys the pictures, page by page, watching Peter wander into Mr. MacGregor's garden, hide in the watering can, and eventually end up drinking his chamomile tea. Picture books show how our brains can process both auditory information (the story) and visual information (the pictures) at the same time. Some children's books (such as *Pat the Bunny*) even introduce a third communication channel—touch. The child can both see the bunny and feel its cotton-soft ears.

But now imagine how we might create cognitive dissonance for the child. Suppose that we told the child the story of Peter Rabbit (which we had memorized), but actually held in our laps the picture book about Jemima Puddleduck. Suddenly the words she was hearing about Peter Rabbit would not match the pictures she was looking at. Or suppose we told the Peter Rabbit story out of sync: While the child looked at Peter drinking his chamomile tea, we told the story of Peter's being chased by Mr. MacGregor. The child would be frustrated by the disconnect between the auditory channel processing words and the visual channel processing images. Our point is that multimodal texts work successfully only when the various modes are in sync.

FUNCTION OF IMAGES IN A MULTIMODAL TEXT   Many multimodal texts rely extensively on images. We examined the power of images in Concept 5.3 and then more fully in Chapter 10 on visual rhetoric. As we explained in these chapters, insights that need to be built up slowly through words in the verbal-processing part of our brains might be grasped almost instantaneously in the visual-processing part of our brains (hence the saying "A picture is worth a thousand words"). An effective image condenses an argument into a memorable scene or symbol that is understandable at a glance and taps deeply into our emotions and values. Images make implicit arguments (*logos*) while also appealing directly to our values and emotions (*pathos*).

The creative challenge of multimodal composing is to find or design images that tell visually the same story that the words tell verbally. Typical images in a multimodal text (say a poster, brochure, advocacy ad, Web page, PowerPoint slide, cartoon, graphic novel, or video) include still or moving photographs, drawings or animations, graphs, charts, maps, or words arranged in meaningful nonlinear designs to show relationships—for example, as components of flow charts, cause-effect diagrams with arrows, circle diagrams showing processes, and so forth.

FUNCTION OF WORDS IN A MULTIMODAL TEXT   In multimodal texts, words are often used to clarify and focus the point of an image. Because images have open-ended or multiple, ambiguous interpretive possibilities, designers of multimodal texts often use words to crystallize the intended meaning, thereby shaping the audience's response. Key words in a successful multimodal text often form a "nutshell statement" that identifies and drives home the text's take-away message. This nutshell serves the same function for a multimodal text as a thesis statement serves for an essay or a topic sentence for a paragraph. Consider as an example the classic World War II poster alerting soldiers in jungle warfare to the dangers of unsafe drinking water (see Figure 5.6, reproduced here in thumbnail).

The poster shows a soldier, a canteen cup in his hand and a look of horror on his face, peering into a pond in search of drinking water. The poster's message is conveyed visually by the reflection of the soldier's face transfigured into a skull—a powerful appeal to *pathos*. But the same message is also conveyed in the verbal channel through the words: "BEWARE . . . Drink Only Approved Water. Never give a germ a break." The words, which appeal primarily to *logos*, serve as a nutshell for the whole argument, making the poster's message unmistakably clear. But note how the words themselves also register in the visual channel through the effect of layout and font size. In the top half of the poster,

the large-font, all-caps "BEWARE" seems to shout a warning to the soldier. In the bottom half of the poster, the text next to the skull—"Drink Only Approved Water"—uses a smaller font and a calm sentence to convey the poster's take-away message. Finally, the words along the bottom border of the poster ("Never Give a Germ a Break!") in yet a different font offer a cause-and-effect explanation of why the water might kill you. Although the images alone convey the message at a glance, the poster's full punch comes when we register the argument in both the visual and verbal parts of our brains.

DUAL CHANNEL EFFECT OF WORDS AND IMAGES   As cognitive scientists researching multimodal learning have shown, multimodal texts achieve their power by combining the strengths of two or more modes of communication. Because each mode or channel is processed in a different area of the brain, each mode contributes its own strengths to the message. This dual-channel effect can be seen in a wide range of multimodal texts. As we have suggested, an effective visual/verbal multimodal text typically has a nutshell claim that summarizes the text's takeaway message combined with images that support the claim through a visual channel. The location of the nutshell claim can vary depending on the design of the text, and it can be emphasized by font size, location on the page, or other means. Table 20.2 shows examples from multimodal posters in this text.

EFFECT OF SOUNDS IN A MULTIMODAL TEXT   Because a print textbook can't accommodate sounds or moving images, our examples have focused primarily on multimodal print genres combining words and images. But sounds can also be a powerful channel for multimedia compositions, particularly the voice qualities in speeches, podcasts, or videos as well as the special powers of music. In our example of a child listening to Peter Rabbit, the parent's voice coming through the auditory channel is simultaneously an auditory experience and a word/verbal experience. The child sees both the pictures of Peter Rabbit and also the words on the page—an important first step in the process of learning to read. A PowerPoint presentation similarly provides words through both an auditory channel (the speech) but also a visual channel (words and images on a slide). In short, the sounds in multimodal compositions can range from the language-centered employment of voice to nonlanguage sounds such as street noise, animal sounds, drums, music, and other sounds with powerful emotional and associational effects.

Using This Design Principle to Revise a Jumbled Multimodal Text

Let's contrast effective multimodal texts with a jumbled one, in this case the "first draft" of a PowerPoint slide developed by student writer Joyce Keeley for an oral presentation of her research on the plight of African refugees (Figure 20.1). It is not quite clear what the function or focus of the slide is. The whole slide seems to be about "Life of a Refugee," but it doesn't make a nutshell claim or assertion. The audience might ask, "What point is this slide making about the life of a refugee?" The top right photograph of a refugee camp seems to make the claim that the life of a refugee is harsh or dismal. But it is uncertain what the other photographs are doing. The top left photo shows refugees being loaded into the back of a truck, while the bottom photo looks like an aerial view of a city, with no apparent connection to the life of a refugee. Additionally, none of the images seems

Table 20.2 Use of Nutshell Claims and Images in Multimodal Texts

Multimodal text	Verbal nutshell, claim, or key assertion (stated in words)	Images used for visual support
 Chapter 9 (Figure 9.2)	Wearing high-heel shoes for an extended time can cause leg and heel damage.	Drawing of leg in high-heel shoe with callouts explaining damage
 Part Opener 3	This glacier was here in 1982. (Implied claim: Global warming is melting the glaciers.)	Photograph showing at a glance the extent to which the glacier has retreated since 1982
 Chapter 10 (Figure 10.11)	Stop wearing Halloween costumes that objectify a culture. (Full argument: Reducing a culture to a costume displays insensitive attitudes that are harmful, even racist.)	Two contrasting, related images illustrate and reinforce the verbal message that it is "not okay" to stereotype a culture. The images and the dramatic display of text create this poster's strong appeal to *pathos*.
 Part Opener 2	Teach your kids how to be more than a bystander. (Full argument: Kids encounter bullying all the time; parents must teach kids how to respond to it.)	Visual impact comes from layout, font size, and shading. Victims of bullying often feel diminished, their identities blurred and less visible. This feeling is carried metaphorically by the shaded, washed-out font of "You're a dumb piece of trash." Adults reading the "piece of trash" text are shocked and turn to the small text in the bottom box for explanation.

connected to the bulleted list on the left side of the slide about political persecution, economic opportunity, violence, kinds of camps, resettlement, repatriation, integration, and naturalization. The slide is trying to do too many things at once. The words and the images aren't working together to send a single meaningful message.

When her peer reviewers expressed confusion about the point of the PowerPoint slide, Joyce decided to redesign it to follow the multimodal principles explained in this lesson:

Figure 20.1 A Jumbled Multimodal Slide

- Political persecution, economic opportunity, flee violence
- Camps (UNHCR supported) or Urban (illegal)
- Resettlement, Repatriation, Integration (Naturalization)

Life of a Refugee

Principles for Effective PowerPoint Slides

- Make sure that each slide has a point that can be stated in a nutshell claim or assertion.
- Make sure the audience knows that point (the presenter can state it in the speech or state it directly on the slide).
- Make sure that the words and images on the slide work together to develop or support that point.

Figure 20.2 shows Joyce's revision of the slide to focus on just one of the points she originally intended.

For more on oral presentations using PowerPoint, see Skill 20.3.

For Writing and Discussion
Purposeful Design of PowerPoint Slides

1. In small groups or as a class, identify the changes that Joyce made when she redesigned her original slide and then speculate on her thinking process. Do you agree that her redesigned slide is more effective than her original one? Why or how? How would you improve it further?

2. Examine student writer Sam Rothchild's multimodal PowerPoint slides, which accompanied his speech outline (Chapter 16). To what extent do Sam's slides follow the design principles outlined in this chapter? How do you imagine that he used each of these slides in his speech?

Figure 20.2 Joyce's Redesign of Her "Jumbled" Slide

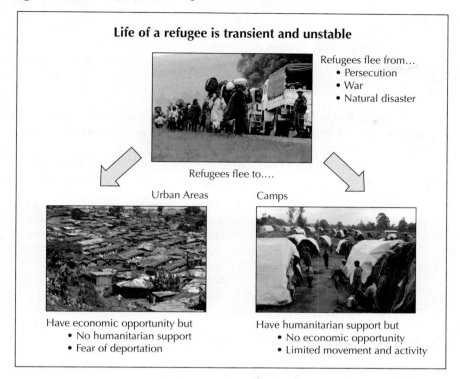

Skill 20.3: Design multimodal texts in a variety of genres, including posters, speeches with visual aids, podcasts, and videos

20.3 Design multimodal texts in a variety of genres, including posters, speeches with visual aids, podcasts, and videos.

In this final lesson, we give some nuts-and-bolts advice connected to specific genres of multimodal texts.

Informational or Advocacy Posters, Brochures, Flyers, and Ads

Posters and their cousin genres such as brochures, flyers, and newspaper ads—all of which can be published in print or posted to Web sites—typically have an informative purpose or a persuasive purpose. Effective posters try to maximize the power of both words and images.

To drive home the message presented in images, designers of posters pay attention to both the content and formatting of verbal text, including type sizes and fonts. Large-type text is frequently used to highlight slogans or condensed thesis statements (nutshells) written in an arresting style. They serve the function of complete sentence assertions, but for purposes of economy or impact may be grammatically incomplete. Here are two examples of large boldfaced copy from advocacy ads that the authors of this text have encountered recently:

- "Abstinence: It works every time . . . . " (from a newspaper advocacy ad sponsored by Focus on the Family, asking readers to donate money to promote abstinence education)
- "Expectant Mothers Deserve Compassionate Health Care—Not Prison!" (an advocacy advertisement from Common Sense for Drug Policy; this one appeared in the *National Review*)

To break up extended blocks of text, designers often put supporting reasons in bulleted lists and sometimes enclose carefully selected facts and quotations in boxed sidebars. To say a lot in a limited space, designers must be efficient in making words, images, and document design work effectively together. Strategies Chart 20.1 will help you design a poster.

Strategies Chart 20.1 Strategies for Designing Posters, Flyers, Brochures, and Ads

Features and Strategies to Consider	Questions to Ask
Purpose, Genre, and Medium: Based on your purpose, choose the most appropriate genre and medium for your targeted audience.	Will your purpose be informative or persuasive? Should your genre be a poster, a flyer, a one-page advertisement, or a brochure? Should you publish it in print or post it on a Web site?
Giving Visual Presence to Your Message: Choose the most effective visual features to create appeals to *pathos*.	What would be the best visual means to establish the urgency and importance of your subject: graphic elements, cartoon images, photos, drawings?
Presenting the "Nutshell" of Your Message: Decide on how you will condense your argument into an assertion or focused point and convey it clearly.	What type size, font, and layout will be the most powerful in presenting your assertion and supporting it for your intended audience? How much verbal text do you want to use? How much will you rely on images alone?
Accentuating Key Phrases: Decide what key phrases could highlight the parts or the main points of this argument.	What memorable phrases or slogans could you use to convey your argument? How condensed or detailed should your argument be?
Clarifying the Call for Action: Decide what you are asking your audience to know or do.	How can document design clarify your poster's take-away message?
Using Color for Impact: Decide whether you will use color. Note: For some media, color might be cost-prohibitive.	If color is an option, how could you use color to enhance the overall impact of your advocacy argument? How could you use black-and-white images effectively?

Scientific Posters

A scientific poster is a common means of disseminating research at a conference.* Unlike a fifteen-minute talk, a poster presentation occurs in a large room where dozens of researchers display their work on posters taped to walls or placed upright on tables. As researchers stand next to their displays, conference participants wander around the room, perusing posters and stopping to talk to researchers whose work particularly interests them.

The content of a scientific poster, like an abstract, follows the same structure as the research report. In fact, a poster is sometimes called an "illustrated abstract" because it presents at a glance the research question, hypothesis, methods, key results, and significance. An example of a scientific poster appears with the reading at the end of Chapter 12.

The function of a scientific poster is to engage viewers' interest in your research project and invite discussion. Professional scientists make posters using special software and plotting printers. A typical poster is thirty-six by fifty-four inches, the largest sheet that most plotting printers can handle. If you don't have access to these professional tools, you can print sections of your poster using regular paper, arrange the sheets on poster board, and tape them in place.

Effective Features of a Scientific Poster

- Is readable from four feet away (text fonts should be at least 24 points; heading fonts should be 36 points)
- Uses the least amount of text possible
- Uses lots of white space with content arranged in columns
- Where appropriate, uses headings to tell your story
- Uses effective visual elements to supplement text, to create a balanced appearance, and to tell your story visually
- Has an easy-to-follow structure; readers know where to start and what sequence to follow

The most common poster mistake is to use small fonts to cram in more text. An effective poster takes a "sound-bite" approach; it entices viewers into discussion with the research team rather than trying to substitute for the whole paper.

To design a poster, begin by blocking sections for your Title, Introduction, Method, Results, and Discussion. Determine what graphics or drawings will make your poster visually attractive and meaningful. Then create sound-bite headings and text, limiting text blocks to fifty words or fewer. Researchers often reword the title and figure captions of the original research report by turning them from phrases into meaning-making assertions, as in the following examples from the reading at the end of Chapter 12:

---

*Our discussion of posters is indebted to two excellent Web sites: G. R. Hess, K. Tosney, and L. Liegel, *Creating Effective Poster Presentations*; C. B. Purrington, *Advice on Designing Scientific Posters*.

	Original Research Report (uses phrases)	Poster (converts phrases to sentences)
Title	A Comparison of Gender Stereotypes in *SpongeBob SquarePants* and a 1930s Mickey Mouse Cartoon	*SpongeBob SquarePants* Has Fewer Gender Stereotypes than Mickey Mouse
Figure caption	Figure 1: Stereotypical Behaviors by Gender in *SpongeBob SquarePants* and Mickey Mouse	Figure 1: Results Show More Non-Stereotypical Behavior for Males and Females in *SpongeBob SquarePants*.

Speeches with Visual Aids (PowerPoint, Prezi, Pechakucha)

Another common multimodal form is a speech supported with visual aids, such as PowerPoint or Prezi. Such presentations are by definition multimodal because the audience receives information through an auditory channel, which processes the speaker's words, and a visual channel, which processes the slides. When the speaker's words and the slides are in sync, they can make the speech memorable and persuasive. But if they are out of sync, the audience will be forced to multitask to make sense of the presentation.

Although PowerPoint remains the most common form of presentation software, Prezi—with its panning, zooming, and rotating features—is becoming increasingly popular. Also becoming popular is a **Pechakucha 20×20** presentation, in which speakers must use exactly twenty slides displayed for twenty seconds each. Developed in Japan and named after the Japanese word for "chitchat," Pechakucha presentations are exactly six minutes and forty seconds long. Whereas in PowerPoint or Prezi presentations the speaker controls the timing of the slides, in Pechakucha the slides are controlled by the computer timer, ensuring that a speaker can't drone on. Pechakucha evenings are now being sponsored in many cities where individuals can present their carefully timed speeches to welcoming audiences.

In all of these genres, the presenter is expected to speak extemporaneously. To speak **extemporaneously** means to spend ample time preparing the speech, but not to read it from a script or to recite it from memory. Instead, the speaker talks directly to the audience with the aid of an outline or note cards.

Long before the delivery of the speech, the speaker should have engaged in the same sort of composing process that produces a finished essay. Effective speakers typically spend an hour of preparation time per minute of speaking time. Much of this work focuses on creating a well-developed sentence outline for the speech. Since you won't be writing out the complete argument in prose, this outline will be the written frame for your speech. Strategies Chart 20.2 suggests strategies for developing your speech outline.

Once you have outlined your speech, you can design slides that follow the design principles that we explain in Skill 20.2 for maximizing the auditory and visual impact of your presentation. Common mistakes are to make too many slides, to overdesign them, or to become enamored with special effects rather than with the ideas in the speech. Particularly avoid text-heavy slides that include passages cut and pasted from a print text. Unlike an image, which is

Strategies Chart 20.2 Strategies for Creating an Effective Speech Outline

Strategies	Rationales and Explanations
Plan the structure and content of your speech with the needs of your audience in mind.	How can you make the question or problem you are addressing come alive for your audience?
	What background information or key vocabulary terms does your audience need?
	What kinds of evidence will you need to support your argument?
	What objections will your listeners raise?
	How can you motivate action?
Create a complete-sentence outline of your argument; use parallel structures, coordination, and subordination to clarify relationships among ideas.	See Skill 18.3 for advice about different kinds of outlines, particularly the advantage of complete-sentence outlines, which state meanings rather than topics. Since you won't be writing out the complete argument in prose, this outline will be the written frame for your speech.
Build into your outline places for explicit signposting to help the audience follow your speech.	Indicate where you are in your speech: "My second reason is that . . . . " "As I stated earlier . . . . "
Early on, practice saying your speech in a normally paced speaking voice to determine its length.	Often speeches can cover much less ground than a written argument. By timing the speech when it is still in its rough-draft stage, you will know whether you must cut or add material.

grasped almost instantaneously in the visual processing part of our brains, a text-heavy slide must be read to be understood. Text-heavy slides force the audience to multitask, moving back and forth between trying to listen to the speech and trying to read the slide. The only way to bring the speaker's words and the slide into sync is for the speaker to read the slide directly (boring!).

Another design flaw is to leave your audience confused about the slide's focus, purpose, or take-away point. This problem is particularly common with PowerPoint because the software encourages users to create short topic phrases for titles rather than complete sentences that assert a point. This topic/subtopic approach violates the meaning-making principle that we emphasize in Skill 18.3, where we advocate complete sentence outlines rather than topic outlines. Meanings are expressed in predicates and thus require complete sentences. In Skill 18.3, we illustrate this distinction in the contrast between "Peanut butter" (a topic) and "Peanut butter is nutritious" (an assertion requiring support). From this meaning-making perspective, PowerPoint's focus on topic phrases for titles often leads to slides that don't assert a nutshell point.

One solution to the problem of topic-only titles, advocated by some rhetoricians, is to make the slide's title a complete sentence rather than a phrase. Examples of assertion titles versus topic titles are shown in the following chart:

Slide Title as Topic	Slide Title as a Claim or Assertion
Gender Stereotypes in Children's Birthday Cards	Children's birthday cards revealed extensive gender stereotyping.
Wage Comparison: CEO Versus Worker	Gap between CEO salaries and average worker salaries is increasing rapidly.

Of course, the designer could choose to articulate the slide's point in the speech itself rather than stating it on the slide as a complete sentence title. Sometimes, too, a title can make an assertion or claim without having to be grammatically complete. The key is to make sure that the audience knows what the slide's take-away point is. (Using a grammatically complete sentence for the title is particularly helpful if you want the slide to stand on its own as an independent multimodal argument.)

Strategies Chart 20.3 provides some additional strategies for creating visual aids for a presentation.

Once you have outlined your speech and developed your slides, you need to practice delivering your speech. You can stand before a mirror, make a video of a practice session, or practice in front of friends until you are confident about the length of your speech and your ability to deliver it with minimal prompting from your notes. In addition, you should think about the important strategies for successful speechmaking listed in Strategies Chart 20.4.

Scripted Speech (Podcasts, Video Voice-overs)

When you speak before a live audience, it is best to speak extemporaneously. However, if you are preparing a podcast or the voice-over on a video, you can read from a completed script. Give your script a tone and voice appropriate for your audience and purpose. For example, part of the drafting/revising process is to read your emerging text aloud to make sure the script sounds effective out

---

Strategies Chart 20.3 Strategies for Creating Effective Visual Aids for a Presentation

Strategies	Rationales and Explanations
Limit the number of words per slide; avoid blocks of text.	Verbal text must be read linearly—a slow process different from the almost instantaneous processing of an image. Viewers can't listen to your speech and read the text on the screen simultaneously.
Use slides to enhance the points in your speech—either images or a very limited number of words.	Effective slides use a visual channel to enhance the points made in your speech. The point of each slide should be quickly apparent through images or rapidly processed words.
Use visual features that enhance meaning; don't use cutesy bells and whistles.	PowerPoint has special effects like exploding figures, words circling into position, and little buses wheeling across the screen. Using these special effects can distract the audience from the content of your speech, creating the *ethos* of a technical whiz rather than a serious presenter of a proposal.
Create your speech first and then design slides to drive home major points. Do not use slides simply to reproduce your speech outline.	If you convert your outline into slides, you simply replicate rather than enhance the speech. Use images (rather than words) wherever possible. Think visually.
Consider using complete sentences for the titles of your slides, particularly if you want them to stand alone as meaning-making arguments.	Complete sentence titles highlight each slide's meaningful point (see Skill 20.2). Note: To have enough room for a complete sentence, you'll need to change the default PowerPoint title font to make room for a complete sentence. It is OK to have a two-line title.
Limit the number of visual aids you use.	Communication experts advise no more than one visual aid per minute of presentation. In many parts of the speech, the screen can be blank.

Strategies Chart 20.4 Strategies for Successfully Delivering a Speech

Strategies	What to Do
Control your volume and pace.	• Speak loudly enough to be heard, and add emphasis by raising or lowering your voice. • Speed up to get through details quickly and slow down for points you want to stress.
Use posture and gestures to your advantage.	• Stand straight and tall to help your breathing and projection. • Use natural gestures or a few carefully planned ones. • Avoid distracting or nervous gestures.
Maintain eye contact with your audience and look at every member of your audience.	• Know your speech well enough that you can look at your audience, not read your note cards. • Make steady and even eye contact with your audience.
Show enthusiasm and passion for the issue of your speech.	• Make your audience care about your issue through your own enthusiasm. • Show your audience that your issue is important by the energy you put into your delivery. • Use your enthusiasm to help control any nervousness you may feel.
Use your slides effectively; turn off the screen if you aren't currently referring to a slide.	• Click on slides at the appropriate time. • Give slides air time. Talking through images and graphs is effective. Reading long text passages is not.
Overcome nervousness by controlling your hands, your breathing, and the volume of your voice.	• Take deep breaths and speak slightly louder than usual to help your body relax. • Use a podium if one is available.

loud, something you wouldn't necessarily do for a print-only paper. Features that might not be appropriate in an academic paper—slang, street language, or less-than-formal grammar—might be just what you need in your script.

You'll also need to practice reading the script so that it sounds spontaneous and natural. If your script includes dialogue, you may need to practice adopting different voices. The most common problems to avoid include reading too rapidly, not enunciating clearly, or swallowing words at the ends of sentences. If you use music in the podcast or video, make sure that it is appropriate to the content of the words and sets an appropriate mood. Don't let the music muffle or overwhelm the words.

Videos

Videos offer a range of production options. At the simplest level, you could make a video of a PowerPoint presentation (yours or a friend's), creating a multimodal text similar to a TED talk or a professor's recorded lecture. You could also make a video that is essentially a screencast of still photos enhanced with background music and voice-over narration. You could even splice in recorded interview segments, captions, or text. At a more complex level, you could make a short documentary or create your own original film with actors and a script. Such productions need to be carefully designed and executed, beginning with preproduction storyboarding, moving through production (where filmmakers often shoot a surprisingly high excess of footage), and concluding with purposeful postproduction editing.

As an example of a simple original production, one of our students, Alex Mullen, was selected to produce a short video to introduce the master of ceremonies at a student award ceremony. He wanted to parody the genre of the humorous "introduction" videos—often used at the Academy Awards or the Grammys—which take the audience backstage to see the Master or Mistress of Ceremonies getting ready. Alex wanted to show the MC getting his official invitation letter, putting on his tux, stopping to talk with friends in a dorm room on his way to the ceremony, forgetting the time, and then racing across campus in goofy circles, arriving breathless at the last moment. Selected scenes from Alex's storyboard are shown in Figure 20.3, and a corresponding screen shot from the video is shown in Figure 20.4. The storyboard, which had more than twenty frames, suggests the kind of advance planning that Alex put into his three-minute video.

If you are contemplating making a video, Strategies Chart 20.5 will help guide your thinking. For discussion of camera shots and angles, see Concept 5.3 and Chapter 10.

Figure 20.3 Scenes from Alex's Storyboard

Figure 20.4 Still Shot of MC Putting on Tux

Strategies Chart 20.5 Strategies for Creating an Effective Video

Strategy	What to Do
Remember the Rhetorical Situation: As always, consider your purpose and audience. What effect do you want your video to have on your targeted audience?	Articulating your rhetorical goal will help you plan appeals to *logos, ethos,* and *pathos* and decide your own role. Do you wish to appear in the video or stay behind the scenes? In some cases, your rhetorical purpose might call for multiple points of view; in other cases your goal is to move your audience toward one view. If your video has a persuasive aim, are you targeting opposing/neutral audiences or appealing to those who already hold your view?
Use a Storyboard Approach: Think about the text in terms of scenes.	Storyboards are like graphic organizers that help you see your video's big picture scene by scene. Organize the video according to individual shots the same way you might use paragraphs or sections in a written text. Also consider ways to transition, using strategies such as zooming, fading, or rapid cuts to a different camera angle. Many narratives seen in literary writing are analogous to film strategies, including flashbacks and sequences of scenes.
Start with Visual Elements First: The text will be dominated by images.	Audiences of video texts expect to be engaged visually at all times. Avoid using monotonous or uninteresting visuals as filler for stretches of voice-over. Use camera angles to create a narrative "story." Consider particularly the use of establishing shots (medium or long shots), point-of-view shots through a character's eyes, and reaction shots (close-ups of faces). Consider also creative juxtapositions of image with graphics or words. For discussion of camera shots and angles, see Concept 5.3 and Chapter 10.
Incorporate Effective Verbal and Written Text: Use graphic and sound design to emphasize main points.	Video technology allows for more versatile text options than just about any other multimodal form. With the use of graphic design and sound options such as voice-overs and captions, you can underscore the intended rhetorical impact of images with written and spoken words to emphasize main points and highlight important information. As in other multimodal texts, present assertions rather than topics by using complete sentences whenever possible.
Use Musical Elements and Other Sound Options to Empha-size the Effect: As appropriate, underscore important rhetorical goals with auditory effects.	Sound can have a subtle but powerful impact on the viewers of a video text. Effective use of music, background sounds (street noise, café buzz, bird chirps, sudden silence), and qualities of voice (accent, pitch, emotional emphasis) can enhance the key ideas of your video. When shooting scenes, consider the placement of microphones as well as cameras.

Part IV
A Rhetorical Guide to Research

This poster for the documentary film *Gasland* (2010) by Josh Fox features an image of Earth connected to a water faucet dripping methane gas. The film focuses on the environmental disruption caused by hydraulic fracturing (fracking), which releases natural gas from shale deep in the earth. The film's claim is that poorly regulated fracking has contaminated many homeowners' water supplies. Although this view is challenged by proponents of fracking, this film and its sequel, *Gasland 2*, build their credibility and authority by explaining scientifically how fracking can contaminate groundwater. Much of the films' persuasive power comes from interviews with people across the country who have experienced problems from fracking. The poster's alarming image of dangerous gas issuing from a water faucet—amplified by the question "Can you light your tap water on fire?"—makes a powerful appeal to *pathos*. Further discussion of the fracking controversy appears in Chapter 22 in our evaluation and rhetorical analysis of advocacy Web sites supporting and opposing fracking.

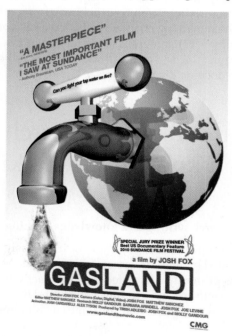

Chapter 21

Asking Questions, Finding Sources

Learning Objectives

21.1 Understand research writing as a knowledge-making activity.

21.2 Argue your own thesis in response to a question.

21.3 Understand differences among kinds of sources.

21.4 Use purposeful strategies for searching libraries, databases, and Web sites.

21.5 Use sources derived from observations, interviews, or questionnaires.

Our goal in Part 4 is to explain the skills you'll need to write successful college-level research papers. In this opening chapter, we help you start on the right track as a college researcher. The remaining chapters in Part 4 show you how to evaluate research sources (Chapter 22), integrate sources into your own arguments and avoid plagiarism (Chapter 23), and create in-text citations and corresponding bibliographic citations to document your sources (Chapter 24).

Skill 21.1: Understand research writing as a knowledge-making activity.

21.1 Understand research writing as a knowledge-making activity.

Although the research paper is a common writing assignment in college, students are often baffled by their professors' expectations. Many students think of research writing as primarily a knowledge-getting activity—choosing a topic and then reporting the information that they have found through research. When well organized, these reports become informative "all about" papers—often interesting, but not what most college professors want. (When poorly organized, they become what one of our colleagues calls "data dumps": The student dumps a ten-page load of information on the professor's desk and says, "Here's what I found out about sweatshops, Professor Jones. Enjoy!")

But a research paper shouldn't be an all-about paper or a data dump. Instead, it should challenge the reader with the writer's own stance on an issue or "best solution" to a problem. Research writing is primarily a knowledge-making activity that requires the writer's own critical thinking, analysis, and argument. It should address a "knowledge-making" question that may not have an agreed-upon answer and that requires attention to counter-arguments, alternative interpretations, or alternative points of view. (See our discussion of **knowledge-getting** versus **knowledge-making** in Concept 1.1; see also discussion of **"all about"** structures versus **problem-thesis-support** structures in Skill 18.2.) A research paper should follow the same principles of writing discussed throughout this text:

- It should pose a problematic and significant question (a "knowledge-making" question).

- It should develop your own answer to your question (your thesis) by bringing your critical thinking to bear on the material you have gathered through research.

- It should position you in a conversation with others who have addressed the same question.

- It should use your research sources purposefully and ethically and document them appropriately.

How does a writer develop a research paper with these characteristics? Early on, your goal is to pose a question that will cause you to "wallow in complexity." You become immersed in alternative points of view, clashing values, different kinds of evidence (often conflicting), and unresolved questions arising from gaps in current knowledge. Through your own critical thinking, you eventually refocus or refine your question and begin to formulate your own thesis. In your completed research paper, some of your sources provide background information, others supply supporting evidence, and still others present alternative points of view that you are pushing against. Throughout, your research data should come from credible sources (see the next chapter on evaluating sources). By documenting your sources according to appropriate conventions, you establish a credible *ethos* and provide a valuable resource for others who wish to locate the same sources. As you begin your research project, make sure that you know your institution's and your teachers' policies on academic honesty and plagiarism. The four chapters in Part 4 will explain fully the knowledge and skills needed for confident and ethical research.

Skill 21.2: Argue your own thesis in response to a question.

21.2 Argue your own thesis in response to a question.

The best way to produce effective, engaged, and ethically responsible research papers is to begin with a good knowledge-making question that requires research. A good question keeps you in charge of your writing. It reminds you that your task is to forge an answer to this question yourself, in your own voice, through your own critical thinking. This approach, which follows the principles explained in Concept 1.1 ("Subject matter problems are the heart of academic writing"), urges you to focus your research on a question rather than a topic. It also helps you avoid the wrong paths of data dumping, strung-together quotations, and uncertainties about why and how you are using sources.

Topic Focus versus Question Focus

To see the difference between a topic focus and a question focus, suppose a friend asks you what your research paper is about. Consider differences in the following responses:

Topic Focus: I am writing a paper on eating disorders.

Question Focus: I'm trying to sort out what the experts say is the best way to treat severe anorexia nervosa. Is inpatient or outpatient treatment more effective?

Topic Focus: I am writing my paper on gender-specific toys for children.

Question Focus: I am puzzled about some of the effects of gender-specific toys. Do boys' toys, such as video games, toy weapons, and construction sets, develop intellectual and physical skills more than girls' toys do?

As these scenarios suggest, a topic focus invites you to collect information without a clear purpose—a sure road toward an all-about paper or a data dump. In contrast, a question focus requires you to be a critical thinker who must assess and weigh data and understand multiple points of view. A topic focus encourages passive collection of information. A question focus encourages active construction of meaning. The more active your thinking, the more likely you will write in your own voice with no worries about purposeless uses of sources or possible plagiarism.

Formulating a Question for a Research Paper

How do you arrive at a good knowledge-making question that requires research? We invite you to look again at Concept 1.1, which introduces the distinction between knowledge-getting and knowledge-making. Table 1.1, which gives examples of knowledge-making questions, is particularly relevant to research writing. Good researchable questions can emerge from puzzles that you pose for yourself or from controversial questions already "out there" that are being actively debated by others. In most cases your initial question will evolve as you do your research. You may make it broader or narrower, or refocus it on a newly discovered aspect of your original problem.

You can test the initial feasibility of your question by considering the following prompts:

- Are you personally interested in this question?
- What makes it a "knowledge-making" question? That is, how does it require you to "make an answer" rather than just "find an answer"? How does it require critical thinking and argument rather than just information-reporting?
- Is there something at stake in the way this question is answered? What makes the question significant?

- Is the question limited enough for the intended length of your paper?
- Is there a reasonable possibility of finding information and alternative points of view on this question based on the time and resources you have available?
- Is the question appropriate for your level of expertise?

Establishing Your Role as a Researcher

After you have formulated your question, you need to consider the possible roles you might play as a researcher. Your role is connected to the aim or purpose of your paper—to explore, to inform, to analyze, or to persuade. The aims of "explore," "analyze," and "persuade" always entail a "knowledge-making" question that requires critical thinking. The aim of "inform" can lead to all-about papers unless the information fills a particular knowledge gap for a targeted audience. In such cases, the writer must exercise critical thinking in selecting and shaping the information for the audience. To appreciate your options, consider Strategies Chart 21.1, which shows typical roles researchers can play.

Strategies Chart 21.1 Establishing Your Role as a Researcher

Aims and Roles	What to Do	Examples of Research Questions
Reporter of information that fills a knowledge gap	Find, synthesize, and report data related to an information question.	• How do Japan and France dispose of nuclear waste from nuclear power plants? • What attitude do elementary math teachers have toward the University of Chicago's *Everyday Math* curriculum?
Reporter of the current best thinking on a problem	Research experts' current thinking on some important problem and report what the experts think.	• What are the views of experts on the causes of homosexuality? • What do researchers consider the possible dangers of online social networks?
Conductor of original field research in response to an empirical question	Pose a problem that requires field research, conduct the research, and present results in a scientific report. Often, include a "review of the literature" section.	• To what extent do pictures of party drinking appear on our students' Facebook profiles? • How do the study habits of humanities majors differ from those of science and engineering majors?
Reviewer of a controversy (primarily an informative aim)	Investigate and report differing arguments on various sides of a controversy.	• What are the arguments for and against granting amnesty and eventual U.S. citizenship to illegal or undocumented immigrants? • What policy approaches have been proposed to the U.S. government for increasing automobiles' fuel economy?
Advocate for a position in a controversy (primarily an analytic and persuasive aim)	Assert a position using research data for background, for support, or for alternative views.	• Should the United States grant amnesty and eventual citizenship to illegal or undocumented immigrants? (Writer argues yes or no.) • What is the best way for the U.S. government to ensure that cars achieve higher fuel economy? (Writer argues for a specific approach.)
Analyzer of an interpretive or evaluative question who also positions himself or herself within a critical conversation	Do your own original analysis of a text, phenomenon, or data source, but also relate your views to what others have said about the same or similar questions.	• To what extent does the film *Avatar* present a Christian worldview? • How effective is microlending at alleviating poverty in developing countries?

For Writing and Discussion
Using Writer's Roles to Generate Questions for a Research Paper

Working individually or in small groups, develop questions on a subject-matter topic such as music, health, sports, use of fossil fuels, a literary work, or some other topic specified by your instructor. Develop questions that would be appropriate for each of the following roles:

1. Reporter of information to fill a knowledge gap
2. Reporter of experts' current best thinking on a problem
3. Original field or laboratory researcher
4. Reviewer of a controversy
5. Advocate in a controversy
6. Critical thinker about an interpretive or evaluative question in conversation with other thinkers
7. Miscellaneous (good questions that don't fit neatly into any of these other roles)

A Case Study: Kent Ansen's Research on Mandatory Public Service

To illustrate how a student writer poses a knowledge-making question and argues his own thesis, let's return to Kent Ansen's investigation of mandatory public service. We first introduced Kent's research in Chapter 2, where we reprinted his initial musings about community service in the form of a five-minute freewrite (Concept 2.2). Kent's original problem was his uncertainty about requiring all young adults to do public service despite its value to young people and communities. In his original freewrite, he pondered his own positive experience with service learning and volunteering in the community but wondered about the wisdom and public acceptance of mandating such service for all young adults.

Later in the course he decided to investigate mandatory public service for a major research project. His research process is narrated in his exploratory essay in Chapter 8. As he began reading articles on the value of public service, he noted that many researchers, participants, and advocates spoke highly of serving the community, arguing that both the individuals involved and the communities in which they served experienced significant benefits. However, Kent remained concerned about public resistance to the government's requiring young people to give a year of their lives to working in the community. He became more and more interested in exploring the arguments on different sides of this question. At the conclusion of his exploratory essay, Kent sums up the status of his thinking and mentions a perspective—nurturing engaged citizenship—that he wants to consider further:

> Looking back over my research, I think the rewards of national service to individual volunteers and the communities they serve are clear. However, I continue to worry about the feasibility of making national service a mandatory program. As I end this exploratory paper, I still have some more research and thinking to do before I am ready to start my proposal argument.

I am leaning in the direction of supporting mandatory public service. I am convinced that such service will benefit America's communities and also help the "Lost Generation" find themselves through learning more about our country's problems and developing valuable job skills. But the clincher for me—if I go in the direction I am leaning—is that mandatory public service would get Americans more involved in their government.

Kent's exploratory research gave him a solid background on public service, enabling him to bring his own critical thinking to bear on his research sources. In order to convert his exploratory narrative into a closed-form research paper, he eventually created a thesis statement proposing mandatory public service based on its benefits to young adults and the nation. You can read his final paper in Chapter 16.

For Writing and Discussion
Following Kent Ansen's Research Process

Working individually, read Kent's exploratory paper (Chapter 8) and his final research paper (Chapter 16). Then, working in small groups or as a class, try to reach consensus answers to the following questions:

1. Trace the steps in Kent's thinking from the time he first becomes interested in mandatory public service to when he finally settles on his proposal to advocate for it. What were the key moments that shaped his thinking? How did his thinking evolve?

2. We have used Kent's story as an example of a student in charge of his own writing. Where do you see Kent doing active critical thinking? Where do you see instances of what we have called "rhetorical reading"—that is, places where Kent asks questions about an author's purpose, angle of vision, and selection of evidence?

3. How is Kent's final paper different from an all-about paper or a data dump? How does it demonstrate ethical use of sources?

Skill 21.3: Understand differences among kinds of sources.

21.3 Understand differences among kinds of sources.

To be an effective researcher, you need to understand the differences among the many kinds of sources that you might use while doing your research. These sources can be classified in different ways. In this section we explain a variety of ways to distinguish among sources. Your payoff will be an increased ability to read sources rhetorically and to use them purposefully in your research writing.

Primary versus Secondary Sources

Researchers often distinguish between primary and secondary sources. **Primary sources** are the original documents, artifacts, or data that a researcher is actively analyzing. **Secondary sources** are works by other people who have analyzed the same or similar documents, artifacts, or data. In short, secondary sources comment upon or analyze primary sources. Table 21.1 presents some examples of primary and secondary sources.

Some research projects are based largely on primary sources. For example, you might analyze the prevalence of gender stereotypes in children's birthday cards. Each birthday card that you examine is a primary source. Or you might analyze the political views expressed in online responses to a news story (each individual response to the news story is a primary source) or the rhetorical strategies employed in an advertising campaign (each print and video ad is a primary source; so are corporate correspondence or press releases about the campaign). Modern libraries together with the Internet now make available a wealth of primary sources—government documents, historical archives, slide collections, population or ethnographic data, maps, health data, and so forth.

For other kinds of research projects—particularly at the undergraduate level—you may need to work primarily or exclusively with secondary sources. For example, in doing research to establish your own stance on nuclear power, single-payer health care, or immigration policy, you will need to enter the civic conversation about these issues carried on in secondary sources (popular magazine articles, scholarly journals, op-ed pieces, advocacy Web sites, and so forth). You'll need to pay attention to what these secondary sources use as evidence in support of their arguments. Are they able to use primary sources for their evidence? Or does their evidence come from other secondary sources? In trying to evaluate each of these secondary sources, you'll need to employ all your rhetorical skills. (Later in this chapter, we offer advice on reading secondary sources rhetorically.)

Distinguishing between primary and secondary sources is sometimes confusing because the distinction depends on context. For example, suppose you are analyzing an advocacy Web site promoting the health benefits of yoga. If your research project is about benefits of yoga, this Web site is a secondary source. However, if your project is about the rhetorical strategies used in advocacy Web sites, the site is a primary source.

Table 21.1 Examples of Primary and Secondary Sources

Field	Examples of Primary Sources	Examples of Secondary Sources
History	Diaries, speeches, newspaper accounts, letters, manuscripts, official records, old photographs, old news reels, archaeological sites	• Scholarly book on European fascism in the 1930s • 1970s documentary film about the rise of the Nazis in Germany
Media studies	Rap lyrics, advertisements, graffiti, episodes of *South Park*, bumper stickers, documentary photographs	• Scholarly journal article analyzing racism in *South Park* • Parenting Web site objecting to *South Park*
Nursing	Minutes of hospital staff meetings, direct observation of patients, research findings on transmission of AIDS virus; public health data on swine flu	• Popular magazine article about nurses working in a hospital in a developing country • Blog site focusing on nursing issues

Stable versus Unstable Sources

Researchers also need to understand the differences between stable and unstable sources. Most print sources (books, journals, magazines, newspapers) are **stable**. Stable sources are archived and can be retrieved by future researchers in the same format. In contrast, many Web sources are **unstable** in that they may change hourly or disappear altogether. If you work from print sources (or stable electronic versions of these sources), you can be sure that others will be able to track down your sources for their own projects. Furthermore, print publications generally go through an editorial review process that helps ensure accuracy and reputability. In contrast, ephemeral Web documents from individuals or organizations may be unedited and may have gone through no review process.

The distinction between stable and unstable documents is sometimes fuzzy. Because the cost of producing, distributing, and storing print materials is high, books and periodicals are now often published in electronic formats. These electronic versions of print materials are usually archived and retrievable by others in the same format and thus can be considered stable. However, when you retrieve print sources electronically, be aware that you may lose important contextual clues about the author's purpose and angle of vision—clues that would be immediately apparent in the original print source. These clues come from such things as statements of editorial policy, other articles in the same magazine or journal, or advertisements targeting specific audiences.

Reading Secondary Sources Rhetorically

It is important to read all sources rhetorically. When you look at a secondary source, you need to think rhetorically about the kind of source you are perusing and about the original author's purpose in producing the source. Your first consideration is to determine whether it is a stable source—that is, one that future researchers will be able to find in an identical format—or whether it is an ephemeral source that might soon disappear. In the rest of this section, we will discuss the rhetorical reading of stable secondary print sources. Later, in Skill 21.4, we look specifically at ways to read Web sources rhetorically.

A RHETORICAL OVERVIEW OF PRINT SOURCES   Table 21.2 shows how print sources can be analyzed according to genre, publisher, author credentials, and angle of vision. The last column in Table 21.2 identifies contextual clues that will help you recognize what category each of these sources belongs to. We suggest that you take a few moments now to peruse the information in this table so that you can begin to appreciate the distinctions we make among types of sources.

As a researcher, you need to understand particularly the differences between peer-reviewed scholarly books and articles versus trade books and magazines, and between secondary sources and tertiary sources such as encyclopedias and other reference works.

SCHOLARLY BOOKS AND JOURNAL ARTICLES VERSUS TRADE BOOKS AND MAGAZINES   Note in Table 21.2 the distinction between scholarly books or journal articles, which are peer-reviewed and published by nonprofit

Table 21.2 A Rhetorical Overview of Print Books and Periodicals

Genre and Publisher	Author and Angle of Vision	How to Recognize Them
BOOKS		
Scholarly Books		
• University/academic presses • Nonprofit • Peer-reviewed	**Author:** Professors, researchers **Angle of vision:** Scholarly advancement of knowledge	• University press on title page • Specialized academic style • Documentation and bibliography • Sometimes available as e-books
Trade Books (Nonfiction)		
• Commercial publishers (for example, PenguinPutnam) • Selected for profit potential	**Author:** Journalists, freelancers, scholars aiming at popular audience **Angle of vision:** Varies from informative to persuasive; often well researched and respected, but sometimes shoddy and aimed for quick sale	• Covers designed for marketing appeal • Popular style • Usually documented in an informal rather than an academic style • Sometimes available as e-books
Reference Books		
• Publishers specializing in reference material • For-profit through library sales	**Author:** Commissioned scholars **Angle of vision:** Balanced, factual overview	• Titles containing words such as *encyclopedia, dictionary, handbook, guide* • Found in reference section of library or online through library Web site
PERIODICALS		
Scholarly Journals		
• University/academic presses • Nonprofit • Peer-reviewed • Examples: *Journal of Abnormal Psychology, Review of Metaphysics*	**Author:** Professors, researchers, independent scholars **Angle of vision:** Scholarly advancement of knowledge; presentation of research findings; development of new theories and applications	• Not sold on magazine racks • No commercial advertising • Specialized academic style • Documentation and bibliography • Cover often has table of contents • Often can be found in online databases
Public Affairs Magazines		
• Commercial, for-profit presses • Manuscripts reviewed by editors • Examples: *Harper's, The Nation, National Review*	**Author:** Staff writers, freelancers, scholars for general audiences **Angle of vision:** Aims to deepen public understanding of issues; magazines often have political bias of left, center, or right	• Long, well-researched articles • Ads aimed at upscale professionals • Often has reviews of books, theater, film, and the arts • Often can be found in online databases or on the Web
Trade Magazines		
• Commercial, for-profit presses • Focused on a profession or trade • Examples: *Advertising Age, Automotive Rebuilder, Farm Journal*	**Author:** Staff writers, industry specialists **Angle of vision:** Informative articles for practitioners; advocacy for the profession or trade	• Title indicating trade or profession • Articles on practical job concerns • Ads geared toward a particular trade or profession
Newsmagazines and Newspapers		
• Newspaper chains and publishers • Examples: *Time, Washington Post, Los Angeles Times*	**Author:** Staff writers and journalists; occasional freelance pieces **Angle of vision:** News reports aimed at balance and objectivity; editorial pages reflect perspective of editors; op-ed pieces reflect different perspectives	• Readily familiar by name, distinctive cover style • Widely available on newsstands, by subscription, and on the Web • Ads aimed at broad, general audience
Popular Niche Magazines		
• Large conglomerates or small presses with clear target audience • Focused on special interests of target audience • Examples: *Seventeen, People, TV Guide, Car and Driver, Golf Digest*	**Author:** Staff or freelance writers **Angle of vision:** Varies—in some cases content and point of view are dictated by advertisers or the politics of the publisher	• Glossy paper, extensive ads, lots of visuals • Popular, often distinctive style • Short, undocumented articles • Credentials of writer often not mentioned

academic presses, and trade books or magazines, which are published by for-profit presses. By **peer review**, which is a highly prized concept in academia, we mean the selection process by which scholarly manuscripts get chosen for publication. When manuscripts are submitted to an academic publisher, the editor sends them for independent review to experienced scholars who judge the rigor and accuracy of the research and the significance and value of the argument. The process is highly competitive and weeds out much shoddy or trivial work.

In contrast, trade books and magazines are not peer-reviewed by independent scholars. Instead, they are selected for publication by editors whose business is to make a profit. Fortunately, it can be profitable for popular presses to publish superbly researched and argued material because college-educated people, as lifelong learners, create a demand for intellectually satisfying trade books or magazines written for the general reader rather than for the highly specialized reader. These can be excellent sources for undergraduate research, but you need to separate the trash from the treasure. Trade books and magazines are aimed at many different audiences and market segments, and they can include sloppy, unreliable, and heavily biased material.

ENCYCLOPEDIAS, WIKIPEDIA, AND OTHER REFERENCE BOOKS AND WIKIS   Another kind of source is an encyclopedia or other kind of reference work. These are sometimes called **tertiary sources** because they provide distilled background information derived from primary and secondary sources. Encyclopedias and reference works are excellent starting places at the beginning of a research project. New researchers, however, should be aware of the difference between a commissioned encyclopedia article and an article in the online source *Wikipedia*. Professional encyclopedia companies such as *Encyclopaedia Britannica* commission highly regarded scholars with particular expertise in a subject to write that subject's encyclopedia entry. Usually the entry is signed so that the author can be identified. In contrast, all forms of wikis—including *Wikipedia*—are communal projects using collaborative wiki software. *Wikipedia, the Free Encyclopedia* (its official name) is written communally by volunteers; anyone who follows the site's procedures can edit an entry. The entry's accuracy and angle of vision depend on collective revisions by interested readers.

Wikipedia is a fascinating cultural product that provides rapid overview information, but it is not a reliable academic source. It is often accused of inaccurate information, editorial bias, and shifting content because of constant revisions by readers. Most instructors will not accept *Wikipedia* as a factual or informative source.

For Writing and Discussion
Identifying Types of Sources

Your instructor will bring to class a variety of sources—different kinds of books, scholarly journals, magazines, and downloaded material. Working individually or in small groups, try to decide which category in Table 21.2 each piece belongs to. Be prepared to justify your decisions on the basis of the cues you used to make your decision.

Skill 21.4: Use purposeful strategies for searching libraries, databases, and Web sites.

21.4 Use purposeful strategies for searching libraries, databases, and Web sites.

In the previous section, we explained differences among the kinds of sources you may encounter in a research project. In this section, we explain how to find these sources by using your campus library's own collection, library-leased electronic databases, and Web search engines for finding material on the World Wide Web.

Checking Your Library's Home Page

We begin by focusing on the specialized resources provided by your campus library. Your starting place and best initial research tool will be your campus library's home page. This portal will lead you to two important resources: (1) the library's online catalog and (2) direct links to the periodicals and reference databases leased by the library. Here you will find indexes to a wide range of articles in journals and magazines and direct access to frequently used reference materials, including statistical abstracts, biographies, dictionaries, and encyclopedias. Furthermore, many academic library sites post lists of good research starting points, organized by discipline, including Web sites that librarians have screened.

In addition to checking your library's home page, make a personal visit to your library to learn its features and especially to note the location of a researcher's best friend and resource: the reference desk. Make use of reference librarians—they are there to help you.

SEARCHING EFFICIENTLY: SUBJECT SEARCHES VERSUS KEYWORD SEARCHES At the start of a research project, researchers typically search an online catalog or database by subject or by keywords. Your own research process will be speedier if you understand the difference between these kinds of searches.

- *Subject searches.* Subject searches use predetermined categories published in the reference work *Library of Congress Subject Headings.* This work informs you that, for example, material on "street people" would be classified under the heading "homeless persons." If the words you use for a subject search don't yield results, seek help from a librarian, who can show you how to use the subject heading guide to find the best word or phrase.

- *Keyword searches.* Keyword searches are not based on predetermined subject categories. Rather, you specify keywords, and the computer locates those keywords in titles, abstracts, introductions, and sometimes bodies of text. Keyword searches in online catalogs are usually limited to finding words and phrases in titles. We explain more about keyword searches in the upcoming section on using licensed databases, whose search engines look for keywords in bodies of text as well as in titles.

Finding Print Articles: Searching a Licensed Database

For many research projects, useful sources are print articles immediately available in your library's periodical collection. You find these articles by searching licensed databases leased by your library.

WHAT IS A LICENSED DATABASE?   Electronic databases of periodical sources are produced by for-profit companies that index articles in thousands of periodicals and construct engines that can search the database by author, title, subject, keyword, date, genre, and other characteristics. In most cases the database contains an abstract of each article, and in many cases it contains the complete text of the article, which you can download and print. These databases go by several different generic names: "licensed databases" (our preferred term), "periodicals databases," or "subscription services." Because access to these databases is restricted to fee-paying customers, they can't be searched through Web search engines like Google. Most university libraries allow students to access these databases from a remote computer by using a password. You can therefore use the Internet to connect your computer to licensed databases as well as to the World Wide Web (see Figure 21.1).

Although the methods of accessing licensed databases vary from institution to institution, we can offer some widely applicable guidelines. Most likely your library has online one or more of the following databases:

- *Academic Search Complete (EBSCO):* Includes citations and abstracts from journals in most disciplines, as well as many full-text articles from thousands of journals.

- *Research Library (ProQuest):* Gives access to full text of articles from scholarly journals, trade publications, magazines, and newspapers.

- *JSTOR:* Offers full text of scholarly journal articles across many disciplines; you can limit searches to specific disciplines.

Given the variability of these and many other resources, we once again refer you to your campus library's Web site and the librarians at the reference desk (who often answer questions by e-mail). There you will find the best advice

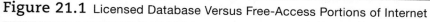

Figure 21.1 Licensed Database Versus Free-Access Portions of Internet

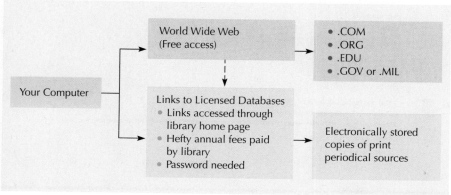

about where to look for what. Then, when you decide to use a specific source for your research project, be sure to include in your notes the names of both the database and the database company because, as we explain in Chapter 23, you will need to include that information when you cite your sources.

MORE ON KEYWORD SEARCHING   To use an online database, you need to be adept at keyword searching, which we introduced earlier. When you type a word or phrase into a search box, the computer will find sources that contain the same words or phrases. If you want the computer to search for a phrase, put it in quotation marks. Thus if you type *"street people"* using quotation marks, the computer will search for those two words occurring together. If you type in *street people* without quotation marks, the computer will look for the word *street* and the word *people* occurring in the same document but not necessarily together. Use your imagination to try a number of related terms. If you are researching gendered toys and you get too many hits using the keyword *toys,* try *gender toys, Barbie, G.I. Joe, girl toys, boy toys, toys psychology,* and so forth.

Illustration of a Database Search

As an illustration of a database search, we'll use student writer Kent Ansen's research on mandatory public service. Figure 21.2 shows the results from Kent's

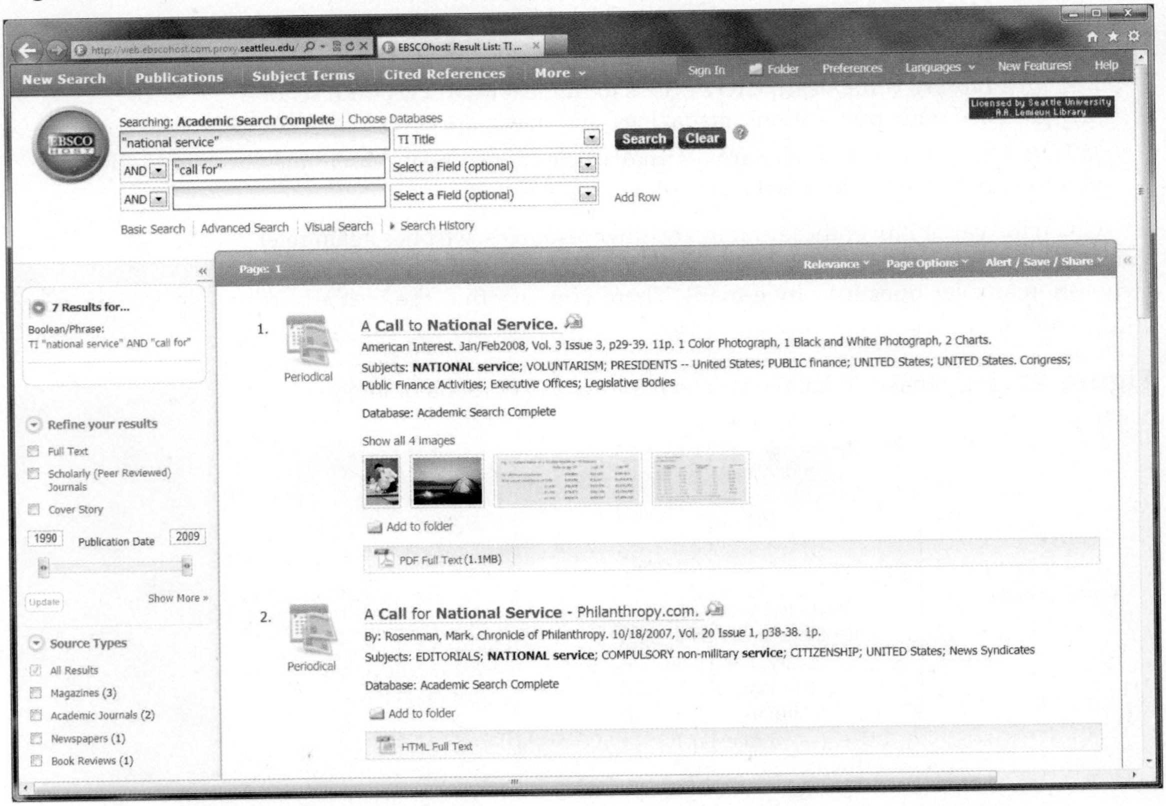

Figure 21.2 Sample Results List from a Search Using EBSCOhost

search using the keywords *national service* and *call for* on the database *Academic Search Complete*. This database host returned a number of articles from news commentary and scholarly journals that deal in some way with national service and voluntary service, both civil and military. When Kent experimented with "national service" in the title of the article, he got the two articles shown in Figure 21.2. The first article, "A Call to National Service," comes from the news commentary journal *American Interest*, and a full text of the article is available online in .pdf format. The second article, "A Call for National Service," comes from the biweekly newspaper *Chronicle of Philanthropy* (affiliated with the reputable *Chronicle of Higher Education*) and is available as a full text .html file. When Kent clicked on that article to get further information, the resulting screen gave an abstract of the article as well as complete data about when and where the article was published in print. Based on the abstract, Kent downloaded the .html file and eventually used this article in his final research paper. (See the entry under "Rosenman" in his Works Cited list.)

A particularly valuable feature of databases is the way that you can limit or expand your searches in a variety of useful ways. Strategies Chart 21.2 shows some strategies for focusing, narrowing, or expanding your list of sources.

After you've identified articles you'd like to read, locate physically all those available in your library's periodical collection. (This way you won't lose important contextual cues for reading them rhetorically.) For those unavailable in your library, print them from the database (if full text is provided), or order them through interlibrary loan.

Finding Cyberspace Sources: Searching the World Wide Web

Another valuable resource is the World Wide Web. To understand the logic of Web search engines, you need to know that the Internet is divided into restricted sections available only to those with special access rights and a "free-access" section. Web engines such as Google search only the free-access portion of the

---

Strategies Chart 21.2 Strategies for Narrowing or Expanding Your Searches on Licensed Databases

What You Want	What to Do
Only scholarly articles in peer-reviewed journals	Check the box for "peer-reviewed" articles in the database search box (different databases have different procedures—ask a librarian).
Only short articles (or only long articles)	Specify length of articles you want in the advanced search feature.
Only magazine articles or only newspaper articles	Specify in the advanced search feature.
Articles within a certain range of dates	Specify the dates in the advanced search feature.
Only articles for which "full text" is available	Check the box for "full text" in the database search box.
Only articles from periodicals carried by your library	Check method used by database. (Most databases accessed through your library will indicate whether your library carries the magazine or journal.)
All articles	Don't check any of the limiting boxes.
To narrow (or expand) the focus of the search	• Experiment with different keywords. • Try different databases. • Ask your reference librarian for help.

Internet. When you type keywords into a Web search engine, it searches for matches in material made available on the Web by all the users of the world's network of computers—government agencies, corporations, advocacy groups, information services, individuals with their own Web sites, and many others. You are likely to receive many more hits in a Web search than in a licensed database search, but the quality of sources may vary. For example, when Kent typed *Call for National Service* into Google, he got more than 500,000 hits. Although it would be impossible for any researcher to examine all these hits, the first few screens often turn up valuable leads. Here, for example, are several sources that showed up in the first two screens of Kent's Google search:

- A Web site "United We Serve" from a government Web address (.gov)
- An article entitled "A Call for National Service" from the Web site of a magazine entitled *The American Interest Magazine*
- A news story from the Web site of William and Mary College (an .edu site) titled "W&M Joins Call for National Service Initiative"
- An article from the Web site of the Aspen Institute (an .org site) describing the "Franklin Project" devoted to promoting voluntary public service
- An op-ed piece from *The Wall Street Journal* by General Stanley McChrystal calling for national public service
- A blog post entitled "General McChrystal's Un-American Call for Universal National Service" from a blog site entitled *The Objective Standard*

For Writing and Discussion
Comparing a Licensed Database Search and a Web Search

Working in small groups or as a class, see if you can reach consensus on the following questions:

1. How does a licensed database search differ from a Web search? Explain what is being searched in each case.
2. Of the six Web items from the first two screens of Kent's Google search (listed above), which might also show up in a licensed database search? Which would never show up in a licensed database search? (For Web-only sites that would not show up in a licensed database, readers must take particular care to analyze the Web site rhetorically. Skill 22.3 in the next chapter will help you do so.)
3. Which of the six items seem particularly valuable for Kent to examine as part of his initial research? Why?

USING WEB SEARCH ENGINES   Different search engines search the Web in different ways, so it is important that you try a variety of search engines when you look for information. Also, most search engines have an "advanced search" feature that allows you to narrow or filter results. There are also special search engines. For example, Google offers "Google Scholar," which allows you to limit a Web search to academic or scholarly sources. (But you will still need to turn to your library's collection or licensed databases for a full text of the source.) On campus, reference librarians and disciplinary experts can give you good advice about what has worked well in the past for particular kinds of searches.

DETERMINING WHERE YOU ARE ON THE WEB   As you browse the Web looking for resources, clicking from link to link, try to figure out what site you are actually in at any given moment. This information is crucial, both for properly documenting a Web source and for reading the source rhetorically.

To know where you are on the Web, begin by identifying the home page, which is the material to the left of the first single slash in the URL (universal resource locator). The generic structure of a typical URL looks like this: http:// www.servername.domain/directory/subdirectory/filename.filetype.

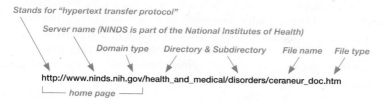

When you click on a link in one site, you may be sent to a totally different site. To determine the home page of a site, simply note the root URL immediately following the "www."* To view the home page directly, delete the codes to the right of the initial home page URL in your computer's location window and hit Enter. You will then be linked directly to the site's home page, where you may be able to find an "About" link through which you can gather information about the purpose and sponsors of the page. As we discuss in later chapters, being able to examine a site's home page helps you read the site rhetorically and document it properly.

Skill 21.5: Use sources derived from observations, interviews, or questionnaires.

21.5   Use sources derived from observations, interviews, or questionnaires.

Although many research projects rely solely on print or Web resources, some projects depend on primary source data gathered from observations, interviews, or questionnaires. **Field research** of this kind is particularly common in the social sciences. In this section, we provide suggestions for conducting these types of field research.

Using Observation to Gather Information

A common method of collecting data is **direct observation** of a phenomenon, whether in a lab or field setting. For example, a psychologist might observe children's play behaviors before and after the children watch a violent cartoon, or a sociologist might observe cell phone usage among people standing in line at a

---

*Not all URLs begin with "www" after the first set of double slashes. Our description doesn't include variations of the most typical URL types. You can generally find the home page of a site by eliminating all codes to the right of the first slash mark after the domain (.com, .edu, and so on) or country name.

coffee bar. The key to successful observation of human behavior or other natural phenomena is having a clear sense of your purpose combined with advance preparation. Strategies Chart 21.3 offers practical strategies for carrying out observational research.

Conducting Interviews

Interviews can be an effective way to gather information. They can range from formal interviews lasting thirty or more minutes to quick, informal interviews. As an example of informal interviews, consider the hypothetical case of a researcher investigating why customers at a local grocery store choose to buy or not buy organic vegetables. This researcher might ask persons buying vegetables if they would be willing to be briefly interviewed. (The researcher would need to be very polite, keep the interviews brief, and get the store manager's permission in advance.)

In other kinds of field research, you might rely on longer, formal interviews with persons whose background or knowledge is relevant to your research question. Although asking a busy professional for an interview can be intimidating, many experts are generous with their time when they encounter a student who is interested in their field. To make interviews as useful as possible, we suggest the strategies listed in Strategies Chart 21.4.

Using Questionnaires

In constructing a questionnaire, your goal is to elicit responses that are directly related to your research question and that will give you the data you need to answer the question. The construction of a questionnaire—both its wording and its arrangement on the page—is crucial to its success. As you design your questionnaire, imagine respondents with only limited patience and time. Keep your questionnaire clear, easy to complete, and as short as possible, taking care to avoid ambiguous sentences and questions. Proofread it carefully, and pilot it on

---

Strategies Chart 21.3 Strategies for Using Observation to Collect Data

Strategies	What to Do	Comments
Determine the purpose and scope of your observation.	Think ahead about the subject of your observation and the details, behaviors, or processes involved. Make a list.	Some phenomena can be observed only once; others can be observed regularly. If you plan on a series of observations, the first one can provide an overview or baseline, while subsequent observations can enable you to explore your subject in more detail or note changes over time.
If permission is required, make arrangements ahead of time.	In making requests, state clearly who you are and what the purpose of your observation is. Be cordial in your requests and in your thanks after your observations.	If you need to ask permission or get clearance for your observation, be sure to do so long before you plan to start the observation.
Take clear, usable notes while observing.	Bring note-taking materials—either a laptop or plenty of paper, a clipboard or binder with a hard surface for writing, and good writing utensils. Document your notes with exact locations, times, and relevant descriptions or data.	Make sure that your notes are easy to read and well labeled with helpful headings.
Go through your notes soon afterward.	Fill in gaps and elaborate where necessary. You might then write a first draft while your observations are still fresh in your mind.	Don't let too much time go by, or you will not be able to reconstruct details or recapture thoughts you had while observing.

Strategies Chart 21.4 Strategies for Conducting an Interview

Strategies	What to Do	Comments
Before the Interview		
Consider your purpose.	Determine what you hope to learn from the interview. Think about your research question and the aim of the paper you are planning to write.	This thinking will help you focus the interview.
Learn about your subject.	Research important subjects related to your research question and the person you will be interviewing. Although you needn't become an expert, you should be conversant about your subject.	Ideally, interviews should give you knowledge or perspectives unavailable in books or articles.
Formulate your questions beginning with some short-answer questions	Develop a range of questions, including short-answer questions like the following: "How long have you been working in this field? What are the typical qualifications for this job?"	Be as thorough with your questions as possible. Most likely you will have only one chance to interview this person. Avoid yes-or-no questions that can stall the conversation with a one-word answer.
Create open-ended questions for the heart of the interview	Once the interview is underway, create open-ended questions. For example: "What changes have you seen in this field? What solutions have you found to be the most successful in dealing with . . . ? What do you see as the causes of . . . ?" Questions framed in this way will elicit the information you need but still allow the interviewee to answer freely.	Avoid leading questions. The more you lead the interviewee to the answers you want, the less valid your research becomes.
Gather your supplies.	If you plan to record the interview, be sure to get your interviewee's permission, and spend time familiarizing yourself with the recording equipment. Bring a laptop, tablet, smartphone, or pad of paper to take notes.	Using a recorder allows you to focus your attention on the substance of the interview. Most likely, you will want to take notes even if you are recording the interview.
During the Interview		
Manage your time.	Arrive on time. Also agree to a time limit for the interview and stick to it. (If necessary, you can request a second interview, or your interviewee may be willing to extend the interview.)	You will show a lack of professionalism if you are not careful to respect the interviewee's time.
Be courteous.	Thank the interviewee for his or her time. During the interview, listen attentively. Don't interrupt.	Your attitude during the interview can help set up a cordial and comfortable relationship between you and the person you are interviewing.
Take notes.	Take down all the main ideas and be accurate with quoted material. Don't hesitate to ask if you are unsure about a fact or statement or if you need to double-check what the person intended to say.	If you are recording the interview, you can double-check quotations later.
Be flexible.	Ask your questions in a logical order, but also be sensitive to the flow of the conversation. If the interviewee rambles away from the question, don't jump in too fast.	You may learn something valuable from the seeming digression. You may even want to ask unanticipated questions if you have delved into new ideas.
After the Interview		
Go through your notes soon after the interview.	No matter how vivid the words are in your mind, take time *very* soon after the interview to go over your notes, fill in any gaps, or transcribe your tape.	What may seem unforgettable at the moment is all too easy to forget later. Do not trust your memory alone.

a few volunteer respondents so that you can eliminate confusing spots. Some specific examples of types of questions often found on questionnaires are shown in Figure 21.3.

When you have designed the questions you will ask, write an introductory comment that explains the questionnaire's purpose. If possible, encourage

Figure 21.3 Types of Questions Used in Questionnaires

1. Fixed-choice question
Compared to other campuses with which you are familiar, this campus's use of alcohol is (mark one):
---- greater than other campuses'
---- less than other campuses'
---- about the same as other campuses'

2. Open-ended question
How would you say alcohol use on this campus compares to other campuses?
Comment: Fixed-choice questions are easier to tabulate and report statistically; open-ended questions can yield a wider variety of insights but are impractical for large numbers of respondents.

3. Question with operationally defined rather than undefined term
Undefined term: Think back over the last two weeks. How many times did you engage in binge drinking?
Operationally defined term: Think back over the last two weeks. How many times have you had four or more drinks in a row?
Comment: An "operational definition" states empirically measurable criteria for a term. In the first version of the question, the term "binge drinking" might mean different things to different persons. Moreover, respondents are apt to deny being binge drinkers given that it is an unflattering categorization. In the revised question, the term "binge drinking" is replaced with an observable and measurable behavior; respondents are more apt to give an honest response.

4. Category question
What is your current class standing?
---- freshman
---- sophomore
---- junior
---- senior
---- other (please specify)
Comment: In category questions, it is often helpful to have an "Other" category for respondents who do not fit neatly into any of the other categories.

5. Scaled-answer question
This campus has a serious drinking problem (circle one):

strongly agree	agree	neither agree nor disagree	disagree	strongly disagree
5	4	3	2	1

How much drinking goes on in your dormitory on Saturday nights?

a lot	some	not much	none

Comment: Although scaled-answer questions are easy to tabulate and are widely used, the data can be skewed by the subjective definitions of each respondent (one person's "a lot" may be another person's "not much").

Figure 21.4 Example of a Questionnaire

Dear Commuter Student:

I am conducting a study aimed at improving the parking situation for commuter students. Please take a few moments to complete the following questionnaire, which will provide valuable information that may lead to specific proposals for easing the parking problems of commuters. If we commuter students work together with the university administration, we may be able to find equitable solutions to the serious parking issues we face. Please return the questionnaires to the box I have placed at the south entrance to the Student Union Building.

1. When do you typically arrive on campus?

   Before 8 a.m. _____   Between 1:00 and 4:59 p.m. _____
   Between 8:01 a.m. and 8:59 a.m. _____   Between 5:00 and 7:00 p.m. _____
   Between 9:00 a.m. and 11:59 a.m. _____   After 7:00 p.m. _____
   Between 12:00 and 12:59 p.m. _____

2. How frequently do you have problems finding a place to park?

   5 days a week ____
   4 days a week ____
   3 days a week ____
   2 days a week ____
   1 day a week ____

3. When the first lot you try is full, how long does it typically take you to find a place to park (for those who buy a commuter parking permit)?

   Less than 10 minutes ___
   10–15 minutes ___
   More than 15 minutes ___

4. For those who use street parking only, how long does it take you to find a place to park?

   Less than 10 minutes ___
   10–15 minutes ___
   More than 15 minutes ___

5. Do you currently carpool?

   Yes ____
   No ____

6. The university is considering a proposal to raise parking fees for single-driver cars and lower them for car pools. If you don't currently carpool, how difficult would it be to find a car-pool partner?

   Impossible ___
   Very difficult ___
   Somewhat difficult ___
   Fairly easy ___

7. If finding a car-pool partner would be difficult, why?

   Few fellow students live in my neighborhood ___
   Few fellow students match my commuting hours ___
   Other ___

8. What suggestions do you have for improving the parking situation for commuter students?

responses by explaining why the knowledge gained from the questionnaire will be beneficial to others. Make your completed questionnaire as professionally attractive and easy to read and fill out as possible. As an example, Figure 21.4 shows a questionnaire, introduced with an explanatory comment, prepared by a student investigating the parking problems of commuter students on her campus.

When you distribute your questionnaire, try to obtain a random sample. For example, if you assessed student satisfaction with a campus cafeteria by passing out questionnaires to those eating in the cafeteria at noon on a particular day, you might not achieve a random sampling of potential cafeteria users. You would miss those who avoid the cafeteria because they hate it or because they eat lunch earlier or later; also, the distribution of noon users of the cafeteria might be different from the distribution of breakfast or dinner users. Another problem with sampling is that people who feel strongly about an issue are more likely to complete a questionnaire than those who don't feel strongly. The student who prepared the parking questionnaire, for example, is likely to get a particularly high rate of response from those most angry about parking issues, and thus her sample might not be representative of all commuter students.

In some situations, random sampling may be unfeasible. If you are using a questionnaire for part of your research, check with your instructor whether a "convenience sample" would be acceptable (for example, you would pass out questionnaires to persons in your dorm or in your class as a matter of convenience, even though these persons would not represent a random sample of the larger population).

Chapter 22
Evaluating Sources

Learning Objectives

22.1 Read sources rhetorically and take purposeful notes.

22.2 Evaluate sources for reliability, credibility, angle of vision, and degree of advocacy.

22.3 Use your rhetorical knowledge to evaluate Web sources.

In Chapter 21, we explained the importance of posing a good research question, of understanding the different kinds of sources, and of using purposeful strategies for searching libraries, databases, and Web sites. In this chapter we explain how to evaluate the sources you find.

Skill 22.1: Read sources rhetorically and take purposeful notes.

22.1 Read sources rhetorically and take purposeful notes.

Once you've located a stack of books and magazine or journal articles, it's easy to feel overwhelmed. How do you begin reading all this material? At times you need to read slowly with analytical closeness. At other times you can skim a source, looking only for its gist or for a needed piece of information. In this section, we offer some advice on how to read your sources with rhetorical savvy and take notes that will help you write your final paper.

Reading with Your Own Goals in Mind

How you read a source depends to a certain extent on where you are in the research process. Early in the process, when you are in the thesis-seeking exploratory stage, your goal is to achieve a basic understanding of your research area. You need to become aware of different points of view, learn what is unknown or controversial about your research question, see what values or assumptions are in conflict, and build up your store of background knowledge. As we saw in the case of Kent Ansen, an initial research question often evolves as knowledge increases and interests shift.

Given these goals, at the early stages of research you should select "over-view" kinds of sources to get you into the conversation. In some cases, even an encyclopedia or specialized reference work can be a good start for getting general background.

As you get deeper into your research, your questions become more focused, and the sources you seek out become more specialized. Once you formulate a thesis and plan a structure for your paper, you can determine more clearly the sources you need. For example, after Kent Ansen decided to focus on the beneficial aspects of mandatory public service, he began following up leads on AmeriCorps volunteers, professional training for young adults, and the effects of public service on participation in democracy. At the same time, he remained open-minded about the costs and drawbacks of mandatory national service.

Reading Your Sources Rhetorically

To read your sources rhetorically, you should keep two basic questions in mind:

1. What was the source author's purpose in writing this piece?
2. What might be my purpose in using this piece?

Let's begin with the first question. Strategies Chart 22.1 sums up the strategies you can use to read your sources rhetorically, along with research tips for answering some of the questions you've posed.

Strategies Chart 22.1 Strategies for Reading Your Sources Rhetorically

Questions to Ask	What to Do	Results
• Who is this author? • What are his or her credentials and affiliations?	• Look for the author's credentials at the end of the article or in the contributors' page. • Google the author's name. • In a database results list, click on the author's name for a list of other articles he/she has written.	• Helps you assess author's *ethos* and credibility. • Helps you establish author's angle of vision.
• What is this source's genre? • Who is the intended audience?	• If the source is downloaded, identify the original publication information. • If the source comes from a periodical, look at the print copy for clues about the audience (titles of other articles, ads, document design). • Use Table 21.2 for further clues about audience and genre. • If a Web-only source, see Skill 22.3.	• Helps you further determine the author's angle of vision as well as the source's reliability and credibility. • Helps explain rhetorical features of the source.
• What is this author's purpose? • How is this author trying to change his/her audience's view of the topic?	• Determine whether the piece is primarily expressive, informational, analytical, or persuasive. • If the source comes from the Web, who is the site's sponsor? Read the "About us" material on the site's home page. • If it is a print source, determine the reputation and bias of the journal, magazine, or press (see Table 22.1).	• Helps you evaluate the source for angle of vision and degree of advocacy. • Helps you decide how you might use the source in your own argument.
• What is this author's angle of vision or bias? • What facts, data, and other evidence does this author cite and what are the sources for the data? • What are this author's underlying values, assumptions, and beliefs? • What is omitted or censored from this text?	• Apply the rhetorical reading strategies explained in Chapter 6. • Evaluate the source for reliability, credibility, angle of vision, and degree of advocacy as explained in Skill 22.2. • If a Web source, evaluate it using strategies explained in Skill 22.3.	• Helps you bring your own critical thinking to bear on your sources. • Keeps your paper intellectually honest and interesting.

This chart reinforces a point we've made throughout this text: All writing is produced from an angle of vision that privileges some ways of seeing and filters out other ways. You should guard against reading your sources as if they present hard, undisputed facts or universal truths. For example, if one of your sources says that "Saint John's wort [an herb] has been shown to be an effective treatment for depression," some of your readers might accept that statement as fact, but many wouldn't. Skeptical readers would want to know who the author is, where his views have been published, and what he uses for evidence. Let's say the author is someone named Samuel Jones. Skeptical readers would ask whether Jones is relying on published research, and if so, whether the studies have been peer-reviewed in reputable, scholarly journals and whether the research has been replicated by other scientists. They would also want to know whether Jones has financial connections to companies that produce herbal remedies and supplements. Rather than settling the question about Saint John's wort as a treatment for depression, a quotation from Jones might open up a heated controversy about medical research.

Reading rhetorically is thus a way of thinking critically about your sources. It influences the way you take notes, evaluate sources, and shape your argument.

Taking Purposeful Notes

Many beginning researchers opt not to take notes—a serious mistake, in our view. Instead, they simply photocopy or print out articles, perhaps using a highlighter to mark passages. This practice, which experienced researchers almost never use, reduces your ability to engage the ideas in a source, to synthesize different sources, and to find your own voice in a conversation. When you begin drafting your paper, you'll have no bibliographic information, no notes to refer to, no record of your thinking-in-progress. Your only recourse is to revisit all your sources, thumbing through them one at a time—a practice that leads to passive cutting and pasting (and possible plagiarism).

RECORDING BIBLIOGRAPHIC INFORMATION To take good research notes, begin by making a bibliographic entry for the source, following the documentation format assigned by your instructor—usually MLA (Modern Language Association) or APA (American Psychological Association). Although you may be tempted to put off doing this mechanical task ("Hey, boring, I can do this documentation stuff later"), there are two reasons to do it immediately:

- Doing it now, while the source is in front of you, will save you time in the long run. Otherwise, you'll have to try to retrieve the source, in a late-night panic, just before the paper is due.
- Doing it now will make you look at the source rhetorically. Is this a peer-reviewed journal article? A magazine article? An op-ed piece? A blog? Making the bibliographic entry forces you to identify the source's genre.

Chapter 24 explains in detail how to make a bibliographic entry.

RECORDING IDEAS AND INFORMATION AND RESPONDING TO EACH SOURCE To take good research notes, follow the habits for "strong reading" discussed in Chapter 6 by weaving back and forth between two modes of writing:

- *Your informational notes on each source:* Summarize each source's argument and record useful information. To avoid the risk of plagiarizing later, make sure that you put quotation marks around any passages that you copy word for word (be sure to copy *exactly*). When you summarize or paraphrase passages, be sure to put the ideas entirely into your own words.

- *Your own exploratory notes as you think of ideas:* Write down your own ideas as they occur to you. Record your thinking-in-progress as you mull over and speak back to your sources.

An approach that encourages both modes of writing is to keep a dialectic or double-entry journal. Divide a page in half; enter your informational notes on one side and your exploratory writing on the other. If you use a computer, you can put your informational notes in one font and your own exploratory writing in another. (An example of double-entry notes appears in Chapter 8.)

Taking effective notes is different from the mechanical process of copying out passages or simply listing facts and information. Rather, make your notes purposeful by imagining how you might use a given source in your research paper. Strategies Chart 22.2 shows the different functions that research sources might play in your argument and lists appropriate note-taking strategies for each function.

Strategies Chart 22.2 Strategies for Taking Notes According to Purpose

Function that Source Might Play in Your Argument	Strategies for Informational Notes	Strategies for Exploratory Notes
Provides background about your problem or issue	• Summarize the information. • Record specific facts and figures useful for background.	• Speculate on how much background your readers will need.
Gives an alternative view that you will mention briefly	• Summarize the source's argument in a couple of sentences; note its bias and perspective. • Identify brief quotations that sum up the source's perspective.	• Jot down ideas on how and why different sources disagree. • Begin making an idea map of alternative views.
Provides an alternative or opposing view that you might summarize fully and respond to	• Summarize the article fully and fairly (see Chapter 6 on summary writing). • Note the kinds of evidence used.	• Speculate about why you disagree with the source and whether you can refute the argument, concede to it, or compromise with it. • Explore what research you'll need to support your own argument.
Provides information or testimony that you might use as evidence	• Record the data or information. • If using authorities for testimony, quote short passages. • Note the credentials of the writer or person quoted.	• Record new ideas as they occur to you. • Continue to think purposefully about additional research you'll need.
Mentions information or testimony that counters your position or raises doubts about your argument	• Note counterevidence. • Note authorities who disagree with you.	• Speculate how you might respond to counterevidence.
Provides a theory or method that influences your approach to the issue	• Note credentials of the author. • Note passages that sparked ideas.	• Freewrite about how the source influences your method or approach.

Skill 22.2: Evaluate sources for reliability, credibility, angle of vision, and degree of advocacy.

22.2 Evaluate sources for reliability, credibility, angle of vision, and degree of advocacy.

When you read sources for your research project, you need to evaluate them as you go along. As you read each potential source, ask yourself questions about the author's reliability, credibility, angle of vision, and degree of advocacy.

Reliability

Reliability refers to the accuracy of factual data in a source. If you check a writer's "facts" against other sources, do you find that the facts are correct? Does the writer distort facts, take them out of context, or otherwise use them unreasonably? In some controversies, key data are highly disputed—for example, the frequency of date rape or the risk factors for many diseases. A reliable writer acknowledges these controversies and doesn't treat disputed data as fact. Furthermore, if you check out the sources used by a reliable writer, they'll reveal accurate and careful research—respected primary sources rather than hearsay or secondhand reports. Journalists of reputable newspapers (not tabloids) pride themselves on meticulously checking their facts, as do editors of serious popular magazines. Editing is often minimal for Web sources, however, and they can be notoriously unreliable. As you gain knowledge of your research question, you'll develop a good ear for writers who play fast and loose with data.

Credibility

Credibility, which is synonymous with the classical term *ethos*, is similar to reliability but is based on internal rather than external factors. It refers to the reader's trust in the writer's honesty, goodwill, and trustworthiness and is apparent in the writer's tone, reasonableness, fairness in summarizing opposing views, and respect for different perspectives. Audiences differ in how much credibility they will grant to certain authors. Nevertheless, a writer can achieve a reputation for credibility, even among bitter political opponents, by applying to issues a sense of moral courage, integrity, and consistency of principle. (For more on ethos, see Concept 4.2.)

Angle of Vision and Political Stance

By *angle of vision*, we mean the way that a piece of writing is shaped by its author's underlying values, assumptions, and beliefs, resulting in a text that reflects a certain perspective, worldview, or belief system. Of paramount importance are the underlying values or beliefs that the writer assumes his or her readers will share. You can get useful clues about a writer's angle of vision and intended audience by doing some quick research into the author's politics and reputation on the Internet or by analyzing the genre, market niche, and political reputation of the publication in which the material appears. (Concept 4.1 discusses angle of vision in detail.)

DETERMINING POLITICAL STANCE Your awareness of angle of vision and political stance is especially important if you are doing research on contemporary cultural or political issues. In Table 22.1, we have categorized some well-known political commentators, publications, policy research institutes

Table 22.1 Angles of Vision in U.S. Media and Think Tanks: A Sampling across the Political Spectrum*

Commentators				
Left	**Left Center**	**Center**	**Right Center**	**Right**
Barbara Ehrenreich	E. J. Dionne	David Ignatius	David Brooks	Charles Krauthammer
Naomi Klein	Leonard Pitts	Thomas Friedman	Peggy Noonan	Michelle Malkin
Michael Moore (film-maker)	Gail Collins	Kathleen Hall Jamieson	Jonah Goldberg	Glenn Beck (radio/TV)
Paul Krugman	Nicholas Kristof	Kevin Phillips	Andrew Sullivan	Rush Limbaugh (radio/TV)
Thom Hartman (radio)	Maureen Dowd	David Broder	George Will	Bill O'Reilly (radio/TV)
Rachel Maddow (television)	Mark Shields	William Saletan	Ruben Navarrette, Jr.	Kathleen Parker
	Frank Bruni	Mary Sanchez	Ross Douthat	Thomas Sowell
	Charles M. Blow		Paul Gigot	Avik Roy
	Froma Harrop			

Newspapers and Magazines**		
Left/Liberal	**Center**	**Right/Conservative**
The American Prospect	*Atlantic Monthly*	*American Spectator*
Harper's	*Business Week*	*Fortune*
Los Angeles Times	*Commentary*	*National Review*
Mother Jones	*Commonweal*	*Reader's Digest*
The Nation	*Foreign Affairs*	*Reason*
New York Times	*New Republic*	*Wall Street Journal*
New Yorker	*Slate*	*Washington Times*
Salon	*Washington Post*	*Weekly Standard*
Sojourners		

Blogs		
Liberal/Left	**Center**	**Right/Conservative**
americablog.com	donklephant.com	firstinthenation.us
crooksandliars.com	newmoderate.blogspot.com	instapundit.com
dailykos.com	politics-central.blogspot.com	littlegreenfootballs.com
digbysblog.blogspot.com	rantingbaldhippie.com	michellemalkin.com
firedoglake.com	stevesilver.net	polipundit.com
huffingtonpost.com	themoderatevoice.com	powerlineblog.com
mediamatters.com	washingtonindependent.com	sistertoldjah.com
talkingpointsmemo.com	watchingwashington.blogspot.com	redstate.com
wonkette.com		townhall.com

Think Tanks		
Left/Liberal	**Center**	**Right/Conservative**
Center for American Progress	The Brookings Institution	American Enterprise Institute
Center for Media and Democracy (sponsors Disinfopedia.org)	Carnegie Endowment for International Peace	Cato Institute (Libertarian)
Institute for Policy Studies	Council on Foreign Relations	Center for Strategic and International Studies
Open Society Institute (Soros Foundation)	Jamestown Foundation	Heritage Foundation (sponsors Townhall.com)
Progressive Policy Institute	National Bureau of Economic Research	Project for the New American Century
Urban Institute		

* For further information about the political leanings of publications or think tanks, ask your librarian about the Gale Directory of Publications and Broadcast Media or NIRA World Directory of Think Tanks.
** Newspapers are categorized according to positions they take on their editorial page; any reputable newspaper strives for objectivity in news reporting and includes a variety of views on its op-ed pages. Magazines do not claim and are not expected to present similar breadth and objectivity.

(commonly known as *think tanks*), and blogs across the political spectrum from left/liberal to right/conservative.

Although the terms *liberal* and *conservative* or *left* and *right* often have fuzzy meanings, they provide convenient shorthand for signaling a person's overall views about the proper role of government in relation to the economy and social values. Liberals, tending to sympathize with those potentially harmed by unfettered free markets (workers, consumers, plaintiffs, endangered species, the world's climate), are typically comfortable with government regulation of economic matters. Conservatives, who tend to sympathize with business interests, typically assert faith in free markets and favor a limited regulatory role for government. On social issues, conservatives tend to espouse traditional family values and advocate laws that would maintain these values (for example, banning abortion, opposing same-sex marriage). Liberals, on the other hand, tend to espouse individual choice regarding marital partnerships and a wide range of other issues. Some persons identify themselves as economic conservatives but social liberals; others side with workers' interests on economic issues but are conservative on social issues.

Finally, many persons regard themselves as "centrists." In Table 22.1 the column labeled "Center" includes commentators who seek out common ground between the left and the right and who often believe that the best civic decisions are compromises between opposing views. Likewise, centrist publications and institutes often approach issues from multiple points of view, looking for the most workable solutions.

Degree of Advocacy

By *degree of advocacy* we mean the extent to which an author unabashedly takes a persuasive stance on a contested position as opposed to adopting a more neutral, objective, or exploratory stance. For example, publications affiliated with advocacy organizations (the Sierra Club, the National Rifle Association) will have a clear editorial bias. When a writer has an ax to grind, you need to weigh carefully the writer's selection of evidence, interpretation of data, and fairness to opposing views.

Although no one can be completely neutral, it is always useful to seek out authors who offer a balanced assessment of the evidence. Evidence from a more detached and neutral writer may be more trusted by readers than the arguments of a committed advocate. For example, if you want to persuade corporate executives on the dangers of global warming, evidence from scholarly journals may be more persuasive than evidence from an environmentalist Web site or from a freelance writer for a leftist popular magazine such as *Mother Jones*.

Skill 22.3: Use your rhetorical knowledge to evaluate Web sources.

22.3 Use your rhetorical knowledge to evaluate Web sources.

In the previous section we focused on reading sources rhetorically by asking questions about a source's reliability, credibility, angle of vision, and degree of advocacy. In this section we focus on evaluating sources from the World Wide Web.

The Web as a Unique Rhetorical Environment

In addition to familiar entertainment and commercial sites, the Web can be a powerful research tool, providing access to highly specialized databases, historical archives, museum collections, governmental documents, blogosphere commentary, scholarly portals useful for academic researchers, and much more. The Web is also a great vehicle for democracy, giving voice to the otherwise voiceless. Anyone with a cause and a rudimentary knowledge of Web design can create a site. The result is a medium that differs in significant ways from print in its creators, composition, and multimodal content.

Criteria for Evaluating a Web Source

When you evaluate a Web source, we suggest that you ask five different kinds of questions about the site in which the source appeared, as shown in Table 22.2. These questions, developed by scholars and librarians as points to consider when you are evaluating Web sites, will help you determine the usefulness of a site or source for your own purposes.

As a researcher, the first question you should ask about a potentially useful Web source should be, "Who placed this piece on the Web and why?" You can begin answering this question by analyzing the site's home page, where you will often find navigational buttons linking to "Mission," "About Us," or other identifying information about the site's sponsors.

Table 22.2 Criteria for Evaluating Web Sites

Criteria	Questions to Ask
1. Authority	• Is the document author or site sponsor clearly identified? • Does the site identify the author's occupation, position, education, experience, or other credentials? • Does the home page or a clear link from the home page reveal the author's or sponsor's motivation for establishing the site? • Does the site provide contact information for the author or sponsor such as an e-mail or organization address?
2. Objectivity or Clear Disclosure of Advocacy	• Is the site's purpose clear (for example, to inform, entertain, or persuade)? • Is the site explicit about declaring its point of view? • Does the site indicate whether the author is affiliated with a specific organization, institution, or association? • Does the site indicate whether it is directed toward a specific audience?
3. Coverage	• Are the topics covered by the site clear? • Does the site exhibit a suitable depth and comprehensiveness for its purpose? • Is sufficient evidence provided to support the ideas and opinions presented?
4. Accuracy	• Are the sources of information stated? • Do the facts appear to be accurate? • Can you verify this information by comparing this source with other sources in the field?
5. Currency	• Are dates included in the Web site? • Do the dates apply to the material itself, to its placement on the Web, or to the time the site was last revised and updated? • Is the information current, or at least still relevant, for the site's purpose? For your purpose?

You can also get hints about the site's purpose by asking, "What kind of Web site is it?" Different kinds of Web sites have different purposes. You should be conscious of the site's purpose, which is often revealed by the domain identifier, such as .com or .org. The most common kinds of sites are as follows:

- **.com** and **.biz** for commercial sites (promoting businesses and marketing services, often with no identified author)

- **.org** sites for nonprofit organizations or advocacy groups (some with balanced coverage but many with distinct angles of vision)

- **.edu** sites for colleges or universities (often complex sites with institutional information as well as scholarly and advocacy links)

- **.gov** or **.mil** sites for government agencies or military units (with a range of data and support for policies)

Analyzing Your Own Purposes for Using Web Sources

Besides analyzing a sponsor's purpose for establishing a Web site, you also need to analyze your own purpose for using the site. To illustrate strategies for evaluating a Web site, we'll use as examples two hypothetical student researchers investigating the civic controversy over hydraulic fracturing (commonly called fracking), an advanced technological process for extracting natural gas from shale buried deep in the earth.

Our first student researcher was interested in doing a rhetorical analysis of arguments for and againt fracking. She did an initial Google search using "fracking" and "natural gas" as her keywords and found dozens of pro-fracking and anti-fracking sites sponsored by the government, energy companies, and advocacy organizations. She found a host of organizations protesting the spread of fracking: Americans Against Fracking, Artists Against Fracking, Students Against Fracking, Farmers Against Fracking, and New Yorkers Against Fracking, among others. She also found a number of sites enthusiastically supporting fracking. One site that caught her attention was EnergyFromShale.org. Fascinated by the way that this organization chose to emphasize economic opportunities for local communities with slideshows and videos of happy Americans, our researcher decided to focus her project on the ways that Web sites on fracking frame the issue and the kinds of arguments they make for and against the benefits and dangers of fracking.

Our second researcher was more directly interested in determining her own stance on the fracking debate. She was trying to decide from a citizen's perspective whether to advocate for fracking or to oppose it, or at least to advocate for more regulation of it. As a researcher, her dilemma was to determine how much she could trust data taken from these advocacy sites. For her, the sites were mostly secondary rather than primary sources.

Let's look at each student's research process in turn.

RESEARCHER 1: DOING A RHETORICAL ANALYSIS OF FRACKING WEB SITES   Our first researcher's goal was to analyze fracking sites rhetorically to understand the ways that stakeholders frame their interests and represent themselves. She discovered that the angle of vision of each site—whether pro-fracking or anti-fracking—led to the filtering of evidence in distinctive ways.

For example, the pro-fracking and natural gas sites emphasize the economic perspective. Appealing to both *logos* and *pathos*, these sites often feature slide-shows and testimonials of smiling people who report that when the oil and shale industry moves into a region, the economic benefits ripple outward, beyond the people who receive royalty checks for wells on their land. These sites claim that the industry brings increased revenue to the government and an infusion of jobs and thus income to boost local businesses such as banks, restaurants, and stores. In addition, the industry draws educational programs to train technicians, pro-viding more jobs. These sites seek to inspire confidence and alleviate fears, mini-mizing the dangers to the environment. On one site, the home page featured a brilliantly lit, aesthetically beautiful drilling rig photographed against a dawn sky and included links to other pages highlighting the economic and social ben-efits of fracking. (Because we were unable to get permission for reprinting screen grabs from these pro-fracking sties, we suggest that you do your own Internet search for them.)

In contrast, she discovered that anti-fracking sites sponsored by citizen activist groups and environmental advocacy organizations don't mention jobs and the economy (although they do mention the loss of property value from the toxicity of fracking wells) but rather focus on the immediate and long-term dangers to the environment, challenging the idea of "safe" processes. They underscore the lag in federal regulation of this extraction process. In addition to describing the gases released into the air in the process, these sites empha-size the millions of gallons of water pumped into the ground for each fracking well; the recent and possible contamination of water supplies for humans, fish, and wildlife from the toxicity of the chemicals mixed with this water; and the lack of environmentally safe disposal procedures. Also, while acknowledging that natural gas is cleaner burning than other fossil fuels, they point out that increased commitment to natural gas does little to lessen the climate-change threat, and may even make it worse (because of large amounts of methane released during the process). It also diverts attention from the need to develop renewable energy.

The anti-fracking sites' appeals to *logos* often focus on the dangers of pol-lution from fracking while their appeals to *pathos* seek to mobilize citizens against corporate power and to encourage stronger governmental regulation before it is too late. To convey the urgency of the issue and the momentum of the opposition to fracking, these anti-fracking sites often list the famous people and the numerous organizations, clubs, groups, businesses, and insti-tutions that support a ban on fracking, show photos of recent protests, and include open letters and news about current campaigns against fracking. The use of red, white, and blue in the Americans Against Fracking site, for example, creates an interesting patriotic appeal, a subtle "protect our coun-try" motif. (See Figure 22.1.) Also as appeals to *pathos*, anti-fracking sites use graphics of the extraction process that highlight the potential for contamina-tion of aquifers. The Part Opener that precedes Chapter 21 features a poster for the anti-fracking documentary film *Gasland* by Josh Fox. The poster por-trays methane, not water, coming out of water faucets, alluding to a problem some people have experienced when fracking gas leaks polluted their wells.

Figure 22.1 A Web Site Portraying Fracking Negatively (from Americans Against Fracking)

For Writing and Discussion

Analyzing the Rhetorical Elements of Advocacy Web Sites

Find advocacy Web sites that take opposing or alternative stands on a current public issue such as gun rights, abortion, immigration, agribusiness, or oil exploration.

Working individually, in small groups, or as a class, explore your answers to these questions:

1. Following this text's emphasis on observation as the first step in analysis, what is your initial impression of the images, information, and layout of the Web pages for the advocacy sites you have found?

2. How would you evaluate these Web sites in terms of authority, objectivity, coverage, accuracy, and currency?

3. How do these advocacy sites use *logos, ethos,* and *pathos* to sway readers toward their point of view?

4. How do these advocacy sites use multimodal arguments (combinations of images and text) to make their case? What do you see as the rhetorical advantages of using photographs, including photos of real people, versus using schematic drawings or graphics?

5. What rhetorical effect do you think the Web page designers were hoping to achieve for each of the sites you have observed?

For other strong appeals to *pathos*, see the promotional material for this film and its sequel on the Web.

RESEARCHER 2: USING ADVOCACY WEB SITES FOR DATA   Researcher 2 is seeking to create her own research-based argument on whether citizens should support or oppose fracking. Her dilemma is to determine to what extent she can use the "facts" presented on these advocacy Web sites. For example, can she trust the pro-fracking sites' statements that drilling companies cooperate with local agencies to protect groundwater and act responsibly in recycling water? On anti-fracking sites, she frequently encountered equivalent statements of fact that raised serious questions about drilling companies' lack of concern for local water, the radioactive and carcinogenic chemicals used, and the failure to clean up water, which is left to seep into the groundwater and eventually into rivers and lakes.

In her initial Web search, she explored the Web site for Energy Citizens, a pro-oil and gas industry site. Searching for information on natural gas and delving into the Web site, she found an article entitled "Freeing Up Energy: Hydraulic Fracturing: Unlocking America's Natural Gas Resources." This article argues that hydraulic fracturing is a process that has been around for decades—although it is improved now—and that it is well monitored by industry itself and by environmental laws. It underscores the lack of confirmed cases of groundwater contamination and the measures involved in the design of wells and the fracking process itself, intended to safeguard groundwater. The purpose of this article and the site is to present fracking as an environmentally safe process, to increase citizens' confidence in the oil and gas industry, and to encourage citizens to relinquish their fears and concerns about the environment and focus on the message of the rest of the article—the benefits of fracking in the form of jobs, revenue, and abundant natural gas resources to last a hundred years.

How should our second researcher proceed in evaluating such an article for her own research purposes? Her first step is to evaluate the site itself. When she reviewed the home page for this site, she found that the site's sponsors targeted a range of energy issues including support for the Keystone XL Pipeline, opposition to the Renewable Fuel Standard, and support for developing domestic oil both on and offshore. The site also emphasized the substantial taxes that oil and gas companies pay to the federal government. This site obviously advocates a pro-corporation stance and boldly links business growth and prosperity with national well-being. It couples an image of the Statue of Liberty with energy security and a photo of a woman worker with the Keystone XL Pipeline. With this perspective in mind, Researcher 2, reconsidering the article about fracking, could easily evaluate this site against the five criteria:

1. *Authority:*   She could clearly tell that this site is an advocacy organization affiliated with the petroleum industry; indeed, the article was written by the American Petroleum Institute.

2. *Advocacy:*   This site clearly promotes removing restrictions from the oil and gas industry and expanding its opportunities for growth, based on the economic philosophy that what is good for American business is good for American citizens.

3. *Coverage:* This site does not cover fracking issues in a complex way. Every aspect of the site and the article is filtered to support the growth of the oil and gas industry.

4. *Accuracy:* At this point, she was unable to check each of the article's assertions about the safety of the fracking process against other sources, but she assumed that all claims and statistics would be rhetorically filtered and selected to accord with the site's angle of vision.

5. *Currency:* Although the article was dated July 19, 2010, one main study cited in it was dated 2004, before recent reports of problems with contamination of water systems by fracking.

Based on this analysis, how might Researcher 2 use the "Freeing Up Energy" article from the Energy Citizens site? Our view is that the article could be very useful as one perspective on the fracking controversy. It is a fairly representative example of the argument that the benefits of fracking far outweigh any possible risk to the environment. It clearly shows the kinds of rhetorical strategies such articles use—claims about the abundance of the resource and the promise of energy independence, the nonexistence of verifiable risks, and the effectiveness of current regulations. A summary of this article's argument could therefore be effective for presenting the pro-fracking point of view.

As a source of factual data, however, this article is unusable. It would be irresponsible for her to use the facts in this article without seeking out other recent sources and reviewing recent legislation regulating fracking. Similarly, it would be irresponsible to adopt the anti-fracking advocacy groups' views of the pollution and contamination of water by fracking wells without researching specific claims and state-by-state records. Researcher 2 should instead seek out governmental data, pending legislation, and scientific sources, including peer-reviewed research articles by scholars, to get a current, larger, more accurate perspective and to find neutral studies, not funded by the oil and gas industry, and not featured by anti-fracking documentary films. One purpose of reading sources rhetorically is to appreciate how much advocates for a given position filter data. Finding and interpreting original data are two challenges of responsible research.

For Writing and Discussion

Analyzing the Use of Information Graphics in Advocacy Web Sites

Pro-fracking Web sites take pains to assure their audiences that fracking is environmentally safe. Conversely, anti-fracking Web sites emphasize the environmental dangers of fracking. Figures 22.2 and 22.3 are examples of information graphics, in this case diagrams, that are similar to those found on pro- and anti-fracking advocacy sites. Figure 22.2 is a typical diagram that aims to persuade viewers that fracking poses no dangers to underground aquifers. In contrast, the diagram in Figure 22.3 emphasizes the dangers of fracking to water supplies.

(continued)

Figure 22.2 Typical Diagram Showing Safety of Fracking

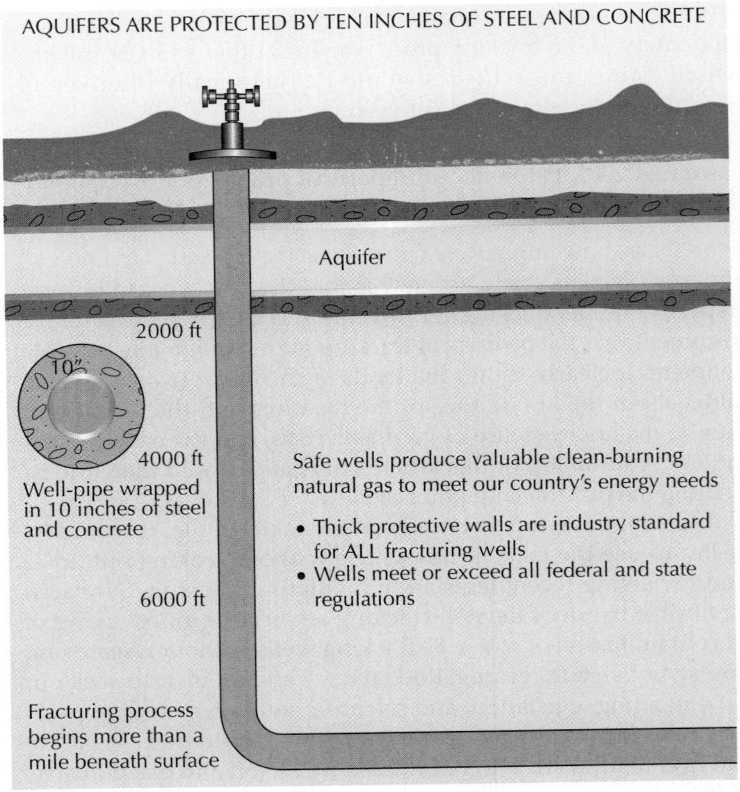

AQUIFERS ARE PROTECTED BY TEN INCHES OF STEEL AND CONCRETE

Aquifer

2000 ft

10"

4000 ft

Well-pipe wrapped
in 10 inches of steel
and concrete

6000 ft

Safe wells produce valuable clean-burning
natural gas to meet our country's energy needs

- Thick protective walls are industry standard
  for ALL fracturing wells
- Wells meet or exceed all federal and state
  regulations

Fracturing process
begins more than a
mile beneath surface

Figure 22.3 Typical Diagram Showing Dangers of Fracking

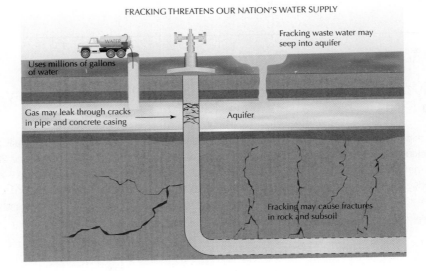

FRACKING THREATENS OUR NATION'S WATER SUPPLY

Fracking waste water may
seep into aquifer

WATER

Uses millions of gallons
of water

Gas may leak through cracks
in pipe and concrete casing

Aquifer

Fracking may cause fractures
in rock and subsoil

Working individually or in groups, examine the diagrams and try to reach consensus on the following questions about the rhetorical effect, accuracy, credibility, and reliability of these graphics.

1. What is the angle of vision of each graphic? How do the visual and verbal features of each graphic contribute to its purpose? What is "seen" in each graphic and what is "not seen"?

2. What rhetorical effect do you think each designer intends the graphic to have on readers? How do these graphics use appeals to *logos, pathos,* and *ethos*? How accurate, credible, and reliable do you find each graphic?

3. What questions do each of these graphics raise that you would want to check through further research?

4. Which graphic do you find more rhetorically effective and why?

Chapter 23
Incorporating Sources Into Your Own Writing

Learning Objectives

23.1 Let your own argument determine your use of sources.

23.2 Know when and how to use summary, paraphrase, and quotation.

23.3 Use attributive tags to distinguish your ideas from a source's.

23.4 Avoid plagiarism by following academic conventions for ethical use of sources.

So far, we have covered strategies for finding and evaluating sources. Now we focus on the skills needed for incorporating sources into your own writing. Many of the examples in this chapter will be based on the following short article from the Web site of the American Council on Science and Health (ACSH)—an organization of doctors and scientists devoted to providing scientific information on health issues and to exposing health fads and myths. Please read the argument carefully in preparation for the discussions that follow.

Is Vegetarianism Healthier than Nonvegetarianism?

Many people become vegetarians because they believe, in error, that vegetarianism is uniquely conducive to good health. The findings of several large epidemiologic studies indeed suggest that the death and chronic-disease rates of vegetarians—primarily vegetarians who consume dairy products or both dairy products and eggs—are lower than those of meat eaters . . . .

The health of vegetarians may be better than that of nonvegetarians partly because of nondietary factors: Many vegetarians are health-conscious. They exercise regularly, maintain a desirable body weight, and abstain from smoking. Although most epidemiologists have attempted to take such factors into account in their analyses, it is possible that they did not adequately control their studies for nondietary effects.

People who are vegetarians by choice may differ from the general population in other ways relevant to health. For example, in Western countries most vegetarians are more affluent than nonvegetarians and thus have better living conditions and more access to medical care.

An authoritative review of vegetarianism and chronic diseases classified the evidence for various alleged health benefits of vegetarianism:

- The evidence is "strong" that vegetarians have (a) a lower risk of becoming alcoholic, constipated, or obese and (b) a lower risk of developing lung cancer.
- The evidence is "good" that vegetarians have a lower risk of developing adult-onset diabetes mellitus, coronary artery disease, hypertension, and gallstones.
- The evidence is "fair to poor" that vegetarianism decreases risk of breast cancer, colon cancer, diverticular disease, kidney-stone formation, osteoporosis, and tooth decay.

For some of the diseases mentioned above, the practice of vegetarianism itself probably is the main protective factor. For example, the low incidence of constipation among vegetarians is almost certainly due to their high intakes of fiber-rich foods. For other conditions, nondietary factors may be more important than diet. For example, the low incidence of lung cancer among vegetarians is attributable primarily to their extremely low rate of cigarette smoking. Diet is but one of many risk factors for most chronic diseases.

Skill 23.1: Let your own argument determine your use of sources.

23.1 Let your own argument determine your use of sources.

How you might use this article in your own writing would depend on your research question and purpose. To illustrate, we'll show you three different hypothetical examples of writers who have reason to cite this article.

WRITER 1: AN ANALYSIS OF ALTERNATIVE APPROACHES TO REDUCING ALCOHOLISM

Writer 1 argues that vegetarianism may be an effective way to resist alcoholism. She uses just one statement from the ACSH article for her own purpose and then moves on to other sources.

Another approach to fighting alcoholism is through naturopathy, holistic medicine, and vegetarianism. Vegetarians generally have better health than the rest of the population and particularly have, according to the American Council on Science and Health, "a lower risk of becoming alcoholic." This lower risk has been borne out by other studies showing that the benefits of the holistic health movement are particularly strong for persons with addictive tendencies. . . . [goes on to other arguments and sources]	*Writer's claim* *Identification of source* *Quotation from ACSH*

WRITER 2: A PROPOSAL ADVOCATING VEGETARIANISM

Writer 2 proposes that people become vegetarians. Parts of his argument focus on the environmental costs and ethics of eating meat, but he also devotes one paragraph to the health benefits of vegetarianism. As support for this point he summarizes the ACSH article's material on health benefits.

Writer's claim

Identification of source

Summary of ACSH material

    Not only will a vegetarian diet help stop cruelty to animals, but it is also good for your health. According to the American Council on Science and Health, vegetarians have longer life expectancy than nonvegetarians and suffer from fewer chronic diseases. The Council cites "strong" evidence from the scientific literature showing that vegetarians have reduced risk of lung cancer, obesity, constipation, and alcoholism. The Council also cites "good" evidence that they have a reduced risk of adult-onset diabetes, high blood pressure, gallstones, and hardening of the arteries. Although the evidence isn't nearly as strong, vegetarianism may also lower the risk of certain cancers, kidney stones, loss of bone density, and tooth decay.

WRITER 3: AN EVALUATION LOOKING SKEPTICALLY AT VEGETARIANISM

Here, Writer 3 uses portions of the same article to make an opposite case from that of Writer 2. She focuses on those parts of the article that Writer 2 consciously excluded.

Writer's claim

Identification of source

Paraphrased points from ACSH

    The link between vegetarianism and death rates is a classic instance of correlation rather than causation. While it is true that vegetarians have a longer life expectancy than nonvegetarians and suffer from fewer chronic diseases, the American Council on Science and Health has shown that the causes can mostly be explained by factors other than diet. As the Council suggests, vegetarians are apt to be more health conscious than nonvegetarians and thus get more exercise, stay slender, and avoid smoking. The Council points out that vegetarians also tend to be wealthier than nonvegetarians and see their doctors more regularly. In short, they live longer because they take better care of themselves, not because they avoid meat.

For Writing and Discussion
Using a Source for Different Purposes

Each of the hypothetical writers uses the short ACSH argument in different ways for different purposes. Working individually or in small groups, respond to the following questions. Be prepared to elaborate on and defend your answers.

1. How does each writer use the original article differently and why?
2. If you were the author of the article from the American Council on Science and Health, would you think that your article is used fairly and responsibly in each instance?
3. Suppose your goal were simply to summarize the argument from the American Council on Science and Health. Write a brief summary of the argument and then explain how your summary is different from the partial summaries by Writers 2 and 3.

Skill 23.2: Know when and how to use summary, paraphrase, and quotation.

23.2 Know when and how to use summary, paraphrase, and quotation.

As a research writer, you need to incorporate sources gracefully into your own prose so that you stay focused on your own argument. Depending on your purpose, you might (1) summarize all or part of a source author's argument, (2) paraphrase a relevant portion of a source, or (3) quote small passages from the source directly. Whenever you use a source, you need to avoid plagiarism by referencing the source with an in-text citation, by putting paraphrases and summaries entirely in your own words, and by placing quotation marks around quoted passages. Strategies Chart 23.1 gives you an overview of summary, paraphrase, and quotation as ways of incorporating sources into your own prose.

For an explanation of avoiding plagiarism in academic writing, see Skill 23.4. For in-text citations, see Chapter 24.

Strategies Chart 23.1 Strategies for Incorporating Sources into Your Own Prose

Strategies	What to Do	When to Use These Strategies
Summarize the source.	Condense a source writer's argument by keeping main ideas and omitting details (see Chapter 6 for instruction on writing summaries).	• When the source writer's whole argument is relevant to your purpose • When the source writer presents an alternative or opposing view that you want to push against • When the source writer's argument can be used in support of your own
Paraphrase the source.	Reproduce an idea from a source writer but translate the idea entirely into your own words; a paraphrase should be approximately the same length as the original.	• When you want to incorporate factual information from a source or to use one specific idea from a source • When the source passage is overly complex or technical for your targeted audience • When you want to incorporate a source's point in your own voice without interrupting the flow of your argument
Quote short passages from the source.	Work brief quotations from the source smoothly into the grammar of your own sentences using quotation marks appropriately. (See explanations of the mechanics of quoting later in this section.)	• When you need testimony from an authority (state the authority's credentials in an attributive tag—see Skill 23.3) • In summaries, when you want to reproduce a source's voice, particularly if the language is striking or memorable • In lieu of paraphrase when the source language is memorable
Quote long passages from the source.	Use the block method without quotation marks (see Skill 23.4). Note that this method creates pages with long blocks of quoted text; use rarely.	• When you intend to analyze or critique the quotation—the quotation is followed by your detailed analysis of its ideas or rhetorical features • When the flavor and language of testimonial evidence is important

With practice, you'll be able to use all these strategies smoothly and effectively.

Summarizing

Detailed instructions on how to write a summary of an article and incorporate it into your own prose are provided in Chapter 6. Summaries can be as short as a single sentence or as long as a paragraph. Make the summary as concise as possible so that you don't distract the reader from your own argument. Writer 2's partial summary of the ACSH article (focusing on the benefits of vegetarianism) is a good example of a summary used in support of the writer's own thesis.

Paraphrasing

Unlike a summary, which is a condensation of a source's whole argument, a **paraphrase** translates a short passage from a source's words into the writer's own words. Writers often choose to paraphrase when the details of a source passage are particularly important or when the source is overly technical and needs to be simplified for the intended audience.

When you paraphrase, be careful to avoid reproducing the original writer's grammatical structure and syntax. If you mirror the original sentence structure while replacing occasional words with synonyms or small structural changes, you will be doing what composition specialists call "**patchwriting**"—that is, patching some of your language into someone else's writing.* Patchwriting is a form of academic dishonesty because you aren't fully composing your own sentences and thus misrepresent both your own work and that of the source writer. An acceptable paraphrase needs to be entirely in your own words. To understand patchwriting more fully, track the differences between unacceptable patchwriting and acceptable paraphrase in the following examples.

ORIGINAL

- The evidence is "strong" that vegetarians have (a) a lower risk of becoming alcoholic, constipated, or obese and (b) a lower risk of developing lung cancer.
- The evidence is "good" that vegetarians have a lower risk of developing adult-onset diabetes mellitus, coronary artery disease, hypertension, and gallstones.

UNACCEPTABLE PATCHWRITING

Identification of source

Note phrases taken word for word from original.

According to the American Council on Science and Health, there is strong evidence that vegetarians have a lower risk of becoming alcoholic, constipated, or obese. The evidence is also strong that they have a lower risk of lung cancer. The evidence is good that vegetarians are less apt to develop adult-onset diabetes, coronary artery disease, hypertension, or gallstones.

---

* We are indebted to the work of Rebecca Moore Howard and others who have led composition researchers to reexamine the use of sources and plagiarism from a cultural and rhetorical perspective. See especially Rebecca Moore Howard, *Standing in the Shadow of Giants: Plagiarists, Authors, Collaborators.* Stamford, CT: Ablex Pub., 1999.

ACCEPTABLE PARAPHRASE

The Council summarizes "strong" evidence from the scientific literature showing that vegetarians have reduced risk of lung cancer, obesity, constipation, and alcoholism. The council also cites "good" evidence that they have a reduced risk of adult-onset diabetes, high blood pressure, gallstones, or hardening of the arteries.

> *Identification of source Doesn't follow original sentence structure*

> *Quotes "strong" and "good" to indicate distinction made in original*

Both the patchwriting example and the acceptable paraphrase reproduce the same ideas as the original in approximately the same number of words. But the writer of the acceptable paraphrase has been more careful to change the sentence structure substantially and not copy exact phrases. In contrast, the patchwritten version contains longer strings of borrowed language without quotation marks.

Among novice writers, the ease of copying Web sources can lead to patchwriting. You may be tempted to copy and paste a Web-based passage into your own draft and then revise it slightly by changing some of the words. Such patchwriting won't occur if you write in your own voice—that is, if you convert information from a source into your own words in order to make your own argument.

When you first practice paraphrasing, try paraphrasing a passage twice to avoid patchwriting:

- The first time, read the passage carefully and put it into your own words, looking at the source as little as possible.

- The second time, paraphrase your own paraphrase. Then recheck your final version against the original to make sure you have eliminated similar sentence structures or word-for-word strings.

We return to the problem of patchwriting in our discussion of plagiarism (Skill 23.4).

Quoting

Besides summary and paraphrase, writers often choose to quote directly in order to give the reader the flavor and style of the source author's prose or to make a memorable point in the source author's own voice. Be careful not to quote a passage that you don't fully understand. (Sometimes novice writers quote a passage because it sounds impressive.) When you quote, you must reproduce the source author's original words exactly without change, unless you indicate changes with ellipses or brackets. Also be careful to represent the author's intention and meaning fairly; don't change the author's meaning by taking quotations out of context.

Because the mechanics of quoting offers its own difficulties, we devote the following sections to it. These sections answer the nuts-and-bolts questions about how to punctuate quotations correctly. Additional explanations covering variations and specific cases can be found in any good handbook.

QUOTING A COMPLETE SENTENCE   In some cases, you will want to quote a complete sentence from your source. Typically, you will include an attributive tag that tells the reader who is being quoted Skill 23.3). At the end of the quotation, indicate its page number in parentheses if it comes from a print or PDF document with stable page numbers (see our discussion of in-text citations, Chapter 24).

ORIGINAL PASSAGE

> Many people become vegetarians because they believe, in error, that vegetarianism is uniquely conducive to good health.

WRITER'S QUOTATION OF THIS PASSAGE

Attributive tag

Quotation introduced with comma. Quotation is a complete sentence, so it starts with a capital letter.

According to the American Council on Science and Health, "Many people become vegetarians because they believe, in error, that vegetarianism is uniquely conducive to good health." [In most cases, a page number in parentheses would come before the final period. However, this example and those that follow have no page number because the original passage came from a Web document without stable page numbers.]

QUOTING WORDS AND PHRASES   Instead of quoting a complete sentence, you often want to quote only a few words or phrases from your source and insert them into your own sentence. In these cases, make sure that the grammatical structure of the quotation fits smoothly into the grammar of your own sentence.

ORIGINAL PASSAGE

> The health of vegetarians may be better than that of nonvegetarians partly because of nondietary factors: Many vegetarians are health-conscious. They exercise regularly, maintain a desirable body weight, and abstain from smoking.

QUOTED PHRASE INSERTED INTO WRITER'S OWN SENTENCE

Attributive tag

Quotation marks show where quotation starts and ends.

No comma or capital letter: Punctuation and capitalization determined by grammar of your own sentence.

The American Council on Science and Health argues that the cause of vegetarians' longer life may be "nondietary factors." The Council claims that vegetarians are more "health-conscious" than meat eaters and that they "exercise regularly, maintain a desirable body weight, and abstain from smoking."

MODIFYING A QUOTATION   Occasionally you may need to alter a quotation to make it fit your own context. Sometimes the grammar of a desired quotation doesn't match the grammar of your own sentence. At other times, the meaning of a quoted word is unclear when it is removed from its original context. In these cases, use brackets to modify the quotation's grammar or to add a clarifying explanation. Place your changes or additions in brackets to indicate that the bracketed material is not part of the original wording. You should also use brackets to show a change in capitalization.

ORIGINAL PASSAGE

Many vegetarians are health-conscious. They exercise regularly, maintain a desirable body weight, and abstain from smoking.

QUOTATIONS MODIFIED WITH BRACKETS

The American Council on Science and Health hypothesizes that vegetarians maintain better health by "exercis[ing] regularly, maintain[ing] a desirable body weight, and abstain[ing] from smoking."

Attributive tag

Brackets show change in quotation to fit grammar of writer's sentence.

According to the American Council on Science and Health, "They [vegetarians] exercise regularly, maintain a desirable body weight, and abstain from smoking."

Attributive tag

Brackets show that writer has added a word to explain what "they" stands for.

OMITTING SOMETHING FROM A QUOTED PASSAGE Another way that writers modify quotations is to leave words out of the quoted passage. To indicate an omission, use three spaced periods called an **ellipsis** (. . .). Placement of the ellipsis depends on where the omitted material occurs. In the middle of a sentence, each of the periods should be preceded and followed by a space. When your ellipsis comes at the boundary between sentences, use an additional period to mark the end of the first sentence. When a parenthetical page number must follow the ellipsis, insert it before the final (fourth) period in the sequence.

ORIGINAL PASSAGE

People who are vegetarians by choice may differ from the general population in other ways relevant to health. For example, in Western countries most vegetarians are more affluent than nonvegetarians and thus have better living conditions and more access to medical care.

QUOTATIONS WITH OMITTED MATERIAL MARKED BY ELLIPSES

According to the American Council on Science and Health, "people who are vegetarians by choice may differ . . . in other ways relevant to health. For example, in Western countries most vegetarians are more affluent than nonvegetarians . . . ."

Three spaced periods mark omitted words in middle of sentence. Note spaces between each period.

Three periods form the ellipsis. (Omitted material comes before the end of the sentence.)

QUOTING SOMETHING THAT CONTAINS A QUOTATION Occasionally a passage that you wish to quote will already contain quotation marks. If you insert the passage within your own quotation marks, change the original double marks (") into single marks (') to indicate the quotation within the quotation. The same procedure works whether the quotation marks are used for quoted words or for a title. Make sure that your attributive tag signals who is being quoted.

ORIGINAL PASSAGE

The evidence is "strong" that vegetarians have (a) a lower risk of becoming alcoholic, constipated, or obese and (b) a lower risk of developing lung cancer.

USE OF SINGLE QUOTATION MARKS TO IDENTIFY A QUOTATION WITHIN A QUOTATION

Double quotation marks enclose the material quoted from the source.

Single quotation marks replace the double quotation marks in the original source.

According to the American Council on Science and Health, "The evidence is 'strong' that vegetarians have (a) a lower risk of becoming alcoholic, constipated, or obese and (b) a lower risk of developing lung cancer."

USING A BLOCK QUOTATION FOR A LONG PASSAGE If you quote a long source passage that will take four or more lines in your own paper, use the block indentation method rather than quotation marks. Block quotations are generally introduced with an attributive tag followed by a colon. The indented block of text, rather than quotation marks, signals that the material is a direct quotation. Block quotations occur rarely in scholarly writing and are used primarily in cases where the writer intends to analyze the text being quoted. If you overuse block quotations, you simply produce a collage of other people's voices.

ORIGINAL PASSAGE

The health of vegetarians may be better than that of nonvegetarians partly because of nondietary factors: Many vegetarians are health-conscious. They exercise regularly, maintain a desirable body weight, and abstain from smoking. Although most epidemiologists have attempted to take such factors into account in their analyses, it is possible that they did not adequately control their studies for nondietary effects.

BLOCK QUOTATION

The American Council on Science and Health suggests that vegetarians may be healthier than nonvegetarians not because of their diet but because of their more healthy lifestyle:

Block quotation introduced with a colon

No quotation marks

Block indented 1/2 inch on left

Many vegetarians are health-conscious. They exercise regularly, maintain a desirable body weight, and abstain from smoking. Although most epidemiologists have attempted to take such factors into account in their analyses, it is possible that they did not adequately control their studies for nondietary effects.

Skill 23.3: Use attributive tags to distinguish your ideas from a source's.

23.3   Use attributive tags to distinguish your ideas from a source's.

Whenever you use sources in your writing, you need to signal to your reader which words and ideas come from your source and which are your own. There are generally two ways of doing so:

- *State source author's name in an attributive tag.*   You can identify the source by using a short phrase (called an **attributive tag** or sometimes a **signal phrase** or **signal tag**) such as "according to the American Council on Science and Health," "Kent Ansen says," "in Ansen's view," and so on. In the humanities, the source author's full name is commonly used the first time the author is mentioned. If the tag refers to a specific passage or quotation in a print or pdf source, then a page number is placed in parentheses at the end of the quotation (see Skill 23.2).

  According to Kent Ansen, a year of public service should be required of all American young adults.

  Attributive tag

  Ansen explains that "mandated national service could be built upon the model of AmeriCorps" (349).

  Attributive tag

  Page number of quotation

- *State source author's name in a parenthetical citation.*   You can identify a source by placing the author's name in parentheses at the end of the material taken from the source (called a **parenthetical citation**).

  A year of public service should be required of all American young adults (Ansen).

  Source identified in parentheses

  "Mandated national service could be built upon the model of AmeriCorps" (Ansen 349).

  Page number of quotation

Of these two methods, attributive tags are generally preferred, especially when you are writing for general rather than specialist audiences. The attributive tag method has three advantages:

- It signals where borrowed material starts and ends.
- It avoids ambiguities about what is "fact" versus what is filtered through a source's angle of vision.
- It allows the writer to frame the borrowed material rhetorically.

  Let's look at each of these methods in turn.

Attributive Tags Mark Where Source Material Starts and Ends

The parenthetical method requires readers to wait until the end of the writer's use of source material before the source is identified. Attributive tags, in contrast, identify the source from the moment it is first used. Here are excerpts from Writer 2's summary of the American Council on Science and Health's article, in which we have highlighted the attributive tags. Note the frequency with which the writer informs the reader that this material comes from the Council. (The complete passage from Writer 2 appears in Skill 23.1.)

USE OF ATTRIBUTIVE TAGS IN WRITER 2's SUMMARY

Not only will a vegetarian diet help stop cruelty to animals, but it is also good for your health. According to the American Council on Science and Health, vegetarians have longer life expectancy than nonvegetarians and suffer from fewer chronic diseases. The Council cites "strong" evidence from the scientific literature showing that vegetarians have reduced risk of lung cancer, obesity, constipation, and alcoholism. They also cite "good" evidence that they have a reduced risk of adult-onset diabetes, high blood pressure, gallstones, or hardening of the arteries.

Here the attributive tags signal the use of the Council's ideas throughout the summary. The reader is never confused about which words and ideas come from the original article.

Attributive Tags Avoid Ambiguities That Can Arise with Parenthetical Citations

Not only does the parenthetical method fail to mark where the source material begins, it also tends to imply that the source material is a "fact" rather than the view of the source author. In contrast, attributive tags always call attention to the source's angle of vision. Note this ambiguity in the following passage, where parenthetical citations are used without attributive tags:

AMBIGUOUS ATTRIBUTIONS

There are many arguments in favor of preserving old-growth forests. First, it is simply unnecessary to log these forests to supply the world's lumber. We have plenty of new-growth forest from which lumber can be taken (Sagoff 89–90). Recently there have been major reforestation efforts all over the United States, and it is common practice now for loggers to replant every tree that is harvested. These new-growth forests, combined with extensive planting of tree farms, provide more than enough wood for the world's needs. Tree farms alone can supply the world's demand for industrial lumber (Sedjo 90).

When confronted with this passage, skeptical readers might ask, "Who are Sagoff and Sedjo? I've never heard of them." It is also difficult to tell how much of the passage is the writer's own argument and how much is borrowed from Sagoff and Sedjo. Is this whole passage a paraphrase? Finally, the writer tends to treat Sagoff's and Sedjo's assertions as uncontested facts rather than as professional opinions. Compare the preceding version with this one, in which attributive tags are added:

CLEAR ATTRIBUTION

There are many arguments in favor of preserving old-growth forests. First, it is simply unnecessary to log these forests to supply the world's lumber. According to environmentalist Carl Sagoff, we have plenty of new-growth forest from which lumber can be taken (89–90). Recently there have been major reforestation efforts all over the United States, and it is common practice now for loggers to replant every tree that is harvested. These new-growth forests, combined with extensive planting of tree farms, provide more than enough wood for the world's needs. According to forestry expert Robert Sedjo, tree farms alone can supply the world's demand for industrial lumber (90).

We can now see that most of the paragraph is the writer's own argument, into which she has inserted the expert testimony of Sagoff and Sedjo, whose views are treated not as indisputable facts but as the opinions of authorities in this field.

Attributive Tags Frame the Source Material Rhetorically

When you introduce a source for the first time, you can use the attributive tag not only to introduce the source but also to shape your readers's attitudes toward the source. In the previous example, the writer wants readers to respect Sagoff and Sedjo, so she identifies Sagoff as an "environmentalist" and Sedjo as a "forestry expert." If the writer favored logging old-growth forests and supported the logging industry's desire to create more jobs, she might have used different tags: "Carl Sagoff, an outspoken advocate for spotted owls over people," or "Robert Sedjo, a forester with limited knowledge of world lumber markets."

When you compose an initial tag, you can add to it any combination of the kinds of information found in Strategies Chart 23.2, depending on your purpose, your audience's values, and your sense of what the audience already knows or doesn't know about the source.

Our point here is that you can use attributive tags rhetorically to help your readers understand the significance and context of a source when you first introduce it and to guide your readers' attitudes toward the source.

Strategies Chart 23.2 Strategies for Modifying Attributive Tags to Shape Reader Response

Add to Attributive Tags	Examples
Author's credentials or relevant specialty (enhances credibility)	Civil engineer David Rockwood, a noted authority on stream flow in rivers
Author's lack of credentials (decreases credibility)	City Council member Dilbert Weasel, a local politician with no expertise in international affairs
Author's political or social views	Left-wing columnist Alexander Cockburn [has negative feeling]; Alexander Cockburn, a longtime champion of labor [has positive feeling]
Title of source if it provides context	In her book *Fasting Girls: The History of Anorexia Nervosa,* Joan Jacobs Brumberg shows that [establishes credentials for comments on eating disorders]
Publisher of source if it adds prestige or otherwise shapes audience response	Dr. Carl Patrona, in an article published in the prestigious *New England Journal of Medicine*
Historical or cultural information about a source that provides context or background	In his 1960s book popularizing the hippie movement, Charles Reich claims that
Indication of source's purpose or angle of vision	Feminist author Naomi Wolfe, writing a blistering attack on the beauty industry, argues that

For Writing and Discussion
Evaluating Different Ways to Use and Cite a Source

What follow are four different ways that a writer can use the same passage from a source to support a point about the greenhouse effect. Working in groups or as a class, rank the four methods from "most effective" to "least effective." Assume that you are writing a researched argument addressed to your college classmates.

1. *Quotation with parenthetical citation* The greenhouse effect will have a devastating effect on the earth's environment: "Potential impacts include increased mortality and illness due to heat stress and worsened air pollution, as in the 1995 Chicago heat wave that killed hundreds of people. . . . Infants, children and other vulnerable populations—especially in already-stressed regions of the world—would likely suffer disproportionately from these impacts" (Hall 19).

2. *Quotation with attributive tag* The greenhouse effect will have a devastating effect on the earth's environment. David C. Hall, president of Physicians for Social Responsibility, claims the following: "Potential impacts include increased mortality and illness due to heat stress and worsened air pollution, as in the 1995 Chicago heat wave that killed hundreds of people. . . . Infants, children and other vulnerable populations—especially in already-stressed regions of the world—would likely suffer disproportionately from these impacts" (19).

3. *Paraphrase with parenthetical citation* The greenhouse effect will have a devastating effect on the earth's environment. One of the most frightening effects is the threat of diseases stemming from increased air pollution and heat stress. Infants and children would be most at risk (Hall 19).

4. *Paraphrase with attributive tag* The greenhouse effect will have a devastating effect on the earth's environment. One of the most frightening effects, according to David C. Hall, president of Physicians for Social Responsibility, is the threat of diseases stemming from increased air pollution and heat stress. Infants and children would be most at risk (19).

Skill 23.4: Avoid plagiarism by following academic conventions for ethical use of sources.

23.4 Avoid plagiarism by following academic conventions for ethical use of sources.

In the next chapter, we proceed to the nuts and bolts of citing and document-ing sources—a skill that will enhance your *ethos* as a skilled researcher and as a person of integrity. Unethical use of sources—called **plagiarism**—is a major concern not only for writing teachers but for writers in all disciplines. To combat plagiarism, many instructors across the curriculum use plagiarism-detection software like turnitin.com. Their purpose, of course, is to discourage students from cheating. But sometimes students who have no intention of cheating can fall into producing papers that look like cheating. That is, they produce papers that might be accused of plagiarism even though the students had no intention of deceiving their readers.* Our goal in this sec-tion is to explain the concept of plagiarism more fully and to sum up the strategies to avoid it.

Why Some Kinds of Plagiarism May Occur Unwittingly

To understand how unwitting plagiarism might occur, consider Table 23.1, where the middle column—"Misuse of Sources"—shows common mistakes of novice writers. Everyone agrees that the behaviors in the "Fraud" column constitute deliberate cheating and deserve appropriate punishment. Everyone also agrees that good scholarly work meets the criteria in the "Ethical Use of Sources" column. Novice researchers, however, may find themselves unwit-tingly in the middle column until they learn the academic community's conven-tions for using research sources.

You might appreciate these conventions more fully if you recognize how they have evolved from Western notions of intellectual property and patent law associated with the rise of modern science in the seventeenth and eighteenth centuries. A person not only could own a house or a horse, but also could own an idea and the words used to express that idea. You can see these cultural con-ventions at work—in the form of laws or professional codes of ethics—whenever a book author is disgraced for lifting words or ideas from another author or whenever an artist or entrepreneur is sued for stealing song lyrics, publishing another person's photographs without permission, or infringing on some inven-tor's patent.

This understanding of plagiarism may seem odd in some non-Western cul-tures where collectivism is valued more than individualism. In these cultures,

---

* See Rebecca Moore Howard, *Standing in the Shadow of Giants: Plagiarists, Authors, Collaborators.* Stamford, CT: Ablex Pub., 1999.

Table 23.1 Plagiarism and the Ethical Use of Sources

Plagiarism		Ethical Use of Sources
Fraud	Misuse of Sources *(Common Mistakes Made by New Researchers)*	
The writer	The writer	The writer
• buys paper from a paper mill • submits someone else's work as his own • copies chunks of text from sources with obvious intention of not being detected • fabricates data or makes up evidence • intends to deceive	• copies passages directly from a source, references the source with an in-text citation, but fails to use quotation marks or block indentation • in attempting to paraphrase a source, makes some changes, but follows too closely the wording of the original ("patchwriting") • fails to indicate the sources of some ideas or data (often is unsure what needs to be cited or has lost track of sources through poor notetaking) • in general, misunderstands the conventions for using sources in academic writing	• writes paper entirely in her own words or uses exact quotations from sources • indicates all quotations with quotation marks or block indentation • indicates her use of all sources through attribution, in-text citation, and an end-of-paper list of works cited

words written or spoken by ancestors, elders, or other authority figures may be regarded with reverence and shared without attribution. Also in these cultures, it might be disrespectful to paraphrase certain passages or to document them in a way that would suggest the audience didn't recognize the ancient wisdom.

However, such collectivist conventions are at odds with the values of research communities committed to advancing knowledge. In the academic world, the conventions separating ethical from unethical use of sources are essential if research findings are to win the community's confidence. Effective research can occur only within ethical and responsible research communities, where people do not fabricate data and where current researchers respect and acknowledge the work of those who have gone before.

Strategies for Avoiding Plagiarism

Strategies Chart 23.3 will help you review the strategies presented throughout Chapters 21 to 23 for using source material ethically and avoiding plagiarism.

Strategies Chart 23.3 Strategies for Avoiding Plagiarism or the Appearance of Plagiarism

What to Do	Why to Do It	Where to Find More Information
	At the beginning	
Read your college's policy on plagiarism as well as statements from your teachers in class or on course syllabi.	Understanding policies on plagiarism and academic integrity will help you research and write ethically.	Skill 21.1
Pose a research question rather than a topic area.	Arguing your own thesis gives you a voice, establishes your *ethos,* and urges you to write ethically.	Skill 21.2
	At the note-taking stage	
Create a bibliographic entry for each source.	This action makes it easy to create an end-of-paper bibliography and encourages rhetorical reading.	Skill 22.1

What to Do	Why to Do It	Where to Find More Information
When you copy a passage into your notes, copy word for word and enclose it within quotation marks.	It is important to distinguish a source's words from your own words.	Skill 22.1
When you enter summaries or paraphrases into your notes, avoid patchwriting.	If your notes contain any strings of a source's original wording, you might later assume that these words are your own.	Skill 22.1 Skill 23.2
Distinguish your informational notes from your personal exploratory notes.	Keeping these kinds of notes separate will help you identify borrowed ideas when it's time to incorporate the source material into your paper.	Skill 22.1 See also "double-entry research notes" in Chapter 8
When writing your draft		
Except for exact quotations, write the paper entirely in your own words.	This strategy keeps you from patchwriting when you summarize or paraphrase.	Skill 23.2 Skill 23.4
Indicate all quotations with quotation marks or block indentation. Use ellipses or brackets to make changes to fit your own grammar.	Be careful to represent the author fairly; don't change meaning by taking quotations out of context.	Skill 23.2
When you summarize or paraphrase, avoid patchwriting.	Word-for-word strings from a source must either be avoided or placed in quotation marks. Also avoid mirroring the source's grammatical structure.	Skill 23.2 Skill 23.4
Never cut and paste a Web passage directly into your draft. Paste it into a separate note file and put quotation marks around it.	Pasted passages are direct invitations to patchwrite.	Skill 23.4
Inside your text, use attributive tags or parenthetical citations to identify all sources. List all sources alphabetically in a concluding Works Cited or References list.	This strategy makes it easy for readers to know when you are using a source and where to find it.	Skill 23.3 Skill 24.2
Cite with attributive tags or parenthetical citations all quotations, paraphrases, summaries, and any other references to specific sources.	These are the most common in-text citations in a research paper.	Skill 23.2 Skill 24.2
Use in-text citations to indicate sources for all visuals and media such as graphs, maps, photographs, films, videos, broadcasts, and recordings.	The rules for citing words and ideas apply equally to visuals and media cited in your paper.	Skill 23.3 Skill 24.1
Use in-text citations for all ideas and facts that are not common knowledge.	Although you don't need to cite widely accepted and noncontroversial facts and information, it is better to cite them if you are unsure.	Skill 24.1 Skill 24.2

For Writing and Discussion

Avoiding Plagiarism

Reread the original article from the American Council on Science and Health at the beginning of this chapter and Writer 3's use of this source in her paragraph about how nondietary habits may explain why vegetarians are healthier than nonvegetarians. Then read the paragraph below by Writer 4, who makes the same argument as Writer 3 but crosses the line from ethical to nonethical use of sources. Why might Writer 4 be accused of plagiarism?

(Continued)

WRITER 4's ARGUMENT (EXAMPLE OF PLAGIARISM)

According to the American Council on Science and Health, the health of vegetarians may be better than that of nonvegetarians partly because of nondietary factors. People who eat only vegetables tend to be very conscious of their health. They exercise regularly, avoid getting fat, and don't smoke. Scientists who examined the data may not have adequately controlled for these nondietary effects. Also, in Western countries most vegetarians are more affluent than nonvegetarians and thus have better living conditions and more access to medical care.

Working in small groups or as a class, respond to the following questions.

1. How does this passage cross the line into plagiarism?
2. The writer of this passage might say, "How can this be plagiarism? I cited my source." How would you explain the problem to this writer?
3. Psychologically or cognitively, what may have caused Writer 4 to misuse the source? How might this writer's note-taking process or composing process have differed from that of Writer 3? In other words, what happened to get this writer into trouble?

Chapter 24
Citing and Documenting Sources

Learning Objectives

24.1 Know what needs to be cited and what doesn't.

24.2 Understand the connection between in-text citations and the end-of-paper list of cited works.

24.3 Cite and document sources using MLA style.

24.4 Cite and document sources using APA style.

In the previous chapter we explained how to incorporate sources into your writing; in this chapter we focus on the nuts and bolts of documenting those sources in a way appropriate to your purpose, audience, and genre, using the systems of the Modern Language Association (MLA) and the American Psychological Association (APA).* Accurate documentation not only helps other researchers locate your sources but also contributes substantially to your own *ethos* as a writer.

Skill 24.1: Know what needs to be cited and what doesn't

24.1 Know what needs to be cited and what doesn't.

Beginning researchers are often confused about what needs to be cited and what doesn't. Table 24.1 will help you make this determination. If you are in doubt, it is better to cite than not to cite.

It is often difficult to determine when a given piece of information falls into the "common knowledge" column of Table 24.1. The answer depends both on

---

* Our discussion of MLA style is based on the *MLA Handbook*, 8th ed. (2016). Our discussion of APA style is based on the *Publication Manual of the American Psychological Association*, 6th ed. (2010) and the *APA Style Guide to Electronic References* (2013).

Table 24.1 Determining What Needs to Be Cited

What Needs to Be Cited	What Does Not Need to Be Cited
You must cite all uses of your research sources as well as any information that is not commonly known by your targeted audience: • Any quotation • Any passage that you paraphrase • Any passage or source that you summarize or otherwise refer to • Any image, photograph, map, drawing, graph, chart, or other visual that you download from the Web (or find elsewhere) and include in your paper • Any sound or video file that you use in a multimedia project • Any idea, fact, statistic, or other information that you find from a source and that is not commonly known by your targeted audience	You do not need to cite commonly shared, widely known knowledge that your target audience will consider factual and noncontroversial: • Commonly known facts (Water freezes at 32 degrees Fahrenheit.) • Commonly known dates (Terrorists flew airplanes into New York's World Trade Center on September 11, 2001.) • Commonly known events (Barack Obama defeated Mitt Romney for the presidency in 2012.) • Commonly known historical or cultural knowledge (Twitter and Facebook are forms of social networking.)

your target audience's background knowledge and on your own ability to speak as an authority. Consider the statement, "Twitter and Facebook are forms of social networking." That information is noncontroversial and well known and therefore doesn't require citation. But if you added, "Twitter is more popular with middle-aged adults than with teenagers," you would need to cite your source (a newspaper article or poll?) unless you are a teenager speaking with authority from your own experience, in which case you would provide personal-experience examples. If you are uncertain, our best advice is this: When in doubt, cite.

Skill 24.2: Understand the connection between in-text citations and the end-of-paper list of cited works

24.2 Understand the connection between in-text citations and the end-of-paper list of cited works.

The most common forms of documentation use in-text citations that match an end-of-paper list of cited works (as opposed to footnotes or endnotes). An **in-text citation** identifies a source in the body of the paper at the point where it is summarized, paraphrased, quoted, inserted, or otherwise referred to. At the end of your paper you include a list—alphabetized by author (or by title if there is no named author)—of all the works you cited. Both the Modern Language Association (MLA) system, used primarily in the humanities, and the American Psychological Association (APA) system, used primarily in the social sciences, follow this procedure. In MLA, your end-of-paper list is called **Works Cited**. In APA it is called **References**.

Whenever you place an in-text citation in the body of your paper, your reader knows to turn to the Works Cited or References list at the end of the paper to get the full bibliographic information. The key to the system's logic is this:

- Every source in Works Cited or References must be mentioned in the body of the paper.
- Conversely, every source mentioned in the body of the paper must be included in the end-of-paper list.

- The first word in each entry of the Works Cited or References list (usually an author's last name) must also appear in the in-text citation. In other words, there must be a one-to-one correspondence between the first word in each entry in the end-of-paper list and the name used to identify the source in the body of the paper.

Suppose a reader sees this phrase in your paper: "According to Debra Goldstein. . . ." The reader should be able to turn to your Works Cited list and find an alphabetized entry beginning with "Goldstein, Debra." Similarly, suppose that in looking over your Works Cited list, your reader sees an article by "Guillen, Manuel." This means that the name "Guillen" has to appear in your paper in one of two ways:

For more on attributive tags, see Skill 23.3.

- As an **attributive tag**: Economics professor Manuel Guillen argues that. . . .
- As a **parenthetical citation**, often following a quotation: ". . . changes in fiscal policy" (Guillen 49)

Because this one-to-one correspondence is so important, let's illustrate it with some complete examples using the MLA formatting style:

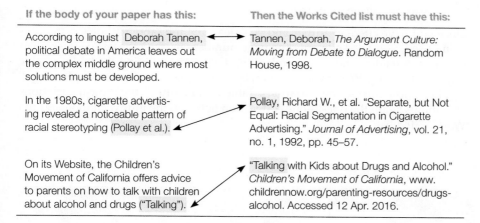

If the body of your paper has this:	Then the Works Cited list must have this:
According to linguist Deborah Tannen, political debate in America leaves out the complex middle ground where most solutions must be developed.	Tannen, Deborah. *The Argument Culture: Moving from Debate to Dialogue.* Random House, 1998.
In the 1980s, cigarette advertising revealed a noticeable pattern of racial stereotyping (Pollay et al.).	Pollay, Richard W., et al. "Separate, but Not Equal: Racial Segmentation in Cigarette Advertising." *Journal of Advertising*, vol. 21, no. 1, 1992, pp. 45–57.
On its Website, the Children's Movement of California offers advice to parents on how to talk with children about alcohol and drugs ("Talking").	"Talking with Kids about Drugs and Alcohol." *Children's Movement of California*, www. childrennow.org/parenting-resources/drugs-alcohol. Accessed 12 Apr. 2016.

How to format an MLA in-text citation and a Works Cited list entry is the subject of the next section. The APA system is similar except that it emphasizes the date of publication in both the in-text citation and the References entry. APA formatting is the subject of Skill 24.4.

Skill 24.3: Cite and document sources using MLA style

24.3 Cite and document sources using MLA style.

An in-text citation and its corresponding Works Cited entry are linked in a chicken-and-egg system: You can't cite a source in the text without first knowing how the source's entry will be alphabetized in the Works Cited list. However, since most Works Cited entries are alphabetized by the first author's last name, for convenience we start with in-text citations.

In-Text Citations in MLA Style

A typical in-text citation contains two elements: (1) the last name of the author and (2) the page number of the quoted or paraphrased passage. However, in some cases a work is identified by something other than an author's last name, and sometimes no page number is required. Let's begin with the most common cases.

Typically, an in-text citation uses one of these two methods:

- *Parenthetical method.* Place the author's last name and the page number in parentheses immediately after the material being cited.

   The Spanish tried to reduce the status of Filipina women who had been able to do business, get divorced, and sometimes become village chiefs (Karnow 41).

- *Attributive tag method.* Place the author's name in an attributive tag at the beginning of the source material and the page number in parentheses at the end.

   According to Karnow, the Spanish tried to reduce the status of Filipina women, who had been able to do business, get divorced, and sometimes become village chiefs (41).

Once you have cited an author and it is clear that the same author's material is being used, you need cite only the page numbers in parentheses in subsequent citations. A reader who wishes to look up the source will find the bibliographic information in the Works Cited section by looking for the entry under "Karnow."

Let's now turn to the variations. Table 24.2 identifies the typical variations and shows again the one-to-one connection between the in-text citation and the Works Cited list.

Table 24.2 In-Text Citations in MLA Style

Type of Source	Works Cited Entry at End of Paper (*Construct the entry while taking notes on each source.*)	In-Text Citation in Body of Paper (*Use the first word of the Works Cited entry in parentheses or an attributive tag; add page number at end of quoted or paraphrased passage.*)
One author	Pollan, Michael. *The Omnivore's Dilemma: A Natural History of Four Meals*. Penguin, 2006.	. . . (Pollan 256). OR According to Pollan, . . . (256).
Two authors	Lewis, Robin, and Michael Dart. *The New Rules of Retail: Competing in the World's Toughest Marketplace*. Macmillan, 2010.	. . . retail" (Lewis and Dart 52). OR Lewis and Dart have argued that "advertisers . . . retail" (52).
More than two authors	Pollay, Richard W., et al. "Separate, but Not Equal: Racial Segmentation in Cigarette Advertising." *Journal of Advertising*, vol. 21, no. 1, 1992, pp. 45-57.	. . . race" (Pollay et al. 52) OR Pollay et al. have argued that "advertisers . . . race" (52). *For the in-text citation, cite the specific page number rather than the whole range of pages given in the Works Cited entry.*

Type of Source	Works Cited Entry at End of Paper (*Construct the entry while taking notes on each source.*)	In-Text Citation in Body of Paper (*Use the first word of the Works Cited entry in parentheses or an attributive tag; add page number at end of quoted or paraphrased passage.*)
Author has more than one work in Works Cited list	Dombrowski, Daniel A. *Babies and Beasts: The Argument from Marginal Cases*. U of Illinois P, 1997. ---. *The Philosophy of Vegetarianism*. U of Massachusetts P, 1984.	. . . (Dombrowski, *Babies* 207). . . . (Dombrowski, *Philosophy* 328). OR According to Dombrowski, . . . (*Babies* 207). Dombrowski claims that . . . (*Philosophy* 328). *Because author has more than one work in Works Cited, include a short version of the title to distinguish between entries.*
Corporate author	American Red Cross. *Standard First Aid*. Mosby Lifeline, 1993.	. . . (American Red Cross 102). OR Snake bite instructions from the American Red Cross show that . . . (102).
No named author (Work is therefore alphabetized by title.)	"Body Piercing. Ouch!" *Menstuff*, www.menstuff.org/issues/byissue/bodypiercing.html. Accessed 12 Apr. 2016.	. . . ("Body"). According to the National Men's Resource Center, . . . ("Body"). • *Add "Body" in parentheses to show that work is alphabetized under "Body" not "National."* • *No page numbers are shown because Web site pages aren't stable. The Web site does not provide a date on which "Body Piercing. Ouch!" was posted. When a Web site does not provide a date of posting or publication, add the access date as the last item in the Works Cited entry.*
Indirect citation of a source that you found in another source *Suppose you want to use a quotation from Peter Singer that you found in a book by Daniel Dombrowski. Include Dombrowski but not Singer in Works Cited.*	Dombrowski, Daniel A. *Babies and Beasts: The Argument from Marginal Cases*. U of Illinois P, 1997.	Animal rights activist Peter Singer argues that . . . (qtd. in Dombrowski 429). • *Singer is used for the attributive tag, but the in-text citation is to Dombrowski.* • *"qtd. in" stands for "quoted in."*

WHEN TO USE PAGE NUMBERS IN IN-TEXT CITATIONS   When the materials you are citing are available in print or in .pdf format, you can provide accurate page numbers for parenthetical citations. If you are working with Web sources or HTML files, however, do not use the page numbers obtained from a printout because they will not be consistent from printer to printer. If the item has numbered paragraphs, cite them with the abbreviation *par.* or *pars.*—for example, "(Jones, pars. 22–24)." In the absence of reliable page numbers for the original material, omit page references from the parenthetical citation. The following chart summarizes the use of page numbers in in-text citations.

Include a page number in the in-text citation:	Do not include a page number:
If the source has stable page numbers (print source or .pdf version of print source): • If you quote something • If you paraphrase a specific passage • If you refer to data or details from a specific page or range of pages in the source	• If you are referring to the argument of the whole source instead of a specific page or passage • If the source does not have stable page numbers (articles on Web sites, HTML text, and so forth)

Works Cited List in MLA Style

In the MLA system, you place a complete Works Cited list at the end of the paper. The list includes all the sources that you mention in your paper. However, it does *not* include works you read but did not use. Entries in the Works Cited list follow these general guidelines:

- Entries are arranged alphabetically by author, or by title if there is no author.
- If there is more than one entry per author, the works are arranged alphabetically by title. For the second and all additional entries, type three hyphens and a period in place of the author's name.

> Dombrowski, Daniel A. *Babies and Beasts: The Argument from Marginal Cases.*
>   U of Illinois P, 1997.
> ---. *The Philosophy of Vegetarianism.* U of Massachusetts P, 1984.

You can see a complete and properly formatted Works Cited list on the last pages of Kent Ansen's paper at the end of Chapter 16.

The remaining pages in this section show examples of MLA citation formats for different kinds of sources and provide explanations and illustrations as needed.

MLA Citation Models

The MLA Handbook provides a set of guidelines to help you format your Works Cited list correctly. You can also visit the MLA's help center online at https://style.mla.org.

The templates in Table 24.3 will help you compile the information you need for your MLA Works Cited list and format your entries correctly. Take note of the punctuation following each element, and use the same punctuation in your entries.

- **Author** can contain other identifying information, such as "editor," "translator," "actor," or "director."
- **Title of source** requires you to use italics and quotation marks correctly. Italicize the titles of books, magazines, newspapers, journals, Web sites, films, albums/CDs, and TV series. Use quotation marks for titles that are part of larger works. Specifically, place quotation marks around article titles, essay titles, episode titles, song titles, and titles of Web posts. When a source is untitled, provide a generic description of it, neither italicized nor in quotation marks. When you document an email, use its subject line as the title.

Table 24.3 Templates for MLA-Style Works Cited

Print Source	
Author.	Herrera-Sobek, Maria.
Title of source.	"Border Aesthetics: The Politics of Mexican Immigration in Film and Art."
Title of container,	*Western Humanities Review*,
Other contributors,	
Version,	
Number,	vol. 60, no. 2,
Publisher,	
Publication date,	2006,
Location.	pp. 60-71.

Online Source	
Author.	Gourlay, Alexander S.
Title of source.	"An Emergency Online Glossary of Terms, Names, and Concepts in Blake."
Title of container,	*The William Blake Archive*,
Other contributors,	
Version,	
Number,	
Publisher,	
Publication date,	
Location.	www.blakearchive.org/exist/blake/archive/glossary.xq?chunk.id=glossary&toc.depth=1&toc.id=0. Accessed 14 Apr. 2016.

- **Container** is a generic term that is intended to capture any type of print or digital medium. A container may be a book, magazine, scholarly journal, TV series, Web site, comic book, any type of social media (Twitter, Facebook), and so on. One container can be nested in a larger container—for example, one blog may be part of a network of blogs. A scholarly journal (the first container) may be retrieved from a larger container—for example, an academic database such as Academic Search Complete (the second container). When a container is nested in a larger container, both containers should be documented, with a period separating the two containers.

- **Other contributors** are people who have played a role in the creation of the source. Other contributions include "Adapted by," "Directed by," "Illustrated by," "Performance by," and "Introduction by."

- **Version** is the version you are citing (for example, the second edition of a work).
- **Number** refers to identifying numbers when a publication is too long to be printed in one book (for example, "vol. 2"). With periodicals, the number is the volume number and the issue number, separated by a comma.
- **Publication date** should be as specific as possible. Provide month, date, and year whenever possible. For books, usually the year alone is sufficient.
- **Location** usually refers to page numbers in a print work and to a URL or DOI in an online source. A **URL** (uniform resource locator) is a Web address. A **DOI** is a digital object identifier. Whenever possible, DOIs are preferred to URLs because DOIs are more stable; that is, DOIs do not change, but URLs may change frequently. To save time and avoid typographical errors, you can cut and paste the URL or DOI from your Internet browser into your source information. Note, however, that "http://" and "https://" are not included in URLs. If a publication date is not provided for a URL, complete the Works Cited entry by listing the date you accessed the URL.

PRINT ARTICLES IN SCHOLARLY JOURNALS

To see what citations look like when typed in a research paper, see Kent Ansen's Works Cited list in Chapter 16.

All scholarly journal entries include both volume number and issue number, regardless of how the journal is paginated.

One author

Herrera-Sobek, Maria. "Border Aesthetics: The Politics of Mexican Immigration in Film and Art." *Western Humanities Review*, vol. 60, no. 2, 2006, pp. 60–71.

Two authors

Kwon, Ohbyung, and Yixing Wen. "An Empirical Study of the Factors Affecting Social Network Service Use." *Computers in Human Behavior*, vol. 26, no. 2, Mar. 2010, pp. 254–263.

Three or more authors

List the first author, and use "*et al.*" (meaning "and others") to replace all but the first author. Your Works Cited entry and the parenthetical citation should match.

Pollay, Richard W., et al. "Separate, but Not Equal: Racial Segmentation in Cigarette Advertising." *Journal of Advertising*, vol. 21, no. 1, 1992, pp. 45–57.

PRINT ARTICLES IN MAGAZINES AND NEWSPAPERS If no author is identified, begin the entry with the title or headline. Distinguish between news stories and editorials by putting the word "Editorial" after the title. If a magazine comes out weekly or biweekly, include the complete date ("27 Sept. 2013"). If it comes out monthly, then state the month only ("Sept. 2013").

Note: If the article begins on one page but continues in another part of the magazine or newspaper, add "+" to the number of the first page to indicate the nonsequential pages: pp. 45+.

Magazine article with named author

Snyder, Rachel L. "A Daughter of Cambodia Remembers: Loung Ung's Journey."
Ms., Aug.–Sept. 2001, pp. 62–67.

Magazine article without named author

"Sacred Geese." *The Economist,* 1 June 2013, pp. 24–25.

Review of book, film, or performance

Schwarz, Benjamin. "A Bit of Bunting: A New History of the British Empire Elevates Expediency to Principle." Review of *Ornamentalism: How the British Saw Their Empire,* by David Cannadine. *The Atlantic,* Nov. 2001, pp. 126–35.

Kaufman, Stanley. "Polishing a Gem." Review of *The Blue Angel,* directed by Josef von Sternberg. *New Republic,* 30 July 2001, pp. 28–29.

Lahr, John. "Nobody's Darling: Fascism and the Drama of Human Connection in *Ashes to Ashes*." Review of *Ashes to Ashes,* by Harold Pinter. The Roundabout Theater Co. Gramercy Theater, New York. *The New Yorker,* 22 Feb. 1999, pp. 182–83.

Newspaper article

Page numbers in newspapers are typically indicated by a section letter or number as well as a page number. The "+" indicates that the article continues on one or more pages later in the newspaper.

Dougherty, Conor. "The Latest Urban Trend: Less Elbow Room." *The Wall Street Journal,* 4 June 2013, pp. A1+.

Newspaper editorial

"Dr. Frankenstein on the Hill." Editorial. *The New York Times,* 18 May 2002, p. A22.

Letter to the editor of a magazine or newspaper

Tomsovic, Kevin. Letter to the editor. *The New Yorker,* 13 July 1998, p. 7.

PRINT BOOKS

One author

Pollan, Michael. *The Omnivore's Dilemma: A Natural History of Four Meals.* Penguin, 2006.

Two authors

Dombrowski, Daniel A., and Robert J. Deltete. *A Brief, Liberal, Catholic Defense of Abortion.* U of Illinois P, 2000.

Lewis, Robin, and Michael Dart. *The New Rules of Retail: Competing in the World's Toughest Marketplace.* Macmillan, 2010.

Three or more authors

List the first author, and use "et al." (meaning "and others") to replace all but the first author. Your Works Cited entry and the parenthetical citation should match.

Belenky, Mary, et al. *Women's Ways of Knowing: The Development of Self, Voice, and Mind.* Basic Books, 1986.

Second, later, or revised edition

Montagu, Ashley. *Touching: The Human Significance of the Skin.* 3rd ed., Perennial, 1986.

In place of "3rd ed.," you can include abbreviations for other kinds of editions: "Rev. ed." (for "Revised edition") or "Abr. ed." (for "Abridged edition").

Republished book (for example, a paperback published after the original hardback edition or a modern edition of an older work)

Hill, Christopher. *The World Turned Upside Down: Radical Ideas During the English Revolution.* 1972. London, Penguin, 1991.

Wollstonecraft, Mary. *A Vindication of the Rights of Woman, with Strictures on Political and Moral Subjects.* 1792. Tuttle, 1995.

The date immediately following the title is the original publication date of the work.

Multivolume work

Churchill, Winston S. *A History of the English-Speaking Peoples.* Dodd, Mead, 1956–58. 4 vols.

Churchill, Winston S. *The Great Democracies.* Dodd, Mead, 1957. *A History of the English-Speaking Peoples,* vol. 4, Dodd, Mead, 1956–58. 4 vols.

Use the first method when you cite the whole work; use the second method when you cite one individually titled volume of the work.

Article in familiar reference work

"Mau Mau." *The New Encyclopaedia Britannica.* 15th ed., 2008, p. 808.

Article in less familiar reference work

Hirsch, E. D., et al. "Kyoto Protocol." *The New Dictionary of Cultural Literacy.* Houghton Mifflin, 2002, pp. 256-57.

Translation

De Beauvoir, Simone. *The Second Sex.* Translated by H. M. Parshley, 1949. Bantam, 1961.

Illustrated book

Jacques, Brian. *The Great Redwall Feast.* Illustrated by Christopher Denise, Philomel, 1996.

Graphic novel

Miyazaki, Hayao. *Nausicaa of the Valley of Wind.* Viz, 1995–97. 4 vols.

Corporate author (a commission, committee, or other group)

American Red Cross. *Standard First Aid.* Mosby Lifeline, 1993.

No author listed

The Complete Cartoons of The New Yorker. Black Dog & Leventhal, 2004.

Whole anthology

O'Connell, David F., and Charles N. Alexander, editors. *Self Recovery: Treating Addictions Using Transcendental Meditation and Maharishi Ayur-Veda.* Haworth, 1994.

Anthology article

Royer, Ann. "The Role of the Transcendental Meditation Technique in Promoting Smoking Cessation: A Longitudinal Study." *Self Recovery: Treating Addictions Using Transcendental Meditation and Maharishi Ayur-Veda*, edited by David F. O'Connell and Charles N. Alexander, Haworth, 1994, pp. 221–39.

ARTICLES OR BOOKS FROM AN ONLINE DATABASE

Article from online database

Matsbuba, Kyle. "Searching for Self and Relationships Online." *CyberPyschology and Behavior, vol. 9, no. 3,* Jun. 2006. *Academic Search Complete*, doi:10.1089/cpb.2006.9.275.

To see where each element in this citation was found, see Figure 24.1, which shows the online database screen from which the Rosenman article was accessed. For articles in databases, you will need to use two containers. The first container is the scholarly journal and its identifying information. The second container is the academic database and its URL.

Article from a scholarly e-journal

Welch, John R., and Ramon Riley. "Reclaiming Land and Spirit in the Western Apache Homeland." *American Indian Quarterly*, vol. 25, no. 4, 2001, pp. 5–14. *JSTOR*, www.jstor.org/stable/1185999?seq=1#.

Broadcast transcript from Web site

Conan, Neal. "Arab Media." *NPR Talk of the Nation,* guest appearance by Shibley Telhami, 2002, www.npr.org/programs/totn/transcripts/2004/may/040504.conan.html. Transcript.

"Transcript" at the end of the entry indicates a text (not audio) version.

E-book from online database

Hanley, Wayne. *The Genesis of Napoleonic Propaganda, 1796–1799.* Columbia UP, 2002. *Gutenberg-e*, www.gutenberg-e.org/haw01. Accessed 12 Apr. 2016.

Figure 24.1 Article Downloaded from an Online Database, with Elements Identified for an MLA-Style Citation

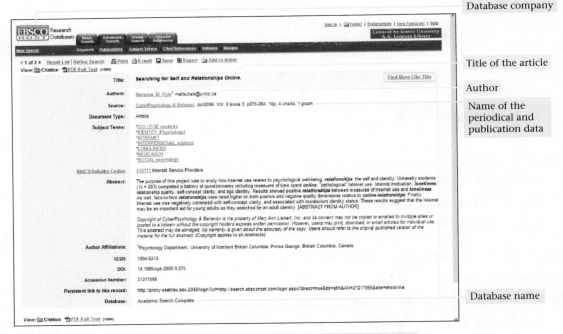

Matsuba, M. Kyle. "Searching for Self and Relationships Online." *CyberPsychology and Behavior* 9.3 (2006): 275-84. *Academic Search Complete*. Web. 14 Apr. 2007.

Paine, Thomas. *Rights of Man.* 1791. *Bibliomania,* www.bibliomania
.com/2/1/327/2414/frameset.html. Accessed 12 Apr. 2016.

Information about the original print version, including a translator if relevant and available, should be provided. Access date should be provided for any sources that are not dated.

E-book on Kindle, iPad, or other e-reader

According to MLA, a book is a book whether you read it in print or on an e-reader (such as a Kindle, Nook, or iPad).

Boyle, T. C. *When the Killing's Done.* Viking Penguin, 2011.

OTHER INTERNET SOURCES

Article on Web site

Saucedo, Robert. "A Bad Idea for a Movie." *theeagle.com,* 13 Mar. 2012, www
.theeagle.com/entertainment/a-bad-idea-for-a-movie/article_00454e59-
7d77-5bc3-9e56-8eec8ca488ee.html.

Date of access is not required because the article is dated (13 Mar. 2012).

Break URLs onto a new line only after a piece of punctuation, such as a hyphen, slash, or period.

Entire Web site

Agatho. *Mysterious Matters*, 2007-16, mysteriousmatters.typepad.com. Accessed
    14 Apr. 2016.

Documents within a Web site

Gourlay, Alexander S. "An Emergency Online Glossary of Terms, Names, and
    Concepts in Blake." *The William Blake Archive*, www.blakearchive.org/
    exist/blake/archive/glossary.xq?chunk.id=glossary&toc.depth=1&toc.
    id=0. Accessed 14 Apr. 2016.

"Body Piercing. Ouch!" *Menstuff*, www.menstuff.org/issues/byissue/
    bodypiercing.html. Accessed 12 Apr. 2016.

Article from a newspaper or newswire site

Brennan, Charlie. "Boulder Scientists over the Moon at Chance to Work on Lunar
    Dust." *Daily Camera Boulder News*, 3 Oct. 2015, www.dailycamera.com/news/
    boulder/ci_28913824/boulder-scientists-over-moon-at-chance-work-lunar.

"Great Lakes: Rwanda Backed Dissident Troops in DRC-UN Panel." *IRIN*, 21
    July 2004, www.irinnews.org/report/50763/great-lakes-rwanda-backed-
    dissident-troops-drc-un-panel.

Broadcast transcript from a Web site

Woodruff, Judy, et al. "Experts Analyze Supreme Court Free Speech Rulings."
    PBS NewsHour, 25 June 2007, www.pbs.org/newshour/bb/law-jan-june07-
    freespeech_06-25. Transcript.

Blog posting

Dsyer, Bob, and Ella Barnes. "The 'Greening' of the Arctic." *Greenversations:*
    The Official Blog of the U.S. Environmental Protection Agency, 7 Oct. 2008,
    blog.epa.gov/blog/2008/10/07/the-greening-of-the-artic.

To see where each element of this citation comes from, refer to Figure 24.2.

Tweet

Identify a short untitled message, such as a tweet, by reproducing its full text, without changes, in place of a title. Enclose the text in quotation marks, and include not only date but also time.

@persiankiwi. "We have report of large street battles in east & west of Tehran
    now - #Iranelection." *Twitter*, 23 June 2009, 11:15 a.m., twitter.com/
    persiankiwi/status/2298106072.

Figure 24.2 A Blog Posting from the Web, with Citation Elements Identified

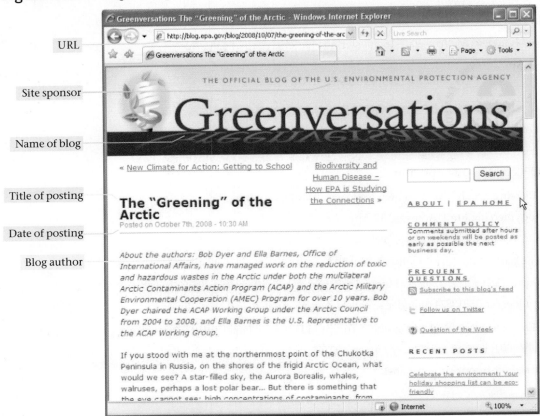

Dyer, Bob, and Ella Barnes. "The 'Greening' of the Arctic." *Greenversations*. U.S. Environmental Protection Agency,
7 Oct. 2008. Web. 11 Oct. 2008. <http://blog.epa.gov/blog/2008/10/07/the-greening-of-the-arctic/>.

Podcast

"The Long and Winding Road: DNA Evidence for Human Migration." *Scientific
American Science Talk*, 7 July 2008, www.scientificamerican.com/podcast/
episode/fe166e6b-f88f-3538-2702d97555f62442.

Web video

"Immigration, World Poverty, and Gumballs." *YouTube*, 10 Sept. 2010, www
.youtube.com/watch?v=LPjzfGChGlE.

Home page

Center for Africana Studies. Home page. School of Advanced International Study,
Johns Hopkins University, krieger.jhu.edu/africana. Accessed 12 Apr. 2016.

E-mail

Start with the sender's name. The title is the subject line.

Rubino, Susanna. "Reasons for Unemployment." Email received by Matthew
Rollins, 12 Dec. 2013.

MISCELLANEOUS SOURCES

Episode of television or radio program

"Lie Like a Rug." *NYPD Blue*, directed by Steven Bochco and David Milch, ABC,
6 Nov. 2001.

Ashbrook, Tom. "Turf Wars and the American Lawn." *On Point*, National Public
Radio, 22 July 2008, onpoint.wbur.org/2008/07/22/turf-wars-and-
american-lawns.

Film or video recording

Use the first format to cite a film on DVD. Use the second format (which uses
a second container) if you watched the film via a rental service such as Netflix or Hulu.

Shakespeare in Love. Directed by John Madden, performances by Joseph Fiennes
and Gwyneth Paltrow, screenplay by Marc Norman and Tom Stoppard.
Universal Miramax, 1998.

Shakespeare in Love. Directed by John Madden, performances by Joseph Fiennes
and Gwyneth Paltrow, screenplay by Marc Norman and Tom Stoppard.
Universal Miramax, 1998. *Netflix*, 9 Mar. 2010.

Song on a CD

Dylan, Bob. "Rainy Day Women #12." *Blonde on Blonde*, Columbia, 1966.

The song title is "Rainy Day Women #12." The CD title is *Blonde on Blonde*. If you
are citing the CD, use the following:

Dylan, Bob. *Blonde on Blonde*, Columbia, 1966.

Cartoon or advertisement (print)

Trudeau, Garry. "Doonesbury." *Seattle Times*, 19 Nov. 2001, p. B4.

Banana Republic. Advertisement. *Details*, Oct. 2001, p. 37.

Cartoon (online)

Sipress, David. "Anger Management Therapy." *The New Yorker*, 14 Mar. 2016,
www.newyorker.com/cartoons/daily-cartoon/monday-march-14th-anger-
management.

Interview

Castellucci, Marion. Personal interview, 7 Oct. 2013.

Lecture, speech, or conference presentation

Sharples, Mike. "Authors of the Future." Conference of European Teachers of
Academic Writing, 20 June 2001, University of Groningen, Netherlands.

Government publications

When a work's publisher and author are separate organizations, give both
names, starting the entry with the author.

When an organization or institution is both publisher and author, begin the entry with the title.

When an entry starts with a government agency as the author, begin with the name of the largest entity, followed by a comma, followed by smaller organizational units within the agency, arranged from largest to smallest and separated by commas.

New York State, Committee on State Prisons. *Investigation of the New York State Prisons.* Arno Press, 1974.

Foreign Direct Investment, the Service Sector, and International Banking. Centre on Transnational Corporations, United Nations, 1987.

Great Britain, Ministry of Agriculture, Fisheries, and Food. *Our Countryside, the Future: A Fair Deal for Rural England.* Her Majesty's Stationery Office, 2000.

MLA Format Research Paper

For an illustration of a student research paper written and formatted in MLA style, see "Engaging Young Adults to Meet America's Challenges: A Proposal for Mandatory National Service" by Kent Ansen (at the end of Chapter 16). Kent's process in producing this paper has been discussed in various places throughout the text.

Skill 24.4: Cite and document sources using APA style

24.4 Cite and document sources using APA style.

In many respects, the APA style and the MLA style are similar and the basic logic is the same. In the APA system, the list where readers can find full bibliographic information is titled "References"; as in MLA format, it includes only the sources cited in the body of the paper. The distinguishing features of APA citation style are highlighted in the following sections.

In-Text Citations in APA Style

A typical APA-style in-text citation contains three elements: (1) the last name of the author, (2) the date of the publication, and (3) the page number of the quoted or paraphrased passage. Table 24.4 identifies some typical variations and shows again the one-to-one connection between the in-text citation and the References list. For an example of as student paper in APA style, see the report by Campbell et al. in Chapter 12.

References List in APA Style

A formatted References list appears in Chapter 12.

The APA References list at the end of a paper presents entries alphabetically. If you cite more than one item for an author, repeat the author's name

Table 24.4 In-Text Citations in APA Style

Type of Source	References Entry at End of Paper	In-Text Citation in Body of Paper
One author	Pollan, M. (2006). *The omnivore's dilemma: A natural history of four meals*. New York, NY: Penguin.	. . . (Pollan, 2006, p. 256). OR According to Pollan (2006), . . . (p. 256).
Two authors	Kwon, O., & Wen, Y. (2010). An empirical study of the factors affecting social network service use. *Computers in Human Behavior, 26*, 254–263. doi:10.1016 /j.chb.2009.04.011	. . . (Kwon & Wen, 2010, p. 262). OR Kwon and Wen (2010) claim that . . . (p. 262).
Three to five authors	Pollay, R. W., Lee, J. S., & Carter-Whitney, D. (1992). Separate, but not equal: Racial segmentation in cigarette advertising. *Journal of Advertising, 21*(1), 45–57.	. . . race" (Pollay, Lee, & Carter-Whitney, 1992, p. 52). OR Pollay, Lee, and Carter-Whitney have argued that "advertisers . . . race" (1992, p. 52). *For subsequent citations, use Pollay et al. For a quotation, use the specific page number, not the whole range of pages.*
Author has more than one work in References list *Note that references are arranged in chronological order, from earliest to latest.*	Dombrowski, D. A. (1984). *The philosophy of vegetarianism*. Amherst, MA: University of Massachusetts Press. Dombrowski, D. A. (1997). *Babies and beasts: The argument from marginal cases*. Urbana: University of Illinois Press.	. . . (Dombrowski, 1984, p. 207). . . . (Dombrowski, 1997, p. 328). OR Dombrowski (1984) claims that . . . (p. 207). According to Dombrowski (1997), . . . (p. 328).
Indirect citation of a source that you found in another source *You use a quotation from Peter Singer from a book by Dombrowski. Include Dombrowski, not Singer, in the References.*	Dombrowski, D. A. (1997). *Babies and beasts: The argument from marginal cases*. Urbana: University of Illinois Press.	Animal rights activist Peter Singer argues that . . . (as cited in Dombrowski, 1997, p. 429). *Singer is used for the attributive tag, but the in-text citation is to Dombrowski.*

each time and arrange the items in chronological order, beginning with the earliest. In cases where two works by an author appeared in the same year, arrange them in the list alphabetically by title, and then add a lowercase "a" or "b" (etc.) after the date so that you can distinguish between them in the in-text citations:

Smith, R. (1999a). *Body image in non-Western cultures, 1750–present*. London, England: Bonanza Press.

Smith, R. (1999b). Eating disorders reconsidered. *Journal of Appetite Studies, 45,* 295–300.

APA Citation Models

PRINT ARTICLES IN SCHOLARLY JOURNALS

General Format for Print Article in Scholarly Journal

Author. (Year of Publication). Article title. *Journal Title, volume number*(issue number), page numbers. doi:xx.xxxx/x.xxxx.xx [or] http://dx.doi.org/10.xxxx/xxxxxx

If there is one, include the **DOI** (digital object identifier), a number that is uniquely assigned to many journal articles, in numeric or URL form. Note the style for capitalizing article titles and for italicizing the volume number.

One author

Herrera-Sobek, M. (2006). Border aesthetics: The politics of Mexican immigration in film and art. *Western Humanities Review, 60,* 60–71. doi:10.1016/j.chb.2009.04.011

Two to seven authors

McElroy, B. W., & Lubich, B. H. (2013). Predictors of course outcomes: Early indicators of delay in online classrooms. *Distance Education, 34*(1). http://dx.doi.org/10.1080/01587919.2013.770433

When a source has more than seven authors, list the first six and the last one by name. Use ellipses (. . .) to indicate the authors whose names have been omitted.

Scholarly journal that restarts page numbering with each issue

Pollay, R. W., Lee, J. S., & Carter-Whitney, D. (1992). Separate, but not equal: Racial segmentation in cigarette advertising. *Journal of Advertising, 21*(1), 45–57.

Note that the issue number and the parentheses are *not* italicized.

PRINT ARTICLES IN MAGAZINES AND NEWSPAPERS

General Format for Print Article in Magazine or Newspaper

Author. (Year, Month Day). Article title. *Periodical Title, volume number,* page numbers.

If page numbers are discontinuous, identify every page, separating numbers with a comma.

Magazine article with named author

Hall, S. S. (2001, March 11). Prescription for profit. *The New York Times Magazine,* 40–45, 59, 91–92, 100.

Magazine article without named author

Sacred geese. (2013, June 1). *Economist,* 24–25.

Review of book or film

Schwarz, B. (2001, November). A bit of bunting: A new history of the British empire elevates expediency to principle [Review of the book *Ornamentalism: How the British saw their empire*]. *Atlantic, 288,* 126–135.

Kaufman, S. (2001, July 30). Polishing a gem [Review of the motion picture *The blue angel*]. *New Republic, 225,* 28–29.

Newspaper article

Dougherty, C. (2013, June 4). The latest urban trend: Less elbow room. *Wall Street Journal,* pp. A1, A12.

Newspaper editorial

Dr. Frankenstein on the hill [Editorial]. (2002, May 18). *The New York Times,* p. A22.

Letter to the editor of a magazine or newspaper

Tomsovic, K. (1998, July 13). Culture clash [Letter to the editor]. *The New Yorker,* 7.

PRINT BOOKS

General Format for Print Books

Author. (Year of publication). *Book title: Subtitle.* City, State [abbreviated]: Name of Publisher.

Brumberg, J. J. (1997). *The body project: An intimate history of American girls.* New York, NY: Vintage.

If the publisher's name indicates the state in which it is located, list the city but omit the state.

Reid, H., & Taylor, B. (2010). *Recovering the commons: Democracy, place, and global justice.* Champaign: University of Illinois Press.

Second, later, or revised edition

Montagu, A. (1986). *Touching: The human significance of the skin* (3rd ed.). New York, NY: Perennial Press.

Republished book (for example, a paperback published after the original hardback edition or a modern edition of an older work)

Wollstonecraft, M. (1995). *A vindication of the rights of woman, with strictures on political and moral subjects.* Rutland, VT: Tuttle. (Original work published 1792)

The in-text citation should read: (Wollstonecraft, 1792/1995).

Multivolume work

Churchill, W. S. (1956–1958). *A history of the English-speaking peoples* (Vols. 1–4). New York, NY: Dodd, Mead.

Citation for all the volumes together. The in-text citation should read: (Churchill, 1956–1958).

Churchill, W. S. (1957). *A history of the English-speaking peoples: Vol. 4. The great democracies.* New York, NY: Dodd, Mead.

Citation for a specific volume. The in-text citation should read: (Churchill, 1957).

Article in reference work

Hirsch, E. D., Kett, J. F., & Trefil, J. (2002). Kyoto protocol. In *The new dictionary of cultural literacy*. Boston, MA: Houghton Mifflin.

Translation

De Beauvoir, S. (1961). *The second sex* (H. M. Parshley, Trans.). New York, NY: Bantam Books. (Original work published 1949)

The in-text citation should read: (De Beauvoir, 1949/1961).

Corporate author (a commission, committee, or other group)

American Red Cross. (1993). *Standard first aid*. St. Louis, MO: Mosby Lifeline.

Anonymous author

The complete cartoons of The New Yorker. (2004). New York, NY: Black Dog & Leventhal.

The in-text citation is (*Complete cartoons*, 2004).

Whole anthology

O'Connell, D. F., & Alexander, C. N. (Eds.). (1994). *Self recovery: Treating addictions using transcendental meditation and Maharishi Ayur-Veda*. New York, NY: Haworth Press.

Anthology article

Royer, A. (1994). The role of the transcendental meditation technique in promoting smoking cessation: A longitudinal study. In D. F. O'Connell & C. N. Alexander (Eds.), *Self recovery: Treating addictions using transcendental meditation and Maharishi Ayur-Veda* (pp. 221–239). New York, NY: Haworth Press.

ARTICLES OR BOOKS FROM AN ONLINE DATABASE

Article from database with a DOI

Scharrer, E., Daniel, K. D., Lin, K.-M., & Liu, Z. (2006). Working hard or hardly working? Gender, humor, and the performance of domestic chores in television commercials. *Mass Communication and Society, 9*(2), 215–238. doi:10.1207/s15327825mcs0902_5

Omit the database name. If an article or other document has been assigned a DOI, include the DOI at the end. To see where the information in the Scharrer citation came from, refer to Figure 24.3.

Article from database without DOI

Highland, R. A., & Dabney, D. A. (2009). Using Adlerian theory to shed light on drug dealer motivations. *Applied Psychology in Criminal Justice, 5*(2), 109–138. Retrieved from http://www.apcj.org

Figure 24.3 Scholarly Journal Article with a Digital Object Identifier (DOI) with Elements Identified for APA-Style Citations

Omit the database name. Instead, use a search engine to locate the publication's home page, and cite that URL. If you need to break a URL at the end of a line, do not use a hyphen. Instead, break it *before* a punctuation mark or *after* http://.

OTHER INTERNET SOURCES

General Format for Web Documents

Author, editor, director, narrator, performer, compiler, or producer of the work,
   if available. (Year, Month Day of posting). *Title of web document, italicized.*
   Retrieved from Name of website if different from author or title: URL of
   home page

Barrett, J. (2007, January 17). *MySpace is a natural monopoly.* Retrieved from
   ECommerce Times website: http://www.ecommercetimes.com

Marks, J. (n.d.). "Overview: Letter from the president." Retrieved June 3, 2010,
   from the Search for Common Ground website: http://www.sfcg.org

Entire Web site

BlogPulse. (n.d.). Retrieved September 3, 2010, from the Intelliseek website:
   http://www.intelliseek.com

Article from a newspaper site

Bounds, A. (2007, June 26). Thinking like scientists. *Daily Camera* [Boulder].
   Retrieved from http://www.dailycamera.com

Article from a scholarly e-journal

Welch, J. R., & Riley, R. (2001). Reclaiming land and spirit in the western Apache homeland. *American Indian Quarterly, 25,* 5–14. Retrieved from muse.jhu .edu/journals/american_indian_quarterly

Reference material

Cicada. (2004). In *Encyclopaedia Britannica.* Retrieved from http://www.britan-nica.com

E-book on the Web

Hoffman, F. W. (1981). *The literature of rock: 1954–1978.* Retrieved from http:// www.netlibrary.com

E-mail, interviews, and personal correspondence

Cite personal correspondence in the body of your text, but not in the References list: "Rubino (personal communication, December 12, 2013) claims that. . . ."

Blog posting

Dyer, B., & Barnes, E. (2008, October 7). The "greening" of the Arctic [Web log post]. Retrieved from blog.epa.gov/blog/2008/10/07/the-greening-of-the-arctic

To see where each element of this citation comes from, refer to Figure 24.2.

Social media posting

Storm King Art Centers. (2013, May 30). Rattlesnake figure (aluminums) by Thomas Houseago. [Facebook update]. Retrieved from http://www .facebook.com/StormKingArtCenter

Web video

Beck, R. (2006, November 2). Immigration gumballs [Video file]. Retrieved from http://www.youtube.com/watch?v=n7WJeqxuOfQ

Podcast

Funke, E. (Host). (2007, June 26). *ArtScene* [Audio podcast]. National Public Radio. Retrieved from http://www.npr.org

MISCELLANEOUS SOURCES

Television program

Bochco, S., & Milch, D. (Directors). (2001, November 6). Lie like a rug [Television series episode]. In *NYPD blue.* New York, NY: American Broadcasting Company.

Film

Madden, J. (Director). (1998). *Shakespeare in love* [Motion picture]. United States: Universal Miramax.

Sound recording

Dylan, B. (1966). Rainy day women #12. *On Blonde on blonde* [Record]. New York, NY: Columbia.

Government publications

U.S. Department of Health and Human Services. (2012). *Preventing tobacco use among youth and young adults: A report of the Surgeon General.* Retrieved from http://www.surgeongeneral.gov/library/reports/preventing-youth-tobacco-use/index.html#Full Report

Student Example of an APA-Style Research Paper

An example of a paper in APA style is shown at the end of Chapter 12.

Part V
Writing
for Assessment

To promote the value of reading, the American Library Association uses posters like this one to protest the banning of books. According to this association, since 1982 more than 11,300 books have been challenged—that is, opposed by groups, usually parents, who object to a book's content or language. Liberal groups might oppose a book, say, for its racial or sexual stereotypes while conservatives might condemn a book for promoting immoral behavior. Opponents of book-banning—whether liberal or conservative—argue that encountering a variety of perspectives and controversial subjects in books encourages critical thinking. Some of this social furor appears indirectly in this poster's appeals to *logos* and *pathos* in the use of bright color, the association of reading with fire, and the claim that books have power to stir the imagination.

Chapter 25
Essay Examinations

Learning Objectives

25.1 Understand how essay exams differ from other essays.

25.2 Use productive strategies to prepare for an essay exam.

25.3 Analyze essay exam questions.

25.4 During the exam, use your allotted time wisely.

When instructors give essay exams, they want to see how well you can restate, apply, and assess course material. Also, they often want to see whether you can think critically about course material by applying it to new problems. These twin demands of college-level learning (both knowledge-getting and knowledge-making—see Concept 1.1) make essay exams doubly challenging. Furthermore, not only must you show mastery of course material, but you must also write about it quickly.

How essay exams differ from other essays

25.1 Understand how essay exams differ from other essays.

Essay exams do share similarities with other writing assignments. Most of the instructions in this book—especially those about closed-form prose—apply to exam writing. Rhetorical knowledge is also helpful. For example, your audience for an essay exam is your instructor, so you need to ask what your instructor values and wants. Does your instructor primarily stress understanding of material (knowledge-getting) or does he or she also emphasize the skills of analysis and argument to address new problems that might not have been discussed in class (knowledge-making)? As we explain later in this chapter, looking at your professor's old exams (if available) will give you clues about what to expect.

However, not all the writing strategies you use for out-of-class papers will serve you well in a test situation. Writing researcher Randall Popken, after reviewing more than two hundred sample exams in various disciplines, identified three skills unique to essay exam writing:

1. The ability to store, access, and translate appropriate knowledge into an organized essay
2. The ability to analyze quickly the specific requirements of an exam question and formulate a response to those requirements
3. The ability to deal with time pressure, test anxiety, and other logistical constraints of the exam situation

The rest of this chapter will help you develop these skills.

Using productive strategies to prepare for an essay exam

25.2 Use productive strategies to prepare for an essay exam.

Preparing for an exam involves finding efficient ways to organize, recall, and apply your knowledge so that you can easily construct an intelligent discussion on paper. Of course, you must first know the material. Even the most brilliant writers will stumble on a test if they haven't bothered to attend class regularly, take notes, participate in class discussions, and keep up with the reading. Familiarity with the material lays the groundwork for a successful exam performance, just as thorough research and exploratory writing grounds a good paper. The preparation strategies described in this section will help you learn the material.

Identifying and Learning Main Ideas

No instructor will expect you to remember every single piece of information covered in class. Most instructors are happy if you can remember main ideas and theories, key terminology, and a few supporting examples. The best strategy when you study for an essay exam is to figure out what is most important and learn it first.

How do you determine the main ideas and key concepts? Sometimes they're obvious. Many professors outline their lectures on the board or distribute or post review sheets before each exam. If your professor does not provide explicit verbal cues, listen for a thesis statement, main points, and transitions in each lecture to determine the key ideas and relationships among them. For example,

The *most important critics* of the welfare state are . . . .

Four developments contributed to the reemergence of the English after the Norman invasion . . . .

Hegel's dialectic was *most influenced by* Kant . . . .

Look for similar signals in your textbook and pay special attention to chapter summaries, subheadings, and highlighted terms. If the course involves class discussion or small group work instead of structured lectures, you can get your cues from the kinds of questions the teacher asks in class or the kinds of student

responses that he or she most encourages. You may have to work harder to identify major points. But streamlining and organizing your knowledge in this way
will keep you from feeling overwhelmed when you sit down to study.

Most instructors expect you to master more than the information they cover
in class. Essay exams in humanities, social science, and fine arts courses often ask
for an individual interpretation, argument, or critique. To prepare for such questions, practice talking back to course readings by developing your own positions
on the viewpoints they express. If the professor has lectured on factors involved
in mainstreaming schoolchildren with physical disabilities, look at your notes
and try to define your own position on mainstreaming. If the textbook identifies
salient features of Caravaggio's art, decide how you think his paintings compare to and differ from his contemporaries' work. Questioning texts and lectures
in this way will help you personalize the material, expand your understanding, and take ownership of your education. Remember, though, that professors
won't be impressed by purely subjective opinions. As you explore your views,
search for evidence and arguments, not just from your own experience but from
the course as well, that you can use to support your ideas in the exam.

Applying Your Knowledge

In business, science, social science, and education courses, professors may ask
you to apply a theory or method to a new situation. For example, they might
ask you to show how "first in, last out" accounting might work in bookkeeping
for a machine parts factory or how you might use psychodynamic concepts to
analyze a hypothetical case study.

If you suspect that such a question might appear, use some study time to
practice this kind of thinking. Brainstorm two or three current situations to
which you could apply the theories or concepts you've been learning. Check
local newspapers or browse the Web for ideas. Then freewrite for a few minutes
on how you might organize an essay that puts the theory to work. For instance,
if you've studied federal affirmative action law in a public administration
course, you might ask the following questions: How did the decision by the U.S.
Supreme Court in regard to the University of Michigan's affirmative action policies affect the use of race as a factor in college admissions? How might it apply
to a local college trying to attract a diverse student body? You won't be able to
predict exactly what will appear on the exam, but you can become skilled at
transferring ideas into new settings.

Making a Study Plan

Once you've identified crucial subject matter, you need to develop a study plan.
If you're a novice at studying for a major exam, try following some tried-and-
true approaches.

- Review your instructor's previous exams. Don't be afraid to ask your
  instructor for general guidelines about the type, length, and format of questions he or she normally includes on tests.
- Generate your own practice questions and compose responses.
- Organize group study sessions with two to four classmates. Meet regularly
  to discuss readings, exchange practice questions, test each other informally,
  and critique each other's essays.

Avoid study techniques that are almost universally ineffective: Don't waste time trying to reread all the material or memorize passages word for word (unless the exam will require you to produce specific formulas or quotations). Don't set an unreasonable schedule. You can seldom learn the material adequately in one or two nights, and the anxiety produced by cramming can hurt your performance even more. Most important, don't stay up all night studying. Doing so can be worse than not studying at all, because sleep deprivation impairs your ability to recall and process information.

Analyzing exam questions

25.3   Analyze essay exam questions.

Whereas paper assignments typically ask you to address broad problems that can be solved in numerous possible ways, essay exams usually require much more narrowly focused responses. Essay exams feature well-defined problems with a very narrow range of right answers. They require you to recall a particular body of information and present it in a highly specific way. However, what your instructors are asking you to recall and how they want it presented will not always be clear to you. Exam questions often require interpretation.

Although the language of essay exams varies considerably across disciplines, professors typically draw on a set of conventional moves when they write exam prompts. Consider the following question from an undergraduate course in the history of the English language:

> Walt Whitman once wrote that English was not "an abstract construction of dictionary makers" but a language that had "its basis broad and low, close to the ground." Whitman reminds us that English is a richly expressive language because it comes from a variety of cultural sources. One of these is African-American culture. Write an essay discussing the major ways in which African-American culture and dialect have influenced the English language in the United States. Identify and illustrate at least three important influences: What were the historical circumstances? What important events and people were involved? What were the specific linguistic contributions?

This question presents an intimidating array of instructions, but it becomes manageable if you recognize some standard organizational features.

Understanding the Use of Outside Quotations

First, like many exam questions, this sample opens with a quotation from an author or work not covered in the course. Many students panic when they encounter such questions. "Whitman?! We didn't even study Whitman. What am I supposed to do now?" Don't worry. The primary function of such quotations is to encapsulate a general issue that the instructor wants you to address in your response.

When you encounter an unfamiliar quotation, look carefully at the rest of the question for clues about what role the quotation should play in your essay. The point of the Whitman quotation is restated in the very next sentence—English is shaped by numerous cultural influences—and the function of the quotation is simply to reinforce that point. Because the rest of the question tells you specifically what kinds of cultural influences your response should address (African-American culture, three major linguistic contributions), you don't need to consider this quotation when you write your essay.

Sometimes professors will ask you to take a position on an unfamiliar quotation and support your argument with material covered in the course. Suppose that the question was, "What is your position on Whitman's view? Do you believe that English is enriched or corrupted by multicultural influences?" In this case the quotation is presented as the basis for a thesis statement, which you would then explain and support. A successful response might begin, "Whitman believes that multicultural influences make our language better, but this view is hopelessly naive for the following reasons . . . ." or "Whitman correctly argues that the contributions of different cultures enrich our language. Take these three examples . . . ."

Recognizing Organizational Cues

The question itself can show you the best way to organize your response. Questions tend to begin with general themes that often suggest a thesis statement. Subsequent divisions tell you how to organize the essay into sections and in what order to introduce supporting points. For example, a successful response that follows the organization of our sample exam question might be arranged as follows:

- A thesis stating that several contributions from African-American language and culture have enriched English
- Three supporting paragraphs, each discussing a different area of influence by
  1. summarizing historical circumstances
  2. noting important people and events
  3. providing one or two examples of linguistic contributions

Interpreting Key Terms

As all exam questions do, our sample question asks you to write about a specific body of information in a specific way. When you encounter a lengthy question such as this, first pick out the *noun phrases* that direct you to specific areas of knowledge: "African-American culture," "major influences on the English language in the United States," "historical circumstances," "important events and people," "linguistic contributions." Pay careful attention to words that modify these noun phrases. Does the question tell you how many influences to discuss? What kinds of examples to cite? Does the instructor include conjunctions, such as *or*, to give you a choice of topics, or does he or she use words such as *and* or *as well as* that require you to address all areas mentioned? Words such as *who, what, where*, and *why* also point to particular kinds of information.

After you've determined the specific areas you need to address, look for *directive verbs* that tell you what to do: *discuss, identify*, or *illustrate*, for example. These verbs define the horizons of your response. Strategies Chart 25.1 defines some key directives that frequently appear in essay exams and provides sample questions for each.

Strategies Chart 25.1 Responding to Common Essay-Question Verbs

Verbs	How to Respond	Example Questions
Analyze	Break an argument, concept, or approach into parts and examine the relations among them; discuss causes and effects; evaluate; or explain your interpretation. Look at the rest of the question to determine which strategies to pursue.	*Analyze* the various technical, acoustic, and aesthetic factors that might lead a musician to choose analog over digital recording for a live performance. Be sure to include the strengths and weaknesses of both methods in your discussion.
Apply	Take a concept, formula, theory, or approach and adapt it to another situation.	Imagine that you've been hired to reengineer the operations of a major U.S. automaker. How might you *apply* the principles of Total Quality Management in your recommendations?
Argue	Take a position for or against an issue and give reasons and evidence to support that position.	*Argue* whether or not cloning should be pursued as a method of human reproduction. Be sure to account for the relationship between cloning and mitosis in your discussion.
Compare/ Contrast	Note the similarities (compare) or differences (contrast) between two or more objects or ideas.	*Compare* and *contrast* the leadership styles of Franklin Delano Roosevelt, John F. Kennedy, and Ronald Reagan, focusing on their uses of popular media and political rhetoric.
Construct	Assemble a model, diagram, or other organized presentation of your knowledge about a subject.	*Construct* a model of the writing process that illustrates the major stages writers go through when developing an idea into a finished text.
Critique	Analyze and evaluate an argument or idea, explaining both strengths and weaknesses.	Dinesh D'Souza's "Illiberal Education" sparked widespread controversy when it was published in 1991. Write an essay *critiquing* D'Souza's arguments against affirmative action, identifying both the strengths and weaknesses of his position. Use examples from the text, class discussion, and other class readings to illustrate your points.
Define	Provide a clear, concise, authoritative meaning for an object or idea. The response may include describing the object or idea, distinguishing it clearly from other objects or ideas, or providing one or more supporting examples.	How was "equality" *defined* by the Supreme Court in *Plessy v. Ferguson* (1896)? How did that definition influence subsequent educational policy in the United States?
Discuss	Comprehensively present and analyze important concepts, supported by examples or evidence. Cover several key points or examine the topic from several perspectives. Check the question for guidelines about what to include.	*Discuss* the controversy that surrounded Stanley Milgram's studies of authority and state your own position on the relevance and validity of the experiments.
Enumerate (or List)	List steps, components, or events pertaining to a larger phenomenon, perhaps briefly explaining and commenting on each item.	A two-year-old child falls from a swing on the playground and lies unconscious. As the head preschool teacher, *enumerate* the steps you would take from the time of the accident until the ambulance arrives.
Evaluate	Make a judgment about the worth of an object or idea, examining strengths and weaknesses.	*Evaluate* William Whyte's "Street Corner Society" as an ethnographic study. What are its methodological strengths and weaknesses? Do you believe the weaknesses make Whyte's research obsolete?
Explain	Clarify and state reasons to show how some object or idea relates to a more general topic.	*Explain* the relationship of centripetal force to mass and velocity and give an example to illustrate this relationship.
Identify	Describe some object or idea and explain its significance to a larger topic.	*Identify* the major phonetic characteristics of each of the following language groups of Africa, and provide illustrative examples: Koisan, Niger-Kordofanian, and Nilo-Saharan.

(continued)

Verbs	How to Respond	Example Questions
Illustrate	Give one or more examples, cases, or other concrete instances to clarify a general concept.	Define "monopoly," "public utility," and "competition," and give specific *illustrations* of each.
Prove	Produce reasons and evidence to establish that a position is logical, supportable, or factual.	Use your knowledge about the findings of the National Assessment of Educational Progress to *prove* that public schools either are or are not doing an adequate job of educating children to become productive U.S. citizens.
Review	Briefly survey or summarize something.	*Review* the major differences between Socrates' conception of ethics and the ethical theories of his contemporaries in the fifth century B.C.E.
Summarize	Lay out the main points of a theory, argument, or event in a concise and organized manner.	*Summarize* Mill's definition of justice and explain how it differs from Kant's. Which definition comes closer to your own, and why?
Trace	Explain chronologically a series of events or the development of an idea.	Write an essay that *traces* the pathway of a nerve impulse through the nervous system, being sure to explain neuron structure, action potential, and the production and reception of neurotransmitters.

Our thanks to Michael C. Flanigan, who suggested some of the terms for this table in his "Processes of Essay Exams" manuscript. University of Oklahoma.

In some questions, directives are implied rather than stated directly. If a question asks, "Discuss the effects of Ronald Reagan's tax policies on the U.S. economy during the 1980s," you'll need to summarize what those policies were before you can assess their effects. Before you can take a position on an issue, you have to define what the controversy is about. In general, when you answer any question, you should include sufficient background information about the topic to convince your instructor that you're making an informed argument, whether or not the question specifically asks for background information.

For Writing and Discussion

Analyze Essay Questions

This exercise will hone your ability to analyze essay questions. The following student essay, which received an A, was a response to one of the four closely related questions that follow it. The essay may address issues raised in two or more questions, but it is an A response to only one of them. Your task is to figure out which question the essay answers best.

Decide on your answer independently; then compare answers in small groups. Try to come to a consensus, referring to the Strategies Chart 25.1 to help resolve disagreements. As you discuss your responses, note any successful strategies that you may be able to adapt to your own writing.

FROM A BRITISH LITERATURE COURSE

Gulliver's Travels and *Frankenstein* portray characters whose adventures bring them face to face with the innate weaknesses and limitations of humankind. Victor Frankenstein and Lemuel Gulliver find out during their travels that humans are limited in reasoning capacity and easily corruptible, traits that cause even their best-intentioned projects to go awry. These characters reflect the critical view that Swift and Shelley take of human nature. Both believe that humans have a "dark side" that leads to disastrous effects.

In *Gulliver's Travels*, Gulliver's sea voyages expose him to the best and worst aspects of human civilization. Through Gulliver's eyes, readers come to share Swift's perception that no matter how good people's original intentions, their innate selfishness corrupts everything they attempt. All the societies Gulliver visits give evidence of this. For example, Lilliput has a system of laws once grounded on justice and morality, but that slowly were perverted by greedy politicians into petty applications. Even the most advanced society, Brobdingnag, has to maintain a militia even though the country is currently peaceful—since they acknowledge that because humans are basically warlike, peace can't last forever. By showing examples of varied cultures with common faults, Swift demonstrates what he believes to be innate human weaknesses. He seems to believe that no matter how much progress we make, human societies will eventually fall back into the same old traps.

Victor Frankenstein also experiences human limitations, this time in his own personality, as he pushes to gain knowledge beyond what any human has ever possessed. When he first begins his experiments to manufacture life in the laboratory, his goals are noble—to expand scientific knowledge and to help people. As he continues, he becomes more concerned with the power that his discovery will bring him. He desires to be a "god to a new race of men." Later, when the creature he creates wreaks havoc, Frankenstein's pride and selfishness keep him from confessing and preventing further deaths. Like the societies Gulliver observed, Frankenstein is a clear example of how human frailties corrupt potentially good projects.

Even though Swift and Shelley wrote during two different historical periods, they share a critical view of human nature. However, several unambiguously good characters in *Frankenstein*—including the old man and his daughter— suggest that Shelley feels more optimism that people are capable of overcoming their weaknesses, while Swift seems adamant that humans will eternally backslide into greed and violence. Basically, however, both works demonstrate vividly to readers the ever-present flaws that prevent people and their societies from ever attaining perfection.

Which of the following questions does this essay address most successfully?

1. Contrast Swift's and Shelley's views of human nature, illustrating your points with specific examples from *Gulliver's Travels* and *Frankenstein*.

2. Analyze the use Swift and Shelley make of scientific knowledge to show the limits of human progress in *Gulliver's Travels* and *Frankenstein*, citing specific illustrations from each work.

3. Discuss the characters of Lemuel Gulliver in *Gulliver's Travels* and Victor Frankenstein in *Frankenstein:* What purpose does each serve in the text? How does each author use the character to illustrate important traits or concepts?

4. Many of the writers we've studied this semester explored the limitations of human potential in their work. Write an essay showing how any two of the following works deal with this idea: William Blake's *Songs of Innocence and Experience*, Jonathan Swift's *Gulliver's Travels*, Mary Shelley's *Frankenstein*, Percy Shelley's "Prometheus Unbound." Does each writer suggest a pessimistic or optimistic view of human nature? Be sure to support your argument with specific illustrations from each text.

Using allotted exam time wisely

25.4   During the exam, use your allotted time wisely.

When the exam begins, note the allotted times for each question. Many students leave an essay exam early, sometimes not using a significant portion of the allotted time. Often these answers are superficial or incomplete. Better use of time might have improved them significantly.

Understanding the Features of a Strong Exam Answer

As you begin planning your exam answer, bear in mind what your professors expect in a strong response. Research suggests that most professors want closed-form, thesis-based prose that develops key ideas fully, drawing on supporting facts and examples. The following list of strong traits can serve as a template for a successful essay:

- *Clear thesis statement.* Show your professor that you understand the big picture that the question addresses by including a thesis statement early on. Many professors recommend that you state your thesis clearly, though not necessarily stylishly, in the very first sentence.

- *Coherent organization.* Although a few instructors will read your essay only to see whether you've included important facts and concepts, most expect a logical presentation. Each paragraph should develop and illustrate one main point. Use transition words and phrases to connect each paragraph clearly to the thesis of the essay: "Another factor that led to the economic decline of the South was . . . ."; "In contrast to Hegel, Mill believed . . . . " Show your instructor that you know where the essay's going, that you're developing your thesis.

- *Support and evidence.* When the question calls for supporting facts and examples, be specific. Don't assert or generalize unless you present names, dates, studies, examples, diagrams, or quotations from your reading as support.

- *Independent analysis and argument.* Your response should not be a pedestrian rehash of the textbook. When the question allows, present your own insights, criticisms, or proposals, making sure to support these statements with course material and relate them clearly to your thesis.

- *Conclusion.* Even if you're running short of time, write a sentence or two to tie together main points and restate your thesis. Your conclusion, even if brief, serves an important rhetorical function. It confirms that you've dealt adequately with the question and proved your point.

Using Your Time Wisely

In essay exams, we suggest that you don't start writing immediately. Instead, spend the first five minutes of so planning your response. Then craft a thesis statement. Imagine that you have time only for a one-sentence answer to the question, so make this sentence a summary of the main points that you intend to cover. Then make a quick scratch outline that will help you organize your ideas and think in advance of the details you will need for evidence. If you run out of time before your answer is complete, your professor will know where you intended to go in the unfinished portion because you forecast it in your opening thesis and because your organizational cues provide a map. If you finish early, reread your answer and make improvements by revising topic sentences, improving transitions, or adding details.

Finally, understand how much teachers appreciate legible handwriting. Begin your answer with the question number from the exam sheet so that the professor knows what question you are answering. Number your pages. Make you exam as easy to read as possible.

Chapter 26

Using Reflective Writing to Promote and Assess Learning

Learning Objectives

26.1 Understand and adopt the habit of reflection to assess learning and promote transfer.

26.2 Use informal reflection to assess a draft-in-progress and plan revision.

26.3 Write a formal portfolio reflection to frame and present your development as a writer.

Reflective writing plays an important role in education and in life. Broadly speaking, **reflective writing** helps you think about a past experience in ways that make it more significant, meaningful, and supportive of future growth. Past experiences can be almost anything, such as the experience of reading an article, writing an essay, performing a work-related task, practicing a new skill, or applying recently acquired knowledge to a new problem. The goal of reflection is to help you understand your experience more fully, to analyze what went well or not so well, to identify and assess your thinking processes as the experience unfolded, and to discover and articulate what was meaningful to you. Reflection furthers your growth as a deep learner—someone who knows how to learn, how to transfer learning from one situation to another, and how to apply and synthesize learning.[1]

---

[1] This chapter is influenced by recent research—from cognitive psychology, learning science, and writing studies—linking reflection to deep learning, metacognition, and transfer of learning. We acknowledge particularly the influence of the following works: Linda Adler-Kassner and Elizabeth Wardle, *Naming What We Know: Threshold Concepts of Writing Studies* (Logan: Utah State University, 2015); Kathleen Blake Yancey, Liane Robertson, and Kara Taczak, *Writing Across Contexts: Transfer, Composition, and Sites of Writing* (Logan, Utah: Utah State University Press, 2014); John D. Bransford, James W. Pelligrino, and M. Suzanne Donovan, eds. *How People Learn: Brain, Mind, Experience, and School, Expanded Edition* (Washington, DC: National Academic Press, 2000); Kathleen Blake Yancey, *Reflection in the Writing Classroom* (Logan, UT: Utah State UP, 1998); and Donna Qualley, *Turns of Thought: Teaching Composition as Reflexive Inquiry* (Portsmouth, NH: Boynton/Cook, Heinemann, 1997).

In this chapter we explain the power of reflective writing and then describe two common types of reflections often assigned in a college writing course.

Understanding the function and value of reflective writing

26.1 Understand and adopt the habit of reflection to assess learning and promote transfer.

In dictionaries, the verb "to reflect" has two meanings: (1) to bounce light off a nonabsorbent surface, and (2) to think deeply about something. Both these meanings are relevant. Reflective writing asks you to think deeply about a past experience. But it also asks you to see the experience from two perspectives—as if the past were reflected in the mirror of the present. Light can be reflected in both directions: your past experience can illuminate your present understanding; your present understanding can illuminate the past. These twin perspectives stimulate dialectic thinking of the kind we discussed in Chapter 8, "Writing an Exploratory Essay or Annotated Bibliography."

A good example of a reflective writing assignment is found in the Brief Writing Project at the end of Chapter 1 (see "An Introductory Learning and Writing Reflection"). This assignment asks students to look back over their high school writing experiences in light of new knowledge about college writing explained in the opening chapter on problem-posing. Another kind of reflective assignment is found in Chapter 6 ("Reading Rhetorically"). This assignment asks you to write a reflection in response to a reading; your aim is make connections between your new insights gained from the reading and your own life's experiences, beliefs, and values. (See the section on "Strong Response as a Reflection," especially Strategies Chart 6.4.)

Whether or not you record your thinking on paper, you think reflectively all the time. Suppose you propose to your boss an idea for improving the efficiency of the front office and your boss ignores you. An hour later, as you vent your frustration over coffee and a doughnut, you think of a better way you might have explained to your boss the problem you were trying to solve. You decide that the next time you are in a similar situation, you will use a different tactic.

On a larger scale, this kind of informal reflective thinking can be made more systematic and purposeful. For example, after you have followed a recipe in a cookbook and tasted the results, you make notes on what you might do differently the next time (add different spices, use a different size pan, and so forth). Or your whole understanding of cooking might change when you take a chemistry course on the science of cooking. For example, you might learn about the chemistry of the *Maillard reaction*, which causes the delicious browning of a seared steak, a piece of toast, or a roasted marshmallow. (You have an "aha" moment when you realize that the same chemical reaction is at work in all three cases.) Once you understand how the right combination of surface temperature and time produces a chemical reaction that releases hundreds of flavor compounds, you understand the science behind lots of recipes and can apply this science to many new cooking situations.

Writing a reflective essay prompts this kind of reflective thinking. It helps you draw together unconnected fragments of knowledge into more coherent wholes and leads to more meaningful understanding.

For Writing and Discussion
Reflecting on a Past Experience

Working individually, think of a past experience that you can evaluate reflectively. This experience could be learning a new skill, wrestling with a difficult concept in a course, having a problematic encounter with another person, or completing a difficult job task. To encourage you to think about the past from the perspective of the present, try asking yourself this question: "How do I see the experience differently now from the way I saw it then?" Working on your own for ten minutes, freewrite reflectively about your performance. What did you do well? What wasn't working for you? What could you have done better?

Then in groups or as a class, share what you have learned through your reflective freewrites. How did the process of looking back give you a new perspective on your experience? How might reflective writing help you bring about changes and improvements in future performances?

Now that you understand the purpose of reflective writing, let's look more closely at its function and value.

How Reflective Thinking Promotes Metacognition

Reflective writing urges you to "think about your own thinking"—a process called **metacognition**. Whereas **cognition** refers to your ability to explain a concept or perform a process, **metacognition** refers to your ability to explore how this concept fits into a broader system of concepts or how this process might be applied to other kinds of problems. To use our marshmallow example, you demonstrate cognition when you show you can successfully roast a marshmallow without burning it. You show metacognition if you can explain why you move the marshmallow closer to or away from the fire (to control temperature), why the temperature matters (the science of the *Maillard reaction*), and why you couldn't brown a marshmallow by putting it in a microwave.

Let's take another example. A common skill taught in college composition courses is how to cite a source, either through parenthetical citation or through attributive tags (see Skill 23.3). If you can use both of these methods, then you demonstrate cognition. But to demonstrate metacognition, you need to think about when and why a writer might choose one method over the other—a choice requiring you to link your knowledge of citation methods to a broader understanding of audience, purpose, and genre. By urging you to think metacognitively—to think about your own thinking—reflection helps you gain this big-picture knowledge of how small bits of information fit into larger systems. The following questions can help you practice metacognition. You can apply them to any college course or subject matter.

QUESTIONS THAT PROMOTE METACOGNITIVE THINKING

- What do I currently know about this subject? (Ask at the beginning of the course.)

- As I got deeper into this subject, how did my understanding change? (Before taking this course, I thought that X was . . . .; but now I think that X is . . . .)

- What was most difficult, challenging, or confusing in this course? What were my thinking and studying strategies when I encountered difficulties? Were these strategies effective?

- How did I do the reading for this course? How effective were my reading strategies? How could I have used the course textbook or other readings more productively?

- Have I had any "aha" moments in this course where something confusing became clear or meaningful or valuable to me? How can I explain this "aha" moment to others?

- How have the ideas, concepts, theories, and values encountered in this course connected to me personally? How does this course connect to previous courses or to other seemingly unrelated courses?

- How would I describe the "big-picture" knowledge that my instructor hopes I will take away from this course? Have I achieved this big-picture knowledge?

How Reflective Writing Promotes Deep Learning and Transfer

One of the goals of reflection is to help you learn knowledge or skills at a deep level so that you can transfer them from one course to another and to your personal and professional life. To illustrate what we mean by a deep level of learning, let's return to the cooking example. Suppose you took the "chemistry of cooking" course with no personal interest in cooking. You might have memorized the definition of the *Maillard reaction,* explained the science adequately on the exam, and then mostly forgotten about it. This kind of learning is often called *surface learning.* But your interest in cooking changes the way you encountered the concepts in the course. You gained power to use this knowledge in future cooking situations. You now know that you can measure and control temperatures to produce the Maillard reaction when you want it and to avoid it when you don't want it. This kind of meaningful knowledge is called **deep learning**. Deep learning is not something transmitted to you by the professor. It is something you make for yourself.

The metacognitive thinking promoted through reflection helps you acquire the deep learning that facilitates transfer. It helps you recognize recurring patterns in different kinds of problems in order to understand what strategies from the past can be best applied to a present problem. You might not know, for example, how to write a nursing care plan. You may therefore assume that a first-year writing course is irrelevant to the kinds of writing required of nurses. But if you take from your writing course a metacognitive awareness that all writing is done for a purpose to an audience within a genre, you will know what questions to ask. What is the purpose of a nursing care plan? Who reads it and why? What does a typical nursing care plan look like? Asking questions like these accelerates your learning when you encounter an unfamiliar writing situation. It is generally not the details of a course that transfer to a new situation, but rather the big-picture knowledge.

Questions to Ask When You Reflect on Your Own Writing

So far, we have discussed the kinds of questions that help you reflect on any past experience. Now we turn to specific questions that will help you reflect on one or more pieces of your own writing. To write an effective reflection, select only a few ideas to focus on, look at specific aspects of a specific paper, explore dialectically your past thinking versus your present thinking, and support your analysis with adequate details. We suggest the following questions as a guide to producing such reflections. You won't answer them all in one reflection. Instead, choose the two or three questions that best apply to your performance and text. (Try to select your questions from at least two different categories.)

PROCESS QUESTIONS:

- What specific writing strategies did I use to complete this work?
- Which strategies were the most or least productive?
- Did this writing project require new strategies, or did I rely on past strategies?
- What was the biggest problem I faced in writing this piece, and how successfully did I solve that problem?
- What has been my major content-level revision so far?
- What were my favorite sentence- or word-level revisions?
- What did I learn about myself as a writer or about writing in general by writing this paper?

SUBJECT-RELATED QUESTIONS:

- How did the subject of my writing cause me to "wallow in complexity"?
- What tensions did I encounter between my ideas/experiences and those of others? Between the competing ideas about the subject in my own mind?
- Did I change my mind or come to see something differently as a result of writing this work?
- What passages show my independent thinking about the subject? My unresolved problems or mixed feelings about it?
- What were the major content problems, and how successfully did I resolve them?
- What did writing about this subject teach me?

RHETORIC-RELATED QUESTIONS:

- How did the audience I imagined influence me in writing this paper?
- How did my awareness of genre influence my choices about subject matter and rhetorical features?
- What do I want readers to take away from reading my work?
- What rhetorical strategies please me most (my use of evidence, my examples, my delayed thesis, etc.)? What effect do I hope these strategies have on my audience?

- How would I describe my voice in this work? Is this voice appropriate? Is it similar to my everyday voice or to the voices I have used in other kinds of writing?
- Did I take any risks in writing this?
- What do readers expect from this genre, and did I fulfill those expectations?

SELF-ASSESSMENT QUESTIONS:
- What are the most significant strengths and weaknesses in this writing?
- Will others also see these as important strengths or weaknesses? Why or why not?
- What specific ideas and plans do I have for revision?

Writing an informal reflection on a draft-in-progress

26.2 Use informal reflection to assess a draft-in-progress and plan revision.

Instructors across the disciplines may ask you to write reflectively about your writing projects in their courses. Many assignments call for an informal reflection in which you think metacognitively about a draft in progress (or about a completed essay that you can imagine revising in the future). Many reflection assignments call for informal, exploratory pieces, similar to other kinds of exploratory writing described in Concept 2.1. Informal reflections are conversational in tone, open in form, and written mainly for yourself and, perhaps, a friendly, nonjudgmental audience. However, informal reflections differ from most other kinds of exploratory writing in timing, focus, and purpose.

Informal reflections can be assigned at any stage of the writing process. The focus in informal reflections is your writing itself, both the product and the processes that produced it. Its aim is to generate critical understanding that will lead to revision—the steps you will take next to improve your draft. In an informal reflection, you think about what's working or not working in the draft, what thinking and writing processes went into producing it, and what possibilities you see for revising it. An example of an informal reflection is Jane Kidder's short reflective piece in the Readings section at the end of this chapter.

Sample Assignments for Informal Reflections

Instructors use a variety of assignments to prompt informal reflections. Some examples of assignments are the following:

- *Process log:* Your instructor asks you to keep a process log in which you describe the writing processes and decisions made for each essay you write throughout the term. In particular, you should offer a detailed and specific account of the problems you encountered (your "wallowing in complexity") and the rhetorical and subject-related alternatives considered and choices made.

- *Writer's memo:* Your instructor asks you to write a memorandum to turn in with your draft. In it, you answer a series of questions: How did you go about composing this draft? What problems did you encounter? What do you see as this draft's greatest strengths? What are its greatest weaknesses? What questions about your draft would you like the instructor to address?

- *Talk-back:* In another type of companion piece, the instructor asks you to respond to his or her comments after you get the paper back: (1) What did I [the instructor] value in this text as a reader? (2) Do you agree with my reading? and (3) What else would you like for me to know?

- *Cover letter:* Your instructor asks you to write a response to your peer reviewers' comments on a draft of your paper to be turned in with a revision of the paper. In your letter, you identify specific feedback you received from your peer reviewers concerning your handling of your subject and the effect of your rhetorical choices on readers. You explain how this feedback influenced your revision. Where did you agree with your reviewers? Which suggestions did you choose not to take and why? How did the responses from a real audience lead you to strengthen this piece of writing?

Example of a Reflective Response to Reader Feedback

The following excerpt from an informal reflection comes from an e-mail message sent by a student writer to her peer reviewers and writing instructor. Her peer reviewers had offered revision advice on her paper about the causes of anorexia. Particularly they had puzzled over a confusing topic sentence and suggested a revised version. However, the writer realizes that the suggested revision didn't match her intentions. Here is her e-mail response:

EXCERPT FROM A STUDENT REFLECTION ON A DRAFT

I agree with my peer reviewers that this sentence is confusing. However, their suggested revision isn't quite what I am trying to say. Most people think that anorexics are trying to be sexually attractive by meeting the media's image of the thin model. But I am arguing that some anorexics are not trying to be beautiful at all. My peer reviewers thought that I am trying to say that anorexics want to be undesirable. But their comments have caused me to try to clarify my thinking. I need to write a new topic sentence something like this: "Perhaps anorexics don't pursue desirability but rather want to avoid the whole issue of being sexual." I am not arguing that anorexics want to be "undesirable" (as my peer reviewers suggest). Rather I am arguing that they want to avoid sexuality altogether. One can feel that, by entering the sexual world of mature adults, one will lose hold of one's essential self. This is the idea I'm trying to express. Anorexia stops menstruation and, in a sense, keeps the anorexic in a pre-adolescent, non-sexual stage. I now see that I need to revise this whole paragraph.

As this example suggests, reflection involves viewing your writing from different perspectives and achieving a critical distance. This process reveals the writer's metacognitive thinking ("What was I really trying to say here?") triggered by her realization that her draft wasn't clear. Reexamining one's writing from a new perspective yields new insights and an enriched, more complicated understanding of one's ideas and writing choices.

Writing a formal reflection to introduce a portfolio

26.3 Write a reflection essay for a portfolio to frame and present your development as a writer.

You may also be asked to write a formal reflection on your development as a writer over a whole term. In such cases you are not looking at a single draft-in-progress but at the whole body of your work. Although end-of-the-term reflective essays differ in scope and audience from single reflections, similar qualities are valued in both: selectivity, specificity, metacognitive thinking, and adequate detail. In many cases, your formal reflection will ask you to self-assess your achievement of certain specified learning goals for the course. Usually, the formal reflection will introduce a portfolio of your work for the course. The goal of the reflection is to help your readers understand how you developed as a writer. Most important, in explaining what you have learned from this review of your work, you also make new self-discoveries.

Preparing a Portfolio of Your Writing

Portfolios offer many advantages to writers. The portfolio process gives you more time to revise before presenting your work for evaluation because many instructors who assign portfolios do not assign grades to individual drafts. Through your comprehensive reflection, you can assess and comment on your writing and learning before someone else passes judgment. Further, the portfolio process helps you develop insights about your thinking and writing processes, insights that you can apply to new writing situations. Finally, this experience can prepare you for work-related tasks because portfolios are increasingly required in job applications as well as in assessments for job promotions or merit-based pay increases.

Specific guidelines for preparing a writing portfolio vary from course to course, so you will need to check with each individual instructor for directions about what to include and how to organize your portfolio. You may be given a lot of leeway in what to include in your portfolio, or you may be required to submit a specific number of assignments or type of work. However, no matter what the specific requirements are, the following general suggestions can help you manage the portfolio process.

COLLECTING WORK   Crucial to your success in assembling a portfolio is careful organization and collection of your work throughout the term. This way, you will avoid the headache and wasted time caused by trying to hunt down lost or misplaced work.

Besides the practical need to keep track of all your work in order to review and select the writing that you will include in your portfolio, the process of saving and organizing your work will cause you to attend to writing processes throughout the term, one of the key goals of portfolio teaching.

SELECTING WORK FOR YOUR PORTFOLIO Even if you are given explicit instructions about the number and type of writing samples to include in your portfolio, you will still have important choices to make about which completed pieces to include or which pieces to revise for inclusion. We suggest three general guidelines to consider as you review your writing and select work for your portfolio presentation.

- *Variety:* One purpose of portfolio assessment is to give a fuller picture of a writer's abilities. Therefore, it is important that you choose work that demonstrates your versatility—your ability to make effective rhetorical choices according to purpose, audience, and genre. What combination of writing samples best illustrates your ability to write effectively for different rhetorical situations and in different genres and media?

- *Course goals:* A second consideration is course goals. The goals are likely to be stated in the course syllabus and may include such objectives as "ability to demonstrate critical thinking in writing"; "ability to use multiple strategies for generating ideas, drafting, revising, and editing"; and "ability to demonstrate control over surface features such as syntax, grammar, punctuation, and spelling." Which pieces of writing most clearly demonstrate the abilities given as your course's goals, or which pieces can be revised to offer such a demonstration?

- *Personal investment:* Finally, be sure to consider which pieces of writing best reflect your personal investment and interest. If you are going to be revising the selected pieces multiple times during the last few weeks of class, you will want to make sure you choose work that holds your interest and has ideas you care about. Which pieces are you proudest of? Which were the most challenging or satisfying to write? Which present ideas you'd like to explore further?

Guidelines for Writing a Portfolio Reflection Essay

Because the portfolio reflection essay self-assesses not only your writing abilities but also your abilities as a reflective learner, it may be one of the most important pieces of writing you do for a writing course. Here we offer some additional guidelines geared specifically toward introducing your writing portfolio:

- Review the informal reflections you have written about specific writing projects during the term. As you reread these process log entries, writer's memos, cover letters, and so on, what do you discover about yourself as a writer?

- Consider key rhetorical concepts that you have learned in this course. Use the detailed table of contents of Chapters 1 through 5 to refresh your memory about these concepts. How can you show that you understand these concepts and have applied them in your writing?

- Take notes on your own writing as you review your work and reconstruct your writing processes for particular writing projects. What patterns do you see? What surprises you? How can you show the process behind the product? How can you show your growth as a writer through specific examples?

- Be honest. Identifying weaknesses is as important as identifying strengths. How can you use this opportunity to discover more about yourself as a writer or learner?

What to Include in the Portfolio Reflection Essay

Instructors look for four kinds of knowledge in formal portfolio reflections: self-knowledge, content knowledge, rhetorical knowledge, and critical knowledge or judgment. Here we suggest questions that you can use to generate ideas for your portfolio reflective essay. Choose only a few of the questions to respond to, questions that allow you to explain and demonstrate your most important learning in the course. Also, choose experiences to narrate and passages to cite that illustrate more than one kind of knowledge.

SELF-KNOWLEDGE   By **self-knowledge**, we mean your understanding of how you are developing as a writer. Think about the writer you were, are, or hope to be. You can also contemplate how the subjects you have chosen to write about (or the way you have approached your subjects) relate to you personally beyond the scope of your papers. Self-knowledge questions you might ask are the following:

- What knowledge of myself as a writer have I gained from the writing I did in this course?

- What changes, if any, have occurred in my writing practices or my sense of myself as a writer?

- What patterns or discontinuities can I identify between the way I approached one writing project versus the way I approached another?

- How can I best illustrate and explain through reference to specific writing projects the self-knowledge I have gained?

CONTENT KNOWLEDGE   **Content knowledge** refers to what you have learned by writing about various subjects. It also includes the intellectual work that has gone into the writing and the insights you gained from considering multiple points of view and grappling with your own conflicting ideas. Perhaps you have grasped ideas about your subjects that you have not shown in your papers. These questions about content knowledge can prod your thinking:

- What kinds of content complexities did I grapple with this term?

- What insights did I arrive at through confronting clashing ideas?

- What new perspectives did I gain about particular subjects from my considerations of multiple or alternate viewpoints?

- What new ideas or perspectives did I gain that may not be evident in the writings themselves?

- What passages from various papers best illustrate the critical thinking I did in my writing projects for this course?

RHETORICAL KNOWLEDGE   Our third category, **rhetorical knowledge**, focuses on your awareness of your rhetorical decisions—how your contemplation of purpose, audience, and genre affected your choices about content, structure, style, and document design. The following questions about rhetorical choices can help you assess this area of your knowledge:

- What important rhetorical choices did I make in various works to accomplish my purpose or to appeal to my audience? What parts of my various works best illustrate these choices? Which of these choices are particularly effective and why? About which choices am I uncertain and why?

- What have I learned about the rhetorical demands of audience, purpose, and genre, and how has that knowledge affected my writing and reading practices?

- How do I expect to use this learning in the future?

CRITICAL KNOWLEDGE OR JUDGMENT   A fourth area of knowledge, **critical knowledge or judgment**, concerns your awareness of significant strengths and weaknesses in your writing. This area also encompasses your ability to identify what you like or value in various pieces of writing and to explain why. You could ask yourself these questions about your critical knowledge:

- Of the works in my portfolio, which is the best and why? Which is the weakest and why?

- How has my ability to identify strengths and weaknesses changed during this course?

- What effect has peer, instructor, or other reader feedback had on my assessments of my work?

- What improvements would I make in these works if I had more time?

- How has my writing changed over the term? What new abilities will I take away from this course?

- What are the most important things I still have to work on as a writer?

- What is the most important thing I have learned in this course?

- How do I expect to use what I've learned from this course in the future?

Readings

Our first reading is a short informal reflection by student Jane Kidder in the form of a cover letter that explains to her instructor how she revised her draft in response to her peer review feedback. Her assignment is to write an "analysis/synthesis" essay in response to several articles by writing theorists about the writing process. Note how Jane explains her choice to write an open-form personal essay rather than a purely academic one and still accomplish the purpose of the assignment.

Jane Kidder (student)
A Reflection on a Draft-in-Progress

My peer reviewers gave me supportive feedback that was helpful in fine-tuning my essay. I took a risk in this project by deciding to write an open-form personal essay rather than a closed-form thesis-driven one. My main question for my peer reviewers was whether my personal essay was an appropriate interpretation of the assignment. My group members helped me to realize that the significant strengths of the essay were my humorous tone and my focus on my personal experiences, while its significant weakness was a lack of deep engagement with the assigned readings. Therefore, the biggest problem that I faced in revising this piece was the challenge of strategically weaving both my personal experiences and the readings throughout, in order to create a cohesive and polished piece of writing. Based on my reviewers' comments, I decided to make several major content revisions: I added more summary of the readings, included attributive tags where needed, and supplemented my personal narrative with two paragraphs of analysis of our course readings. The subject for my essay caused me to wallow in complexity because I struggled to analyze and evaluate the writing strategies discussed in the readings and to connect those strategies to my own personal experiences as a writer.

In revising this piece, I also made several key rhetorical choices. For instance, in crafting my narrative about my experience as a writer, I was influenced by my awareness of my audience, which was not only my instructor, but my fellow students as well. I assumed that my audience would be engaged by an amusing personal essay but would also take interest in my analysis of the assigned readings. Additionally, I was influenced by my keen awareness of the genre in which I was writing: I aimed to write an engaging narrative because readers expect the genre of open-form nonfiction to be compelling and entertaining. Overall, through the process of writing and revising this piece, I learned about myself as a writer: that I can take risks in my writing, because risks allow me to make creative and pleasing rhetorical choices while still engaging deeply with my sources.

THINKING CRITICALLY
About "A Reflection on a Draft-in-Progress"

1. To what extent does this reflection show that Jane has deepened her thinking about her analysis/synthesis-reflection task and herself as a writer?

2. Where does Jane show an awareness of audience and purpose in her self-reflection on her essay?

3. To what extent does Jane show us that she can identify strengths and weaknesses of her essay?

4. What are her most important insights about her essay?

5. How would you characterize Jane's voice in this reflection? Does this voice seem appropriate for this kind of reflective writing? Why or why not?

Our second reading is a reflective essay written by a student writer Annabelle Forster to introduce her end-of-term portfolio for a first-year composition course. One of the learning objectives for the course was to demonstrate rhetorical knowledge by writing for different audiences within different genres.

Annabelle Forster (student)
A Portfolio Reflection Cover Letter

Dear Portfolio Reader:

In the attached portfolio, I have chosen three writing assignments from this course to show my progress working with the learning goals of this class. I think these samples show that I have gained basic competency in sentence structure and grammar as well as fundamental skills for citing and documenting sources. In this reflective cover letter I hope to display my growth in rhetorical skills. This course has given me the opportunity to write in different genres for different audiences—difficult tasks that tested my flexibility as a writer and that encouraged me to think metacognitively about my writing and thinking processes concerning rhetorical choices.

My first selection for this portfolio is an example from early in the course when I became conscious of the relationship between writing and rhetorical context. This assignment asked us to research how writing functions in a discipline other than our majors and to use that research to contribute to a conversation about the purpose of writing. I interviewed an astronomy professor, read a style guide for scientific writing, and studied an article in an astronomy journal. I started with no content or relevant rhetorical knowledge at all: What did I know about astronomy or scientific writing? However, my roommate, a biology major, explained to me that in the scientific community the charts and tables are as important to the piece as the text itself in accomplishing the ultimate goal of conveying as much verifiable information as possible to the readers. The more I learned about writing in the discipline of astronomy, the more I learned about the conventions of an unfamiliar field and saw that there isn't just one way to write a paper. Although I struggled in making rhetorical choices to present my research in the genre of an informal report, trying this genre and exploring writing in another discipline showed me that I write more comfortably to analyze and evaluate than to report.

My second selection, a multimodal assignment to explain to or persuade an audience of our choice, required us to approach rhetoric in a new way. I worked with a friend to make an educational video for outdoor leaders to give women information about female hygiene in the backcountry. As an outdoor trip leader, I enjoyed this opportunity to cross communities and use media I was unfamiliar with. This project was easier for me. My growing content knowledge and self-knowledge with writing combined with my experience backpacking and leading women in the backcountry made me feel confident in my ethos and in touch with my audience. My experience gave me authority, and I think that translated well in my selection and presentation of key points. The rhetorical challenges came from working in a new mode (I had never made a video before) and from addressing a large audience without being redundant or exclusive. My instructor, class members, and Outdoor Recreation supervisor all responded well to the video, validating my rhetorical appeals to *ethos* and *pathos*.

My final selection, written late in the course, stretched me as a writer but was ultimately successful. For the assignment I had to take a piece of writing from another course and rewrite it in a new genre for a new audience. I used an interpretive argument I had written for my literature class about Mary Shelley's *Frankenstein* and turned it into a letter to my mom that recommended this book to her book club. When making my argument for my literature class, I had a strong thesis concerning the different frames of narration in the novel. However, my mom had only seen the *Frankenstein* movies and had an interpretation of the story that differed greatly from mine. It was an interesting challenge to both defend my original thesis and layer it with a new thesis defending the value of the book. In my early drafts I struggled to adapt my content knowledge to the interests and understanding of a different audience, but my rhetorical knowledge helped me stay true to the letter genre, and my mom agreed to propose the book to her book club.

This course has expanded my understanding of how writers make choices to best fit their audience and genre. I learned that having content knowledge and a strong thesis is only one part of creating a strong argument. The writer also has to adjust content to the audience and the genre. In the future, I will use my confidence in my ability to analyze and understand content to give me more time to focus on rhetorical choices.

THINKING CRITICALLY

About "A Portfolio Reflection Cover Letter"

1. What kinds of self-knowledge does Annabelle display in her reflective letter?
2. How does Annabelle demonstrate a journey of wrestling with different rhetorical situations, new content and genres, and herself as a writer?
3. What specifics does Annabelle include to show she has engaged in dialectical thinking and "earned her insights"? If you were a reader of her portfolio, would you say she has included adequate details to demonstrate her growth as a writer?
4. How does Annabelle demonstrate her ability to make judgments about her essays' strengths and weaknesses?

What learning from this course do you think Annabelle is likely to transfer to new writing situations in the future?

Part VI
A Guide to Editing

This poster, sponsored by the Ad Council and StopBullying.gov, is part of an ongoing campaign to curtail bullying among young people. The ad is aimed at parents, urging them to encourage their children to be active in opposing bullying. Although the ad's creators chose to use lettering—not an image—to illustrate bullying, the poster has both visual and verbal rhetorical effects. It makes strong appeals to *pathos* in its use of shocking abusive language and disturbing lettering style. Note how the blurry presentation of the type makes a visual statement about both perception and psychological damage. It reinforces the idea that not everyone is aware of bullying and suggests that bullying dims the personhood of victims. Together with the line about parents' unawareness of the hostility present in their kids' environment, this ad presents a powerful message to parents.

Chapter 1
Improving Your Editing Skills

Learning Objectives

H1.1 Practice strategies for improving your editing processes.

In our discussion of the writing process in Chapter 17, we recommend saving editing for last. We do so not because editing is unimportant but because fine-tuning a manuscript requires that the main features of the text—its ideas and organization—be relatively stable. There is no point in correcting mistakes in a passage that is going to be deleted or completely rewritten.

This late-stage concern for clarity and correctness is a crucial part of the writing process because editing and proofreading errors reflect directly on your *ethos*, that is, on the reader's image of you as a writer. They make you seem careless and unprofessional. If you're writing something with real-world consequences—a job application letter, a grant proposal, a letter to a client, a field report for your boss—then typos, misspellings, sentence fragments, and dangling participles are like a piece of lettuce between your teeth. Instead of focusing on your message, your readers may not even take you seriously enough to finish reading what you have written.

Strategies for improving your editing and proofreading processes

H1.1 Practice strategies for improving your editing and proofreading processes.

You can become a more attentive editor and proofreader of your own prose if you practice the editing strategies we suggest in this section.

Keep a List of Your Own Characteristic Errors

When one of your papers is returned, look carefully at the kinds of sentence-level errors noted by your instructor. A paper with numerous errors might actually contain only two or three *kinds* of errors repeated several times. For example, some writers consistently omit apostrophes from possessives or add them to plurals; others regularly create comma splices when they use such words as *therefore* or *however*. Try to classify the kinds of errors you made on the paper, and then try to avoid these errors on your next paper.

Do a Self-Assessment of Your Editing Knowledge

Look over the detailed table of contents for this editing guide and note the various topics covered. Which of these topics are familiar to you from previous instruction? In which areas are you most confident? In which areas are you most shaky? We generally recommend that students study the topics in Handbook Chapter 3 early in a course because the chapter explains the main punctuation rules for placing commas and avoiding fragments and comma splices. The remaining handbook chapters can function as handy references when specific questions arise. Become familiar with the organization of this guide so that you can find information rapidly.

Read Your Draft Aloud

A key to good editing is noting every word. An especially helpful strategy is to read your paper aloud—really aloud, not half-aloud, mumbling to yourself, but at full volume, as if you were reading to a room full of people. When you stumble over a sentence or have to go back to fit sound to sense, mark the spot. Something is probably wrong there and you will want to return to it later.

Make sure that the words you read aloud are actually on the page. When reading aloud, people often unconsciously fill in missing words or glide over mispunctuated passages, so check carefully to make sure that what you say matches what you wrote. Some writers like to read aloud into a recorder and then reread their draft silently while playing back the recording. If you haven't tried the recording technique, consider doing so at least once. It is a surprisingly powerful way to improve your editing skills.

Read Your Draft Backward

Another powerful editing technique—strange as it might seem—is to read your paper backward, word by word, from end to beginning. When you read forward, you tend to focus on meaning and often read right past mistakes. Reading backward estranges you from the paper's message and allows you to focus on the details of the essay—the words and sentences. As you read backward, keep a dictionary and this handbook close by. Focus on each word, looking for typos, spelling errors, misused apostrophes, pronoun case errors, and so forth, and attend to each sentence unit, making sure that it is a complete sentence and that its boundaries are properly marked with punctuation.

Use a Spell-Checker and (Perhaps) Other Editing Programs

With spell-checkers, you have almost no excuse for including misspelled words or typos in a formal paper. Become a skilled operator of your computer's spell-checker, and always run the program before printing your final draft.

Be aware, however, that a spell-checker isn't foolproof. These programs match strings of letters in a document against strings stored in memory. A spell-checker may not contain some of the specialized words you use (authors' names or special course terms), nor can it tell whether a correctly spelled word is used correctly in context (*it's, its; their, there,* or *they're; to, too,* or *two*).

Many writers use "grammar" checkers, also called "style" or "usage" checkers. We place "grammar" in quotation marks because these programs do not really check grammar. They can perform only countable or matchable functions such as identifying *be* verbs and passive constructions, noting extremely long sentences, identifying clichés and wordy expressions, and so forth. Although these programs can draw your attention to some areas where you may be able to tighten or enliven your prose, you must use them with caution. So-called grammar-checkers can't catch most of the most common errors in usage and grammar that writers make, and they often flag nonexistent problems.

Microtheme Projects on Editing

The following microtheme assignments focus on selected problems of editing and style. Since you never know a concept as well as when you have to teach it to someone else, these assignments place you in a teaching role. They ask you to solve an editing problem and to explain your solution in your own words to a hypothetical audience that has turned to you for instruction.

Your instructor can use these microtheme assignments as individual or group writing projects or as prompts for classroom discussion.

MICROTHEME 1: APOSTROPHE MADNESS   Your friend Elmer Fuddnick has decided to switch majors from engineering to creative writing. Poor Elmer has a great imagination, but he forgot to study basic punctuation when he was in high school. He's just sent you the first draft of his latest short story, "The Revenge of the Hedgehogs." Here are his opening sentences:

> The hedgehogs' scrambled from behind the rock's at the deserts edge, emitted what sounded like a series of cats scream's and then rolled themselve's into spiny balls. One of the hedgehogs hunched it's back and crept slowly toward a cactus' shadow.

Although you can't wait to finish reading Elmer's story, you are a bit annoyed by his misuse of apostrophes. Your job is to explain to Elmer how to use apostrophes correctly. Begin by correcting Elmer's sentences; then explain to Elmer the principles you used to make your corrections. Your explanation of apostrophes should be clear enough so that Elmer can learn their use from your explanation. In other words, you are the teacher. Use your own language and make up your own examples.

MICROTHEME 2: STUMPED BY HOWEVER   You are putting yourself through college by operating an online grammar hot line and charging people for your advice. One day you see the following post:

> Dear Grammarperson:
> I get really confused on how to punctuate words like "however" and "on the other hand." Sometimes these words have commas on both sides of them, but at other times they have a comma in back and a semicolon in

front. What's the deal here? How can I know whether to use a comma or a semicolon in front of a "however"?

Bewildered in Boston

Write a response to Bewildered explaining why words such as *however* are sometimes preceded by a comma and sometimes by a semicolon (or a period, in which case *however* starts with a capital letter). Use your own language and invent your own examples.

MICROTHEME 3: THE COMIC DANGLER   Here is another message received at the grammar hot line (see Microtheme 2):

Dear Grammarperson:

My history teacher was telling us the other day that editing our papers before we submitted them was really important. And then she mentioned in passing that some editing mistakes often create comic effects. She said that the dangling participle was her favorite because it often produced really funny sentences. Well, maybe so, but I didn't know what she was talking about. What are dangling participles and why are they funny?

Not Laughing in Louisville

Explain to Not Laughing what dangling participles are and why they are often funny. Illustrate with some examples of your own and then show Not Laughing how to correct them.

MICROTHEME 4: HOW'S THAT AGAIN?   The grammar hot line is doing a great business (see Microtheme 2). Here is another query:

Dear Grammarperson:

It has often been said by some instructors that I have had in the various educational institutions that I have attended that a deadening effect is achievable in the prose produced by writers through the transformation of verbs into nouns and through the overuse of words that are considered empty in content or otherwise produce a redundant effect by the restating of the same idea in more words than are necessary for the reader's understanding of the aforementioned ideas. Could these teachers' allegations against the sentence structure of many writers be considered to be at least partially applicable to my own style of writing prose?

Verbose in Vermont

Help Verbose out by rewriting his or her question in a crisper style. Then explain briefly, using your own language and examples, the concepts of wordiness and nominalization.

MICROTHEME 5: THE INTENTIONAL FRAGMENT   Advertisers frequently use sentence fragments purposely. Find an advertisement that makes extensive use of fragments. Rewrite the copy to eliminate all sentence fragments. Then write a one-paragraph microtheme in which you speculate why the advertiser used fragments rather than complete sentences. Try to suggest at least two possible reasons.

Chapter 2
Understanding Sentence Structure

Learning Objectives

H2.1 Explain what a sentence is.
H2.2 Identify basic sentence patterns.
H2.3 Identify parts of speech.
H2.4 Identify types of phrases.
H2.5 Identify types of clauses.
H2.6 Identify simple, compound, complex, and compound-complex sentences.

The concept of the sentence

H2.1 Explain what a sentence is.

A *sentence* is a group of related words with a complete subject and a complete predicate. The subject names something, and the predicate makes an assertion about the thing named.

Name Something	Make an Assertion about It
Cheese	tastes good on crackers.
Lizards and snakes	are both kinds of reptiles.
Capital punishment	has been outlawed in many countries.

Every sentence must include at least one subject and one predicate. These components answer two different questions: (1) Who or what is the sentence about? (subject); and (2) What assertion does the sentence make about the subject? (predicate). Consider the following example:

Tree ants in Southeast Asia construct nests by sewing leaves together.

What is this sentence about? *Tree ants in Southeast Asia* (subject). What assertion is made about tree ants? (They) *construct nests by sewing leaves together* (predicate).

Ordinarily a sentence begins with the subject, followed by the verb. Sometimes, however, word order can be changed. In the following examples, the subjects are underlined once and the verbs are underlined twice.

Normal Word Order   The most terrifying <u>insects</u> <u>wander</u> through the countryside seeking prey.

Question   <u>What</u> <u>are</u> the most terrifying insects?

Imperative   <u>Watch</u> for the driver ants. ("You" is understood as the subject.)

"There" Opening   There <u>are</u> various <u>kinds</u> of terrifying insects.

Inverted Order   Across the jungles of Africa <u>marched</u> the driver <u>ants</u>.

Sentences can also have more than one subject or predicate.

Compound Subject   The army <u>ants</u> of South America and the driver ants of Africa <u>march</u> in long columns.

Compound Predicate   The <u>hunters</u> at the head of a column <u>discover</u> a prey, <u>swarm</u> all over it, and eventually <u>cut</u> it apart.

Basic sentence patterns

H2.2   Identify basic sentence patterns.

All sentences must have a complete subject and a complete predicate. However, the predicates of sentences can take several different shapes, depending on whether the verb needs a following noun, pronoun, or adjective to complete its meaning. These words are called *complements*. The four kinds of complements are *direct objects, indirect objects, subject complements,* and *object complements.*

Pattern One: Subject + Verb (+ Optional Adverb Modifiers)

adverb modifiers

The <u>eagle</u> <u>soared</u> gracefully across the summer sky.

In this pattern, the predicate contains only a verb and optional adverbial modifiers. Because the verb in this pattern does not transfer any action from a doer to a receiver, it is called *intransitive.*

Pattern Two: Subject + Verb + Direct Object (DO)

DO

<u>Peter</u> <u>was</u> <u>fixing</u> a flat tire over in Bronco County at the very moment of the crime.

Direct objects occur with *transitive verbs*, which transfer action from a doer (the subject) to a receiver (the direct object). Transitive verbs don't seem complete in themselves; they need a noun or pronoun following the verb to answer the question What? or Whom? Peter was fixing *what*? The *flat tire*.

Pattern Three: Subject + Verb + Subject Complement (SC)

My <u>mother</u> <u>is</u> a professor.
SC

The <u>engine</u> in this car <u>seems</u> sluggish.
SC

In this pattern, verbs are *linking verbs,* which are followed by subject complements rather than direct objects. Unlike direct objects, which receive the action of the verb, subject complements either rename the subject (a noun) or describe the subject (an adjective). You can best understand a subject complement if you think of the linking verb as an equals sign (=).

Pattern Four: Subject + Verb + Direct Object + Object Complement (OC)

That <u>woman</u> <u>called</u> me an idiot.

Whereas a subject complement describes the subject of the sentence, an object complement describes the direct object, either by modifying it or by renaming it. Compare the patterns.

Pattern Three   I <u>am</u> an idiot.

Pattern Four   The <u>woman</u> <u>called</u> me an idiot.

Pattern Five: Subject + Verb + Indirect Object (IDO) + Direct Object

My <u>mother</u> <u>sent</u> the professor an angry letter.

My <u>father</u> <u>baked</u> me a cake on Valentine's Day.

Sometimes transitive verbs take an *indirect object* as well as a direct object. Whereas the direct object answers the question What? or Whom? following the verb, the indirect object answers the question To what or whom? or For what or whom? My mother sent *what*? *A letter* (direct object). She sent a letter *to whom*? *The professor* (indirect object). My father baked *what*? *A cake* (direct object). My father baked a cake *for whom*? For *me* (indirect object).

Parts of speech

H2.3 Identify parts of speech.

Although linguists argue about the best way to classify the functions of words in a sentence, the traditional eight parts of speech listed here are most often used in dictionaries and basic introductions to grammar.

Parts of Speech

nouns (N)	adverbs (Adv)
pronouns (PN)	prepositions (P)
verbs (V)	conjunctions (C)
adjectives (Adj)	interjections (I)

Each part of speech serves a different function in a sentence and also possesses structural features that distinguish it from the other parts of speech. Because many words can serve as different parts of speech in different circumstances, you can determine what part of speech a word plays only within the context of the sentence you are examining.

Nouns

Nouns are the names we give to persons (*Samuel, mechanic*), places (*Yellowstone, the forest*), things (*a rock, potatoes*), and abstract concepts (*love, happiness*). Nouns can be identified by structure as words that follow the articles *a, an,* or *the*; as words that change their form to indicate number; and as words that change their form to indicate possession.

   a rock   several rock*s*   the rock*'s* hardness

But not: a *from*; several *froms*; the *from's* coat.

Pronouns

Pronouns take the place of nouns in sentences. The noun that a pronoun replaces is called the pronoun's *antecedent*. English has the following types of pronouns:

Type of Pronoun	Examples
Personal	I, me, you, he, him, she, her, it, we, us, they, them
Possessive (with Noun)	my, your, his, her, its, our, their
Possessive (no Noun)	mine, yours, his, hers, ours, theirs
Demonstrative	this, that, these, those
Indefinite	any, anybody, someone, everyone, each, nobody
Reflexive/Intensive	myself, yourself, himself, herself, itself, ourselves, yourselves, themselves
Interrogative	who, what, whom, whose, which, whoever, whomever
Relative	who, whom, whose, which, that

Verbs

Verbs are words that express action (*run, laugh*) or state of being (*is, seem*). Structurally, they change form to indicate tense and sometimes to indicate person and number. A word can function as a verb if it can fit the following frames:

I want to _____. I will _____.
I want to *throw.*   I will *throw.*
But not: I want to *from*; I will *from.*

Verbs are used as complete verbs or as incomplete verbs, often called *verbals.* When used as complete verbs, they fill the predicate slot in a sentence. When used as incomplete verbs, they fill a noun's, adjective's, or adverb's slot in a sentence. Verbs often require helping verbs, also called *auxiliary verbs*, to fulfill their function.

PRINCIPAL PARTS   Verbs have five principal parts, which vary depending on whether the verb is *regular* or *irregular.*

Principal Part	Regular Verb Examples	Irregular Verb Examples
Infinitive or Present Stem (infinitives begin with *to*; the word following the *to* is the *present stem*)	to love to borrow	to begin to get
Present Stem + s (used for third-person singular, present tense)	loves borrows	begins gets
Past Stem (regular verbs add *ed* to present stem; irregular verbs have different form)	loved borrowed	began got
Past Participle (same as past stem for regular verbs; usually a different form for irregular verbs)	loved borrowed	begun gotten
Present Participle (add *ing* to present stem)	loving borrowing	beginning getting

The irregular verb *to be* has more forms than other verbs.

Infinitive	to be
Present Forms	am, is, are
Past Forms	was, were
Past Participle	been
Present Participle	being

TENSES   Verbs change their forms to reflect differences in time. A verb's time is called its *tense.* There are six main tenses, each with three forms, sometimes called *aspects*—simple, progressive, and emphatic. For two of the tenses—the simple present and simple past—a complete verb is formed by using one word only. For all other tenses, two or more words are needed to form a complete verb. The additional words are called *helping* or *auxiliary* verbs. In some tenses the main verb or one of the helping verbs changes form to agree with its subject in person and number.

Simple Form.   Here are regular and irregular examples of the simple form of the six main tenses:

Simple Present	She *enjoys* the pizza. They *begin* the race.
Simple Past	She *enjoyed* the pizza. They *began* the race.
Simple Future	She *will enjoy* the pizza. They *will begin* the race.
Present Perfect	She *has enjoyed* the pizza. They *have begun* the race.
Past Perfect	She *had enjoyed* the pizza. They *had begun* the race.
Future Perfect	She *will have enjoyed* the pizza. They *will have begun* the race.

Progressive Form.   Each tense also has a progressive form to indicate actions that are ongoing or in-process.

Present Progressive	Shanice *is eating* her sandwich.
Past Progressive	Shanice *was eating* her sandwich.
Future Progressive	Shanice *will be eating* her sandwich.
Present Perfect Progressive	Shanice *has been eating* her sandwich.
Past Perfect Progressive	Shanice *had been eating* her sandwich.
Future Perfect Progressive	Shanice *will have been eating* her sandwich.

Emphatic Form.   Several tenses have an emphatic form, which uses the helping verb *to do* combined with the present stem. The emphatic form is used for giving special stress, for asking questions, and for making negations.

I *do go*. I *did go*.

Did the dog *bark*?

Do you *like* peanuts?

The child *does* not *sit* still.

Modal Forms.   Additionally, a variety of other helping verbs, often called *modals*, can be used to form complete verbs with different senses of time and attitude.

will, would	may, might
can, could	must
shall, should	

MOOD   Verbs have three moods: indicative (by far the most common), subjunctive, and imperative.

Indicative Mood.   The indicative mood is used for both statements and questions.

The dog *rode* in the back of the pickup. Where *is* Shanice?

Subjunctive Mood.   The subjunctive mood is used to indicate that a condition is contrary to fact and, in certain cases, to express desire, hope, or demand. The subjunctive is formed in the present tense by using the infinitive stem.

I request that Joe *pay* the bill.

Compare with the indicative: Joe *pays* the bill.

In the past tense, only the verb *to be* has a distinctive subjunctive form, which is always *were*.

If I *were* the teacher, I would give you an A for that project.

Here the subjunctive *were* means "I am *not* the teacher"; it expresses a condition contrary to fact.

Imperative Mood.   Finally, the imperative mood conveys a command or request. For most verbs the imperative form is the same as the second-person present tense. An exception is the verb *to be*, which uses *be*.

Be here by noon. *Pay* the bill immediately.

VOICE   The *voice* of a verb indicates whether the subject of the verb acts or is acted on. The concept of voice applies only to *transitive* verbs, which transfer action from a doer to a receiver. In the active voice, the subject is the doer of the action and the direct object is the receiver.

Active Voice   The professor graded the paper.

In the passive voice, the subject is the receiver of the action; the actor is either omitted from the sentence or made the object of the preposition *by*. The passive voice is formed with the past participle and some form of the helping verb *to be*.

Passive Voice   The paper was graded (by the professor).

Adjectives and Adverbs

Adjectives and adverbs describe or *modify* other words.

ADJECTIVES   Adjectives modify nouns by answering such questions as Which ones? (*those* rabbits); what kind? (*gentle* rabbits); how many? (*four* rabbits); what size? (*tiny* rabbits); what color? (*white* rabbits); what condition? (*contented* rabbits); and whose? (*Jim's* rabbits).

Articles (*a, an, the*) form a special class of adjectives. *A* and *an* are indefinite and singular, referring to any representative member of a general class of objects.

I would like *an* apple and *a* sandwich.

The is definite and can be singular or plural. It always specifies that a particular object is meant.

I want *the* apple and *the* sandwich that were sitting on my desk a few minutes ago.

ADVERBS   Adverbs modify verbs, adjectives, or other adverbs. They answer the questions How? (he petted the rabbit *gently*); how often? (he petted the rabbit *frequently*); where? (he petted the rabbit *there* in the corner of the room); when? (he petted the rabbit *early*); and to what degree? (he petted the rabbit *very* gently).

Conjunctive adverbs, such as *therefore, however*, and *moreover*, modify whole clauses by showing logical relationships between clauses or sentences.

POSITIVE, COMPARATIVE, AND SUPERLATIVE FORMS   Adjectives and adverbs have positive, comparative, and superlative forms.

Positive	This is a *quick* turtle. It moves *quickly*.
Comparative	My turtle is *quicker* than yours. It moves *more quickly* than yours.
Superlative	Of the three turtles, mine is the *quickest*. Of all the turtles in the race, mine moves *most quickly*.

Conjunctions

Conjunctions join elements within a sentence. *Coordinating* conjunctions (*and, or, nor, but, for, yet*, and *so*) join elements of equal importance.

John *and* Hida went to town.

The city rejoiced, *for* the rats had finally been exterminated.

Subordinating conjunctions (such as *when, unless, if, because, after, while, although*) turn an independent sentence into a subordinate clause and then join it to an independent clause.

After I get off work, I will buy you a soda.

You will need to borrow an umbrella *if* it is raining.

Prepositions

Prepositions show the relationship between a noun or pronoun (the object of the preposition) and the rest of the sentence. The preposition and its object together are called a *prepositional phrase*. Common prepositions include *about, above, across, among, behind, between, from, in, into, of, on, toward*, and *with*.

The cat walked *under* the table.

The table is a mixture *of* cherry and walnut woods.

Interjections

Interjections (*Yippee! Sweet! Ouch!*) are forceful expressions, usually followed by exclamation marks, that express emotion.

Hooray, school's out! *Ugh,* that's disgusting!

Types of phrases

H2.4   Identify types of phrases.

A *phrase* is a group of related words that does not contain a complete subject and a complete verb. There are four main kinds of phrases: prepositional, appositive, verbal (participial, gerund, and infinitive), and absolute.

Prepositional Phrases

A preposition connects a noun, pronoun, or group of words acting as a noun to the rest of the sentence, thereby creating a *prepositional phrase* that serves as a modifying element within the sentence. Prepositional phrases usually begin with the preposition and end with the noun or noun substitute, called the *object of the preposition*.

> We watched the baby crawl *under the table*.
>
> The man *in the gray suit* is my father.

Appositive Phrases

Appositive phrases give additional information about a preceding noun or pronoun. They sometimes consist of only one word.

> Jill saw her friend *Theresa* in the café.
>
> We stopped for a mocha latte at Adolpho's, *the most famous espresso bar in the city*.

Verbal Phrases

Verbals are incomplete forms of verbs that can't function as predicates in a sentence. Rather, they fill noun, adjective, or adverb slots in a sentence. Similar to verbs, verbals can show tense and can take complements. When a verbal is accompanied by modifiers or complements, the word group is called a *verbal phrase*. There are three kinds of verbals and verbal phrases: participial, gerund, and infinitive.

PARTICIPIAL PHRASES Participles have two forms: the present participle and the past participle. The present participle is the *ing* form (*swimming, laughing*); the past participle is the *ed* form for regular verbs (*laughed*) and an irregular form for irregular verbs (*swum*). Participles and participial phrases always act as adjectives in a sentence. In the following examples, the noun modified by the participle is indicated by an arrow.

> I saw some ducks *swimming in the lake*.
>
> *Laughing happily*, Gloria squeezed Franco's arm.
>
> The 100-meter freestyle, a race *swum by more than twenty competitors last year*, was won by a thirteen-year-old boy.

GERUND PHRASES Gerunds are always the *ing* form of the verb, and they always serve as nouns in a sentence.

> *Swimming* is my favorite sport. [*serves as subject*]
>
> I love *swimming in the lake*. [*serves as direct object*]
>
> I am not happy about *losing my chemistry notebook in the student union*. [*serves as object of preposition*]

INFINITIVE PHRASES An *infinitive* is the dictionary form of a verb preceded by the word *to* (*to run, to swim, to laugh*). Infinitives or infinitive phrases can serve as nouns, adjectives, or adverbs.

To complete college with a major in electrical engineering is my primary goal at the moment.

The person *to help you with that math* is Lyonis Martine.

Absolute Phrases

An *absolute phrase* is composed of a noun or noun substitute, followed by a participle. It is *absolute* because it doesn't act as a noun, adverb, or adjective; rather, it modifies the whole clause or sentence to which it is attached.

Her face flushed with sweat, the runner headed down Grant Street.

The assistant hunched over the keyboard, *his fingers typing madly*.

Types of clauses

H2.5   Identify types of clauses.

Clauses have complete subjects and complete predicates. Some clauses can stand alone as sentences (*independent*, or *main*, clauses), whereas others (*dependent*, or *subordinate*, clauses) cannot stand alone as sentences because they are introduced by a *subordinating conjunction* or a *relative pronoun*.

Here are two independent sentences that could serve as independent clauses:

Darnell had a sore throat.

Lucia studied the violin for thirteen years.

Now here are the same two sentences converted to subordinate clauses:

because Darnell had a sore throat

who studied the violin for thirteen years

In the first example, the subordinating conjunction *because* reduces the independent clause to a subordinate clause. In the second example, the relative pronoun *who*, which replaces *Lucia*, also reduces the independent clause to a subordinate clause.

Finally, here are these subordinated clauses attached to independent clauses to form complete sentences.

Because Darnell had a sore throat, he decided to miss the party.

Lucia, who studied the violin for thirteen years, won a music scholarship to a prestigious college.

Subordinate clauses always act as nouns, adjectives, or adverbs in another clause.

Noun Clauses

A *noun clause* is a subordinate clause that functions as a noun in a sentence. Noun clauses act as subjects, objects, or complements.

He promised *that he would study harder.* [*serves as direct object*]

Why he came here is a mystery. [*serves as subject*]

He lied about *what he did last summer.* [*serves as object of preposition*]

Adjective Clauses

An *adjective clause* is a subordinate clause that modifies a noun or a pronoun. Adjective clauses are formed with the relative pronouns *who, whom, whose, which,* and *that.* For this reason they are sometimes called *relative clauses.*

Kyle, *who is a star athlete,* has trouble with reading.

The future threat *that I most fear* is a global food shortage.

Adverb Clauses

An *adverb clause* is a subordinate clause that modifies a verb, an adjective, or another adverb. Adverb clauses begin with subordinating conjunctions, such as *although, because, if,* and *when.*

Because he had broken his leg, he danced all night using crutches.

When he got home, he noticed unusual blisters.

Types of sentences

H2.6   Identify simple, compound, complex, and compound-complex sentences.

Sentences are often classified by the number and kinds of clauses they contain. There are four kinds of sentences: simple, compound, complex, and compound-complex.

Simple Sentences

A sentence is *simple* if it consists of a single independent clause. The clause may contain modifying phrases and have a compound subject and a compound predicate.

John laughed.
John and Maria laughed and sang.

modifying phrase

Laughing happily and holding hands in the moonlight, John and Maria

independent clause (with compound subject and predicate)

walked along the beach, wrote their names in the sand, and threw pebbles

into the crashing waves.

Compound Sentences

A sentence is *compound* if it consists of two independent clauses linked either by a semicolon or by a comma and a coordinating conjunction. Each clause may contain modifying phrases as well as compound subjects and predicates.

independent clause   independent clause

John laughed, and Maria sang.

modifying phrase   independent clause (with compound subject)

Laughing happily, John and Maria walked hand in hand toward the kitchen,

independent clause

but they weren't prepared for the surprise on the countertop.

Complex Sentences

A sentence is *complex* if it contains one independent clause and one or more subordinate clauses.

independent clause   subordinate clause

John smiled to himself while Maria sang.

subordinate clause   independent clause

When John and Maria saw the surprise on the countertop, they screamed

subordinate clause

uncontrollably until John fainted.

Compound-Complex Sentences

A *compound-complex sentence* has at least one subordinate clause and two or more independent clauses joined by a semicolon or by a comma and a coordinating conjunction.

independent clause   subordinate clause   independent clause

John smiled to himself while Maria sang, for he was happy.

subordinate clause   independent clause

When John and Maria saw the surprise on the countertop, they screamed

independent clause

uncontrollably; soon John collapsed on the floor in a dead faint.

Chapter 3
Punctuating Boundaries of Sentences, Clauses, and Phrases

Learning Objectives

H3.1 Use standard conventions for punctuating clauses and phrases within a sentence.

H3.2 Identify and correct sentence fragments.

H3.3 Identify and correct comma splices and run-on sentences.

Rules for punctuating clauses and phrases within a sentence

H3.1 **Use standard conventions for punctuating clauses and phrases within a sentence.**

This section explains four main punctuation rules for marking the boundaries of clauses and phrases within a sentence. The rules will help you avoid fragments, run-ons, and comma splices.

RULE 1: JOIN TWO INDEPENDENT SENTENCES WITH A SEMICOLON OR WITH A COMMA AND A COORDINATING CONJUNCTION. You can join two complete sentences to form a compound sentence in two ways: (1) with a semicolon, or (2) with a comma and a coordinating conjunction. You should learn the seven coordinating conjunctions:

      and   but   or   nor   for   yet   so

When you join two sentences using either of these methods, each sentence becomes an independent clause in the compound sentence; the punctuation signals the joining point.

Two Sentences	Melissa hasn't changed the oil in her car. However, she is still willing to take it to the game.
Joined with Semicolon	Melissa hasn't changed the oil in her car; however, she is still willing to take it to the game.
Joined with Comma and Coordinating Conjunction	Melissa hasn't changed the oil in her car, but she is still willing to take it to the game.

RULE 2: USE A SINGLE COMMA TO SET OFF AN INTRODUCTORY ADVERB CLAUSE.   Another common way to join sentences is to use a subordinating conjunction to convert one sentence to an adverb clause. Subordinating conjunctions are words such as *because, when, if, although*, and *until*. If the resulting adverb clause comes at the start of the sentence, set it off from the independent clause with a comma. If it follows the independent clause, don't set it off.

| **Adverb Clause Preceding Independent Clause** | If the sun is shining in the morning, we'll go for the hike. |
| **Adverb Clause Following Independent Clause** | We'll go for the hike if the sun is shining in the morning. |

Note that no comma is used in the second example because the adverb clause follows, rather than precedes, the independent clause.

An exception to this rule occurs with the subordinating conjunction *although*. You should use a comma to set off a clause introduced by *although* even if it comes at the end of a sentence.

> The police officer still gave me a ticket, although I explained to her that my speedometer was broken.

RULE 3: INSIDE A SENTENCE CORE, USE PAIRS OF COMMAS TO SET OFF INTERRUPTING ELEMENTS.   The core of a sentence consists of the subject, verb, and direct object or subject complement. Within the core of a sentence, never use a single comma; either omit commas or use commas *in pairs* to set off interrupting elements.

| **Sentence Core** | My dog chased the cat around the room. |
| **Interrupting Element Inside the Core** | My dog, barking loudly and snapping his teeth, chased the cat around the room. |

Note that *a pair* of commas—a comma preceding the element and a comma following the element—marks the boundaries of the interrupting element.

| **Sentence Core** | The police officer still gave me a ticket. |
| **Interrupting Element Inside the Core** | The police officer, however, still gave me a ticket. |

RULE 4: USE A SINGLE COMMA TO SET OFF SOME INTRODUCTORY OR CONCLUDING PHRASES.   An introductory phrase often precedes the core of a sentence. Set off an introductory phrase if it is long or if your voice pauses noticeably between the phrase (or single word such as *however*) and the start of the sentence core. Similarly, use a single comma to set off long concluding

elements if your voice pauses noticeably after the core. In either case, the comma signals the boundary between the sentence core and the introductory or concluding element.

INTRODUCTORY ELEMENT

Barking loudly and snapping his teeth, my dog chased the cat around the room.

According to the defense attorney, the officer's use of force was justified.

CONCLUDING ELEMENT

My dog chased the cat around the room, his jaws snapping angrily.

The scholar's claim bothered Jensen, leaving him bewildered and possibly angry.

Identifying and correcting sentence fragments

H3.2 Identify and correct sentence fragments.

A *sentence fragment* is a nonsentence (any structure lacking a complete subject or a complete predicate) that is punctuated either as a sentence or as an independent clause.

Types of Fragments

There are two kinds of sentence fragments.

1. *Phrase fragments* may lack either a subject or a complete predicate or both. In the following passage, the phrase fragments are italicized.

   Caleb and Harper love their mountain home. *Going fishing in the morning. Watching the deer graze in the meadows.* Outside their cabin, a pair of majestic eagles nest in the top of a lone pine; *with only the starry sky as a night roof.*

   The first two fragments are participial phrases punctuated as complete sentences. The last fragment is a prepositional phrase punctuated as an independent clause. The semicolon signals to readers that two independent clauses are joined together.

2. *Subordinate clause fragments* have a subject and a complete predicate, but they begin with either a subordinating conjunction or a relative pronoun, which prevents them from standing alone as a sentence. In the following examples, the subordinate clause fragments are italicized.

   Caleb and Harper often go for a hike. *As soon as the sun comes up.* At night they love to watch the eyes of owls. *Which blink at them from the branches of nearby trees.*

   The first fragment is created by the subordinating conjunction *as soon as*; the second is created by the relative pronoun *which*.

Methods for Correcting Sentence Fragments

There are various ways to correct a fragment; each method produces a slightly different variation in meaning and emphasis.

METHOD 1: CHANGE A PHRASE FRAGMENT TO A COMPLETE SENTENCE BY CONVERTING AN INCOMPLETE VERB INTO A COMPLETE VERB OR BY ADDING A VERB. This method emphasizes the material in the fragment by giving it the weight of a full sentence.

> **Fragment** The buffalo began to stampede. Their heads flailing wildly.
>
> **Revised** The buffalo began to stampede. Their heads flailed wildly.

The fragment has been converted to a complete sentence by changing the participle *flailing* to the complete verb *flailed*.

METHOD 2: CHANGE A CLAUSE FRAGMENT TO A COMPLETE SENTENCE BY REMOVING THE SUBORDINATOR. This method also emphasizes the ideas in the original fragment.

> **Fragment** For Native Americans, killing buffalo was very dangerous. Because the stampeding buffalo herd had to be guided toward the cliff by men shaking wolf skins.
>
> **Revised** For Native Americans, killing buffalo was very dangerous. The stampeding buffalo herd had to be guided toward the cliff by men shaking wolf skins.

Removing the subordinating conjunction *because* converts the fragment into a complete sentence.

METHOD 3: CORRECT THE FRAGMENT BY JOINING IT TO THE SENTENCE THAT PRECEDES OR FOLLOWS IT, WHICHEVER MAKES MORE SENSE. This method subordinates the material in the fragment and can work for either phrase or clause fragments. With this method, you may need to use a comma to signal the joining point.

> **Fragment** The buffalo crashed to their deaths. Although the men killed the animals that were still alive. The women did most of the work in preparing the hides and meat.
>
> **Revised** The buffalo crashed to their deaths. Although the men killed the animals that were still alive, the women did most of the work in preparing the hides and meat.

The original passage contains a subordinate clause fragment beginning with *although*. The revised passage attaches the *although* clause to the second sentence.

Identifying and correcting run-ons and comma splices

H3.3 Identify and correct comma splices and run-on sentences.

Writers make run-on errors or comma splices whenever they fail to show where one sentence ends and the next begins.

A *run-on error* occurs when two sentences are fused together without any punctuation.

I explained to the police officer that my speedometer was broken she still gave me a ticket.

Two sentences come together between *broken* and *she*, but no period and capital letter or semicolon marks the boundary.

A *comma splice* occurs when a writer marks the end of a sentence with a comma instead of with a period and a capital letter or a semicolon.

I explained to the police officer that my speedometer was broken, she still gave me a ticket.

A comma by itself cannot mark the boundary between two sentences.

Methods for Correcting Run-Ons and Comma Splices

Run-ons and comma splices can be corrected in a variety of ways, depending on the meaning you wish to convey. You may choose to separate the ideas by placing them in two separate sentences, or you may wish to join the ideas into a single sentence. To choose the most appropriate method, consider the rhetorical context of the passage you are writing.

METHOD 1: SEPARATE THE SENTENCES WITH A PERIOD AND A CAPITAL LETTER. This method gives equal emphasis to both sentences. If you wish to indicate a logical relationship between the two sentences, you can add a conjunctive adverb (such as *therefore* or *nevertheless*) somewhere in the second sentence.

Revised   I explained to the police officer that my speedometer was broken. She still gave me a ticket.

Revised   I explained to the police officer that my speedometer was broken. However, she still gave me a ticket.

METHOD 2: JOIN THE SENTENCES WITH A SEMICOLON. This method creates a compound sentence with two equally strong independent clauses.

Revised   I explained to the police officer that my speedometer was broken; however, she still gave me a ticket.

METHOD 3: JOIN THE SENTENCES WITH A COMMA AND A COORDINATING CONJUNCTION. This method also creates a compound sentence with two equally strong independent clauses.

Revised   I explained to the police officer that my speedometer was broken, but she still gave me a ticket.

METHOD 4: JOIN THE SENTENCES WITH A SUBORDINATING CONJUNCTION OR A RELATIVE PRONOUN. This method creates a complex sentence with an independent clause and a subordinate clause. The material in the independent clause receives more emphasis than the subordinated material does.

Revised   Although I explained to the police officer that my speedometer was broken, she still gave me a ticket.

METHOD 5: CONVERT ONE OF THE SENTENCES INTO A PHRASE.   This method creates a simple sentence with an added or embedded phrase. The phrase has less importance than the rest of the sentence.

Revised   Despite my explanation of the broken speedometer, the police officer gave me a ticket.

Thinking Rhetorically When Correcting Run-Ons and Comma Splices

Although each of the previous methods of correcting run-ons and comma splices will produce a grammatically correct solution, the method to be used in a given situation depends on the meaning and emphasis you intend. Consider the following example:

Comma Splice   The weather is beautiful, my neighbor is washing her car.

To determine the best way to correct this comma splice, you need to consider the passage in which it occurs. Different correction methods create different effects.

Revised   It is a great day. The weather is beautiful. My neighbor is washing her car. Kids are playing in the street. The dog is sleeping in the sun.

Here the focus is on the writer's sense of a great day. The beautiful weather and the neighbor washing her car are only two of four separate pieces of evidence the writer uses to support the feeling. By putting them all in separate sentences, the writer emphasizes each one.

But consider how the comma splice might be corrected in a different context:

Revised   I was hoping to invite my neighbor over to watch the football game with me this afternoon. But because the weather is beautiful, she is washing her car.

In this version, the main point is the writer's disappointment that the neighbor isn't coming over to watch football. The beautiful weather is the cause of her washing the car, but the subordinating conjunction *because* makes that information secondary. The writer isn't interested in the beautiful weather for its own sake, so a separate sentence such as the one in the first revised example would be inappropriate.

These differences illustrate that punctuation is a way of controlling and signaling meaning for readers. As you learn ways of correcting comma splices and run-ons, you will also become aware of the wide variety of options available to convey subtleties of thought and feeling.

Chapter 4
Editing for Standard English Usage

Learning Objectives

H4.1 Correct mixed constructions and faulty predication.

H4.2 Avoid shifts in verb tense and person and number of pronouns.

H4.3 Correct subject-verb and pronoun-antecedent agreement errors.

H4.4 Maintain parallel constructions.

H4.5 Avoid dangling or misplaced modifiers.

H4.6 Use correct pronoun cases.

H4.7 Use adjectives and adverbs correctly.

Fixing grammatical tangles

H4.1 Correct mixed constructions and faulty predication.

Among the most frequent errors in rough drafts are grammatically tangled sentences that result in *mixed constructions* or *faulty predication*.

Mixed Constructions

In the heat of composing a first draft, a writer sometimes starts a sentence with one kind of construction and shifts midway to another construction.

Faulty   By buying a year's supply of laundry soap at one time saves lots of money.

This sentence opens with a prepositional phrase that cannot serve as a sentence subject. The writer can correct the error by eliminating the preposition or by supplying a subject.

Revised   Buying a year's supply of laundry soap at one time saves lots of money.

　　　　　.or

　　　　　By buying a year's supply of laundry soap at one time, the average consumer can save lots of money.

Faulty Predication

Another kind of grammatical tangle, called *faulty predication*, occurs when the action specified by the verb can't logically be performed by the subject.

> **Faulty**   Throughout *The Scarlet Letter*, Hester Prynne's "A" is imbibed with symbolic significance.
>
> *Imbibe* means "to drink," so its use makes no sense in this sentence.
>
> **Revised**   Throughout *The Scarlet Letter*, Hester Prynne's "A" is invested with symbolic significance.

Maintaining consistency

H4.2   Avoid shifts in verb tense and person and number of pronouns.

Consistency errors occur whenever a writer illogically shifts verb tenses or shifts the person or number of pronouns.

Shifts in Tense

Readers can become confused when writers change tenses without explanation. You should avoid shifting verb tenses in a passage unless you mean to signal a shift in time.

> **Faulty**   The display cases of the little bakery were filled with cakes, pies, doughnuts, and special pastries. From the heated ovens against the back wall *drifts* the aroma of buttery croissants.
>
> The verbs in the first sentence are all in the past tense. The verb in the second sentence shifts to the present without an explanation.
>
> **Revised**   The display cases of the little bakery were filled with cakes, pies, doughnuts, and special pastries. From the heated ovens against the back wall *drifted* the aroma of buttery croissants.

Shifts in the Person and Number of Pronouns

Pronouns have three persons: first (*I, we*); second (*you*); and third (*he, she, it, one, they*). Keep your point of view consistent by avoiding confusing shifts from one person to another or from singular to plural.

> **Confusing**   As readers, we are not prepared for Hamlet's change in the last act. When one sees Hamlet joking with the grave diggers, you forget momentarily about his earlier despair.
>
> The pronouns shift from first to third to second person.
>
> **Revised**   As readers, we are not prepared for Hamlet's change in the last act. When *we* see Hamlet joking with the grave diggers, *we* forget momentarily about his earlier despair.

Maintaining agreement

H4.3   Correct subject-verb and pronoun-antecedent agreement errors.

Writers often have to choose between singular and plural forms of verbs and pronouns to ensure that verbs match their subjects and pronouns match their antecedents. In some cases, special rules determine whether a subject or an antecedent is singular or plural.

Subject-Verb Agreement

In most cases, it is easy to determine whether the subject is singular or plural, but some cases are tricky. The following rules cover most of these tricky cases.

PLURAL WORDS BETWEEN SUBJECT AND VERB   It may be difficult to find the subject when it is separated from the verb by intervening words, phrases, or embedded clauses or when an indefinite word such as *one, each,* or *kind* is followed by a prepositional phrase beginning with *of.* In the latter case the object of the preposition is often mistaken for the subject.

Faulty	One of the recent shipments of boxes containing computers, printers, and monitors *were* delayed.
Revised	One of the recent shipments of boxes containing computers, printers, and monitors *was* delayed.

In this sentence, *one* is the subject, not any of the intervening plural words.

Similarly, prepositional phrases beginning with *as well as, in addition to, along with,* and *including* can trick writers into thinking that a singular subject is plural.

Faulty	My mother, along with several of her coworkers, *are* getting a special award for excellence in customer relations.
Revised	My mother, along with several of her coworkers, *is* getting a special award for excellence in customer relations.

In this sentence the subject is *mother*; the intervening prepositional phrase should be ignored.

COMPOUND SUBJECTS JOINED BY AND   Use a plural verb for singular or plural subjects joined by *and* unless the nouns joined by *and* are thought of as one unit, in which case the verb is singular. Notice the different meanings of the following sentences:

My brother and my best friend *is* with me now.

This sentence means that my brother is with me now and that my brother is my best friend.

My brother and my best friend *are* with me now.

This sentence means that two people are with me—my brother and my best friend.

COMPOUND SUBJECTS JOINED BY *OR, NOR, EITHER . . . OR,* *NEITHER . . . NOR* The coordinating conjunctions *or, nor, either . . . or,* and *neither . . . nor* take singular verbs if they join singular subjects and plural verbs if they join plural subjects. If they join a singular subject to a plural subject, the verb agrees with the nearer subject.

> Either a raccoon or a dog *is* getting into the garbage pails.
>
> Both subjects are singular, so the verb is singular.
>
> Either raccoons or dogs *are* getting into the garbage pails.
>
> Both subjects are plural, so the verb is plural.
>
> Either some raccoons or a dog *is* getting into the garbage pails.
>
> The subject closer to the verb is singular, so the verb is singular.

INDEFINITE PRONOUN AS SUBJECT Some indefinite pronouns are always singular; others can be singular or plural depending on context.

Always Singular		Singular or Plural
anybody	none	all
anyone	each	any
anything	everybody	some
either	neither	
nobody		

The indefinite pronouns in the left-hand columns are always singular.

> **Faulty**   Each of the dogs *are* thirsty.
>
> **Revised**   Each of the dogs *is* thirsty.

The indefinite pronouns in the right-hand column can be singular or plural. These words are generally followed by a prepositional phrase beginning with *of.* The number of the pronoun depends on whether the object of the preposition is singular or plural.

> Some of the table *is* sanded.
>
> The object of the preposition (*table*) is singular, so the verb is singular.
>
> Some of the tables *are* sanded.
>
> The object of the preposition (*tables*) is plural, so the verb is plural.

INVERSION OF SUBJECT AND VERB Locating the subject may be tricky in *inverted sentences*, in which the subject comes after the verb.

> Just beyond the fence line on the other side of the road are some pheasants.
>
> The subject is *pheasants*, so the verb is plural.

Be especially careful with inverted sentences that begin with *here, there,* or *where.* Errors occur most frequently when a writer uses these words in contractions or in questions.

Faulty   Where's my belt and sweater?

The subject is *belt and sweater*, so the verb should be plural.

Revised   Where are my belt and sweater?

RELATIVE PRONOUN AS SUBJECT   Relative pronouns used as subjects (*who, that, which*) are singular or plural depending on their antecedents.

A person who *builds* glass houses shouldn't throw stones.

Who is singular because its antecedent, *person*, is singular; hence the verb should be singular.

People who *build* glass houses shouldn't throw stones.

Who is plural because its antecedent, *people*, is plural; hence the verb should be plural.

Be especially careful when the antecedent is the object of the preposition *of*.

One of the reasons that *are* frequently given is inflation.

The verb of the main clause (*is*) is singular because its subject is the singular pronoun *one*. But the verb of the relative clause (*are*) is plural because its subject (*that*) has a plural antecedent (*reasons*).

SUBJECT FOLLOWED BY LINKING VERB AND SUBJECT COMPLEMENT   Linking verbs should agree with the subject of the sentence, not with the subject complement.

Sleeping, eating, and drinking *are* his whole life.

The verb *are* agrees with the plural subject, not with the singular subject complement.

His whole life *is* sleeping, eating, and drinking.

In this case, the verb agrees with the singular subject, not with the plural subjective complement.

COLLECTIVE NOUN AS SUBJECT   With collective nouns such as *group, committee, crew, crowd, faculty, majority*, and *audience*, use a singular verb if the collective group acts as one unit; use a plural verb if the members of the group act individually.

The faculty at Hogwash College *is* delighted with the new president.

Here the faculty functions as a single unit.

The faculty at Hogwash College *are* arguing at this very moment.

Here *faculty* refers to individuals who act independently.

Some collective nouns present special problems or follow special rules— for instance, *a number* versus *the number*. *A number* refers to a collection of individual items and takes a plural verb. *The number* refers to a unit and takes a singular verb.

A number of students *are* studying grammar this semester.

The number of students studying grammar *is* declining every year.

Titles or words referred to as words use singular verbs.

Snow White and the Seven Dwarfs is a famous Disney movie.

The italics indicate a title, which takes a singular verb. If you were referring to the characters rather than the title, the verb would be plural: "Snow White and the seven dwarfs are my favorite Disney characters."

Pronoun-Antecedent Agreement

Just as a subject must agree in number with its verb, so must a pronoun agree in number with its antecedent (the noun that the pronoun stands for). To apply this rule, you must first determine the antecedent of the pronoun and then decide whether the antecedent is singular or plural, following the rules presented in the previous section. Pronoun-antecedent agreement occasionally presents some difficulties. The following rules cover most cases.

COMPOUND CONSTRUCTION AS ANTECEDENT If a compound antecedent is joined by *and*, choose a plural pronoun; if a compound antecedent is joined by *or*, the pronoun should agree in number with the closer antecedent.

Gabriela and Levi invited us to their party.

Either Brian or Luis will bring his volleyball to the party.

Either Brian or his sisters will bring their volleyball.

COLLECTIVE NOUN AS ANTECEDENT Use a singular pronoun to refer to a collective noun that acts as one unit; use a plural pronoun if members of the group act individually.

The committee reported its opinion.

The committee began arguing among themselves.

INDEFINITE PRONOUN AS ANTECEDENT Generally, if the antecedent is an indefinite pronoun such as *either, neither, everyone, everybody, someone, somebody, anyone,* or *anybody*, you use a singular pronoun.

Everybody coming to the party should bring his or her own drinks.

Maintaining parallel structure

H4.4 Maintain parallel constructions.

A nonparallel construction occurs whenever a writer fails to maintain the same grammatical structure for each item in a series.

Faulty Shanelle likes playing soccer and to roller-skate.

Here the writer has joined a gerund phrase (*playing soccer*) to an infinitive (*to roller-skate*). The problem can be solved by making both items gerunds or both infinitives.

Revised	Shanelle likes playing soccer and roller-skating.
	or
	Shanelle likes to play soccer and to roller-skate.
Faulty	As a teacher, he was a courteous listener, helpful during office hours, and he lectured in an exciting way.
Revised	As a teacher, he was a courteous listener, a good helper during office hours, and an exciting lecturer.

In this revision the writer converts all items in the series to nouns.

Faulty	This term paper is illogical, poorly documented, and should have used more primary sources.

Here the first two items are parallel (the adjectives *illogical* and *poorly documented*), but the last item is a verb phrase (*should have used more primary sources*).

Revised	This term paper is illogical, poorly documented, and poorly researched.
	or
	This term paper, which should have used more primary sources, is illogical and poorly documented.

To increase clarity, writers often repeat function words such as articles, prepositions, conjunctions, or the infinitive word *to* at the beginning of each item in a parallel series.

Confusing	The drill sergeant told the recruits that there would be no weekend passes and they would be on KP instead.
Revised	The drill sergeant told the recruits that there would be no weekend passes and that they would be on KP instead.

The repetition of *that* clarifies the writer's intention: to report two things the drill sergeant told the recruits.

Placement of Correlative Conjunctions

When using *correlative conjunctions* (two-part conjunctions such as *either . . . or, neither . . . nor, both . . . and,* and *not only . . . but also*), make sure that each unit of the correlative precedes the same grammatical structure.

Faulty	I not only like ice cream but also root beer.

Here the writer places *not only* in front of a verb (*like*), but places *but also* in front of a noun (*root beer*).

Revised	I like not only ice cream but also root beer.

Use of *and which/that* or *and who/whom*

Be sure that a clause beginning with *and which, and that, and who,* or *and whom* is preceded by a parallel clause beginning with *which, that, who,* or *whom.*

Faulty   Of all my friends, Jayden is the one with the greatest sense of courage and who most believes in honesty.

The writer links a pronoun (*one*) to a relative clause (*who most believes*), creating a nonparallel structure.

Revised   Of all my friends, Jayden is the one who has the greatest sense of courage and who most believes in honesty.

Avoiding dangling or misplaced modifiers

Dangling Modifiers

H4.5   **Avoid dangling or misplaced modifiers.**

When a sentence opens with a modifying phrase, the phrase must be followed immediately by the noun it modifies, which is usually the grammatical subject of the sentence; otherwise, the phrase is said to *dangle*. You can correct a dangling modifier by (a) recasting the sentence so that the subject is the word modified by the opening modifier, or (b) expanding the modifying phrase into a clause that has its own subject.

                                  modifier   subject

Faulty   Walking down the street, a flowerpot fell on my head.

This sentence brings to mind a walking flowerpot.

                                  modifier   subject

Revised   Walking down the street, I was struck on the head by a flowerpot.

                  or

modifying clause with subject

While *I* was walking down the street, a flowerpot fell on my head.

                                modifier   subject

Faulty   With only a dollar in change, the meal was too expensive.

Does the meal have only a dollar in change?

                                  modifier   subject

Revised   With only a dollar in change, I couldn't afford the meal.

                  or

modifying clause with subject

Because *I* had only a dollar in change, the meal was too expensive.

Misplaced Modifiers

A modifier is said to be *misplaced* when a modifying word or phrase is separated from the element it modifies. To correct this type of error, change the location of the modifier so that it is next to the word or phrase it modifies.

Faulty   The students gave a present to their teacher in a big box.

This sentence suggests that the teacher is in a big box.

Revised   The students gave their teacher a present in a big box.

Note: Be careful to place limiting adverbs, such as *only, just,* and *merely,* next to the words they limit. As the following example shows, changing the location of *only* can often change the meaning of a sentence.

Only I baked the cake. (I am the person solely responsible for baking the cake.)

I only baked the cake. (I baked it, but I didn't put the frosting on it.)

I baked only the cake. (Someone else baked the cookies.)

Place limiting adverbs *directly in front of* the words they modify.

Faulty   I should get a higher grade because I only failed one exam.

The writer intends to modify *one exam* rather than *failed* and thus needs to move *only.*

Revised   I should get a higher grade because I failed only one exam.

Choosing correct pronoun cases

H4.6   Use correct pronoun cases.

Many pronouns change their form according to the grammatical slot they fill in a sentence.

Case Name	Used for These Slots	Personal Pronouns	Relative Pronouns
subjective	subject, subject complement	I, we, he, she, they	who, whoever
objective	direct object, indirect object, object of preposition, subject of infinitive	me, us, him, her, them	whom, whomever
possessive	adjective showing possession	my, our, his, her, their	whose

The case of a pronoun is determined by its slot in the sentence.

She and *I* are good friends. *[subjects]*
Lucas likes *her* and *me*. *[direct objects]*
Give *her* and *me* the present. *[indirect objects]*
Lucas did it for *her* and *me*. *[objects of preposition]*
The winners were *she* and *I*. *[subject complements]*

Although writers generally handle pronoun cases accurately, the following instances can create confusion.

Cases of Relative Pronouns

In relative or noun clauses, the pronouns *who, whom, whoever,* or *whomever* take their case from their function in their own clause, not from the function of that clause in the rest of the sentence.

Faulty	Give the prize to *whomever* says the secret word.

Although *whomever* at first seems to be the object of the preposition *to,* it is actually the subject of the verb *says* and should be in the subjective case. The object of the preposition *to* is actually the whole noun clause.

Revised	Give the prize to *whoever* says the secret word.
Faulty	I voted against Ralph Winkley, *who* big business especially supports.

In this case the relative pronoun fills a direct object slot in its own clause. Compare: Big business especially supports *him.* The writer should choose *whom.*

Revised	I voted against Ralph Winkley, *whom* big business especially supports.

Intervening Parenthetical Clauses

When choosing the case of relative pronouns, don't let such words as *I think* or *he supposes* influence your choice. These are parenthetical expressions that can be discarded from the sentence.

Faulty	I voted for Marion Fudge, *whom* I think is the most honest candidate.

Here the relative pronoun is the subject of the verb *is,* not the direct object of *I think,* and hence it should be subjective.

Revised	I voted for Marion Fudge, *who* I think is the most honest candidate.

Pronouns as Parts of Compound Constructions

Case errors are especially frequent in compound constructions. Pronouns that fill object slots (or subjects of infinitives) must be in the objective case. You can usually avoid case errors in compound constructions by choosing the same case that you would select if you were using the pronoun alone.

Faulty	Isobel appointed Ralph and *I* to the committee.

The pronoun is a direct object and should be in the objective case. Compare: Isobel appointed *me* to the committee.

Revised	Isobel appointed Ralph and *me* to the committee.

Note that subjects of infinitives are in the objective case.

Faulty	The dean of students wants *she* and *I* to represent the student council at the convention.

Compare: The dean of students wants *me* to represent the student council. . . .

Revised	The dean of students wants *her* and *me* to represent the student council at the convention.

Be especially careful with pronouns appearing in front of infinitives that omit the *to*.

Faulty	Let's you and I go to the show this evening.

The pronoun is the subject of the infinitive *(to) go* and should be in the objective case. Compare: Let *me* go to the show.

Revised	Let's you and *me* go to the show this evening.

Pronouns in Appositive Constructions

In appositive constructions, in which the pronoun is followed by an identifying noun, use the pronoun case that would be correct if the noun were not there:

The principal told *us* boys to go home.

Compare: The principal told us to go home.

We boys hid around the corner until the principal went back to her office.

Compare: We hid around the corner.

Pronouns as Parts of Implied Clauses

When a pronoun occurs after a *than* that is introducing an implied clause, choose the pronoun's case according to the pronoun's use in the implied clause. Both of the following sentences are correct, but their meanings are different.

I like Paul better than he.

This sentence means "I like Paul better than he likes Paul."

I like Paul better than him.

This sentence means "I like Paul better than I like him."

Pronouns Preceding Gerunds or Participles

Use the possessive case before gerunds (-*ing* verbals used as nouns) and the subjective or objective case before present participles (-*ing* verbals used as adjectives).

I saw *him* running away from the police.

In this sentence, *running* is a participle modifying the direct object *him*.

I think *his* running away from the police was his biggest mistake.

Here, *running* is a gerund, the subject of *was*.

Choosing correct adjective and adverb forms

H4.7   Use adjectives and adverbs correctly.

Although adjectives and adverbs are both modifiers, they cannot be used inter-changeably because adjectives modify nouns or pronouns whereas adverbs modify verbs, adjectives, other adverbs, and sometimes whole phrases, clauses, or sentences.

Problems with adjectives and adverbs can occur in the following cases.

Confusion of Adjective and Adverb Forms

Do not use adjectives when adverbs are warranted.

> **Faulty**   I did *real good* on that test.
>
> *The adverb form is well, not good. Similarly, real is an adjective, which cannot modify an adverb.*
>
> **Revised**   I did *really well* on that test.

Be careful to use the appropriate modifier after verbs that can be either linking verbs or action verbs. Linking verbs (such as *is, are,* and *seem*) take subject com-plements, which are either nouns or adjectives. Certain linking verbs, especially the sense verbs *feel, look, taste, smell, sound,* and a few others, can also be action verbs. After such verbs, choose an adjective if the word modifies the subject and an adverb if it modifies the verb.

> The captain looked *angry.*
>
> *Here, angry is an adjective modifying captain. Compare: The angry captain . . .*
>
> The captain looked *angrily* at the crew.
>
> Here, *angrily* is an adverb telling how the captain did the looking.

Problems with Comparative and Superlative Forms

Short adjectives (with one syllable or two syllables ending in *y* or *le*) form their comparative and superlative degrees by adding *er* and *est* to the simple form. Other adjectives and most adverbs generally use *more* (or *less*) for the compara-tive and *most* (or *least*) for the superlative. A few modifiers are irregular.

CHOOSING COMPARATIVES VERSUS SUPERLATIVES   Use the comparative degree for two persons or things and the superlative for three or more.

> Of the two players, Maria is the *better.*
> Of the whole team, Maria is the best.

MISUSE OF COMPARATIVES WITH ABSOLUTE ADJECTIVES   Do not use comparative and superlative degrees with absolute adjectives, such as *unique* or *impossible.*

Faulty	Her dress was the *most unique* one I had ever seen.

Unique already means "one of a kind" and can't be further modified.

Revised	Her dress was *unique*.
or	
	Her dress was the *most unusual* one I had ever seen.

DOUBLE COMPARATIVES Do not use double comparatives or superlatives.

Faulty	Raphael is *more smarter* than George.
Revised	Raphael is *smarter* than George.

ILLOGICAL COMPARISONS Avoid making illogical comparisons between items that are not actually comparable. Sometimes illogical comparisons result from a missing word such as *other*.

Faulty	Our Volvo is better than any car on the road.

This sentence inadvertently implies that this Volvo isn't a car on the road.

Revised	Our Volvo is better than any *other* car on the road.

At other times an illogical comparison arises when the grammar of the sentence mixes apples and oranges.

Faulty	Handwritten papers are harder to read than typing.

Papers cannot be compared with typing.

Revised	Handwritten papers are harder to read than typed papers.

Chapter 5
Editing for Style

Learning Objectives

H5.1 Edit for conciseness.

H5.2 Use strategies to enliven your prose.

H5.3 Avoid unclear pronoun references.

H5.4 Use the active and passive voices effectively.

H5.5 Use inclusive language.

Pruning your prose

H5.1   Edit for conciseness.

In most rhetorical contexts, conciseness is a virtue. Readers like efficient prose that makes its point without padding.

Cutting Out Deadwood

Good writers typically write first drafts that are much longer than their final versions. Eliminating unneeded words and phrases is an essential part of revision.

Wordy	Ilana was interested in finding out the answer to a question that she had recently been puzzling about. The question was this: What is the important and essential difference between a disease that most people would call "mental illness" and a disease that is simply a disease of the brain?
Revised	Ilana was puzzled by the difference between "mental illness" and "brain disease."

When eliminating deadwood, watch out for common wordy phrases such as the following:

at the present time (use *now*)
because of the fact that (use *because*)
are of the opinion that (use *believe*)
have the ability to (use *can*)
in spite of the fact that (use *although*)

You can easily delete these expressions—and dozens more like them—without sacrificing meaning.

Combining Sentences

Another cause of wordiness is the inefficient use of short, choppy sentences. Try to recast a choppy passage by combining sentences, thus saving words while creating more complex and graceful structures.

Wordy	Jim Maxwell took two years to build his solar building. Building his solar building included nearly one year of planning. His solar building was intended mainly as a grain drier. But it also provided a warm winter shop. Additionally he had the advantage of a machinery shed. This shed kept his machinery dry. His new solar building would pay dividends for years to come.
Revised	It took two years to build, including nearly one year of planning, but when Jim Maxwell finished his solar building, he had a grain drier, a warm winter shop, and a dry machinery shed that would pay dividends for years to come.

Enlivening your prose

H5.2   **Use strategies to enliven your prose.**

You can often revise your prose to make it livelier and more interesting.

Avoiding Nominalizations

Lively writers express actions with verbs. Lifeless writers often *nominalize* their sentences by converting actions into nouns (for example, by writing, "arrive at a conclusion" rather than "conclude"). Nominalizations make much bureaucratic and administrative prose sound stilted, impersonal, and dead.

Nominalized	For the production of effective writing, the expression of an action through the use of a verb is the method most highly preferred.
Revised	Effective writers express actions with verbs.

A nominalized sentence is not only long and dull, but also confusing. Nominalized sentences often include two additional problems: overuse of the verb *to be* and a pileup of prepositional phrases. To revise a nominalized sentence, ask yourself who is doing what; then make the doer of the action the subject and make the action a verb.

Nominalized	Jim's receiving of this low grade was the result of his reading of the material too quickly.
Revised	Jim received a low grade because he read the material too quickly.

By putting *Jim* in the subject slot, the writer eliminates the weak verb *was* as well as three prepositional phrases.

Avoiding Noun Pileups

Noun pileups result from the tendency, again common in bureaucratic prose, to use nouns as adjectives.

> **Noun Pileup** Consideration of an applicant physical disability access plan by the student services reform committee will occur forthwith.
>
> **Revised** The committee to reform student services will soon consider a plan for improving access to buildings for physically disabled applicants.

Avoiding Pretentious Language

Unless you are intentionally imitating a long-winded style, strive for language that sounds natural and clear rather than pretentious (or developed through overuse of a thesaurus).

> **Stilted** The tyro in the field of artistic endeavors commenced to ascertain the suitability of different constituencies of pigment.
>
> **Revised** The student artist began wondering which color paint would be most suitable.

Avoiding Clichés, Jargon, and Slang

Clichés are tired, frequently repeated phrases such as "last but not least," "easier said than done," or "a chill ran up my spine." Replace them with fresh language.

Deciding when to avoid jargon and slang is more problematic because their use may be appropriate depending on your audience, purpose, and genre. Technical jargon is acceptable if you are writing for an audience who understands it within a genre that uses it; slang is also fine if it suits your purpose, audience, and genre. In general, you should avoid jargon that may not be understood by your audience, and you should avoid slang in most formal contexts.

Inappropriate Jargon for a Teacher's Letter to Parents

> Your child displays maladaptive socialization behaviors.
>
> **Revised** Your child is sometimes rude to classmates.

Inappropriate Slang for a College Essay

> The gods are all bent out of shape because Oedipus killed his dad.
>
> **Revised** The gods are angry because Oedipus killed his father.

Creating Sentence Variety

Prose can feel wooden or choppy if each sentence has the same construction and length. Skilled writers combine sentences in various ways for emphasis and grace.

Abstract	The poor are often stereotyped as beggars, drunks, or people with uncared-for children.
Revised	We often stereotype poor people as panhandlers demanding our spare change, as scruffy drunks holding a bottle in a paper bag, or as barefoot children with matted hair, filthy clothes, and tears streaking down their dirty faces as they tug on their mother's arm.
Monotonous	Martin watched carefully for loose rocks. He picked his way along the edge of the cliff. Martin didn't hear the rattles at first. Then he suddenly froze with fear when he heard them. A timber rattler was about two feet away. It was coiled like a garden hose. The rattler's neck was arched. Its fangs looked like twin needles of death.

In this passage, each sentence starts with the subject, and all the sentences are approximately the same length.

Revised	Watching carefully for loose rocks as he picked his way along the edge of the cliff, Martin suddenly froze with fear. At first he didn't hear the rattles. Then he heard them for sure. About two feet away, coiled like a garden hose, was a timber rattler, its neck arched, its fangs looking like twin needles of death.

Here the longest sentence is twenty-four words and the shortest is six words. The two short sentences emphasize dramatically important moments.

Writing Low on the Ladder of Abstraction

Except in philosophical or theoretical writing, which uses abstract language precisely, too much abstract prose can be dull. You can enliven abstract prose by moving down the ladder of abstraction from the general to the specific. These strategies—using specific details, appealing to the senses, "showing" rather than "telling"—are so important rhetorically that we discuss them in earlier sections of the text. (See the ladder of abstraction in Concept 4.3. See also Skill 19.5 about using open-form narrative strategies to enliven closed-form prose.)

Avoiding broad or unclear pronoun reference

H5.3   Avoid unclear pronoun references.

Each time you use a pronoun, make sure that the noun to which it refers, its *antecedent*, is clearly apparent. Unclear use of pronouns can confuse readers.

Avoiding Broad Reference

A broad reference occurs whenever a pronoun—usually *this*, *that*, or *it*—stands for an idea or a whole group of words rather than for a single noun. Although this usage is sometimes acceptable, it is often ambiguous or vague.

Broad Reference	Harold Krebs in Hemingway's "Soldier's Home" rebels against his parents. He does *this* by refusing to accept their values, and *this* is why his parents are so upset by *it*.

In this sentence the italicized pronouns refer not to specific nouns but to ideas, which shift with each pronoun, confusing the reader.

Revised	Harold Krebs in Hemingway's "Soldier's Home" rebels against his parents by refusing to accept their way of life. His rejection of their values explains why his parents are so upset by his later actions.

Do not make broad references with the pronoun *which*, which must have a single noun for its antecedent.

Faulty	He drinks a lot, which is something I disapprove of.
Revised	I disapprove of his heavy drinking.

In the original sentence, *which* has no noun antecedent.

Avoiding Unclear Antecedents

To avoid confusing your readers, make sure that every pronoun has a clear antecedent. Avoid using pronouns that seem to stand for two different antecedents.

Unclear Antecedent	Chris explained to his son the reasons he couldn't go to the meeting.
Revised	Chris explained the reasons his son couldn't go to the meeting.

In the original sentence, *he* could stand for either *Chris* or *son*, making it unclear whether Chris or his son couldn't go to the meeting.

Deciding between active and passive voice

H5.4   Use the active and passive voices effectively.

Experienced writers usually prefer the active voice because it is stronger and more economical. The passive voice requires *to be* helping verbs and prepositional phrases for the doer of the action.

Weak	The cake and ice cream were eaten, and then games were played.
Revised	The children ate the cake and ice cream and then played games.

However, the passive voice isn't always inappropriate. Writers sometimes choose the passive voice to create appropriate emphasis or to be intentionally vague.

PASSIVE VOICE WHEN DOER IS UNIMPORTANT The passive voice is appropriate whenever the receiver of the action is more important than the doer. It is often used in scientific writing, which tends to emphasize the material acted on rather than the doer of the action.

The distillate is then removed from the liquid.

PASSIVE VOICE TO PLACE OLD INFORMATION BEFORE NEW   The passive voice is often required to follow the old/new contract. (See Concept 18.7.) If the old information from a preceding sentence is the receiver of the action in your current sentence, the passive voice is appropriate.

> Graphs are essential tools for economic analysis. They *are* commonly *used by* economists to display both concrete economic data and abstract economic concepts.
>
> In the second sentence, the passive voice allows the writer to begin with old information. The pronoun *they* refers to *graphs* in the previous sentence.

PASSIVE VOICE TO CREATE VAGUENESS   Sometimes writers use the passive voice intentionally to be vague or evasive rather than direct. This practice is ethically questionable. Avoid it when you can.

Evasive	The decision has been made to raise the dues.
Forthright	The president and the treasurer have decided to raise the dues.

Using inclusive language

H5.5   Use inclusive language.

For much of the history of the English language, grammarians accepted the use of masculine pronouns ("Everyone should bring *his* own lunch") and the use of *man* ("Peace and goodwill to *men* everywhere") as generic references for both men and women. Most contemporary writers believe that these usages reflect gender bias. Many writers are also now aware of other ways in which language subtly reflects attitudes toward gender, culture, class, and ethnicity. In this section, we offer suggestions that will help you construct sentences free of biased language.

Avoiding Sexist Labels and Stereotypes

Avoid language that labels or stereotypes women. Let the same considerations guide you whether you are describing a man or a woman.

Sexist	Janet Peterson, stunning in her new, blue-sequined evening gown, gave the keynote address at the annual mayors' conference.
	Would you say, "Robert Peterson, stunning in his new tuxedo, ruffled shirt-front, and cummerbund, gave the keynote address at the annual mayors' conference"?
Revised	Janet Peterson, newly elected mayor of the state's third-largest city, gave the keynote address at the annual mayors' conference.

Avoiding Use of Masculine Pronouns to Refer to Both Sexes

Whenever possible, revise sentences to avoid using the masculine pronouns *he*, *him*, *his*, and *himself* to refer to people of both sexes. Often you can use plural pronouns (*they, them, their,* and *themselves*), which do not indicate gender.

Problematic	If a student wants to bring his text to the exam, he may.
Revised	If students want to bring their texts to the exam, they may.

In informal writing, you can also use *you* and *your* to avoid sexist language; in formal prose you can use *one* and *one's*, although this usage sometimes sounds stilted.

Revised	If you want to bring your texts to the exam, you may.
Revised	If one wants to bring one's text to the exam, one may.

Avoid bureaucratic constructions such as *him/her* or *s/he*, which are cumbersome and inelegant. Occasional use of the combined forms *he or she* or *him or her* is acceptable, but overuse of this construction is tiresome.

Respecting Pronoun Wishes for Transgender Persons

The transgender and genderqueer communities have raised public consciousness about the way pronouns in English promote a binary view of gender. In many circles new acquaintances tell each other what gender pronoun they prefer. When in doubt, choose the pronoun that matches the person's chosen identity. Many members and allies of the LGBT community have argued that English needs a gender-neutral pronoun (candidates include *zie, zem, zir* or *ey, em, eir*) and hope that these words will catch on in the way that *Ms* caught on to replace *Mrs.*

Avoiding Inappropriate Use of the Suffix *-man*

Use of *-man* as a suffix in such words as *repairman, mailman*, and *policeman* or as a prefix in *mankind* seems to ignore the presence of women in the workforce and in the human race. The suffix *-person* may be an acceptable substitute; *chairperson* and *salesperson* are common in formal usage. However, *weatherperson* still sounds odd, as does "Joan is a new *freshperson* at state college." Look for alternative expressions.

Avoid	Prefer
congressman	representative, member of Congress
forefathers	ancestors
mailman	mail carrier
man (generic)	person, people, humans, human beings
wives, husbands	spouses
manmade	synthetic

Avoiding Language Biased Against Ethnic or Other Minorities

As a writer, you need to be sensitive to the subtle ways in which language can make people feel included and welcomed or excluded and insulted. Nowhere is the evolving and charged nature of language more evident than in the connotations of words referring to cultural minorities.

Avoid language that reflects stereotypes against ethnic or other minorities. Language referring to minorities evolves rapidly. In the 1980s black and *Afro-American* were preferred terms, but in the 1990s these largely gave way to *African-American* and, more recently, *Black*. Similarly, the terms *Latino* and *Latina* are replacing *Hispanic*. Homosexual people now prefer the terms *gay man* and *lesbian* and in some contexts are reviving the word *queer*. Today the term *people of color* is in favor, but the term *colored person* is an intense insult.

Chapter 6
Editing for Punctuation and Mechanics

Learning Objectives

H6.1   Use periods, question marks, and exclamation points correctly.

H6.2   Use commas correctly.

H6.3   Use semicolons correctly.

H6.4   Use colons, dashes, and parentheses correctly.

H6.5   Use apostrophes correctly.

H6.6   Use quotation marks correctly.

H6.7   Use italics (underlining) correctly.

H6.8   Use brackets, ellipses, and slashes correctly.

H6.9   Use capital letters correctly.

H6.10 Use numbers appropriately.

H6.11 Use abbreviations appropriately.

Periods, question marks, and exclamation points

H6.1   **Use periods, question marks, and exclamation points correctly.**

Periods, question marks, and exclamation points, sometimes called *terminal punctuation* or *endmarks*, signal the end of a sentence. These marks generally raise few problems for writers except in the case of sentence fragments (when an endmark follows a nonsentence), comma splices (when a comma is substituted for an endmark), and run-ons (when two sentences are fused together without an endmark).

A few other situations that sometimes pose problems for writers are discussed next.

Courtesy Questions

Courtesy questions—mild commands phrased politely as questions—normally end with a period.

> Would you please return the form in the enclosed envelope.

Indirect Questions

Direct questions require a question mark, but indirect questions end with a period.

Direct Question	He asked me, "Where are you going?"
Indirect Question	He asked me where I was going.

Placement of Question Marks with Quotations

If quotation marks and a question mark appear together, the question mark goes inside the quotation marks when only the quotation is a question and outside when the whole sentence is a question.

QUOTATION IS QUESTION

> The professor asked, "Can you solve the fox-and-chicken puzzle?"

ENTIRE SENTENCE IS QUESTION

> Did you hear the professor talk about the "fox-and-chicken puzzle"?

Note: When the question mark goes inside the quotation marks, do not follow the question mark with a comma or period.

Faulty	"Can we go with you?," she asked.
Revised	"Can we go with you?" she asked.

Exclamation Points

An exclamation point is used after a sentence or word group to express strong emotion. Exclamation points are used primarily in dialogue to indicate shouting or an especially strong feeling. Avoid using them in most other instances—especially academic prose—because they rarely have the effect on a reader that the writer intends. Expressing emotion through word choice, sentence structure, and tone is more effective. When an exclamation point goes inside a quotation, do not follow the exclamation point with a comma or period.

Commas

H6.2   Use commas correctly.

The comma is the most frequently used mark of internal punctuation. A comma mistakenly used as an endmark creates a comma splice.

Using Commas

USING COMMAS WITH COORDINATING CONJUNCTIONS   Use a comma and a coordinating conjunction (*and, or, nor, for, but, yet,* and *so*) to join two independent clauses.

> I released the dog's leash, and the dog trotted off across the field.

If the main clauses are very short, it is acceptable to omit the comma before the coordinating conjunction, but it is never acceptable to omit the coordinating conjunction; doing so will create a comma splice.

Comma Splice	We crossed the meadow, then we headed toward the mountain.
Revised	We crossed the meadow, and then we headed toward the mountain.

COMMA AFTER INTRODUCTORY ADVERB CLAUSES AND LONG INTRODUCTORY PHRASES   Use a comma to set off introductory adverb clauses and long introductory phrases from the rest of the sentence.

Introductory Adverb Clause	When I get home from work, I always fix myself a big sardine sandwich.
Introductory Phrase	Having lost my balance, I began waving my arms frantically.

Note: Initial gerund phrases or infinitive phrases used as sentence subjects should not be set off because they are part of the sentence core.

Faulty	To know him, is to love him. Playing her guitar every evening, is Sally's way of relaxing.

These introductory phrases serve as the subjects of their sentences and should not be set off.

Revised	To know him is to love him. Playing her guitar every evening is Sally's way of relaxing.

COMMA AFTER INTRODUCTORY TRANSITIONAL WORDS AND EXPRESSIONS   Set off most introductory transitional words and phrases such as *on the other hand, in sum, however, moreover,* and *for example* with a comma.

> On the other hand, bicycle racing involves an astonishing amount of strategy.

Writers often do not use a comma to set off *thus* and *therefore* and some other transitional expressions that do not noticeably interrupt the flow of the sentence. In such cases let your voice be your guide. If you pause noticeably after the transitional expression, set it off with a comma.

COMMAS TO SET OFF ABSOLUTE PHRASES   An absolute phrase comprises a noun followed by a participle or participial phrase. These phrases are *absolute* because they are complete in themselves; they modify the entire sentence rather than an individual word within the sentence. Absolute phrases are always set off with commas.

His hand wrapped in a blanket, Harvey hobbled toward the ambulance.

The bear reared on its hind legs, *its teeth looking razor sharp in the glaring sun.*

COMMA BEFORE CONCLUDING PARTICIPIAL PHRASES Use commas to set off participial phrases at the ends of sentences if they modify the subjects.

The doctor rushed quickly toward the accident victim, fumbling to open his black bag.

In this example, it is the doctor who fumbles to open his bag. The comma indicates that *fumbling* modifies *doctor* (the sentence subject) and not *victim* (the noun immediately preceding the participle).

Do not use a comma to set off a participial phrase at the end of a sentence if the phrase modifies the immediately preceding noun.

The doctor rushed quickly toward the accident victim lying face forward on the soft shoulder of the road.

Here the participial phrase modifies the preceding noun, *victim*, instead of the sentence subject. It is not set off with commas.

COMMAS TO AVOID CONFUSION Use commas to separate sentence elements if failure to separate them would create confusion.

Confusing	Every time Manny ate his dog wanted to be fed too.
Revised	Every time Manny ate, his dog wanted to be fed too.

COMMAS TO SET OFF NONRESTRICTIVE CLAUSES AND PHRASES Adjective modifiers following a noun are either *restrictive* or *nonrestrictive*, depending on whether they are needed to identify the noun they modify. Use commas to set off nonrestrictive clauses and phrases.

RESTRICTIVE AND NONRESTRICTIVE CLAUSES. An adjective clause is *nonrestrictive* if it is not needed to identify the noun it modifies. In such cases, set off the clause or phrase with commas.

Nonrestrictive Clause	My roommate dislikes my friend Corby, who rides a Harley motorcycle.

In this case, you know whom the roommate dislikes: a person named Corby. The fact that Corby rides a Harley motorcycle is additional information about him.

If the modifying clause is needed to identify the noun it is modifying, then it is *restrictive* and is not set off with commas.

Restrictive Clause	My roommate dislikes people who ride Harley motorcycles.

Here the meaning is this: "My roommate doesn't dislike all people, just those people who ride Harley motorcycles." The adjective clause restricts the meaning of *people*; that is, it narrows down the class "people" to the subclass of "people who ride Harley motorcycles." Because the phrase is needed to identify which people the roommate dislikes, it is a restrictive clause used *without* commas.

To help you remember this rule, think of this saying: Extra information, extra commas; needed information, no commas.

Nonrestrictive Clause	My grandmother, who graduated from college when she was eighty-two years old, deserves a special award.
Restrictive Clause	Anyone who graduates from college at age eighty-two deserves a special award.

RESTRICTIVE AND NONRESTRICTIVE PHRASES.   The same extra information/needed information rule holds for adjective phrases.

Restrictive Phrase	The man wearing the double-breasted suit is an accountant.

Here the phrase *wearing the double-breasted suit* identifies which man is an accountant, so it is not set off with commas.

Nonrestrictive Phrase	Elvis Dweezle, wearing a double-breasted suit, looked at himself briefly in the mirror before knocking on his boss's door.

Here the phrase *wearing a double-breasted suit* merely adds extra information about the already-identified Elvis Dweezle.

COMMAS TO SET OFF NONRESTRICTIVE APPOSITIVES   An *appositive* is a noun or noun phrase that immediately follows another noun, renaming it or otherwise referring to it. Appositives also follow the extra information/needed information rule. An appositive is restrictive (needed information) if it serves to identify the preceding noun; it is nonrestrictive (extra information) if it simply contributes additional information to an already-identified noun. As with nonrestrictive adjective clauses and phrases, set off nonrestrictive appositives with commas.

Nonrestrictive Appositive	Angela, a good friend of mine, has just been promoted to chief accountant.

In this example you know who has just been promoted: Angela. The appositive *a good friend of mine* adds extra information about Angela.

Restrictive Appositive	My friend Angela offered to do my income taxes for me.

Here the appositive *Angela* is needed to identify which friend offered to do the taxes. No commas are used.

COMMAS TO SEPARATE ITEMS IN A SERIES   Use commas to separate items in a series of three or more words, phrases, or clauses. The first comma leads readers to anticipate a list, with the last two elements joined by *and* or *or*. Place commas after each item in the series except the last.

He especially likes golf, jogging, and swimming.

We went to the movies, had dinner downtown, and then went bowling.

Note: Although British writers and some American writers and journalists omit the comma before the coordinating conjunction in a series, sentences are generally clearer if the comma is included.

Confusing	I like three kinds of pizza: pepperoni, Canadian bacon and pineapple and Italian sausage.
Clearer	I like three kinds of pizza: pepperoni, Canadian bacon and pineapple, and Italian sausage.

In the first version, the reader initially thinks that the first *and* marks the end of the series when, in fact, it simply joins one of the elements (*Canadian bacon and pineapple*). Placing a comma before the final *and* in the series clarifies the sentence.

COMMAS TO SEPARATE COORDINATE ADJECTIVES PRECEDING A NOUN   Coordinate adjectives in a series are separated by commas. Adjectives are coordinate if they can be separated by *and* or if they can be placed in a different order.

Coordinate Adjectives	A nearsighted, tall, thin, grumpy-looking man walked slowly down the street.

In this case you could say a "thin and grumpy-looking and nearsighted and tall man," thus separating the elements with *and* and placing them in a different order. These are coordinate adjectives separated by commas.

Noncoordinate Adjectives	Three copper-plated frying pans sat on the shelf.

These adjectives are not coordinate because you cannot say "frying and copper-plated and three pans." Hence these adjectives are not separated by commas.

COMMAS TO SET OFF PARENTHETICAL OR INTERRUPTING ELEMENTS   Use commas to set off parenthetical words, phrases, or clauses and other similar elements that interrupt the flow of the sentence. By reading your sentences aloud in a natural voice, you can generally identify parenthetical material that interrupts the flow of a sentence. Such material should be set off by pairs of commas. The following are common examples of interrupting material:

CONTRASTING ELEMENTS INTRODUCED BY *BUT*, *NOT*, OR *ALTHOUGH*

The man at the front desk, not the mechanic, was the one who quoted me the price.

WORDS OF DIRECT ADDRESS, *YES* AND *NO*, AND MILD INTERJECTIONS

I tell you, Jennifer, your plan won't work.

TRANSITION WORDS AND EXPRESSIONS

She will, however, demand more money.

TAG PHRASES CITING SOURCES

This new car, according to the latest government reports, gets below-average mileage.

ATTRIBUTIVE TAGS IDENTIFYING SPEAKERS

"To be a successful student," my adviser told me, "you have to enjoy learning."

COMMAS TO SET OFF ELEMENTS OF PLACES, ADDRESSES, AND DATES Use commas to set off each separate element in a date, place, or address.

He drove to Savannah, Georgia, on July 5, 1971, in an old blue Ford.

Omitting Commas

Many writers tend to use too many commas rather than too few. Do not use a comma unless a specific rule calls for one. "When in doubt, leave it out" is a good rule of thumb for comma usage. Learn to recognize the following situations that do *not* require commas. These are frequently sources of error in student papers.

DO NOT USE A COMMA TO SEPARATE A SUBJECT FROM ITS VERB OR A VERB FROM ITS COMPLEMENTS

Faulty   The man in the apartment next to mine, swallowed a goldfish.

Here a comma mistakenly separates the subject from the verb.

Revised   The man in the apartment next to mine swallowed a goldfish.

DO NOT USE A SINGLE COMMA WITHIN A SENTENCE CORE

Faulty   My brother, who recently won a pole-sitting contest swallowed a goldfish.

Here a comma occurs on one side of a nonrestrictive clause but not on the other side.

Revised   My brother, who recently won a pole-sitting contest, swallowed a goldfish.

DO NOT USE A COMMA BEFORE and **IF IT JOINS ONLY TWO WORDS OR PHRASES**

Faulty   She pedaled uphill for twenty minutes, and won the race by several lengths.

The *and* joins two verbs rather than two main clauses.

Revised   She pedaled uphill for twenty minutes and won the race by several lengths.

DO NOT USE A COMMA AFTER *SUCH AS*

Faulty   They forgot some key supplies such as, candles, matches, and trail mix.
Revised   They forgot some key supplies such as candles, matches, and trail mix.

Semicolons

H6.3   Use semicolons correctly.

A semicolon is stronger than a comma. It can be used to join two independent clauses to form a single sentence or to separate the main items in a list that already contains commas.

Semicolon to Join Main Clauses

When a semicolon is used to join main clauses, it signals a close relationship between the meanings of the two main clauses and creates a sentence with two balanced, equal parts.

> I asked the professor for an extension on my essay; she told me I was out of luck.

Semicolons are frequently used to connect main clauses when the second clause contains a conjunctive adverb or transitional phrase such as *however, therefore, nevertheless,* and *on the other hand.*

Comma Splice	He spent all morning baking the pie, however, nobody seemed to appreciate his efforts.
Revised	He spent all morning baking the pie; however, nobody seemed to appreciate his efforts.

Note: Joining two main clauses with only a comma creates a comma splice.

Semicolon in a Series Containing Commas

Use a semicolon to separate elements in a series when some of those elements already contain commas.

> On vacation we went to Laramie, Wyoming; Denver, Colorado; Salt Lake City, Utah; and Boise, Idaho.

Colons, dashes, and parentheses

Colons

H6.4   Use colons, dashes, and parentheses correctly.

The most frequent uses of a colon are to introduce a list; to announce a word, clause, or phrase predicted in a preceding main clause; or to introduce a block quotation. Colons are generally preceded by main clauses and are not used as internal punctuation within a clause.

COLON TO INTRODUCE A LIST   Use a colon to introduce a list when the list follows a grammatically complete independent clause.

> We can win in two ways: changing our defense or adding Jones to the offensive lineup.

Do not use a colon in the middle of a clause or after the words *such as, for example,* or *including.*

Faulty	The things you should bring to the party are: chips, salsa, and your own drinks.
Revised	The things you should bring to the party are chips, salsa, and your own drinks.
	or
	Please bring to the party the following: chips, salsa, and your own drinks.

In the first example the offending colon is removed. In the second, the structure preceding the colon has been expanded to a main clause by adding *the following*, which serves as the direct object of *bring*.

COLON TO INTRODUCE A PREDICTED ELEMENT FOLLOWING AN INDEPENDENT CLAUSE   Following an independent clause, use a colon to introduce a predicted element, which can be a word, a phrase, or a clause.

> The professor agreed to something remarkable: grading contracts for all students.
>
> The professor agreed to something remarkable: He allowed Jack to submit a late paper.

Note on capitalization: If what follows the colon is a main clause, you have the option of beginning the clause with a capital letter. If what follows the colon is not a complete sentence, use a lowercase letter.

COLON TO INTRODUCE BLOCK QUOTATIONS OR QUOTATIONS RECEIVING SPECIAL EMPHASIS   A colon is used to introduce a block quotation if what precedes the colon is a main clause. You can also use a colon to introduce a short quotation that you want to emphasize.

> His father replied slowly, carefully, thoughtfully: "Buying the SUV now, when we are already too deeply in debt, is not a good idea."

A comma could also be used to introduce this quotation; a colon is more formal and emphatic.

COLON IN SALUTATIONS, TIME NOTATIONS, TITLES, AND BIBLICAL CITATIONS   Colons are sometimes used in letter salutations and within titles. They are also used in time expressions and biblical notations.

Salutation	Dear Sarah:
Time Notation	4:30 A.M.
Titles	*Teaching Critical Thinking Skills: Theory and Practice*
Biblical Citations	Proverbs 3:16

Dashes

Think of the dash as a strong comma that gives special emphasis to the material being set off. (To make a dash, type two hyphens; leave no space before, after, or between the hyphens.)

> Sir Walter Raleigh brought the potato—as well as tobacco—to Queen Elizabeth I on his return from Virginia.

In this example, a pair of commas could replace the pair of dashes. The dashes emphasize the material between them by calling for a greater pause when reading.

Parentheses

Parentheses are used to enclose nonessential, supplemental information and to enclose citations or list numbers.

SUPPLEMENTAL INFORMATION   The most common use of parentheses is to enclose supplemental information.

> I wanted to know if my first computer (an old Kaypro from the early 1980s) could be placed in a museum of technology.

CITATIONS AND NUMBERED ITEMS IN A LIST   Parentheses are also used to enclose citations in many documentation systems and to enclose numbers or letters identifying parts of a list.

> To graduate, a student must fill out three forms: (1) the transcript summary, (2) the request form, and (3) the adviser's sign-off sheet (*Junebug State Bulletin* 32).

PUNCTUATING SENTENCES THAT INCLUDE PARENTHESES   When you place a complete sentence within parentheses, the concluding endmark goes inside the parentheses. When you end a sentence with parenthetical elements, the endmark goes outside the parentheses.

> When visiting England, we watched a lot of cricket. (Cricket is a British game something like American baseball.)

> When visiting England, we watched a lot of cricket (a British game somewhat similar to American baseball).

Apostrophes

H6.5   Use apostrophes correctly.

The apostrophe is used mainly for showing possession, but it is also used to indicate missing letters in contractions and to form special plurals.

Apostrophe to Show Possession

Use the apostrophe to indicate possession of nouns and indefinite pronouns. Possessive constructions show both a possessor and a thing possessed. The thing possessed occurs last in the construction; the person or thing that possesses (the possessor) comes first and contains an apostrophe.

Possessor	Thing Possessed	Alternative Construction
Luciana's	car	car belonging to Luciana
men's	coats	coats for men
cats'	fur	fur of cats
three minutes'	work	work lasting three minutes

Because plurals and possessives both add an *s* sound to words, they are identical to the ear. To the eye, however, they are easily distinguished by the use of the apostrophe in the possessive. Be sure that you don't confuse your reader by mixing possessives and plurals.

> **Faulty**   Our neighbor's have two horse's and ten cat's on their grandfathers old farm.

> **Revised**   Our neighbors have two horses and ten cats on their grandfa-
> ther's old farm.

Neighbors, horses, and *cats* are plurals, not possessives; *grandfather's* is a possessive, not a plural.

Forming the Possessive

To make a noun possessive, you must first determine whether it is singular or
plural. Add an apostrophe and an *s* (*'s*) to singular nouns and to plural nouns
that do not end in *s;* add an apostrophe only (*'*) to plural nouns that end in *s*.

> The man's car [*the car belonging to the man*]
>
> The men's cars [*the cars belonging to the men*]
>
> The cats' food dish [*the food dish belonging to the cats*]
>
> The cat's food dish [*the food dish belonging to the cat*]

To form the possessive of hyphenated words, compound words, and word
groups, add an apostrophe and an *s* (*'s*) to the last word only.

> her mother-in-law's lawn mower
>
> the ladies-in-waiting's formal gowns

**DO NOT USE APOSTROPHES FOR POSSESSIVES OF PERSONAL PRO-
NOUNS**   Do not use apostrophes with the possessive forms of personal and
relative pronouns (*yours, his, hers, ours, theirs, its, whose*). When an apostrophe is
used with personal or relative pronouns, it indicates a contraction. Be especially
careful to distinguish between *it's* ("it is") and *its* (possessive).

Possessive	Contraction
The dog chases its tail.	It's (it is) a funny dog.
Your tie is crooked.	You're (you are) a sloppy dresser.
Whose dog is that?	Who's (who is) at the door?

Apostrophes with Contractions

Use an apostrophe (*'*) to indicate omitted letters in contractions.

> you're (you are)   isn't (is not)
>
> it's (it is)   spring of '34 (spring of 1934)

Note: Be sure to insert the apostrophe exactly where the missing letters would
be.

> Faulty   is'nt
>
> Revised   isn't

Apostrophes to Form Plurals

Use an apostrophe and an *s* (*'s*) to form the plural of letters and words used as
words. Underline (italicize) the letter or word but not the plural ending.

> On your test I can't distinguish between your *t*'s and your *E*'s. You also
> use too many *very*'s and *extremely*'s.

Quotation marks

H6.6   Use quotation marks correctly.

Use quotation marks to enclose words, phrases, and sentences that are someone's spoken words or that you have copied from a source. Also use quotation marks to set off titles of short works and to indicate words used in a special sense. Quotation marks always occur in pairs, one marking the beginning and the other the ending of the quoted material.

Punctuating the Start of a Quotation

When a quotation is introduced with an attributive tag (such as "my instructor says" or "Teresa Ortega acknowledges"), the tag can be followed by a comma, a colon, or *that*. If you use a comma or a colon, begin the quotation with a capital letter. If you introduce a quotation with *that*, do not capitalize the first letter of the quotation even if it is capitalized in the original. In this case, you do not precede the quotation with a comma.

> Columnist E. J. Dionne says, "Terror is designed to paralyze."
> Columnist E. J. Dionne says that terror is "designed to paralyze."

If you work a short quotation into the structure of your own sentence, use no punctuation other than quotation marks around the quoted passage.

> According to E. J. Dionne, all acts of terror are "designed to paralyze."

Placement of Attributive Tags

Attributive tags can be placed before, inside, or after the quotation. When an attributive tag is placed between the two halves of a quotation, the second half is not capitalized unless it begins a new sentence.

> Michael Karnok says, "To be a father is to know the meaning of failure."
> "To be a father," says Michael Karnok, "is to know the meaning of failure."
> "To be a father is to know the meaning of failure," says Michael Karnok.

Punctuating the End of a Quotation

Put commas and periods inside quotation marks.

> He told me to "buzz off," and then he went about his business.
> He told me to "buzz off." Then he went about his business.

> Note that both the comma (first sentence) and the period (second sentence) go inside the quotation marks.

In documented papers that place citations inside parentheses at the end of the quotation, put the comma or period after the parenthetical citation.

> According to Immunex Chief Executive Edward Fritzky, "Genetic Institute is doing very, very well" (Lim C5).

> Note the order: quotation mark, parenthetical citation, final period.

Place colons and semicolons outside the ending quotation mark.

> He told me to "buzz off"; then he went about his business.
> My sexist husband wants his "privileges": Monday night football and no household chores.

Note that the semicolon (first sentence) and the colon (second sentence) go outside the quotation marks.

Place question marks and exclamation points inside quotation marks if they belong to the quotation; place them outside the ending quotation marks if they belong to the whole sentence.

Indirect Quotations

Use quotation marks for *direct* quotations—the actual words spoken by someone— but not for *indirect* quotations, which report what someone said without using the exact words.

Direct Quotation   "Do you want to go to the library?" Tyler asked Julio.

Indirect Quotation   Tyler asked Julio whether he wanted to go to the library.

Indented Block Method for Long Quotations

When quoting more than four typed lines (MLA style) or forty words (APA style), use the indented block method rather than quotation marks to indicate direct quotations. Double-space the quotation for both styles. For the MLA style, indent each line ten spaces from the left margin. Indent five spaces for the APA style. Do *not* put quotation marks around the blocked passage.

Single Quotation Marks

In American practice, use single quotation marks, made with an apostrophe on most keyboards, to enclose a quotation within a quotation.

> Molly angrily told her discussion group, "Every time I ask my husband to help me with the ironing, he says that 'men don't iron clothes' and stalks out of the room in a huff."

Inside Molly's directly quoted words is a direct quotation from Molly's husband: *men don't iron clothes*. The husband's words in this case are enclosed in single quotation marks.

With the block indentation method, use regular quotation marks to enclose a quotation within a quotation.

Quotation Marks for Titles of Short Works

Use quotation marks for titles of essays, short stories, short poems, songs, book chapters, and other sections that occur within books or periodicals.

> I liked Spenser's sonnet "Most Glorious Lord of Lyfe" better than *The Faerie Queene*.

In this sentence, both the sonnet and *The Faerie Queene* are poems, but the former is in quotation marks because it is short, and the latter is italicized (underlined) because it is long.

Quotation Marks for Words Used in a Special Sense

Use quotation marks to call attention to a word or phrase used in a special sense. Often your intention is to show that you disagree with how someone else uses the word or phrase.

> My husband refuses to do what he considers "woman's work."
>
> In this example, the quotation marks indicate that the writer would not use the phrase *woman's work* and that she and her husband have different ideas about what the phrase means.

Although you may set off words used in a special sense with quotation marks, avoid using quotation marks for slang and clichés as an attempt to apologize for them. Rephrase your sentence to eliminate the triteness.

Weak	I've been "busy as a bee" all week, so I'm exhausted.
Revised	I've been so busy this week that I'm exhausted.

Italics (underlining)

H6.7 Use italics (underlining) correctly.

In handwritten papers, indicate italics with underlining. In papers prepared using a computer, italicizing is usually preferable. Check with your instructor.

Italics for Titles of Long Complete Works

Use italics for titles of books, magazines, journals, newspapers, Web sites, plays, films, works of art, long poems, pamphlets, and musical works. Capitalize and italicize *a*, *an*, and *the* only if they are part of the title.

Moby-Dick	Michaelangelo's *David*	*YouTube*
Newsweek	the *Encyclopaedia Britannica*	*Facebook*
Star Wars	*The Sound and the Fury*	*The Jupiter Symphony*

Note: The Bible and its books, as well as the Qur'an (Koran), are not underlined or italicized.

the Bible	Exodus	Revelations	the Qur'an

Italics for Foreign Words and Phrases

Use italics for foreign words and phrases.

> You should avoid the *post hoc ergo propter hoc* fallacy.

Italics for Letters, Numbers, and Words Used as Words

Use italics for letters, for numbers, and for words when they are referred to as words and phrases and not as what they represent.

> To spell the word *separate* correctly, remember there is *a rat* in *separate*.

Brackets, ellipses, and slashes

H6.8 **Use brackets, ellipses, and slashes correctly.**

Brackets and ellipses (three spaced dots) indicate changes within quotations and occasionally have other uses. Slashes are used primarily to indicate line breaks in quoted poetry.

Brackets

Brackets [ ] are made with straight lines and should not be confused with parentheses ( ), which use curved lines.

BRACKETS TO SET OFF EXPLANATORY MATERIAL INSERTED INTO QUO-TATIONS Use brackets to set off explanatory material inserted into a quotation.

> According to Joseph Menosky, "Courses offered to teach these skills [computer literacy] have popped up everywhere."

The original source of this quotation did not contain the words *computer literacy*, since the context of the original source explained what *these skills* meant. In this example, *computer literacy* is inserted in brackets to make up for the missing context. The brackets indicate that the material they enclose did not occur in the original version.

BRACKETS TO INDICATE THE WRITER'S ALTERATION OF THE GRAMMAR OF A QUOTATION Use brackets when you need to change the grammar of a quotation to make it fit the grammar of your own sentence.

Original Source	I see electric cars as our best hope for reducing air pollution.
	—Jean Haricot
Correct Use of Brackets	Jean Haricot says that "electric cars [are] our best hope for reducing air pollution."

In this example the writer has to change the original *as* to *are* to make the quotation fit the grammar of his or her own sentence. This change is placed in brackets.

BRACKETS TO ENCLOSE SIC TO INDICATE A MISTAKE IN A QUOTATION If you quote a source that contains an obvious mistake, you can insert *sic* in brackets to indicate that the mistake is in the original source and is not your own.

> According to Vernon Tweeble, not your greatest sportswriter, the home-run king is still "Baby [*sic*] Ruth."

Here the *sic* indicates that Tweeble said "Baby Ruth," not "Babe Ruth." The mistake belongs to Tweeble, not to the writer.

Ellipses

An ellipsis, made with three spaced periods (. . .), is used to indicate an omission within a quotation. When an ellipsis occurs at the end of a sentence, a period is used before the ellipsis to mark the sentence boundary.

Original	Before the dam, a float trip down the river through Glen Can-yon would cost you a minimum of seven days' time, well within anyone's vacation allotment, and a capital outlay of about forty dollars—the prevailing price of a two-man rubber boat with oars, available at any army-navy surplus store. A life jacket might be useful but not required, for there were no dangerous rapids in the 150 miles of Glen Canyon. —Edward Abbey, "The Damnation of a Canyon"
Correct Use of Ellipses	According to Edward Abbey, before the dam was built "a float trip down the river through Glen Canyon would cost you a minimum of seven days' time . . . and a capital outlay of about forty dollars . . . . A life jacket might be useful but not required . . . " (351).

Here the first ellipsis indicates words omitted in the middle of a sentence. The second ellipsis shows words omitted at the end of a sentence and hence includes a period to mark the sentence boundary. In the last example, the period marking the sentence boundary goes after the parenthetical citation, which indicates the page number of the source.

When quoting poetry, use a line of dots to indicate that one or more full lines of the poem have been omitted, as in this example using Ben Jonson's "Come, My Celia":

Come, my Celia, let us prove,
While we can, the sports of love;

. . . .

Why should we defer our joys?

Fame and rumor are but toys.

Slashes

The main use of the slash is to divide lines of poetry written as a quotation within a sentence.

Ben Jonson evokes the *carpe diem* tradition when he says: "Come, my Celia, let us prove, / While we can, the sports of love."

If you quote more than four lines of poetry, use the indented block method rather than quotation marks with slashes.

Slashes are sometimes used to indicate options, but this use is too informal for most essays.

Informal	He told me to take algebra and/or trigonometry.
Formal	He told me to take either algebra or trigonometry or both.

Capital letters

H6.9   Use capital letters correctly.

When in doubt about whether to capitalize a particular word, consult a good dictionary.

Capitals for First Letters of Sentences and Intentional Fragments

Capitalize the first letter of the first word in every sentence and also in sentence fragments used intentionally for effect. In fragmentary questions in a series, initial capital letters are optional.

> That man is a liar and a scoundrel. What do you want me to do? Like him? Invite him to dinner? Offer him my money?
>
> **or**
>
> What do you want me to do? like him? invite him to dinner? offer him my money?

Capitals for Proper Nouns

Use capitals for all proper nouns. The following rules cover most cases you will encounter.

Capital Letters	Miguel Cabrera, Barack Obama, Jennifer Lawrence
Capitalize titles of people when the title precedes the name or when the title follows the name without an article.	Doctor Teodora Koskov; John Jones, Professor of Mathematics
Do not capitalize titles of people that include an article (*a* or *an*).	Teodora Koskov, a medical doctor; John Jones, a mathematics professor
Capitalize family relationship names (Mother, Uncle) when used with a name. When used in place of a name, capitalization is optional.	Please, Aunt Eloise, tell Grandfather (or grandfather) that dinner is ready.
Do not capitalize relationship words when not used with a name or as a name.	I hear that my uncle and your father are going to visit Tony's grandfather.
Capitalize the names of specific geographic locations, areas, and regions, including compass directions if they are part of a name.	Mount Everest; the Pacific Northwest; Main Street; the Hudson River; the South; Illinois
Do not capitalize geographic locations indicated by compass directions but not considered actual names.	the northeast part of the United States; a mountain south of here
Capitalize historical events, names, movements, and writings.	the Korean War; the Oregon Territory; Articles of Confederation; the Renaissance; the Impressionist Period
Capitalize the names of ships and buildings and capitalize brand names.	USS *Missouri*; the Empire State Building; Pepsi

Capitalize specific academic courses but not academic subject areas, except "English" and foreign languages.	This term I am taking Chemistry 101, Integral Calculus 414, and French. But: This term I am taking chemistry, calculus, and French. (In the first sentence, the writer names specific courses; in the second sentence, the writer names subject areas only.)
Capitalize specific times, days, months, and holidays, but not names of seasons.	Monday; the Fourth of July; Halloween; last year; autumn; winter
Capitalize abbreviations derived from proper names.	NFL; U.S.A.; RCA; NAFTA; U. of W.

Capitals for Important Words in Titles

In titles of books, articles, plays, musical works, and so forth, capitalize the first and last words, any word following a colon or a semicolon, and all other words except articles, prepositions, and conjunctions of fewer than five letters.

> "Ain't No Such Thing as a Montana Cowboy"
> *Famous Myths and Legends of the World: Stories of Gods and Heroes*

Capitals in Quotations and Spoken Dialogue

Capitalize the first word of spoken dialogue, but do not capitalize the first word in the second half of a broken quotation that follows an attributive tag.

> She said, "Because it is raining, we won't go."
> "Because it is raining," she said, "we won't go."

Do not capitalize indirect quotations.

> She said that we wouldn't go because it is raining.

Numbers

H6.10   Use numbers appropriately.

Writers often have to decide whether to write numbers as words (ten) or as numerals (10). Follow the conventions of the genre in which you are writing.

Numbers in Scientific and Technical Writing

Scientific and technical writers generally use numerals for all numbers. Check with your instructor about how to handle numbers in lab reports and other formal papers in science, mathematics, and engineering.

Numbers in Formal Writing for Nontechnical Fields

In the humanities and other nontechnical fields and in most business and professional writing, writers usually adhere to the following conventions:

Use Words Instead of Numerals

For single-word number	eight dogs; a hundred doughnuts
For common fractions	one-third of a cup; half a pie
In the humanities, for two-word numbers	twenty-three students (however, business and professional writers prefer numerals for two-word numbers—23 students)
For numbers greater than a million, use a combination of words and numerals.	72 billion dollars

Use Numerals Instead of Words

For addresses	1420 Heron Street
For times and dates	I'll be there at 10:00 A.M. on November 5th.
For percentages and statistics	At least 30 percent of the students scored above 15 on the standardized test.
With decimals	The average score was 29.63
For amounts of money that include cents	That notebook cost around $3.95.
With symbols	20°C, 5'4"
For scores	The Yankees beat the Indians 5 to 3.
To refer to chapters, pages, and lines	You'll find that statistic in Chapter 12 on page 100 at line 8.

Numbers at the Beginning of a Sentence

Spell out in words any number that begins a sentence. If the result is awkward, rewrite the sentence.

Faulty	375 students showed up for the exam.
Revised	Three hundred seventy-five students showed up for the exam.
	Or
	We counted 375 students at the exam.

Abbreviations

H6.11   Use abbreviations appropriately.

Whenever it is necessary to save space, such as in tables, indexes, and footnotes, you may use abbreviations. In the main text of formal writing, however, you should generally spell out rather than abbreviate words. Abbreviations are acceptable in the following cases.

Abbreviations for Academic Degrees and Titles

Use abbreviations for academic degrees and for the following common titles when used with a person's name: *Mr., Ms., Mrs., Dr., Jr., Sr., St.* (*Saint*). Other titles, such as *governor, colonel, professor,* and *reverend*, are spelled out.

> The doctor asked Colonel Jones, Ms. Hemmings, and Professor Pruitt to present the portrait of St. Thomas to Judge Hogkins on the occasion of her receiving a Ph.D. in religious studies.

Abbreviations for Agencies, Institutions, and Other Entities

Use abbreviations for agencies, groups, people, places, or objects that are commonly known by capitalized initials.

FBI	UCLA
IOOF	DNA molecules
Washington, DC	CD-ROM

If you wish to use a specialized abbreviation that may be unclear to your audience, write out the term in full the first time it appears and place in parentheses the abbreviation that you will use subsequently.

> The Modern Language Association (MLA) recently issued new guidelines for citing electronic sources.
>
> This example indicates that the writer will henceforth use the abbreviation *MLA*.

Abbreviations for Common Latin Terms

Use abbreviations for common Latin terms used in footnotes, bibliographies, or parenthetical comments. In the main text, spell out the English equivalents.

e.g.	for example
i.e.	that is
c.f.	compare

This rule also applies to *etc.* (*et cetera*, meaning "and so forth"). Avoid using *etc.* in formal writing. Instead, use the English *and so forth* or *and so on*, or rewrite your sentence to make it more inclusive, thus eliminating the need for *and so forth*. Never write *and etc.*, because *et* is Latin for "and."

Weak	During my year in London I went to ballets, the opera, Shakespeare plays, etc.
Revised	During my year in London I saw many cultural events, including two ballets, one opera, and four Shakespeare plays.

Plurals of Abbreviations

Do not use an apostrophe when forming the plural of an abbreviation.

Faulty	I've misplaced two of my CD's.
Revised	I've misplaced two of my CDs.

Credits

Text

Page 2. Reprinted by permission from Rodney Kilcup.

Page 4. Cohan, Mark, Ph.D. Passage concerning nature vs. nurture in regards to sexual behavior of adolescents. Used with permission.

Page 14. A. Kimbrough Sherman, Management Professor, Quoted by Barbara E. Walvoord and Lucille P. McCarthy. Walvoord, Barbara E. and McCarthy, Lucile P., "Thinking and Writing in College: A Naturalistic Study of Students in Four Disciplines." Urbana, IL: National Council of Teachers of English (NCTE), 1990, p. 51.

Page 22. The Male Myth by Paul Theroux, November 27, 1983. *The New York Times*. Retrieved from http://www.nytimes.com/1983/11/27/magazine/the-male-myth.html

Page 36. *The Oregonian*, January 1, 1993. Reprinted by permission from Rosalie Rockwood Bean.

Page 37. "Listen to the Lizards" by Kris Saknussemm, 2014. Copyright ©2014. Originally published in *World Literature Today*. Used by permission.

Page 46. Edward Abbey, The Damnation of a Canyon in *The Glen Canyon Reader* edited by Mathew Barrett Gross. University of Arizona Press, 2003

Page 53. Kenneth Burke, Rhetorician. Kenneth Burke. From *Permanence and Change: An Anatomy of Purpose* by Kenneth Burke, 1984. University of California Press and The Kenneth Burke Literary Trust.

Page 58. Arctic Power, "Which One is the REAL ANWR?". Retrieved from http://www.anwr.org/features/pdfs/realanwr.pdf. Used with permission (top). Description of Arctic National Wildlife Refuge. Used with permission (Bottom).

Page 61. Michael A. Chaney, "Representations of Race and Place in Static Shock, King of the Hill, and South Park". Coloring Whiteness and Blackvoice Minstrelsy: Representations of Race and Place in Static Shock, King of the Hill, and South Park. *Journal of Popular Film and Television* Volume 31, Issue 4, 2004,DOI:10.3200/JPFT.31.4.167-184Michael A. Chaney pages 167-184 http://www.tandfonline.com/doi/abs/10.3200/JPFT.31.4.167-184

Page 85. Marche, Stephen. "The Epidemic of Facelessness" from *The New York Times*, February 14, 2015. Copyright © 2015. Used by permission. Stephen Marche is a Novelist and Columnist at Esquire Magazine.

Page 93, 95, 96, 107, 111. Used with permission from Scott Lindquist.

Page 115. Reprinted by permission from Stephanie Malinowski.

Page 121. *Black Boy* (2009) by Richard Wright, HarperCollins Publishers.

Page 124. Reprinted by permission from Megan Lacy (top). Reprinted by permission from Jeffrey J. Cain (bottom).

Page 128. Kris Saknussemm "Phantom Limb Pain". Reprinted by permission from Kris Johnson.

Page 130. Reprinted by permission from Patrick Jose.

Page 132. Reprinted by permission from Stephanie Whipple.

Page 136. When Writers Can't Write: Studies in Writer's Block and Other Composing Process Problems. Ed. Mike Rose, *Guilford Press*, 1985: pp. 273–85. Reprinted with permission of Guilford Press.

Page 168, 170. Used with permission from Kristen Smock.

Page 172. Reprinted by permission from Shannon King.

Page 200. Reprinted by permission from Lydia Wheeler.

Page 208. Alison Townsend, "The Barbie Birthday" from *The Blue Dress*. Copyright © 2003, 2008 by Alison Townsend. Reprinted with the permission of The Permissions Company, Inc., on behalf of White Pine Press, www.whitepine.org.

Page 217. Jubal Tiner (Eds.), Pisgah Review. Winter 2006 Volume: 1 Issue: 2; http://www.pisgahreview.com/?p=22. Used with permission from Jacquelyn Kolosov.

Page 219. Reprinted by permission from Michelle Eastman.

Page 234. LeAnne M. Forquer, Ph.D., et al. "Sleep Patterns of College Students at a Public University" by LeAnne M. Forquer, Ph.D., Adrain E. Camden, B.S., Krista M. Gabriau, B.S., C. Merle Johnson, Ph.D., *Journal of American College Health*, Vol. 56, No. 5, March/April 2008. Reprinted by permission from LeAnne M. Forquer. Department of Psychology at Central Michigan University in Mount Pleasant. Copyright © 2008 Heldref Publications

Page 239, 246. Campbell, Lauren, Charlie Bourain and Tyler Nishida, "SpongeBob SquarePants has Fewer Gender Stereotypes than Mickey Mouse." Used with permission.

Page 278. A Bug's Death by Olivia Judson, September 25, 2003. *The New York Times Company.*

Page 297, 383. Reprinted by permission from Ross Taylor.

Page 301. *Insisting on gun-control laws that don't work, then registration, then confiscation* by E. Gregory Wallace, December 12, 2015. Used with permission from E. Gregory Wallace.

Page 303. Fascitelli, Ralph and Jordan Royer. "3 Ways to Dramatically Cut Gun Violence" from *Seattle Times*, October 11, 2015. Copyright © 2015. Used by permission of Washington Ceasefire. Link at http://www.seattletimes.com/opinion/3-ways-to-dramatically-cut-gun-violence/.

Page 305. Used with permission from Theda Hovind.

Page 307. Reprinted by permission from Claire Giordano.

Page 326. Reprinted by permission from Jackie Wyngaard.

Page 328. Used with permission from Katy Lapinski.

Page 341. Reprinted by permission from Sarah Bean.

Page 345, 346. Reprinted by permission from Stephen Bean.

Page 388, 397, 398. Reprinted by permission from Dao Do.

Page 395. "Where's Papa?" from *Life Without Father: Compelling New Evidence that Fatherhood and Marriage Are Indispensable for the Good of Children and Society*. Reprinted by permission from David Popenoe.

Page 403. Data from Degrees conferred by degree-granting institutions, by *level of degree and sex of student: Selected years, 1869-70 through 2016–17*, Table 258. U.S Department of Education, National Center for Education statistics.

Page 407. Graves, Michael E., et al., from "Some Characteristics of Memorable Expository Writing: Effects of Revisions by Writers with Different Backgrounds," *Research in the Teaching of English*, 1988, Vol. 22, No. 3, pp. 242–265. Urbana, IL: National Council of Teachers of English, 1988.

Page 415. The Strange Case of the Queen-Post Truss: John McPhee on Writing and Reading, *College Composition and Communication* 42: 2 (May 1991), 200-210]. http://www.stthomasu.ca/~hunt/qptruss.htm

Page 416. New Journalism by Tom Wolfe, 1973. HarperCollins Publishing Company.

Page 418. Loren Eisley, "The Bird and the Machine" Eiseley, Loren. The Immense Journey. New York: Vintage Books, 1959, Knopf Doubleday Publishing Group, page 179.

Page 419. Annie Dillard (1982). Teaching a Stone to Talk: Expeditions and Encounters. Harper Collins Publishers LLC.

Page 420. Isak Dinesen, "The Iguana," *Out of Africa* was first published in 1937 by Putnam & Co. Ltd. http://www.whiterabbit.net/@port03/Dinesen/Iguana/iguana.htm

Page 422. Victoria Register-Freeman, "My Turn: Hunks and Handmaidens" *Newsweek*; 11/4/1996, Vol. 128 Issue 19, p16.

Page 423. Beryl Markham, "Flying Elsewhere," *West with the Night*, ISBN 1453237917, 9781453237915 Open Road Media (top). Barbara Tuchman, "This Is the End of the World," A Distant Mirror Random House (bottom).

Page 429, 430, 431. Reprinted by permission from Joyce Keeley.

Page 438. Reprinted by permission from Alex Mullen.

Page 454. Reprinted by permission from EBSCO Industries, Inc.

Page 473. Image Courtesy of Food & Water Watch / Americans Against Fracking.

Page 478. Is Vegetarianism Healthier Than Nonvegetarianism? (July 1, 1997) . Retrieved from http://acsh.org/1997/07/is-vegetarianism-healthier-than-nonvegetarianism/. Reprinted by permission from American Council on Science and Health (ACSH).

Page 490. Pro – Are Greenhouse Gases A Threat? by David C. Hall, Tim K. Takaro, Jane Koenig, December 3, 1997. *The Seattle Times*. Retrieved from http://community.seattletimes.nwsource.com/archive/?date=19971203&slug=2575805

Page 506. EBSCO Host research database screenshot includes abstract of "Searching for Self and Relationships Online by M. Kyle Matsuba" *CyberPsychology & Behavior*; Jun 2006, Vol. 9 Issue 3. Reprinted by permission (top). Reprinted with permission from CyberPsychology & Behavior, 9/3, June 2006, published by Mary Ann Liebert Inc., New Richelle, NY (bottom).

Page 507. Twitter, 23 June 2009, 11:15 a.m., twitter.com/persiankiwi/status/2298106072.

Page 508. Greenversations EPA blog posting; http://www3.epa.gov/

Page 515. Reprinted by permission from EBSCO Host (top). Erica Scharrer, D. Daniel Kim, Ke-Ming Lin & Zixu Liu. Working Hard or Hardly Working? Gender, Humor, and the Performance of Domestic Chores in Television Commercials. *Mass Communication and Society* Volume 9, Issue 2, 2006. pages 215–238 (bottom).

Page 540. Used with permission from Jane Kidder.

Page 541. Used with permission from Annabelle Forster.

Images

Page 1. Billie G. Lynn

Page 7. ©2013 Artists Rights Society (ARS), New York/ADAGP, Paris. CNAC/MNAM/Dist. RMN-Grand Palais/Art Resource, NY

Page 38. Olesya Karakotsya/123RF

Page 51. Roz Chast/The New Yorker Collection/The Cartoon Bank

Page 55. Jonathan Carr

Page 74. Peter Sobolev/Shutterstock

Page 76. Lars Thulin/Getty Images (top left). 4FR/E+/Getty Images (top right). Design Pics Inc/Alamy Stock Photo (middle left). Image Source/Getty Images (middle right).

Page 79. John Bean (3 images)

Page 163. Mary T Nguyen/Columbus Dispatch

Page 176. Steven James Silva/Reuters/Landov

Page 177. Jim Sulley/AFP/Getty Images (top center). David Turnley/Corbis (bottom center).

Page 181. Peter Turnley/Corbis

Page 183. AFP/Getty Images (middle center). Armend Nimani/AFP/Getty Images (bottom center).

Page 185. Peter Macdiarmid/Getty Images

Page 187. Natalie M Ball

Page 191, 194. Pearson Education

Page 195. Courtesy of Ohio University's Students Teaching About Racism in Society (STARS) organization

Page 196. The Story of Stuff Project. www.storyofstuff.org

Page 201. Stephen Crowley/The New York Times/Redux Pictures

Page 202. Library of Congress Prints and Photographs Division [Dorothea Lange/LC-DIG-fsa-8b29516]

Page 318. David R. Frazier Photolibrary, Inc./Alamy Stock Photo

Page 336. a katz/Shutterstock

Page 345. arinahabich/Fotolia (middle center). Spencer Platt/Getty Images (bottom center).

Page 346. Don Jon Red/Alamy Stock Photo

Page 355. Zou Zheng/Landov

Page 428. National Library of Medicine

Page 429. Mary T Nguyen/Columbus Dispatch (top left). Zou Zheng/Landov (middle left). The Advertising Council (middle left and bottom left).

Page 430. Erich Schlegel/KRT/Newscom (top left). Cynthia Jones/World Food Programme/Getty Images (top right). dbimages/Alamy Stock Photo (middle right).

Page 431. Lionel Healing/AFP/Getty Images (top center). dbimages/Alamy Stock Photo (middle left). Eddie Gerald/Alamy Stock Photo (middle right).

Page 439. June Johnson

Page 441. INTERNATIONAL WOW COMPANY/Newscom

Page 454. Karramba Production/Fotolia (bottom center). 123rf (bottom center).

Page 519. Wetta, Molly, Banned book display: "Set Your Imagination On Fire: Read a Banned Book." Copyright © 2012. Used by permission.

Index